# The Longwood Reader

## Third Edition

Edward A. Dornan
Charles W. Dawe

*Orange Coast College*

Allyn and Bacon
Boston London Toronto Sydney Tokyo Singapore

*Vice President, Humanities:* Joseph Opiela
*Editorial Assistant:* Kate Tolini
*Marketing Manager:* Lisa Kimball
*Production Administrator:* Rowena Dores
*Editorial Production Service:* York Production Services
*Text Designer:* Pat Torelli
*Cover Administrator:* Linda Dickinson
*Composition Buyer:* Linda Cox
*Manufacturing Buyer:* Megan Cochran


A Viacom Company
160 Gould Street
Needham Heights, MA 02194

Internet: www.abacon.com
America Online: Keyword: College Online



**Library of Congress Cataloging-in-Publication Data**

The Longwood reader / [edited by] Edward A. Dornan, Charles W. Dawe. -
- 3rd ed.
p. cm.
Includes bibliographical references.
ISBN 0-205-26233-3
1. College readers. 2. English language—Rhetoric. I. Dornan, Edward A. II. Dawe, Charles W.
PE1417.L66 1997
808'.0427—dc21

96-46390
CIP



Printed in the United States of America

10 9 8 7 6 5 4 3 2 1 99 98 97 96

# *Contents*

# *Thematic Table of Contents*

***Current Issues***



***Family Life***

### *Growing Up*



### *History*



### *Human Behavior*

### *Leisure*



### *Media*



### *Men and Women*



### *Minority Experiences*

## *Personal Experiences*



## *Politics and Government*



## *Work*

# *Pairs of Essays*

Although the selections in *The Longwood Reader* are arranged by rhetorical patterns, we have included a Thematic Table of Contents grouping the selections under sixteen subject areas.

In addition, we offer the following suggestions for those who wish to assign pairs of essays. Such pairing may be useful for discussion of contrary and/or complementary views of similar subjects or situations, choices of style and presentation strategies, as well as different ways of using a particular rhetorical strategy.

Individual teachers will, of course, discover additional pairings equally valid and informative.

# *Preface to the Third Edition*

This third edition of *The Longwood Reader* maintains the rhetorical arrangement of the first two editions but also includes several new features. We have added guidelines for peer evaluation in the chapter titled "The Writing Process" and collaborative learning activities at the end of each subsequent chapter, both designed to be unobtrusive so that individual instructors may use them as appropriate.

In this edition, one-third of the essays are new to *The Longwood Reader.* While selecting these essays, we were guided by the same principle that guided our selections for the first edition: the assumption that "good reading influences good writing."

By "good reading" we mean the activity that engages a reader's imagination when he or she picks up a text. We mean the ability to question an author's ideas, to subject an author's argument to skeptical scrutiny, to use a pencil to note disagreements and counterpoints in a text's margins. By good reading we also mean the ability to read with a "critical eye," that is, to read with the ability to see an author's strategies: the way paragraphs are shaped, the way sentences create rhythm and impact, and the way images create feeling. Every writing course must then also be a course in reading with a second sight that sees beneath a text's skin to examine its bones and vital organs. Unfortunately, reading like a writer, reading with a critical eye, does not come naturally; students must acquire the ability.

How?

They must gather information about the writing craft, and they must study the craft at work. As we perceive the process, student writers must go into "training" much like student actors, dancers, musicians, or painters must train. A vital part of this training is studying the works of those who have mastered the art of writing, writers like Maya Angelou, E. B. White, George Orwell, Maxine Hong Kingston, Gretel Ehrlich, and others represented in *The Longwood Reader.*

You will notice that Chapter 1 of *The Longwood Reader* also prepares students to read with a critical eye. We explain the reader–writer contract: a reader must assume that a writer has created an understandable work; a writer must assume that a reader wants to understand the work. Together the reader and writer create meaning, relying on writing conventions to aid their effort. We explain the importance of reading to understand a writer's purpose, strategy, and style, a framework that establishes the pattern for the discussion questions that follow each essay. We also present five tips for the first reading of an essay. We illustrate the practice of reading with a pencil in hand with Williard Gaylin's "What You See Is the Real You" accompanied by student notes. We close the Introduction with five tips for rereading an essay.

Chapter 2. "The Writing Process," features a student essay, one we use throughout the chapter to illustrate key concepts. In "The Writing Process" we define the essay, place essay writing in the college classroom context, and then discuss the composing process. The discussion begins with ways to find subjects and follows with an explanation of prewriting techniques that help writers explore their subjects.

We then offer methods for sorting and grouping information in rough form by using clusters or informal outlines. Next we explain the thesis statement—how to find one and shape it to serve as an essay's guiding principle. We go on to explain and illustrate formal planning with a clear sense of a reader in mind (a step many students resist). We then discuss essay structure in detail—a discussion that concentrates on strategies for writing introductions, discussions, and conclusions. We also present guidelines for maintaining unity, coherence, and for developing content.

We conclude "The Writing Process" with Five Tips for Revision. These are practical tips, ones we believe will not overwhelm students writers with technical detail but still provide them with enough direction to polish their essays.

We arranged the next nine chapters that follow the first two according to traditional writing methods, beginning with description and ending with argumentation. We believe there is a slight risk in teaching rhetorical modes. When misunderstood, they may generate "cookie-cutter" prose, but we believe the benefit of mastering rhetorical modes outweighs the risk. When students understand these common development patterns, they can examine them at work in professional essays, thus sharpening their critical reading skills. By way of caution, however, throughout *The Longwood Reader* we discuss essays as having a dominant mode. We point out that during the composing process writers respond primarily to their material by selecting paragraph and essay patterns that best suit their subject and purpose instead of trying to fit their material into preselected patterns.

Each chapter that concentrates on a rhetorical mode begins with a detailed discussion that explains the writing method, offers strategies for using the method, and presents a sample of student work, several paragraphs in length, that illustrates the method at work in college writing. Here we wish to emphasize "detailed," for *The Longwood Reader* offers a thorough, though economical, discussion of each rhetorical mode and uses ample examples to illustrate major concepts. In Chapter 4, Narration, for instance, you will find an explanation of narrative effect illustrated by a brief tale from Zen Buddhist lore. You will find advice on writing the opening, body, and climax of a narrative as well as a discussion of conflict, point of view, chronological and psychological time, and scene and summary. We use several examples to illustrate these concepts to help students understand them in the essays that comprise this chapter. In Chapter 5, Examples, you will find a detailed discussion of specific, typical, and hypothetical examples as well as the practice of mixing different types of examples in an essay. The discussion is amply illustrated by eight paragraph examples. We continue this practice throughout the text. Moreover, the student essays that conclude each chapter are fully annotated to reveal the writer's strategy and to illustrate editing techniques.

Eight chapters have five essays each, while Chapter 11,

Persuasion and Argument, has six. Each essay is introduced with a brief biography of the author, brief comments to place the essay in context, and a prompt to initiate attentive reading. Each essay is followed by questions grouped under the headings of Meaning and Purpose, Strategy, and Style. Two writing assignments follow the study questions, and each chapter closes with additional writing assignments, one designed to generate a response to a photograph, developed to challenge students with a wide range of essay topics from which to choose.

*The Longwood Reader* offers several important reference features. The Glossary defines rhetorical terms that appear throughout the text. When a term first appears, it is highlighted in bold type to signal its appearance in the Glossary. *The Longwood Reader* also offers a thematic table of contents for readers who wish to read several essays on a common subject and a list of paired readings for those who wish to read for similarities or differences in perspective and style.

Of all the reference features, A Guide to Editing and Revising Sentences will have the most direct influence on a student's writing. The guide is arranged by rules: "Eliminate pretentious language," "Use technical language with care," "Consider the denotation and connotation of words," "Revise for proper coordination," "Place modifiers with care," "Provide variety in your sentences," and so on. Each of the rules is fully explained and illustrated, thus allowing students to use this appendix independently.

We thank those colleagues from colleges and universities around the country who reviewed the third edition of *The Longwood Reader:* Maggie Berdine, West Virginia University—Parksburg; Leigh Boyd, Temple Junior College; Patricia Creed, Temple Junior College; Judith Haberman, Phoenix College; Michael J. Meils, El Paso Community College; Ruth Peña, El Paso Community College; Rebecca Phillips, Western Virginia University—Parksburg; Ann Spurlock, Mississippi State University; Donna Tobin, Bucks County Community College.

Once again we thank those who advised us on previous editions: Kathleen L. Bell, Univrsity of Central Florida; Michael

Bobkoff, Westchester Community College; Judith M. Boschult, Phoenix College; Shirley Curtis, Polk Community College; Charles Dodson, University of North Carolina—Wilmington; Jane Dugan, Cleveland State University; Janet Eber, County College of Morris; Leslie Harris, Georgia State University; Elaine Sheridan Horne, Manchester Community College; Gloria Johnson, Broward Community College; Peggy Jolly, University of Alabama—Birmingham; Robert A. Kelly, Macon College; Joseph LaBriola, Sinclair Community College; Russell R. Larson, Eastern Michigan University; Barry Maid, University of Arkansas—Little Rock; Thomas E. Martinez, Villanova University; Jerry McElveen, Richland College; Gratia Murphy, Youngstown State University; Beth Richards, University of Nebraska; Connie Rothwell, University of North Carolina—Charlotte; Gerald Schiffhorst, University of Central Florida; David E. Schwalm, Arizona State University; Carole M. Sherman, College of DuPage; Laurence J. Starczyk, Kent State University; Jo Koster Tarvers, Rutgers University; Eugene Wright, University of North Texas.

We also thank the professionals at Allyn and Bacon who guided the first edition through the production process: Alicia Reilly, Amy Capute, and Rowena Dores. And we continue to appreciate Kathy Daniel's and David Lynch's fine work on the final manuscript for the first edition.

For all three editions we owe a special debt of gratitude to our sponsoring editor Joe Opiela for his advice throughout the process. We also thank Editorial Assistants Brenda Conaway and Kate Tolini, Permissions Editor Laurie Frankenthaler, and Production Administrator Rowena Dores for their help in preparing the third edition manuscript for publication.

We also wish to acknowledge an immense debt to our colleagues Don Pierstorff and Mike Finnegan for their extensive contributions to both the first, second, and third editions of *The Longwood Reader.* Finally, a special thank you is due John Finnegan for his ability to translate illegible handwriting into finished copy.

# 1

# *The Reading Process*

We heard a story recently about an event that occurred at a nearby campus. Campus officials, faculty members, and a contingent of dissatisfied students had been haggling over curriculum changes. Months of negotiation ended in deadlock. Frustrated, the students called a rally. A representative from administration began to speak, offering the "official" view. Suddenly, a student leader leaped to the platform and grabbed the microphone. Veins pulsed in his neck; his face turned crimson; his eyes spurted with anger. Everyone became excited, ready for a fiery attack on the administration and faculty, but instead he shouted, "Words, Words, Words! I'm sick of words!" He dug into a bag and began tossing lecture notes, essay shreds, and pages torn from textbooks at the astonished crowd. "If words were feathers," he bellowed, "everyone on this campus would smother before anything changed." And then he stormed to the admissions office and promptly withdrew from his classes.

Or so the story goes.

A true story? Who knows for sure? It does, nevertheless, illustrate a common belief that words slow action. Indeed, taking direct action seems much easier than agonizing over a thoughtful, well-reasoned argument. But education relies primarily on words, written words—words *you* read and words *you* write. Reading and writing are sometimes slow, frustrating activities that at first glance may seem to oppose each other. On the contrary, though, reading and writing complement each other. The better reader you are, the better writer you can become.

Of course, you've been reading since grammar school. You might even spend some leisure time reading for pleasure, perhaps becoming engrossed in the psychological twists and turns of a popular thriller or enthralled by the intricate social weaving of a historical narrative. But you probably spend more time reading for information, gleaning facts from history, psychology, and science textbooks. While reading textbooks, you concentrate on a goal, which often has something to do with a midterm or final examination. In other words, you've learned efficient reading techniques. You've learned to approach a textbook as if it were a lake in which to trawl for facts and theories instead of bass or trout.

Certainly, reading in this way helps you prepare for tests. It will also help after graduation when you face the heaps of memoranda, reports, and research every profession generates. It won't, however, help you become a better writer. For your writing to improve, you must learn to read like a writer. You can begin by learning to read with a "critical eye." The critical eye reveals a writer's purpose and strategies. It scrutinizes the way words work in sentences. The critical eye pierces a work's surface and reveals its bones and heart.

We offer the essays in this anthology as a means to help you develop a critical eye. The essay is often described as a well-organized nonfiction composition in which the author concentrates on a single aspect of a subject. Usually this kind of essay is written in formal English and designed to convey information. But essays as a group cover a much broader territory. Many are impressionistic or exploratory. Often they express personal feelings or attitudes based on the writer's experience.

Because essays are so varied, these selections represent a great range, all the better, we believe, to help you sharpen your critical eye. They include works by such well-known essayists as George Orwell, Joan Didion, and E. B. White, as well as works by less-known, rising essayists, such as Gretel Ehrlich and Phyllis Rose. The essays are from varied sources: newspapers, magazines, academic and scientific journals, and nonfiction books. They cover many subjects: crime and violence, men and women, work and play, country and city life, even culture and customs. The collection embodies several styles, ranging from the newswriter's objective report to the poet's subjective expression. Some are serious. Some are playful. All are worth your attention.

To deepen your understanding of the essay, we have arranged *The Longwood Reader* by rhetorical patterns, that is, according to the dominant strategies writers use to organize the content of their essays. These are common strategies—narration, description, examples, comparison and contrast, cause and effect, process analysis, classification and division, definition, and argument. Perhaps you already have a casual acquaintance with a few of these patterns. Good—but now you can get to know them intimately. *The*

*Longwood Reader* examines them closely by beginning each chapter with a detailed explanation of a pattern and a student example of the pattern at work. As you study them, hold one idea in mind: You are reading like a writer; that is, reading to develop your writing skill—reading with a critical eye.

## *The Writer–Reader Contract*

Pause for a moment. Imagine an essayist pushing back from a typewriter desk. The writer stretches and yawns before slipping a final manuscript into an envelope and sending it off for publication. You might think this is the critical moment—when the essay is completed and in the mail to the publisher.

But it isn't.

The critical moment comes when the work falls into a reader's hands—your hands. To begin reading an essay is the first act in a dynamic interaction—not between you and the writer, as you might guess—but between you and the essay itself.

This is not to deny that a relationship connects you and the writer. In fact, readers and writers are joined by an implicit agreement, a "contract." To meet the writer–reader contract a writer agrees to create an understandable work; a reader agrees to try to understand the work.

Unfortunately, communicating in written language is often difficult. A writer cannot gaze over your shoulder and whisper into your ear to make understanding an essay any easier. Only the essay speaks to you. To fulfill the writer–reader contract, a writer employs principles known as "conventions" to help you understand the essay. Even if the essay is difficult, you must trust that the writer has kept the reader in mind during the writing. You must trust that the writer has seen the essay through *your* eyes. In other words, you must trust that the writer has used the conventions of essay writing to help you understand the work.

Generally, these conventions dictate that essays have a purpose, use clear strategies to achieve the purpose, and employ an appropriate style. Understanding these conventions will help you decipher most nonfiction texts. Indeed, understanding the conventions will help sharpen your critical eye.

## *Reading for Purpose*

Writers know that readers expect a purpose to be at work behind a piece of writing. They tend to view purpose from two perspectives: the general purpose of the entire essay and the particular purpose of a paragraph or passage.

### *General Purpose*

A general purpose gives an essay direction. It provides a destination. It keeps a reader on the track. Some writers, especially when the primary intent is to convey information, state a general purpose: "My purpose is to explain the ways in which human beings have decorated their bodies through the ages: by tattooing, by scarring, and by reshaping bone structure." Other writers, especially those writing personal narration and description, do not state a general purpose as directly, thus encouraging the reader to become more deeply involved in interpretation. You must then formulate the general purpose in your own way: "The writer narrates an early childhood experience to show how important imaginative play is." When an essay is rich enough to invite interpretation, much like a careful reading of an intricate poem or short story, then all that you have heard, tasted, touched, smelled, seen, and thought; all your knowledge of people, books, music, art, culture, and language; literally everything you have lived through, is the raw material at your disposal. Drawing on that rich resource, you apply your knowledge to interpret the essayist's general purpose.

### *Particular Purpose*

The particular purpose refers to what a writer intends in a single paragraph or short passage that helps to develop the general purpose. Consider a short passage from Norman Mailer's *Fire on the Moon*, a work in which he concentrates on America's space program. In this passage astronauts Neil Armstrong and Buzz Aldrin have completed their historic moon walk on the Sea of Tranquility. The event takes place at the end of their first day on the moon.

> It was about three-thirty in the morning when the astronauts finally prepared for sleep. They pulled down the shades and Aldrin stretched out on the floor, his nose near the moon dust. Armstrong sat on the cover of the ascent engine, his back leaning against one of the walls, his legs supported in a strap he had tied around a vertical bar. In front of his face was the eyepiece of the telescope. The earth was in its field of view, and the earth "like a big blue eyeball" stared back at him. They could not sleep. Like the eye of a victim just murdered, the earth stared back at him.

One clear purpose is to describe the astronauts' preparations for sleep, but toward the end of the passage, Mailer compares the earth to a murder victim. Moreover, he suggests that Armstrong is haunted by the image of the earth "like the eye of a victim" staring at him. Is the comparison merely a dramatic flourish? We doubt it. The description will lead a sensitive reader to explore the deeper purpose in Mailer's comparison. Mailer does not spell out what the passage means. Instead he invites the reader to interpret it. That puts the reader in an interesting spot, for just as Mailer has drawn on his knowledge and experience to create the image, readers must draw on theirs to interpret it, to find a meaning.

The meaning may vary from reader to reader, depending on each one's knowledge and experience. One reader may recall Edgar Allan Poe's macabre tale of murder, "The Tell-Tale Heart." In Poe's story the murder victim's eye—"a pale blue eye"—haunted the murderer, as the blue earth seems to haunt Armstrong. Does the image suggest, therefore, that the earth has been abandoned like a corpse by astronauts who seek other worlds?

Another reader may explore technological associations. The 1969 Apollo II flight was history's most advanced scientific achievement. But at what price? Isn't the human thirst for scientific achievement and the technology it generates sapping mother earth's natural resources? In a metaphorical sense, therefore, isn't technology killing the earth? And couldn't Mailer be using the moon landing to suggest that "ecological crime"? Who, then, are the perpetrators? Perhaps all humankind, represented by the astronaut who, Mailer suggests, feels accused by the "big blue eyeball" staring at him.

Not all essays invite a careful interpretation of purpose, but the many that do are rich in detail and express a personal vision.

## *Reading for Strategy*

A *strategy* is composed of the various approaches, plans, or methods writers rely on to construct their essays. Any writer must develop a strategy to execute an essay's purpose.

### ***Audience***

A writer might first develop a sense of audience and a strategy for addressing them: To whom is the essay directed? How much do they know about the subject? How much time are they likely to spend with the essay? Will they want a straightforward treatment of the subject or an exploration through richly textured prose? Answering questions such as these will give a writer a sense of the audience, a feel for the person sitting at a desk or in an easy chair reading the essay.

### ***Structure***

Having acquired a sense of the audience, the writer may next develop a strategy for the essay's structure, knowing that readers want essays to have clear organization. Usually writers choose a dominant rhetorical pattern to organize their work. Rhetorical patterns are not formulas. They don't offer a magic recipe for success in writing. Moreover, professional writers seldom stick to any one pattern, choosing instead to use several within a dominant structure. We suggest you see rhetorical patterns as tools to guide your writing and to provide effective ways to fulfill a reader's desire for structure.

To see how rhetorical patterns can work, imagine that you are a film critic and want to compare and contrast two movies. You pick thrillers and narrow your subject to plot structure. You decide to explain the similarities and differences in each director's way of hooking an audience, generating suspense, building to a climax, and constructing the resolution. Thorough knowledge of comparison-and-contrast patterns will help you balance the similarities and differences in your analysis.

While composing your essay, however, you find yourself bringing the plot of a third movie into the discussion, one that represents still another structure. A warning light flashes in the back of your mind. You pause to think through what you're doing. Your knowledge of rhetorical patterns helps you realize you're drifting into classification, which is a pattern different from comparison and contrast, perhaps one best avoided for this writing situation. You stop. You return to your original strategy or reconsider, and in fact move to classification.

At still another stage, you drift into discussing the effects of thriller plots on an audience. It makes sense—an exciting plot does affect an audience, right? Of course it does. But you would be employing yet another rhetorical pattern, cause and effect. After some thought, though, you may decide to explore the effect on the audience, but you will do it in another section of your paper, and you will arrange it according to cause-and-effect technique.

Our point is quite simple: Knowledge of rhetorical patterns helps writers organize their work. These aren't cookie-cutter patterns that writers press into the dough of their thought. They are effective strategies that writers use to organize their material and guide a reader through an essay. They also help writers remain flexible, shifting smoothly from pattern to pattern according to the demands of the subject. The best way we know for you to build knowledge of rhetorical patterns is to examine how professional writers use them—that is, to read with a critical eye.

## *Reading for Style*

People usually think of style as appearance. Imagine a punk rocker walking across your campus. To what kinds of things are you referring when you speak of his or her "style"? Perhaps it's the black leather jacket and silver studs; the hair dyed black, swept into a peak, and shaved at the sides; the defiant swagger; even the throaty voice, rasping across the quad—all these details, and more, create the image, the "style" this person generates.

### *Word Selection*

Writing also embodies many details that work together to generate a "style." To identify a writer's style, you might begin by examining word selection. Are the words abstract or concrete? Do the words lull you into inattention like the speech of a politician trying to obscure past transgressions, or do they catch your attention like pebbles pinging against a window? Are the words common, found in everyone's vocabulary? Or are they scholarly, obscure words used by specialists? Or does the writer mix common with scholarly language?

### *Sentence Structure*

You might also study a writer's sentences. Notice how the writer builds sentences and varies their structure. We have no simple rules for this technique. Writers learn a feel for sentences, as potters develop a feel for clay. They shape them. They vary their length. They alter their rhythm to increase or slow the pace of reading for emphasis.

### *Figures of Speech*

Writers use sentences to create figures of speech, the bits and pieces of colorful language sparkling through the essay. A writer may use figurative language to compare two things that are essentially different but alike in some way. With a crisp simile, Flannery O'Connor compares a woman's determination to a truck: Mrs. Freeman's "forward expression was steady and driving like the advance of a heavy truck." In another memorable simile, Ralph Waldo Emerson offers a fresh way to see a child: "A sleeping child gives me the impression of a traveler in a very far country." With figurative language, writers not only help their readers understand what is being said but also add vigor to their prose.

### *Tone*

Word choice, sentence variety, and figurative language combine to create another element of style—tone. Begin to think of tone as an expression of a writer's attitude, much as tone of voice may reflect a speaker's attitude. Imagine, for a moment, that you have given a speech. The next day you receive this note:

> That was an effective speech. You carefully covered the main points. We all thank you.

A straightforward compliment? We think so, don't you? But with a few word substitutions and additions and by altering emphasis, the tone changes dramatically:

> That was . . . *some* speech. You *lingered* on all the points—at least three times each. Thanks a lot.

The message no longer expresses appreciation. It now expresses snide criticism. In other words, the tone has changed.

Some kinds of writing are dominated by well-defined tones. News reporters seem to share a tone, an objective presentation of events—just the facts, please. Thriller and romance writers seem to favor a breathless, frenzied tone. Essayists, however, struggle to find the exact tone to fit the subject, audience, and attitude. The same writer may use one tone for one subject and another tone for another subject. The tone may be formal, informal, flippant, conversational, intimate, solemn, playful, or ironic. The tone may even reveal the writer's awe of the subject. Consider the opening lines from Richard Selzer's essay on skin:

> I sing of skin, layered fine as baklava, whose colors shame the dawn, at once the scabbard upon which is writ our only signature, and the instrument by which we are thrilled, protected, and kept constant in our natural place.

Selzer brings to his essay years of experience as a surgeon and medical-school teacher. A reader with knowledge of Selzer's background might expect him to treat the skin in a matter-of-fact way, as merely a thin barrier that must be sliced through to reach the vital organs. But this is clearly not his attitude. He writes rhapsodically, "I sing of skin"; he makes a rich comparison, "layered fine as baklava"; and he claims its "colors shame the dawn." The sentence is a tribute to skin, and the tone expresses his sense of awe.

Style is difficult territory to explore, no doubt about it. If you devote time to reading for style, you will achieve a *feel* for it. Study a writer's words and you will learn to choose the right words. Study a writer's sentences and you will learn to shape your sentences. Study a writer's figurative language and you will soon be writing colorfully. Study a writer's tone and soon a voice will rise from your pages.

## *Five Tips for a First Reading*

When reading to improve your writing, you cannot sweep through an essay and then set it aside. You should be prepared to read it several times. The first reading may be quick, designed to give you a view of the content, a sense of the purpose, and a feeling for the style. When you begin the first reading, we suggest you keep five tips in mind.

### *1. Know the Writer*

Whatever you learn about an author will help you anticipate his or her biases. If the author is identified as a liberal politician and the subject is poverty, then you might anticipate an argument supporting government aid to the poor. If the author is an environmentalist and the subject is the greenhouse effect, then you might expect a plea to save the world's rain forests. Many periodicals and essay anthologies include information about an author, usually on the first page of the essay or in a section often titled "Notes on Contributors." In this collection, each essay is introduced by a headnote, which includes an author profile and brief comments on the essay. Read each profile with care; it will prepare you for your first reading of the essay.

### *2. Consider the Place and Year of Publication*

Knowing where the essay was first published is necessary in establishing a writer's credentials. An essay titled "Bigfoot: Hoax or Hysteria?" would have more credibility if published in *Media, Culture, and Society* than it would if it were published in *The National Enquirer*. Why? *Media, Culture, and Society* is a highly respected periodical known for its analysis of the influence exerted by newspapers, television, and cinema on reader and viewer perceptions. In contrast, *The National Enquirer* is a popular tabloid known for its sensationalism. Knowing when an essay was first published will also give you clues about the social environment it was written in. Certainly an essay on civil liberty written in the early 1960s is going to display different assumptions from those in one written in the late 1980s.

### *3. Examine the Title*

Sounds obvious, right? Well, you would be surprised at how many readers mistakenly believe an essay begins with its first line. It doesn't. It begins with a title.

A title can help you anticipate what is to follow. It may announce the writer's subject, suggest the dominant rhetorical pattern, or hint at the writer's attitude. The title "A Hanging" lets you know you won't be going to a tea party. It makes sense to anticipate an essay about an execution, which will not be a pretty experience. The title "Cyclone! Rising to the Fall" is a little more ambiguous. Does "cyclone" refer to the destructive natural phenomenon? Or does it mean a roller coaster? Or could "Cyclone" be the name of a bronco? Anyway, you probably expect a description of a thrilling, or even frightening, experience so get a tight grip on the book. "I Want a Wife" seems like a straightforward title. But if you know that a feminist author wrote the essay, you might expect an ironic tone.

### *4. Take Quick Notes*

Always read with a pencil in hand. Don't just chew on the eraser: star key passages, underline startling images, bracket shifts in thought, and scribble notes in the margins. Roughly trace your reactions to the text, questions that come to mind, even disagreements with the writer. Ah yes, circle words you don't know so that you can refer to a dictionary for their meaning before the second reading.

Why go to all this trouble for a first reading? We don't suggest that you linger on any page for very long, but a first reading is like traveling in new territory. Much like markings on a map, markings on an essay will help your exploration during the return visit.

### *5. Record Your First Impressions*

We urge you to record your first impressions after the first reading and before going on to a second reading. Write down what you think the writer was trying to achieve—the purpose. Identify the dominant strategies. Describe the audience. Jot down your thoughts on style. Record any impressions you have.

Now let's look at an essay, Willard Gaylin's "What You See Is the Real You," with notes that reflect the guidelines for a first reading.

Gaylin is a psychiatrist and psychoanalyst—that is, his profession concentrates on the mind and behavior. As well as teaching and lecturing at colleges and universities around the world, he has also written several books on psychiatry and the law. This 1977 essay, published in *The New York Times*, a highly respected newspaper, deals with an interesting question: Should people be judged primarily by their outward behavior rather than their inward potential?

What does this brief description add up to? Clearly Gaylin seems to be an informed authority in psychiatry, thus his observations on the mind and behavior should be respected (which doesn't mean you have to agree with his position). The article was published in a newspaper known for its high standards, but it was published over twenty years ago, which suggests that it might be dated.

With the author's background in mind, read the essay and the handwritten observations based on the suggestions in "Five Tips for a First Reading." Remember, the observations were jotted down for the reader herself, not for an audience. Even though they are often elliptical, maybe even cryptic, they clearly represent a reader's encounter with a serious essay.

A bit of advice: Since book margins are seldom wide enough for extensive notes, place a sheet of paper along the side of the margin and jot down your notes on the paper. Indicate paragraphs by number in your notes to help you track your observations.

## ❦ Willard Gaylin ❦

# *What You See Is the Real You*

What does title mean? Do clothes represent the "real" "person"? A smiling face?

A priest who established a home for "wayward" boys. Why does G. call him "financier"?

It was, I believe, the distinguished Nebraska financier Father Edward J. Flanagan who professed to having "never met a bad boy." Having, myself, met a remarkable number of bad boys, it might seem that either our experiences were drastically different or we were using the word "bad" differently. I suspect neither is true, but rather that the Father was appraising the "inner man," while I, in fact, do not acknowledge the existence of inner people. 1

*Key point? Inner vs outer person.

Interesting Conflict suggested: Doctor of the mind (psychoanalyst) vs Doctor of the soul (priest) — Inner/outer Conflict. Sexist language — "person" written '70's.

Since we psychoanalysts have unwittingly contributed to this confusion, let one, at least, attempt a small rectifying effort. Psychoanalytic data —which should be viewed as supplementary information—are, unfortunately, often viewed as alternative (and superior) explanation. This has led to the prevalent tendency to think of the "inner" man as the real man and the outer man as an illusion or pretender. 2

While psychoanalysis supplies us with an incredibly useful tool for ex- 3

Idea: motives are not moral or immoral—behavior is!

plaining the motives and purposes underlying human behavior, most of this has little bearing on the moral nature of that behavior.

Analogy: points out that the underlying structure is less important than the outward appearance.

Like roentgenology, psychoanaly- 4
sis is a fascinating, but relatively new, means of illuminating the person. But few of us are prepared to substitute an X-ray of Grandfather's head for the portrait that hangs in the parlor. The inside of the man represents another view, not a truer one. A man may not always be what he appears to be, but what he appears to be is always a significant part of what he is. A man is the sum total of *all* his behavior. To probe for unconscious determinants of behavior and then define *him* in their terms exclusively, ignoring his overt behavior altogether, is a greater distortion than ignoring the unconscious completely.

* repeats key idea established above.

Writer: ~~Cat's Cradle~~ & ~~Slaughter-house Five.~~ Dark humor. Supports view: a person is what a person does.

Kurt Vonnegut has said, "You are 5
what you pretend to be," which is simply another way of saying, you are what we (all of us) perceive you to be, not what you think you are.

Example supporting idea that people are what they do, not what they think. Good people have/has bad thoughts.

Consider for a moment the case 6
of the ninety-year-old man on his deathbed (surely the Talmud must deal with this?) joyous and relieved over the success of his deception. For ninety years, he has shielded his evil nature from public observation. For ninety years he has affected courtesy, kindness, and generosity—suppressing all the malice he knew was

within him while he calculatedly and artificially substituted grace and charity. All his life he had been fooling the world into believing he was a good man. This "evil" man will, I predict, be welcomed into the Kingdom of Heaven.

Contrasting example: bad person has good thoughts.

7 Similarly, I will not be told that the young man who earns his pocket money by mugging old ladies is "really" a good boy. Even my generous and expansive definition of goodness will not accommodate that particular form of self-advancement.

*Echoes point of view.

8 It does not count that beneath the rough exterior he has a heart—or, for that matter, an entire innards—of purest gold, locked away from human perception. You are for the most part what you seem to be, not what you would wish to be, nor, indeed, what you believe yourself to be.

Tone: ironic, sounds as if he is exhausted by hearing the same old tales. Spare me! a plea to stop.

9 Spare me, therefore, your good intentions, your inner sensitivities, your unarticulated and unexpressed love. And spare me also those tedious psychohistories which—by exposing the goodness inside the bad man, and the evil in the good—invariably establish a vulgar and perverse egalitarianism, as if the arrangement of what is outside and what inside makes no moral difference.

Alludes to 1 Saint — Francis

10 Saint Francis may, in his unconscious, indeed have been compensating for, and denying, destructive, unconscious Oedipal impulses identi-

2. Conqueror—Attilla

cal to those which Attilla projected and acted on. But the similarity of the unconscious constellations in the two men matters precious little, if it does not distinguish between them.

3. Nazi—Hitler only behavior can be judged.

I do not care to learn that Hitler's heart was in the right place. A knowledge of the unconscious life of the man may be an adjunct to understanding his behavior. It is *not* a substitute for his behavior in describing him. 11

Only behavior causes joy or suffering.

The inner man is a fantasy. If it helps you to identify with one, by all means, do so; preserve it, cherish it, embrace it, but do not present it to others for evaluation or consideration, for excuse or exculpation, or, for that matter, for punishment or disapproval. 12

Restates key idea/central point.

Echoes the title.

Like any fantasy, it serves your purposes alone. It has no standing in the real world which we share with each other. Those character traits, those attitudes, that behavior—that strange and alien stuff sticking out all over you—*that's the real you!* 13

Final Notes—

Purpose: to show that people should be judged by what they do, not by what they think.

Strategy: argues the point, sets up opposites, Good vs bad; inner vs outer. Problem—no shades of grey between black and white.

Style: Tone is ironic at times and authoritarian. He seems to be shaking a finger at the reader. Sexist use of Pronouns &x "Man".

After the first reading you should be familiar with the essay's content and purpose. You should have a sense of the writer's strategies and the tone. You also should have jotted down general impressions and responses to the essay. In other words, you've left your markings. Now you're ready to return to the territory.

## *Five Tips for Rereading*

Before reading the essay, review your notes and reconsider the title: Did it accurately reflect the content or purpose of the essay? Did it embody the tone? If not, how does it function? Now you're ready to begin. Once again you should read with pencil in hand, ready to explain or change your previous observations and make new ones. Remember, too, that you're attempting to read like a writer examining another writer's techniques—that is, you're reading with the critical eye.

### *1. Review the Beginning and End*

The beginning and end are critical sections. The opening paragraphs usually will, directly or indirectly, establish the purpose of the essay. Sometimes the purpose will be immediately clear, as it is in Gaylin's "What You See Is the Real You." Clearly, his purpose is to argue that people should be judged by the sum total of their behavior, not by their "unconscious determinants." The end will often restate, or in a narrative, dramatize the purpose. Gaylin's essay ends by restating the purpose, thus making his intent unmistakable.

### *2. Reread with the Purpose in Mind*

The purpose can serve as a beacon that will guide you as you reread the essay. Knowing the purpose will clarify the strategies the writer uses to achieve that purpose. For example, two of Gaylin's examples become clear on a rereading—the X-ray of

Granddad's head and the anecdote about who suppressed his "evil" nature and lived a good life.

### 3. Examine the Style

You'll already have a sense of the style from the first reading. Now's the time to pin it down. Notice the selection of words. Pay close attention to the shapes and rhythms of sentences. Underline phrases that embody the tone. Gaylin has the tone of a highly educated but authoritative writer. He sometimes uses erudite vocabulary, which might be difficult for the average reader—"roentgenology," referring to the use of film in X-rays; "overt behavior," referring to action; and "exculpation," referring to having been declared innocent of a crime. He also makes several literate allusions, which demonstrate his wide knowledge and which he expects his reader to know—Father Edward J. Flanagan, founder of a home for wayward boys he called "Boys Town"; Kurt Vonnegut, the author of such satiric novels as *Cat's Cradle* and *Slaughterhouse Five*; the Talmud, the Jewish book of spiritual laws; Francis of Assisi, who renounced his wealth and founded the Franciscan order, and was made a Saint in 1228.

Sometimes his authoritative tone sounds exasperated—"I will not be told that the young man who earns his pocket money by mugging old ladies is 'really' a good boy." At other times he sounds ironic—"Even my generous and expansive definition of goodness will not accommodate *that particular form of self-advancement*," which is an ironic way to say, "mugging." Always he sounds pompous, especially when he uses "man" and all its pronouns to refer to people in general.

### 4. Linger on Interesting Passages

Pause while rereading to examine passages that catch your attention. What's an interesting passage? That, of course, is a judgment call. Perhaps a passage will be an interestingly structured paragraph or a series of paragraphs. Later, you might want us use it as a model to emulate in your writing practice.

For example, in one interesting paragraph, Gaylin makes a point through; metaphor that is, he makes a brief comparison between dissimilar subjects.

> Like roentgenology, psychoanalysis is a fascinating, but relatively new, means of illuminating the person. *But few of us are prepared to substitute an X-ray of Grandfather's head for the portrait that hangs in the parlor.* The inside of the man represents another view, not a truer one. A man may not always be what he appears to be, but what he appears to be is a significant part of what he is. A man is the sum total of *all* his behavior. To probe for unconscious determinants of behavior and then define *him* in their terms exclusively, ignoring his overt behavior altogether, is a greater distortion than ignoring the unconscious completely.

The metaphor comparing an X-ray and a portrait to the concept of the inner and outer person makes the abstract discussion concrete, that is, something that the reader can visualize and that reflects Gaylin's point.

### *5. Record Your Closing Impressions*

Your impressions may be related to purpose, strategy, and style. They may also include your associations with the essay: Does it bring to mind any experiences you've had? Do you associate it with something you've learned or something you've seen or heard about? Does it stir a specific meaning in you? And, perhaps most important, does it call to mind any ideas you might like to explore in writing?

The guidelines for a first reading and for rereading give you a procedure to follow when reading any essay or written work that deserves your attention. In *The Longwood Reader* we've also added questions on purpose, strategy, and style after each essay—all written to help you understand an author's methods. Your instructor might assign the questions and ask you to respond to them in writing. But if they are not assigned, we suggest you review them on your own as an independent way to become a more critically minded reader.

# 2

# *The Writing Process*

The situation has changed. The writer–reader roles are reversed. You are no longer the reader. You are now the writer, in this case the essayist. The writer–reader contract still applies to the situation, but now you must meet the obligation you have to your reader, which is to compose an understandable work. You, in other words, will be using writing conventions to guide your reader, and your reader will rely on these conventions to decipher your essay. Bluntly, you, like every successful writer, must fulfill your half of the writer–reader contract—you must use what you have learned from reading with a critical eye.

Remember, essays are relatively brief nonfiction compositions. Essays concentrate on a single aspect of a topic. Effective essays always have a well-defined purpose, use clear strategies to achieve their purpose, and employ an appropriate style. Sometimes essays, especially in college writing, integrate research, but usually they tend to be personal, embodying a writer's voice and analyzing or interpreting a subject from a writer's personal perspective. Keep in mind, however, that even though an essay embodies a writer's perspective, it is not necessarily about the writer. Instead, essays gain their personal character from the individual writer's insights and values as manifested in the discussion.

## *Rhetorical Patterns*

Although a writer may combine several rhetorical patterns in an essay (each discussed in a separate chapter in this text), one of nine common patterns will usually dominate the overall work, depending on the subject and the writer's approach.

1. *Description* captures the sense of an experience. Description renders what something looks like, its characteristics, the impressions it makes. (See Chapter 3.)
2. *Narration* relates events. Narration shows what happened, when and where it took place, who was involved, and why it happened. (See Chapter 4.)

3. *Examples* illustrate ideas. Examples offer typical cases and concrete instances to develop a point. (See Chapter 5.)
4. *Comparison and Contrast* presents similarities and differences. Comparison relates how something is like something else. Contrast relates how something is different from something else. Combined, the pattern relates how two things are both alike and different. (See Chapter 6.)
5. *Cause and Effect* identifies reasons and results. Cause and effect explores why something happened, what the consequences are, how something is related to something else. (See Chapter 7.)
6. *Process Analysis* explains experience step by step. Process analysis shows how something happens, how it works, how it is made. (See Chapter 8.)
7. *Classification and Division* establishes categories. Classification and division sorts things by their common components and characteristics. (See Chapter 9.)
8. *Definition* limits meaning. Definition explains what something is, what it means, how it is alike and different from other members in its class. (See Chapter 10.)
9. *Persuasion and Argument* convinces readers. Persuasion and argument attempts to move people to action or to convince them to change their opinions. (See Chapter 11.)

Writers use rhetorical patterns to help them make writing choices. Imagine, for a moment, that you have been assigned an essay on advertising. Once you decide on your essay's purpose, you will then decide on which rhetorical pattern would best help to achieve the purpose; thus the pattern dominates the essay's development. For example, if your purpose is to relate consumer stories, you would choose narration. If your purpose is to reveal the subliminal messages in advertising images, you would choose description. If your purpose is to explain the similarities and differences between two advertising campaigns, you would choose comparison and contrast. Or if your purpose is to convince a reader that film directors should stop including "disguised" cigarette advertisements in movies, then you would choose argumentation. No matter which choice you make, your final essay will reflect the rhetorical conventions of the pattern you choose, thus helping the reader trace the development of the essay's central purpose.

## *Essay Structure*

Once you decide on a dominant rhetorical pattern and are ready to write, you can employ another conventional essay strategy by structuring your essay with a clear introduction, discussion, and conclusion.

Introductions are composed of one or more paragraphs, all designed to introduce an essay's central purpose. An introduction should arouse a reader's curiosity, provide appropriate background information, and clarify any questions the reader might need to have answered in order to understand the central purpose. An introduction should also display the thesis, which is a clear, limited statement of the essay's general purpose. You might think of the thesis statement as a direct promise to a reader, a promise that clearly sets the course for the rest of the essay.

Discussions fulfill the promise made in the thesis. An essay's discussion should be several paragraphs in length, all organized by topic sentences that identify subpoints of the thesis statement. The topic sentences should also *echo* the thesis to show the promise is being fulfilled and to rivet the reader's attention to the essay's central purpose.

Conclusions bring an essay to a satisfactory close. At the very least, a conclusion should show that the promise made in the thesis statement has been fulfilled. One point to keep in mind: A conclusion should never apologize for covering the subject inadequately.

Typically, a college essay is between 500 and 1,500 words, but more appropriately the length should be determined by the complexity of the subject and the amount of detailed discussion necessary to support the thesis.

Please don't get the wrong impression. Effective essays are not as mechanically contrived as our brief description might suggest, a fact you can quickly substantiate by thumbing through several selections in this text. Our purpose here, before discussing the process involved in composing an essay, is to emphasize that writers employ a few common conventions to help them meet their part of the writer–reader contract. How well writers use those conventions depends on their skills.

### *A Student Essay for Study*

Now, with this brief description in mind, study the following essay on one aspect of the topic *propaganda*. The student author Lane Williams has the following to say about his essay:

> For me composing an essay is a chaotic activity. Whenever I reread a final draft and it makes sense, I'm always surprised. The development of this essay was especially chaotic. I created it from my own ideas, class notes, and by looking at magazine and television advertisements.
>
> One major problem I had to overcome was to think about an essay in more complicated ways than I had been taught in high school where I learned to write five-paragraph essays. For this project I had too much information to fit into a simple five-paragraph structure, so I needed to work very hard at organization. But once I had all my material gathered, the central purpose emerged and the actual writing process began to organize itself. What is my purpose? I wanted to explain some ways advertisers use propaganda devices to trick us into spending our money. Clearly my essay had to define some important terms, but overall I knew the rhetorical pattern would be dominated by examples.

Now study Williams's essay. After reading the essay through once, reread it along with the marginal notes, which point out some of the conventional strategies Williams uses.

*Title suggests subject-advertising*

## Who's Come a Long Way, Consumers?

*Opens with a dramatic Catalogue*

*Explains how abstract terms work*

*Glittering generalities named and linked to other propaganda devices, which will be discussed*

No doubt you have seen advertisements such as these: A savings and loan company claiming that an investment in a retirement account is an investment in "the American way"; a food producer associating its cake mix with "motherhood"; a men's clothing manufacturer relating its *roughware* to "manhood." "The American way," "motherhood," and "manhood" are all abstract concepts that elicit emotional responses in our psyches. Many other concepts create a similar response: "liberty," "freedom," "constitutional rights," "free speech," "the democratic process," "the right to life," "freedom of choice." All these words suggest a virtue or quality most Americans hold dear. Sometimes their use is designed to trigger an unexamined response that bypasses intellectual analysis. Among people who manipulate this kind of language these virtue words are called glittering generalities. Glittering generalities are often used to gain unquestioned support for a cause or product. In fact, glittering generality is one among several potent propaganda devices.

*Opening sentence sets up propaganda definition*

*Begins to define propaganda*

*Introduces Key word, "trick"*

When most of us think of propaganda, we think of politicians or dictators, people who want to control the masses. We might even think of official or political lying. But propaganda does not have to be used to perpetuate lies. It can also be used for positive ends, such as moving people to protect endangered species or rain forests or voting rights. Nevertheless, whether in support of a good cause or a bad cause, the propagandist appeals to a target audience's emotion rather than to its powers of reason, unlike an educator who explores all sides of an issue. In other words, the propagandist works by tricking us, not by informing us.

*This paragraph links propaganda to advertising; the general purpose begins to emerge*

For good or evil, propaganda pervades our daily lives, helping to shape our attitudes on thousands of subjects. Nowhere is the propagandist more active than in the advertising business. For example, why is investing in a retirement account an investment in "the American way?" Or how can buying a cake mix confirm a sense of "motherhood?" Or how can a feeling of "manhood" be gained from wearing a brand of clothes? When examined critically, these advertisements have no relationship between the service or product they offer and the glittering generalities associated with them. They are merely an advertiser's obvious attempts to manipulate consumers by appealing to emotion rather than to reason. Glittering generality is only one propaganda device. Advertisers use several other propaganda devices to trick consumers into buying their products.

*Ties back to glittering generalities*

*Thesis statement makes a promise to the reader. Reuses key word, "trick"*

*Topic sentence presents one subpoint of thesis Bandwagon briefly defined*

Bandwagon is another technique advertisers use to trick consumers into buying their products. Through bandwagon, they urge people to buy a product because it is popular—that is, because everyone is doing it together. This call to "get on the bandwagon" appeals to the strong desire to join the crowd rather than be an outsider. A recent television advertisement for Plymouth's mini van uses bandwagon to motivate car buyers. The advertisement features a group of people working out in a gym. A message over the loudspeaker announces, "There is a Plymouth mini van parked in the street." The message is clear: If you want to be part of the crowd, buy a mini van. A recent magazine advertisement for Cuervo Gold tequila also makes use of bandwagon. The advertisement features sixteen young party people either sitting on the edge or standing in an empty

*Example 1*

*Example 2*

swimming pool. They are clearly enjoying themselves, each holding a margarita and toasting the viewer outside the advertisement. Clearly, a Cuervo Gold party is fun. The message is that the consumer can join the party. How? Quite obviously, buy Cuervo Gold . . . and hop on the bandwagon.

*This brief paragraph links bandwagon discussion with next subpoint, testimonial*

The Cuervo Gold tequila advertisement also features a prominent television personality—Dennis Miller. Miller stands in the group's center and also holds a Cuervo margarita. His presence adds prestige to the product, suggesting that if Cuervo Gold is good enough for a celebrity like Dennis Miller, it certainly is good enough for the average consumer. The technique of using a celebrity to sell a product is called testimonial, another method advertisers use to entice consumers.

*Brief definition of testimonial*

*Opening sentence sets up a more detailed discussion of testimonial*

Testimonial is a commonly used advertising ploy. Many celebrities from motion pictures, music, and sports lend (more accurately, sell) the use of their names to pitch products: music performer Michael Jackson for soft drinks, basketball star Michael Jordan for athletic shoes, retired actress June Allyson for adult diapers, comedienne Martha Raye for denture cleaner, and, among advertising's more clever use of testimonial, former Jets quarterback Broadway Joe Namath's classic advertisement for pantyhose. What do these celebrities know about the products they pitch? Probably very little, but advertisers bank on consumers being attracted to products because a celebrity claims to use it. The appeal is to emotion, not to reason.

*Presents a Catalogue of celebrities*

*This paragraph begins with a clear topic sentence and defines "Plain folks" with a brief comparison to testimonial*

Another device advertisers use to trick consumers is plain folks. In one way plain folks is like testimonial. Both involve someone standing up to praise a product, urging consumers to rely on his or her word, not on sound evidence, to make a product decision. But whereas testimonial features a respected celebrity, plain folks features someone "just like ourselves" to promote confidence in a product. Often plain folks takes the form of a dentist praising a toothpaste or a friendly neighbor recommending a brand of coffee or a Little League coach explaining that a detergent is powerful enough to remove grass stains. Of course what advertisers do not reveal is that these are all actors who are paid (just as celebrities are paid) to pitch the toothpaste, coffee, and detergent.

*Examples of "Common folks" who praise products*

A recent advertisement for Solgar Vitamin Supplements features a potent use of the plain folks device. This advertisement features a young attractive working mother, who is obviously a single parent trying to make ends meet. In the middle of the advertisement, she stands behind her son, smiling with her arms wrapped around him in a protective embrace, and looks directly at the viewer. The son, about eight years old, is also smiling and holding on to his mother's arm. Both seem to be healthy and to care deeply for each other. Above the photograph is the phrase "First Things First," suggesting that loved ones come first. Below the photograph, the son is quoted as saying, "You're the most important thing to me, Mom. Please take care of yourself." Featured next to the comment is a bottle of Solgar vitamins. Implicitly, the average working mother and son are testifying to the power of Solgar Vitamins to maintain their health and their loving relationship.

*This opening sentence signals that the "plain folk" discussion will continue*

*An extended example*

Also at work in this Solgar advertisement and in most advertisements, for that matter, is another propaganda device called transfer. Through transfer advertisers at-

*Effective transition into next paragraph*
*Briefly defines transfer*

tempt to lure consumers into buying their products by associating them with something consumers love, desire, or respect. No manufacturer uses transfer more effectively than Philip Morris, Inc. For over two decades Philip Morris has effectively transferred the desire for the rugged cowboy's outdoor life to smoking Marlboro cigarettes. Marlboro advertisements feature images of cowboys herding cattle or riding horses across open spaces. More recently, Marlboro has concentrated less on cowboys at work and more on equipment these Marlboro men use: worn boots, spurs, lariats, saddles—each item designed to remind the reader of a life spent on open prairies with snow capped mountains in the background. And, in case the consumer misses the point, Marlboro advertisements usually include the slogan, "Come to Marlboro Country." How can consumers reach "Marlboro Country?" By lighting up a Marlboro cigarette, of course, thus completing the transfer.

*Example 1*

*Opening sentence connects with previous discussion of transfer*

Philip Morris also makes effective use of transfer in its Virginia Slims magazine campaign. Each advertisement features a beautiful woman staring boldly into the camera. Clearly, she is in charge of her life, the embodiment of the 1990s image of an independent woman. In a box placed in the corner of these advertisements is a contrasting image, a photograph of a woman from an earlier historical period serving a man. An ironic slogan links the two images, "You've come a long way, baby" (ironic because "baby" echoes sexism). Without much analysis the advertiser's ploy here is clear. Philip Morris hopes to entice women into smoking Virginia Slims by transferring a desire for personal independence to its product.

*Example 2 of transfer (echoes title)*

*Conclusion opens with a "question"*

Do these propaganda ploys work? Can advertisers actually trick unwary consumers into buying their products? When

*Emphasizes critical thinking*

*Echoes title "A long way"*

*Ends with a provocative question*

subjected to critical examination, propaganda seems to be obvious perhaps even ludicrous . . . certainly too clumsy to allow any manufacturer to pick a consumer's pocket. But the power of propaganda is emotional. Advertisers use propaganda techniques to operate beneath the level of intellect where images and concepts are not subjected to critical analysis. They work through suggestion, association, image. They seduce and their seductions have taken advertisers "a long way." Why else would they use these propaganda tactics to trick consumers year after year and decade after decade?

Williams's essay is effectively executed. He has established a strong purpose and expressed it in a clear thesis statement, which serves as his promise to the reader. He develops an ample discussion section by arranging his information around subpoints of the thesis statement, thus fulfilling his promise. And his conclusion successfully brings the essay to a close. In other words, Williams has met his part of the writer–reader contract.

Let's now examine the process Williams and other writers follow to create their essays. We don't want to give you the impression that experienced writers sit down and write a perfect first draft—they don't. They struggle with subjects, shuffle rough notes, doodle with outlines, all in an effort to shape their material effectively into finished form. Generally, a finished essay unfolds according to a writer's unique composing methods—that is, the phases of the composing process that begin with finding a subject and end with a final draft.

## *Find a Subject*

"What should I write about?" is an all too familiar question that often signals a writer is blocked. If you find yourself asking this question, you must immediately turn the question to your advantage. Instead of "What should I write about?" ask, "How can I find a subject to write about?" The rephrased question gives you direction. You can stop chewing the pencil eraser and go to work.

Here's how to start.

Begin by keeping this writing principle firmly in mind: You will write your best essays on subjects you know and care about. We urge you, therefore, to examine your own experience for subjects. Look at your interests, your work, your values, your leisure activities. Watch the news, a film, or a television show for ideas. Browse through a newspaper or magazine for subject possibilities. Any of these sources can give you plenty to write about.

You must pursue this search actively. Engage yourself in the process by picking up a pencil and going to work. Try one of the following strategies:

1. *Create idea lists*. Time management experts urge busy people to keep lists of commitments—action lists. Action lists begin as random collections of upcoming events, commitments, or tasks. Once the list is complete, the list maker evaluates the entries, ranks them, and establishes a work schedule. The list provides the person with some clarity and direction for his or her activities.

   An idea list like an action list helps to bring your activity into focus. In this case the activity is writing. You can use an idea list to compile possible writing topics. Begin by setting a minimum time limit—perhaps thirty, forty, sixty minutes—and stick to it. Your goal is to develop a *spontaneous* series of brief entries that capture your ideas and responses to them.
2. *Use a journal*. If you have kept a journal at any time in your life, browse through it for ideas. There is always a good chance that if an entry engages your interest you can develop it into a full essay that will engage a reader's interest.
3. *Record from memory*. If a recent class discussion or lecture stimulated your curiosity or stirred a strong opinion you

hold, record the details you recall. Either the discussion or lecture could inspire an essay.

4. *Browse through current reading material.* Glance through a newspaper or magazine until a subject catches your attention, perhaps merely a headline or an article title. Jot down your responses. A response to an article can make an effective essay, especially if the article ignites a strong value you hold.

Often college writing is initiated by class assignments. At first, you might think an assignment makes the writing task simple, but it usually does not. In fact, an assigned task might be harder to complete than one you generate yourself. It might create a sense of false security by leading you to skip the exploration process and plunge directly into the first draft.

As a way of defending yourself from this mistake, remember a second writing principle: An assignment is not a subject. You must create a subject from the assignment.

For example, consider Lane Williams's essay. He wrote it in response to the following assignment: "In four to five typed pages, discuss the role of propaganda in political or commercial communication." To the experienced writer this assignment is much too large to be addressed successfully in a single essay. It must be placed in a more limited focus, reduced to a manageable subject. So instead of plunging into a first draft without exploring the assignment, he used the assignment wisely. Williams says,

> The assignment was just too broad to cover in a five-page essay. I would have to write about propaganda in politics and advertising. I immediately knew it had to be narrowed to manageable size so I decided to explore the assignment by writing an idea list. I knew if I listed enough of my interests I would eventually find something that would give me more direction.

Williams's idea list took the form of phrases capturing the flow of his thought. He put down whatever came to mind. Later he would judge the entries to see how they related.

Politicians and lying . . .
Campaign propaganda in the presidential race . . .
Local council members and land developers . . .
Advertisements and the consumer . . .
Why do people vote for politicians?
Why do people buy certain products?
How do advertisements get attention?
What propaganda techniques are effective in ads?
How can we protect ourselves from propaganda?
  In political decisions?
  In the marketplace?
I'm the victim of propaganda.
  In voting?
  In buying products?
What do advertisements reveal about consumers?
What does propaganda use reveal about politicians?
Propaganda undermines the democratic process.
Master propagandists—political "spin doctors."

Writing the list helped Williams place his subject in focus. Although no single entry represented a clear subject, he was able to combine several ideas to shape a general subject, the role of propaganda in advertising.

## *Use Prewriting Techniques to Explore a Subject*

You, like all writers, must place your subject in focus and clarify your purpose, often a long and difficult process. The most effective way to start the process is by using prewriting techniques to discover what you know and do not know about the subject.

What is prewriting and how does it work?

Well, prewriting is easy to understand. But first, consider how some writers talk about the mind in relation to writing—a simplified view, but one that will help you understand the writing process.

When discussing how they compose their works, writers often talk of intuition and intellect. They associate intuition with creativity. The creative part of the mind generates ideas, events, and metaphors, the raw material that makes fresh, interesting writing. In contrast, they associate intellect with criticism. The critical part of the mind judges content, organization, and logic, the refined evaluation that makes accurate, coherent writing. Intuition fuels the creative process; intellect guides the critical process. Through the creative process writers *invent* their material; through the critical process they evaluate and organize it for readers.

Both creative and critical abilities are necessary to write successfully. The creative process, however, is less self-conscious than the critical process. As a consequence, prewriting activities use the creative process while restraining the more self-conscious critical process.

### *Freewriting*

Freewriting, or brainstorming, is valuable during any phase of the writing process. Freewriting is a method of free association for generating ideas. Freewriting can help you frame a subject more accurately, generate material, clarify a purpose, and even develop a thesis. But perhaps its most important use is to start the actual writing process.

Once you have a subject, no matter how tentative, set aside some time for a writing session (as we advised you to do when compiling a memory list). While freewriting, abandon the urge to criticize yourself. Instead the creative process take over, especially if you have a little voice in your head that automatically judges your writing efforts.

To direct the process, write your subject at the top of the page. Then go at it, writing down everything that comes to mind. Associate one idea to another. Don't judge your ideas or shut them out. Often the unexpected will present itself, ideas connecting to ideas in ways you could have never planned. Don't be concerned with the technical aspects of writing—grammar, punctuation, sentence structure, or logic. Merely enter the creative flow of your own thought, excluding the critical process. Remember—this draft is for your eyes only, not for your reader's. It is a rough map of your thought process, a chart of your mental meanderings, not a paper to be graded. About his freewriting process, Lane Williams says,

> Freewriting helps me gain perspective on my subject. The process releases a great deal of information I have somehow stored in my memory. By free writing, that is, merely following the pattern of my thought, I gain access to that information. The hard part, of course, is sorting through all that I have written.

The examination of freewriting can be difficult. You will quickly discover that much of your freewriting will not help you develop an effective essay, such as obvious observations, clichéd thinking, dead-end ideas, stalled musings, odd digressions, but other parts will be valuable—"hot" ideas you can pursue. Evaluating the material in freewriting involves the intellect more directly; that is, now apply the "critical eye" to decide what material will help develop an effective paper and what will not.

While reading your prewritten draft, mark passages that seem to be hot leads for further exploration. Once you have the leads, you can use them to start another freewriting session to generate more new material.

Freewriting will also reveal what you do not know about a subject. This knowledge can direct your search to the library, to class notes, to discussions with relatives, friends, or teachers, to any number of sources that will be helpful. All these activities will help define a general purpose and generate material for your final essay.

## *Sort and Group Your Material*

The freewriting is complete. Now is the time to sort and group your ideas in a logical arrangement. Here, one of two common strategies will help—clustering and informal outlining.

### *Clustering*

Clustering visually shows the relationship between ideas. Often freewriting appears to create a hodgepodge of unrelated material, but if you rearrange the material around the central purpose that emerges from the free written draft, then you can begin to see connections. In one sense, a cluster brings order to the creative chaos.

Begin a cluster in a simple fashion. Write what you have determined to be your essay's purpose in the center of the page. Draw a circle around the purpose. As you examine the prewritten draft, arrange major ideas around the central purpose in "orbits" connected by lines. Also circle the major ideas. As you discover (or develop) ideas related to the major ideas, create another orbiting system. All this is done in single words or brief phrases. Remember you can always return to the prewritten draft to examine the full entry. Through this process, you are simply dividing and subdividing your roughly drafted material, becoming more specific as you isolate facts, opinions, examples, and specific details that could be used effectively to develop your purpose.

Here is a tip: Be prepared to create more than one cluster. Clustering, like freewriting, often generates even more material. We also suggest you develop your cluster on a large piece of drawing paper, or at least be prepared to tape several sheets of notebook paper together to accommodate all your material.

Lane Williams created a cluster from his prewritten material. Examine part of it reproduced on page 40.

### *Informal Outlining*

The second approach to sorting and grouping your material involves arranging the major ideas related to your purpose under broad headings in an informal fashion. The complexity of the outline depends on how you like to work. It may include only the broadest heading or it may include broad headings followed by more specific points, even phrases that capture specific information.

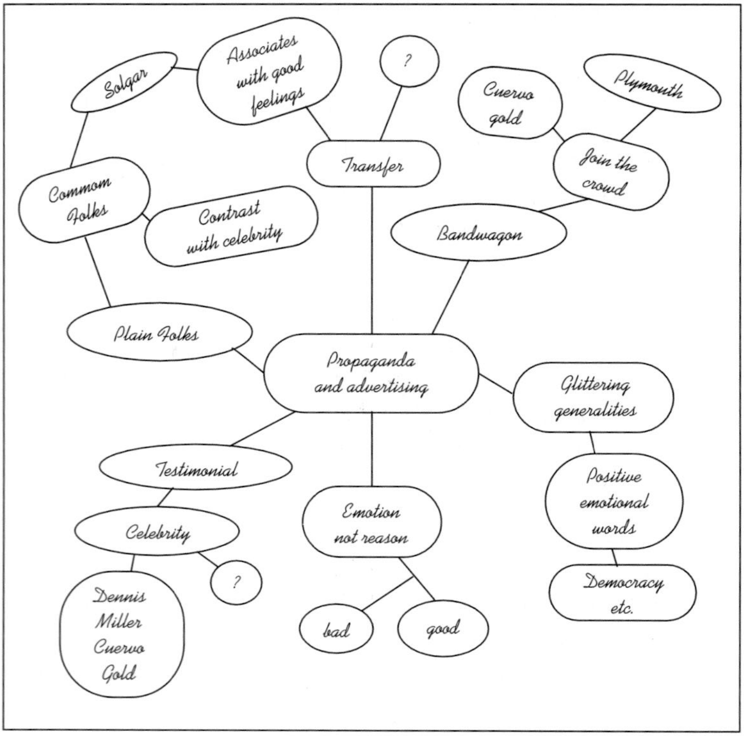


*Figure 2–1*

You may create several drafts of informal outlines, each becoming more specific. Gradually drafts of informal outlines may suggest your essay's final development pattern.

If you find yourself dissatisfied with your outlines, rather than spending a great deal of time rewriting them, photocopy them and then cut and paste the photocopies until you have one that satisfies you.

The following example shows part of the detailed informal outline Lane Williams developed from his cluster. About this informal outline Williams writes,

I wasn't happy with just clustering. Eventually I have to develop a sense of my material as I imagine it will unfold in the essay. I'm not obsessed with detail or perfection at this stage of the writing process, but I do need to create a strong impression of how the development takes place. The cluster didn't give me the space to add the detail I wanted. For me, an informal outline is a strong preliminary plan that helps me to see where I need to delete information or develop more information.

<u>Propaganda and advertising</u>
<u>What is it</u>: appeals to emotion
rather than reason.
Use for good and bad causes.

<u>Methods</u>:
(1) Glittering Generalities: Positive words to
stir strong values.
"Motherhood"
"Manhood"
"American Way"

Develop a list of G. G.

(2) Bandwagon: Invites consumers to
join the crowd.
Plymouth minivan – Health Club
Cuervo Gold – Yuppie Crowd standing in an
empty pool, drinking margaritas

Link to Testimonial – Dennis Miller

(3) Testimonial: Celebrities praise products
Dennis Miller/Cuervo Gold – two methods
working together.
Develop extensive list of celebrities...
include old Joe Namath ad for
laughs.

Figure 2–2

## *Develop a Thesis Statement*

Always keep in mind that any essay you write unfolds through a process. Although throughout this discussion we describe the writing process as if it follows a predictable pattern, in actual practice you will find it does not always do so. An essay evolves, often changing its direction as you encounter new information and uncover new relationships in your material. Nevertheless, if there is a point where an essay's final direction and shape become clear, it is at the point where you form a clear thesis statement.

A thesis statement embodies your essay's central purpose. It is the statement that all the following paragraphs support, argue for, or illustrate. The thesis statement should be broad enough to serve as an umbrella for the discussion that follows it while at the same time it should limit the discussion to a manageable size. In other words, the thesis statement marks the territory of the essay.

Pause for a moment to consider how useful a clearly stated thesis statement is for writers and readers.

For writers, a thesis statement articulates the central purpose and keeps the essay unified. Once you have a clear thesis statement, you will find it easier to make decisions about what to include and exclude. If you have trouble developing your thesis statement, then you know you must seek more information to flesh out your content.

For readers, a thesis statement tells where the essay is headed. A clearly phrased thesis statement helps them put your discussion paragraphs in perspective. Imagine the burden you place on a reader if you develop several paragraphs but fail to provide the perspective to understand their purpose. A thesis statement provides that perspective.

### *Limit the Thesis*

What are the characteristics of an effective thesis statement? An effective thesis statement, usually expressed in a single sentence, limits the central purpose of your essay. If you were writing about crime, for example, and tried to develop this thesis statement, "Crime is destroying the social fabric of America," you would soon discover the impossibility of your task. This thesis statement is much too broad for a three-or four-page essay. At best you could only develop a few general—very general—observations, all unsupported by specific detail.

This thesis statement could be limited, however. Writers limit their thesis statements in two ways. First, they limit the subject. As it now stands, the subject of this thesis statement is "crime." But "crime" covers a large territory—murder, robbery, swindles, shoplifting, and so on. If the writer were to concentrate on one aspect of crime, then the subject would be limited. For example, "Violent crime is destroying the social fabric of America" or "Gang crime is destroying the social fabric of America" or "Crime against children is destroying the social fabric of America."

These thesis statements are still too broad, much too broad for a brief essay even though the subjects are now narrow. Another way to limit a thesis is to narrow the predicate part, in this example the part that reads "is destroying the social fabric of America." "The social fabric of America" covers a great deal of territory, but if the writer were to write about his or her direct experience, this might be narrowed to a city, town, or neighborhood. After narrowing the predicate part, the thesis statement might read, "Violent crime is destroying the social fabric of my neighborhood" or "Gang crime is destroying the social fabric of my hometown" or "Crime against children is destroying the social fabric of schools."

These thesis statements are now manageable. A writer could develop them from personal observation, police reports, and newspaper articles.

### *State a Thesis Precisely*

An effective thesis statement is always stated precisely and lends itself to development. Vague language and overly general assertions misguide your reader. Use precise language, not fuzzy words, to phrase your thesis statement.

*Not*: The study of people in prisons is fascinating.

*But*: Psychological studies of imprisoned murderers reveal that the death penalty is no deterrent to killers.

The second example, phrased precisely in specific language, leaves no room for the reader to be confused about the purpose of this paper.

Finally, an effective thesis statement makes a promise to the reader to fulfill the essay's purpose, a promise the writer must keep or risk writing an unsuccessful essay.

For example, consider the following three thesis statements:

> If a thug has the firepower, holding up a mom and pop grocery store is a simple process.

*The promise*: to explain the easy process of robbing the innocent.

> Although there were over 450 arrests in my neighborhood last year, crime can be categorized into three groups.

*The promise*: to classify local crime.

> Some people think the political buzz phrase "law and order" has something to do with putting criminals behind bars, but in reality it has a racist definition.

*The promise*: to redefine the political phrase "law and order."

Lane Williams developed his thesis statement in several phases. He says,

> By the time I had finished freewriting and grouping my material, I had a pretty clear idea of my general purpose. I wanted to expose how some advertisers misguide consumers. After I developed more material by reviewing class notes and finding some typical advertisements, I decided it was time to formulate a more specific purpose, that is, a thesis statement that would keep me on track.
>
> I began with this statement: "The public needs to become aware of how advertisers deceive them." Sounds

lame, doesn't it? At least that's what I thought. Just too vague. I rephrased it: "The public needs to know how advertisers use propaganda to deceive them." I didn't like this either. What was I, the public guardian? Mr. District Attorney? The statement made me feel pretentious. But when I had written the word "propaganda," my mind started firing. The assignment called for a discussion of propaganda so the word had to be in my thesis. Moreover, the word stirred up my anger. I hate to be tricked by people, and bottom line, that's what advertisers do—they trick people. So now I was on to my thesis, which finally became "Advertisers use propaganda devices to trick consumers into buying their products." I wasn't sure this statement would be phrased this way in my final draft, but I knew it would help me arrange my paper—and announce what to expect to the reader.

## *Develop a Formal Plan with a Reader in Mind*

If you have not done so already, now is the time to imagine your reader. The reader you conceive in your imagination will influence choices you make about the content and vocabulary of your essay. If you were separately to report the events at an accident scene to a friend, your parents, a police officer, an insurance agent, or as a witness in court you would select different details and words for each occasion. In speech you make this adjustment quite easily. In writing you have to give this adjustment some thought. It is essential, therefore, that before you get too far into the writing process, you imagine who your reader will be so you can determine how much he or she might already know about your subject, which will help you decide what to include and exclude.

For example, although Lane Williams was writing a paper for a critical thinking course, he decided his reader would be the "average consumer," one who did not know the meaning of propaganda and would not understand the way advertisers use it. This decision and the formulation of his thesis statement meant that he was ready to develop a more formal plan for his essay.

One method to plan your essay is to create a formal outline. Whereas an informal outline will help you sort and group prewriting around ideas, a formal outline will help you see the final arrangement of the material. A formal outline will include the thesis statement, the subpoints, and various levels of detail depending on the subject's complexity.

A formal outline can be written in topic or sentence form. The main items will be identified by roman numerals, the first sublevel of items by capital letters, the second sublevel by arabic numerals, the third sublevel by lowercase letters, the fourth sublevel by arabic numerals enclosed in parentheses, and the fifth sublevel by lowercase letters enclosed in parentheses. All letters and numbers at the same level are indented to fall directly under one another.

I. ____________________

    A. ____________________<br>
    B. ____________________<br>
        1. ____________________<br>
        2. ____________________<br>
            a. ____________________<br>
            b. ____________________<br>
                (1) ____________________<br>
                (2) ____________________<br>
                    (a) ____________________<br>
                    (b) ____________________

II. ____________________

You will rarely need all six levels, especially for college essays. But notice that each level is a division of the level above it. Therefore, there must be two items at every level because, logically, a topic cannot be divided into one item. You cannot have an A without a B or a 1 without a 2, for example. Of course, there may be more than two items at any level.

Also keep in mind that all items at the same level must be

expressed in parallel grammatical structure and the first word in each item must be capitalized. The following example is a formal topic outline for "Who's Come a Long Way, Consumers?"

Thesis: Advertisers use propaganda devices to trick consumers into buying their products.

I. Propaganda appeals to emotion not reason
   A. Glittering generalities
   B. Good and bad propaganda
   C. Advertisers and propaganda

II. Bandwagon says join the crowd
   A. Plymouth mini van
   B. Cuervo Gold and bandwagon

III. Testimonial features celebrities
   A. Cuervo Gold and Dennis Miller
   B. All-star list
      1. Michael Jackson for soft drink
      2. Michael Jordan for shoes
      3. June Allyson for diapers
      4. Martha Raye for denture cleaner
      5. Joe Namath for pantyhose

IV. Plain folks features the common people
   A. Common folks list
      1. Dentist for toothpaste
      2. Neighbor for coffee
      3. Coach for detergent
   B. Solgar Vitamin Supplements

V. Transfer associates with good feelings
   A. Marlboro cigarettes and the outdoors
      1. Cowboys
      2. Western gear
   B. Virginia Slims and female independence
      1. Today's woman
      2. Yesterday's woman

VI. Advertising works

Developing a formal outline forces you to arrange your material for a reader. Throughout the process of constructing a formal outline, you will draw on the informal outline you constructed earlier, your prewritten material, and any other material you collected. About his outlining process, Williams says,

> This is the first outline I have written. Before I finished I had my rough outline, prewriting, class notes, and the advertisements I planned to use as examples in a pile on my desk. I kept moving through the material, thinking how it should be arranged. I ended up with some surprises.
>
> For instance, I had planned to use glittering generalities as the topic for a discussion paragraph, but while outlining, I realized I didn't have enough material for a full discussion. As a result, I used it in the introduction.
>
> I decided to discuss transfer last because I thought my readers would be familiar with the Marlboro and Virginia Slims advertisements, and I also found them to be the most interesting.
>
> All in all, I discovered that writing a formal outline forced me to think through the actual essay before I started my first full draft. Looking back on the experience, I believe it saved me time overall.

Too often beginning writers want to skip formal planning, yet it is an important part of the writing process, one that will force you to figure out the final arrangement of your material.

## *Develop Parts of the Essay*

At this point in the writing process you should be aware of your reader and the conventions you will use to guide your reader. In other words, you are consciously trying to meet the writer–reader contract by seeing and shaping your material with a "critical eye."

To start, reread the final draft of Lane Williams's essay (pp.

28–33). Study how the material from his formal plan was developed into a full essay. Clearly, his initial strategy was to arrange his material in a traditional fashion—that is, to structure his essay with a clear introduction, discussion, and conclusion.

### *Write the Introduction*

The introduction presents the thesis statement. Actually, "presents" is not dramatic enough. Let's say the introduction "showcases" a thesis statement, because to showcase is to display in a way the reader cannot miss. Remember your thesis statement is your promise to the reader. Don't let the reader miss the promise.

Also remember the introduction is your chance to grab the reader's interest, but too often student writers waste their introductions. They offer sweeping generalizations. They write aimless, dull comments. They end the sequence with an ill-phrased thesis statement. You should make your introductions do much more. Professional writers tend to use one of six strategies to begin their essays.

1. Relate a dramatic anecdote;
2. Expose a commonly held belief;
3. Present surprising facts and statistics;
4. Use a provocative quotation or question;
5. Create a dramatic narrative example;
6. Define a key term.

Any of these is an effective strategy to begin your essay—if it fits your purpose. That's the key to writing an effective introduction: It must grow from the essay's purpose and lead to the thesis statement.

Often introductions are only a paragraph long and end with the thesis statement. But an introduction can be one, two, three, or any number of paragraphs in length. We suggest, however, that it be no longer than a fifth of the length of your entire essay, a reasonable length which should be determined by the complexity of your purpose.

For example, the introduction Lane Williams wrote for his final draft of "Who Has Come a Long Way, Consumers?" is three paragraphs long and ends with the thesis statement. About his final introduction Williams says,

> I expected to write a single-paragraph introduction, a convention I had learned in high school. I imagined that introduction would formally define propaganda and end with the thesis statement that claimed advertisers use propaganda devices to trick consumers into buying their products.
>
> But while planning the introduction I saw I would have to cover too much territory. I would have had trouble making the leap from the general use of propaganda to advertising. So I decided to integrate my material on glittering generalities, which was skimpy anyway, into the introduction while preparing my reader for the thesis statement, which now comes after paragraph 3.

Whatever approach you choose for your introduction, remember it is an integral part of the essay. It should grow from your purpose, arouse a reader's interest, and showcase the thesis statement, usually by placing it in the closing sentences of the introduction.

### *Write the Discussion*

The discussion develops the thesis statement. Discussion paragraphs present the subpoints and supporting detail necessary to convince your reader that the thesis statement is reasonable. In other words, the discussion keeps the promise implied in the thesis.

To be effective, discussion paragraphs should follow three paragraph conventions—they should be unified, coherent, and well developed.

**Unity.** Discussion paragraphs are unified when the information they present is clearly related to the main idea in the paragraph, which some writers shape in the form of a topic sentence.

For example, consider the following paragraph from Olivia Vlahos's *Human Beginnings*. Vlahos opens with a clearly stated topic sentence, "Nearly all living creatures manage some form of communication," and follows with a series of examples, each clearly related to the topic sentence.

*Topic sentence sets a direction*

*Series of examples clearly relates to the main idea*

*Nearly all living creatures manage some form of communication.* The dance patterns of bees in their hive help to point the way to distant flower fields or announce successful foraging. Male stickleback fish regularly swim upside-down to indicate outrage in a courtship contest. Male deer and lemurs mark territorial ownership by rubbing their own body secretions on boundary stones or trees. Everyone has seen a frightened dog put his tail between his legs and run in panic. We, too, use gestures, expressions, postures, and movement to give our words point.

Keep in mind also that the main idea or topic sentence is one step in fulfilling your promise to the reader. It identifies one subpoint of the thesis and supports that subpoint. For example, Lane Williams begins this process in his first discussion paragraph. He clearly relates his opening topic sentence to his thesis statement, which maintains that advertisers use propaganda devices to trick consumers into buying their products.

*Williams' topic sentence establishes the subpoint "bandwagon."*

Bandwagon is another technique advertisers use to trick consumers into buying their products. Through bandwagon, they

*Brief definition of "bandwagon"*

urge people to buy a product because it is popular—that is, because everyone is doing it together. This call to "get on the bandwagon" appeals to the strong desire to join the crowd rather than be an outsider.

*Bandwagon example*

A recent television advertisement for Plymouth's mini van uses bandwagon to motivate car buyers. The advertisement features a group of people working out in a gym. A message over the loudspeaker announces, "There is a Plymouth mini van parked in the street." The message is clear: If you want to be part of the crowd, buy a mini van.

*Bandwagon example 2*

A recent magazine advertisement for Cuervo Gold tequila also makes use of bandwagon. The advertisement features sixteen young party people either sitting on the edge or standing in an empty swimming pool. They are clearly enjoying themselves, each holding a margarita and toasting the viewer outside the advertisement. Clearly, a Cuervo Gold party is fun. The message is that the consumer can join the party. How? Quite obviously, buy Cuervo Gold . . . and hop on the bandwagon.

While this paragraph is unified because the entire discussion relates to its topic sentence, it also adds to the overall unity of the essay because the topic sentence refers back to the thesis statement. Echoing the thesis statement in topic sentences is an effective strategy to use throughout an essay. The technique reminds the reader of your thesis and shows how the subpoints are connected.

Coherence. Guide your readers smoothly and logically from one sentence to another. Don't let them stray from the direction you establish in the paragraph's opening. If they do stray, you risk losing their attention. When a paragraph flows smoothly and logically, the paragraph is coherent; that is, the main idea advances from sentence to sentence in a well-constructed verbal web.

You can create coherence in your paragraphs in three conventional ways.

1. By repeating and rephrasing key words and concepts;
2. By using pronouns to refer to key nouns in previous sentences;
3. By using transitional expressions that guide your reader through a paragraph.

Poet and novelist Erica Jong repeats a key word to create coherence in the following paragraph from "The Artist as Housewife." The paragraph's main idea deals with a poet's problem of creating a personal voice in her work. Jong then associates with *authenticity* in the second sentence. She then repeats or rephrases the key word *authenticity* throughout the paragraph.

*Writer maintains coherence by effectively repeating "Key word"*

The main problem of the poet is to raise a voice. We can suffer all kinds of kinks and flaws in a poet's work except lack of authenticity. Authenticity is a difficult thing to define, but roughly it has to do with our sense of the poet as a mensch, a human being, an author (with the accent on authority). Poets arrive at authenticity in very different ways. Each poet finds her own road by walking it—sometimes backward, sometimes at a trot. To achieve authenticity you have to know who you are and approximately why. You have to know yourself not only as defined by the roles you play but also

*Rephrase this "Key idea"*

as a creature with an inner life, a creature built around an inner darkness. Because women are always encouraged to see themselves as role players and helpers ("help-mate" as a synonym for "wife" is illuminating here), rather than as separate beings, they find it hard to grasp this authentic sense of self. They have too many easy cop-outs.

In the following paragraph, conservationist Cleveland Amory repeats a key noun—coyotes—and uses pronouns to refer back to it.

*Coherence is created by the effective use of Key nouns and their pronouns.*

The coyote's only hope lies in his cleverness. And stories of coyotes outwitting hunters are legion. Coyotes will work in teams, alternately resting and running to escape dogs set upon them. They have even been known to jump on automobiles and flat cars to escape dogs. And they have also successfully resisted bombing. Lewis Nordyke reports that once when a favorite coyote haunt in Texas became a practice range for bombing, the coyotes left—temporarily. Soon they were back to investigate and found that the bombing kept people out. They decided to stay. Meanwhile, they learned the bombing schedule and avoided bombs.

Conscious and careful repetition of key words and ideas is a subtle way to keep a paragraph coherent. A more direct strategy is to use transitional words and phrases. In "Who's Come a Long Way, Consumers'?" Lane Williams uses overt transitions effectively in one paragraph.

*Williams uses overt transitions to create coherence*

A recent advertisement for Solgar Vitamin Supplements features a potent use of the plain folks device. This advertisement features a young attractive working mother, who is obviously a single parent trying to make ends meet. In the middle of the advertisement, she stands behind her son, smiling with her arms wrapped around him in a protective embrace, and looks directly at the viewer. The son, about eight years old, is also smiling and holding on to his mother's arm. Both seem to be healthy and to care deeply for each other. Above the photograph is the phrase "First Things First," suggesting that loved ones come first. Below the photograph, the son is quoted as saying, "You're the most important thing to me, Mom. Please take care of yourself." Featured next to the comment is a bottle of Solgar vitamins. Implicitly, the average working mother and son are testifying to the power of Solgar Vitamins to maintain their health and their loving relationship.

No matter what strategy you use to create coherence, remember the purpose is to direct the reader's attention as he or she reads from sentence to sentence.

**Development.** Beginning writers often ask the question, how long should a paragraph be? Paragraph length depends on several considerations: the complexity of material, the rhetorical method, and the length of preceding and following paragraphs.

But most importantly, a paragraph should be developed enough to do justice to the main idea.

Well-developed paragraphs might contain examples, definitions, comparisons, causes, effects, facts, statistics—all presented in enough detail to make a paragraph several hundred words long, or a paragraph might serve as a transition between subpoints of a thesis statement and be only a sentence or two long. When a paragraph becomes exceptionally long, writers will often separate the material into two or more paragraphs to ease the reading process, even though the information amplifies the main idea in a single subpoint. For example, Williams breaks up several exceptionally long paragraphs in "Who's Come a Long Way, Consumers?" as the following example illustrates.

*Topic sentence introduces transfer*

*First extended example of transfer*

Also at work in this Solgar advertisement and in most advertisements, for that matter, is another propaganda device called transfer. Through transfer advertisers attempt to lure consumers into buying their products by associating them with something consumers love, desire, or respect. No manufacturer uses transfer more effectively than Philip Morris, Inc. For over two decades Philip Morris has effectively transferred the desire for the rugged cowboy's outdoor life to smoking Marlboro cigarettes. Marlboro advertisements feature images of cowboys herding cattle or riding horses across open spaces. More recently, Marlboro has effectively transferred the desire for the rugged cowboy's outdoor life to smoking Marlboro cigarettes. Marlboro advertisements feature images of cowboys herding cattle or riding horses across open spaces. More recently, Marlboro has concentrated less on cowboys at work and more on equipment these Marlboro men use: worn boots, spurs, lariats, saddles—each item designed to remind the reader of a life spent on open prairies with snow-capped mountains in the background. And, in case the consumer misses the point, Marlboro advertisements usually include the slogan, "Come to Marlboro Country." How can consumers reach "Marlboro Country?" By lighting up a Marlboro cigarette, of course, thus completing the transfer.

*Opening sentence continues the main idea*

Philip Morris also makes effective use of transfer in its Virginia Slims magazine campaign. Each advertisement features a beautiful woman staring boldly into the camera. Clearly, she is in charge of her life, the embodiment of the 1990s image of an independent woman. In a box placed in the corner of these advertisements is a contrasting image, a photograph of a woman from an earlier historical period serving a man. An ironic slogan links the two images, "You've come a long way, baby" (ironic because "baby" echoes sexism). Without much analysis the advertiser's ploy here is clear. Philip Morris hopes to entice women into smoking Virginia Slims by transferring a desire for personal independence to its product.

*Second extended example of transfer*

In the opening sentence, Williams sets up the transition from one paragraph to another by referring to the previous discussion of Solgar Vitamin Supplements. He then develops the main paragraph idea with a brief definition of the transfer device. He follows with the analysis to two extended examples to show transfer at work in advertisements. But since the examples are long, he breaks the paragraph into parts, yet both parts amplify a single main idea—that is, advertisers use the transfer device to trick consumers. Williams is careful to begin the second paragraph with an opening statement that clearly shows the discussion of transfer is continuing, even though he has begun a new paragraph.

While composing an essay, you might discover that you need

more information to develop an effective paragraph. You have three actions to take. First, you can return to your freewriting draft for an idea. Second, you can actually develop more freewriting. Third, you can consult outside sources for more information. The process of inventing and acquiring material continues until the final draft is complete.

### *Write the Conclusion*

Too often beginning writers treat their conclusions in a perfunctory manner—a couple of general statements about the subject and a rapid "That's all, folks" to close. Experienced writers, in contrast, use a different strategy based on the simple principle that readers remember best what they read last. They, therefore, treat their conclusions as a challenge, one that demands skill and concentration. Generally, writers use one of four common strategies to close their essays:

1. Review the subpoints and restate the essay's thesis statement.
2. Recommend a course of action.
3. Offer a prediction based on the discussion.
4. Present an appropriate quotation or anecdote that leads a reader to reflect about the subject.

Keep in mind that a conclusion must flow logically from the essay. If it does not, it will merely seem tacked on.

### *Create a Title*

Titles are not afterthoughts, a phrase hastily typed at the top of the page before rushing to class. A title actually begins the essay. Titles should suggest the general subject and serve as an invitation to read the essay.

The best time to compose a title is after you have written your essay. Only then will you know the complete content. The title should be brief but interesting and may be taken directly from the essay. Often, however, it will echo a thought that runs through the essay. About his title, "Who's Come a Long Way, Consumers?" Lane Williams says,

> I usually have a hard time thinking of titles, but if I reread the essay or parts of it enough, a title will eventually come to mind . . . persistence, I guess, is my method.
>
> The title "Who's Come a Long Way, Consumers?" is my way of reworking the Virginia Slims slogan. I hope it is read ironically, since my essay's purpose is to make unaware consumers conscious of ploys advertisers use to get their hard-earned cash.

So how should you proceed in composing a title? Well, we can offer no clear guidelines because the process involves more intuition than logic. But once you have a title follow this rule: Never underline or place quotation marks around your own title. Use quotation marks or underlining for other people's titles, not yours.

## *Revise Your Essay for Style and Clarity*

Once you have a well-structured essay in hand, you can begin the revision process that will lead to the final draft. You might think each phase of the writing process refines the material for the final draft . . . and each does . . . but the final draft is the only part of the process your reader will see. We suggest, therefore, that you approach revision with care.

During the early phases of the composing process, we mentioned that you should imagine your reader. Now the reader becomes a major part of the process, as if he or she is sitting on your shoulder as you make revision decisions.

As you reread your essay with a eye toward revision, consider its style (see p.9). Style, as you probably recall, has to do with word selection, sentence length and variety, and tone. For college papers, we suggest you employ a plain style that communicates your purpose clearly and directly. You should write in standard American English, which is taught in schools and used in mainstream magazines and newspapers. In most writing situations, standard English is appropriate.

Standard American English can be formal or informal. Informal writing is characterized by common expressions taken from spoken English and makes use of contractions such as "don't," "can't," "won't," and "could've," which are contractions of "do not," "cannot," "will not," and "could have." Formal written English seldom uses contractions and avoids other characteristics of informal writing, such as abbreviations and the personal point of view. About his style decision, Lane Williams says,

> I tried to conform to my instructor's view of English, which leans toward the formal. You may have noticed for instance that I avoided using some common abbreviations. I wrote out "television" and "advertisement" instead of using the more common "TV" and "ad." I also avoided using contractions, which helps create a more formal tone. I did, however, address my reader as "you" now and then and used the personal pronouns "we" and "our" several times, decisions some instructors might discourage.

To further develop your sense of style, consult "A Guide to Editing and Revising Sentences" (pp. 709–735). We offer the Guide along with the following tips with the hope that they will help you meet your bargain with the reader.

## *Five Tips for Revision*

1. Reread to see if your purpose is clear. Examine the thesis statement. Does it suggest a rhetorical pattern? Does it make a promise to the reader?
2. Reread to determine if your strategy is effective. Does your paper have an introduction, a discussion, and a conclusion? Have you organized your discussion paragraphs around topic sentences or main ideas? Do you use transitions to connect paragraphs?

3. Reread the discussion paragraphs. Are they clearly unified? Are they coherent? Are they adequately developed?
4. Reread for style. Have you selected words for accuracy? Are the sentences varied? Is the tone consistent?
5. Reread to correct technical errors. Is the grammar correct? Are punctuation marks used correctly? Is the spelling correct?

## *Peer Review*

Having other class members review your work can be helpful before completing a final draft. We all have blind spots, but when several sets of eyes examine our essays, the blind spots will usually be revealed.

Some writing instructors organize formal peer-review sessions, that is, they require their writers to submit early drafts of their essays for other class members to comment on. Often peer review, such as this, is done in established writers groups whose members work together throughout the semester. Other times instructors reform writers groups every few weeks to give everyone in class a chance to work together. In either case, writing instructors usually set aside some class time for the groups to complete their reviews. For these peer review sessions, they will generally provide review guidelines based on the particular requirements of the assignment, thus establishing clear directions for the evaluation process.

If your instructor does not require formal peer review, you and other classmates may wish to form an informal writers group to help revise early essay drafts. Or you may wish to merely work with another class member to review each other's work. But no matter if you work in a formal or in an informal writing group or in pairs, the goal will be the same: to see your work through another reader's eyes, for often an essay that may be perfectly clear to you will be confusing to a reader who has intellectual and emotional distance from the material.

### *Peer Review Responsibilities*

You have two responsibilities during the peer review process: To receive advice and to give advice in a collegial manner.

Receiving Advice. Writing isn't easy, and sometimes it's in the flawed piece of writing that writers place the most emotional energy. When someone criticizes it, then, quite naturally, the tendency is to become combative, willing to defend each paragraph, each sentence, each word against what may be perceived as an attack. Of course, when writers look at responses to their work unemotionally, it is easy to see reviewer comments are offered as suggestions for improvement, not challenges. So relax when receiving advice—judge the observations by what you are trying to accomplish and how well your effort is executed.

Once your work has been reviewed, read all written responses with care. Although they may be brief, they may still be valuable. Moreover, you can follow up written responses to a draft by asking the reviewer questions to help clarify or amplify any written advice. Be sure to consider all oral responses and note the advice you feel will help improve your draft. If a group member asks you a question, answer, but don't feel you have to justify the decisions you made during the writing process. Most importantly, don't become defensive. Always remember that your reviewers will be evaluating the effectiveness of a piece of writing, not your character.

While revising should you incorporate suggestions? To do so is your decision. Sometimes the responses will conflict, often reflecting a reviewer's inexperience or misconceived information. Other times the responses will agree, giving you a clear direction for revision. Remember, only you can decide which responses are appropriate and which are inappropriate. The responsibility for a final draft is all yours, not your group's nor your partner's.

Giving Advice. When reviewing another writer's work, keep in mind that your task is not to rewrite the draft but to respond as a reader and offer advice for improvement. It's up to the writer to write the next draft.

What kind of advice should you offer?

First, know the assignment. Each draft you read will be written in response to a writing assignment. To respond intelligently, you must be familiar with the assignment. The chances are you will be writing an essay for the same assignment, but if not, then it's your job to know what the assignment calls for and keep the requirements in mind when reviewing a writer's early draft.

Second, apply your knowledge of writing strategies when giving advice. You will have studied essay strategies, both as we will present them in the following chapters and as your instructor will present them in class. These strategies will help you make accurate observations and give you a vocabulary to describe your observations in a way the writer will be able to understand.

Third, offer specific advice. Identify a draft's strengths and weaknesses as specifically as you can. Vague and general observations don't help a writer. For example, the following two responses represent the extremes. One is ineffective and one is effective.

*Ineffective Response*

> Good work. I like the way it reads, even though it isn't clear. Also good use of words. I like it. Keep it up.

Clearly, this is an ineffective response. Why? Perhaps the reviewer fears hurting the writer's feelings? Or perhaps he has not read the assignment the writer is responding to? Or perhaps he's just plain lazy? Who knows? Still this fact remains: The student offers only vague, "feel-good" responses that avoid giving specific advice to improve the writer's draft.

*Effective Response*

> Discussion paragraph 2 is particularly strong. Using a question as a topic sentence followed by an answer clearly sets the pattern that follows: "How many situation comedies

> currently run on television? Only three, but they are broadcast under 23 different titles." This paragraph opening is effective, but the three categories that follow overlap—you should fix them.
>
> One problem though is unity. You seldom refer to your thesis in topic sentences. To fix it wouldn't take much. I suggest you add a key word to your thesis, such as "dysfunctional" and work it, or synonyms for it, into your topic sentences. For example, "The dysfunctional family lurks behind all the antics in "I Love Lucy." Just a suggestion. Take it or leave it, but you still need to improve unity one way or another.
>
> Another strong point is your use of active verbs: "shrieked," "maul," "cavort" and so on. They all add specific detail—good.

This reviewer's response is effective. She identifies strengths and weaknesses in specific language. Where she can, she gives advice to help the writer revise. She does all this specifically and clearly.

Fourth, don't be distracted by surface errors when giving advice. Do not spend your time correcting grammar, punctuation, and mechanics. Tell the writer that the errors exist, but remember it's the writer's job to proofread carefully and correct surface errors. Instead, concentrate on the larger elements.

### *Five General Questions to Guide Peer Review*

In order to stay on track, use the following five questions to guide your review:

1. Does the draft reflect the concepts presented in the assignment?
2. What is the dominant purpose and is the organization logical?
3. At what points is the draft confusing?
4. Is the draft adequately developed? Does it need more information or examples?
5. What is the draft's main strength? Weakness?

The first step in the review process is usually done in writing, then the reviewer will discuss the written review with the writer.

### *Five Guidelines to Discuss a Review*

Always respond sensitively. Most beginning writers have no experience submitting their work for peer review. They may misconstrue genuine advice for criticism. To avoid sounding critical, make objectively descriptive comments instead of subjectively evaluative comments. Keep in mind that your responsibility is to help other writers, not to criticize them for their mistakes. When discussing your responses with a writer, keep in mind the following guidelines.

1. A review session should be a dialogue not a debate;
2. Ask questions that might help you develop a clear understanding of the writer's goals;
3. Take notes while reading a draft and use them to discuss the draft's strengths and weaknesses. Emphasize the strengths, but remember the writer needs to know the weaknesses;
4. Make suggestions for improvement related to the writer's intent;
5. Close your response by summarizing ways the writer can improve the draft.

Remember, the emphasis is on improvement—both for the writer as a writer and for the reviewer as a reader.

# 3

# *Description*

## *Capturing Sensory Details*

## *The Method*

To describe is to create a picture with words—the people we meet, the places we visit, the conversations we hear, the infinite number of things we encounter. Description, like narration, is often associated with imaginative literature: children's tales, short stories, and novels. In fiction, narrative events provide a story's bones; description adds flesh to the skeletal structure, helping a reader to imagine the narrative events: "The wind rattled the windows . . . a tall figure wearing a cape emerged from the darkness . . . a pasty white face . . . black hair plastered like a swimmer's cap to his head . . . red lips curled in a sneer . . . the air smelling of rotting meat. . . ." For a descriptive passage to be effective, fiction writers know they must involve their readers' senses to create a reaction to the words. This requirement also applies to essayists who use description as a dominant essay pattern. They, too, must involve a reader's senses—that is, make their readers see, hear, smell, feel, and taste.

### *Sight*

*The streets boiled with shoppers . . .*
*His sunburned face was grim, heavily lined, and ringed with a gray beard . . .*
*Flames lashed the sky . . .*

### *Sound*

*The breath rasped from his lungs . . .*
*Water trickled from the faucet in a steady beat . . .*
*The silence was broken by clicks of forks against plates and the crunching of lettuce . . .*
*The soft lilt of voices carried across the river . . .*

### *Smell*

*The streets smelled of ripe fruit and straw . . .*
*The aroma of curry floated above the cooking pots . . .*
*The perfume was full of musk . . .*

*His breath, laced with garlic and onions, could stop a bloodhound . . .*

### Touch

*The fur, soft and silky, touched my skin . . .*
*Sharp pebbles covered the path . . .*
*The cold shower felt like a gust of Arctic air . . .*
*His fingers said the wound was gaping . . .*

### Taste

*The potion had a sharp, coppery flavor . . .*
*She held the bite of sweet melon in her mouth, then began to chew, the juice, like rich syrup, trickling down her throat . . .*

Beyond the specific senses is a source that writers also use to involve their readers in a descriptive passage. It might be called a writer's "impression" of an experience, his or her own reaction or perception. Or more simply, a writer's *feelings*.

### Feelings

*The air was fresh, cool, and clean, as I walked up the trail, feeling as if I had been reborn . . .*
*Around and around the park the motorcyclists buzzed like deadly black bees, and I was afraid to move . . .*
*I feel happy when I am curled up in bed with a good book . . .*

## Strategies

When reading with a critical eye, study the techniques writers use to involve your senses. Remember that serious writers calculate each detail in a descriptive passage, shaping the words to touch a circuit in your imagination. Study this passage from

*Teaching a Stone to Talk* by naturalist and essayist Annie Dillard. Dillard describes a jungle encampment by appealing to our senses of sight, touch, sound, and smell. She closes by expressing her feelings about the site.

> It was February, the middle of summer. Green fireflies spattered lights across the air and illuminated for seconds, now here, now there, the pale trunks of enormous, solitary trees. Beneath us the brown Napo River was rising, in all silence; it coiled up the sandy bank and tangled its foam in vines that trailed from the forest and roots that looped the shore.
>
> Each breath of night smelled sweet, more moistened and sweet than any kitchen, or garden, or cradle. Each star in Orion seemed to tremble and stir with my breath. All at once, in the thatch house across the clearing behind us, one of the village's Jesuit priests began playing an alto recorder, playing a wordless lyric, in a minor key, that twined over the village clearing, that caught in the big trees' canopies, muted our talk on the bankside, and wandered over the river, dissolving downstream.
>
> This will do, I thought. This will do, for a weekend, or a season, or a home.

Dillard describes a concrete scene full of details directly perceived by the senses. But writers don't limit their descriptive passages to that which can be perceived. Often they describe abstract experiences, such as love, hate, joy, or anger. But to fire a reader's imagination, they must describe the abstract in concrete words. Anger might be described as "a fire in the blood." In this passage from *Dispatches*, a collection of essays about the Vietnam War, Michael Herr captures the fear that comes when an enemy-filled jungle suddenly goes silent. Notice how Herr uses concrete words to describe the abstract and weaves his feelings and earlier experiences into the descriptive fabric.

> There were times during the night when all the jungle sounds would stop at once. There was no dwindling down

> or falling away, it was all gone in a single instant as though some signal had been transmitted out to the life; bats, birds, snakes, monkeys, insects, picking up on a frequency that a thousand years in the jungle might condition you to receive, but leaving you as it was to wonder what you weren't hearing now, straining for sound, one piece of information. I had heard it before in other jungles, the Amazon and the Philippines, but those jungles were "secure," there wasn't much chance that hundreds of Viet Cong were coming and going, moving and waiting, living out there just to do you harm. The thought of that one could turn any sudden silence into a space that you'd fill with everything you thought was quiet in you. It could even put you on the approach to clairvoyance. You thought you heard impossible things: damp roots breathing, fruit sweating, fervid bug action, the heartbeat of tiny animals.

### *Subjective and Objective Description*

Descriptive writing is likely to be either subjective or objective. The passage above from Herr's *Dispatches* is subjective. Herr describes a personal encounter with fear, trying to picture his response to the threat an utterly silent jungle foreshadows in a war zone. Subjective description, like that in Herr's passage, embodies a writer's personal vision. Throughout a passage of subjective description, writers mix personal responses with concrete detail to reflect an attitude toward the experience. For example, in another paragraph from *Teaching a Stone to Talk*, Annie Dillard creates a subjective portrait of village life in an Ecuadorian rain forest.

> We would eat chicken that night in the village, and rice, yucca, onions, beets, and heaps of fruit. The sun would ring down, pulling darkness after it like a curtain. Twilight is short, and the unseen birds of twilight wistful, uncanny, catching the heart. The two nuns in their dazzling white habits—the beautiful-boned young nun and the warm-faced old—would glide to the open cane-and-thatch schoolroom in darkness, and start the children singing. The children

> would sing in piping Spanish, highpitched and pure; they would sing "Nearer My God to Thee" in Quechua, very fast. (To reciprocate, we sang for them "Old MacDonald Had a Farm"; I thought they might recognize the animal sounds. Of course they thought we were out of our minds.) As the children became excited by their own singing, they left their log benches and swarmed around the nuns, hopping, smiling at us, everyone smiling, the nuns' faces bursting in their cowls, and the clear-voiced children still singing, and the palm-leafed roofing stirred.

Here, Dillard has mixed personal responses with concrete detail to create an idyllic portrait of village life—unseen birds are "uncanny, catching the heart"; two benevolent nuns—one young, one old—lead the children in song until they become overwhelmed with joy and hop from their benches to swarm playfully around the nuns, still laughing and singing. Clearly, Dillard has colored these descriptive details to reflect her emotional view of the scene.

In contrast to subjective description, objective description renders a subject in a straightforward, literal way. In objective description, writers withhold their personal attitudes and let the concrete details speak for themselves. For example, in the following paragraph from *Voices in the Mirror*, photographer Gordon Parks creates an objective portrait of a slum called a *favela* where 700,000 impoverished *flavados* live.

> Billowing clouds blanketed Mount Corcovado as we approached the favela the following morning. Suddenly the sun burst through, silhouetting Cristo Redentor, the towering sculpture of Christ with arms extended, its back turned against the slopes of Catacumba. The square at the entrance to the favela bustled with hundreds of favelados. Long lines waited at the sole water spigot. Others waited at the only toilet on the entire mountainside. Women, unable to pay for soap, beat dirt from their wash at laundry tubs. Men, burdened with lumber, picks and shovels and tools important to their existence threaded their way through the noisy

throngs. Dogs snarled, barked and fought. Woodsmoke mixed with the stench of rotting things. In the mist curling over the higher paths, columns of favelados climbed like ants with wood and water cans on their heads.

Unlike Dillard, Parks does not mix his responses with concrete detail. Instead he presents his subject objectively, allowing readers to draw their own conclusions. Purely objective writing is rare in essays with description as the dominant pattern. It is found mainly in scientific reports and encyclopedias. Of course, we find degrees of subjectivity and objectivity in most descriptive essays, as your reading will confirm.

### *Dominant Impression*

To create an effective description, you might think writers do nothing more than record all they perceive. They do much more. As a critical reader, keep in mind that descriptive writing is not a haphazard activity. With so much detail available for any description, writers must select descriptive details with care and shape them with precision to achieve a **dominant impression**.

In subjective description, selecting detail to create a dominant impression is even more critical than in objective description. Writers must not only select but also embellish descriptive details to create the impression they want. When describing a desert, a writer might want to show that the land is hostile: "the harsh sunlight reflecting from the bleached sand like needles plunging into the hiker's eyes." Describing a politician, a writer might want to show him to be untrustworthy: "his face heavily lined from years of calculating behind closed doors, his eyes skipping around the crowd like those of a criminal about to be exposed." Writers seldom directly state the dominant impression they wish to create; they suggest it.

Consider this passage from Gretel Ehrlich's "A Season of Portraits." Ehrlich, who is an essayist, a novelist, and a Wyoming rancher, describes the dry summer of 1988, when raging fires consumed much of Yellowstone National Park forests. In this passage she concentrates on the wind, suggesting that it is a wind from hell, savage and ghostly, perhaps even isolating her as souls are isolated in a mythical underworld.

> A breeze stiffens. Gusts are clocked at forty-five, sixty, eighty-five miles per hour. Rainless thunderclouds crack above, shaking pine pollen down. *La bufera infernale*—that's what Dante calls winds that lashed at sinners in hell. I decide to go out in the infernal storm. "This is hell," a herder moving his sheep across the mountain says, grinning, then clears his parched throat and rides away. Wind carries me back and forth, twisting, punching me down.
>
> I'm alone here for much of the summer, these hot winds my only dancing partner. The sheep and their herder vanish over the ridge. I close my eyes, and the planet is auditory only: tree branches twist into tubas and saxes, are caught by large hands that press down valves, and everywhere on this ranch I hear feral music—ghostly tunes made not by animals gone wild but by grasses, sagebrush, and fence wire singing.

Once writers decide on a dominant impression and select the appropriate details to suggest it, they must arrange the details in an effective order. Often a structure will become visible during the writing and revision, one that will be unique for that passage. Ehrlich arranges the passage above in two parts: the world she sees and the world she hears, which are clearly separated when she writes, "I closed my eyes." She continues by suggesting that the wind plays the branches of trees like musical instruments and creates ghostly music by rushing through grasses, sagebrush, fence wire. By shutting her eyes, and yours as a sensitive reader, she transforms the world into a mysterious place.

### *Arrangement of Details*

Although you will find no strict formulas for arranging descriptive details, writers do, however, follow some general principles. In visual description, a writer will usually structure the details in the way that the eye would record them; that is, by spatial arrangement—from left to right, right to left, near to far, far to near, center outward. A writer might begin with a broad picture and narrow to the particulars, like a film opening with a panoramic view of a landscape or city and gradually moving into the scene, finally focusing on one specific image.

To describe a person, a writer might begin with a general descriptive statement: "She looked as if she had stepped from the pages of *Vogue*, a stylish woman," and then move downward from head to toe, "Her hair was the color of straw and cropped short; her neck seemed carved from ivory. . . ." Or this writer might begin by describing an unusual physical feature and work from there: "Her nose didn't fit her stylish appearance: it was a bit long and bent slightly to the left, as if it had stopped a boxer's left cross. Otherwise, she was unflawed. . . ." As you read descriptive passages, keep in mind that writers have many ways in which to organize a description. Critical readers examine writers' varied ways of structuring descriptive details and apply the techniques.

## *Description in College Writing*

Vivid description supplements all but the most scientifically objective papers, often bringing life to arguments, explanations, and narrations. For example, if you were to take a position against allowing cigarettes to be sold in public vending machines where underage teens can easily buy them, your essay's dominant purpose would be to argue a position, but you might supplement your argument with a vivid description of a lung cancer victim. Or if you wanted to explain the effects of proposed cutbacks in medical aid to the poor, your essay's dominant purpose would be cause and effect, but you might supplement the explanation with a dramatic description of the impact on one impoverished family. If you wanted to write a personal narrative of the events that led to a dramatic insight, you would no doubt use some description to bring alive the people and places in the story. And finally, you might find yourself relying on description to write college reports for such courses as marine biology and art history, where descriptive accuracy will be an important part of the assignment.

### *Guidelines for Writing Description*

1. Select a subject that lends itself to description and examine it closely to decide whether your description will be subjective or objective.
2. Establish the dominant purpose, whether it is a supporting passage in an explanation or argument essay or the dominant method of development in a descriptive report.
3. Develop an extended list of descriptive details, then select the appropriate details from the list and arrange them for effect.
4. Decide on an appropriate structure and then write your essay, using concrete language.
5. Revise your essay, making sure that the dominant purpose is clear.

### *A Student Essay Developed by Description*

In Contemporary Art History, Clarita Tan wrote a descriptive report in response to the following class assignment:

> This assignment will require you to do minor background research and to attend a current art exhibit at a local gallery or museum. Select a contemporary artist currently being exhibited as your subject. Then review representative works on display and describe the artist's method of working.

Now examine Tan's essay. First read it through once, then reread it along with the notes in the margin to see how effectively Tan employs descriptive writing techniques. Finally, read the comments that follow the essay.

*Tan's title suggests the purpose.*

## Imaginatively Chaotic Art

*Introduction gives background—the who, what, where, and when.*

*Closing sentence suggests the purpose.*

The Fine Arts Gallery is featuring George McNeil, a figurative Abstract Expressionist who lived and worked his entire life in New York City. The ten canvases, drawn together from local collections, are stunning for their color and imagery. It is hard to separate color and imagery in McNeil's work, for from pools of purple, orange, and yellow emerge massive faces, airplanes, bodies, and cryptic scrawls. The color and imagery magically emerge from the method McNeil uses to compose his canvases. The result is that viewer's mind is pulled from the real world into a imaginatively chaotic world.

*Tan begins the discussion. Remember she has two tasks to achieve in this assignment:*
*1. describe the artist's working method; 2. review the work that results.*

*Tan begins to present the method by describing the first photograph of the artist in a series of photographs.*

*Notice how Tan arranges her discussion: She begins with an overall impression, then presents descriptive details by moving upward from the boots to the watch cap.*

In the foyer before entering the show, the curator has a series of photographs showing McNeil at work. The first photograph shows him walking into his studio to begin his day. A muted gray light streams from a skylight and McNeil stands in the doorway. At first glance he looks like a retiree getting ready to putter in a garden. He wears heavy work boots, tattered oversized jeans that ride on his hip bones, a chambray shirt open at the neck with a T-shirt underneath, and a watch cap against the morning chill. But unlike a gardener's work clothes stained with soil and grass, McNeil's are splattered with paint. In fact, his boots are so crusted with paint they look like art objects.

*Tan concentrates on two strong physical characteristics—hands and eyes.*

*Dominant impression begins to emerge—McNeil is a mischievous devil.*

Two of McNeil's physical features are dramatically riveting: his massive hands, gnarled from arthritis, that hang at the ends of long arms and his riveting eyes, set in the eighty-five-year-old face, that sparkle mischievously as if they belong to a spirited ten-year-old possessed by a humorous demon.

The next three photographs capture the first phase of McNeil's painting method. Like other abstract expressionists, such as Jackson Pollock, who is noted for his drip and splatter paintings, McNeil begins by stapling his canvas to a plywood sheet and laying it on the studio floor. The first photograph in this sequence shows him in action. McNeil leans over the canvas, dripping paint from a styrofoam cup taken from a nearby table covered with other styrofoam cups running over with paint. The next photograph shows him aggressively slashing the air with a brush as if it were a weapon, paint arcing toward the canvas. The third photograph shows him whipping the brush back, lashing downward, a mischievous grin on his face, his eyes twinkling.

*Strong transition sentence sets up the next photo sequence.*
*Active verbs add action to the artist-at-work portrait.*

*Dominant impression enhanced.*

The final phase of McNeil's method is captured in the fifth photograph. The canvas is now raised upright on the plywood base, a practice that deviates from Pollock's and that of other Abstract Expressionists. Here McNeil stands with his back to the camera and faces the massive canvas. He is hunched forward with an upraised brush held like a symphony conductor's baton, and I think of composer Paul Dukas' "Sorcerer's Apprentice." Indeed McNeil is performing artistic sorcery, for he is creating images that suggest themselves from the splattered configurations on the canvas.

*Tan uses this paragraph to set up the close of the artist-at-work sequence.*

*This allusion reinforces the "artist as magician" impression.*

The images themselves are startling to view, often suggesting the untainted imagination of a child who knows none of technical restraints of someone who is "trained" to paint. Two images affected me the most. "Kennedy Airport" (1989, 78 × 64 inches) is awash in color—patches of blues, reds, purples, yellows, whites, oranges and blacks. McNeil has created the feeling that the viewer is looking down from the sky at a flat surface. Nothing is to scale—a huge head dominates the upper left-hand corner and a smaller head, its mouth agape, fills the lower

*The opening sentences announce a shift from artist's method to his work.*
*First painting: vivid detail creates a sense of chaos, the second impression Tan wants to create. The careful arrangement of detail helps the reader imagine the painting.*

right-hand corner. In between floats a mysterious, cartoonish world—a woman in high heels and net hose, two tiny airplanes, and many spirals and circles. All is aswirl, as if the images have been whipped into the sky by an infernal wind that has brought havoc to the airport.

*Second painting: Description reflects the first—vivid and cartoon-like, the painting suggests chaos.*

"Diablo Disco" (1986, 78 × 64 inches) is as dramatic as "Kennedy Airport." It, too, is alive with clashing colors. The central figure is a massive lime green dancer, whose high-heeled feet touch the canvas bottom and tilted head touches the canvas top. The figure is an abstraction, the lips and eyes smeared on with thick layers of blue, red, purple paint. The hair, a massive mop, shoots upward. It is painted in orange, red, and yellow that suggest flames. In the center of the dancer's body McNeil has painted what appears to be a small city. The dancer herself is surrounded by other dancing figures, all much smaller, but all equally bizarre, perhaps even devilish.

*Tan closes paragraph by reinforcing the impression of devilishness.*

Every canvas in the show is powerful, offering a unique vision of contemporary life. But perhaps the most important element in the show is the opening photographs that reveal this artistic magician at work. Without an understanding of how his paintings evolve from colorful splatters and pools to chaotic figures, I would have merely been distracted by the question, "How does anyone think of these images?" No doubt this question is the wrong one to ask when responding to art.

*Tan ends by reminding the reader of what's been covered and of the two dominant images: artist as creative sorcerer and the chaotic world he creates.*

### *Comments*

A careful reading of Tan's descriptive essay shows that she responds to both parts of her assignment—that is, she describes McNeil's working method and reviews his work. She uses description as her dominant method of development, carefully selecting and describing details from the photographs and paintings to support her interpretation. She organizes this descriptive essay with a clear introduction that provides readers with background information they might need and indicates her purpose. Basically, Tan promises to write an explanation and review of contemporary artist George McNeil's creative method and work, which is currently displayed in the Fine Arts Gallery, to show that it is "imaginatively chaotic." She develops her purpose in a discussion of several paragraphs, separate paragraphs devoted to each important element. She ends with a conclusion that emphasizes her dominant impression of McNeil and his work.

Now let's take a closer look at how Tan effectively employs description strategies to develop the inner-workings of her essay.

**Descriptive Details.** Tan's selection of vivid detail that appeals mainly to the eye will help readers imagine the actual images. Knowing that too much detail will bog down a reader, she selects dominant details to create the image she wants. For example, she concentrates on his hands and eyes to describe McNeil physically.

Two of McNeil's physical features are dramatically riveting:

> his massive hands, gnarled from arthritis, which hang at the ends of long arms and his eyes, set in the eighty-five-year-old face, that sparkle mischievously as if they belong to a spirited ten-year old possessed by a humorous demon.

In contrast, she describes the paintings in bolder strokes, capturing the cartoon quality in McNeil's work, especially when describing "Kennedy Airport" where massive heads, distorted figures, spirals, and circles are all aswirl with color.

> "Kennedy Airport" is awash in color—patches of blues, reds, purples, yellows, whites, oranges and blacks . . . Nothing is to scale—a huge head dominates the upper left-hand corner and a smaller head, its mouth agape, fills the right-hand corner. In between floats a mysterious cartoonish world—a woman in high heels and net hose, two tiny airplanes, and many spirals and circles. All is aswirl, as if the images have been whipped

into the sky by an infernal wind that has brought havoc to the airport.

**Subjective Description.** Like Dillard's paragraphs in the opening discussion, Tan's essay is highly subjective. She infuses the essay with her personal vision of McNeil and his work. This vision emerges in the two *dominant impressions* she creates—that is, McNeil as artistic sorcerer and his world as imaginatively chaotic, two visions reflected by the descriptive detail and by direct commentary she weaves throughout the description. Tan is careful not to overstate these impressions and always supports them with description.

**Arrangement.** Tan has carefully arranged the detail so her reader can easily move through the essay. When describing the photographs of McNeil at work, she presents the images in step-by-step sequence, which is the logical way to proceed. But to describe the two paintings, she had to invent an arrangement since there was no logical pattern to the chaotic imagery. For example, she begins the "Kennedy Airport" description with an overview that moves from large to small details. To describe "Diablo Disco," she begins with the large central figure and then relates other figures to it. Throughout each section, Tan guides her readers by using clear transitional techniques.

**Revision.** Always revise a descriptive essay with an eye on arrangement and detail. For example, when Tan reread the following passage as it was written in an early draft, she knew it was weak.

Three more photographs show McNeil's painting method. Like other abstract expressionists, such as Jackson Pollock, who is known for his drip and splatter paintings, McNeil staples his canvas to a plywood sheet and lays it on the floor. Then he leans over the canvas and drips paint from a styrofoam cup. Nearby is a table covered with other styrofoam cups running over with paint. Mischievously, he then flips paint from a brush he swings at the canvas, all of which speckles the canvas with paint.

She realized she had jammed the photographs together instead of describing them separately. She also felt the paragraph lacked visual action and fell short of the energy McNeil put into his work. As a result of her analysis, she decided to rearrange the description to emphasize the sequence of events. She also decided to add more detail and active verbs to create a sense of movement.

*The next three) Capture the first phase of*

~~Three more~~ photographs ~~show~~ his painting method. Like

other abstract expressionists, such as Jackson Pollock, who

is known for his drip and splatter paintings, McNeil

*begins by stapling*   *laying*

~~staples~~ his canvas~~es~~ to a plywood sheet and ~~lays~~ it on the

*The first photograph in the sequence shows him in action. McNeil*

floor. ~~Then he~~ leans over the canvas ~~and drips~~ paint ~~from a~~

*taken from a nearby*   *dripping out of a*

styrofoam cup ~~Nearby is a~~ table covered with other styro-

*The next*

foam cups running over with paint. ~~Mischievously, he then~~

*photograph shows him aggresively slashing the*

~~flips paint from a brush he swings at the canvas, all of which~~

*air with a brush as if it were a weapon,*

~~speckles the canvas with paint.~~

*paint arcing toward the canvas.*

*The third photograph shows him whipping the brush back, lashing downward, a mischievous grin on his face, his eyes twinkling.*

Once the line editing was done, she typed out the paragraph adding the changes.

The next three photographs capture the first phase of McNeil's painting method. Like other abstract expressionists, such as Jackson Pollock, who is noted for his drip and splatter paintings, McNeil begins by stapling his canvas to a plywood sheet and laying it on the studio floor. The first

> photograph in this sequence shows him in action. McNeil leans over the canvas, dripping paint from a styrofoam cup taken from a nearby table covered with other styrofoam cups running over with paint. The next photograph shows him aggressively slashing the air with a brush as if it were a weapon, paint arcing toward the canvas. The third photograph shows him whipping the brush back, lashing downward, a mischievous grin on his face, his eyes twinkling.

Most of us share senses—sight, sound, smell, touch, taste—and we have feelings. Professional writers know that by evoking

### *Peer Review*

You may be asked to write an essay about one of the readings that follow. Before you meet with your writing group, review this introduction. As you read your group papers, use these general principles of description to help guide your comments.

1. A description should involve a reader's senses of sight, sound, smell, touch, and taste as appropriate for the subject being described.
2. A description should have an appropriate balance between the objective and the subjective. Look for a writer's feelings about what is described as well as the details of the description.
3. Concrete details make a description come alive. A reader cannot feel an experience conveyed only with general statements.
4. Details should be presented within an overall structure, usually, but not necessarily, in some variation of a spatial arrangement.
5. Except for purely objective descriptions, the paper should communicate some dominant impression. Without a dominant impression, what is the purpose of the description?

sensory experience and feelings in their readers' minds, they will enrich the reading experience. Read the essays in the following section. See how the authors evoke the senses; analyze their selection of descriptive details; and examine how they shape descriptive passages to achieve a dominant impression. Take notes as you read, mark an interesting passage, underline a vivid phrase. When you write your own descriptive passages, apply the principles you've learned from reading as a writer. Don't be timid about using a professional writer's passage for a model. The techniques of effective description are universal—available for everyone to use. Professional writers are challenged by the demands of description; certainly you, while developing writing skills, should also feel challenged.

# ❦ Maxine Hong Kingston ❦

*Maxine Hong Kingston was born and raised in a Chinese-American community in Stockton, California, where her parents ran a laundry. She grew up listening to stories about China from her parents and relatives, who were first-generation immigrants. She attended the University of California at Berkeley and currently teaches creative writing at the University of Hawaii. Her stories, essays, and poems have been published in* Ms., The New Yorker, *and* American Heritage. The Woman Warrior: Memoirs of a Girlhood among Ghosts *(1975), Kingston's award-winning autobiography, describes her memories and retells the stories she heard as a child. Her second book,* China Men *(1980), won the National Book Award.*

# *Photographs of My Parents*

*In this selection from* The Woman Warrior, *Kingston looks at much more than photographs. Her searching descriptions of mundane objects reveal some of the deep differences between the culture she grew up in and the China her parents left. In writing of both the familiarity and the strangeness in the photographs of her parents, she reaches into the past to better understand the present.*

*Try to visualize as vividly as you can the differences between the Chinese and the Chinese-American photographs that Kingston describes. Consider how these differences contribute to the essay's central meaning.*

---

Once in a long while, four times so far for me, my mother brings out the metal tube that holds her medical diploma. On the tube are gold circles crossed with seven red lines each—"joy" ideographs in abstract. There are also little flowers that look like gears for a gold machine. According to the scraps of labels with Chinese and American addresses, stamps, and postmarks, the family airmailed the can from Hong Kong in 1950. It got crushed in the middle, and whoever tried to peel the labels off stopped because the red and gold paint came off too, leaving silver scratches 1 that rust. Somebody tried to pry the end off before discovering that the tube pulls apart. When I open it, the smell of China flies out, a thousand-year-old bat flying heavy-headed out of the Chinese caverns where bats are as white as dust, a smell that comes from long ago, far back in the brain. Crates from Canton, Hong Kong, Singapore, and Taiwan have that smell too, only stronger because they are more recently come from the Chinese.

Inside the can are three scrolls, one inside another. The 2
largest says that in the twenty-third year of the National Republic, the To Keung School of Midwifery, where she has had two years of instruction and Hospital Practice, awards its Diploma to my mother, who has shown through oral and written examination her Proficiency in Midwifery, Pediatrics, Gynecology, "Medecine," "Surgary," Therapeutics, Ophthalmology, Bacteriology, Dermatology, Nursing and Bandage. This document has eight stamps on it: one, the school's English and Chinese names embossed together in a circle; one, as the Chinese enumerate, a stork and a big baby in lavender ink; one, the school's Chinese seal; one, an orangish paper stamp pasted in the border design; one, the red seal of Dr. Wu Pak-liang, M.D., Lyon, Berlin, president and "Ex-assistant étranger à la clinique chirugicale et d'accouchement de l'université de Lyon"; one, the red seal of Dean Woo Yin-kam, M.D.; one, my mother's seal, her chop mark larger than the president's and the dean's; and one, the number 1279 on the back. Dean Woo's signature is followed by "(Hackett)." I read in a history book that Hackett Medical College for Women at Canton was founded in the nineteenth century by European women doctors.

The school seal has been pressed over a photograph of my 3
mother at the age of thirty-seven. The diploma gives her age as twenty-seven. She looks younger than I do, her eyebrows are thicker, her lips fuller. Her naturally curly hair is parted on the left, one wavy wisp tendrilling off to the right. She wears a scholar's white gown, and she is not thinking about her appearance. She stares straight ahead as if she could see me and past me to her grandchildren and grandchildren's grandchildren. She has spacy eyes, as all people recently from Asia have. Her eyes do not

focus on the camera. My mother is not smiling; Chinese do not smile for photographs. Their faces command relatives in foreign lands—"Send money"—and posterity forever—"Put food in front of this picture." My mother does not understand Chinese-American snapshots. "What are you laughing at?" she asks.

The second scroll is a long narrow photograph of the gradu- 4
ating class with the school officials seated in front. I picked out my mother immediately. Her face is exactly her own, though forty years younger. She is so familiar, I can only tell whether or not she is pretty or happy or smart by comparing her to the other women. For this formal group picture she straightened her hair with oil to make a chinlength bob like the others'. On the other women, strangers, I can recognize a curled lip, a sidelong glance, pinched shoulders. My mother is not soft; the girl with the small nose and dimpled underlip is soft. My mother is not humorous, not like the girl at the end who lifts her mocking chin to pose like Girl Graduate. My mother does not have smiling eyes; the old woman teacher (Dean Woo?) in front crinkles happily, and the one faculty member in the western suit smiles westernly. Most of the graduates are girls whose faces have not yet formed; my mother's face will not change anymore, except to age. She is intelligent, alert, pretty. I can't tell if she's happy.

The graduates seem to have been looking elsewhere when 5
they pinned the rose, zinnia, or chrysanthemum on their precise black dresses. One thin girl wears hers in the middle of her chest. A few have a flower over a left or right nipple. My mother put hers, a chrysanthemum, below her left breast. Chinese dresses at that time were dartless, cut as if women did not have breasts; these young doctors, unaccustomed to decorations, may have seen their chests as black expanses with no reference points for flowers. Perhaps they couldn't shorten that far gaze that lasts only a few years after a Chinese emigrates. In this picture too my mother's eyes are big with what they held—reaches of oceans beyond China, land beyond oceans. Most emigrants learn the barbarians' directness—how to gather themselves and stare rudely into talking faces as if trying to catch lies. In America my mother has eyes as strong as boulders, never once skittering off a face, but she has

not learned to place decorations and phonograph needles, nor has she stopped seeing land on the other side of the oceans. Now her eyes include the relatives in China, as they once included my father smiling and smiling in his many western outfits, a different one for each photograph that he sent from America.

He and his friends took pictures of one another in bathing 6
suits at Coney Island beach, the salt wind from the Atlantic blowing their hair. He's the one in the middle with his arms about the necks of his buddies. They pose in the cockpit of a biplane, on a motorcycle, and on a lawn beside the "Keep Off the Grass" sign. They are always laughing. My father, white shirt sleeves rolled up, smiles in front of a wall of clean laundry. In the spring he wears a new straw hat, cocked at a Fred Astaire angle. He steps out, dancing down the stairs, one foot forward, one back, a hand in his pocket. He wrote to her about the American custom of stomping on straw hats come fall. "If you want to save your hat for next year," he said, "you have to put it away early, or else when you're riding the subway or walking along Fifth Avenue, any stranger can snatch it off your head and put his foot through it. That's the way they celebrate the change of seasons here." In the winter he wears a gray felt hat with his gray overcoat. He is sitting on a rock in Central Park. In one snapshot he is not smiling; someone took it when he was studying, blurred in the glare of the desk lamp.

There are no snapshots of my mother. In two small portraits, 7
however, there is a black thumbprint on her forehead, as if someone had inked in bangs, as if someone had marked her.

"Mother, did bangs come into fashion after you had the pic- 8
ture taken?" One time she said yes. Another time when I asked, "Why do you have fingerprints on your forehead?" she said, "Your First Uncle did that." I disliked the unsureness in her voice.

The last scroll has columns of Chinese words. The only 9
English is "Department of Health, Canton," imprinted on my mother's face, the same photograph as on the diploma. I keep looking to see whether she was afraid. Year after year my father did not come home or send for her. Their two children had been dead for ten years. If he did not return soon, there would be no

more children. ("They were three and two years old, a boy and a girl. They could talk already.") My father did send money regularly, though, and she had nobody to spend it on but herself. She bought good clothes and shoes. Then she decided to use the money for becoming a doctor. She did not leave for Canton immediately after the children died. In China there was time to complete feelings. As my father had done, my mother left the village by ship. There was a sea bird painted on the ship to protect it against shipwreck and winds. She was in luck. The following ship was boarded by river pirates, who kidnapped every passenger, even old ladies. "Sixty dollars for an old lady" was what the bandits used to say. "I sailed alone," she says, "to the capital of the entire province." She took a brown leather suitcase and a seabag stuffed with two quilts.

---

## *Meaning and Purpose*

1. Have you ever looked through old photographs of your parents or grandparents? What feelings did you have when you looked at them? What questions did you ask? What do the photographs tell you about yourself?
2. What are the contrasts between Chinese and Chinese-American photographs and what do these contrasts suggest about the meaning of "Photographs of My Parents"?
3. In paragraph 3, Kingston writes that "the school seal has been pressed over a photograph of my mother"; in paragraph 7, Kingston describes a small portrait of her mother, "there is a black thumbprint on her forehead . . . as if someone had marked her"; and in paragraph 9, she reports that another photograph has the English words, "Department of Health, Canton," printed over her face. How do these descriptive details work in the essay?
4. What does paragraph 6 reveal about Kingston's father?
5. Discuss the significance of flowers pinned awkwardly on the graduates' dresses.

6. In the first paragraph, what does the "thousand-year-old bat" signify?

## Strategy

1. What is Kingston's general organizational strategy for description? Where are the three transition points at which Kingston moves from one section to another?
2. Identify some descriptions that involve the senses, and some that evoke impressions or feelings. What kinds of figures of speech are they—metaphor, simile, personification, descriptive image?
3. Is this descriptive essay subjective or objective, and how do you know?
4. What impression does Kingston give of the metal tube in the first paragraph? How does her description prepare you for the rest of the essay?

## Style

1. How would you describe the tone of the essay or the narrator's feelings about the contents of the metal tube?
2. Consider the metal tube to be a symbol for Kingston's mother. What qualities does it suggest about her?
3. Kingston uses some medical terms. Be sure you know their meanings: *ophthalmology, pediatrics, gynecology, dermatology, therapeutics* (2).

## Writing Tasks

1. Study Kingston's essay to see how she uses photographs to reveal bits and pieces of her parents' history. Then select photographs of two friends or relatives who have both similar and

opposing character traits. Use the photographs to write a description that reveals their character traits without stating them directly.

2. Describe a significant possession of someone you know, and show how it characterizes the person.

## ❦ Sallie Tisdale ❦

*Sallie Tisdale, born in 1957, earned her nursing degree in 1983 from the University of Portland. A Buddhist, she was Schoenfeldt Distinguished Writer at the University of Portland, and a visiting writer at the University of California, Davis, both appointments in 1992. Among her works are* The Sorcerer's Apprentice: Tales of the Modern Hospital *(McGraw-Hill, 1986),* Harvest Moon: Portrait of a Nursing Home *(Holt, 1987), and* Talk Dirty to Me: An Intimate Philosophy of Sex *(Doubleday, 1994). She has contributed to such periodicals as the* New York Times, Vogue, Esquire, The New Yorker, *and* Outside, *and she is one of* Harper's *contributing editors.* Chicago Tribune *contributor Victoria Jenkins has said that "Tisdale's voice is fluid and richly varied," and Alex Raskin in the* Los Angeles Times Book Review *claimed that "Tisdale joins writers such as Tess Gallagher and Gary Snyder [by] . . . capturing the spiritual in the environment and viewing nature as a kind of secular religion."*

# *Sins of the Flesh*

*This essay is from "Meat," the larger work having appeared in the Summer 1994 issue of* The Antioch Review. *In this part of that larger work, Tisdale moves from accepting unquestioningly the innocence of childhood to recognizing, equally unquestioningly, that things are not always what they seem. Behind every fact, no matter how trivial, is a cause for that fact. This is an initiation essay, when "initiation" refers to a person's awakening to her capacity for independent actions, knowing that those actions can start a series of events.*

*As you read the essay, pay particular attention to Tisdale's describing her actions while she was growing up, maturing both physically and mentally. Also, note how the verb tense changes in several paragraphs, helping to quicken the actions in such a way that you, the reader, feel more deeply involved with them.*

---

I went to the butcher's several times a week as a child. Meat was always in my life. The butcher shop was just down the street 1 from our house, past the old, squat Carnegie Library, the Elks Club, the Groceteria, the bakery, and the big stucco fire department with its long driveway. I loved the Meat Market best; it was orderly, with the hushed front room encased in windows. The floor was golden oak, shiny and clean, facing a horseshoe of white metal display cases curving away like the fabric of space. The air held the scent of clean skin.

I would lay my hot cheeks against the cool glass and gaze at the meat inside: flaccid steaks, roasts, and sausages in neat rows like tile or shingles laid atop one another in patterns of soft red, pink, and maroon. I knew the textures—they were my textures. I liked to examine the down on my legs, the way the irises of my eyes opened and closed when I turned the light above the bathroom mirror off and on, the intricate maze of my belly button. I pulled scabs off and chewed them, and licked the ooze that followed. The rump roast in the glass case made a delicate curve, the curve of my own pliable buttocks. Me, but not me. 2

On panting summer days our basement beckoned, crowded and lifeless, the air cool, musty, and dim after the glazed sunlight. No one would find me there, if anyone cared to look for me. Most of the small basement was filled with a freezer, which my mother, one in a long line of carefully organized women, kept filled as a hedge against catastrophe. (Distantly, my mother's voice at the top of the stairs: "Shut the freezer!"—trailing off into words I didn't bother to hear.) Its heavy white lid seemed to lift from the stiff latch with relief and swing up so that a waft of the freezer's queer fog blew in my face. My taut, tanned skin could breathe again in the damp. There was often a whole side of beef and more in the freezer, broken up among the TV dinners and the quarts of bean soup and ice cream. Each cut was wrapped in white freezer paper and labeled with a red wax crayon in strange abbreviations: "FLK STK 4 #" and "P CHOPS–6." The irregular, heavy packets sat in the cold trough like a haphazard pile of white rocks littered with food. 3

There was never a meal without meat; every afternoon the house filled with the scents of frying oil and roasting flesh. The long dining table leaned toward my father's end, anticipating the 4 heavy cuts on the platter beside him—the pot roast, the round roast beef, the piles of rust-colored chops dripping juice. He carved. At Thanksgiving he leaned over the enormous turkey to get a good purchase, the double blades of the electric carving knife slicing in a noisy blur.

My father was a volunteer fireman, and every few weeks the 5
town alarm would sound during dinner, and he would move so fast, so instinctively, that time seemed to stand still: the knife or fork or bite of food falls to the table, his chair scrapes back along the floor, we children scoot out of his way as he thunders past, "Goddammit!" trails him out the back door, the door slams, and seconds later his pickup roars out of the driveway.

On quiet nights we squabbled for drumsticks, thick ham- 6
burger patties, the fatty end of the roast. I always had the chicken's back with its fat, heart-shaped tail, which my grandmother called the pope's nose, and when we were done our plates were littered with the rags of bones.

Buying meat was like this every time: I am with my mother, 7
an efficient, plain woman with the smell of academics around her. She much preferred reading to cooking, but she cooked every day. The butcher, Mr. Bryan, is my father's best friend; like all my father's friends, he is a fireman. He stands behind the counter, a tall, jolly man with a hard, round stomach covered in a white apron streaked with blood. He has saved his best meat for my mother, kept it apart for her inspection: a pot roast, a particular steak, perhaps giblets for her special dressing, the hard nubbins of chicken hearts and kidneys, the tiny livers purple-red like gems in his palm.

Now and then Mr. Bryan went to the back of the store and 8
brought my mother something really special: a whole beef heart, balanced like a waxy pyramid on his hands, or a cow's tongue, one of my favorite things. Sometimes I would come into the kitchen in the morning and find a tongue set out waiting for the pot, an enormous apostrophe of flesh covered in pale papillae. Tongue takes forever to cook, boiling for many hours on the stove, and it filled the kitchen with a tender mist and steamed the windows gray. When it was done, my mother sliced the tongue as soft as angel

cake into thin, delicious strips unlike anything else, melting, perfumed. When all the rest of the world wouldn't bend, flesh would bend.

You will think me disingenuous if I tell you now that I didn't 9
know what meat was. I couldn't know; the shift from cow to beef is a shift so monumental and sudden that it's hard to conceive. Perhaps small children cannot know this even when they are witnesses, and I was never a witness. I have never seen an animal slaughtered for meat. And if you had leaned over me when I was four or five or six and suggested I eat an animal, I might have been shocked. I loved animals more, and more easily, than I loved my parents. I held my old dog, a dour mongrel Lab, for hours in my room sometimes, telling him what I couldn't tell anyone else; I was weak with him because he kept my secrets. I loved horses, goats, deer, and the cattle chewing stupidly by the back-road fences; in my bedroom I kept lizards, snakes, chameleons, and a rat, and that was all my mother allowed. And it was my mother who one day told me where meat came from, as though it were the most natural thing.

I was about seven when I asked, that age when one begins to 10
see the depth of betrayal in the world, that one can't really count on things after all. And my mother answered yes, the chicken we ate for dinner was the same as the chickens down the street I would cluck at through the fence, the ones with the thick white feathers that filled the breeze. The peeled skin of the wieners Mr. Bryan gave me were loops of intestine washed clean, and their pulp a ground mash of bodies and bones. The unbelievable objects had a name, a face, a history; the sweet and salty taste was the taste of blood, the same as my blood. It came all at once, like a blow, that pickled pigs' feet was not a colorful metaphor but the very thing, that I had eaten a *pig's* foot, and much more.

I lived on bare noodles and peanut-butter sandwiches for a 11
long time after that. I wouldn't allow my mother to spoon the sausage-flavored spaghetti sauce onto my plate. A few years later it seemed less important, the resistance too hard. Perhaps I had had other surprises; it's hard to remember whole sections of those years. I've gone years without eating meat as an adult, and years

when I was too tired not to eat whatever was in front of me. And there have been times when I craved flesh, when I broiled and roasted, made scratch gravy and giblet dressing like my mother's, or sat at my long dining table with steamed clams clattering against my fork, times when I longed for the irreducible flavors of meat, to be full of meat. Yet I will even now find myself knocked flat sometimes when I see meat in front of me and realize what I'm doing. It's a heartfelt knowledge; it is visceral, gutlevel, organic. I hold the steak with a fork and begin to cut a slice, and my stomach turns upside down; it feels as if I'm cutting my own flesh off and that I'll choke to death upon it, like a prisoner fed his own treacherous, boiled tongue.

One shock after another. Breasts and hips and hair, more of the pleasures and debts of flesh. I began to bleed several days a month, and when I sat to pee the smell rose up yeasty and rich. I found furtive darting touches: I found lips, saliva, tongues, sweat, fingers. My dog decayed from the inside out, and stank and stumbled and licked the mysterious lumps under his fur. I traced his ribs so near the surface the day before he died. Then my mother yellowed and thickened and wept and died, and my father's big arms hung loose and his black hair turned gray . . . I moved out to the fleshy edges of things, and finally I grew wings like angel wings, and I flew away. 12

The word "butcher" comes—a long way down the years—from the word "buck." He-goat. They are set aside, butchers, into their own unions, their own neighborhoods, their own bars, set aside. I don't know if it means anything that besides Mr. Bryan, my father's closest friend was the undertaker; it may not be anything more than the limits of a small town. But I think of the Butcher's Mass, their special blessing, and the *shehitah* of the Jews. The *shochet*, the slaughterer, who must be pious and above reproach, must be as swift and painless as he can be in the killing, murmuring a benediction near the animal's ear and following with a graceful stroke across the throat. I think of Mr. Bryan's cleaver. 13

The Meat Market burned down on a hot day under a blank blue sky. It was apocalypse. It was a great fire. I stood at the end of the alley and watched the flames spurt out the back door in 14 gouty bursts. I heard a shriek of metal inside and guessed the white metal cooler had turned red and ignited its own frost. The smoke billowed out the back door in a cottony black cloud, and I clapped my hands. Men in turnouts and boots rushed past and paid me no attention, and I saw my father paying out the hose from the pumper with great speed.

The meat burned; the water washed it clean. I learned later 15
that Mr. Bryan had inherited the Meat Market from his father, and he'd secretly hated it all those years, going home at night with the stink of blood on his hands and hair. He is still jolly and thick-fingered, and he still comes by to visit my father, who is tired and gruff and without cheer. They have been retired from fires, too old to go into the heat and pull things out. For myself, I know you can't be cleansed until you know how dirty you really are. I still live far away, still seek salvation from my many sins.

---

## *Meaning and Purpose*

1. How does Tisdale's description of the butcher shop, in paragraph 1, help to cause her shock, described in paragraphs 9 and 10?
2. What was the long-term effect on Tisdale when she learned where meat came from?
3. Paragraph 13 contains a definition of *butcher* followed by a discussion of butchers. How are the definition and the discussion important to the essay?
4. Given the evidence in paragraph 14, what is the author's opinion of the Meat Market's burning down?

## *Strategy*

1. Why does the first sentence in paragraph 7 begin in the past tense—"Buying meat was like this every time"—and then immediately shift to the present tense—"I *am* with my mother" . . .?

2. In paragraph 3, why are summer days described as "panting"?
3. What single paragraph best describes how much the author's family likes to eat meat? Explain why you chose that paragraph.
4. What evidence is there in the essay to show that cow's tongue was one of the author's favorite meat dishes?

## *Style*

1. In paragraph 2, steaks are described as "flaccid." Why, in your opinion, did the author use that adjective?
2. Why is "pig's" italicized, in paragraph 10?
3. Paragraph 12 ends with "finally I grew wings like angel wings, and I flew away." What does that image suggest about the author's attitude towards leaving her family's home?
4. The meat market eventually burned down. The author describes the fire as an "apocalypse." In your opinion, why did she choose that word?
5. In paragraph 14, what does the word *turnouts* mean?

## *Writing Tasks*

1. All of us have experienced a shock of recognition that has caused us to react emotionally and to change our thinking. (Remember what happened when you found out about Santa Claus?) In an essay, describe an idea, belief, or opinion you once held, that you later discovered was not valid. Be sure to tell the reader how you discovered the truth or the facts and how that discovery affected you at the time you realized you had been wrong.
2. Describe an event in your life that helped you to make a major decision. For example, if you have already chosen a vocation, what single cause, more than any other, affected that choice?

## ❦ E. B. White ❦

*Born in Mount Vernon, New York, in 1899, Elwyn Brooks White is considered one of America's finest essayists. At Cornell University he studied English composition with Edmund Strunk, and years later revised Strunk's concise book of writing guidance, now known as Strunk and White's* Elements of Style. *He was for many years a staff writer at* The New Yorker, *where he first earned his reputation as a master essayist. He also wrote a regular column for* Harper's *magazine for several years. His essay collections include* One Man's Meat *(1944),* The Second Tree from the Corner *(1953), and* The Essays of E. B. White *(1977). Two of his books—*Stuart Little *(1945) and* Charlotte's Web *(1952)—have become classics of children's literature. He died in 1985 at his farm in coastal Maine, to which he had retired in 1957.*

# *Once More to the Lake*

*In this essay, first published in* Harper's *in 1941 and collected in* One Man's Meat *(1944), White uses the force of reminiscence to enhance a meticulous description of a recent event. On a fishing trip to a lake in Maine with his young son, the author recalls his own childhood summers at the same lake. He inevitably begins to see himself in his son and is jolted into awareness of his own mortality.*

*White, in this essay, ranges in time—from the present, to the past, to the present, and back again. Be alert to those changes.*

---

*August 1941*

One summer, along about 1904, my father rented a camp on a lake in Maine and took us all there for the month of August. We all got ringworm from some kittens and had to rub Pond's Extract on our arms and legs night and morning, and my father rolled over in a canoe with all his clothes on; but outside of that the vacation was a success and from then on none of us ever thought there was any place in the world like that lake in Maine. We returned summer after summer—always on August 1 for one 1 month. I have since become a salt-water man, but sometimes in summer there are days when the restlessness of the tides and the fearful cold of the sea water and the incessant wind that blows across the afternoon and into the evening make me wish for the placidity of a lake in the woods. A few weeks ago this feeling got so strong I bought myself a couple of bass hooks and a spinner and returned to the lake where we used to go, for a week's fishing and to revisit old haunts.

I took along my son, who had never had any fresh water up 2
his nose and who had seen lily pads only from train windows. On the journey over to the lake I began to wonder what it would be like. I wondered how time would have marred this unique, this holy spot—the coves and streams, the hills that the sun set behind, the camps and the paths behind the camps. I was sure that the tarred road would have found it out, and I wondered in what other ways it would be desolated. It is strange how much you can remember about places like that once you allow your mind to return into the grooves that lead back. You remember one thing, and that suddenly reminds you of another thing. I guess I remembered clearest of all the early mornings, when the lake was cool and motionless, remembered how the bedroom smelled of the lumber it was made of and of the wet woods whose scent entered through the screen. The partitions in the camp were thin and did not extend clear to the top of the rooms, and as I was always the first up I would dress softly so as not to wake the others, and sneak out into the sweet outdoors and start out in the canoe, keeping close along the shore in the long shadows of the pines. I remembered being very careful never to rub my paddle against the gunwale for fear of disturbing the stillness of the cathedral.

The lake had never been what you would call a wild lake. 3
There were cottages sprinkled around the shores, and it was in farming country although the shores of the lake were quite heavily wooded. Some of the cottages were owned by nearby farmers, and you would live at the shore and eat your meals at the farmhouse. That's what our family did. But although it wasn't wild, it was a fairly large and undisturbed lake and there were places in it that, to a child at least, seemed infinitely remote and primeval.

I was right about the tar; it led to within half a mile of the shore. But when I got back there, with my boy, and we settled into a camp near a farmhouse and into the kind of summertime I had known, I could tell that it was going to be pretty much the same as it had been before—I knew it, lying in bed the first morning, smelling the bedroom and hearing the boy sneak quietly out and go off along the shore in a boat. I began to sustain the illusion that he was I, and therefore, by simple transposition, that I was my father. This sensation persisted, kept cropping up all the time we were there. It was not an entirely new feeling, but in this setting it grew much stronger. I seemed to be living a dual existence. I would be in the middle of some simple act, I would be picking up a bait box or laying down a table fork, or I would be saying something, and suddenly it would be not I but my father who was saying the words or making the gesture. It gave me a creepy sensation. 4

We went fishing the first morning. I felt the same damp moss covering the worms in the bait can, and saw the dragonfly alight 5 on the tip of my rod as it hovered a few inches from the surface of the water. It was the arrival of this fly that convinced me beyond any doubt that everything was as it always had been, that the years were a mirage and that there had been no years. The small waves were the same, chucking the rowboat under the chin as we fished at anchor, and the boat was the same boat, the same color green and the ribs broken in the same places, and under the floorboards the same fresh-water leavings and débris—the dead hellgrammite, the wisps of moss, the rusty discarded fishhook, the dried blood from yesterday's catch. We stared silently at the tips of our rods, at the dragonflies that came and went. I lowered the tip of mine into the water, tentatively, pensively dislodging the fly, which darted two feet away, poised, darted two feet back, and came to rest again a little farther up the rod. There had been no years between the ducking of this dragonfly and the other one—the one that was part of memory. I looked at the boy, who was silently watching his fly, and it was my hands that held his rod, my eyes watching. I felt dizzy and didn't know which rod I was at the end of.

We caught two bass, hauling them in briskly as though they 6 were mackerel, pulling them over the side of the boat in a businesslike manner without any landing net, and stunning them with a blow on the back of the head. When we got back for a swim before lunch, the lake was exactly where we had left it, the same number of inches from the dock, and there was only the merest suggestion of a breeze. This seemed an utterly enchanted sea, this lake you could leave to its own devices for a few hours and come back to, and find it had not stirred, this constant and trustworthy body of water. In the shallows, the dark, water-soaked sticks and twigs, smooth and old, were undulating in clusters on the bottom against the clean ribbed sand, and the track of the mussel was plain. A school of minnows swam by, each minnow with its small individual shadow, doubling the attendance, so clear and sharp in the sunlight. Some of the other campers were in swimming, along the shore, one of them with a cake of soap, and the water felt thin and clear and unsubstantial. Over the years there had been this person with the cake of soap, this cultist, and here he was. There had been no years.

Up to the farmhouse to dinner through the teeming, dusty field, the road under our sneakers was only a two-track road. The middle track was missing, the one with the marks of the hooves and the splotches of dried, flaky manure. There had always been three tracks to choose from in choosing which track to walk in; now the choice was narrowed down to two. For a moment I missed terribly the middle alternative. But the way led past the tennis court, and something about the way it lay there in the sun reassured me; the tape had loosened along the backline, the alleys were green with plantains and other weeds, and the net (installed in June and removed in September) sagged in the dry noon, and the whole place steamed with midday heat and hunger and emptiness. There was a choice of pie for dessert, and one was blueberry and one was apple, and the waitresses were the same country girls, there having been no passage of time, only the illusion of it as in a dropped curtain—the waitresses were still fifteen; their hair had been washed, that was the only difference—they had been to the movies and seen the pretty girls with the clean hair. 7

Summertime, oh summertime, pattern of life indelible, the fade-proof lake, the woods unshatterable, the pasture with the sweetfern and the juniper forever and ever, summer without end; 8

this was the background, and the life along the shore was the design, their tiny docks with the flagpole and the American flag floating against the white clouds in the blue sky, the little paths over the roots of the trees leading from camp to camp and the paths leading back to the outhouses and the can of lime for sprinkling, and at the souvenir counters at the store the miniature birch-bark canoes and the postcards that showed things looking a little better than they looked. This was the American family at play, escaping the city heat, wondering whether the newcomers in the camp at the head of the cove were "common" or "nice," wondering whether it was true that the people who drove up for Sunday dinner at the farmhouse were turned away because there wasn't enough chicken.

It seemed to me, as I kept remembering all this, that those 9 times and those summers had been infinitely precious and worth saving. There had been jollity and peace and goodness. The arriving (at the beginning of August) had been so big a business in itself, at the railway station the farm wagon drawn up, the first smell of the pine-laden air, the first glimpse of the smiling farmer, and the great importance of the trunks and your father's enormous authority in such matters, and the feel of the wagon under you for the long ten-mile haul, and at the top of the last long hill catching the first view of the lake after eleven months of not seeing this cherished body of water. The shouts and cries of the other campers when they saw you, and the trunks to be unpacked, to give up their rich burden. (Arriving was less exciting nowadays, when you sneaked up in your car and parked it under a tree near the camp and took out the bags and in five minutes it was all over, no fuss, no loud wonderful fuss about trunks.)

Peace and goodness and jollity. The only thing that was 10 wrong now, really, was the sound of the place, an unfamiliar nervous sound of the outboard motors. This was the note that jarred, the one thing that would sometimes break the illusion and set the years moving. In those other summertimes all the motors were inboard; and when they were at a little distance, the noise they made was a sedative, an ingredient of summer sleep. They were one-cylinder and two-cylinder engines, and some were make-and-break and some were jump-spark, but they all made a sleepy sound across the lake. The one-lungers throbbed and fluttered, and the twin-cylinder ones purred and purred, and that was a quiet sound, too. But now the campers all had outboards. In the daytime, in the hot mornings, these motors made a petulant, irritable sound; at night, in the still evening when the afterglow lit the water, they whined about one's ears like mosquitoes. My boy loved our rented outboard, and his great desire was to achieve single-handed mastery over it, and authority, and he soon learned the trick of choking it a little (but not too much), and the adjustment of the needle valve. Watching him I would remember the things you could do with the old one-cylinder engine with the heavy flywheel, how you could have it eating out of your hand if you got really close to it spiritually. Motorboats in those days didn't have clutches, and you would make a landing by shutting off the motor at the proper time and coasting in with a dead rudder. But there was a way of reversing them, if you learned the trick, by cutting the switch and putting it on again exactly on the final dying revolution of the flywheel, so that it would kick back against the compression and begin reversing. Approaching a dock in a strong following breeze, it was difficult to slow up sufficiently by the ordinary coasting method, and if a boy felt he had complete mastery over his motor, he was tempted to keep it running beyond its time and then reverse it a few feet from the dock. It took a cool nerve, because if you threw the switch a twentieth of a second too soon you would catch the flywheel when it still had speed enough to go up past center, and the boat would leap ahead, charging bull-fashion at the dock.

We had a good week at camp. The bass were biting well and 11
the sun shown endlessly, day after day. We would be tired at night and lie down in the accumulated heat of the little bedrooms after the long hot day and the breeze would stir almost imperceptibly outside and the smell of the swamp drift in through the rusty screens. Sleep would come easily and in the morning the red squirrel would be on the roof, tapping out his gay routine. I kept remembering everything, lying in bed in the mornings—the small steamboat that had a long rounded stern like the lip of a Ubangi, and how quietly she ran on the moonlight sails, when the older

boys played their mandolins and the girls sang and we ate doughnuts dipped in sugar, and how sweet the music was on the water in the shining night, and what it had felt like to think about girls then. After breakfast we would go up to the store and the things were in the same place—the minnows in a bottle, the plugs and spinners disarranged and pawed over by the youngsters from the boys' camp, the Fig Newtons and the Beeman's gum. Outside, the road was tarred and cars stood in front of the store. Inside, all was just as it had always been, except there was more Coca-Cola and not so much Moxie and root beer and birch beer and sarsaparilla. We would walk out with the bottle of pop apiece and sometimes the pop would backfire up our noses and hurt. We explored the streams, quietly, where the turtles slid off the sunny logs and dug their way into the soft bottom; and we lay on the town wharf and fed worms to the tame bass. Everywhere we went I had trouble making out which I was, the one walking at my side, the one walking in my pants.

One afternoon while we were there at that lake a thunder- 12
storm came up. It was like the revival of an old melodrama that I had seen long ago with childish awe. The second-act climax of the drama of the electrical disturbance over a lake in America had not changed in any important respect. This was the big scene, still the big scene. The whole thing was so familiar, the first feeling of oppression and heat and a general air around camp of not wanting to go very far away. In mid-afternoon (it was all the same) a curious darkening of the sky, and a lull in everything that had made life tick; and then the way the boats suddenly swung the other way at their moorings with the coming of a breeze out of the new quarter, and the premonitory rumble. Then the kettle drum, then the snare, then the bass drum and cymbals, then crackling light against the dark, and the gods grinning and licking their chops in the hills. Afterward the calm, the rain steadily rustling in the calm lake, the return of light and hope and spirits, and the campers running out in joy and relief to go swimming in the rain, their bright cries perpetuating the deathless joke about how they were getting simply drenched, and the children screaming with delight at the

new sensation of bathing in the rain, and the joke about getting drenched linking the generations in a strong indestructible chain. And the comedian who waded in carrying an umbrella.

When the others went swimming, my son said he was going in, too. He pulled his dripping trunks from the line where they had hung all through the shower and wrung them out. Languidly, and with no thought of going in, I watched him, his hard little body, skinny and bare, saw him wince slightly as he pulled up around his vitals the small, soggy, icy garment. As he buckled the swollen belt, suddenly my groin felt the chill of death. 13

---

## *Meaning and Purpose*

1. Have you a special place about which you feel nostalgic that you've visited recently? If so, has anything changed? If not, what are you afraid might have changed? Do any of White's descriptions remind you of this place?
2. As you read the opening paragraph of "Once More to the Lake," what do you understand White's purpose to be?
3. How does the title relate to the essay? After you've read the essay, does the title become more significant?
4. What do you think White comes to understand about time and change during his visit to the lake?
5. In the closing paragraph, White describes his son pulling on his wet swimming trunks. At that moment, White says he feels "the chill of death." What do you believe he means? Has anything in the essay prepared you for this conclusion?

## *Strategy*

1. What is the dominant impression that White creates in paragraph 12? How does he use language to create it?
2. White mixes description of his recent trip to the lake with details from past trips. How does he avoid confusion? What transitions does he use to go back and forth in time?

3. Could White's essay have significance for you even if you have never been to Maine, or camped by a lake, or fished? Does the essay transcend its subject? If so, how does White accomplish this feat? Does the lake have a larger meaning?
4. Why does White call his son his "boy" and not name him or give him strong identifying characteristics?

## *Style*

1. Identify in the opening three paragraphs the words that White uses to describe the lake. What impressions do they create? How does the closing sentence in paragraph 3 reinforce this impression?
2. White's essay is clearly subjective, amply mixing descriptive details about the lake with his personal thoughts. How would you describe the essay's tone? What frame of mind does White seem to be in?
3. If necessary, check the dictionary for the meaning of these words: *gunwale* (2); *primeval* (3); *transposition* (4); *hellgrammite* (5); *undulating* (6); *petulant* (10); *premonitory* (12); *languidly* (13). What do these words reveal about White's intended audience?

## *Writing Tasks*

1. Describe a place such as a camp, a farm home, a relative's house, or a childhood haunt, to which you returned after long absence. Structure your description so that it captures how the place appears in your memory and how it appears now. Select the descriptive details carefully and include your subjective thoughts.
2. Write a short descriptive essay (about any subject) in which you appeal to all five senses.

## ❦ George Simpson ❦

*Born in Virginia in 1950, George Simpson studied journalism at the University of North Carolina. He wrote for the* Carolina Financial Times *in North Carolina and for the News-Gazette in Virginia before joining the staff at* Newsweek *in 1972. In 1978 he was appointed* Newsweek's *director of public affairs. For a series of articles about the football program at the University of North Carolina, he won the Sigma Delta Chi Best Feature Writing Award in 1972. He has contributed stories to* The New York Times, Sport, Glamour, *and other major publications.*

# *The War Room at Bellevue*

*In this essay, first published in* New York *magazine in 1983, George Simpson uses objective description of events during one night at Bellevue Hospital to achieve immediacy. Arranging the emergency-room scenes in strict (by-the-clock) chronological order creates the impression of a minute-by-minute account and contributes to the power of the description.*

*Simpson describes the staff at the Bellevue trauma center speedily responding to emergencies with both efficiency and care. Notice how they maintain commonplace relationships among themselves even amid the chaos.*

---

Bellevue. The name conjures up images of an indoor war zone: the wounded and bleeding lining the halls, screaming for help while harried doctors in blood-stained smocks rush from stretcher to stretcher, fighting a losing battle against exhaustion and the crushing number of injured. "What's worse," says a long-time Bellevue nurse, "is that we have this image of being a hospital only for . . .". She pauses, then lowers her voice; "for crazy people." 1

Though neither battlefield nor Bedlam is a valid image, there is something extraordinary about the monstrous complex that spreads for five blocks along First Avenue in Manhattan. It is said 2 best by the head nurse in Adult Emergency Service: "If you have any chance for survival, you have it here." Survival—that is why they come. Why do injured cops drive by a half-dozen other hospitals to be treated at Bellevue? They've seen the Bellevue emergency team in action.

9:00 P.M. It is a Friday night in the Bellevue emergency room. 3
The after-work crush is over (those who've suffered through the day, only to come for help after the five-o'clock whistle has blown) and it is nearly silent except for the mutter of voices at the admitting desk, where administrative personnel discuss who will go for coffee. Across the spotless white-walled lobby, ten people sit quietly, passively, in pastel plastic chairs, waiting for word of relatives or to see doctors. In the past 24 hours, 300 people have come to the Bellevue Adult Emergency Service. Fewer than 10 percent were true emergencies. One man sleeps fitfully in the emergency ward while his heartbeat, respiration, and blood pressure are monitored by control consoles mounted over his bed. Each heartbeat trips a tiny bleep in the monitor, which attending nurses can hear across the ward. A half hour ago, doctors in the trauma room withdrew a six-inch stiletto blade from his back. When he is stabilized, the patient will be moved upstairs to the twelve-bed Surgical Intensive Care Unit.

9:05 P.M. An ambulance backs into the receiving bay, its red 4
and yellow lights flashing in and out of the lobby. A split second later, the glass doors burst open as a nurse and an attendant roll a mobile stretcher into the lobby. When the nurse screams, "Emergent!" the lobby explodes with activity as the way is cleared to the trauma room. Doctors appear from nowhere and transfer the bloodied body of a black man to the treatment table. Within seconds his clothes are stripped away, revealing a tiny stab wound in his left side. Three doctors and three nurses rush around the victim, each performing a task necessary to begin treatment. Intravenous needles are inserted into his arms and groin. A doctor draws blood for the lab, in case surgery is necessary. A nurse begins inserting a catheter into the victim's penis and continues to feed in tubing until the catheter reaches the bladder. Urine flows through the tube into a plastic bag. Doctors are glad not to see

blood in the urine. Another nurse records pulse and blood pressure.

The victim is in good shape. He shivers slightly, although the 5
trauma room is exceedingly warm. His face is bloodied, but shows no major lacerations. A third nurse, her elbow propped on the treatment table, asks the man a series of questions, trying to quickly outline his medical history. He answers abruptly. He is drunk. His left side is swabbed with yellow disinfectant and a doctor injects a local anesthetic. After a few seconds another doctor inserts his finger into the wound. It sinks in all the way to the knuckle. He begins to rotate his finger like a child trying to get a marble out of a milk bottle. The patient screams bloody murder and tries to struggle free.

Meanwhile in the lobby, a security guard is ejecting a derelict 6
who has begun to drink from a bottle hidden in his coat pocket. "He's a regular, was in here just two days ago," says a nurse. "We checked him pretty close then, so he's probably okay now. Can you believe those were clean clothes we gave him?" The old man, blackened by filth, leaves quietly.

9:15 P.M. A young Hispanic man interrupts, saying his preg- 7
nant girl friend, sitting outside in his car, is bleeding heavily from her vagina. She is rushed into an examination room, treated behind closed doors, and rolled into the observation ward, where, much later in the night, a gynecologist will treat her in a special room—the same one used to examine rape victims. Nearby, behind curtains, the neurologist examines an old white woman to determine if her headaches are due to head injury. They are not.

9:45 P.M. The trauma room has been cleared and cleaned mer- 8
cilessly. The examination rooms are three-quarters full—another overdose, two asthmatics, a young woman with abdominal pains. In the hallway, a derelict who has been sleeping it off urinates all over the stretcher. He sleeps on while attendants change his clothes. An ambulance—one of four that patrol Manhattan for Bellevue from 42nd Street to Houston, river to river—delivers a middle-aged white woman and two cops, the three of them soaking wet. The woman has escaped from the psychiatric floor of a nearby hospital and tried to drown herself in the East River. The

cops fished her out. She lies on a stretcher shivering beneath white blankets. Her eyes stare at the ceiling. She speaks clearly when an administrative worker begins routine questioning. The cops are given hospital gowns and wait to receive tetanus shots and gamma globulin—a hedge against infection from the befouled river water. They will hang around the E.R. for another two hours, telling their story to as many as six other policemen who show up to hear it. The woman is rolled into an examination room, where a male nurse speaks gently: "They tell me you fell into the river." "No," says the woman, "I jumped. I have to commit suicide." "Why?" asks the nurse. "Because I'm insane and I can't help [it]. I have to die." The nurse gradually discovers the woman has a history of psychological problems. She is given dry bedclothes and placed under guard in the hallway. She lies on her side, staring at the wall.

The pace continues to increase. Several more overdose vic- 9
tims arrive by ambulance. One, a young black woman, had done a striptease on the street just before passing out. A second black woman is semiconscious and spends the better part of her time at Bellevue alternately cursing it and pleading with the doctors. Attendants find a plastic bottle coated with methadone in the pocket of a Hispanic O.D. The treatment is routinely the same, and sooner or later involves vomiting. Just after doctors begin to treat the O.D., he vomits great quantities of wine and methadone in all directions. "Lovely business, huh?" laments one of the doctors. A young nurse confides that if there were other true emergencies, the overdose victims would be given lower priority. "You can't help thinking they did it to themselves," she says, "while the others are accident victims."

10:30 P.M. A policeman who twisted his knee struggling 10
with an "alleged perpetrator" is examined and released. By 10:30, the lobby is jammed with friends and relatives of patients in various stages of treatment and recovery. The attendant who also functions as a translator for Hispanic patients adds chairs to accommodate the overflow. The medical walk-in rate stays steady—between eight and ten patients waiting. A pair of derelicts, each with battered eyes, appear at the admitting desk. One has a dramatically swollen face laced with black stitches.

11:00 P.M. The husband of the attempted suicide arrives. He thanks the police for saving his wife's life, then talks at length with doctors about her condition. She continues to stare into the void and does not react when her husband approaches her stretcher. 11

Meanwhile, patients arrive in the lobby at a steady pace. A young G.I. on leave has lower-back pains; a Hispanic man complains of pain in his side; occasionally parents hurry through the adult E.R. carrying children into the pediatric E.R. A white woman of about 50 marches into the lobby from the walk-in entrance. Dried blood covers her right eyebrow and upper lip. She begins to perform. "I was assaulted on 28th and Lexington, I was," she says grandly, "and I don't have to take it *anymore*. I was a bride 21 years ago, and, God, I was beautiful then." She has captured the attention of all present. "I was there when the boys came home—on Memorial Day—and I don't have to take this kind of treatment." 12

As midnight approaches, the nurses prepare for the shift change. They must brief the incoming staff and make sure all reports are up-to-date. One young brunet says, "Christ, I'm gonna go home and take a shower—I smell like vomit." 13

11:50 P.M. The triage nurse is questioning an old black-man about chest pains, and a Hispanic woman is having an asthma attack, when an ambulance, its sirens screaming full tilt, roars into the receiving bay. There is a split-second pause as everyone drops what he or she is doing and looks up. Then all hell breaks loose. Doctors and nurses are suddenly sprinting full-out toward the trauma room. The glass doors burst open and the occupied stretcher is literally run past me. Cops follow. It is as if a comet has whooshed by. In the trauma room it all becomes clear. A half-dozen doctors and nurses surround the lifeless form of a Hispanic man with a shotgun hole in his neck the size of your fist. Blood pours from a second gaping wound in his chest. A respirator is slammed over his face, making his chest rise and fall as if he were breathing. "No pulse," reports one doctor. A nurse jumps on a stool and, leaning over the man, begins to pump his chest with her palms. "No blood pressure," screams another nurse. The ambulance driver appears shaken. "I never thought I'd get here in time," he stutters. More doctors from the trauma team upstairs arrive. Wrappings from syringes and gauze pads fly through the air. 14

The victim's eyes are open yet devoid of life. His body takes on a yellow tinge. A male nurse winces at the gunshot wound. "This guy really pissed off somebody," he says. This is no ordinary shooting. It is an execution. IV's are jammed into the body in the groin and arms. One doctor has been plugging in an electrocardiograph and asks everyone to stop for a second so he can get a reading. "Forget it," shouts the doctor in charge. "No time." "Take it easy, Jimmy," someone yells at the head physician. It is apparent by now that the man is dead, but the doctors keep trying injections and finally they slit open the chest and reach inside almost up to their elbows. They feel the extent of the damage and suddenly it is all over. "I told 'em he was dead," says one nurse, withdrawing. "They didn't listen." The room is very still. The doctors are momentarily disgusted, then go on about their business. The room clears quickly. Finally there is only a male nurse and the still-warm body, now waxy-yellow, with huge ribs exposed on both sides of the chest and giant holes in both sides of the neck. The nurse speculates that this is yet another murder in a Hispanic political struggle that has brought many such victims to Bellevue. He marvels at the extent of the wounds and repeats, "This guy was really blown away."

Midnight. A hysterical woman is hustled through the lobby into an examination room. It is the dead man's wife, and she is nearly delirious. "I know he's dead, I know he's dead," she screams over and over. Within moments the lobby is filled with anxious relatives of the victim, waiting for word on his condition. The police are everywhere asking questions, but most people say they saw nothing. One young woman says she heard six shots, two louder than the other four. At some point, word is passed that the man is, in fact, dead. Another woman breaks down in hysterics; everywhere young Hispanics are crying and comforting each other. Plainclothes detectives make a quick examination of the body, check on the time of pronouncement of death, and begin to ask questions, but the bereaved are too stunned to talk. The rest of the uninvolved people in the lobby stare dumbly, their injuries suddenly paling in light of a death. 15

12:30 A.M. A black man appears at the admission desk and says he drank poison by mistake. He is told to have a seat. The 16 ambulance brings in a young white woman, her head wrapped in white gauze. She is wailing terribly. A girl friend stands over her, crying, and a boyfriend clutches the injured woman's hands, saying, "I'm here, don't worry, I'm here." The victim has fallen downstairs at a friend's house. Attendants park her stretcher against the wall to wait for an examination room to clear. There are eight examination rooms and only three doctors. Unless you are truly an emergency, you will wait. One doctor is stitching up the elbow of a drunk who's been punched out. The friends of the woman who fell down the stairs glance up at the doctors anxiously, wondering why their friend isn't being treated faster.

1:10 A.M. A car pulls into the bay and a young Hispanic asks if a shooting victim has been brought here. The security guard blurts out, "He's dead." The young man is stunned. He peels his tires leaving the bay. 17

1:20 A.M. The young woman of the stairs is getting stitches in a small gash over her left eye when the same ambulance driver who brought in the gunshot victim delivers a man who has been stabbed in the back on East 3rd Street. Once again the trauma room goes from 0 to 60 in five seconds. The patient is drunk, which helps him endure the pain of having the catheter inserted through his penis into his bladder. Still he yells, "That hurts like a bastard," then adds sheepishly, "Excuse me, ladies." But he is not prepared for what comes next. An X-ray reveals a collapsed right lung. After just a shot of local anesthetic, the doctor slices open his side and inserts a long plastic tube. Internal bleeding had kept the lung pressed down and prevented it from reinflating. The tube releases the pressure. The ambulance driver says the cops grabbed the guy who ran the eight-inch blade into the victim's back. "That's not the one," says the man. "They got the wrong guy." A nurse reports that there is not much of the victim's type blood available at the hospital. One of the doctors says that's okay, he won't need surgery. Meanwhile blood pours from the man's knife wound and the tube in his side. As the nurses work, they chat about personal matters, yet they respond immediately to orders from either doctor. "How ya doin'?" the doctor asks the patient. "Okay," he says. His blood spatters on the floor. 18

So it goes into the morning hours. A Valium overdose, a woman who fainted, a man who went through the windshield of his car. More overdoses. More drunks with split eyebrows and chins. The doctors and nurses work without complaint. "This is nothing, about normal, I'd say," concludes the head nurse. "No big deal." 19

---

## *Meaning and Purpose*

1. Have you ever been in a hospital emergency room? How would you describe the experience? Were you aware of the attitude of the doctors and nurses? Of the people waiting with the patients? Do any of Simpson's descriptions compare to what you saw?
2. What do you believe to be Simpson's purpose in "The War Room at Bellevue"?
3. What impressions of the hospital and its staff grow from the description? What details give you that impression?
4. Although Simpson does not describe the city that surrounds the hospital, what impression of the city does he leave you with? Support your answer with details from the essay.
5. Why does Simpson capitalize "Bedlam" in paragraph 2? What are the denotation and connotation of the word?

## *Strategy*

1. What is the structure of this descriptive essay?
2. Many internal workings of "The War Room at Bellevue" are constructed on a "stimulus-response" pattern—that is, an event takes place and people respond. You'll find a stimulus-response pattern in paragraph 4: it opens with the arrival of an ambulance; a patient is rolled into the lobby on a mobile stretcher; a nurse screams "Emergent!" and the scene explodes with action. Find a stimulus-response pattern in other passages of the essay.

3. Often Simpson has to describe simultaneous events—that is, separate actions that take place at the same time. Find at least four overt transitions at the beginning of paragraphs that capture the sense of simultaneous action.
4. Simpson describes the Bellevue emergency room in the present tense. What is the effect of using this tense?
5. Comment on the spatial arrangement of some of the descriptions. Is it broad to narrow? near to far? center outward? Give examples.

## *Style*

1. How would you describe the narrator of "The War Room at Bellevue"? Is the material presented objectively or subjectively?
2. What words and images help create the sense of a battle in the first two paragraphs?
3. How does the tone of the final paragraph differ from the tone Simpson creates through most of the essay?
4. Identify phrases that help create the sense of sound in paragraph 3. Find words that create a dominant sense impression in one or two other paragraphs.

## *Writing Tasks*

1. Describe a scene in which a great deal of action takes place—a sports event, a shopping mall, an intersection, a park, or a school yard. Keep your description objective, carefully selecting the details to create, without emotion or judgment, a dominant impression.
2. Compare the subjective description in "Once More to the Lake" with the objective description in "The War Room at Bellevue." What words make the essays predominantly subjective or objective? What is the overall effectiveness of each strategy and its suitability to the subject? Could each essay be told from the other point of view?

# ❦ Gretel Ehrlich ❦

*Journalist, poet, fiction writer, and documentary film maker, Gretel Ehrlich was born in California and studied at Bennington College, UCLA Film School, and the New School for Social Research. After a journey to Wyoming to make a documentary film, Ehrlich decided to live there, doing various kinds of ranch work including branding, sheep herding, and helping with the births of lambs and calves. Her many books include a collection of essays,* The Solace of Open Spaces *(1985);* Drinking Dry Clouds: Stories from Wyoming *(1991);* Arctic Heat: A Poem Cycle *(with David Buckland, 1992); and* A Match to the Heart: One Woman's Story of Being Struck by Lightning *(1994; paperback, 1995), in which the work below appears.*

# *Struck by Lightning*

*This essay, from a larger work, imitates an ancient mystical journal from death or near-death to rebirth. While describing all of the events that occur as a result of her being struck by lightning, the essay also stirs emotions far below the event's surface, entering the realm of thoughts of death and how it is possible to describe that which one has not yet endured.*

*As you read this essay, pay particular attention to how Ehrlich uses time as a device to bring the reader in and out of the experience, just as Ehrlich herself mentally traveled through those events. And note how she uses description to appeal to the image-making qualities of a reader's mind. You not only can mentally "see" many events in this essay, but you can also "feel" many of its parts.*

---

Deep in an ocean. I am suspended motionless. The water is gray. That's all there is, and before that? My arms are held out straight, cruciate, my head and legs hang limp. Nothing moves. Brown kelp lies flat in mud and fish are buried in liquid clouds of dust. There are no shadows or sounds. Should there be? I don't know if I am alive, but if not, how do I know I am dead? My body 1 is leaden, heavier than gravity. Gravity is done with me. No more sinking and rising or bobbing in currents. There is a terrible feeling of oppression with no oppressor. I try to lodge my mind against some boundary, some reference point, but the continent of the body dissolves . . .

A single heartbeat stirs gray water. Blue trickles in, just a tiny 2
stream. Then a long silence.

Another heartbeat. This one is louder, as if amplified. Sound 3
takes a shape: it is a snowplow moving grayness aside like a heavy snowdrift. I can't tell if I'm moving, but more blue water flows in. Seaweed begins to undulate, then a whole kelp forest rises from the ocean floor. A fish swims past and looks at me. Another heartbeat drives through dead water, and another, until I am surrounded by blue.

Sun shines above all this. There is no pattern to the way its 4
glint comes free and falls in long knives of light. My two beloved dogs appear. They flank me like tiny rockets, their fur pressed against my ribs. A leather harness holds us all together. The dogs climb toward light, pulling me upward at a slant from the sea.

I have been struck by lightning and I am alive. 5

Before electricity carved its blue path toward me, before the 6
negative charge shot down from cloud to ground, before "streamers" jumped the positive charge back up from ground to cloud, before air expanded and contracted producing loud pressure pulses I could not hear because I was already dead, I had been walking.

When I started out on foot that August afternoon, the thun- 7
derstorm was blowing in fast. On the face of the mountain, a mile ahead, hard westerly gusts and sudden updrafts collided, pulling black clouds apart. Yet the storm looked harmless. When a distant thunderclap scared the dogs, I called them to my side and rubbed their ears: "Don't worry, you're okay as long as you're with me."

I woke in a pool of blood, lying on my stomach some distance 8
from where I should have been, flung at an odd angle to one side of the dirt path. The whole sky had grown dark. Was it evening, and if so, which one? How many minutes or hours had elapsed

since I lost consciousness, and where were the dogs? I tried to call out to them but my voice didn't work. The muscles in my throat were paralyzed and I couldn't swallow. Were the dogs dead? Everything was terribly wrong: I had trouble seeing, talking, breathing, and I couldn't move my legs or right arm. Nothing remained in my memory—no sounds, flashes, smells, no warnings of any kind. Had I been shot in the back? Had I suffered a stroke or heart attack? These thoughts were dark pools in sand.

The sky was black. Was this a storm in the middle of the day 9 or was it night with a storm traveling through? When thunder exploded over me, I knew I had been hit by lightning.

The pain in my chest intensified and every muscle in my body 10 ached. I was quite sure I was dying. What was it one should do or think or know? I tried to recall the Buddhist instruction regarding dying—which position to lie in, which direction to face. Did the "Lion's position" taken by the Buddha mean lying on the left or the right? And which sutra to sing? Oh yes, the Heart Sutra . . . gaté, gaté, paragaté . . . form and formlessness. Paradox and cosmic jokes. Surviving after trying to die "properly" would be truly funny, but the chances of that seemed slim.

Other words drifted in: how the "gateless barrier" was the gate 11 through which one passes to reach enlightenment. Yet if there was no gate, how did one pass through? Above me, high on the hill, was the gate on the ranch that lead nowhere, a gate I had mused about often. Now its presence made me smile. Even when I thought I had no aspirations for enlightenment, too much effort in that direction was being expended. How could I learn to slide, yet remain aware?

To be struck by lightning: what a way to get enlightened. That 12 would be the joke if I survived. It seemed important to remember jokes. My thinking did not seem connected to the inert body that was in such terrible pain. Sweep the mind of weeds, I kept telling myself—that's what years of Buddhist practice had taught me. . . . But where were the dogs, the two precious ones I had watched being born and had raised in such intimacy and trust? I wanted them with me. I wanted them to save me again.

It started to rain. Every time a drop hit bare skin there was an 13 explosion of pain. Blood crusted my left eye. I touched my good hand to my heart, which was beating wildly, erratically. My chest was numb, as if it had been sprayed with novocaine. No feeling of peace filled me. Death was a bleakness, a grayness about which it was impossible to be curious or relieved. I loved those dogs and hoped they weren't badly hurt. If I didn't die soon, how many days would pass before we were found, and when would the scavengers come? The sky was dark, or was that the way life flew out of the body, in a long tube with no light at the end? I lay on the cold ground waiting. The mountain was purple, and sage stirred against my face. I knew I had to give up all this, then my own body and all my thinking. Once more I lifted my head to look for the dogs but, unable to see them, I twisted myself until I faced east and tried to let go of all desire.

When my eyes opened again I knew I wasn't dead. Images from World War II movies filled my head: of wounded soldiers dragging themselves across a field, and if I could have laughed—that is, made my face work into a smile and get sounds to discharge from my throat—I would have. God, it would have been good to laugh. Instead, I considered my options: either lie there and wait for someone to find me—how many days or weeks would that take?—or somehow get back to the house. I calmly assessed what might be wrong with me—stroke, cerebral hemorrhage, gunshot wound—but it was bigger than I could understand. The instinct to survive does not rise from particulars; a deep but general misery rollercoasted me into action. I tried to propel myself on my elbows but my right arm didn't work. The wind had swung around and was blowing in from the east. It was still a dry storm with only sputtering rain, but when I raised myself up, lightning fingered the entire sky. 14

It is not true that lightning never strikes the same place twice. I had entered a shower of sparks and furious brightness and, worried that I might be struck again, watched as lightning touched down all around me. Years before, in the high country, I'd been hit by lightning: an electrical charge had rolled down an open meadow during a fearsome thunderstorm, surged up the legs of my horse, coursed through me, and bounced a big spark off the 15 top of my head. To be struck again—and this time it was a direct hit—what did it mean?

The feeling had begun to come back into my legs and after many awkward attempts, I stood. To walk meant lifting each leg up by the thigh, moving it forward with my hands, setting it down. The earth felt like a peach that had split open in the middle; one side moved up while the other side moved down and my legs were out of rhythm. The ground rolled the way it does during an earthquake and the sky was tattered book pages waving in different directions. Was the ground liquifying under me, or had the molecular composition of my body deliquesced? I struggled to piece together fragments. Then it occurred to me that my brain was torn and that's where the blood had come from. 16

I walked. Sometimes my limbs held me, sometimes they didn't. I don't know how many times I fell but it didn't matter because I was making slow progress toward home. 17

Home—the ranch house—was about a quarter of a mile away. I don't remember much about getting there. My concentration went into making my legs work. The storm was strong. All the way across the basin, lightning lifted parts of mountains and sky into yellow refulgence and dropped them again, only to lift others. The inside of my eyelids turned gold and I could see the dark outlines of things through them. At the bottom of the hill I opened the door to my pickup and blew the horn with the idea that someone might hear me. No one came. My head had swollen to an indelicate shape. I tried to swallow—I was so thirsty—but the muscles in my throat were still paralyzed and I wondered when I would no longer be able to breathe. 18

Inside the house, sounds began to come out of me. I was doing crazy things, ripping my hiking boots off because the bottoms of my feet were burning, picking up the phone when I was finally able to scream. One of those times, someone happened to be on the line. I was screaming incoherently for help. My last conscious act was to dial 911. 19

Dark again. Pressing against sore ribs, my dogs pulled me out of the abyss, pulled and pulled. I smelled straw. My face was on 20 tatami. I opened my eyes, looked up, and saw neighbors. Had they come for my funeral? The phone rang and I heard someone give directions to the ambulance driver, who was lost. A "first responder," an EMT from town who has a reputation with the girls, leaned down and asked if he could "touch me" to see if there were any broken bones. What the hell, I thought. I was going to die anyway. Let him have his feel. But his touch was gentle and professional, and I was grateful.

I slipped back into unconsciousness and when I woke again two EMTs were listening to my heart. I asked them to look for my dogs but they wouldn't leave me. Someone else in the room went outside and found Sam and Yaki curled up on the porch, frightened but alive. Now I could rest. I felt the medics jabbing needles into the top of my hands, trying unsuccessfully to get IVs started, then strapping me onto a backboard and carrying me out the front door of the house, down steps, into lightning and rain, into what was now a full-blown storm. 21

The ambulance rocked and slid, slamming my bruised body against the metal rails of the gurney. Every muscle was in violent spasm and there was a place on my back near the heart that burned. I heard myself yell in pain. Finally the EMTs rolled up towels and blankets and wedged them against my arms, shoulders, hips, and knees so the jolting of the vehicle wouldn't dislodge me. The ambulance slid down into ditches, struggled out, bumped from one deep rut to another. I asked to be taken to the hospital in Cody, but they said they were afraid my heart might stop again. As it was, the local hospital was thirty-five miles away, ten of them dirt, and the trip took more than an hour. 22

Our arrival seemed a portent of disaster—and an occasion for comedy. I had been struck by lightning around five in the afternoon. It was now 9:00 P.M. Nothing at the hospital worked. Their one EKG machine was nonfunctional, and jokingly the nurses blamed it on me. "Honey, you've got too much electricity in your body," one of them told me. Needles were jammed into my hand—no one had gotten an IV going yet—and the doctor on call hadn't arrived, though half an hour had elapsed. The EMTs kept assuring me: "Don't worry, we won't leave you here." When an- 23 other nurse, who was filling out an admission form, asked me how tall I was, I answered: "Too short to be struck by lightning."

> "Electrical injury often results in ventricular fibrillation and injury to the medullary centers of the brain. Immediately after electric shock patients are usually comatose, apneic, and in circulatory collapse. . . ." 24

When the doctor on call—the only doctor in town, waddled into what they called the emergency room, my aura, he said, was yellow and gray—a soul in transition. I knew that he had gone to medical school but had never completed a residency and had been barred from ER or ICU work in the hospitals of Florida, where he had lived previously. Yet I was lucky. Florida has many lightning victims, and unlike the doctors I would see later, he at least recognized the symptoms of a lightning strike. The tally sheet read this way: I had suffered a hit by lightning which caused ventricular fibrillation—cardiac arrest—though luckily my heart started beating again. Violent contractions of muscles when one is hit often causes the body to fly through the air: I was flung far and hit hard on my left side, which may have caused my heart to start again, but along with that fortuitous side effect, I sustained a concussion, broken ribs, a possible broken jaw, and lacerations above the eye. The paralysis below my waist and up through the chest and throat—called kerauno-paralysis—is common in lightning strikes and almost always temporary, but my right arm continued to be almost useless. Fernlike burns—arborescent erythema—covered my entire body. These occur when the electrical charge follows tracings of moisture on the skin—rain or sweat—thus the spidery red lines. 25

> "Rapid institution of fluid and electrolyte therapy is essential with guidelines being the patient's urine output, hematocrit, osmolality, central venous pressure, and arterial blood gases. . . ." 26

The nurses loaded me onto a gurney. As they wheeled me down the hall to my room, a front wheel fell off and I was slammed into 27 the wall. Once I was in bed, the deep muscle aches continued, as did the chest pains. Later, friends came to visit. Neither doctor nor nurse had cleaned the cuts on my head, so Laura, who had herded sheep and cowboyed on all the ranches where I had lived and whose wounds I had cleaned when my saddle horse dragged her across a high mountain pasture, wiped blood and dirt from my face, arms, and hands with a cool towel and spooned yogurt into my mouth.

I was the only patient in the hospital. During the night, sheet lightning inlaid the walls with cool gold. I felt like an ancient, mummified child who had been found on a rock ledge near our ranch: bound tightly, unable to move, my dead face tipped backwards toward the moon. 28

In the morning, my regular doctor, Ben, called from Massachusetts, where he was vacationing, with this advice: "Get yourself out of that hospital and go somewhere else, anywhere." I was too weak to sign myself out, but Julie, the young woman who had a summer job on our ranch, retrieved me in the afternoon. She helped me get dressed in the cutoffs and torn T-shirt I had been wearing, but there were no shoes, so, barefoot, I staggered into Ben's office, where a physician's assistant kindly cleansed the gashes in my head. Then I was taken home. 29

Another thunderstorm slammed against the mountains as I limped up the path to the house. Sam and Yaki took one look at me and ran. These dogs lived with me, slept with me, understood every word I said, and I was too sick to find them, console them—even if they would have let me. 30

The next day my husband, who had just come down from the mountains where he worked in the summer, took me to another hospital. I passed out in the admissions office, was loaded onto a gurney, and taken for a CAT scan. No one bothered to find out why I had lost consciousness. Later, in the emergency unit, the doctor argued that I might not have been struck by lightning at all, as if I had imagined the incident. "Maybe a meteor hit me," I said, a suggestion he pondered seriously. After a blood panel and a brief neurological exam, which I failed—I couldn't follow his finger with my eyes or walk a straight line—he promptly released me. 31

> "Patients should be monitored electrocardiographically for at least 24 hours for significant arrhythmias which often have delayed onset. . . ." 32

It was difficult to know what was worse: being in a hospital where nothing worked and nobody cared, or being alone on an isolated ranch hundreds of miles from decent medical care. 33

In the morning I staggered into the kitchen. My husband, from whom I had been separated for three months, had left at 4:00 A.M. to buy cattle in another part of the state and would not be back for a month. Alone again, it was impossible to do much for myself. In the past I'd been bucked off, stiff and sore plenty of times but this felt different: I had no sense of equilibrium. My head hurt, every muscle in my body ached as if I had a triple dose of the flu, and my left eye was swollen shut and turning black and blue. Something moved in the middle of the kitchen floor. I was having difficulty seeing, but then I did see: a rattlesnake lay coiled in front of the stove. I reeled around and dove back into bed. Enough tests of character. I closed my eyes and half-slept. Later, when Julie came to the house, she found the snake and cut off its head with a shovel. 34

My only consolation was that the dogs came back. I had chest pains and all day Sam lay with his head against my heart. I cleaned a deep cut over Yaki's eye. It was half an inch deep but already healing. I couldn't tell if the dogs were sick or well, I was too miserable to know anything except that Death resided in the room: not as a human figure but as a dark fog rolling in, threatening to cover me; but the dogs stayed close and while my promise to keep them safe during a thunderstorm had proven fraudulent, their promise to keep me alive held good. 35

---

## *Meaning and Purpose*

1. If you had read this essay's first paragraph only, what would you have imagined the rest of the essay to be about? What evidence do you have for your answer?

2. In paragraph 14, “Images from World War II movies” filled the author’s head. Why do you suppose she would be mentally seeing such images?
3. What evidence is there to show that the author is interested in non-Western thought?
4. Why are paragraphs 24, 26, and 32 in quotation marks?

## *Strategy*

1. Paragraph 2 begins with “A single heartbeat stirs gray water.” Paragraph 3 begins with “Another heartbeat.” What is the author descriptively emphasizing by this strategy?
2. What is the main purpose of the dogs in this essay? What do they illustrate?
3. In paragraph 25, Erlich says that the first doctor she saw had a poor professional medical background. Yet she was fortunate that that doctor was the first to see her. Why?
4. In paragraph 27, Erlich describes equipment and activities at the hospital. What do those descriptions tell you about the conditions at the hospital? Where else in the essay is evidence to strengthen your answer to this question? What is that evidence?

## *Style*

1. What is humorous about the first sentence in paragraph 12?
2. Reread paragraph 15 and then read the definition of “rhetorical question” in this book’s glossary. Is the question in paragraph 15 a rhetorical question? Give a reason for your answer.
3. In paragraph 19, the author says “sounds began to come out of me.” Why didn’t she simply say, “I began to make sounds”?
4. Paragraph 22 has the phrase “ten of them dirt.” To what does that phrase refer?

## *Writing Tasks*

1. Write an essay that thoroughly describes someone whom you know well. In the first paragraph, of not fewer than 100 words,

begin your description by detailing a characteristic of that person in such a way that you purposely mystify your essay's audience. For example, one student described her uncle, an automobile mechanic. Her first paragraph began with, "No one in this neighborhood can hear a car being started on a cold morning without thinking about my uncle." Then she went on to describe three cars briefly: One was an oil-burning clunker belonging to the next-door neighbor; one was a brand-new model that had blue smoke puffing from it every time its driver shifted gears; and one was an eight-year-old sedan that belonged to the elderly couple who lived across the street. It ran beautifully. Naturally, the elderly couple entrusted their car to the girl's uncle. After she pointed out that fact, the student described her uncle's other characteristics, habits, and physical features. Follow this strategy in your essay.

2. A small incident in a life can have an effect for a long time. The incident can be a happy one, a sad one, a thoughtful one, a reflective one, a cheerful one—almost any kind, in other words. If a small incident has strongly affected you, then describe that incident. Be sure to use details. Remember that you are trying to reinvent the incident in the reader's mind. To do that, use abstract words or broad-meaning words, such as "large," "pretty," "big," "great," and "nice" sparingly. When you use such words excessively, readers can only guess at what you saw. Be sure, therefore, to use specific and concrete words to help readers see in their mind's eye what you saw.

## ❦ *Responding to Photographs* ❦

### *Description*

Woman Brushing Her Hair

Before children speak, they see. A child looks and recognizes before it can form words. At an early age we learn to respond to visual experience and interpret it. A smiling or scowling face, a closed or open hand, an erect or slumped body—all are gestures that invite our interpretation.

As we move through life, our interpretations of visual experiences become more complex. A young man walking down the street might go unnoticed. But add spiked hair, a leather coat, and torn jeans held up by a chain belt. Put a safety pin through one earlobe and thread an earring in his pierced nose, and this visual experience catches our attention. We examine the details of the young man's attire and perhaps draw conclusions about his character, lifestyle, personal values, or musical taste.

Photographs, unlike spontaneous visual experience, arrange details for a viewer. They are not, as is often assumed, a realistic record of an experience, but an arranged and reproduced moment of experience. Whenever we look at a photograph we are being guided by the hand that held the camera. And whenever we look at a photograph we are being invited to respond to the image—to interpret it.

At first glance, "Woman Brushing Her Hair" seems to be a snapshot that captures a spontaneous moment in this woman's day. But on closer examination, the image seems to be carefully arranged, the hand of the photographer reaching to pull a response from the viewer.

With description as a dominant method of development, complete one of the following writing tasks. Before beginning your essay, reread "Description: Capturing Sensory Details" at the beginning of this chapter to familiarize yourself with the conventions of effective descriptive writing.

1. Write a "fly-on-the-wall" description, one that strictly reports the arrangement and content of "Woman Brushing Her Hair." After studying the contents of the photograph, decide on how you wish to arrange your description. Through your essay, be sure to follow the arrangement consistently.
2. Use "Woman Brushing Her Hair" as the basis of an *objective* description that creates a dominant impression of this woman's life. Like any writer, or photographer for that matter, you must select details, gestures, objects, arrangements that help generate the dominant impression you wish to create. Remember, your task is not to describe everything in the photo, but to use material from the photo for your purpose.
3. Use "Woman Brushing Her Hair" as the basis of a *subjective* description that creates a dominant impression of this woman's life. You, as in assignment 1, must select material from the photo that leads readers to a single impression, but because you are approaching the photograph subjectively, you may color the details with your feelings.
4. Select a photograph that engages your interest. Title the photograph, and then using it as the basis of your description, complete one of the writing tasks just outlined. Be sure to include the photograph as part of your final draft.

## ❦ *Additional Writing Tasks* ❦

### *Description*

1. Recall a spot you visited when younger, not far from your home. It should be a place you remember well but not one you visit constantly. Once you have selected the spot, draw upon your strength of recollection: visualize yourself in this place, seeing the physical features, hearing the sounds, and smelling the odors and aromas. Jot down your memories. What details do you recall, and in what order of importance? Record your memories just as the place was at that time in your life. How would you tell what you saw if you were describing the scene for a stranger? Which details would create images in this stranger's mind? Try to write this part of the description from a child's perspective.

   Once you have described the place as you recall it, write a description of how the place appears now, after years have passed. This part of the description should be done from an adult's perspective. Perhaps the place has not held up under time's pressure. Perhaps your view of it has changed. Perhaps you colored this place with romantic illusions.

   Once the second rough description is completed, begin the first draft. Develop a structure that shifts between past and present, revealing both the child's and the adult's attitude.
2. Select several photographs that represent milestones in your life. Describe them as if you were a reporter relating the events that are taking place in the photo. Keep your description objective but vivid. Or, if you wish, use several magazine ads as the basis for a description. Here, too, describe the events in the advertisement objectively, merely reporting the image you see on the page, not interpreting it.
3. Describe an animal you have encountered, perhaps a wild animal such as a coyote, wolf, deer, bear, or whale. Begin with a description of the animal from folklore, which will probably require a visit to the library. Then follow with a description of the animal as you experienced it. Seek a connection between the two elements in this description.

4. Do something slightly out of the ordinary and describe the experience. Perhaps you will climb a tree and sit among the branches. Maybe you will sit in a closed closet for half an hour. You might roller skate, stand on your head, dance a waltz, lie on the grass and stare at the clouds—the possibilities are endless. Once you have had the experience, describe it in detail.
5. Select a physical event and describe it in detail: the fog rolling through the woods or city streets; a storm gathering in the distance and sweeping toward you; a cloudburst; wind roaring through the trees and rattling the windows; an earthquake. In your description capture a sense of motion, sound, and smell, as well as visual detail.
6. Describe people at work in various settings:
   - A supermarket
   - A fast-food restaurant
   - A newsstand
   - A factory
   - A car wash
   - A pizza parlor

   In your description create a dominant impression.

# 4

# *Narration*

## *Relating Events*

## *The Method*

*Once upon a time* is the phrase that begins countless childhood narratives. *To narrate* is to tell a story. Our lives are full of stories, some exciting, some dull. These stories might be as brief as an anecdote—"A funny thing happened to me today while dissecting a frog in biology." They might seem as simple as a fairy tale, such as "Little Red Riding Hood," or as complex as a novel, such as James Joyce's *Ulysses*.

Narratives are so common in human experience that some psychologists have claimed that their patterns are etched on the human psyche, that people actually *need* stories. Absurd? Well, it is difficult to imagine that some people might require stories in the same way as they require affection. One fact, though, is certain: effective narratives embody a few known characteristics, and good writers keep this fact in mind when composing their stories.

The most common of these characteristics is the **narrative effect**, which you may conceive as the narrative purpose, or, as some writers call it, the "payoff." Readers want a payoff—a moral, an insight, a message, a point, or just good entertainment. Often the narrative effect will be subtle, nothing more than getting the reader to utter a soft "Aha!" Consider this narrative, a teaching tale from Zen Buddhist lore. At first glance, it may seem to lack a narrative effect.

> A man traveling across a field encountered a tiger. He fled, the tiger after him. Coming to a precipice, he caught hold of the root of a wild vine and swung himself down over the edge. The tiger sniffed at him from above. Trembling, the man looked down to where, far below, another tiger was waiting to eat him. Only the vine sustained him.
>
> Two mice, one white and one black, little by little started to gnaw away the vine. The man saw a luscious strawberry near him. Grasping the vine with one hand, he plucked the strawberry with the other. How sweet it tasted!

What is the payoff? is a fair question that every reader has the right to ask. Clearly the narrative effect the storyteller might wish to achieve is not spelled out; the story reveals no thesis. But it certainly has something to do with being involved in the present and, perhaps, not worrying about what can't be controlled. One student suggests that fear of the past (represented by the first tiger pacing above the traveler) or fear of the future (the second tiger pacing below the traveler) should not interfere with our enjoyment of the present (the strawberry). But what about the mice? They're a detail that needs to be considered in any interpretation. Soon they will gnaw through the vine, sending the monk to his death. Perhaps the tale suggests that when death is imminent, life becomes inordinately sweet.

Why create a story to illustrate a point, you might ask, even one as brief as this Zen tale? Why not just hold up a finger, smile sagely, and directly state a purpose? "Do not let fear of the past or future interfere with your enjoyment of the moment" or "Enjoy life now, for death may be near." In other words, "Why all the mystery?"

Not all narratives are packed with hidden meanings or intended to provoke emotional responses. Many are factual reports, such as news reports or police reports, which simply recount events as they unfold, but narrative essays often deal with subjects that go beyond the limits of a report. Like the treasures in many children's tales, the purpose in many narratives—especially works of imagination such as tales, short stories, and novels—is therefore buried. In this way, the narrative essay offers its readers the opportunity to experience anything the storyteller has experienced—love, anger, fear, hate, prejudice, outrage, confusion, hope, disappointment—all the emotional states we encounter in life. The events, therefore, must be dramatized, not explained, thus recreating, rather than reporting, events: first you live through a string of related experiences and then you get the meaning—well, maybe you get the meaning.

## *Strategies*

Because of the nature of narrative essays, the relationship between you and the storyteller is complex. Storytellers will entice you to use your imagination to re-create the experience. You should join, not resist, a writer in this effort. If the effort fails, then you will not make the creative leap that allows a narrative essay to achieve its emotional effect. Even if the purpose behind a narrative essay seems murky after a first reading, trust that the writer who chooses narration as a dominant essay pattern will always keep an eye on the purpose, usually dramatizing rather than stating it.

### *Narrative Structure*

Every storyteller knows that readers love narratives to be driven by conflict between opposing forces, such as two figures in the narrative pitted against each other in a battle of wills or a single figure in conflict with his or her own feelings. But just as important, they also know that readers crave order, a sense that the action has direction, movement. To meet this need, many narrative essays are divided into three parts:

1. The **orientation**. The beginning sentences in a short narrative or the opening paragraphs in a long narrative are designed to establish the situation, identify the key figures, and suggest the conflict. The narrative purpose may be suggested, but the outcome should not be revealed.
2. The **complication**. The narrative should move forward through a series of scenes that intensifies the conflict and builds to a climax. The climax is the narrative's point of highest drama and sets up the narrative effect, that is, the writer's purpose, which always lurks within the climactic moment.
3. The **resolution**. The issues in the narrative should be resolved before the story ends. The resolution may be brief, often suggesting rather than directly stating the effect the writer has tried to create. At times the resolution will be ambiguous, thus forcing readers to reinterpret the narrative events in light of the closing observation.

You will find that most effective narrative essays follow this loose pattern. You can usually count on a storyteller to establish a story's situation in the orientation by providing information that answers these questions: Who? What? Where? and When? They will suggest a **conflict** as well. Consider this opening from Martin Gansberg's "Thirty-eight Who Saw Murder Didn't Call the Police."

> For more than half an hour thirty-eight respectable, law-abiding citizens in Queens watched a killer stalk and stab a woman in three separate attacks in Kew Gardens.
>
> Twice their chatter and the sudden glow of their bedroom lights interrupted him and frightened him off. Each time he returned, sought her out, and stabbed her again. Not one person telephoned the police during the assault; one witness called after the woman was dead.
>
> That was two weeks ago today.

Whom does the situation involve? A murder victim, the murderer, and, most important, the "thirty-eight respectable, law-abiding citizens" who didn't call the police. What does the situation involve? Crime in the streets. Where did it take place? An area in Queens, a New York City borough. When did it happen? Two weeks before the date of the newspaper narrative. And the conflict? Gansberg clearly suggests a conflict related to social obligation—the indifference of the thirty-eight bystanders who fail to meet their legal and moral responsibility.

### *Point of View*

Also in the orientation section of narrative essays, writers establish the **point of view**—that is, they reveal who is telling the story. As generally used in narrative essays, point of view is easy to understand. Stories are told either by a participant in the events (first-person point of view) or by a nonparticipant (third-person point of view).

Most often readers associate stories with the first-person point of view, which seems to give narrative essays authenticity: "I swear this is true—I was there! I lived it!" Often the events have directly affected the first-person storyteller in some emotional or intellectual way. At other times, the storyteller acts as a spectator, reporting events he or she saw others experience. In either case, first-person narratives usually are more subjective than third-person narratives. They embody the storyteller's attitudes throughout the essay, directly in overt statements or indirectly in style. Writers almost always establish the point of view in the first paragraph. Consider the opening paragraph in Flannery O'Connor's essay, "The King of Birds."

> When I was five, I had an experience that marked me for life. Pathé News sent a photographer from New York to Savannah to take a picture of a chicken of mine. This chicken, a buff Cochin Bantam, had the distinction of being able to walk either forward or backward. Her fame had spread through the press, and by the time she reached the attention of Pathé News, I suppose there was nowhere left for her to go—forward or backward. Shortly after that she died, as now seems fitting.

O'Connor's opening paragraph illustrates one more bit of advice we can give you when reading first-person narratives: watch for the storyteller's own perspective. Notice that O'Connor begins by relating the emotional effect of an event that took place when she was five, but the first and last sentences clearly indicate that she is writing from an adult's perspective, not a five-year-old's, thus adding complexity, perhaps even irony, to the tone.

A writer who uses the third-person point of view usually relates events as accurately, and sometimes objectively, as possible. As a nonparticipant, the third-person narrator develops the story from reports by others, much as a journalist collects information for a story. This approach doesn't mean a third-person narration lacks power or drama. It merely means that the storyteller is not part of the action. Consider the opening paragraph in Maxine Hong Kingston's brief narrative "The Wild Man of the Green Swamp."

> For eight months in 1975, residents on the edge of Green Swamp, Florida, had been reporting to the police that

> they had seen a Wild Man. When they stepped toward him, he made strange noises as in a foreign language and ran back into the saw grass. At first, authorities said the Wild Man was a mass hallucination. Maneating animals lived in the swamp, and a human being could hardly find a place to rest without sinking. Perhaps it was some kind of a bear the children had seen.

Kingston's point of view is clearly **objective,** even dispassionate. We don't want to leave you with the impression, though, that third-person narrations are always objective and dispassionate. Review the opening from Gansberg's "Thirty-eight Who Saw Murder Didn't Call the Police," presented above. Gansberg's attitude toward the "thirty-eight respectable, law-abiding citizens" who watched a killer stalk his victim is clearly **subjective** and very passionate.

### *Chronological and Psychological Time*

Because narratives unfold in time, storytellers must arrange the events so that the connections between them are clear. As you begin to read a narrative, notice the writer's narrative arrangement: Are the events arranged according to **chronological time**; that is, in sequence as they happened, step by step? Or are they arranged according to **psychological time**; that is, the way in which events might be connected in memory, shifting back and forth in time while keeping a sense of forward movement?

The decision a writer makes about the arrangement of a narrative essay is often determined by the subject. A historical essay, such as a narrative about a battle, usually marches along in chronological time. But if the subject comes from personal experience then the essay may be arranged in psychological time, beginning *in medias res*, "in the middle of things," with an event that comes near the end of the actual chronology. This opening event can be highly dramatic, designed to keep readers in suspense until the essay closes, when its purpose becomes clear.

Writers use *flashback* and *flashforward* to shift the narrative action from one time frame to another. Flashback skips to the past to dramatize a previous event that has some bearing on the present. Flashforward skips to the future to help create suspense by showing a consequence that might result from present events. Although writers mainly use flashback and flashforward in psychologically arranged narratives, they can also use them, but to a much lesser extent, in narratives dominated by chronological development to add depth and variety to the predictable, step-by-step arrangement of events.

Whichever arrangement the writer chooses, he or she is obliged to guide you through the story. While reading with a critical eye, you should, therefore, watch for transitions in time. They may be complete sentences designed to smooth your way from one event to another: "My social life began to crumble into pieces like a stale oatmeal cookie after we settled in Santa Fe." They may take the form of brief phrases: "Two weeks later," "Only one year ago," "Soon I was to learn." Or they may be single words that help a writer cut through time: "Now, Then," "Before, Today." Identifying the transitional tactics will help you follow the most complex narrative.

### *Scene and Summary*

While crafting a narrative essay, the storyteller has two methods to use in presenting the events: **scene** and **summary**. You'll recognize scene because it directly portrays an event on the page. Like a scene in film or drama, a narrative-essay scene is played before your eyes. Summary is a synopsis of an event. It relates the high points but leaves out much of the specific detail that a scene usually includes. Many narratives include both scene and summary, with summary serving as the glue that holds the scenes together. It might help if you think of scene and summary as showing and telling: scene shows, summary tells. Consider this scene from a student's narrative that shows the writer's battle with fear:

> I stood paralyzed on the dock, my hands clenched and my knees locked tight. Bobby was flailing at the water, trying

> to pull himself to the overturned boat. He shouted for help, his voice rising to a shrill pitch and carrying beyond the boathouse and into the empty woods.
>
> I wanted to plunge into the lake, but my body would not unlock, and the horrible, empty spot in my mind threatened me like a black pit I might fall into. It was the water and all it symbolized—darkness, suffocation, a murky death.

The narrator presents this dramatic moment as if it were taking place before your eyes. He is showing it to you. Now compare this scene to a summarized version:

> When my brother Bobby overturned the rowboat and fell into the lake, I panicked. You see, I had almost drowned once in this very lake. The experience left me with the deep, irrational fear that if I ever swam in it again, I would be swallowed up. Although I knew he needed help, fear of the water paralyzed me.

Here the writer tells about the event. This summary lacks the immediacy of the scenic version, yet it, too, is effective.

Writers often, but not always, use dialogue in scenes, which helps to dramatize an event. Usually dialogue will reflect the give-and-take that takes place between two speakers and is integrated with action. For example,

> Raymond leaned forward, jabbing a finger into Chico's chest, "You will never see Ellen again," he said. "Never!"
>
> "You are wrong," Chico said, "We are going to be married."
>
> Raymond, his face frozen in an angry mask, stared at Chico, who was much smaller and looked frail. Then Raymond glanced around the crowded locker room where the rest of the team had stopped to watch. "If you live," Raymond said, before storming out the door.

In summary, writers will sometimes add key snatches of dialogue to create authenticity while moving on to more dramatic scenes. For example,

When Raymond confronted Chico in the locker room, their teammates watched in dismay. They had never seen Raymond so angry when he told Chico that he would never see Ellen again. Chico remained calm and told Raymond that he was wrong and then revealed that he and Ellen were to be married. Raymond could not hide his anger and said, "If you live," before storming out the door.

Whether writers use scene and summary, or both, depends on the effect they wish to create. Often narrative essayists present the dramatic moments in scenes and use summary to move from scene to scene, thus skipping through the less significant events.

## *Narration in College Writing*

College writers sometimes work brief narrative passages into an essay with other dominant patterns. In such papers, narrative passages may be used to create an interesting opening or to illustrate a point. In either case, the narrative must have a clear structural purpose to justify its use. More frequently, however, narratives based on personal experience are frequent assignments in college courses. In cultural anthropology or social psychology you may be assigned a narrative report that requires your own observations. In history you may be asked to write from imagination a narrative about a historical event from a historical figure's point of view. In English you may be assigned an informal narrative essay based on personal experience that brought some insight.

### *Guidelines for Narrative Writing*

1. Select an experience that lends itself to narrative development and identify the narrative effect you wish to achieve.
2. Determine the point of view to use—first person for a narrative based on experience and third person for a narrative compiled from outside information.
3. In prewriting, limit the events in your narrative. Pick out the highlights, then enrich them with descriptive detail.

Remember, not every event should be presented in a scene. By dramatizing the emotional peaks, you will sustain your reader's interest.

4. Compose your first draft.

   Write an *orientation* that sets the situation, identifies the key figures, establishes the conflict, and arouses interest.

   Structure the *complication* by arranging events in climactic order with the most dramatic and revealing event serving as the climax.

   Create a *resolution* that reveals, directly or indirectly, the narrative effect, that is, the narrative purpose or "payoff."
5. Revise your first draft with an eye for scene and summary. If you use dialogue, examine it to see if you should present it in scene or summary. Be sure that your narrative has a strong forward movement with enough descriptive detail to engage the reader's senses.

### *A Student Essay Developed by Narration*

Richard McKnight, a freshman composition student, wrote the following narrative in response to this class assignment:

> In "A Hanging," George Orwell uses narrative to communicate ideas without stating them directly. Write a 750 to 1000 word narrative in which you make a point without explicitly stating it. Tell a story of an event that illustrates your point, such as (1) how a stylish wedding shows that we care too much about money and appearance, or (2) how a charismatic speaker shows that we are easily persuaded to believe something, or (3) how a sports event shows that old age is not the end of active living.

For his narrative, McKnight chose the third option. Examine his essay to see how effectively he uses narrative conventions to tell his story. After reading it through once, read it again along with the notes in the margin. Then read the comments that follow the essay.

The Last Ride

*McKnight begins the orientation with the opening sentence, which immediately sets up the situation, establishes the first person point of view, and suggests the conflict.*

*Here McKnight suggests the narrative purpose.*

I watched a gray-haired surfer sitting on the longest board I had ever seen, waiting for a wave in Candle Cove. He was forty yards beyond the edge of a reef that seemed to rise and fall dangerously as the sea sucked to and from the shore. Connie stood nearby, a senior year-round lifeguard who patrolled the beaches in a jeep during winter. I wondered why a man his age was surfing alone on such dangerous winter swells.

*McKnight's vivid description helps readers visualize the dangerous reef.*

At Candle Cove a winter swell can sometimes rise to twelve feet. Twelve feet is not a remarkable height for waves at sandy beaches where they break slowly and leave plenty of room for surfers to maneuver. But at the Cove waves break quickly and crash over a reef crusted with razor-sharp barnacles. Surfers must race across a wave's face to clear the reef and reach the sandy beach. Only the best surfers will risk being swept over the rocks, even for a spectacular ride. But sometimes even the best do not make it safely to the beach.

*First flashback—notice that McKnight introduces it with the phrase, "Just two weeks earlier," which clearly indicates the narrative will skip back in time. McKnight wants to dramatize the danger in a way the last paragraph did not. He shows a surfer being washed over the reef, thus concretely establishing the danger.*

Just two weeks earlier, a hot-shot from Hawaii paddled out in heavy surf that a Mexican storm had kicked up. He sat on his board beyond the break and waited for the big swells to roll in. Suddenly, he swung his board's nose toward shore to catch the day's biggest wave. He seemed to do everything right: He quickly leaped to his feet, cut sharply left, moved to the board's nose to gain speed as he shot ahead of the curl—but not in time. The massive wave broke over his shoulder and tossed him into the roiling foam. The breaking wave's force snapped his board in half and swept him over the reef. He survived, but barely. Lifeguards raced him to an emergency ward where doctors hovered above his body for two hours with needles and thread.

*In this sentence McKnight links the old surfer to a specific danger, echoes the narrative purpose, and ends the orientation. The complication begins with dialogue, which helps vary the narrative pace.*

Now the old man was in that kind of danger but with one difference—he was well past his prime, much too old to be riding riding in dangerous waters.

"Better call him in," I said. "He's going to get hurt."

"He won't come in," Connie said.

"You're in charge of the beach."

"Don't you know who he is?" she said.

*Excellent use of scene and summary throughout this section. McKnight wisely mixed dramatic dialogue with information presented in summarized dialogue. Never use dialogue merely to give information; use it to suggest conflict.*

I said I didn't. She asked if I had ever seen *Slippery When Wet.* The film, made by an amateur photographer thirty years earlier, had become a surfing classic in the late 1950s. I told her I had. She said that when he was a young man, the old surfer had been featured in it. She said he was shown riding long boards on waves over twenty-five feet high at Sunset Beach in Hawaii and that he was even shown riding shore break at this beach. I vaguely remembered him, but there were many surfers in the film agilely maneuvering their boards as they rode waves.

"He's a living legend," Connie said.

"A living legend should know when to quit."

"If it's in your blood, you don't quit."

*Once again, McKnight suggests the narrative purpose.*

"Look," I said, "the living legend's going to need an ambulance."

*The climax begins to build. "He's tanked" is the most dramatic moment. McKnight's vivid, carefully arranged description helps readers visualize the event.*

The old surfer was paddling to catch a wave, the largest to roll into the cove since I had been watching. His arms dug three, four times into the water before the wave swept him up, the reef rising dangerously close before him. He sprang to his feet, arched his back, and turned the board left as he raced down the wave's face. Taking short, choppy steps, he made his way to the board's nose to gain more speed and crouched low, avoiding the curl as it cracked behind him.

Suddenly he was out of sight. The wave had tossed forward and the curl folded over his crouching body.

"He's tanked," I said, looking at the white water as it washed over the reef. "Better get him."

"Wait." she said.

"Now!" I said, but didn't know why. I wasn't a lifeguard or her boss.

She looked at me, "Show a little courage," she said. "He is."

*McKnight uses the second flashback to show readers what the old surfer could do in his youth in a way that leads to the resolution.*

She was right. Still bent low on the front of the board, the old surfer shot out of the curl, well ahead of the white water. And then an image from the film came to me: A young man, over thirty years younger than this man, riding waves at this same beach. He, too, shot out of the curl and cleared the reef on a massive wave, bigger than this one, that was crashing behind him, spraying twenty feet into the air. In the film, the beach was crowded with cheering spectators. They had seen a ride beyond their belief, but that was when surfing was new and still viewed as an astounding feat.

*In the resolution McKnight returns to the present and links the flashback directly to this moment, thus suggesting the narrative purpose. The last sentence strongly suggests the purpose without stating it directly.*

Now, this time as an old man with only two people watching, he once again cleared the reef and guided his board toward shore. In shallow water he stepped from the board, and swung it up under his arm, striding toward the sand where we stood. He walked passed us, nodding to Connie, who smiled at him. He looked ancient, his skin thick from years of sun, his hair gray and thin, his face wrinkled, and his belly growing thick. Yet his blue eyes were full of life, full of future rides. I knew that I, like that crowd in the film, had seen something special, an astounding feat, not just for someone with gray hair and wrinkled skin, but for anyone, young or old.

### *Comments*

Now let's examine some of the significant elements in McKnight's essay.

**The Orientation.** McKnight quickly establishes the situation—that is, he and a lifeguard watch an old surfer in dangerous waters. He also establishes a first person point of view, which is appropriate for this essay even though he is not the center of attention. He is, however, observing the experience, and he is the one who learns a lesson, which suggests that to grow old does not necessarily mean one must grow weak. The conflict emerges from McKnight's attitude about growing old as reflected in his comments about the old surfer riding a big wave.

**The Complication.** McKnight builds his narrative slowly while working-in background information to intensify the danger. The climax occurs when the old man catches the wave, disappears in the curl, and then shoots out of the curl, clearing the reef.

**The Resolution.** McKnight resolves the action when he remembers having seen the old surfer in a film made some thirty years earlier. Even though he is wrinkled and paunchy, the old surfer repeats an earlier feat, thus showing that age has not destroyed his physical capacity.

**The Narrative Effect.** McKnight leaves his purpose unstated but heavily suggested. First, by juxtaposing the Hawaiian surfer's accident with the old surfer's success, he suggests that the old man can compete with anyone. Second, by recalling the old surfer's youthful performance, McKnight shows that he can surf as well as he did thirty years earlier. Finally, at first McKnight creates the sense that the old surfer has "passed his prime," but the closing sentence indicates that he was mistaken, thus suggesting the narrative purpose.

**Time Arrangement.** McKnight arranges the events chronologically but makes effective use of flashback in two spots—each one bearing on the present action. In the orientation, he recalls the accident that sent the Hawaiian surfer to an emergency ward, thus highlighting the danger the old surfer faces. In the resolution, McKnight recalls having seen the old surfer on film, thus demonstrating that over thirty years later he still has his physical skills. Both flashbacks come at critical moments in the chronology and add significance to the action.

**Revision.** When you revise a narrative, look for places that seem flat. Then try to dramatize them. For example, McKnight's essay had been polished and ready to turn in. Then he reread it and noticed that his initial description was flat, that is, it lacked drama. He was merely telling about the danger rather than showing just how dangerous the reef was.

At the cove a winter swell can sometimes rise to twelve
a remarkable height
feet ~~and be very dangerous to ride~~. Twelve feet is not ~~high~~ for
they
waves at sandy beaches where ~~waves~~ break slowly and leave
plenty of room for surfers to maneuver. But at the cove
waves break quickly and crash over a reef crusted with
race across a wave's
razor-sharp barnacles. Surfers ~~who are willing to risk the~~
face to clear the reef and reach the sandy
~~danger must catch that wave quickly, leap up, and cut left to~~
beach. Only the best surfers will risk being
~~shoot ahead of the curl until safely passed the reef. If surfers~~
swept over the rocks, even for a spectacular
~~are not fast or if they take a misstep, they might end up in~~
ride. But sometimes even the best do not
~~emergency wards with doctors hovering over them with~~
make it safely to the beach.
~~noddles and thread~~.

Just two weeks earlier, a hot-shot from Hawaii paddled out in heavy surf that a mexican storm had kicked up. He sat on his board beyond the break and waited for the big swells to roll in. Suddenly, he swung his board's nose toward shore to Catch the day's biggest wave. He seemed to do everything right: He quickly leaped to his feet, cut sharply left, moved to the board's nose to gain speed as he shot ahead of the curl—but not in time. The massive wave broke over his shoulder and tossed him into the roiling foam. The breaking wave's force snapped his board in half and swept him over the reef. He survived, but barely. Lifeguards raced him to an emergency ward where doctors hovered above his body for two hours with needles and thread.

Revised, with detail added and with a flashback that shows how dangerous the reef is, McKnight's final draft reads as follows:

At the Cove a winter swell can sometimes rise to twelve feet. Twelve feet is not a remarkable height for waves at sandy beaches where they break slowly and leave plenty of room for surfers to maneuver. But at the Cove waves break quickly and crash over a reef crusted with razor sharp barnacles. Surfers must race across a wave's face to clear the reef and reach the sandy beach. Only the best surfers will risk being swept over the rocks, even for a spectacular ride. But sometimes even the best do not make it safely to the beach.

Just two weeks earlier, a hot-shot from Hawaii paddled out in heavy surf that a Mexican storm had kicked up. He sat on his board beyond the break and waited for the big swells to roll in. Suddenly, he swung his board's nose toward shore

## Peer Review

You may be asked to write an essay about one of the readings that follow. Before you meet with your writing group, review this introduction. As you read the group papers, use these general principles of narration to help guide your comments.

1. The situation should be clear, that is, the who, what, when, and why of the story.
2. Some sort of conflict should be suggested early. If there is no conflict, the paper may be flat and uninteresting.
3. The point of view (who is telling the story) should be clear.
4. People in the narrative should be carefully distinguished, one from another.
5. The time sequence should be clear. Readers must be guided carefully through any changes in chronological order.
6. The narrative should have a purpose. Readers want a payoff.

to catch the day's biggest wave. He seemed to do everything right: He quickly leaped to his feet, cut sharply left, moved to the board's nose to gain speed as he shot ahead of the curl—but not in time. The massive wave broke over his shoulder and tossed him into the roiling foam. The breaking waves force snapped his board in half and swept him over the reef. He survived, but barely. Lifeguards raced him to an emergency ward where doctors hovered above his body for two hours with needles and thread.

This dramatized version, though longer, creates visual action for the reader, thus showing the danger, *not* just telling about it.

What follows is a collection of narrative essays by professional writers. As you read them, keep in mind that you are reading as a writer who is learning the craft, not merely reading to gather information for a test.

# ❦ Maya Angelou ❦

*Maya Angelou's talents and accomplishments span many fields, but she is perhaps best known for* I Know Why the Caged Bird Sings *(1970), the first volume in her five-part autobiography, in which she recounts her childhood years living with her grandmother in Stamps, Arkansas and for the stirring poem she composed and read at the 1993 presidential inauguration. Born Marguerita Johnson in 1928, Angelou surmounted the hardships and disadvantages of her youth—raped at age eight, unwed mother at sixteen—to write a joyful account of her own life and to achieve distinction as a dancer, actress, director, poet, scriptwriter, civil-rights activist, and television writer and producer. She acted in the television series "Roots," and has written several television specials, including a BBC–TV documentary called* Trying to Make It Home *(1988). She has received numerous awards and honorary degrees for her accomplishments and her continued service to the cause of civil rights.*

# *Finishing School*

*This story describes a brief time in Maya Angelou's childhood in Arkansas, where she was sent to work in a white woman's house to learn "mid-Victorian values" as a black woman was supposed to know them. In the story, taken from* I Know Why the Caged Bird Sings, *the author mixes chronological and psychological narrative to relate her growing awareness of the subtleties in white domination.*

*Notice, as you read, how Maya Angelou's attitudes toward her employer, Mrs. Cullinan, change. What specific events occasion those changes?*

---

Recently a white woman from Texas, who would quickly describe herself as a liberal, asked me about my hometown. When I told her that in Stamps my grandmother had owned the only Negro general merchandise store since the turn of the century, she exclaimed, "Why, you were a debutante." Ridiculous and even ludicrous. But Negro girls in small Southern towns, whether 1 poverty-stricken or just munching along on a few of life's necessities, were given as extensive and irrelevant preparations for adulthood as rich white girls shown in magazines. Admittedly the training was not the same. While white girls learned to waltz and sit gracefully with a tea cup balanced on their knees, we were lagging behind, learning the mid-Victorian values with very little money to indulge them. . . .

We were required to embroider and I had trunkfuls of colorful dishtowels, pillowcases, runners and handkerchiefs to my credit. I mastered the art of crocheting and tatting, and there was a lifetime's supply of dainty doilies that would never be used in sacheted dresser drawers. It went without saying that all girls could iron and wash, but the finer touches around the home, like setting a table with real silver, baking roasts and cooking vegetables without meat, had to be learned elsewhere. Usually at the source of those habits. During my tenth year, a white woman's kitchen became my finishing school. 2

Mrs. Viola Cullinan was a plump woman who lived in a three-bedroom house somewhere behind the post office. She was singularly unattractive until she smiled, and then the lines around her eyes and mouth which made her look perpetually dirty disappeared, and her face looked like the mask of an impish elf. She usually rested her smile until late afternoon when her women friends dropped in and Miss Glory, the cook, served them cold drinks on the closed-in porch. 3

The exactness of her house was inhuman. This glass went here and only here. That cup had its place and it was an act of impudent rebellion to place it anywhere else. At twelve o'clock the table was set. At 12:15 Mrs. Cullinan sat down to dinner (whether her husband had arrived or not). At 12:16 Miss Glory brought out the food. 4

It took me a week to learn the difference between a salad plate, a bread plate and a dessert plate. 5

Mrs. Cullinan kept up the tradition of her wealthy parents. She was from Virginia. Miss Glory, who was a descendant of slaves that had worked for the Cullinans, told me her history. She had married beneath her (according to Miss Glory). Her 6 husband's family hadn't had their money very long and what they had "didn't 'mount to much."

As ugly as she was, I thought privately, she was lucky to get a husband above or beneath her station. But Miss Glory wouldn't let me say a thing against her mistress. She was very patient with me, however, over the housework. She explained the dishware, silverware and servants' bells. The large round bowl in which soup was served wasn't a soup bowl, it was a tureen. There were goblets, sherbet glasses, ice-cream glasses, wine glasses, green glass coffee cups with matching saucers, and water glasses. I had a glass to drink from, and it sat with Miss Glory's on a separate shelf from the others. Soup spoons, gravy boat, butter knives, salad forks and carving platter were additions to my vocabulary and in fact almost represented a new language. I was fascinated with the novelty, with the fluttering Mrs. Cullinan and her Alice-in-Wonderland house. 7

Her husband remains, in my memory, undefined. I lumped him with all the other white men that I had ever seen and tried not to see. 8

On our way home one evening, Miss Glory told me that Mrs. Cullinan couldn't have children. She said that she was too delicate-boned. It was hard to imagine bones at all under those layers of fat. Miss Glory went on to say that the doctor had taken out all her lady organs. I reasoned that a pig's organs included the lungs, heart, and liver, so if Mrs. Cullinan was walking around without those essentials, it explained why she drank alcohol out of unmarked bottles. She was keeping herself embalmed. 9

When I spoke to Bailey about it, he agreed that I was right, but he also informed me that Mr. Cullinan had two daughters by a colored lady and that I knew them very well. He added that the girls were the spitting image of their father. I was unable to remember what he looked like, although I had just left him a few hours before, but I thought of the Coleman girls. They were very light-skinned and certainly didn't look very much like their mother (no one ever mentioned Mr. Coleman). 10

My pity for Mrs. Cullinan preceded me the next morning like the Cheshire cat's smile. Those girls, who could have been her 11 daughters, were beautiful. They didn't have to straighten their hair. Even when they were caught in the rain, their braids still hung down straight like tamed snakes. Their mouths were pouty little cupid's bows. Mrs. Cullinan didn't know what she missed. Or maybe she did. Poor Mrs. Cullinan.

For weeks after, I arrived early, left late and tried very hard to make up for her barrenness. If she had her own children, she wouldn't have had to ask me to run a thousand errands from her back door to the back door of her friends. Poor old Mrs. Cullinan. 12

Then one evening Miss Glory told me to serve the ladies on the porch. After I set the tray down and turned toward the kitchen, one of the women asked, "What's your name, girl?" It was the speckled-faced one. Mrs. Cullinan said, "She doesn't talk much. Her name's Margaret." 13

"Is she dumb?" 14

"No. As I understand it, she can talk when she wants to but she's usually quiet as a little mouse. Aren't you, Margaret?" 15

I smiled at her. Poor thing. No organs and couldn't even pronounce my name correctly. 16

"She's a sweet little thing, though." 17

"Well, that may be, but the name's too long. I'd never bother myself. I'd call her Mary if I was you." 18

I fumed into the kitchen. That horrible woman would never have the chance to call me Mary because if I was starving I'd never work for her. . . . 19

That evening I decided to write a poem on being white, fat, old and without children. It was going to be a tragic ballad. I would have to watch her carefully to capture the essence of her loneliness and pain. 20

The very next day, she called me by the wrong name. Miss Glory and I were washing up the lunch dishes when Mrs. Cullinan came to the doorway. "Mary?" 21

Miss Glory asked, "Who?" 22

Mrs. Cullinan, sagging a little, knew and I knew. "I want Mary to go down to Mrs. Randall's and take her some soup. She's not been feeling well for a few days." 23

Miss Glory's face was a wonder to see. "You mean Margaret, ma'am. Her name's Margaret." 24

"That's too long. She's Mary from now on. Heat that soup from last night and put it in the china tureen and, Mary, I want you to carry it carefully." 25

Every person I knew had a hellish horror of being "called out of his name." It was a dangerous practice to call a Negro anything that could be loosely construed as insulting because of the centuries of their having been called niggers, jigs, dinges, blackbirds, crows, boots and spooks. 26

Miss Glory had a fleeting second of feeling sorry for me. Then as she handed me the hot tureen she said, "Don't mind, don't pay that no mind. Sticks and stones may break your bones, but words . . . You know, I been working for her for twenty years." 27

She held the back door open for me. "Twenty years. I wasn't much older than you. My name used to be Hallelujah. That's what Ma named me, but my mistress give me 'Glory,' and it stuck. I likes it better too." 28

I was in the little path that ran behind the houses when Miss Glory shouted, "It's shorter too." 29

For a few seconds it was a tossup over whether I would laugh (imagine being named Hallelujah) or cry (imagine letting some white woman rename you for her convenience). My anger saved me from either outburst. I had to quit the job, but the problem was going to be how to do it. Momma wouldn't allow me to quit for just any reason. 30

"She's a peach. That woman is a real peach." Mrs. Randall's maid was talking as she took the soup from me, and I wondered what her name used to be and what she answered to now. 31

For a week I looked into Mrs. Cullinan's face as she called me Mary. She ignored my coming late and leaving early. Miss Glory was a little annoyed because I had begun to leave egg yolk on the dishes and wasn't putting much heart in polishing the silver. I hoped that she would complain to our boss, but she didn't. 32

Then Bailey solved my dilemma. He had me describe the contents of the cupboard and the particular plates she liked best. Her favorite piece was a casserole shaped like a fish and the green glass 33 coffee cups. I kept his instructions in mind, so on the next day when Miss Glory was hanging out clothes and I had again been told to serve the old biddies on the porch, I dropped the empty serving tray. When I heard Mrs. Cullinan scream, "Mary!" I picked up the casserole and two of the green glass cups in readiness. As she rounded the kitchen door I let them fall on the tiled floor.

I could never absolutely describe to Bailey what happened next, because each time I got to the part where she fell on the floor and screwed up her ugly face to cry, we burst out laughing. She actually wobbled around on the floor and picked up shards of the cups and cried, "Oh, Momma. Oh, dear Gawd. It's Mamma's china from Virginia. Oh, Momma, I sorry." 34

Miss Glory came running in from the yard and the women from the porch crowded around. Miss Glory was almost as broken up as her mistress. "You mean to say she broke our Virginia dishes? What we gone do?" 35

Mrs. Cullinan cried louder. "That clumsy nigger. Clumsy little black nigger." 36

Old speckled-face leaned down and asked, "Who did it, Viola? Was it Mary? Who did it?" 37

Everything was happening so fast, I can't remember whether her action preceded her words, but I know that Mrs. Cullinan said, "Her name's Margaret, goddamn it, her name's Margaret." And she threw a wedge of broken plate at me. It could have been the hysteria which put her aim off, but the flying crockery caught Miss Glory right over her ear and she started screaming. 38

I left the front door wide open so all the neighbors could hear. 39

Mrs. Cullinan was right about one thing. My name wasn't Mary. 40

---

## *Meaning and Purpose*

1. The message you take from this selection will be influenced by your own experiences and attitudes. Think of an experience from your life, a movie or television program, reading, or knowledge of others' experiences, which in some way parallels Marguerita's experience. In what ways was this experience similar and different?

2. How would you describe Marguerita's feelings about Mrs. Cullinan before Mrs. Cullinan calls her Mary, and then after? What actions or events does Angelou use in her narrative to show those feelings?
3. Do you think Angelou's primary purpose is to give information or to evoke emotion? Examine your own response to this selection as you decide. What words and sentences convince you of your choice?
4. How would you describe Angelou's intended audience? Does she expect that audience to be empathetic with the young black girl? How do you know?
5. What does Angelou reveal about the significance of being "called out of [one's] name" (26)?
6. Why do you think Angelou included the story about Hallelujah's name being changed to "Glory"?

## *Strategy*

1. What is the payoff in this narrative essay—that is, the moral, point, or message?
2. The first two paragraphs in this selection serve as introduction to the narrative, which begins in the third paragraph. How does this introduction prepare you for the narrative?
3. In the last scene, how does Angelou's telling you she has trouble remembering exactly what happened affect the credibility of the narrative? How does this admission help establish point of view?
4. The entire narrative covers several weeks. List some of the transitional phrases that Angelou uses to help her readers follow the passage of time.
5. What significance has the last sentence? How does it pull the essay together and conclude it?

## *Style*

1. Several times Angelou presents the thoughts of the young girl. In paragraph 16, after being called Margaret instead of Marguerita,

the girl thinks "Poor thing. No organs and couldn't even pronounce my name correctly." Find other examples of Marguerita's thoughts and discuss what they tell us about her.

2. Irony describes our recognizing a reality different from the one that appears to us. It can be expressed in words that actually mean the opposite of what they say. Explain the irony in these items:
   a. "During my tenth year, a white woman's kitchen became my finishing school."
   b. The careful attention to lists of names Marguerita had to learn (soup spoons, gravy boat, butter knives, and so on).
   c. "I would have to watch her carefully to capture the essence of her loneliness and pain."
   d. Mrs. Cullinan's reaction to Marguerita's breaking the dishes. Can you find other ironies in the selection?
3. How does humor work in this essay? Find examples.

## *Writing Tasks*

1. Consider whether you think Mrs. Cullinan has learned a lesson from Marguerita's actions at the end of the selection. Write a narrative essay about an event in which the "payoff" (moral, point) involves a subordinate or "weaker" person's taking revenge on an authority figure or "stronger" person. End your narrative so that the person in authority either learns a lesson or not, according to whether or not you think Mrs. Cullinan does.
2. Write an essay expressing your feelings about the way in which Marguerita deals with prejudice. Before writing, consider these questions and others of your own: What choices do you think Marguerita had? Was she naive to empathize with Mrs. Cullinan's lack of children? Is Mrs. Cullinan merely a product of her culture's attitudes toward blacks? What responsibility do you think she has for what happens in the final scene?

## ❦ George Orwell ❦

*George Orwell is the pen name of Eric Arthur Blair, who was born in Bengal, India, the son of a British civil servant. At age four, he was sent to England, where he attended prestigious schools, but before finishing his university education he returned to India to serve in the British Imperial Police in Burma. Already scornful of British high society, he was soon disillusioned with imperialism as well. He returned to Europe in 1927 to spend several impoverished years in Paris and London before his writing began to bring him financial and critical rewards. His experience living among and writing about the poor workers and coal miners in urban northwest England confirmed his political stand as a socialist, which led him to fight in the Spanish Civil War against the fascists. Many of his essays and his nonfiction works relate in narrative form the first-hand experiences that shaped his political views, and in his best-known novels,* Animal Farm *(1945) and 1984 (1949), he uses fiction to elaborate the dangers of totalitarianism.*

# *A Hanging*

*In "A Hanging," Orwell uses a simple story to examine the complexity of his personal involvement in the British imperialistic occupation of India early in the twentieth century. Taken from the collection,* Shooting an Elephant and Other Essays *(1950), it is a straight chronological narrative that conveys Orwell's deep sympathy for the oppressed in society.*

*Notice the simplicity and understatement of Orwell's language and how it contrasts with the enormity of the event it describes. Notice, too, how this contrast emphasizes and dramatizes that event.*

---

It was in Burma, a sodden morning of the rains. A sickly light, like yellow tinfoil, was slanting over the high walls into the jail yard. We were waiting outside the condemned cells, a row of sheds fronted with double bars, like small animal cages. Each cell measured about ten feet by ten and was quite bare within except for a plank bed and a pot for drinking water. In some of them 1 brown, silent men were squatting at the inner bars, with their blankets draped round them. These were the condemned men, due to be hanged within the next week or two.

One prisoner had been brought out of his cell. He was a 2
Hindu, a puny wisp of a man, with a shaven head and vague liquid eyes. He had a thick, sprouting mustache, absurdly too big for his body, rather like the mustache of a comic man on the films. Six tall Indian warders were guarding him and getting him ready for the gallows. Two of them stood by with rifles and fixed bayonets, while the others handcuffed him, passed a chain through his handcuffs and fixed it to their belts, and lashed his arms tight to his sides. They crowded very close about him, with their hands always on him in a careful, caressing grip, as though all the while feeling him to make sure he was there. It was like men handling a fish which is still alive and may jump back into the water. But he stood quite unresisting, yielding his arms limply to the ropes, as though he hardly noticed what was happening.

Eight o'clock struck and a bugle call, desolately thin in the wet 3
air, floated from the distant barracks. The superintendent of the jail, who was standing apart from the rest of us, moodily prodding the gravel with his stick, raised his head at the sound. He was an army doctor, with a grey toothbrush mustache and a gruff voice. "For God's sake, hurry up, Francis," he said irritably. "The man ought to have been dead by this time. Aren't you ready yet?"

Francis, the head jailer, a fat Dravidian in a white drill suit and 4
gold spectacles, waved his black hand. "Yes sir, yes sir," he bubbled. "All iss satisfactorily prepared. The hangman iss waiting. We shall proceed."

"Well, quick march, then. The prisoners can't get their break- 5
fast till this job's over."

We set out for the gallows. Two warders marched on either 6
side of the prisoner, with their rifles at the slope; two others marched close against him, gripping him by arm and shoulder, as though at once pushing and supporting him. The rest of us, magistrates and the like, followed behind. Suddenly, when we had gone ten yards, the procession stopped short without any order or warning. A dreadful thing had happened—a dog, come goodness

knows whence, had appeared in the yard. It came bounding among us with a loud volley of barks and leapt around us wagging its whole body, wild with glee at finding so many human beings together. It was a large woolly dog, half Airedale, half pariah. For a moment it pranced around us, and then, before anyone could stop it, it had made a dash for the prisoner, and jumping up tried to lick his face. Everybody stood aghast, too taken aback even to grab the dog.

"Who let that bloody brute in here?" said the superintendent 7 angrily. "Catch it, someone!"

A warder detached from the escort, charged clumsily after the 8 dog, but it danced and gambolled just out of his reach, taking everything as part of the game. A young Eurasian jailer picked up a handful of gravel and tried to stone the dog away, but it dodged the stones and came after us again. Its yaps echoed from the jail walls. The prisoner, in the grasp of the two warders, looked on incuriously, as though this was another formality of the hanging. It was several minutes before someone managed to catch the dog. Then we put my handkerchief through its collar and moved off once more, with the dog still straining and whimpering.

It was about forty yards to the gallows. I watched the bare 9 brown back of the prisoner marching in front of me. He walked clumsily with his bound arms, but quite steadily, with that bobbing gait of the Indian who never straightens his knees. At each step his muscles slid neatly into place, the lock of hair on his scalp danced up and down, his feet printed themselves on the wet gravel. And once, in spite of the men who gripped him by each shoulder, he stepped lightly aside to avoid a puddle on the path.

It is curious; but till that moment I had never realized what 10 it means to destroy a healthy, conscious man. When I saw the prisoner step aside to avoid the puddle, I saw the mystery, the unspeakable wrongness, of cutting a life short when it is in full tide. This man was not dying, he was alive just as we are alive. All the organs of his body were working—bowels digesting food, skin renewing itself, nails growing, tissues forming—all toiling away in solemn foolery. His nails would still be growing when he stood on the drop, when he was falling through the air with a tenth-of-a-second to live. His eyes saw the yellow gravel and the grey walls, and his brain still remembered, foresaw, reasoned—even about puddles. He and we were a party of men walking together, seeing, hearing, feeling, understanding the same world; and in two minutes, with a sudden snap, one of us would be gone—one mind less, one world less.

The gallows stood in a small yard, separate from the main 11
grounds of the prison, and overgrown with tall prickly weeds. It was a brick erection like three sides of a shed, with planking on top, and above that two beams and a crossbar with the rope dangling. The hangman, a greyhaired convict in the white uniform of the prison, was waiting beside his machine. He greeted us with a servile crouch as we entered. At a word from Francis the two warders, gripping the prisoner more closely than ever, half led, half pushed him to the gallows and helped him clumsily up the ladder. Then the hangman climbed up and fixed the rope around the prisoner's neck.

We stood waiting, five yards away. The warders had formed 12
in a rough circle round the gallows. And then, when the noose was fixed, the prisoner began crying out to his god. It was a high, reiterated cry of "Ram! Ram! Ram! Ram!" not urgent and fearful like a prayer or cry for help, but steady, rhythmical, almost like the tolling of a bell. The dog answered the sound with a whine. The hangman, still standing on the gallows, produced a small cotton bag like a flour bag and drew it down over the prisoner's face. But the sound, muffled by the cloth, still persisted, over and over again: "Ram! Ram! Ram! Ram! Ram!"

The hangman climbed down and stood ready, holding the 13
lever. Minutes seemed to pass. The steady, muffled crying from the prisoner went on and on, "Ram! Ram! Ram!" never faltering for an instant. The superintendent, his head on his chest, was slowly poking the ground with his stick; perhaps he was counting the cries, allowing the prisoner a fixed number—fifty, perhaps, or a hundred. Everyone had changed colour. The Indians had gone grey like bad coffee, and one or two of the bayonets were wavering. We looked at the lashed, hooded man on the drop, and listened to his cries—each cry another second of life; the same

thought was in all our minds; oh, kill him quickly, get it over, stop that abominable noise!

Suddenly the superintendent made up his mind. Throwing up his head he made a swift motion with his stick. "Chalo!" he shouted almost fiercely. 14

There was a clanking noise, and then dead silence. The prisoner had vanished, and the rope was twisting on itself. I let go of the dog, and it galloped immediately to the back of the gallows; but when it got there it stopped short, barked, and then retreated into a corner of the yard, where it stood among the weeds, looking timorously out at us. We went round the gallows to inspect the prisoner's body. He was dangling with his toes pointed straight downwards, very slowly revolving, as dead as a stone. 15

The superintendent reached out with his stick and poked the bare brown body; it oscillated slightly. "*He's* all right," said the superintendent. He backed out from under the gallows, and blew out a deep breath. The moody look had gone out of his face quite suddenly. He glanced at his wrist-watch. "Eight minutes past eight. Well, that's all for this morning, thank God." 16

The warders unfixed bayonets and marched away. The dog, sobered and conscious of having misbehaved itself, slipped after them. We walked out of the gallows yard, past the condemned cells with their waiting prisoners, into the big central yard of the prison. The convicts, under the command of warders armed with lathis, were already receiving their breakfast. They squatted in long rows, each man holding a tin pannikin, while two warders with buckets marched around ladling out rice; it seemed quite a homely, jolly scene, after the hanging. An enormous relief had come upon us now that the job was done. One felt an impulse to sing, to break into a run, to snigger. All at once everyone began chattering gaily. 17

The Eurasian boy walking beside me nodded towards the way we had come, with a knowing smile: "Do you know, sir, our friend (he meant the dead man) when he heard his appeal had been dismissed, he pissed on the floor of his cell. From fright. Kindly take one of my cigarettes, sir. Do you not admire my new 18 silver case, sir? From the boxwallah, two rupees eight annas. Classy European style."

Several people laughed—at what, nobody seemed certain. 19

Francis was walking by the superintendent, talking garrulously: "Well, sir, all has passed off with the utmost satisfactoriness. It was all finished—flick! Like that. It iss not always so—oah, no! I have known cases where the doctor was obliged to go beneath the gallows and pull the prissoner's legs to ensure decease. Most disagreeable!" 20

"Wriggling about, eh? That's bad," said the superintendent. 21

"Ach, sir, it iss worse when they become refractory! One man, I recall, clung to the bars of hiss cage when we went to take him out. You will scarcely credit, sir, that it took six warders to dislodge him, three pulling at each leg. We reasoned with him, 'My dear fellow,' we said, 'think of all the pain and trouble you are causing to us!' But no, he would not listen! Ach, he wass very troublesome!" 22

I found that I was laughing quite loudly. Everyone was laughing. Even the superintendent grinned in a tolerant way. "You'd better all come out and have a drink," he said quite genially. "I've got a bottle of whisky in the car. We could do with it." 23

We went through the big double gates of the prison into the road. "Pulling at his legs!" exclaimed a Burmese magistrate suddenly, and burst into a loud chuckling. We all began laughing again. At that moment Francis' anecdote seemed extraordinarily funny. We all had a drink together, native and European alike, quite amicably. The dead man was a hundred yards away. 24

---

## *Meaning and Purpose*

1. Orwell titles his essay simply "A Hanging." How effective is this title? Is it different in meaning from "*the* hanging"? Would a more descriptive title, such as "A Horrible Experience in Burma" or "The Cruelty of Capital Punishment," be better? Why or why not?

2. Why do you think the narrator describes the sudden presence of the dog as a "dreadful thing"?
3. Why does the condemned man's sidestepping a puddle make the narrator realize "what it means to destroy a healthy, conscious man"?
4. How would you characterize the behavior of the men after "the job was done"? How do you explain the behavior?
5. What is the purpose of Orwell's essay? Is it just a riveting story, or does it have a larger meaning?

## *Strategy*

1. What is the point of view in this essay, and how well does it work?
2. What time order does Orwell use in telling his story? Does he depart from this order anywhere?
3. Why do you think Orwell doesn't tell us the crime the man is being hanged for? Does it matter? Why or why not?

## *Style*

1. How would you describe the tone established in the first paragraph? What words create it? Is this tone sustained throughout the essay, or does it change? Explain.
2. Understatement is a form of irony that represents something as less than it actually is. Find some sentences that are examples of understatement. How does this technique serve Orwell's purpose?
3. Explain the irony in the last two sentences.

## *Writing Tasks*

1. In "A Hanging," Orwell uses narrative to communicate ideas without stating them directly. Write a brief narrative in which you make a point without explicitly stating it. Tell the story of an

event that illustrates your point, such as how a stylish wedding shows that we care too much about money and appearance, or how a charismatic speaker shows that we are easily persuaded to believe something.

2. Write a first-person narrative in which you tell about an exciting or moving event in a detached, dispassionate voice. Let understatement emphasize the excitement or other emotion in the story.

## ❦ Richard Selzer ❦

*Richard Selzer is a surgeon who writes essays and stories, aimed at a general audience, about the practice of medicine. Born in New York state in 1928, he studied at Union College and Albany Medical School and later at Yale University. He subsequently taught writing at Yale and both taught and practiced surgery at the Yale University Medical School. His articles, for which he received the National Magazine Award in 1975 and an American Medical Writer's Award in 1985, have appeared in* Harper's, Esquire, *and* Redbook. *He has published a book of short stories,* Rituals of Surgery *(1975), and a collection of autobiographical essays,* Mortal Lessons: Notes on the Art of Surgery *(1976), in addition to his collections of essays about the medical profession. His most recent book is* Raising the Dead: A Doctor's Encounter With His Own Mortality (1994).

# *The Masked Marvel's Last Toehold*

*Told in the first person, this narrative reveals the anguish of a patient through the eyes of his doctor, Richard Selzer. Selzer finds himself treating a man he had seen fight in a wrestling match many years earlier, when he was a boy. The author's perspective changes as he moves from the present to the childhood memory and back again to the present. The essay is from Selzer's* The Confessions of a Knife *(1979).*

---

On the fifth floor of the hospital, in the west wing, I know that a man is sitting up in his bed, waiting for me. Elihu Koontz is seventy-five, and he is diabetic. It is two weeks since I amputated his left leg just below the knee. I walk down the corridor, but I do not go straight into his room. Instead, I pause in the doorway. He is not yet aware of my presence, but gazes down at the place in the bed where his leg used to be, and where now there is the collapsed leg of his pajamas. He is totally absorbed, like an athlete apprais- 1 ing the details of his body. What is he thinking? I wonder. Is he dreaming the outline of his toes? Does he see there his foot's incandescent ghost? Could he be angry? Feel that I have taken from him something for which he yearns now with all his heart? Has he forgotten so soon the pain? It was a pain so great as to set him apart from all other men, in a red-hot place where he had no kith or kin. What of those black gorilla toes and the soupy mess that was his heel? I watch him from the doorway. It is a kind of spying, I know.

Save for a white fringe open at the front, Elihu Koontz is bald. 2
The hair has grown too long and is wilted. He wears it as one would wear a day-old laurel wreath. He is naked to the waist, so that I can see his breasts. They are the breasts of Buddha, inverted triangles from which the nipples swing, dark as garnets.

I have seen enough. I step into the room, and he sees that I am 3
there.

"How did the night go, Elihu?" 4

He looks at me for a long moment. "Shut the door," he says. 5

I do, and move to the side of the bed. He takes my left hand 6
in both of his, gazes at it, turns it over, then back, fondling, at last holding it up to his cheek. I do not withdraw from this loving. After a while he relinquishes my hand, and looks up at me.

"How is the pain?" I ask. 7

He does not answer, but continues to look at me in silence. I 8
know at once that he has made a decision.

"Ever hear of The Masked Marvel?" He says this in a low voice, 9
almost a whisper.

"What?" 10

"The Masked Marvel," he says. "You never heard of him?" 11

"No." 12

He clucks his tongue. He is exasperated. 13

All at once there is a recollection. It is dim, distant, but com- 14
ing near.

"Do you mean the wrestler?" 15

Eagerly, he nods, and the breasts bob. How gnomish he looks, 16
oval as the huge helpless egg of some outlandish lizard. He has very long arms, which, now and then, he unfurls to reach for

things—a carafe of water, a get-well card. He gazes up at me, urging. He *wants* me to remember.

"Well, . . . yes," I say. I am straining backward in time. "I saw 17
him wrestle in Toronto long ago."

"Ha!" He smiles. "You saw *me*." And his index finger, held 18
rigid and upright, bounces in the air.

The man has said something shocking, unacceptable. It must 19
be challenged.

"You?" I am trying to smile. 20

Again that jab of the finger. "You saw *me*." 21

"No," I say. But even then, something about Elihu Koontz, 22
those prolonged arms, the shape of his head, the sudden agility with which he leans from his bed to get a large brown envelope from his nightstand, something is forcing me toward a memory. He rummages through his papers, old newspaper clippings, photographs, and I remember . . .

It is almost forty years ago. I am ten years old. I have been sent 23
to Toronto to spend the summer with relatives. Uncle Max has bought two tickets to the wrestling match. He is taking me that night.

"He isn't allowed," says Aunt Sarah to me. Uncle Max has 24
angina.

"He gets too excited," she says. 25

"I wish you wouldn't go, Max," she says. 26

"You mind your own business," he says. 27

And we go. Out into the warm Canadian evening I am not 28
only abroad, I am abroad in the *evening*! I have never been taken out in the evening. I am terribly excited. The trolleys, the lights, the horns. It is a bazaar. At the Maple Leaf Gardens, we sit high and near the center. The vast arena is dark except for the brilliance of the ring at the bottom.

It begins. 29

The wrestlers circle. They grapple. They are all haunch and 30
paunch. I am shocked by their ugliness, but I do not show it. Uncle Max is exhilarated. He leans forward, his eyes unblinking, on his face a look of enormous happiness. One after the

other, a pair of wrestlers enter the ring. The two men join, twist, jerk, tug, bend, yank, and throw. Then they leave and are replaced by another pair. At last it is the main event. "The Angel vs. The Masked Marvel."

On the cover of the program notes, there is a picture of The Angel hanging from the limb of a tree, a noose of thick rope around his neck. The Angel hangs just so for an hour every day, it is explained, to strengthen his neck. The Masked Marvel's trade mark is a black stocking cap with holes for the eyes and mouth. He is never seen without it, states the program. No one knows who The Masked Marvel really is! 31

"Good," says Uncle Max. "Now you'll see something." He is fidgeting, waiting for them to appear. They come down separate aisles, climb into the ring from opposite sides. I have never seen anything like them. It is The Angel's neck that first captures the eye. The shaved nape rises in twin columns to puff into the white hood of a sloped and bosselated skull that is too small. As though strangled by the sinews of that neck, the skull had long since withered and shrunk. The thing about The Angel is the absence of any mystery in his body. It is simply *there*. A monosyllabic announcement. A grunt. One looks and knows everything at once, the fat thighs, the gigantic buttocks, the great spine from which hang knotted ropes and pale aprons of beef. And that prehistoric head. He is all of a single hideous piece, The Angel is. No detachables. 32

The Masked Marvel seems dwarfish. His fingers dangle kneeward. His short legs are slightly bowed as if under the weight of the cask they are forced to heft about. He has breasts that swing when he moves! I have never seen such breasts on a man before. 33

There is a sudden ungraceful movement, and they close upon one another. The Angel stoops and hugs The Marvel about the waist, locking his hands behind The Marvel's back. Now he straightens and lifts The Marvel as though he were uprooting a tree. Thus he holds him, then stoops again, thrusts one hand through The Marvel's crotch, and with the other grabs him by the neck. He rears and . . . The Marvel is aloft! For a long moment, The Angel stands as though deciding where to make the toss. Then throws. Was that board or bone that splintered there? 34

Again and again, The Angel hurls himself upon the body of The Masked Marvel.

Now The Angel rises over the fallen Marvel, picks up one 35
foot in both of his hands, and twists the toes downward. It is far beyond the tensile strength of mere ligament, mere cartilage. The Masked Marvel does not hide his agony, but pounds and slaps the floor with his hand, now and then reaching up toward The Angel in an attitude of supplication. I have never seen such suffering. And all the while his black mask rolls from side to side, the mouth pulled to a tight slit through which issues an endless hiss that I can hear from where I sit. All at once, I hear a shouting close by

"Break it off! Tear off a leg and throw it up here!" 36

It is Uncle Max. Even in the darkness I can see that he is gray. 37
A band of sweat stands upon his upper lip. He is on his feet now, panting, one fist pressed at his chest, the other raised warlike toward the ring For the first time I begin to think that something terrible might happen here. Aunt Sarah was right.

"Sit down, Uncle Max," I say. "Take a pill, please." 38

He reaches for the pillbox, gropes, and swallows without tak- 39
ing his gaze from the wrestlers. I wait for him to sit down.

"That's not fair," I say, "twisting his toes like that." 40

"It's the toehold," he explains. 41

"But it's not *fair*," I say again. The whole of the evil is laid open 42
for me to perceive. I am trembling.

And now The Angel does something unspeakable. Holding 43
the foot of The Marvel at full twist with one hand, he bends and grasps the mask where it clings to the back of The Marvel's head. And he pulls. He is going to strip it off! Lay bare an ultimate carnal mystery! Suddenly it is beyond mere physical violence. Now I am on my feet, shouting into the Maple Leaf Gardens.

"Watch out," I scream. "Stop him. Please, somebody, stop 44
him."

Next to me, Uncle Max is chuckling. 45

Yet The Masked Marvel hears me, I know it. And rallies 46
from his bed of pain. Thrusting with his free heel, he strikes The Angel at the back of the knee. The Angel falls. The Masked

Marvel is on top of him, pinning his shoulders to the mat. One! Two! Three! And it is over. Uncle Max is strangely still. I am gasping for breath. All this I remember as I stand at the bedside of Elihu Koontz.

Once again, I am in the operating room. It is two years since I amputated the left leg of Elihu Koontz. Now it is his right leg which is gangrenous. I have already scrubbed. I stand to one side wearing my gown and gloves. And . . . *I am masked.* Upon the table lies Elihu Koontz, pinned in a fierce white light. Spinal anesthesia has been administered. One of his arms is taped to a board placed at a right angle to his body. Into this arm, a needle has been placed. Fluid drips here from a bottle overhead. With his other hand, Elihu Koontz beats feebly at the side of the operating table. His head rolls from side to side. His mouth is pulled into weeping. It seems to me that I have never seen such misery. 47

An orderly stands at the foot of the table, holding Elihu Koontz's leg aloft by the toes so that the intern can scrub the limb 48 with antiseptic solutions. The intern paints the foot, ankle, leg, and thigh, both front and back, three times. From a corner of the room where I wait, I look down as from an amphitheater. Then I think of Uncle Max yelling, "Tear off a leg. Throw it up here." And I think that forty years later I am making the catch.

"It's not fair," I say aloud. But no one hears me. I step forward to break The Masked Marvel's last toehold. 49

---

## *Meaning and Purpose*

1. The last sentence in this essay includes the words of the title. How does that sentence help you interpret the title? In what sense does the doctor "break The Masked Marvel's last toehold"?
2. What is Selzer's purpose in telling the story of The Masked Marvel? How do you interpret the meaning of the essay?
3. How does the surgeon describe the pain he believes Elihu Koontz experiences during the wrestling match, and as a patient?

How does the surgeon's awareness of pain help you understand him (the surgeon)?

4. The boy and his uncle have different reactions to the evening of wrestling. Discuss how this contrast enriches the essay.
5. In the last three paragraphs, the surgeon takes on the role of wrestler. What details tell you so, and how effective are they in unifying the essay?

## *Strategy*

1. Selzer departs from strict chronological order in this narrative. What order does he put the events in, and how does it affect the story?
2. Each of the three sections gives us a piece of The Masked Marvel's story, making a natural connection among them. But Selzer has taken pains to further connect the sections by repeating details from section one in section two and details from section two in section three. Examine these parallels. How do they affect your reading of the essay?
3. How does Selzer use transitions to let you know when the time order changes? Are the transitions clear and effective?
4. Though the surgeon narrates the whole essay, his perspective, or point of view, changes in each section. What picture do you have of his character because of these three perspectives?

## *Style*

1. What does dialogue do for the story? How effective do you think the story would be without dialogue?
2. Authors don't always tell of past events in the past tense. Look at the tense used in each section. How does Selzer's choice of tense influence your experience of the events in the narrative and your understanding of the chronology?
3. In paragraph 36, when Uncle Max yells, "Tear off a leg and throw

it up here!" you already know Elihu Koontz has lost a leg to diabetes. How is this irony sustained in the final section?

## *Writing Tasks*

1. Think of a person or event that impressed you as a child and has some significant connection to your later life. Write a narrative about it, using the same tense to describe both the past and the present, but also clearly separating past from present.
2. Write a narrative, incorporating somewhere in the story the exact words of the title you give it. How can you make the title significant?

## ❦ Art Harris ❦

*Art Harris is an award-winning journalist based in Atlanta. After graduating from Duke University, he began his journalism career with the* Atlanta Constitution. *He later worked for the* San Francisco Examiner *before joining the staff of the* Washington Post, *the paper for which he has since covered the South. His articles have appeared in* Reader's Digest, GQ, Esquire, *and* Rolling Stone. *Harris covered the downfall of evangelical preacher Jimmy Swaggart for the* Washington Post *and wrote the well-known article about Swaggart's demise for* Penthouse *magazine. He has won two National Headliner Awards for outstanding feature writing. He is on the staff at CNN news as a contributing correspondent for their investigative unit.*

# *Trapped in Another Life*

*This newspaper article, from the* Los Angeles Times, *February 23, 1989, tells the story of a woman who led two distinctly separate lives, one as a drug-abusing prostitute with a criminal record and the other as a model wife and mother. Because of the remarkable turnaround in this woman's life, the story raises questions about justice and punishment.*

*Harris carefully outlines the causes that led the woman who is the subject of this essay to live two diametrically opposed lives. Pay particularly close attention to those causes.*

---

JESSUP, MD. She stares out the window past twin 12-foot fences topped with razor wire, watchtowers manned by armed guards, steel electronic gates, past the stand of hardwoods, the nearby men's prison and up the road. 1

It's dusting snow, cold, bleak. Just over the hill, a 10-minute drive if she could just drive out of here, and she would be home in her split-level house with a devoted but baffled brood: her husband, Ray, two teen-age sons. 2

Kay Smith was the very model of a Severn, Md., housewife and working mother, so perfect that no one around here can 3 believe she was once a hard-drinking, pill-popping criminal with a gun.

## Dark Secrets Come to Light

But for a decade, until her capture last spring, she was a fugitive from a South Carolina mill town. She had been imprisoned for a string of armed robberies until she walked away from work release and disappeared. Her first husband was a convicted killer. 4

These were secrets Kay Smith buried deep as she recast her life. Over the years, she had become a doting mom to her two boys and foster daughters. She ferried her sons to school and sports, took courses at Anne Arundel Community College. As a real estate agent for Gary Hart Realty in Glen Burnie, she sold house after house—$1 million in sales last year. 5

Who could have suspected that she really was an outlaw named Pamela Rodgers? 6

Kay Smith wore subdued suits and slacks, a bare wisp of Max Factor. In her home, she warned her sons about drinking. She spurned even a glass of wine, and politely insisted that friends take half-empty bottles home after parties. 7

"I can't imagine for the life of me how this woman could do anything remotely resembling what happened," says Bill Cashman, who coached her sons in track at Old Mill High. "She'd ask me what I thought about her sons' grades, their sports performance, the people they hung around with. Her family was always first." 8

Somehow, she managed to keep it together as she lived in fear and hid her past, even from her husband. "I just wanted to get my boys through school," she says, "then I was going to straighten it all out." 9

But detectives disrupted her plan last May. And when they came for her, she had run so long and hard, she barely knew the woman, handcuffed and under arrest. All at once, she again was Pamela Rodgers—the woman she thought she had left behind. In three months, she was on her way back to prison in South Carolina. 10

11 Just before Christmas, a routine interstate swap allowed her to serve out the rest of her 12-year sentence for armed robbery near home. She found herself in this stark red-brick campus, the Maryland Correctional Institute for Women.

12 "At least I don't have to carry that terrible secret any more," she says, wrapping a sweater about her to ward off the chill. Suddenly she looks panicked. "Oh, God, I'm so sorry my sons were cheated."

13 She wears a purple prison jumpsuit, works in the prison library, clips recipes and frets about her family. Figuring "someday they'll want honest answers," she writes letters she never mails.

14 Based on her record of violent crime and escape, Kay Smith was classified by Maryland prison officials as a security risk. So she awaits the outcome of early release pleas—by her reckoning she could be here until March, 1993, unless authorities grant an unlikely pardon, premature parole or work release.

15 Family and friends have canvassed the community, collecting at least 3,000 signatures petitioning South Carolina's Pardon and Parole Board for leniency.

16 "I'm not saying she ought to get a medal, but she's paid her debt to society," argues John Hassett, a former prosecutor, who took her case for expenses only.

17 In South Carolina, former prosecutor Dick Harpootlian took up her cause too, saying, "I take other cases for money. Kay's case is among those I take because I believe in the folks."

18 But sniffs Jim Anders, the South Carolina prosecutor who put Kay Smith back in jail: "Don't make me cry. If we cut slack for her, we encourage people to escape."

19 Jean Gilbert, Kay Smith's mother, says of her daughter in a telephone interview from Greenville, S.C.: "If people could just understand what brought her to this point. She was just a woman desperate to have her kids, who was terrorized by bad men."

20 Kay Smith was born Pamela Annette Gilbert on Oct. 1, 1951, the second of six children raised by a trucker and a grocer's daughter in the Blue Ridge foothills of Greenville, S.C. She remembers her father's belt, his guns, his whiskey, his temper.

21 Her father declines to discuss the past, but other family members confirm her memories; her mother recalls stepping in to take "many of those licks."

22 "I watched him whip her . . . when she was just 15 months old," says her grandmother, Mary Hinton, 83.

23 Kay says of her father: "He just didn't know how to show affection. I can't remember ever hearing him say 'I love you.' "

24 When Kay was a 10th-grader, she dropped out and took a job at a convenience store, where she met stock boy Danny Rodgers, another dropout.

25 "I knew I didn't love Danny," Kay reflects. "I married him to get out. I thought I could make it work."

26 She was 16.

27 Bouncing between Rodgers' modest family farm in Cullman, Ala., and her hometown in Greenville, they moved into a dinky Greenville trailer.

28 "First time I ever saw him slap her," Kay's mother says, "I hit him back. He said, 'You hit me,' and I said, 'You hit my daughter.' So he informed me, 'It's not your daughter any more; it's my wife.' "

29 They moved to Florida, where Danny found construction work at Disney World, but preferred hanging out. Danny Jr. was born Dec. 17, 1969, as Pam was learning fast about her mercurial husband, who relished "playing with guns and knives, very nice one day and the next day beating the heck out of you."

30 Six months later, out of work, he ran off with a neighbor's wife, she says. So Pam headed home again, hired on the midnight shift as a cotton mill weaver. Danny returned, but she refused to make up.

31 Then, one night, when she was at work, he snatched the baby and ran, a tactic he repeatedly used to keep her in line. And it worked: She kept going back to him. "It was the only way to keep my baby," she says. Another son, James, was born in September, 1972, but life was only getting worse.

32 Kay moved home to Greenville, and in 1973 won temporary custody of the boys. Rodgers stalked her, she says, and one day showed up and fired a pistol into the roof of her trailer.

Days later, he snatched the boys again. Only this time Pam couldn't find them.

"She had dreams he'd drowned them because he swore he'd 33
do it before he'd let her have them," her mother says. "She woke up at night screaming and fell into drugs and alcohol."

She boxed up their toys, reminders of her "failure," and 34
dumped them at Goodwill. She reported her husband to the police, but no one offered any hope.

She found a kind of solace at the Little Darling, a Greenville 35
bar that drew hustlers such as Arthur Broome Jr., a distant cousin.

She was 22. 36

Broome was 43, owned a tile company, but never seemed to 37
work. He promised to help track her boys, and she moved into his trailer—a place police say attracted the local criminal fringe. Broome, she says, had money, and drugs to kill her pain.

Life was going badly for her. During the 1974 Masters golf 38
tournament, she drove to Augusta, Ga., to hang out with a bar mate—a former hooker, she says. A man approached them at a local restaurant. They began flirting. Suddenly, she says, she was under arrest for possessing amphetamines and soliciting an undercover cop for prostitution. Police records suggest that case was never prosecuted.

Meanwhile, back home, Broome was teaching her how to use 39
a gun—and everything a country girl needed to know about stick-ups. Together they held up stores in the Greenville area.

"I didn't really care if I got caught," she says. "I thought if I got 40
in enough trouble, Danny would tell me where the boys were. I wasn't thinking straight."

On Sept. 14, 1974, they hit Paces Jewelers just before closing. 41
Pulling a pistol from a large black bag, she ordered customers to the floor and grabbed 18 watches and $400 in cash.

Because witnesses had caught her license plate numbers, po- 42
lice easily tracked her to Broome's trailer, where both were arrested. But she got out on bail, and, high on uppers, hit a liquor store alone. Later, she drove the rolling countryside for hours, realizing she would never get her sons back now. She went

home and gobbled pills to end it all, then raced to find her mother.

"She said, 'Mama, I took a handful of pills and I'm gonna die,' " her mother recalls. "I called an ambulance, they pumped her stomach and took her to the state hospital." 43

Rodgers got the news at his California apartment, where he had taken the boys. He phoned, invited his wife to join him and try again. Ignoring bail rules against leaving the state, her mother put her on a plane. "I had to do it to save her," she says. 44

But it didn't work out. 45

Danny began knocking her around, but for the first time, she fought back. When she called the police for help, Danny told them his wife was a bail jumper from South Carolina. 46

Detectives flew her home, where she pleaded guilty in state court to five armed robberies. In October, 1975, she drew a 121/2-year sentence. Broome got 25 years; Kay wound up in Columbia's women's prison. 47

Rodgers filed for divorce and won permanent custody of the children, but in March, 1977, he shot a man in California, for which he was convicted of second-degree murder and sentenced to five years in prison. The boys, 6 and 8, were dispatched to live with his family in Alabama. 48

Pam, who was told Danny was in a hospital, was being a model inmate. After 18 months, she made work release and labored in a printing plant. But she fell off the wagon on the job—using pills and whiskey, she says. And she feared further setbacks would let Danny keep her children forever. There was only one way out: Take a walk. 49

With six or so months left to serve, in January, 1978, she hitched as far as Glen Burnie, Md., rented a room, took a job as a waitress in a Greek diner. To avoid confusion with a waitress named Pam, she became Kay Smith. Days later, just after midnight, a short, balding trucker plopped down, spied the sad-eyed brunette in a white apron and fell in love. 50

She was crying. A cook was screaming at her. The trucker asked her name. 51

"Ray and Kay," Ray Smith joked. "Pretty neat. We ought to get 52
along fine. We got the same names."

He was gentle, optimistic. He told her he had two daughters 53
by a woman he never had married, that he was lonely on the road and looking for a co-pilot. At quitting time, she threw down her apron and climbed aboard his snorting '74 Peterbilt.

High in the cab, hauling steel and furniture over the next 54
three months, they became friends. Ray talked of a hardscrabble life, raised by grandparents in the West Virginia hollows. She was amazed. He had suffered, yet was so happy. Kay hedged about her past.

After three months on the road, he proposed marriage at the 55
Truck Stop of America in Knoxville. Her dilemma was right out of some country song: How could she let someone she loved marry an outlaw with a fake name? She had forged a birth certificate, gotten a Social Security card and a Maryland driver's license. "There was no right answer," she says. "So I just decided to block out the past."

On July 1, 1978, Ray's family and drinking buddies, about 56
500 in all, crowded into a Pasadena, Md., church, and went from there to a dance hall. "I was happier than anyone could be," he says. "I knew she loved me."

Kay was determined to change her life. That Christmas, gam- 57
bling on her former in-laws to keep her secret, she drove to Alabama with Ray to see her boys.

Studying on the road, she passed a high school equivalency 58
exam, enrolled in Anne Arundel Community College, began driving on her own.

In 1980, the Smiths bought a three-bedroom house in Severn, 59
outfitting bedrooms for the boys. Life without them still drove her into the bedroom with a bottle.

When Ray drew the line over her drinking, she found a ther- 60
apist in Baltimore, and her story tumbled out for the first time. She looked inside, read Norman Vincent Peale, tried biofeedback and stopped drinking.

She made friends, becoming close to neighbor Cathy Moore, 61
a divorced mother who once rescued her dog. When Moore's

daughter left to live with her father in Wyoming, Kay "reassured me," she says. "I wondered, 'How comes she's so smart about life?' "

On one visit to Alabama, she learned her former husband was in prison. But she knew there was nothing she could do to get her boys back without giving herself away. 62

And there was nothing she could do when Danny got out, remarried, reclaimed the boys and resettled in his new wife's hometown, Boise, Idaho. 63

But she stayed in touch, sent money, opened local charge accounts for the boys, saw them at Boise's Flying J truck stop on trips west. 64

Meanwhile, she hired a Baltimore attorney to square her past. But he reported there was no record, raising her hopes. Only later did she discover her name had been misspelled in the search. 65

She grew more concerned for her sons. They had told her that Danny had recruited them to steal from the Salvation Army to furnish his yard sales. Then, in January, 1985, James attempted suicide; young Dan got into a fight with his father. One night, James sneaked out for a ride with a teen-ager who wrapped his car around a telephone pole, killing the driver. 66

Rodgers threw in the towel. "Come get them," he told his former wife. "They're yours." 67

She flew west the next day to claim them before he changed his mind. Back in Severn, the boys made friends quickly, reveled in their rooms, Reeboks and new jeans. When Ray wheeled in, they sat grinning at the kitchen table. For the first time, he saw Kay was happy. Curfews were set; grades improved. It was a "Leave It to Beaver" home, they liked to say. 68

She seized on real estate as a way to sock away money for college. 69

But she remained haunted by the past and present. In 1987, her former husband was charged again with murder for shooting a 21-year-old Boise man over a drug deal, chopping him into 13 pieces and dumping them into a reservoir. Now he was 70 calling collect from jail; he wanted to see the boys, afraid he might get the chair.

After Rodgers was convicted last March, an Idaho pre-sentencing investigator ran a routine computer check of his former wife, discovered she was a fugitive and alerted South Carolina. 71

But the investigator, puzzling over an unlisted Maryland phone number in the killer's wallet, dialed it. He reached James, who confirmed his mother's maiden name and her hometown without knowing what he had done. 72

Now police had the tip they had been after. The phone rang and when she answered, it was Danny. "I guess we're in the same boat," he said. "They know about you." 73

She was numb, near hysterics. 74

Without alarming the boys, she hinted she "might have to go away for a little while" and phoned her attorney, who suggested she find a criminal lawyer. She found Hassett. 75

Then, on May 10, 1988, a patrolman knocked on her door. After her arrest, with handcuffs on, she turned white, broke into tears. "It's been 101/2 years," she said. "Why now?" 76

Ray was loading in New Jersey when he got the word. The boys were in school. The next day, out on $25,000 bail, she told the boys the rest of the story, then sat down with Ray, alone. 77

"She told me everything," he says. "She was crying. She said, 'I hope this doesn't break us up. I love you so much.' " 78

Now the house feels empty. Danny, a well-mannered 6-footer who has briefly curtailed college to work in a hospital billing department, cheers on James, who takes his anger out on a punching bag and works to stay afloat at Old Mill. Most Saturdays, they visit their mother for an hour in a communal room at the prison. 79

With Ray on the road, working double time to pay the bills, friends like Pam McLane, an Old Mill senior, drop by to fix dinner, help clean up and remember Kay. 80

As for Kay herself, "there wasn't any freedom for the last 10 years, not for anyone with a conscience," she reflects on this bleak Maryland winter day. "You overcome depression, drinking and 81 negative forces, but you're not free. I was 21 when it happened. I made a terrible, terrible mistake. I feel horrible about it. . . ."

But, she adds, "I am not Pam Rodgers any more. I just don't want my children destroyed. That's my sense of urgency. Why destroy a family when it's on the verge of changing the cycle?" 82

---

## *Meaning and Purpose*

1. Taking the entire article into consideration and paying close attention to the last section (79–82), what do you think Harris's purpose is in this article?
2. How does the title relate to the story?
3. Examine the statements by John Hassett in paragraph 16 and Jim Anders in paragraph 18. Which statement more closely agrees with your thinking about reformed criminals in general? About Kay Smith-Pamela Rodgers in particular? Has Harris led you to a specific view? If so, how?
4. What does Harris mean by "a bare wisp of Max Factor" in paragraph 7?
5. What is the emotional effect of describing Kay as both "the very model of a Severn, Md., housewife and working mother," and "a hard-drinking, pill-popping criminal with a gun" in the same paragraph (3)?

## *Strategy*

1. How do the first three paragraphs pull the reader into Kay Smith's story?
2. Harris summarizes Kay's life in paragraphs 4–19, then begins her story again at an earlier time and in more detail, starting with paragraph 20. Why does he choose this order of events? Why doesn't he begin the article with "Kay Smith was born Pamela Annette Gilbert on Oct. 1, 1951 . . ." (20)?

3. Does Harris use the scene or summary method to present the events of the story? Give examples to support your answer.
4. Harris alternates between present and past tense in this essay. What logic do you think he uses in choosing tenses?

## *Style*

1. What is Harris's attitude toward Kay's situation? How does he establish this attitude in the tone of the essay?
2. What do words in paragraphs 53–56 such as "co-pilot," "snorting," and "hardscrabble" tell you about Harris's intended audience? This article originally appeared in a mass-circulation newspaper. Does that background explain his choice of words?
3. This essay is a news article, and most news writers try to claim objectivity in reporting. Does Harris care about objectivity? How do you know?

## *Writing Tasks*

1. The Kay Smith-Pamela Rodgers article begins in the present and then goes back in time to retrace her history. Write a narrative beginning with a description of a present situation as Harris does. Then go back to record the events leading to that situation. At the end of your narrative, return to the present.
2. Write an essay in which you compare style and effectiveness of the opening situations in this chapter's first four selections. Ask yourself how well each author grabs readers, establishes a situation and a conflict, and begins to create a mood. If necessary, read the chapter introduction again for some elements of narrative openings.

# ❦ Richard Rodriguez ❦

*Richard Rodriguez was born in San Francisco in 1944 to Mexican-American parents who spoke only Spanish at home. Rodriguez nonetheless mastered the English language and went on to study at Stanford, Columbia, and the University of California at Berkeley, where he earned a Ph.D. in English literature. He also received a Fulbright fellowship to study English literature in London. In spite of several offers for teaching positions, Rodriguez made writing and journalism his profession. In* The Hunger of Memory *(1982), a collection of autobiographical essays, he examines the American educational system from the point of view of an immigrant who has gone all the way through it, and he strongly opposes bilingual education.*

# *Los Pobres*

*In this autobiographical essay from* The Hunger of Memory, *Rodriguez describes his first experience of working at hard labor. The summer after he graduates from Stanford University, he takes a construction job that leads him to a vital insight about his relationship to the Mexican immigrant community he "left behind" because of his education.*

*Be aware as you read how closely Rodriguez examines himself, particularly how he examines himself in relation to others.*

---

I went to college at Stanford, attracted partly by its academic reputation, partly because it was the school rich people went to. I found myself on a campus with golden children of western America's upper middle class. Many were students both ambitious for academic success and accustomed to leisured life in the sun. In the afternoon, they lay spread out, sunbathing in front of the library, reading Swift or Engels or Beckett. Others went by in convertibles, off to play tennis or ride horses or sail. Beach boys dressed in tank-tops and shorts were my classmates in undergraduate seminars. Tall tan girls wearing white strapless dresses sat directly in front of me in lecture rooms. I'd study them, their 1 physical confidence. I was still recognizably kin to the boy I had been. Less tortured perhaps. But still kin. At Stanford, it's true, I began to have something like a conventional sexual life. I don't think, however, that I really believed that the women I knew found me physically appealing. I continued to stay out of the sun. I didn't linger in mirrors. And I was the student at Stanford who remembered to notice the Mexican-American janitors and gardeners working on campus.

It was at Stanford, one day near the end of my senior year, that a friend told me about a summer construction job he knew was available. I was quickly alert. Desire uncoiled within me. My friend said that he knew I had been looking for summer employment. He knew I needed some money. Almost apologetically he explained: It was something I probably wouldn't be interested in, but a friend of his, a contractor, needed someone for the summer to do menial jobs. There would be lots of shoveling and raking and sweeping. Nothing too hard. But nothing more interesting either. Still, the pay would be good. Did I want it? Or did I know someone who did? 2

I did. Yes, I said, surprised to hear myself say it. 3

In the weeks following, friends cautioned that I had no idea how hard physical labor really is. ("You only *think* you know what it is like to shovel for eight hours straight.") Their objections seemed to me challenges. They resolved the issue. I became happy with my plan. I decided, however, not to tell my parents. I wouldn't tell my mother because I could guess her worried reaction. I would tell my father only after the summer was over, when I could announce that, after all, I did know what "real work" is like. 4

The day I met the contractor (a Princeton graduate, it turned out), he asked me whether I had done any physical labor before. "In high school, during the summer," I lied. And although he seemed to regard me with skepticism, he decided to give me a try. Several days later, expectant, I arrived at my first construction site. I would take off my shirt to the sun. And at last grasp desired sensation. No longer afraid. At last become like a *bracero*. "We need those tree stumps out of here by tomorrow," the contractor said. I started to work. 5

I labored with excitement that first morning—and all the days after. The work was harder than I could have expected. But it was never as tedious as my friends had warned me it would be. There was too much physical pleasure in the labor. Especially early in the day, I would be most alert to the sensations of movement and straining. Beginning around seven each morning (when the air was still damp but the scent of weeds and dry earth anticipated the heat of the sun), I would feel my body resist the first thrusts of the shovel. My arms, tightened by sleep, would gradually loosen; after only several minutes, sweat would gather in beads on my forehead and then—a short while later—I would feel my chest silky with sweat in the breeze. I would return to my work. A nervous spark of pain would fly up my arm and settle to burn like an ember in the thick of my shoulder. An hour, two passed. Three. My whole body would assume regular movements; my shoveling would be described by identical, even movements. Even later in the day, my enthusiasm for primitive sensation would survive the heat and the dust and the insects pricking my back. I would strain wildly for sensation as the day came to a close. At three-thirty, quitting time, I would stand upright and slowly let my head fall back, luxuriating in the feeling of tightness relieved. 6

Some of the men working nearby would watch me and laugh. Two or three of the older men took the trouble to teach me the right way to use a pick, the correct way to shovel. "You're doing it wrong, too fucking hard," one man scolded. Then proceeded to show me—what persons who work with their bodies all their lives quickly learn—the most economical way to use one's body in labor. 7

"Don't make your back do so much work," he instructed. I stood impatiently listening, half listening, vaguely watching, then noticed his work-thickened fingers clutching the shovel. I was annoyed. I wanted to tell him that I enjoyed shoveling the wrong way. And I didn't want to learn the right way. I wasn't afraid of back pain. I liked the way my body felt sore at the end of the day. 8

I was about to, but, as it turned out, I didn't say a thing. Rather it was at that moment I realized that I was fooling myself if I expected a few weeks of labor to gain me admission to 9 the world of the laborer. I would not learn in three months what my father had meant by "real work." I was not bound to this job; I could imagine its rapid conclusion. For me the sensations of exertion and fatigue could be savored. For my father or uncle, working at comparable jobs when they were my age, such sensations were to be feared. Fatigue took a different toll on their bodies—and minds.

10 It was, I know, a simple insight. But it was with this realization that I took my first step that summer toward realizing something even more important about the "worker." In the company of carpenters, electricians, plumbers, and painters at lunch, I would often sit quietly, observant. I was not shy in such company. I felt easy, pleased by the knowledge that I was casually accepted, my presence taken for granted by men (exotics) who worked with their hands. Some days the younger men would talk and talk about sex, and they would howl at women who drove by in cars. Other days the talk at lunchtime was subdued; men gathered in separate groups. It depended on who was around. There were rough, good-natured workers. Others were quiet. The more I remember that summer, the more I realize that there was no single type of worker. I am embarrassed to say I had not expected such diversity. I certainly had not expected to meet, for example, a plumber who was an abstract painter in his off hours and admired the work of Mark Rothko. Nor did I expect to meet so many workers with college diplomas. (There were the ones who were not surprised that I intended to enter graduate school in the fall.) I suppose what I really want to say here is painfully obvious, but I must say it nevertheless: The men of that summer were middle-class Americans. They certainly didn't constitute an oppressed society. Carefully completing their work sheets; talking about the fortunes of local football teams; planning Las Vegas vacations; comparing the gas mileage of various makes of campers—they were not *los pobres* my mother had spoken about.

11 On two occasions, the contractor hired a group of Mexican aliens. They were employed to cut down some trees and haul off debris. In all, there were six men of varying age. The youngest in his twenties, the oldest (his father?) perhaps sixty years old. They

came and they left in a single old truck. Anonymous men. They were never introduced to the other men at the site. Immediately upon their arrival, they would follow the contractor's directions, start working—rarely resting—seemingly driven by a fatalistic sense that work which had to be done was best done as quickly as possible.

I watched them sometimes. Perhaps they watched me. The 12 only time I saw them pay me much notice was one day at lunchtime when I was laughing with the other men. The Mexicans sat apart when they ate, just as they worked by themselves. Quiet. I rarely heard them say much to each other. All I could hear were their voices calling out sharply to one another, giving directions. Otherwise, when they stood briefly resting, they talked among themselves in voices too hard to overhear.

The contractor knew enough Spanish, and the Mexicans—or 13 at least the oldest of them, their spokesman—seemed to know enough English to communicate. But because I was around, the contractor decided one day to make me his translator. (He assumed I could speak Spanish.) I did what I was told. Shyly I went over to tell the Mexicans that the *patrón* wanted them to do something else before they left for the day. As I started to speak, I was afraid with my old fear that I would be unable to pronounce Spanish words. But it was a simple instruction I had to convey. I could say it in phrases.

The dark sweating faces turned toward me as I spoke. They 14 stopped their work to hear me. Each nodded in response. I stood there. I wanted to say something more. But what could I say in Spanish, even if I could have pronounced the words right? Perhaps I just wanted to engage them in small talk, to be assured of their confidence, our familiarity. I thought for a moment to ask them where in Mexico they were from. Something like that. And maybe I wanted to tell them (a lie, if need be) that my parents were from the same part of Mexico.

I stood there. 15

Their faces watched me. The eyes of the man directly in front 16 of me moved slowly over my shoulder, and I turned to follow his glance toward *el patrón* some distance away. For a moment I felt swept up by that glance into the Mexicans' company. But then I heard one of them returning to work. And then the others went back to work. I left them without saying anything more.

When they had finished, the contractor went over to pay them in cash. (He later told me that he paid them collectively—"for the job"—though he wouldn't tell me their wages. He said something quickly about the good rate of exchange "in their own country.") I can still hear the loudly confident voice he used with the Mexicans. It was the sound of the *gringo* I had heard as a very young boy. And I can still hear the quiet, indistinct sounds of the Mexican, the oldest, who replied. At hearing that voice I was sad for the Mexicans. Depressed by their vulnerability. Angry at myself. The adventure of the summer seemed suddenly ludicrous. I would not shorten the distance I felt from *los pobres* with a few weeks of physical labor. I would not become like them. They were different from me. 17

After that summer, a great deal—and not very much really—changed in my life. The curse of physical shame was broken by the sun; I was no longer ashamed of my body. No longer would I deny myself the pleasing sensations of my maleness. During those years when middle-class Black Americans began to assert with pride, "Black is beautiful," I was able to regard my complexion without shame. I am today darker than I ever was as a boy. I have taken up the middle-class sport of long-distance running. Nearly every day now I run ten or fifteen miles, barely clothed, my skin exposed to the California winter rain and wind or the summer sun of late afternoon. The torso, the soccer player's calves and thighs, the arms of the twenty-year-old I never was, I possess now in my thirties. I study the youthful parody shape in the mirror: the stomach lipped tight by muscle; the shoulders rounded by chin-ups; the arms veined strong. This man. A man. I meet him. He laughs to see me, what I have become. 18

The dandy. I wear double-breasted Italian suits and custom made English shoes. I resemble no one so much as my father—the man pictured in those honeymoon photos. At that point in life when he abandoned the dandy's posture, I assume it. At the point when my parents would not consider going on vacation, I register 19 at the Hotel Carlyle in New York and the Plaza Athénée in Paris. I am as taken by the symbols of leisure and wealth as they were. For my parents, however, those symbols became taunts, reminders of all they could not achieve in one lifetime. For me those same symbols are reassuring reminders of public success. I tempt vulgarity to be reassured. I am filled with the gaudy delight, the monstrous grace of the nouveau riche.

In recent years I have had occasion to lecture in ghetto high schools. There I see students of remarkable style and physical grace. (One can see more dandies in such schools than one ever will find in middle-class high schools.) There is not the look of casual assurance I saw students at Stanford display. Ghetto girls mimic high-fashion models. Their dresses are of bold, forceful color; their figures elegant, long; the stance theatrical. Boys wear shirts that grip at their overdeveloped muscular bodies. (Against a powerless future, they engage images of strength.) Bad nutrition does not yet tell. Great disappointment, fatal to youth, awaits them still. For the moment, movements in school hallways are dancelike, a procession of postures in a sexual masque. Watching them, I feel a kind of envy. I wonder how different my adolescence would have been had I been free. . . . But no, it is my parents I see—their optimism during those years when they were entertained by Italian grand opera. 20

The registration clerk in London wonders if I have just been to Switzerland. And the man who carries my luggage in New York guesses the Caribbean. My complexion becomes a mark of my leisure. Yet no one would regard my complexion the same way if I entered such hotels through the service entrance. That is only to say that my complexion assumes its significance from the context of my life. My skin, in itself, means nothing. I stress the point because I know there are people who would label me "disadvantaged" because of my color. They make the same mistake I made as a boy, when I thought a disadvantaged life was circumscribed by particular occupations. That summer I worked in the sun may have made me physically indistinguishable from the Mexicans working nearby. (My skin was actually darker because, unlike 21 them, I worked without wearing a shirt. By late August my hands were probably as tough as theirs.) But I was not one of *los pobres*. What made me different from them was an attitude of *mind*, my imagination of myself.

22 I do not blame my mother for warning me away from the sun when I was young. In a world where her brother had become an old man in his twenties because he was dark, my complexion was something to worry about. "Don't run in the sun," she warns me today. I run. In the end, my father was right—though perhaps he did not know how right or why—to say that I would never know what real work is. I will never know what he felt at his last factory job. If tomorrow I worked at some kind of factory, it would go differently for me. My long education would favor me. I could act as a public person—able to defend my interests, to unionize, to petition, to speak up—to challenge and demand. (I will never know what real work is.) I will never know what the Mexicans knew, gathering their shovels and ladders and saws.

23 Their silence stays with me now. The wages those Mexicans received for their labor were only a measure of their disadvantaged condition. Their silence is more telling. They lack a public identity. They remain profoundly alien. Persons apart. People lacking a union obviously, people without grounds. They depend upon the relative good will or fairness of their employers each day. For such people, lacking a better alternative, it is not such an unreasonable risk.

24 Their silence stays with me. I have taken these many words to describe its impact. Only: the quiet. Something uncanny about it. Its compliance. Vulnerability. Pathos. As I heard their truck rumbling away, I shuddered, my face mirrored with sweat. I had finally come face to face with *los pobres*.

---

## *Meaning and Purpose*

1. What picture of Rodriguez do you get from the first paragraph? How does he see himself?

2. Why is he surprised to hear himself say yes (3) to the offer of a summer job at manual labor? What is his motive for taking the job? Why doesn't he tell his parents?
3. Rodriguez talks about many things in this essay: being a student at Stanford, physical labor, the Italian suits he wears, and ghetto high-school students. What do you think his main point is, and where does he state it?
4. Paragraph 10 begins with "It was, I know, a simple insight." What is the insight and what triggers it? How does this insight connect with his later statement, "But I was not one of *los pobres*"?
5. Is it significant that the Mexican workers were paid as a group rather than individually? Explain.
6. Rodriguez begins paragraphs 23 and 24 with the words, "Their silence stays with me." What does the silence signify?

## Strategy

1. Rodriguez's narrative begins with one summer while he is a student at Stanford, then jumps to the vague time frame of "After that summer" (18), then to "In recent years" (20). Why does he choose to arrange the events and skip to the periods that he does?
2. Why does Rodriguez draw out details of his summer construction job and compress the details of the longer periods in sections 2 and 3?
3. Does Rodriguez use summary or scene to tell his story? Give examples.
4. What is Rodriguez's point of view? Give evidence from the essay of how effective it is.

## Style

1. Locate the words *los pobres*, *bracero*, *patrón*, and *gringo* in the text. Can you define them using only the context of the narrative?

2. Rodriguez occasionally uses sentence fragments purposely. Find at least three in the first two paragraphs and explain how they affect the tone of the introduction.
3. A good narrative re-creates life. Does "Los Pobres" do so? Explain.

## *Writing Tasks*

1. At some time in your life you have undoubtedly been an "outsider." It may have been in another country or at a new school, in a new neighborhood, or on a new job. Write a narrative about that time. As Rodriguez does in "Los Pobres," blend the details of the situation with your thoughts and insights from a later perspective.
2. Choose an event to narrate, and write it in two ways. In one version, use the scene method to dramatize the event and make it immediate. In the other version, use summary to tell more than show. Which version is more effective?

## ❦ *Responding to Photographs* ❦

*Narration*

The Storyteller

Ancient cultures viewed storytellers as being touched with divine madness. These storytellers had tales that explained life's mysteries.

But times have changed

Astronauts have soared through space. The deepest rainforests and highest mountain peaks have been photographed. What mysteries need to be explained? What lessons need to be taught? What is the role of the storyteller in an age when movie and television production companies create visual stories by formula?

Is the photograph "The Storyteller" commenting on the role of storytellers today?

The Storyteller's outfit suggests he indeed might be touched by divine madness. He wears ribbons, balloons, streamers, a whimsical laurel around his head, and a banner that identifies him.

Displayed on a wall are hundreds of photographs, many of African-American and Native-American leaders, perhaps each embodying a story of its own. Behind his head, slightly obscured, are the words of Martin Luther King, "I have a dream."

This storyteller stands in the classroom, but where are the students who might be eager to hear a meaningful story? He is looking and pointing outside the photographic frame, but at what or whom? From the viewer's perspective he is alone . . . or is he?

In a unified narrative respond to one of the following writing tasks. Before you begin the first draft, review effective narrative conventions described at the beginning of the chapter.

1. Create your own tale about the storyteller in this photograph. Begin by studying the photograph. Imagine how the storyteller feels in his attire. Imagine how he feels during his performance. Imagine what his life is like when he is not being a storyteller. What does he do? Where does he live? What do his friends think of his storytelling? Is he a fulfilled person? A happy person? A sad person?

   As you imagine the storyteller, list your observations. Once this exploratory phase of the assignment is complete, review your observations and determine what dominant impression you wish to create.

   Finally, to start your first draft, you might begin this way: "Once upon a time an ordinary man who lived in our city decided to become a storyteller." Throughout your draft integrate physical details from the photograph.
2. Imagine that the storyteller in the photograph is fully aware that ancient mysteries have been clarified scientifically. He is still compelled to tell tales, meaningful tales designed to give people insight into a society which some see as growing more and more chaotic.

   For this task, tell how the storyteller became successful. Include in your narrative a summary of one tale that gave his listeners insight into contemporary life.

## ❦ *Additional Writing Tasks* ❦

### *Narration*

1. All of us have had experiences that can be retold in narrative form. Often these experiences stay with us much longer than impersonal events we have merely observed. For this writing task, select an incident from your early years that involves a simple action that you can recall clearly and vividly. The incident does not have to be exceptionally dramatic, but it should be interesting enough to move from the opening through the body to the climax—the major components of narrative. The incident may involve you alone or it may involve others as well. It must have enough action with connected events to be developed as a narration.

   Because this is to be an incident from your early years, you might begin by setting aside time to explore your past. Begin by spontaneously jotting down memories from your early past as a way to begin the selection procedure. Make a list by devoting no more than three or four sentences to each experience you recall. These three entries are from one student's memory list:

   > I remember walking home from school one June morning. Hot. Humid. A man with a Bible and wearing a black suit stopped me and asked, "Have you been saved, Sonny?" I was frightened.
   >
   > When I was ten I visited my grandfather in the hospital. He was very ill, dying. I recalled all the wonderful and all the horrible fishing trips we took together.
   >
   > Why was my dog shot? The killer was never found. I remember searching the faces of strangers for looks of guilt.

   Each writer, of course, will have his or her own memories: an automobile accident, a mystery, a sudden appearance, a victory, a defeat, a meeting with a famous person, and so on.

   Once you have compiled a list, select one of the memories, perhaps the one that stirs the most emotion in you when you recall it, and use it as the basis for your narration. Before starting your first draft, take at least an uninterrupted hour to compose a rough sketch of the incident, capturing the movement of events and the people. Then you will be prepared to start the first draft. Begin by arranging the material in dramatic order to serve as a loose outline.

2. Select an incident to narrate that you have not directly experienced yourself. The incident may come from what you have seen, heard, or read. Perhaps you will select an incident from a television show, film, short story, news article, or friend's experience. If you select a newspaper article as your source, you may want to retell it as though you had witnessed the incident. If you want to convey a friend's story, you may add observations of your own. If you select an incident from a film or short story, you may want to concentrate on an incident involving one character and rearrange the events to suit your purpose. Keep in mind, though, that your task is not to merely summarize the story line; your task is to select material for your own narrative.

# 5

# *Examples*

## *Illustrating Ideas*

## *The Method*

Examples bring the vague and abstract down to earth. They clarify the historian's lectures. They make concrete the philosopher's abstractions. They electrify the politician's arguments. By using examples effectively you will not only help your readers understand your point, but you will also improve your chances of holding their attention because vivid, concrete examples can make your writing more interesting to read.

Examples are much used, even in everyday conversation. If someone claims that advertisers use fear of rejection to manipulate consumers, you might say, "Show me."

Examples such as these would follow: "What about those mouthwash commercials? One actually shows a salesman rejected because he has bad breath. And then after a quick rinse, Presto! he makes the sale, and the customer drives away smiling. And what about the commercial that shows a young female banker passed over for a promotion? A wiser, older colleague whispers in her ear. In the next scene she is scrubbing her head with the advertiser's shampoo, and the commercial closes with the smiling banker now managing her own department."

The speaker is using examples to clarify the general observation that advertisers use fear of rejection to manipulate consumers into buying their products. Writers use examples with the same intent—to illustrate a generalization; that is, to select one thing from many to represent the *whole*. In fact, the word *example* derives from the Latin *exemplum*, which refers to "one thing selected from the many." Examples used to represent ideas are essential to clear communication because they give readers something concrete to visualize. It might be difficult for a reader to understand what social critic Jack Solomon means by this statement.

> No matter how you look at it, in the scant space of some forty years, television has revolutionalized our lives. First introduced as a novelty alternative to radio, television has rapidly evolved into the most profound invention of the age. Nothing is immune from its influence.

For the sake of clarity, Solomon immediately provides several examples to illustrate his idea for the reader:

> Politicians play for the cameras, and so do international terrorists. Physicians call news conferences, and judges host courtroom dramas. Television, through its hyping of the Olympic Games, has transformed sport into politics and politics into sport, treating everything from presidential elections to military conflicts as prime-time entertainment. What is not televised is hardly thought of at all in a world in which television creates reality as much as it records.

These examples add clarity to Solomon's statement. Without them the reader would have only a vague understanding of Solomon's point in this paragraph, which would amount to a slip in communication.

## *Strategies*

Professional writers use three kinds of examples—specific, typical, and hypothetical—to support their ideas. They can be used in any combination and are often mixed within one paragraph.

### *Specific Examples*

**Specific examples** capture an experience, event, incident, or fact. Banesh Hoffman, in "My Friend, Albert Einstein," uses a specific example (an **anecdote**) to support the general comment that the essence of Einstein's personality was simplicity.

> He was one of the greatest scientists the world has ever known, yet if I had to convey the essence of Albert Einstein in a single word, I would choose *simplicity*. Perhaps an anecdote will help. Once, caught in a downpour, he took off his hat and held it under his coat. Asked why, he explained,

> with admirable logic, that the rain would damage the hat, but his hair would be none the worse for its wetting. This knack for going instinctively to the heart of the matter was the secret of his major scientific discoveries.

Hoffman selects this specific example with a clear purpose in mind. He wants to make concrete the generalization in the topic sentence. The example is vivid and interesting, capturing Einstein's essence.

Hoffman's specific example illustrating Einstein's simplicity is a short narrative, but writers often shape examples in other ways. Sometimes the writer will use several specific examples in one paragraph. A series of brief examples might function like verbal snapshots, freezing in time several events or experiences. In this paragraph, naturalist Jane van Lawick-Goodall uses seven short visual examples to illustrate social behavior among the chimpanzees she studied in Tanzania.

> While many details of their [the chimpanzees'] social behavior were hidden from me by the foliage, I did get occasional fascinating glimpses. I saw one female, newly arrived in a group, hurry up to a big male and hold her hand toward him. Almost regally he reached out, clasped her hand in his, drew it toward him, and kissed it with his lips. I saw two adult males embrace each other in greeting. I saw youngsters having wild games through treetops, chasing around after each other or jumping again and again, one after the other, from a branch to a springy bough below. I watched small infants dangling happily by themselves for minutes on end, patting at their toes with one hand, rotating gently from side to side. Once two tiny infants pulled on opposite ends of a twig in a gentle tug-of-war. Often during the heat of midday or after a long spell of feeding, I saw two or more adults grooming each other, carefully looking through the hair of their companions.

Sometimes writers will create a *list* or a *catalogue* of specific examples to illustrate their observations. In this paragraph from *The*

*Distant Mirror*, historian Barbara Tuchman catalogues how people in fourteenth-century England might imagine the distant places they had heard of but never seen.

> Faraway lands, however—India, Persia, and beyond—were seen through a gauze of fabulous fairy tales revealing an occasional nugget of reality: forests so high they touch the clouds, horned pygmies who move in herds and grow old in seven years, brahmins who kill themselves on funeral pyres, men with dogs' heads and six toes, "cyclopeans" with only one eye and one foot who move as fast as the wind, the "monoceros" which can be caught only when it sleeps in the lap of a virgin, Amazons whose tears are of silver, panthers who practice the caesarean operation with their own claws, trees whose leaves supply wool, snakes 300 feet long, snakes with precious stones for eyes, snakes who so love music that for prudence they stop up one ear with their tail.

Tuchman's and Goodall's paragraphs also illustrate another point: examples can come from various sources. Tuchman finds her specific examples by researching historical documents; Goodall gets hers by observing chimpanzees in their natural habitat. Both writers use their examples for the same purpose, however: to illustrate a general observation.

### *Typical Examples*

In contrast to specific examples, writers compose **typical examples** by generalizing from many experiences, events, incidents, or facts. Consider this paragraph from Jonathan Kozol's essay "The Human Cost of an Illiterate Society." Kozol uses a typical example to develop the point that illiterates, people who cannot read, lead a precarious existence, even when they are in the care of professionals trained to provide for their health. As you read Kozol's paragraph, keep in mind that this typical example represents the experience of many people, not that of one specific person.

> Illiterates live, in more than literal ways, an uninsured existence. They cannot understand written details on a health insurance form. They cannot read the waivers that they sign preceding surgical procedures. Several women I have known in Boston have entered a slum hospital with the intention of obtaining a tubal ligation and have emerged a few days later after having been subjected to a hysterectomy. Unaware of their rights, incognizant of jargon, intimidated by the unfamiliar air of fear and atmosphere of ether that so many of us find oppressive in the confines even of the most attractive and expensive medical facilities, they have signed their names to documents they could not read and which nobody, in the hectic situation that prevails so often in those overcrowded hospitals that serve the urban poor, had even bothered to explain.

Kozol begins with a general statement that establishes the dangers illiterate patients face. He follows with two sentences of background: illiterate patients cannot understand insurance forms or the legal documents that give away their rights during surgery. He then supports his general statement with an extended typical example, thus illustrating, even dramatizing, the result of being unable to read: several illiterate Boston women signed papers permitting hysterectomies when they wanted tubal ligations.

Typical examples, as Kozol's illustrates, are composites of many experiences. They are not rooted in specific times but compiled after many observations over an extended period. In the next paragraph cultural anthropologist Edward T. Hall uses typical examples developed after extended observation to illustrate how people react when their sense of space is violated:

> People are very sensitive to any intrusion into their spatial bubble. If someone stands too close to you, your first instinct is to back up. If that's not possible, you lean away and pull yourself in, tensing your muscles. If an intruder doesn't respond to these body signals, you may then try to protect yourself, using a briefcase, umbrella, or raincoat. Women—especially when traveling alone—often plant their pocketbook in such a way that no one can get very close to them.

As a last resort, you may move to another spot and position yourself behind a desk or a chair that provides screening. Everyone tries to adjust the space around himself in a way that's comfortable for him; most often, he does this unconsciously.

### *Hypothetical Examples*

Sometimes writers create **hypothetical examples** from their imagination. Hypothetical examples are similar to typical examples, usually composed from bits and pieces of experience or information. Often a writer will use a hypothetical example where something concrete is needed to tie down an abstraction and no *actual* example is available. In the opening paragraph of *The White Album*, essayist and novelist Joan Didion uses hypothetical examples to illustrate why stories are important in life.

> We *tell* ourselves stories in order to live. The princess is caged in a consulate. The man with candy will lead the children to the sea. The naked woman on the ledge outside the window on the sixteenth floor is a victim of *accidie*, or the naked woman is an exhibitionist, and it would be "interesting" to know which. We *tell* ourselves that it makes some difference whether the naked woman is about to commit a mortal sin or is about to register a political protest or is about to be, the Aristophanic view, snatched back to the human condition by the fireman in priest's clothing just visible in the window behind her, the one smiling at the telephoto lens. We *look* for the sermon in the suicide, for the social or moral lesson in the murder of five. We *interpret* what we see, select the most workable of the multiple choices. We *live* entirely, especially if we are writers, by the imposition of a narrative line upon disparate images, by the "ideas" with which we have learned to freeze the shifting phantasmagoria which is our actual experience.

Didion has clearly drawn these brief examples from her imagination, yet they are effective because they make her observation more concrete. With these conjectures, she hopes to stir her readers' interest by appealing to typical experiences they might have encountered in fairy tales and newspapers, the mysterious experiences for which many seek explanations.

### *Mixing Examples*

When studying professional writing, you'll notice that writers use different strategies to develop their examples. You'll find specific, typical, and hypothetical examples mixed, and you'll notice that sometimes examples illustrating one point will be presented in several paragraphs. In this passage from *No House Calls*, Peter Gott, a practicing physician and medical columnist, develops his point in several paragraphs and mixes examples with explanation to reveal the scientific facts behind the commercial claims of mouthwash and disinfectant companies.

> With people's increasing knowledge about bacteria, it was inevitable that some companies would, with success, try to play upon the fear that we have all developed about "bacterial infection." For instance, Listerine and Lysol are currently being advertised to produce "clean breath" and a clean environment, respectively, as a result of their bacteria-killing properties. While it is true that these compounds do, in fact, kill bacteria, the consumer would do well to demand more precision in evaluating their claims.
>
> As an example, the mouth contains billions of harmless bacteria. Some forms of bad breath are caused by bacterial decomposition of food between teeth. Listerine—and many other mouthwashes—will kill millions of bacteria on contact, but only a tiny proportion of the *total*. Furthermore, as soon as the Listerine has been spit out, billions of bacteria are reintroduced into the mouth during breathing and eating. So while the consumer's mouth will feel "fresh," in fact the bacterial count rapidly rises to "pretreatment" levels; essentially, nothing has been accomplished.
>
> Lysol spray when applied to surfaces will kill some bacteria, but most of these are nonpathogens and would do us

> no harm anyway. Bacteria that cause venereal disease die quickly outside the body and would be unlikely to reside on public toilet seats long enough for the spray to make any difference. The Lysol spray will scent the air, however, and that seems to be the important consideration. Somehow, if we don't see or smell the germs, we assume they're all gone. The room must be safe. The evil has been repelled. We can take a shower.

Peter Gott's passage establishes an important principle to keep in mind: every writer, whether a professional writer or a student writer, must develop an eye for examples. The most effective way we know of developing that eye is to read critically; that is, read as a writer reads. Study how professional writers shape their examples. Study how their examples relate to their generalizations. And study the kinds of examples they develop.

## *Examples in College Writing*

Examples are so effective in clarifying an idea that you will probably use them in every college essay you write. The vivid, specifically written example brings to life the most abstract concept. Without examples, an expository essay will lack vigor. In fact, turning in an essay without effectively using examples may indicate to your reader that your understanding of the subject is deficient, especially if you write a string of unsubstantiated generalizations.

### *Guidelines for Writing Examples*

1. Select a subject that can be developed through examples and determine if you have enough information to develop examples.
2. Decide on a dominant purpose of the essay. Then use the dominant purpose to focus your prewriting to generate as many examples as you can.

3. Review your prewritten material, compose a thesis, and then select appropriate examples from your prewriting to develop it.
4. Decide on appropriate structure and arrange the examples to create the strongest effect. Vary the examples in length and type, while keeping in mind the purpose they serve.
5. Revise your essay, making sure that the examples are adequately developed for your purpose.

### *A Student Essay Developed by Examples*

In a Law and Society course, Rick Yocum used examples as the dominant development pattern in response to the following assignment:

> From articles distributed in class, from lecture notes, and from your general knowledge, write a 750-to-1000-word essay on "stalkers" that concentrates on an area listed below:
>
> 1. reasons more men than women are stalkers;
> 2. the long term psychological effects of being stalked;
> 3. how stalkers operate, who they are, who the victims are;
> 4. the difficulty police face in pursuing stalker complaints;
> 5. the effect of recent laws created to make investigating and controlling stalkers easier.

Rick Yocum decided to write on item 3. He had plenty of material from lecture notes and articles the instructor distributed as background material to develop examples. Moreover, he knew of a stalking case in his community that involved a businessman and a female attorney. As you read Yocum's essay, notice how he uses a mixture of examples—that is, a combination of specific examples, including catalogs, typical examples, and hypothetical examples.

No Safe Place

*Notice how Yocum announces his subject—stalkers—in the first sentence. He then presents a hypothetical example for dramatic effect.*

How do stalkers operate? They can be flattering at first, especially if you are young and inexperienced. Imagine this scenario: You meet an interesting person at a social function. The next morning you receive a phone message from your new acquaintance, saying that because of you an ordinary evening became special. Indeed, the two of you should become special friends. The conversation makes you feel special. Then more phone calls follow with more flattering messages. Soon the calls become annoying, and you ignore them, hoping they will go away. But they don't. This special friend continues to declare how much you are loved. Love letters follow, maybe even gifts—all unsolicited. By this point, a casual encounter that turned into an annoyance has become harassment. One phone call will end it, you think, but it doesn't. In fact, the harassment intensifies, and the messages turn threatening: "We are destined to be together"; "If I can't have you, no one will"; "Love me or we both must die"; "Our love is God's will. God punishes those who defy His will." Then at night, you see your special friend following you. Now you are being stalked.

*The quotations add a touch of reality to the example.*

*The last two sentences make the subject clear, promising to tell the reader about stalking and stalkers.*

Sound absurd? It's not. Since 1987 stalking cases are up over 300 percent. Stalking is predicted to be the growth crime of the late 1990s. This fact leads to two obvious questions—"Who are stalkers?" and "Who are victims?" Although there is no psychological description of stalkers that can predict who they are, one stalker characteristic is certain—they are delusional and anyone can become the center of their delusions.

*This paragraph ends the introduction. It reveals how serious stalking has become and ends with the thesis.*

*Thesis.*

Merely looking into someone's eyes will

*This paragraph explains "delusions." Yocum uses a brief catalogue to list some examples of delusions.*

not tell you what imaginary scenarios might be unfolding in the brain. These scenarios can seem farfetched—assassination schemes, government conspiracies, the United Nations invading the U.S. generals plotting military revolution, or even foreign aliens occupying the bodies of politicians—but to someone who cannot separate imaginary from actual events, they are real, just as real as a hamburger you might have had for lunch. In other words, they are what psychiatrists call "delusions," that is, the belief in something that is contrary to what is objectively experienced. The single trait stalkers share is that they are delusional; they believe in the cinema unreeling in their minds, not in the facts before their eyes. But, of course, many people who are not stalkers share the same trait.

*The opening sentence announces that typical examples will follow. Yocum arranges the information in this paragraph in two catalogues of typical stalker characteristics.*

In a more general sense, however, stalkers may typically share several other behavior traits: an intense interest in being famous, a history of failure in relationships, a severely flawed self-identity, a pathological desire to have one person's full attention, and a preoccupation with others who have been identified as stalkers. Moreover, the messages they send their victims typically have common characteristics: expressions of obsessive love, reverence for weapons, intimations of death, threats of suicide, allusions to religious themes, and claims that the stalker and victim share a common destiny.

*Yocum follows the topic sentence with a series of brief specific examples of celebrity stalking victims. He then closes the paragraph with an extended example.*

In the mind of the public, stalking victims are usually perceived to be celebrities who are pursued by delusional fans. Just recently, Madonna received a restraining order to keep an obsessive fan at bay. When he trespassed on her Southern California estate, police arrested him. Obsessive fans menacing celebrities gained full-media attention in the 1980's. For example, in 1980

Mark Chapman, a disturbed fan, murdered the former Beatle John Lennon. In 1981 John W. Hinkley, Jr. stalked actress Jodie Foster before he tried to kill President Reagan. In 1988 a woman falsely claimed to be talk-show host David Letterman's wife and kept trying to move into his home. In 1989 a delusional fan named Robert Bardo stalked and murdered Rebecca Schaeffer, star of the television series "My Sister Sam." After "worshipping" Schaeffer since 1986, Bardo saw the actress perform a movie bedroom scene and believed she had become "another Hollywood whore."

*Yocum uses another extended example of a celebrity being stalked to emphasize how far stalkers will go to pursue their quarry.*

Delusional fans who become stalkers are not restrained by national borders. In 1989 before Schaeffer's murder, Arthur Jackson became obsessed with actress Theresa Saldana. He traveled from Scotland under the belief that the two of them shared a common destiny and had to be "united." When he finally met Saldana, he attacked her with a knife. She survived, and he was arrested and jailed. Even in prison his delusions continued. When he was about to be paroled, Saldana objected and prosecutors kept him in custody by filing new charges that he had threatened her from jail.

*A clear topic sentence signals a shift from celebrities to ordinary people.*

*After some typical examples of categories of people who might become stalking victims, Yocum concentrates on a specific case to show just how difficult it is to stop a stalker.*

People other than the rich and famous can also become the target of delusional stalkers. They could be local elected officials, such as county supervisors, council members, or mayors. They could be teachers, community activists, or business people. For example, consider the case of a little-known Westminster attorney, Barbara Evens, just two years out of law school: A potential client, let's call him Mr. Smith, met her on a business matter. Although the meeting concentrated on his business concerns, Smith apparently decided that Evens fell in love with him during this first meeting, and he with her. To acknowledge her love for him and to declare his love for her, he besieged her with telephone calls, love letters, and flowers. She was stunned, of course, and denied any interest in Smith, finally filing harassment charges with the police. He seems to have interpreted her reactions as a "test of love." He became so obsessed he soon left his wife and abandoned his business to pursue the lawyer. When she continued to rebuff his advances, he sent her threatening letters and demanded to see her. Evens now has a restraining order that prevents Smith from coming within 100 yards of her. But the restraining order provides little comfort. The behavior of a stalker is difficult to predict. She fears he will become violent.

*Yocum closes by showing how being stalked can change someone's life. The closing clause provides the title.*

Whether a stalking victim is a celebrity or an ordinary person, being stalked is a life-changing experience. Every stranger seems to be a threat. Each time the doorbell rings, the stalker could be on the other side with a knife. Crowds are often seen as camouflage for the stalker. Whether rich and famous or poor and anonymous, stalking victims learn a universal lesson—there is no safe place to hide.

## *Comments*

In a unified, coherent fashion, Yocum addresses each requirement of this writing assignment. He creates an impression of how a stalker might operate; he develops a portrait of a stalker's mind and overt obsessions; he identifies stalker victims—that is, anyone—high profile celebrities or ordinary citizens. He clarifies the purpose of his discussion with three questions: How do stalkers operate? Who are stalkers? and Who are victims? And he ends the introductory paragraph with a thesis sentence: "Although there is no psychological description of stalkers that can predict who they are, one stalker characteristic is certain—they are delusional and anyone can become the center of their delusions."

Now let's closely examine other elements of Yocum's essay.

**Development Strategy.** Yocum uses examples effectively. Boldly, he uses an example in answer to the opening question: "How do stalkers operate?" The example is hypothetical, one that is created from the general knowledge he has of stalkers, and clearly illustrates how a stalker might move into the life of a victim. In the second paragraph he gives some general statistics and states his thesis. In the third paragraph, he creates an impression of how a stalker might think, using specific references to common delusions to serve as brief examples.

In the fifth paragraph Yocum uses a catalogue of examples to extend the impression of a stalker by referencing some typical characteristics, such as a desire for fame, failure in relationships, and flawed self-identity. In the fifth, sixth, and seventh paragraphs he concentrates on well-known victims of stalking, first in a series of brief specific examples and then in a single extended example. In the eighth paragraph he concentrates on the ordinary citizen as victim by first giving brief typical examples of who that person might be and then providing a well-developed specific example of an attorney in his community who apparently is being stalked by a businessman. He ends the essay with a brief paragraph that emphasizes the psychological effect on stalking victims.

By mixing examples—hypothetical, typical, and specific—and varying their length, Yocum avoids monotonous repetition in the essay's structure. Remember, like Yocum, always try to vary the type and length of examples you use.

**Revision.** In an early draft, Yocum referred to a stalker as "he," thus creating the impression that stalkers are always men and that the victims are always women. Members of his reading group pointed out the discrepancy, and he decided to change it. The group also pointed out that the opening needed to be more specific so the reader would have a clear understanding of how delusional a stalker could be. Yocum decided they were right and, therefore, added quotations that reflect a stalker's psychological make-up.

Adding specifics was easy, but changing the focus from women without shifting it to men was difficult. Finally, he realized he could address his reader directly by using "you" and avoid gender references by restructuring some sentences and using the phrase "special friend," which turned out to add an ironic dimension to the introduction. To his surprise, addressing the reader as "you" deepened the reader's involvement by placing him or her in the role of victim.

Now read Yocum's edited draft, paying particular attention to the changes.

How do stalkers operate? ~~At first a woman might find them~~ They can be flattering at first, especially if ~~she is~~ you are young and inexperienced. Imagine this scenario: ~~A college student~~ You meet~~s~~ an interesting person at a social function. The next morning ~~she~~ you receive~~s~~ a phone message ~~from him~~ from your new acquaintance, saying that because of ~~her~~ you an ordinary evening became special. Indeed, ~~they~~ the two of you should become special friends. And ~~she~~ you feel~~s~~ special. Then more phone calls follow, and more flattering messages. Now the calls seem annoying, and ~~she~~ you ignore~~s~~ them, hoping ~~he will stop~~ they will go away. But ~~he~~ they ~~doesn't~~ don't, and soon ~~he~~ this special friend declares how much ~~he loves her~~ you are loved. Love letters follow, maybe even gifts—all unsolicited. By this point, a casual encounter that turned into an annoyance has become harassment. One phone call will end it, ~~she~~ you think~~s~~, but it doesn't. In fact, the harassment intensifies, and the messages turn threatening.: ~~Now she knows she is being stalked.~~ "We are destined to be together"; If I can't have you, no one will"; "Love me or we both must die"; "Our love is God's will. God punishes those who defy His Will." Then at night you see your <u>special friend</u> following you. Now you are being stalked.

Once finished with the line editing, Yocum reviewed it with a group member and wrote the final polished draft. Study the differences, especially noting how he avoids referring to gender.

> How do stalkers operate? They can be flattering at first, especially if you are young and inexperienced. Imagine this scenario: You meet an interesting person at a social function. The next morning you receive a phone message from your new acquaintance, saying that because of you an ordinary evening became <u>special</u>. Indeed, the two of you should become <u>special friends</u>. And you feel special. Then more phone calls follow, and more flattering messages. Now the calls seem annoying, and you ignore them, hoping they will go away. But they don't, and soon this <u>special friend</u> declares how much you are loved. Love letters follow, maybe even gifts—all unsolicited. By this point, a casual encounter that turned into an annoyance has become harassment. One phone call will end it, you think, but it doesn't. In fact, the harassment intensifies, and the messages turn threatening: "We are destined to be together"; If I can't have you, no one will"; "Love me or we both must die"; "Our love is God's will. God punishes those who defy His will." Then at night you see your <u>special friend</u> following you. Now you are being stalked.

As you read the essays in the following section, you will see the variety of ways writers develop examples. Sometimes a writer

## *Peer Review*

You may be asked to write an essay about one of the readings that follow. Before you meet with your writing group, review this introduction. As your read the papers of your group, use these general principles of using examples to help guide your comments.

1. All examples should clearly relate to the general statements they illustrate.
2. The number of examples should be enough to validate the general statement, but not so many that the reader feels overwhelmed and loses interest. There is no mathematical way to measure this balance, so rely on your own judgment as you read the paper.
3. The examples should be combined with explanations to guide the reader to the desired conclusion.

will use a single extended example to develop a point. At other times, a writer will combine short and extended examples, specific and typical examples, and will include personal observations and background information.

Sometimes examples will serve as the dominant development pattern, but, like narration and description, examples also function in essays with other dominant patterns, such as comparison and contrast, cause and effect, classification, and argumentation. Always, however, writers use examples with one fundamental purpose in mind: *to make the general more specific and the abstract more concrete.*

## ❦ Lewis Thomas ❦

*Lewis Thomas, born in 1913, studied at Princeton University and Harvard Medical School. He has had a distinguished career as research pathologist, medical doctor, biologist, professor, and writer, but is best known for his collections of essays, many of which first appeared in* The New England Journal of Medicine. *He has been a professor of pathology and medicine at the Cornell University Medical School and has served as both president and chief executive officer of the Memorial Sloan-Kettering Cancer Center in New York City. His first collection,* Notes of a Biology Watcher: The Lives of a Cell *(1975), won the National Book Award and was followed by* More Notes of a Biology Watcher: The Medusa and the Snail *(1979).*

# *On Natural Death*

*In this short essay from* The Medusa and the Snail, *Lewis Thomas invites the reader to consider a new way of thinking about death. His examples are taken from his own observations and from medical research, from the professional realm as well as the personal, from the extraordinary and the mundane.*

*Keep in mind the essay's title, "On Natural Death," as you read. Apply the title to each paragraph to determine exactly how convincing Thomas's contentions about death are.*

---

There are so many new books about dying that there are now special shelves set aside for them in bookshops, along with the health-diet and home-repair paperbacks and the sex manuals. Some of them are so packed with detailed information and step-by-step instructions for performing the function that you'd think this was a new sort of skill which all of us are now required to learn. The strongest impression the casual reader gets, leafing through, is that proper dying has become an extraordinary, even an exotic experience, something only the specially trained get to do. 1

Also, you could be led to believe that we are the only creatures capable of the awareness of death, that when all the rest of nature is being cycled through dying, one generation after another, it is a different kind of process, done automatically and trivially, more "natural," as we say. 2

An elm in our backyard caught the blight this summer and dropped stone dead, leafless, almost overnight. One weekend it was a normal-looking elm, maybe a little bare in spots but nothing alarming, and the next weekend it was gone, passed over, departed, taken. Taken is right, for the tree surgeon came by yesterday with his crew of young helpers and their cherry picker, and took it down branch by branch and carted it off in the back of a red truck, everyone singing. 3

The dying of a field mouse, at the jaws of an amiable household cat, is a spectacle I have beheld many times. It used to make me wince. Early in life I gave up throwing sticks at the cat to make him drop the mouse, because the dropped mouse regularly went ahead and died anyway, but I always shouted unaffections at the cat to let him know the sort of animal he had become. Nature, I thought, was an abomination. 4

Recently I've done some thinking about that mouse, and I wonder if his dying is necessarily all that different from the passing of our elm. The main difference, if there is one, would be in the matter of pain. I do not believe that an elm tree has pain receptors, and even so, the blight seems to me a relatively painless way to go even if there were nerve endings in a tree, which there are not. But the mouse dangling tail-down from the teeth of a gray cat is something else again, with pain beyond bearing, you'd think, all over his small body. 5

There are now some plausible reasons for thinking it is not like that at all, and you can make up an entirely different story about the mouse and his dying if you like. At the instant of being trapped and penetrated by teeth, peptide hormones are released by cells in the hypothalamus and the pituitary gland; instantly these substances, called endorphins, are attached to the surface of other cells responsible for pain perception; the hormones have the pharmacologic properties of opium; there is no pain. Thus it is that the mouse seems always to dangle so languidly from the jaws, 6 lies there so quietly when dropped, dies of his injuries without a struggle. If a mouse could shrug, he'd shrug.

7 I do not know if this is true or not, nor do I know how to prove it if it is true. Maybe if you could get in there quickly enough and administer naloxone, a specific morphine antagonist, you could turn off the endorphins and observe the restoration of pain, but this is not something I would care to do or see. I think I will leave it there, as a good guess about the dying of a cat-chewed mouse, perhaps about dying in general.

8 Montaigne had a hunch about dying, based on his own close call in a riding accident. He was so badly injured as to be believed dead by his companions, and was carried home with lamentations, "all bloody, stained all over with the blood I had thrown up." He remembers the entire episode, despite having been "dead, for two full hours," with wonderment:

> It seemed to me that my life was hanging only by the tip of my lips. I closed my eyes in order, it seemed to me, to help push it out, and took pleasure in growing languid and letting myself go. It was an idea that was only floating on the surface of my soul, as delicate and feeble as all the rest, but in truth not only free from distress but mingled with that sweet feeling that people have who have let themselves slide into sleep. I believe that this is the same state in which people find themselves whom we see fainting in the agony of death, and I maintain that we pity them without cause. . . . In order to get used to the idea of death, I find there is nothing like coming close to it.

Later, in another essay, Montaigne returns to it:

> If you know not how to die, never trouble yourself: Nature will in a moment fully and sufficiently instruct you; she will exactly do that business for you; take you no care for it.

9 The worst accident I've ever seen was on Okinawa, in the early days of the invasion, when a jeep ran into a troop carrier and was crushed nearly flat. Inside were two young MPs, trapped in bent steel, both mortally hurt, with only their hands and shoulders visible. We had a conversation while people with the right tools were

prying them free. Sorry about the accident, they said. No, they said, they felt fine. Is everyone else okay, one of them said. Well, the other one said, no hurry now. And then they died.

Pain is useful for avoidance, for getting away when there's 10
time to get away, but when it is end game, and no way back, pain is likely to be turned off, and the mechanisms for this are wonderfully precise and quick. If I had to design an ecosystem in which creatures had to live off each other and in which dying was an indispensable part of living, I could not think of a better way to manage.

---

## *Meaning and Purpose*

1. The first paragraph may make readers think they are going to read an essay about "books on dying." What is the topic of the essay, and where does it first appear?
2. In the second paragraph, Thomas suggests that most of us think the deaths of things or creatures other than human beings are "natural," or trivial. How does Thomas use the example of a mouse's death to turn that notion around? Is nature necessarily trivial?
3. What kind or kinds of examples does Thomas use—specific, typical, hypothetical, or a combination of these—to support his ideas? Explain.
4. What does Thomas tell you that is important for you to know about death? Do you agree with him?
5. The author quotes Montaigne, who says elsewhere, "Let us give Nature a chance; she knows her business better than we do." How is this quotation important to the essay?

## *Strategy*

1. In the last sentence of paragraph 3, why does everyone sing?
2. Why do you think Thomas devotes four paragraphs to his thoughts about details in the mouse's death, and only one to the soldiers' deaths? How does the former example set you up for the latter?

3. Despite the topic, this essay has some humor. How is this humor appropriate to the essay?
4. Would you call this a "personal" essay? Which specific sentences in the essay support your answer?

## Style

1. Reread the first sentence in paragraph 4. The author uses the word "amiable" instead of "friendly," "spectacle" instead of "sight," and "beheld" instead of "seen." How are these words more appropriate than their synonyms? Look up the words in a good dictionary before you answer this question.
2. The first sentence in paragraph 8 is written in an informal style. Reread the sentence and then tell how a reader would know that it is informal.
3. The final paragraph includes the chess expression "end game," which means "the final stage of a game, usually after the exchange of queens and the serious reduction of forces." How is this phrase appropriate to the paragraph and to the essay?

## Writing Tasks

1. Your views on death may be strengthened or changed by this essay, even if only a little. In an essay, discuss your views on death and then tell how Thomas's essay has strengthened those views or changed them. If you believe that death is "normal" to all things, including human beings, what do you mean by "normal"? If you believe that human beings somehow die differently, what do you think makes their deaths different from those of other creatures?
2. Think of something—an experience, a situation—which at first appears unpleasant or distressing, but which actually has redeeming or beneficial features. Write an essay exploring these ideas and use examples to support your statements. Decide whether to use specific, typical, or hypothetical examples, or a mixture.

# ❦ Amy Tan ❦

*Amy Tan was born in Oakland, California, in 1952, two and a half years after her parents emigrated to the United States from China. Her parents expected her to become a neurosurgeon, but instead she became a consultant to programs for disabled children and then a free-lance writer. She visited China for the first time in 1987 and felt an instant cultural identity with her parents' homeland. Her first novel,* The Joy Luck Club *(1989), spent several weeks on American bestseller lists and earned much critical acclaim. It sensitively explores the relationships between young Chinese-American women and their immigrant mothers. Her second novel,* The Kitchen God's Wife *(1991), further explores this theme. Tan has also written two books for children, The Moon Lady and* The Siamese Cat. *Her latest novel is* The Hundred Secret Senses *(1995).*

## *Mother Tongue*

*In the following essay, first published in* Threepenny Review, *Tan describes how her use of English changes according to the needs of the circumstance and moment. During her exploration of language she also manages to paint an affectionate portrait of her mother and the relationship she has with her.*

*Tan uses example after example to demonstrate her points. Notice how specific those examples are, how they aptly illustrate her generalizations, and how they lend interest to what she says.*

---

I am not a scholar of English or literature. I cannot give you much more than personal opinions on the English language and its variations in this country or others. 1

I am a writer. And by that definition, I am someone who has always loved language. I am fascinated by language in daily life. I spend a great deal of my time thinking about the power of language—the way it can evoke an emotion, a visual image, a complex idea, or a simple truth. Language is the tool of my trade. And I use them all—all the Englishes I grew up with. 2

3 Recently, I was made keenly aware of the different Englishes I do use. I was giving a talk to a large group of people, the same talk I had already given to half a dozen other groups. The nature of the talk was about my writing, my life, and my book, *The Joy Luck Club*. The talk was going along well enough, until I remembered one major difference that made the whole tale sound wrong. My mother was in the room. And it was perhaps the first time she had heard me give a lengthy speech, using the kind of English I have never used with her. I was saying things like, "The intersection of memory upon imagination" and "There is an aspect of my fiction that relates to thus-and-thus"—a speech filled with carefully wrought grammatical phrases, burdened, it suddenly seemed to me, with nominalized forms, past perfect tenses, conditional phrases, all the forms of standard English that I had learned in school and through books, the forms of English I did not use at home with my mother.

4 Just last week, I was walking down the street with my mother, and I again found myself conscious of the English I was using, the English I do use with her. We were talking about the price of new and used furniture and I heard myself saying this: "Not waste money that way." My husband was with us as well, and he didn't notice any switch in my English. And then I realized why. It's because over the twenty years we've been together I've often used that same kind of English with him, and sometimes he even uses it with me. It has become our language of intimacy, a different sort of English that relates to family talk, the language I grew up with.

5 So you'll have some idea of what this family talk I heard sounds like, I'll quote what my mother said during a recent conversation which I videotaped and then transcribed. During this conversation, my mother was talking about a political gangster in Shanghai who had the same last name as her family's, Du, and how the gangster in his early years wanted to be adopted by her family, which was rich by comparison. Later, the gangster became more powerful, far richer than my mother's family, and one day showed up at my mother's wedding to pay his respects. Here's what she said in part.

6 "Du Yusong having business like fruit stand. Like off the street

kind. He is Du like Du Zong—but not Tsung-ming Island people. The local people call putong, the river east side, he belong to that side local people. That man want to ask Du Zong father take him in like become own family. Du Zong father wasn't look down on him, but didn't take seriously, until that man big like become a mafia. Now important person, very hard to inviting him. Chinese way, came only to show respect, don't stay for dinner. Respect for making big celebration, he shows up. Mean gives lots of respect. Chinese custom. Chinese social life that way. If too important won't have to stay too long. He come to my wedding. I didn't see, I heard it. I gone to boy's side, they have YMCA dinner. Chinese age I was nineteen."

You should know that my mother's expressive command of English belies how much she actually understands. She reads the *Forbes* report, listens to *Wall Street Week*, converses daily with her stockbroker, reads all of Shirley MacLaine's books with ease—all kinds of things I can't begin to understand. Yet some of my friends tell me they understand 50 percent of what my mother says. Some say they understand 80 to 90 percent. Some say they understand none of it, as if she were speaking pure Chinese. But to me, my mother's English is perfectly clear, perfectly natural. It's my mother tongue. Her language, as I hear it, is vivid, direct, full of observation and imagery. That was the language that helped shape the way I saw things, expressed things, made sense of the world. 7

Lately, I've been giving more thought to the kind of English my mother speaks. Like others, I have described it to people as "broken" or "fractured" English. But I wince when I say that. It has always bothered me that I can think of no way to describe it other than "broken," as if it were damaged and needed to be fixed, as if it lacked a certain wholeness and soundness. I've heard other terms used, "limited English," for example. But they seem just as bad, as if everything is limited, including people's perceptions of the limited English speaker. 8

I know this for a fact, because when I was growing up, my mother's "limited" English limited *my* perception of her. I was ashamed of her English. I believed that her English reflected the 9 quality of what she had to say. That is, because she expressed them imperfectly her thoughts were imperfect. And I had plenty of empirical evidence to support me: the fact that people in department stores, at banks, and at restaurants did not take her seriously, did not give her good service, pretended not to understand her, or even acted as if they did not hear her.

My mother has long realized the limitations of her English as well, When I was fifteen, she used to have me call people on the phone to pretend I was she. In this guise, I was forced to ask for information or even to complain and yell at people who had been rude to her. One time it was a call to her stockbroker in New York. She had cashed out her small portfolio and it just so happened we were going to go to New York the next week, our very first trip outside California. I had to get on the phone and say in an adolescent voice that was not very convincing, "This is Mrs. Tan." 10

And my mother was standing in the back whispering loudly, "Why he don't send me check, already two weeks late. So mad he lie to me, losing me money." 11

And then I said in perfect English, "Yes, I'm getting rather concerned. You had agreed to send the check two weeks ago, but it hasn't arrived." 12

Then she began to talk more loudly. "What he want, I come to New York tell him front of his boss, you cheating me?" And I was trying to calm her down, make her be quiet, while telling the stockbroker, "I can't tolerate any more excuses. If I don't receive the check immediately, I am going to have to speak to your manager when I'm in New York next week." And sure enough, the following week there we were in front of this astonished stockbroker, and I was sitting there red-faced and quiet, and my mother, the real Mrs. Tan, was shouting at his boss in her impeccable broken English. 13

We used a similar routine just five days ago, for a situation that was far less humorous. My mother had gone to the hospital for an appointment, to find out about a benign brain tumor a CAT scan had revealed a month ago. She said she had spoken very good English, her best English, no mistakes. Still, she said, the hospital did not apologize when they said they had lost the CAT scan and she had come for nothing. She said they did not seem to 14 have any sympathy when she told them she was anxious to know the exact diagnosis, since her husband and son had both died of brain tumors. She said they would not give her any more information until the next time and she would have to make another appointment for that. So she said she would not leave until the doctor called her daughter. She wouldn't budge. And when the doctor finally called her daughter, me, who spoke in perfect English—lo and behold—we had assurances the CAT scan would be found, promises that a conference call on Monday would be held, and apologies for any suffering my mother had gone through for a most regrettable mistake.

I think my mother's English almost had an effect on limit- 15
ing my possibilities in life as well. Sociologists and linguists probably will tell you that a person's developing language skills are more influenced by peers. But I do think that the language spoken in the family, especially in immigrant families which are more insular, plays a large role in shaping the language of the child. And I believe that is affected my results on achievement tests, IQ tests, and the SAT. While my English skills were never judged as poor, compared to math, English could not be considered my strong suit. In grade school I did moderately well, getting perhaps B's, sometimes B-pluses, in English and scoring perhaps in the sixtieth or seventieth percentile on achievement tests. But those scores were not good enough to override the opinion that my true abilities lay in math and science, because in those areas I achieved A's and scored in the ninetieth percentile or higher.

This was understandable. Math is precise; there is only one 16
correct answer. Whereas, for me at least, the answers on English tests were always a judgment call, a matter of opinion and personal experience. Those tests were constructed around items like fill-in-the-blank sentence completion, such as, "Even though Tom was ______, Mary thought he was ______." And the correct answer always seemed to be the most bland combinations of thoughts, for example, "Even though Tom was shy, Mary thought he was charming," with the grammatical structure "even though" limiting the correct answer to some sort of semantic opposites, so you wouldn't get answers like, "Even though Tom was foolish, Mary

thought he was ridiculous." Well, according to my mother, there were very few limitations as to what Tom could have been and what Mary might have thought of him. So I never did well on tests like that.

The same was true with word analogies, pairs of words in which you were supposed to find some sort of logical, semantic relationship—for example, "*Sunset* is to *nightfall* as _____ is to _____." And here you would be presented with a list of four possible pairs, one of which showed the same kind of relationship: *red* is to *stoplight, bus* is to *arrival, chills* is to *fever, yawn* is to *boring*. Well, I could never think that way. I knew what the tests were asking, but I could not block out of my mind the images already created by the first pair, "*sunset* is to *nightfall*"—and I would see a burst of colors against a darkening sky, the moon rising, the lowering of a curtain of stars. And all the other pairs of words—red, bus, stoplight, boring—just threw up a mass of confusing images, making it impossible for me to sort out something as logical as saying: "A sunset precedes nightfall" is the same as "a chill precedes a fever." The only way I would have gotten that answer right would have been to imagine an associative situation, for example, my being disobedient and staying out past sunset, catching a chill at night, which turns into feverish pneumonia as punishment, which indeed did happen to me. 17

I have been thinking about all this lately, about my mother's English, about achievement tests. Because lately I've been asked, as a writer, why there are not more Asian Americans represented in American literature. Why are there few Asian Americans enrolled in creative writing programs? Why do so many Chinese students go into engineering? Well, these are broad sociological questions I can't begin to answer. But I have noticed in surveys—in fact, just last week—that Asian students, as a whole, always do significantly better on math achievement tests than in English. And this makes me think that there are other Asian-American students whose English spoken in the home might also be described as "broken" or "limited." And perhaps they also have teachers who are steering them away from writing and into math and science, which is what happened to me. 18

Fortunately, I happen to be rebellious in nature and enjoy the challenge of disproving assumptions made about me. I became an English major my first year in college, after being enrolled as pre-med. I started writing nonfiction as a freelancer the week after I was told by my former boss that writing was my worst skill and I should hone my talents toward account management. 19

But it wasn't until 1985 that I finally began to write fiction. And at first I wrote using what I thought to be wittily crafted sentences, sentences that would finally prove I had mastery over the English language. Here's an example from the first draft of a story that later made its way into *The Joy Luck Club*, but without this line: "That was my mental quandary in its nascent state." A terrible line, which I can barely pronounce. 20

Fortunately, for reasons I won't get into today, I later decided I should envision a reader for the stories I would write. And the reader I decided upon was my mother, because these were stories about mothers. So with this reader in mind—and in fact she did read my early drafts—I began to write stories using all the Englishes I grew up with: the English I spoke to my mother, which for lack of a better term might be described as "simple"; the English she used with me, which for lack of a better term might be described as "broken"; my translation of her Chinese, which could certainly be described as "watered down"; and what I imagined to be her translation of her Chinese if she could speak in perfect English, her internal language, and for that I sought to preserve the essence, but neither an English nor a Chinese structure. I wanted to capture what language ability tests can never reveal: her intent, her passion, her imagery, the rhythms of her speech and the nature of her thoughts. 21

Apart from what any critic had to say about my writing, I knew I had succeeded where it counted when my mother finished reading my book and gave me her verdict: "So easy to read." 22

---

## *Meaning and Purpose*

1. What is Tan's thesis? Where does she state it?
2. Tan asserts that her mother's lack of command of standard

English ". . . belies how much she actually understands" (7). How is this so?

3. Explain how her mother's "limited" English limited Tan's perception of her.
4. Explain how her mother's lack of English skills nearly limited some of the author's life possibilities.

## *Strategy*

1. Tan uses anecdotes to illustrate her points, yet this is not a narrative essay. Why?
2. How effectively do Tan's examples illustrate her points?
3. Why does Tan distinctly break her essay at the end of paragraph 8 and again at the end of paragraph 17?

## *Style*

1. In paragraph 7 Tan says that some of her friends claim to understand little of her mother's speech, while some others claim to understand none of it. Translate the transcription of her mother's language in paragraph 6. Can it be accurately described as an "expressive command of English" (7)?
2. How many "Englishes" does Tan speak?
3. Tan says she eliminated the line "That was my mental quandary in its nascent state" from her novel *The Joy Luck Club* and labels the line "terrible." Why?
4. If necessary, look up the following in a good dictionary: *wrought, nominalized* (3); *transcribed* (5); *belies* (7); *empirical* (9); *guise* (10); *impeccable* (13); *benign* (14); *insular* (15); *semantic* (16); *quandary, nascent* (19).

## *Writing Tasks*

1. Using Amy Tan's essay as a model, write an essay in which you examine the various Englishes you use. What do you talk about

when you speak with friends of the same sex? Of the opposite sex? With both sexes? With your co-workers? With your parents? How does your language change? Make sure your examples are many and specific.

2. If you work in a job that has specialized jargon, or if you play a sport or participate in any social activity that has its own slang, write an essay in which you categorize and explain that language.

## ❦ Brent Staples ❦

*Brent Staples, born in 1951 in Chester, Pennsylvania, attended Widener University in his home town, where he received a B.A. in behavioral sciences. He then pursued graduate school at the University of Chicago, earning a Ph.D. in psychology. He has been a writer and editor for the* Chicago Sun-Times, *the* Chicago Reader, Chicago *magazine, and* Down Beat. *Since 1985 he has been on the editorial board of the* New York Times, *where he writes regularly on politics and culture. He has also been a regular contributor to the* New York Times Magazine, New York Woman, Ms., *and* Harper's. *He published* Parallel Time: A Memoir *in 1991.*

# *Black Men and Public Space*

*"Black Men and Public Space" appeared in a slightly different form in the September 1986 issue of* Ms. *magazine. The current version of the essay subsequently appeared in the December 1987 issue of* Harper's. *The essay is a provocative account of the ironic power and the real pain connected to being a young, black man in our race-conscious society.*

*As you read, pay close attention to the number and kinds of examples Staples uses to make his points vivid and alive.*

---

My first victim was a woman—white, well dressed, probably in her late twenties. I came upon her late one evening on a deserted street in Hyde Park, a relatively affluent neighborhood in an otherwise mean, impoverished section of Chicago. As I swung onto the avenue behind her, there seemed to be a discreet, uninflammatory distance between us. Not so. She cast back a worried glance. To her, the youngish black man—a broad six feet two inches with a beard and billowing hair, both hands shoved into the pockets of a bulky military jacket—seemed menacingly close. After a few more quick glimpses, she picked up her pace and was 1 soon running in earnest. Within seconds she disappeared into a cross street.

That was more than a decade ago. I was twenty-two years old, a graduate student newly arrived at the University of Chicago. It was in the echo of that terrified woman's footfalls that I first began to know the unwieldy inheritance I'd come into—the ability to alter public space in ugly ways. It was clear that she thought herself the quarry of a mugger, a rapist, or worse. Suffering a bout of insomnia, however, I was stalking sleep, not defenseless wayfarers. As a softy who is scarcely able to take a knife to a raw chicken—let alone hold one to a person's throat—I was surprised, embarrassed, and dismayed all at once. Her flight made me feel like an accomplice in tyranny. It also made it clear that I was indistinguishable from the muggers who occasionally seeped into the area from the surrounding ghetto. That first encounter, and those that followed, signified that a vast, unnerving gulf lay between nighttime pedestrians—particularly women—and me. And I soon gathered that being perceived as dangerous is a hazard in itself. I only needed to turn a corner into a dicey situation, or crowd some frightened, armed person in a foyer somewhere, or make an errant move after being pulled over by a policeman. Where fear and weapons meet—and they often do in urban America—there is always the possibility of death. 2

In that first year, my first away from my hometown, I was to become thoroughly familiar with the language of fear. At dark, shadowy intersections, I could cross in front of a car stopped at a traffic light and elicit the *thunk, thunk, thunk, thunk* of the driver—black, white, male, or female—hammering down the door locks. On less traveled streets after dark, I grew accustomed to but never comfortable with people crossing to the other side of the street rather than pass me. Then there were the standard unpleasantries with policemen, doormen, bouncers, cabdrivers, and others whose business it is to screen out troublesome individuals *before* there is any nastiness. 3

I moved to New York nearly two years ago and I have remained an avid night walker. In central Manhattan, the near- 4 constant crowd cover minimizes tense one-on-one street encounters. Elsewhere—in SoHo, for example, where sidewalks are narrow and tightly spaced buildings shut out the sky—things can get very taut indeed.

After dark, on the warrenlike streets of Brooklyn where I live, 5
I often see women who fear the worst from me. They seem to have set their faces on neutral, and with their purse straps strung across their chests bandolier-style, they forge ahead as though bracing themselves against being tackled. I understand, of course, that the danger they perceive is not a hallucination. Women are particularly vulnerable to street violence, and young black males are drastically overrepresented among the perpetrators of that violence. Yet these truths are no solace against the kind of alienation that comes of being ever the suspect, a fearsome entity with whom pedestrians avoid making eye contact.

It is not altogether clear to me how I reached the ripe old age 6
of twenty-two without being conscious of the lethality nighttime pedestrians attributed to me. Perhaps it was because in Chester, Pennsylvania, the small, angry industrial town where I came of age in the 1960s, I was scarcely noticeable against a backdrop of gang warfare, street knifings, and murders. I grew up one of the good boys, had perhaps a half-dozen fistfights. In retrospect, my shyness of combat has clear sources.

As a boy, I saw countless tough guys locked away; I have since 7
buried several, too. They were babies, really—a teenage cousin, a brother of twenty-two, a childhood friend in his mid-twenties—all gone down in episodes of bravado played out in the streets. I came to doubt the virtues of intimidation early on. I chose, perhaps unconsciously, to remain a shadow—timid, but a survivor.

The fearsomeness mistakenly attributed to me in public 8
places often has a perilous flavor. The most frightening of these confusions occurred in the late 1970s and early 1980s, when I worked as a journalist in Chicago. One day, rushing into the office of a magazine I was writing for with a deadline story in hand, I was mistaken for a burglar. The office manager called security and, with an ad hoc posse, pursued me through the labyrinthine

halls, nearly to my editor's door. I had no way of proving who I was. I could only move briskly toward the company of someone who knew me.

Another time I was on assignment for a local paper and killing time before an interview. I entered a jewelry store on the city's affluent Near North Side. The proprietor excused herself and returned with an enormous red Doberman pinscher straining at the end of a leash. She stood, the dog extended toward me, silent to my questions, her eyes bulging nearly out of her head. I took a cursory look around, nodded, and bade her good night. 9

Relatively speaking, however, I never fared as badly as another black male journalist. He went to nearby Waukegan, Illinois, a couple of summers ago to work on a story about a murderer who was born there. Mistaking the reporter for the killer, police officers hauled him from his car at gunpoint and but for his press credentials would probably have tried to book him. Such episodes are not uncommon. Black men trade tales like this all the time. 10

Over the years, I learned to smother the rage I felt at so often being taken for a criminal. Not to do so would surely have led to madness. I now take precautions to make myself less threatening. I move about with care, particularly late in the evening. I give a wide berth to nervous people on subway platforms during the wee hours, particularly when I have exchanged business clothes for jeans. If I happen to be entering a building behind some people who appear skittish, I may walk by, letting them clear the lobby before I return, so as not to seem to be following them. I have been calm and extremely congenial on those rare occasions when I've been pulled over by the police. 11

And on late-evening constitutionals I employ what has proved to be an excellent tension-reducing measure: I whistle melodies from Beethoven and Vivaldi and the more popular classical composers. Even steely New Yorkers hunching toward nighttime destinations seem to relax, and occasionally they even join in the tune. Virtually everybody seems to sense that a mugger wouldn't be warbling bright, sunny selections from Vivaldi's *Four Seasons*. It 12 is my equivalent of the cowbell that hikers wear when they know they are in bear country.

---

## *Meaning and Purpose*

1. Staples claims he has the power "to alter public space in ugly ways" (2). How and from where did he derive that power?
2. In what ways has this "ability to alter public space" affected Staples?
3. Does Staples suggest any solutions for the profound problems he describes in the essay?
4. Does Staples speak only for himself when he says in paragraph 11 that he "learned to smother [his] rage"? Explain.

## *Strategy*

1. Staples begins his essay with an anecdote (see the term *anecdote* in the Glossary). Comment on the effectiveness of this introduction.
2. What is the function of paragraph 2?
3. Staples' claim that he has the "ability to alter public space in ugly ways" is rather abstract and vague. How does he make the term fully understandable to the reader?

## *Style*

1. Is there a discrepancy between the language that Staples uses and the subject he describes? If there is, describe the effect that discrepancy creates.
2. In the first paragraph Staples calls a woman who walked in front of him his "victim." Why is that designation ironic (see *irony* in the Glossary)? Is there any real victim described in the essay?

3. Explain the analogy Staples uses in the final sentence.
4. If necessary, look up the following in a dictionary: *affluent, mean, impoverished, discreet* (1); *unwieldy, quarry, dicey, foyer* (2); *taut* (4); *warrenlike, bandolier, forge, solace* (5); *bravado* (7); *ad hoc, labyrinthine* (8); *cursory* (9); *skittish* (11); *constitutionals, steely, warbling* (12).

## Writing Tasks

1. Using Staples' essay as a model, write an essay that describes how you or someone else have altered public space, how you or someone else, in other words, have changed other people's behavior or attitudes by merely being present. Make sure you use as many examples as you can to demonstrate your points.
2. Write an essay in which you argue for or against Staples' point of view. Whatever position you take, make sure your thesis is clear, and be sure to refer to Staples' points in your essay. Be sure, too, to use plenty of examples to illustrate the validity of your observations.

## ❦ Phyllis Rose ❦

*Phyllis Rose was born in 1926 in New Jersey and attended Connecticut College, Duke University, and the University of Wisconsin, where she earned her Ph.D. in English. She has been a professor of English at the University of Hawaii and a member of the board of several Hawaiian councils for the arts and humanities. She has published two works of biography—*Woman of Letters: A Life of Virginia Woolf *and* Parallel Lives: Five Victorian Marriages*—and a collection of essays,* Writing of Women. *She wrote the "Hers" column for* The New York Times *for ten weeks and has contributed to numerous national publications, including* The Atlantic, Vogue, *and* The Nation. *She is an English professor at Wesleyan University.*

# *Tools of Torture*

*In this work, first published in* The Atlantic *in 1968, Phyllis Rose takes an uncompromising look at the social and psychological sources of and rationalizations for torture. She uses specific examples from an exhibit in Paris of torture instruments to draw conclusions about the relation of pleasure to pain.*

*Determine, as precisely as you can, the answers to these questions: Why are there so many torture devices? Why were they invented in the first place? What are the justifications for institutionalized torture? What is the relation of pleasure to pain?*

---

In a gallery off the rue Dauphine, near the *parfumerie* where I get my massage, I happened upon an exhibit of medieval torture instruments. It made me think that pain must be as great a challenge to the human imagination as pleasure. Otherwise there's no accounting for the number of torture instruments. One would be quite enough. The simple pincer, let's say, which rips out flesh. Or the head crusher, which breaks first your tooth sockets, then your skull. But in addition I saw tongs, thumbscrews, a rack, a ladder, ropes and pulleys, a grill, a garrote, a Spanish horse, a Judas cra- 1 dle, an iron maiden, a cage, a gag, a strappado, a stretching table, a saw, a wheel, a twisting stork, an inquisitor's chair, a breast breaker, and a scourge. You don't need complicated machinery to cause incredible pain. If you want to saw your victim down the middle, for example, all you need is a slightly bigger than usual saw. If you hold the victim upside down so the blood stays in his head, hold his legs apart, and start sawing at the groin, you can get as far as the navel before he loses consciousness.

Even in the Middle Ages, before electricity, there were many things you could do to torment a person. You could tie him up in an iron belt that held the arms and legs up to the chest and left no point of rest, so that all his muscles went into spasm within minutes and he was driven mad within hours. This was the twisting stork, a benign-looking object. You could stretch him out backward over a thin piece of wood so that his whole body weight rested on his spine, which pressed against the sharp wood. Then you could stop up his nostrils and force water into his stomach through his mouth. Then, if you wanted to finish him off, you and your helper could jump on his stomach, causing internal hemorrhage. This torture was called the rack. If you wanted to burn someone to death without hearing him scream, you could use a tongue lock, a metal rod between the jaw and collarbone that prevented him from opening his mouth. You could put a person in a chair with spikes on the seat and arms, tie him down against the spikes, and beat him, so that every time he flinched from the beating he drove his own flesh deeper onto the spikes. This was the inquisitor's chair. If you wanted to make it worse, you could heat the spikes. You could suspend a person over a pointed wooden pyramid and whenever he started to fall asleep, you could drop him onto the point. If you were Ippolito Marsili, the inventor of this torture, known as the Judas cradle, you could tell yourself you had invented something humane, a torture that worked without burning flesh or breaking bones. For the torture here was supposed to be sleep deprivation. 2

The secret of torture, like the secret of French cuisine, is that nothing is unthinkable. The human body is like a foodstuff, to be grilled, pounded, filleted. Every opening exists to be stuffed, all 3 flesh to be carved off the bone. You take an ordinary wheel, a heavy wooden wheel with spokes. You lay the victim on the ground with blocks of wood at strategic points under his shoulders, legs, and arms. You use the wheel to break every bone in his body. Next you tie his body onto the wheel. With all its bones broken, it will be pliable. However, the victim will not be dead. If you want to kill him, you hoist the wheel aloft on the end of a pole and leave him to starve. Who would have thought to do this with a man and a wheel? But, then, who would have thought to take the disgusting snail, force it to render its ooze, stuff it in its own shell with garlic butter, bake it, and eat it?

Not long ago I had a facial—only in part because I thought I needed one. It was research into the nature and function of pleasure. In a dark booth at the back of the beauty salon, the aesthetician put me on a table and applied a series of ointments to my face, some cool, some warmed. After a while she put something into my hand, cold and metallic. "Don't be afraid, madame," she said. "It is an electrode. It will not hurt you. The other end is attached to two metal cylinders, which I roll over your face. They break down the electricity barrier on your skin and allow the moisturizers to penetrate deeply." I didn't believe this hocus-pocus. I didn't believe in the electricity barrier or in the ability of these rollers to break it down. But it all felt very good. The cold metal on my face was a pleasant change from the soft warmth of the aesthetician's fingers. Still, since Algeria it's hard to hear the word "electrode" without fear. So when she left me for a few minutes with a moist, refreshing cheesecloth over my face, I thought, What if the goal of her expertise had been pain, not moisture? What if the electrodes had been electrodes in the Algerian sense? What if the cheesecloth mask were dipped in acid? 4

In Paris, where the body is so pampered, torture seems particularly sinister, not because it's hard to understand but because—as the dark side of sensuality—it seems so easy. Beauty care is among the glories of Paris. *Soins esthétiques* include makeup, facials, massages (both relaxing and reducing), depilations (partial and complete), manicures, pedicures, and tanning, in addition to 5 the usual run of *soins* for the hair: cutting, brushing, setting, waving, styling, blowing, coloring, and streaking. In Paris the state of your skin, hair, and nerves is taken seriously, and there is little of the puritanical thinking that tries to persuade us that beauty comes from within. Nor do the French think, as Americans do, that beauty should be offhand and low-maintenance. Spending time and money on *soins esthétiques* is appropriate and necessary, not self-indulgent. Should that loving attention to the body turn malevolent, you have torture. You have the procedure—the aesthetic, as it were—of torture, the explanation for the rich diversity of torture instruments, but you do not have the cause.

Historically torture has been a tool of legal systems, used to get 6 information needed for a trial or, more directly, to determine guilt or innocence. In the Middle Ages confession was considered the best of all proofs, and torture was the way to produce a confession. In other words, torture didn't come into existence to give vent to human sadism. It is not always private and perverse but sometimes social and institutional, vetted by the government and, of course, the Church. (There have been few bigger fans of torture than Christianity and Islam.) Righteousness, as much as viciousness, produces torture. There aren't squads of sadists beating down the doors to the torture chambers begging for jobs. Rather, as a recent book on torture by Edward Peters says, the institution of torture creates sadists: the weight of a culture, Peters suggests, is necessary to recruit torturers. You have to convince people that they are working for a great goal in order to get them to overcome their repugnance to the task of causing physical pain to another person. Usually the great goal is the preservation of society, and the victim is presented to the torturer as being in some way out to destroy it.

From another point of view, what's horrifying is how easily 7 you can persuade someone that he is working for the common good. Perhaps the most appalling psychological experiment of modern times, by Stanley Milgram, showed that ordinary, decent people in New Haven, Connecticut, could be brought to the point of inflicting (as they thought) severe electric shocks on other people in obedience to an authority and in pursuit of a goal, the advancement of knowledge, of which they approved.

Milgram used—some would say abused—the prestige of science and the university to make his point, but his point is chilling nonetheless. We can cluck over torture, but the evidence at least suggests that with intelligent handling most of us could be brought to do it ourselves.

In the Middle Ages, Milgram's experiment would have had no point. It would have shocked no one that people were capable of cruelty in the interest of something they believed in. That was as it should be. Only recently in the history of human thought has the avoidance of cruelty moved to the forefront of ethics. "Putting cruelty first," as Judith Shklar says in *Ordinary Vices*, is comparatively new. The belief that the "pursuit of happiness" is one of man's inalienable rights, the idea that "cruel and unusual punishment" is an evil in itself, the Benthamite notion that behavior should be guided by what will produce the greatest happiness for the greatest number—all these principles are only two centuries old. They were born with the eighteenth-century democratic revolutions. And in two hundred years they have not been universally accepted. Wherever people believe strongly in some cause, they will justify torture—not just the Nazis, but the French in Algeria. 8

Many people who wouldn't hurt a fly have annexed to fashion the imagery of torture—the thongs and spikes and metal studs—hence reducing it to the frivolous and transitory. Because torture has been in the mainstream and not on the margins of history, nothing could be healthier. For torture to be merely kinky would be a big advance. Exhibitions like the one I saw in Paris, which presented itself as educational, may be guilty of pandering to the tastes they deplore. Solemnity may be the wrong tone. If taking one's goals too seriously is the danger, the best discouragement of torture may be a radical hedonism that denies that any goal is worth the means, that refuses to allow the nobly abstract to seduce us from the sweetness of the concrete. Give people a good croissant and a good cup of coffee in the morning. Give them an occasional facial and a plate of escargots. Marie Antoinette picked a bad moment to say "Let them eat cake," but I've often thought she was on the right track. 9

All of which brings me back to Paris, for Paris exists in the imagination of much of the world as the capital of pleasure—of 10 fun, food, art, folly, seduction, gallantry, and beauty. Paris is civilization's reminder to itself that nothing leads you less wrong than your awareness of your own pleasure and a genial desire to spread it around. In that sense the myth of Paris constitutes a moral touchstone, standing for the selfish frivolity that helps keep priorities straight.

---

## Meaning and Purpose

1. What is the thesis of the essay and where is it explicitly stated?
2. Rose gives a long list of garish torture devices in the first paragraph. What do you think her purpose is in using examples in this way? Do you feel that they overwhelm and discourage the reader, or hook the reader?
3. In paragraph 3, the author says "The secret of torture, like the secret of French cuisine, is that nothing is unthinkable." How is this statement both a compliment and a condemnation?
4. According to the author, what is the primary cause of human torture? What does this idea imply about social values and human nature? What examples does the author give to demonstrate that those social and psychological tendencies are still with us?
5. In the last two paragraphs the author argues that hedonistic, selfish frivolity is just the thing to keep our moral priorities straight. Why?

## Strategy

1. The author says in the opening sentence of paragraph 2 that even before electricity many ways had been devised to torture a person. Why does the author bring in the idea of electricity?
2. Can you point out one specific and one typical example in the essay? How effective is each?
3. Reread paragraphs 7, 8, and 9. Describe the focus of each paragraph and the logic of moving from one to the other.

4. In informative (some might say academic) essays like this one, writers use examples "to make the general more specific and the abstract more concrete" (chapter introduction [page 218]). What effect overall does Rose accomplish with her graphic examples of torture? Read as a writer and assess how her examples affect tone and the reader's senses.

## *Style*

1. Two French expressions go untranslated: *parfumerie* (1) and *soins esthétiques* (5). Presumably, the author thinks their meanings should be evident from the context. Are they? What effect is created by leaving the words in the original French?
2. In the final paragraph, Rose generalizes when she uses Paris as *the* example of a place of pleasure, a "moral touchstone." How does this general paragraph, following as it does many paragraphs of specific and even graphic examples and facts, serve to close the essay?
3. Explain how the expression "puritanical thinking" is used in paragraph 5.
4. If necessary, check a dictionary for the meaning of these words: *benign* (1); *aesthetician* (4); *malevolent* (5); *vetted* (6); *inalienable* (8); *transitory* (9); *touchstone* (10).

## *Writing Tasks*

1. In "Tools of Torture," Rose uses an event in her life to generate a thesis. Can you think of an event or incident in your life that you can expand into an essay? Make the essay informative, developing your thesis with specific, concrete examples; you may have to do some research.
2. In a few paragraphs, write about a typical example of something—that is, a composite. You might write about a typical day at the beach, a typical American traveler overseas, a typical pet, a typical birthday, and so on.

## ❦ Neil Postman ❦

*Neil Postman has written widely on education, often examining how language relates to education and calling for radical reform in the field. His books include* Crazy Talk, Stupid Talk: How We Defeat Ourselves by the Way We Talk and What to Do about It *(1976),* Teaching as a Conserving Activity *(1980),* The Disappearance of Childhood *(1982), and* Amusing Ourselves to Death: Public Discourses in the Age of Show Business *(1985). He is also coauthor of several books on educational reform, including* Linguistics: A Revolution in Teaching *(1966),* Teaching as a Subversive Activity *(1969), and* The End of Education: Redefining the Value of Schools *(1995). He was born in 1931 and has been a professor of media ecology at New York University. His articles have appeared in major periodicals, including* The Atlantic *and* The Nation.

# *Future Shlock*

*In "Future Shlock," from his* Conscientious Objections: Stirring up Trouble about Language, Technology and Education *(1988), Postman uses a string of examples—from politics, religion, film, and literature—to illustrate the dangers of eroding intelligence in a society hooked on entertainment. He mentions in particular the danger of television, which presents everything, from news reports to religion, as entertainment.*

*Keep Postman's contention that "We will become . . . a people amused into stupidity" in mind while you read the essay and his claim that such serious subjects as news broadcasting, politics, and religion have been reduced in this country to mere entertainment.*

---

Human intelligence is among the most fragile things in nature. It doesn't take much to distract it, suppress it, or even annihilate it. In this century, we have had some lethal examples of how easily and quickly intelligence can be defeated by any one of its several nemeses: ignorance, superstition, moral fervor, cruelty, cowardice, neglect. In the late 1920s, for example, Germany was, 1 by any measure, the most literate, cultured nation in the world. Its legendary seats of learning attracted scholars from every corner. Its philosophers, social critics, and scientists were of the first rank; its humane traditions an inspiration to less favored nations. But by the mid-1930s—that is, in less than ten years—this cathedral of human reason had been transformed into a cesspool of barbaric irrationality. Many of the most intelligent products of German culture were forced to flee—for example, Einstein, Freud, Karl Jaspers, Thomas Mann, and Stefan Zweig. Even worse, those who remained were either forced to submit their minds to the sovereignty of primitive superstition, or—worse still—willingly did so: Konrad Lorenz, Werner Heisenberg, Martin Heidegger, Gerhardt Hauptmann. On May 10, 1933, a huge bonfire was kindled in Berlin and the books of Marcel Proust, André Gide, Emile Zola, Jack London, Upton Sinclair, and a hundred others were committed to the flames, amid shouts of idiot delight. By 1936, Joseph Paul Goebbels, Germany's Minister of Propaganda, was issuing a proclamation which began with the following words: "Because this year has not brought an improvement in art criticism, I forbid once and for all the continuance of art criticism in its past form, effective as of today." By 1936, there was no one left in Germany who had the brains or courage to object.

Exactly why the Germans banished intelligence is a vast and 2 largely unanswered question. I have never been persuaded that the desperate economic depression that afflicted Germany in the 1920s adequately explains what happened. To quote Aristotle: Men do not become tyrants in order to keep warm. Neither do they become stupid—at least not *that* stupid. But the matter need not trouble us here. I offer the German case only as the most striking example of the fragility of human intelligence. My focus here is the United States in our own time, and I wish to worry you about the rapid erosion of our own intelligence. If you are confident that such a thing cannot happen, your confidence is misplaced, I believe, but it is understandable.

After all, the United States is one of the few countries in the 3 world founded by intellectuals—men of wide learning, of extraordinary rhetorical powers, of deep faith in reason. And although we have had our moods of anti-intellectualism, few people have been more generous in support of intelligence and learning than Americans. It was the United States that initiated the experiment in mass education that is, even today, the envy of the world. It was America's churches that laid the foundation of our admirable system of higher education; it was the Land-Grant Act of 1862 that made possible our great state universities; and it is to America that scholars and writers have fled when freedom of the intellect became impossible in their own nations. This is why the great historian of American civilization Henry Steele Commager called America "the Empire of Reason." But Commager was referring to the United States of the eighteenth and nineteenth centuries. What term he would use for America today, I cannot say. Yet he has observed, as others have, a change, a precipitous decline in our valuation of intelligence, in our uses of language, in the disciplines of logic and reason, in our capacity to attend to complexity. Perhaps he would agree with me that the Empire of Reason is, in fact, gone, and that the most apt term for America today is the Empire of Shlock.

In any case, this is what I wish to call to your notice: the frightening displacement of serious, intelligent public discourse in American culture by the imagery and triviality of what may be called show business. I do not see the decline of intelligent discourse in America leading to the barbarisms that flourished in Germany, of course. No scholars, I believe, will ever need to flee America. There will be no bonfires to burn books. And I cannot imagine any proclamations forbidding once and for all art criticism, or any other kind of criticism. But this is not a cause for complacency, let alone celebration. A culture does not have to force scholars to flee to render them impotent. A culture does not have to burn books to assure that they will not be read. And a culture does not need a Minister of Propaganda issuing proclamations to silence criticism. There are other ways to achieve stupidity, and it appears that, as in so many other things, there is a distinctly American way. 4

To explain what I am getting at, I find it helpful to refer to two films, which taken together embody the main lines of my argu- 5 ment. The first film is of recent vintage and is called *The Gods Must Be Crazy*. It is about a tribal people who live in the Kalahari Desert plains of southern Africa, and what happens to their culture when it is invaded by an empty Coca-Cola bottle tossed from the window of a small plane passing overhead. The bottle lands in the middle of the village and is construed by these gentle people to be a gift from the gods, for they not only have never seen a bottle before but have never seen glass either. The people are almost immediately charmed by the gift, and not only because of its novelty. The bottle, it turns out, has multiple uses, chief among them the intriguing music it makes when one blows into it.

But gradually a change takes place in the tribe. The bottle becomes an irresistible preoccupation. Looking at it, holding it, thinking of things to do with it displace other activities once thought essential. But more than this, the Coke bottle is the only thing these people have ever seen of which there is only one of its kind. And so those who do not have it try to get it from the one who does. And the one who does refuses to give it up. Jealousy, greed, and even violence enter the scene, and come very close to destroying the harmony that has characterized their culture for a thousand years. The people begin to love their bottle more than they love themselves, and are saved only when the leader of the tribe, convinced that the gods must be crazy, returns the bottle to the gods by throwing it off the top of a mountain. 6

The film is great fun and it is also wise, mainly because it is about a subject as relevant to people in Chicago or Los Angeles or New York as it is to those of the Kalahari Desert. It raises two questions of extreme importance to our situation: How does a culture change when new technologies are introduced to it? And is it always desirable for a culture to accommodate itself to the demands of new technologies? The leader of the Kalahari tribe is forced to confront these questions in a way that Americans have refused to do. And because his vision is not obstructed by a belief in what Americans call "technological progress," he is able with minimal discomfort to decide that the songs of the Coke bottle are not so alluring that they are worth admitting envy, egotism, and greed to a serene culture. 7

The second film relevant to my argument was made in 1967. It is Mel Brooks's first film, *The Producers. The Producers* is a rather raucous comedy that has at its center a painful joke: An unscrupulous theatrical producer has figured out that it is relatively easy to turn a buck by producing a play that fails. All one has to do is induce dozens of backers to invest in the play by promising them exorbitant percentages of its profits. When the play fails, there being no profits to disperse, the producer walks away with thousands of dollars that can never be claimed. Of course, the central problem he must solve is to make sure that his play is a disastrous failure. And so he hits upon an excellent idea: he will take the most tragic and grotesque story of our century—the rise of Adolf Hitler—and make it into a musical. 8

Because the producer is only a crook and not a fool, he assumes that the stupidity of making a musical on this theme will be immediately grasped by audiences and that they will leave the theater in dumbfounded rage. So he calls his play *Springtime for Hitler*, which is also the name of its most important song. The song begins with the words: 9

*Springtime for Hitler and Germany;*
*Winter for Poland and France.*

The melody is catchy, and when the song is sung it is accompanied by a happy chorus line. (One must understand, of course, that *Springtime for Hitler* is no spoof of Hitler, as was, for example, Charlie Chaplin's *The Great Dictator*. The play is instead a kind of denial of Hitler in song and dance; as if to say, it was all in fun.) 10

The ending of the movie is predictable. The audience loves the play and leaves the theater humming *Springtime for Hitler*. The musical becomes a great hit. The producer ends up in jail, his joke having turned back on him. But Brooks's point is that the joke is on us. Although the film was made years before a movie actor became President of the United States, Brooks was making a kind of prophecy about that—namely, that the producers of American culture will increasingly turn our history, politics, religion, commerce, and education into forms of entertainment, and that we 11 will become as a result a trivial people, incapable of coping with complexity, ambiguity, uncertainty, perhaps even reality. We will become, in a phrase, a people amused into stupidity.

For those readers who are not inclined to take Mel Brooks as seriously as I do, let me remind you that the prophecy I attribute here to Brooks was, in fact, made many years before by a more formidable social critic than he. I refer to Aldous Huxley, who wrote *Brave New World* at the time that the modern monuments to intellectual stupidity were taking shape: Nazism in Germany, fascism in Italy, communism in Russia. But Huxley was not concerned in his book with such naked and crude forms of intellectual suicide. He saw beyond them, and mostly, I must add, he saw America. To be more specific, he foresaw that the greatest threat to the intelligence and humane creativity of our culture would not come from Big Brother and Ministries of Propaganda, or gulags and concentration camps. He prophesied, if I may put it this way, that there is tyranny lurking in a Coca-Cola bottle; that we could be ruined not by what we fear and hate but by what we welcome and love, by what we construe to be a gift from the gods. 12

And in case anyone missed his point in 1932, Huxley wrote *Brave New World Revisited* twenty years later. By then, George Orwell's *1984* had been published, and it was inevitable that Huxley would compare Orwell's book with his own. The difference, he said, is that in Orwell's book people are controlled by inflicting pain. In *Brave New World*, they are controlled by inflicting pleasure. 13

The Coke bottle that has fallen in our midst is a corporation of dazzling technologies whose forms turn all serious public business into a kind of *Springtime for Hitler* musical. Television is the principal instrument of this disaster, in part because it is the medium Americans most dearly love, and in part because it has become the command center of our culture. Americans turn to television not only for their light entertainment but for their news, their weather, their politics, their religion, their history—all of which may be said to be their serious entertainment. The light entertainment is not the problem. The least dangerous things on television are its junk. What I am talking about is television's pre- 14 emption of our culture's most serious business. It would be merely banal to say that television presents us with entertaining subject matter. It is quite another thing to say that on television all subject matter is presented as entertaining. And that is how television brings ruin to any intelligent understanding of public affairs.

Political campaigns, for example, are now conducted largely in the form of television commercials. Candidates forgo precision, complexity, substance—in some cases, language itself—for the arts of show business: music, imagery, celebrities, theatrics. Indeed, political figures have become so good at this, and so accustomed to it, that they do television commercials even when they are not campaigning. Even worse, political figures appear on variety shows, soap operas, and sitcoms. *Where* is the line that one ought to be able to draw between politics and entertainment? I would suggest that television has annihilated it. 15

But politics is only one arena in which serious language has been displaced by the arts of show business. We have all seen how religion is packaged on television, as a kind of Las Vegas stage show, devoid of ritual, sacrality, and tradition. Today's electronic preachers are in no way like America's evangelicals of the past. Men like Jonathan Edwards, Charles Finney, and George Whitefield were preachers of theological depth, authentic learning, and great expository power. Electronic preachers such as Jimmy Swaggart, Jim Bakker, and Jerry Falwell are merely performers who exploit television's visual power and their own charisma for the greater glory of themselves. 16

We have also seen "Sesame Street" and other educational shows in which the demands of entertainment take precedence over the rigors of learning. And we well know how American businessmen, working under the assumption that potential customers require amusement rather than facts, use music, dance, comedy, cartoons, and celebrities to sell their products. 17

Even our daily news, which for most Americans means television news, is packaged as a kind of show, featuring handsome news readers, exciting music, and dynamic film footage. Most especially, film footage. When there is no film footage, there is no story. Stranger still, commercials may appear anywhere in a news 18 story—before, after, or in the middle. This reduces all events to trivialities, sources of public entertainment and little more. After all, how serious can a bombing in Lebanon be if it is shown to us prefaced by a happy United Airlines commercial and summarized by a Calvin Klein jeans commercial? Indeed, television newscasters have added to our grammar a new part of speech—what may be called the "Now . . . this" conjunction, a conjunction that does not connect two things, but disconnects them. When newscasters say, "Now . . . this," they mean to indicate that what you have just heard or seen has no relevance to what you are about to hear or see. There is no murder so brutal, no political blunder so costly, no bombing so devastating that it cannot be erased from our minds by a newscaster saying, "Now . . . this." He means that you have thought long enough on the matter (let us say, for forty seconds) and you must now give your attention to a commercial. Such a situation is not "the news." It is merely a daily version of *Springtime for Hitler*, and in my opinion accounts for the fact that Americans are among the most ill-informed people in the world. To be sure, we know *of* many things; but we know *about* very little.

I do not mean to say that the trivialization of American public 19
discourse is all accomplished on television. Rather, television is the paradigm for all our attempts at public communication. It conditions our minds to apprehend the world through fragmented pictures and forces other media to orient themselves in that direction. You know the standard question we put to people who have difficulty understanding even simple language: we ask them impatiently, "Do I have to draw a picture for you?" Well, it appears that, like it or not, our culture will draw pictures for us, will explain the world to us in pictures. As a medium for conducting public business, language had receded in importance; it has been moved to the periphery of culture and has been replaced at the center by the entertaining visual image.

Please understand that I am making no criticism of the visual 20
arts in general. That criticism is made by God, not by me. You will remember that in His Second Commandment, God explicitly states that "Thou shalt not make unto thee any graven image, nor

any likeness of anything that is in Heaven above, or that is in the earth beneath, or the waters beneath the earth." I have always felt that God was taking a rather extreme position on this, as is His way. As for myself, I am arguing from the standpoint of a symbolic relativist. Forms of communication are neither good nor bad in themselves. They become good or bad depending on their relationship to other symbols and on the functions they are made to serve within a social order. When a culture becomes overloaded with pictures; when logic and rhetoric lose their binding authority; when historical truth becomes irrelevant; when the spoken or written word is distrusted or makes demands on our attention that we are incapable of giving; when our politics, history, education, religion, public information, and commerce are expressed largely in visual imagery rather than words, then a culture is in serious jeopardy.

Neither do I make a complaint against entertainment. As an 21
old song has it, life is not a highway strewn with flowers. The sight of a few blossoms here and there may make our journey a trifle more endurable. But in America, the least amusing people are our professional entertainers. In our present situation, our preachers, entrepreneurs, politicians, teachers, and journalists are committed to entertaining us through media that do not lend themselves to serious, complex discourse. But these producers of our culture are not to be blamed. They, like the rest of us, believe in the supremacy of technological progress. It has never occurred to us that the gods might be crazy. And even if it did, there is no mountaintop from which we can return what is dangerous to us.

We would do well to keep in mind that there are two ways in 22
which the spirit of a culture may be degraded. In the first—the Orwellian—culture becomes a prison. This was the way of the Nazis, and it appears to be the way of the Russians. In the second—the Huxleyan—culture becomes a burlesque. This appears to be the way of the Americans. What Huxley teaches is that in the Age of Advanced Technology, spiritual devastation is more likely to come from an enemy with a smiling countenance than from one whose face exudes suspicion and hate. In the Huxleyan prophecy, Big Brother does not watch us, by his choice; we watch him, by

ours. When a culture becomes distracted by trivia; when political and social life are redefined as a perpetual round of entertainments; when public conversation becomes a form of baby talk; when a people become, in short, an audience and their public business a vaudeville act, then—Huxley argued—a nation finds itself at risk and culture-death is a clear possibility. I agree.

---

## *Meaning and Purpose*

1. The purpose of an essay is like a goal that the writer sets. The writer has to keep the reader reminded of the purpose and pointed in the right direction. What do you think Postman's purpose is in "Future Shlock," and does he achieve it? How does he do so, and if he doesn't, why does he fail?
2. Postman states his general thesis in a number of ways. Paragraphs 2, 3, 4, 11, and 12 have sentences that sound like thesis statements. Reread these paragraphs and find the statement that you think best summarizes the essay as a whole.
3. What is the main point in *The Gods Must Be Crazy* example? In *The Producers* example?
4. How convincing is Postman? Does his view of our culture coincide with yours? In what ways? Do you disagree with portions of his argument?

## *Strategy*

1. Postman often ends paragraphs with strong statements. See paragraphs 1, 2, and 3. Find other strong statements that end paragraphs and discuss the purpose they serve.
2. Why does Postman begin with a pre-World War II German example in an essay about the United States? Why does he turn away from the example without examining its causes?
3. Whom do you think Postman had in mind as his audience when he wrote "Future Shlock"? What kind of reader does he appeal

to? Do you think he wants to provoke readers with his criticisms of television and American culture and intelligence? Discuss.

4. Trace the use of examples in the essay. Are they specific or typical? extended or brief? Are different types of examples put to different uses?

## Style

1. In Postman's opening example, Germany, he says, "this cathedral of human reason had been transformed into a cesspool of barbaric irrationality." Comment on the effectiveness of this metaphor, especially the words "cathedral," "cesspool," and "barbaric."
2. The Coca-Cola bottle so vital to Postman's discussion of *The Gods Must Be Crazy* is used as a metaphor for what? Comment on the connection between these statements and the original metaphor:

   ". . . there is tyranny lurking in a Coca-Cola bottle" (12).

   ". . . we could be ruined . . . by what we welcome and love" (12).

   "The Coke bottle that has fallen in our midst is a corporation of dazzling technologies" (14).

   "Television . . . is the medium Americans most dearly love" (14).
3. If necessary, check a dictionary for the meaning of these words: *shlock*; *nemeses* (1); *rhetorical*; *precipitous* (3); *preemption* (14); *banal* (14); *sacrality* (16); *paradigm* (19); *countenance* (22).

## Writing Tasks

1. In paragraph 1, Postman says, "In this century, we have had some lethal examples of how easily and quickly intelligence can be defeated by any one of its several nemeses: ignorance, superstition, moral fervor, cruelty, cowardice, neglect." Have you ever

seen these forces at work in your studies or in your own experience? Consider your own behavior, your friends' behavior, the workings of your city or community, national or international affairs, your college, your clubs and organizations. Write an essay about one of these forces as you have seen it at work in one or more situations. Develop your essay with either typical or specific examples.

2. Postman argues that "serious matters of public concern" have been turned into entertainment. Write an essay in which you agree or disagree with his view in relation to one serious matter of public concern. Use one or more specific, extended examples to support your assertions.

## ❦ *Responding to Photographs* ❦

### *Examples*

Style Is the Man

What is style? If we say a certain person has style, what exactly do we mean? Is it behavior? Clothing? Speech? Posture? Grooming? All of these? Some other things? Does everyone have style or only a few?

Style may be hard to define precisely, but we know it when we see it, right? And most people would undoubtedly agree that the young man in the photograph "Style Is the Man" has it.

Style communicates. Before interacting with a person we form impressions based on some elements at least of his or her personal style. We may be able to trace this impression to very specific things, or we may say we just have a feeling but are unable to specify particulars. A style may be created consciously and purposefully (perhaps to deceive) or it may simply grow out of the true values and accumulated experiences of the individual.

After reviewing "Examples: Illustrating Ideas" at the beginning of this chapter, complete one of the following writing tasks.

1. Using specific examples from the photograph as your method of development, write a paper that characterizes the style portrayed by the young man. Begin with a short physical description of the man leading to a generalization about his style and the attitude and values it communicates to you. Then examine various items and aspects of his appearance and discuss each as a specific example which led you to your interpretation of his message.
2. Write a paper combining typical and specific examples. Find three photographs of humans, each showing a different sense of style. These need not be as dramatic as the style illustrated in "Style Is the Man," though they may be. As in number 1, begin with a short description of the three photographs leading to a generalization about each style and what it communicates to you. In the discussion section of your paper, point to specific examples in each photograph that support your generalization and then relate typical examples of the expected behavior, dress, and attitudes of a member of each style group. Include the photographs when you submit your final draft.

## ❦ *Additional Writing Tasks* ❦

*Examples*

1. Write an essay on one of the general statements listed here or on a general statement you compose. Throughout your essay use examples to illustrate your main idea or thesis. Your discussion should include a mixture of typical and specific examples. Remember: you are not bound by any of these statements; you may rewrite them to reflect your interests, or you may compose your own.
   a. People must assume responsibility for their actions.
   b. Success comes from 5 percent talent and 95 percent hard work.
   c. Vandals control the night in local neighborhoods.
   d. Teenagers can learn both positive and negative lessons about economic survival from part-time jobs.
   e. Graffiti scrawled on walls throughout the city carry psychological messages about human behavior.
   f. Books I have read have taught me a great deal about life.
   g. Bumper stickers reveal a person's values.
   h. Public obscenity is objectionable.
   i. Life in the fast lane leads to head-on collisions.
2. Write a full essay related to one of these situations. Be sure examples serve as the dominant essay pattern of development.
   a. Some contemporary political figures have demonstrated courage in office. Using examples from recent history, write an essay illustrating how important political courage is.
   b. Society seems to require more and more cooperation among individuals and groups to function effectively. Write an essay illustrating how cooperation is needed for success.
   c. Although society seems to require more and more cooperation among individuals and groups, the values of the "rugged individualist" are still required for success. Write an essay illustrating how much "rugged individualism" helps in becoming successful.

d. Often the better moments in life go unnoticed. Recollect some of your better moments and write an essay making use of them to illustrate what they have taught you.

e. Magazine advertisers attempt to entice customers to buy products not by high quality but by associating the products with selected "life-styles." Write an essay illustrating that some magazine advertisements encourage consumers to buy products for the wrong reasons.

3. Read this paragraph from Jack Solomon's *The Signs of Our Time*, in which he generally concentrates on the messages that clothing communicates in American society.

> The complexity of the dress code in America, the astonishing range of styles that are available to us in our choice of clothing designs, directly reflects the cultural diversity of our country. Americans are differentiated by ethnic, regional, religious, and racial differences that are all expressed in the clothing they wear. Age differences, political differences, class differences, and differences in personal taste further divide us into finer and finer sub-cultures that maintain, and even assert, their sense of distinct identity through their characteristic clothing. From the severe black suits of the Amish to the safety-pinned T-shirts and chains of punk culture, Americans tell one another who they are through the articles of their dress.

Write an essay, with examples as the dominant method of development, illustrating Solomon's general observation that "Americans tell one another who they are through the articles of their dress."

# 6

# *Comparison and Contrast*

## *Presenting Similarities and Differences*

## *The Method*

In conversation we often hear comments that could lead to **comparison and contrast**:

"I eat vegetables, fruits, grains, nuts, and dairy products. It is a lot healthier than a diet that includes red meat, fowl, and even fish."

"Strip away the rhetoric and compare their economic platforms; you will see few differences between Republicans and Democrats."

"The effects of marijuana are no more harmful than those of alcohol. In fact they may be less harmful."

No doubt in class discussions, at family gatherings, or during arguments at the local pizza parlor you have heard similar comments. How such comparisons are developed in conversation probably depends on the group's mood and analytical talent. Nevertheless, a fundamental principle is at work: We all make decisions by comparing and contrasting our options.

To compare is to point out similarities; to contrast is to point out differences. Poems and song lyrics are often similar in some ways: both often rhyme; they are constructed on rhythmic patterns; sometimes they repeat key lines. They also have one major difference: poems are written to be spoken; songs are written to be sung to music. Presenting similarities and differences is a common technique not only in conversation but also in all forms of writing, including essays, research papers, reports, and examinations.

Commonly, writers include informal comparisons that are merely incidental to the dominant essay pattern. Often such brief comparisons are implied rather than fully developed, merely suggesting a comparison. This paragraph opens an essay explaining the causes directing new trends in city planning.

> In southern California, historically known for its suburban sprawl, city planning seems to have come full circle. Using the concept of the traditional village, planners are designing new urban villages that feature a main street and a mix of stores, offices, town halls, and parks. They are trying

> to re-create the traditional village by designing neighborhoods where thousands of residents can live and work, where they can walk to shopping and stroll to places of entertainment.

The writer, Jack Scott, does not intend to compare traditional with contemporary city design; he alludes to traditional design merely to place his reader in familiar territory.

When writers use comparison and contrast as a dominant essay pattern, they explore their subjects in detail, applying several principles to guide the composition. To sharpen your critical eye and read as a writer reads, be aware of these general principles.

## *Strategies*

Professional writers know they need a basis for the comparison: any subjects they choose to compare must belong to the same general category. If the subjects do not belong to that category, the writers have no logical reason to enumerate the similarities and differences. Usually, but not always, the general categories are obvious. For such a discussion, consider hammerhead sharks, great white sharks, chimpanzees, and dolphins.

Comparing and contrasting a hammerhead with a great white shark is clearly logical because although they are similar, they differ in several distinctive ways. But to compare and contrast a chimpanzee to a great white shark is clearly illogical. Yes, they belong to a category we might call "living creatures," but do you see any other basis for a comparison? The chimpanzee is a mammal, the great white shark a fish. One lives on land, the other in the sea. One is a hunter, the other a forager. To compare and contrast them just would not make much sense.

To compare and contrast a dolphin and a great white shark, however, does make sense. Even though the dolphin is a mammal, it is a marine mammal. The dolphin and the great white shark are also shaped roughly alike, but with significant differences. Perhaps most important, both the dolphin and the great white shark are significant in sea lore. In fact, Hollywood films featuring a dolphin and a great white shark have been box-office hits, as in *Flipper* and *Jaws*.

What about comparing a dolphin and a chimpanzee? Although they are not obvious selections, both are categorized as mammals. A writer might ask if their both being mammals makes them subjects worth comparing and contrasting. What else do they have in common? Close examination reveals that scientists are studying communication patterns of both chimpanzees and dolphins. Perhaps they are in the limited category of animals that communicate with human beings. Taking up this similarity, a writer might explore the possibility of comparing chimpanzees and dolphins.

Now we must consider an exception to the principle that subjects should belong to the same general category if they are to be logically compared. This figurative comparison is called **analogy**. Writers use analogy to explain something difficult to understand by describing it as if it were something familiar. A writer might choose to explain life by comparing it with a river, watching a situation comedy with taking a narcotic, or being in love with riding a roller coaster. Writers of analogy are interested only in using one subject to explain another; they are not out to explain the major similarities and differences of both subjects equally as they would be when writing a typical comparison-and-contrast passage.

In this following paragraph, humorist James Thurber develops an analogy by comparing his editor Harold Ross to a skilled auto mechanic.

> Having a manuscript under Ross's scrutiny was like putting your car in the hands of a skilled mechanic, not an automotive engineer with a bachelor of science degree, but a guy who knows what makes a motor go, and sputter, and wheeze, and sometimes come to a dead stop; a man with an ear for the faintest body squeak as well as the loudest engine rattle. When you first gazed, appalled,

> upon an uncorrected proof of one of your stories or articles, each margin had a thicket of queries and complaints—one writer got a hundred and forty-four on one profile. It was as though you beheld the works of your car spread all over the garage floor, and the job of getting the thing together again and making it work seemed impossible. Then you realized that Ross was trying to make your Model T or old Stutz Bearcat into a Cadillac or Rolls-Royce. He was at work with the tools of his unflagging perfectionism, and, after an exchange of growls or snarls, you set to work to join him in his enterprise.

Clearly, Thurber has stuck to the principle of analogy: he uses the familiar work of an auto mechanic to explain the unfamiliar work of a magazine editor.

Professional writers are always wary of confusing their readers. As you study comparison-and-contrast essays, notice how writers immediately orient their readers by informing them that a comparison and contrast follows.

Read the opening paragraph in Russell Baker's "From Song to Sound: Elvis and Bing." Baker quickly establishes that he will compare two eras and the popular singers who represent them.

> The grieving for Elvis Presley and the commercial exploitation of his death were still not ended when we heard of Bing Crosby's death the other day. Here is a generational puzzle. Those of an age to mourn Elvis must marvel that their elders could really have cared about Bing, just as the Crosby generation a few weeks ago wondered what all the to-do was about when Elvis died.

Baker's opening paragraph gives a clear idea that the essay is headed into comparison and contrast. Most professional writers do likewise, thus keeping their readers on the track.

Professional writers also use clear—and we emphasize that word—stylistic techniques to keep their readers from becoming confused. Sometimes they use parallel structure to balance the similarities and differences of their subjects. They also use such transitional words and phrases as *on the one hand*, *on the other hand*, *in contrast*, *like*, and *unlike*, words with which they delineate similarities and differences.

In a paragraph from an essay contrasting crows and ravens, Barry Lopez applies both transitional phrases and parallel structures.

> The raven is larger than the crow and has a beard of black feathers at his throat. He is careful to kill only what he needs. Crows, on the other hand, will search out the great horned owl, kick and punch him awake, and then for roosting too close to their nests, they will kill him. They will come out of the sky on a fat, hot afternoon and slam into the head of a dozing rabbit and go away laughing. They will tear out a whole row of planted corn and eat only a few kernels. They will defecate on scarecrows and go home and sleep with 200,000 of their friends in an atmosphere of congratulation. Again, it is only a game; this should not be taken to mean that they are evil.

In his paragraph Lopez concentrates primarily on the crow's destructive behavior, contrasting it sharply to the raven in the two sentences describing that black bird. Usually, writers will develop both subjects in more detail. They generally employ one of two organizational strategies when comparing and contrasting: **subject-by-subject** development or **point-by-point** development.

### *Subject-by-Subject Development*

Developing a subject-by-subject comparison is quite simple: all the details of one side of the comparison or contrast are presented first, followed by all the details of the other side. Anthropologist Edward T. Hall uses subject-by-subject development to contrast Arab and American attitudes in a paragraph from *The Hidden Dimension*.

> Another silent source of friction between Americans and Arabs is in an area that Americans treat very informally—the

> manners and rights of the road. In general, in the United States we tend to defer to the vehicle that is bigger, more powerful, faster, and heavily laden. While a pedestrian walking along a road may feel annoyed he will not think it unusual to step aside for a fast-moving automobile. He knows that because he is moving he does not have the right to the space around him that he has when he is standing still. It appears that the reverse is true with the Arabs who apparently *take on rights to space as they move*. For someone else to move into a space an Arab is also moving into is a violation of his rights. It is infuriating to an Arab to have someone else cut in front of him on the highway. It is the American's cavalier treatment of moving space that makes the Arab call him aggressive and pushy.

Hall contrasts these subjects in one paragraph, but sometimes a writer will divide the subjects into separate contrasting paragraphs, as Noel Perrin does in these two discussion paragraphs from his essay "The Two Faces of Vermont."

> On the one hand, it's to the interest of everyone in the tourist trade to keep Vermont (their motels, ski resorts, chambers of commerce, etc., excepted) as old-fashioned as possible. After all, it's weathered red barns with shingle roofs the tourists want to photograph, not concrete-block barns with sheet aluminum on top. Ideally, from the tourist point of view, there should be a man and two boys inside, milking by hand, not a lot of milking machinery pumping directly into a bulk tank. Out back, someone should be turning a grindstone to sharpen an ax—making a last stand, so to speak, against the chainsaw.
>
> On the other hand, the average farmer can hardly wait to modernize. He wants a bulk tank, a couple of arc lights, an automated silo, and a new aluminum roof. Or in a sense he wants these things. Actually, he may like last-stand farming as well as any tourist does, but he can't make a living at it. In my town it's often said that a generation ago a man could raise and educate three children on fifteen cows and

still put a little money in the bank. Now his son can just barely keep going with 40 cows. With fifteen cows, hand-milking was possible, and conceivably even economic; with 40 you need all the machinery you can get. But the tourists don't want to hear it clank.

### *Point-by-Point Development*

Subject-by-subject development is effective for an essay of a few paragraphs, but when an essay is longer the reader may lose track of the information about the first subject while reading about the second. The point-by-point development solves this shortcoming by alternately presenting each point under consideration. Alison Lurie, in a paragraph from *The Language of Clothes*, uses the point-by-point method to compare and contrast boys' and girls' clothes.

> In early childhood girls' and boys' clothes are often identical in cut and fabric, as if in recognition of the fact that their bodies are much alike. But the T-shirts, pull-on slacks and zip jackets intended for boys are usually made in darker colors (especially forest green, navy, red and brown) and printed with designs involving sports, transportation and cute wild animals. Girls' clothes are made in paler colors (especially pink, yellow and green) and decorated with flowers and cute domestic animals. The suggestion is that the boy will play vigorously and travel over long distances; the girl will stay home and nurture plants and small mammals. Alternatively, these designs may symbolize their wearers: the boy is a cuddly bear or a smiling tiger, the girl a flower or a kitten. There is also a tendency for boys' clothes to be fullest at the shoulders and girls' at the hips, anticipating their adult figures. Boys' and men's garments also emphasize the shoulders with horizontal stripes, epaulets or yokes of contrasting color. Girls' and women's garments emphasize the hips and rear through the strategic placement of gathers and trimmings.

Lurie's strategy is quite simple. She organizes the discussion around three points: the different colors in girls' and boys' clothes; the different designs that decorate them; and the different cut. She presents the details point by point, carefully balancing one with the other.

## *Comparison and Contrast in College Writing*

Generally, in college writing, you will compare the similarities and contrast the differences of subjects for one of two reasons: to describe two subjects in order to clarify them or to evaluate two subjects in order to determine which is better. For either reason, you must consider the outstanding features of each subject, and when the purpose is evaluation, you must carefully delineate both positive and negative aspects of the subjects.

### *Guidelines for Writing a Comparison and Contrast Essay*

1. Select two subjects from the same general category to compare and contrast (unless, of course, you are developing an analogy).
2. With each subject as a focus, use prewriting techniques to generate a list of similarities and differences.
3. Establish your purpose and develop a thesis that does the following:

    - Names the subjects being compared and contrasted;
    - Clearly indicates whether the essay will compare, contrast, or both.

4. Select the points to be compared and contrasted and decide which should be developed in a subject-by-subject arrangement and which should be developed in a point-by-point arrangement. Organize the paragraphs by placing the most dramatic point last in the sequence.

5. Revise your essay, making sure that you've used clear transitions to keep your reader on track as you move from one subject to the other.

### *A Student Essay Developed by Comparison and Contrast*

For a Freshman Composition class, Jim Cartozian responded to the following assignment:

> Write an essay with comparison and contrast as the dominant development pattern on one of the following topics:
>
> a. two athletes
> b. two film directors
> c. two artists
> d. two writers
> e. two politicians
> f. two newscasters

Cartozian selected item "d" and compared and contrasted writers Ernest Hemingway and William Faulkner. He had studied them in a high school American literature course, and recalled how different the two writers seemed to be. He knew he would have plenty of material.

Two American Writers: Hemingway and Faulkner

*Cartozian opens with a comparison and contrast pattern that establishes his subjects. He arranges his material in a subject-by-subject pattern*

If American writers Ernest Hemingway and William Faulkner were to attend the same party, both would command attention for different reasons. Hemingway, a big bear of a man, seemed gregarious, and liked to hold the center of attention. He was handsome, and some have said he prided himself on being a lady's man. Faulkner, a frail, soft-spoken man, tended to be reclusive. He would not seek the attention Hemingway seemed to thrive on, but would probably find a mantel to lean on. Speaking in a gentle,

*He ends the introduction with the thesis statement that clearly signals a comparison and contrast essay will follow.*

lilting voice, Faulkner would tell a story about the rural South while holding the attention of everyone within earshot. No two modern American writers have gained as much worldwide critical recognition as Ernest Hemingway and William Faulkner; moreover, no two are so obviously different while at the same time sharing significant similarities.

*Because this paragraph presents both similarities and differences, point-by-point works better than subject-by-subject. Notice how Cartozian structures the information effectively by using parallel structure throughout the paragraph, the words "both" and "each," and by indicating the shift from one author to the next by beginning sentences with their names.*

They each won the coveted Nobel Prize for literature, but when the mild-mannered Faulkner won first, the boisterous Hemingway is said to have lost his temper and then sulked. Both were publishing at a young age, but Hemingway attracted popular attention early in his career while Faulkner worked in near obscurity. Hemingway became America's first modern literary media star. Magazines featured spreads of his war exploits, his African safaris, and his bullfighting adventures. Faulkner, in contrast, was never a media celebrity. Instead, he seemed to embody the lifestyle of small-town Southern gentry, spending most of his quiet existence in Oxford, Mississippi. Hemingway set his novels and stories in exotic locales like France, Spain, and Cuba; Faulkner set his works in the South, in the mythical Yoknapatawpha County. Each dealt with very different visions: Hemingway's work displays psychologically wounded characters struggling to establish a personal value code in an absurd world. Faulkner's work displays characters who are victims of history, suffering because of the sins of their ancestors, the men who wrenched the land from Native Americans and enslaved Native Africans. In 1961 Hemingway died violently by his own hand; in 1962 Faulkner died peacefully.

The qualities that made such different men successful novelists are difficult to iden-

*The first sentence of this paragraph indicates a shift to more abstract qualities.*

*First Cartozian states they both were determined and worked hard, then explains the role of inspiration. He develops an analogy by comparing spiritual practices with Hemingway's and Faulkner's working practices.*

tify. No doubt their success came from determination and hard work, for both men were dedicated to their craft. But another quality—inspiration—must be figured into the equation. Inspiration that comes from pursuing the creative process is perhaps similar to the spiritual insight that comes from participating in a mystical practice, such as meditation, which is usually performed daily in psychological isolation. Most successful novelists pursue their creative inspiration by isolating themselves, too. Faulkner and Hemingway were no different. Both created special spaces to write in. When Faulkner wrote, he isolated himself in an upstairs bedroom located in the family house. Although Hemingway was more nomadic than Faulkner, he still created a "space apart" to write in no matter where he was living, the most famous one in the tower at his Cuban hacienda.

*He continues the analogy in this paragraph, suggesting that their inspiration came from ritually pursuing their work routines.*

Too often spiritual insight and creative inspiration are thought to arrive like a bolt of lightning. But mystics claim insight comes from the relentless pursuit of routines. As writers, Faulkner and Hemingway ritually pursued their routines. Hemingway would rise at first light and spend the morning writing with a hand-sharpened pencil while standing at a high desk or bookcase top. Faulkner would also rise early, but he would sit at a desk and plunk away at an old typewriter. The routines seldom varied, but perhaps it was routine pursued with the fervor of a mystic that generated their inspiration and led to their recognition.

*In the conclusion, Cartozian fulfills the thesis promise to show how Hemingway and Faulkner share*

It is the creative process that unites Hemingway and Faulkner. Beneath Hemingway's distasteful machismo and existential sophistication was a sensitive and insightful artist who depicted the modern *significant similarities—that is, their creative process and ability to connect with readers.*

epoch full of all its horror and despair. Yet he continued to explore the value and capacity of the individual's faith in Self. Beneath Faulkner's deceptive regionalism and self-doubts was a socially committed artist who explored the impact of history's dark events on a culture and the individual psyche. Both were remarkable in their ability to connect with their readers—even readers who were born the after authors' deaths.

### *Comments*

The assignment was very broad, which left Cartozian plenty of room for interpretation. At first he considered comparing and contrasting a novel by each writer, but quickly realized that doing so would be too difficult in a short essay. Since his psychology class had been studying the creative process, he decided to work in some observations from his instructor's lectures and from class discussions. After prewriting activities, he planned his essay: First, he would concentrate on the external characteristics that embodied Hemingway's and Faulkner's differences; second, he would speculate about the creative behavior that embodied their similarities.

Development Strategy. The principles of comparison and contrast are clearly at work. Obviously, Cartozian's subjects are members of the same logical category of critically acclaimed American writers, thus making them valid subjects for a comparison and contrast essay.

Cartozian decided to open the introduction by showing the most obvious difference between the two writers: their personalities. He used subject-by-subject development, first showing that Hemingway was gregarious then showing that Faulkner was reclusive. These differences could have been presented in the discussion section of the essay, and Cartozian could have opened with a more traditional introduction, one that mainly announced the subjects and presented the thesis. But since he had so much material to use in this short essay, Cartozian decided to get right into a comparison, thus showing the reader what the paper would be about, before stating the thesis. The result is eye-catching, immediately thrusting the reader into the specifics of the discussion.

Cartozian arranges the second paragraph point by point. He covers several aspects of these two writers, pointing out how their careers, attitudes, and work differed. In the third and fourth paragraphs, Cartozian introduces an implicit analogy—creative writing pursuits are similar to spiritual pursuits. He points out in these two paragraphs how Hemingway and Faulkner shared certain practices yet were still very different. He closes with some general observations about the two writers, emphasizing that although their creative processes were similar, they were still very different.

Cartozian has carefully mixed the two main methods of comparison and contrast development, that is, subject-by-subject development and point-by-point development, thus showing that he not only understands the two methods, but can also use them effectively. Throughout his essay, Cartozian maintains his neutrality, primarily describing the writers' differences and similarities without evaluating them.

**Revision.** Cartozian's writers group pointed out several weak areas in the first draft, especially a weak thesis. Since the assignment required him to write about both differences and similarities, he composed a working thesis statement to reveal his intent. Group members pointed out that it needed more specific information. Clearly, it indicated that a comparison and contrast essay would follow, but gave very little other information. For instance, why are these writers significant? How important are these differences and similarities? Cartozian revised the thesis so it would reflect their concerns. First he wrote,

> Two well-known American writers are very different and similar in some ways.

Revised, the thesis reads as follows:

no two have gained as
~~Two well known~~ American writers ~~are very different and~~
much worldwide critical recognition as
~~similar in some ways.~~
Ernest Hemingway and William Faulkner; moreover, no two are so obviously different while at the same time sharing significant similarities.

Now the thesis has more specific information while still signaling that a comparison and contrast essay will follow. Cartozian placed it at the close of the introductory paragraph. Remember, he revised his thesis after the first draft. Seldom do writers begin with a highly polished thesis. Instead, once they write a draft and can

## *Peer Review*

You may be asked to write an essay about one of the readings that follow. Before you meet with your writing group, review this introduction. As you read the papers, use these general principles of comparison and contrast to help guide your comments.

1. Unless the paper is an analogy, the subjects should belong to the same general category.
2. The reader should be informed early in the paper that a comparison and contrast will follow.
3. The choice of point-by-point or subject-by-subject development (or a combination of both) should be appropriate to the content. A long paper with complex points of comparison and contrast usually requires a point-by-point method or a combination of both methods.
4. Clear transitions between subjects or points should guide the reader through the paper.

"see" what they've said, they refine the thesis, sometimes writing several drafts before they are satisfied.

As you read the essays that follow, keep in mind that the most effective way to develop skill in comparison and contrast is to study the professionals. Analyze their choices. Ask yourself why a writer chooses point-by-point development over subject-by-subject for a particular passage. Notice how writers mix the two development patterns. Study the kinds of transitional techniques they use. This kind of careful reading—that is, reading with a critical eye—will prepare you to write your own comparisons.

# Bruce Catton

*Bruce Catton (pronounced Cayton) was one of those rare historians who could bring the past to life. Born in Michigan in 1899, he grew up hearing Civil War stories from the many Civil War veterans in his small midwestern town. After attending Oberlin College he was a reporter for newspapers in Boston and Cleveland, served as director of information for government agencies in Washington, D.C., and finally accepted a position as full-time editor and writer for* American Heritage *magazine, which he kept until his death in 1978. Considered one of the foremost authorities on the American Civil War era, he published many books on the subject. The most popular of those books is* A Stillness at Appomattox *(1953), which won both the Pulitzer Prize for history and, in 1954, the National Book Award.*

# *Grant and Lee:*
## *A Study in Contrasts*

*In this essay, first published in* The American Story, *an anthology of essays by noted historians, Catton describes the similarities and differences in style and character between the opposing Civil War generals. It was their coming together and their ability to put aside their extreme differences that marked the end of the war and a turning point in American history.*

*Catton claims in this essay that Ulysses S. Grant and Robert E. Lee represent two different American cultures. Make sure while you read, then, to distinguish the various facets of their personalities as well as the differences of the two societies they personified.*

---

When Ulysses S. Grant and Robert E. Lee met in the parlor of a modest house at Appomattox Court House, Virginia, on April 9, 1865, to work out the terms for the surrender of Lee's Army of Northern Virginia, a great chapter in American life came to a close, and a great new chapter began. 1

These men were bringing the Civil War to its virtual finish. To be sure, other armies had yet to surrender, and for a few days the fugitive Confederate government would struggle desperately and vainly, trying to find some way to go on living now that its chief support was gone. But in effect it was all over when Grant and Lee signed the papers. And the little room where they wrote out the terms was the scene of one of the poignant, dramatic contrasts in American history. 2

They were two strong men, these oddly different generals, and they represented the strengths of two conflicting currents that, through them, had come to final collision. 3

Back of Robert E. Lee was the notion that the old aristocratic concept might somehow survive and be dominant in American life. 4

Lee was tidewater Virginia, and in his background were family, culture, and tradition . . . the age of chivalry transplanted to a New World which was making its own legends and its own myths. He embodied a way of life that had come down through the age of knighthood and the English country squire. America was a land that was beginning all over again, dedicated to nothing much more complicated than the rather hazy belief that all men had equal rights and should have an equal chance in the world. In such a land Lee stood for the feeling that it was somehow of advantage to human society to have a pronounced inequality in the social structure. There should be a leisure class, backed by ownership of land; in turn, society itself should be keyed to the land as the chief source of wealth and influence. It would bring forth (according to this ideal) a class of men with a strong sense of obligation to the community; men who lived not to gain advantage for themselves, but to meet the solemn obligations which had been laid on them by the very fact that they were privileged. From them the country would get its leadership; to them it could look for the higher values—of thought, of conduct, of personal deportment—to give it strength and virtue. 5

Lee embodied the noblest elements of this aristocratic ideal. Through him, the landed nobility justified itself. For four years, the Southern states had fought a desperate war to uphold the 6 ideals for which Lee stood. In the end, it almost seemed as if the Confederacy fought for Lee; as if he himself was the Confederacy . . . the best thing that the way of life for which the Confederacy stood could ever have to offer. He had passed into legend before Appomattox. Thousands of tired, underfed, poorly clothed Confederate soldiers, long since past the simple enthusiasm of the early days of the struggle, somehow considered Lee the symbol of everything for which they had been willing to die. But they could not quite put this feeling into words. If the Lost Cause, sanctified by so much heroism and so many deaths, had a living justification, its justification was General Lee.

Grant, the son of a tanner on the Western frontier, was everything Lee was not. He had come up the hard way and embodied nothing in particular except the eternal toughness and sinewy fiber of the men who grew up beyond the mountains. He was one of a body of men who owed reverence and obeisance to no one, who were self-reliant to a fault, who cared hardly anything for the past but who had a sharp eye for the future. 7

These frontier men were the precise opposites of the tidewater aristocrats. Back of them, in the great surge that had taken people over the Alleghenies and into the opening Western country, there was a deep, implicit dissatisfaction with a past that had settled into grooves. They stood for democracy, not from any reasoned conclusion about the proper ordering of human society, but simply because they had grown up in the middle of democracy and knew how it worked. Their society might have privileges, but they would be privileges each man had won for himself. Forms and patterns meant nothing. No man was born to anything, except perhaps to a chance to show how far he could rise. Life was competition. 8

Yet along with this feeling had come a deep sense of belonging to a national community. The Westerner who developed a farm, opened a shop, or set up in business as a trader could hope to prosper only as his own community prospered—and his community ran from the Atlantic to the Pacific and from Canada down to Mexico. If the land was settled, with towns and highways and accessible markets, he could better himself. He saw his fate in 9 terms of the nation's own destiny. As its horizons expanded, so did his. He had, in other words, an acute dollars-and-cents stake in the continued growth and development of his country.

And that, perhaps, is where the contrast between Grant and 10
Lee becomes most striking. The Virginia aristocrat, inevitably, saw himself in relation to his own region. He lived in a static society which could endure almost anything except change. Instinctively, his first loyalty would go to the locality in which that society existed. He would fight to the limit of endurance to defend it, because in defending it he was defending everything that gave his own life its deepest meaning.

The Westerner, on the other hand, would fight with an equal 11
tenacity for the broader concept of society. He fought so because everything he lived by was tied to growth, expansion, and a constantly widening horizon. What he lived by would survive or fall with the nation itself. He could not possibly stand by unmoved in the face of an attempt to destroy the Union. He would combat it with everything he had, because he could only see it as an effort to cut the ground out from under his feet.

So Grant and Lee were in complete contrast, representing two 12
diametrically opposed elements in American life. Grant was the modern man emerging; beyond him, ready to come on the stage, was the great age of steel and machinery, of crowded cities and a restless burgeoning vitality. Lee might have ridden down from the old age of chivalry, lance in hand, silken banner fluttering over his head. Each man was the perfect champion of his cause, drawing both his strengths and his weaknesses from the people he led.

Yet it was not all contrast, after all. Different as they were—in 13
background, in personality, in underlying aspiration—these two great soldiers had much in common. Under everything else, they were marvelous fighters. Furthermore, their fighting qualities were really very much alike.

Each man had, to begin with, the great virtue of utter tenacity 14
and fidelity. Grant fought his way down the Mississippi Valley in spite of acute personal discouragement and profound military handicaps. Lee hung on in the trenches at Petersburg after hope itself had died. In each man there was an indomitable quality . . .

the born fighter's refusal to give up as long as he can still remain on his feet and lift his two fists.

Daring and resourcefulness they had, too: the ability to think faster and move faster than the enemy. These were the qualities which gave Lee the dazzling campaigns of Second Manassas and Chancellorsville and won Vicksburg for Grant. 15

Lastly, and perhaps greatest of all, there was the ability, at the end, to turn quickly from war to peace once the fighting was over. Out of the way these two men behaved at Appomattox came the possibility of a peace of reconciliation. It was a possibility not wholly realized, in the years to come, but which did, in the end, help the two sections to become one nation again . . . after a war whose bitterness might have seemed to make such a reunion wholly impossible. No part of either man's life became him more than the part he played in their brief meeting in the McLean house at Appomattox. Their behavior there put all succeeding generations of Americans in their debt. Two great Americans, Grant and Lee—very different, yet under everything very much alike. Their encounter at Appomattox was one of the great moments of American history. 16

---

## *Meaning and Purpose*

1. The essay begins with a brief description of the negotiations at Appomattox that led to the end of the Civil War. Can you think of any countries today so torn by civil strife and bitterness that reunion and reconciliation seem difficult or nearly impossible? What are the differences between their condition now and that of the United States at the time of the Civil War?
2. Describe the social structure of the Confederacy that Lee defended. The author claims that Lee was also a symbol of that social order (6). In what way was he such a symbol?
3. In paragraph 5, Catton states, "Lee stood for the feeling that it was somehow of advantage to human society to have a pronounced inequality in the social structure." Apparently, one

underclass in that society consisted of the "Thousands of tired, underfed, poorly clothed Confederate soldiers, long since past the simple enthusiasm of the early days of the struggle," but who, nonetheless, "somehow considered Lee the symbol of everything for which they had been willing to die" (6). Discuss the apparent contradictions in this situation.

4. Describe the social structure that Grant represented.
5. How were the two men the same? What was their most important similarity? What was their key difference?
6. What is the meaning of "tidewater Virginia" (5), and what is its significance in this essay?

## *Strategy*

1. Identify the introduction in Catton's essay and state his thesis. How do you know where the introduction ends? How does the information in the introduction differ from that in the rest of the essay; in other words, what characterizes Catton's introductory remarks?
2. Paragraph 2 consists of four sentences. Describe the function of each.
3. What new rhetorical technique does Catton begin to apply in paragraph 13?
4. Examine the first sentence in each paragraph. What transitional devices does the author use in each? What effect do these devices have?
5. Study Catton's method or methods of comparison and contrast in the essay. Does he use the subject-by-subject method, the point-by-point method, or a combination of the two? Discuss the effectiveness of his rhetorical structure.

## *Style*

1. In paragraph 1, Catton uses a metaphor comparing the negotiations to end the Civil War to a concluding chapter in the larger

book of American life How effective is that metaphor? What are its implications?

2. In paragraph 12, the author says that "Lee might have ridden down from the old age of chivalry, lance in hand, silken banner fluttering over his head." What effect does this language have? Is it satirical?
3. Check the dictionary for the meaning of these words: *virtual, poignant, chivalry, legends, myths, embodied, deportment, obeisance, static, tenacity, fidelity, indomitable.*
4. In the final paragraph, Catton brings the reader back to the setting he describes in the opening paragraph. What is the stylistic effect of this technique?
5. What is Catton's attitude toward Lee and Grant? How is this attitude shown?

## *Writing Tasks*

1. Write an essay in which you compare and contrast two historical or literary characters who represent two ways of life or value systems. The structure of your essay should include an introduction in which you set the scene for the two people you will discuss; that is, put them in the same category or on the same basis. Choose the subject-by-subject method, point-by-point method, or a combination to set up your comparison and contrast. Pay attention to transitions. Conclude your essay by bringing the two characters together again.
2. Write a brief dialogue between the two characters you chose for the assignment above, or any other two people you want to compare and contrast. Put them in a scene and let their conversation illustrate clearly the differences and similarities between them. You might enjoy presenting this exercise as a dramatic reading with fellow students.

## ❦ Richard Rodriguez ❦

*Richard Rodriguez was born in San Francisco in 1944 to Mexican-American parents who spoke only Spanish at home. Rodriguez nonetheless mastered the English language and went on to study at Stanford, Columbia, and the University of California at Berkeley, where he earned a Ph.D. in English literature. He also received a Fulbright fellowship to study English literature in London. In spite of several offers to teach, Rodriguez made writing and journalism his profession. In* The Hunger of Memory *(1982), a collection of autobiographical essays, he examines the American educational system from the point of view of an immigrant who has gone all the way through it, and he strongly opposes bilingual education.*

# *Los Otros, Mis Hermanos*

*This exerpt from Richard Rodriguez's autobiography,* The Hunger of Memory, *portrays one of the conflicts he felt growing up as a Hispanic in an Anglo culture. He concentrates here on his youthful sensitivity to language and how he identified his Spanish-speaking world with the comfort and security of family and the English-speaking world that surrounded him as alien and threatening.*

*In the essay Rodriguez explains the different ways that language formed his identity. While you read, imagine as vividly as you can how he perceived people, and his relationship to them, in the way that they spoke. Notice the various ways he isolated in his mind the Spanish-speaking world from the English.*

---

I grew up in a house where the only regular guests were my relations. For one day, enormous families of relatives would visit and there would be so many people that the noise and the bodies would spill out to the backyard and front porch. Then, for weeks, no one came by. (It was usually a salesman who rang the doorbell.) Our house stood apart. A gaudy yellow in a row of white bungalows. We were the people with the noisy dog. The people 1 who raised pigeons and chickens. We were the foreigners on the block. A few neighbors smiled and waved. We waved back. But no one in the family knew the names of the old couple who lived next door; until I was seven years old, I did not know the names of the kids who lived across the street.

In public, my father and mother spoke a hesitant, accented, not always grammatical English. And they would have to strain—their bodies tense—to catch the sense of what was rapidly said by *los gringos*. At home they spoke Spanish. The language of their Mexican past sounded in counterpoint to the English of public society. The words would come quickly, with ease. Conveyed through those sounds was the pleasing, soothing, consoling reminder of being at home. 2

During those years when I was first conscious of hearing, my mother and father addressed me only in Spanish; in Spanish I learned to reply. By contrast, English (*inglés*), rarely heard in the house, was the language I came to associate with *gringos*. I learned my first words of English overhearing my parents speak to strangers. At five years of age, I knew just enough English for my mother to trust me on errands to stores one block away. No more. 3

I was a listening child, careful to hear the very different sounds of Spanish and English. Wide-eyed with hearing, I'd listen to sounds more than words. First, there were English (*gringo*) sounds. So many words were still unknown that when the butcher or the lady at the drugstore said something to me, exotic polysyllabic sounds would bloom in the midst of their sentences. Often, the speech of people in public seemed to me very loud, booming with confidence. The man behind the counter would literally ask, "What can I do for you?" But by being so firm and so clear, the sound of his voice said that he was a *gringo*; he belonged in public society. 4

I would also hear then the high nasal notes of middle-class American speech. The air stirred with sound. Sometimes, even now, when I have been traveling abroad for several weeks, I will hear what I heard as a boy. In hotel lobbies or airports, in Turkey or Brazil, some Americans will pass, and suddenly I will hear it 5 again—the high sound of American voices. For a few seconds I will hear it with pleasure, for it is now the sound of my society—a reminder of home. But inevitably—already on the flight headed for home—the sound fades with repetition. I will be unable to hear it anymore.

When I was a boy, things were different. The accent of *los gringos* was never pleasing nor was it hard to hear. Crowds at Safeway or at bus stops would be noisy with sound. And I would be forced to edge away from the chirping chatter above me. 6

I was unable to hear my own sounds, but I knew very well that I spoke English poorly. My words could not stretch far enough to form complete thoughts. And the words I did speak I didn't know well enough to make into distinct sounds. (Listeners would usually lower their heads, better to hear what I was trying to say.) But it was one thing for *me* to speak English with difficulty. It was more troubling for me to hear my parents speak in public; their high-whining vowels and guttural consonants; their sentences that got stuck with 'eh' and 'ah' sounds; the confused syntax; the hesitant rhythm of sounds so different from the way *gringos* spoke. I'd notice, moreover, that my parents' voices were softer than those of *gringos* we'd meet. 7

I am tempted now to say that none of this mattered. In adulthood I am embarrassed by childhood fears. And, in a way, it didn't matter very much that my parents could not speak English with ease. Their linguistic difficulties had no serious consequences. My mother and father made themselves understood at the county hospital clinic and at government offices. And yet, in another way, it mattered very much—it was unsettling to hear my parents struggle with English. Hearing them, I'd grow nervous, my clutching trust in their protection and power weakened. 8

There were many times like the night at a brightly lit gasoline station (a blaring white memory) when I stood uneasily, hearing my father. He was talking to a teenaged attendant. I do not recall what they were saying, but I cannot forget the sounds my father made as he spoke. At one point his words slid together to form one word—sounds as confused as the threads of blue and green oil in the puddle next to my shoes. His voice rushed through what 9 he had left to say. And, toward the end, reached falsetto notes, appealing to his listener's understanding. I looked away to the lights of passing automobiles. I tried not to hear anymore. But I heard only too well the calm, easy tones in the attendant's reply. Shortly afterward, walking toward home with my father, I shivered when he put his hand on my shoulder. The very first chance that I got, I evaded his grasp and ran on ahead into the dark, skipping with feigned boyish exuberance.

But then there was Spanish. *Español*: my family's language. 10
*Español*: the language that seemed to me a private language. I'd hear strangers on the radio and in the Mexican Catholic church across town speaking in Spanish, but I couldn't really believe that Spanish was a public language, like English. Spanish speakers, rather, seemed related to me, for I sensed that we shared—through our language—the experience of feeling apart from *los gringos*. It was thus a ghetto Spanish that I heard and I spoke. Like those whose lives are bound by a barrio, I was reminded by Spanish of my separateness from *los otros*, *los gringos* in power. But more intensely than for most barrio children—because I did not live in a barrio—Spanish seemed to me the language of home. (Most days it was only at home that I'd hear it.) It became the language of joyful return.

A family member would say something to me and I would 11
feel myself specially recognized. My parents would say something to me and I would feel embraced by the sounds of their words. Those sounds said: *I am speaking with ease in Spanish. I am addressing you in words I never use with los gringos. I recognize you as someone special, close, like no one outside. You belong with us. In the family.*

*(Ricardo.)* 12

At the age of five, six, well past the time when most other chil- 13
dren no longer easily notice the difference between sounds uttered at home and words spoken in public, I had a different experience. I lived in a world magically compounded of sounds. I remained a child longer than most; I lingered too long, poised at the edge of language—often frightened by the sounds of *los gringos*, delighted by the sounds of Spanish at home. I shared with my

family a language that was startlingly different from that used in the great city around us.

For me there were none of the gradations between public and private society so normal to a maturing child. Outside the house was public society; inside the house was private. Just opening or closing the screen door behind me was an important experience. I'd rarely leave home all alone or without reluctance. Walking down the sidewalk, under the canopy of tall trees, I'd warily notice the—suddenly—silent neighborhood kids who stood warily watching me. Nervously, I'd arrive at the grocery store to hear there the sounds of the gringo—foreign to me—reminding me that in this world so big, I was a foreigner. But then I'd return. Walking back toward our house, climbing the steps from the sidewalk, when the front door was open in summer, I'd hear voices beyond the screen door talking in Spanish. For a second or two, I'd stay, linger there, listening. Smiling, I'd hear my mother call out, saying in Spanish (words): "Is that you, Richard?" All the while her sounds would assure me: *You are home now; come closer; inside. With us.* 14

"*Si*," I'd reply. 15

Once more inside the house I would resume (assume) my place in the family. The sounds would dim, grow harder to hear. Once more at home, I would grow less aware of that fact. It required, however, no more than the blurt of the doorbell to alert me to listen to sounds all over again. The house would turn instantly still while my mother went to the door. I'd hear her hard English sounds. I'd wait to hear her voice return to soft-sounding Spanish, which assured me, as surely as did the clicking tongue of the lock on the door, that the stranger was gone. 16

Plainly, it is not healthy to hear such sounds so often. It is not healthy to distinguish public words from private sounds so easily. I remained cloistered by sounds, timid and shy in public, too dependent on voices at home. And yet it needs to be emphasized: I was an extremely happy child at home. I remember many nights when my father would come back from work, and I'd hear him call out to my mother in Spanish, sounding relieved. In Spanish, he'd sound light and free notes he never could manage in English. 17

Some nights I'd jump up just at hearing his voice. With *mis hermanos* I would come running into the room where he was with my mother. Our laughing (so deep was the pleasure!) became screaming. Like others who know the pain of public alienation, we transformed the knowledge of our public separateness and made it consoling—the reminder of intimacy. Excited, we joined our voices in a celebration of sounds. *We are speaking now the way we never speak out in public. We are alone—together*, voices sounded, surrounded to tell me. Some nights, no one seemed willing to loosen the hold sounds had on us. At dinner, we invented new words. (Ours sounded Spanish, but made sense only to us.) We pieced together new words by taking, say, an English verb and giving it Spanish endings. My mother's instructions at bedtime would be lacquered with mock-urgent tones. Or a word like si would become, in several notes, able to convey added measures of feeling. Tongues explored the edges of words, especially the fat vowels. And we happily sounded that military drum roll, the twirling roar of the Spanish r. Family language: my family's sounds. The voices of my parents and sisters and brother. Their voices insisting: *You belong here. We are family members. Related. Special to one another. Listen!* Voices singing and sighing, rising, straining, then surging, teeming with pleasure that burst syllables into fragments of laughter. At times it seemed there was steady quiet only when, from another room, the rustling whispers of my parents faded and I moved closer to sleep.

---

## *Meaning and Purpose*

1. What are Rodriguez's childhood feelings about Spanish and English? Use examples from the essay to illustrate your answer.
2. In paragraph 7 the author says he felt differently about his own inability to speak fluent English and his parents' inability to do so. Why does he feel so differently? How strong are his feelings? Explain.

3. Rodriguez says in paragraph 8 that his parents' difficulties with English didn't matter in some ways but did in others. Explain this.
4. "I remained a child longer than most . . ." says the author in paragraph 13. What does he mean by this? What does he consider the characteristics of childhood? How did language affect his slow development?

## *Strategy*

1. Where and how does the author make clear what he intends to compare and contrast?
2. Paragraph 5 is an example. What function does it serve?
3. Paragraph 9 is also an example. What is its function?
4. Paragraph 15 consists of a short, single sentence. Why does Rodriguez separate it from the preceding paragraph?

## *Style*

1. Examine the essay closely and point out some places where Rodriguez uses point-by-point development and where he uses subject-by-subject development. Why do you think he chose those methods when and where he did?
2. Rodriguez uses Spanish words and phrases to demonstrate "private" language. Are the meanings clear in context? What effect do they create even if you are unable to translate them?
3. What does the word *gringo* mean? What are its connotations? How does the author want the word to affect you? Explain.

## *Writing Tasks*

1. If English is not your first language, write an essay in which you compare aspects of your native culture to those of American cul-

ture. If you are a native American but have encountered foreign cultures, compare some aspects of those cultures to your own. What were things you liked or disliked? Why?

2. Think about where you grew up. Did the place, the people, and your family affect the way you learned to think of yourself? How? Write an essay in which you enumerate and describe those things that formed your sense of identity.

## ❦ Alleen Pace Nilsen ❦

*Alleen Pace Nilsen was born in 1936 and attended Brigham Young University as an undergraduate and American University as a masters student. She received her doctorate from the University of Iowa, where she studied linguistic sexism in children's literature. She is coauthor, with her husband, of two books:* Pronunciation Contrasts in English *(1971) and* Semantic Theory: A Linguistic Perspective *(1975). Continuing her work in linguistic sexism and children's literature, she has coedited a book of essays,* Sexism and Language *(1977), and a textbook,* Literature for Today's Young Adults *(1980). Currently she is a professor of English and assistant vice president for academic affairs at Arizona State University.*

# *Sexism in English*

## *A 1990s Update*

*In an essay written in the early 1970s, Nilsen examined the sexist biases inherent in numerous words of the English language. The article was published as part of a series sponsored by the Modern Language Association's Commission on the Status of Women. Nilsen wrote this following essay, in which she looks at how language use has changed since then, and adds new examples to her old list. "A 1990s Update" first appeared in* Language Awareness, *a composition anthology.*

*Nilsen establishes a powerful case on how our current use of language still promotes sexual stereotypes. Watch for those places where she thinks our language may be changing to help remedy those stereotypes.*

---

1 Twenty years ago I embarked on a study of the sexism inherent in American English. I had just returned to Ann Arbor, Michigan, after living for two years (1967–69) in Kabul, Afghanistan, where I had begun to look critically at the role society assigned to women. The Afghan version of the *chaderi*

prescribed for Moslem women was particularly confining. Few women attended the American-built Kabul University where my husband was teaching linguistics because there were no women's dormitories, which meant that the only females who could attend were those whose families happened to live in the capital city. Afghan jokes and folklore were blatantly sexist, for example this proverb, "If you see an old man, sit down and take a lesson; if you see an old woman, throw a stone."

But it wasn't only the native culture that made me question women's roles; it was also the American community. Nearly six hundred Americans lived in Kabul, mostly supported by U.S. taxpayers. The single women were career secretaries, school teachers, or nurses. The three women who had jobs comparable to the American men's jobs were textbook editors with the assignment of developing reading books in Dari (Afghan Persian) for young children. They worked at the Ministry of Education, a large building in the center of the city. There were no women's restrooms, so during their two-year assignment whenever they needed to go to the bathroom they had to walk across the street and down the block to the Kabul Hotel. 2

The rest of the American women were like myself—wives and mothers whose husbands were either career diplomats, employees of USAID, or college professors who had been recruited to work on various contract teams including an education team from Teachers College, Columbia University and an agricultural team from the University of Wyoming. These were the women who were most influential in changing my way of thinking. We were suddenly bereft of our traditional roles; some of us became alcoholics; others got very good at bridge, while others searched desperately for ways to contribute either to our families or to the Afghans. The local economy provided few jobs for women and certainly none for foreigners; we were isolated from former friends and the social goals we had grown up with. Most of us had three servants (they worked for $1.00 a day) because the cook refused to wash dishes and the dishwasher refused to water the lawn or sweep the sidewalks—it was their form of unionization. Occasionally, someone would try to get along without servants, 3 but it was impossible because the houses were huge and we didn't have the mechanical aids we had at home. Drinking water had to be brought from the deep well at the American Embassy, and kerosene and wood stoves had to be stocked and lit. The servants were all males, the highest-paid one being the cook who could usually speak some English. Our days revolved around supervising these servants. One woman's husband got so tired of hearing her complain about such annoyances as the *bacha* (the housekeeper) stealing kerosene and needles and batteries, and about the cook putting chili powder instead of paprika on the deviled eggs, and about the gardener subcontracting his work and expecting her to pay all his friends that he scheduled an hour a week for listening to complaints. The rest of the time he wanted to keep his mind clear to focus on his important work with his Afghan counterparts and with the president of the university and the Minister of Education. What he was doing in this country was going to make a difference! In the great eternal scheme of things, of what possible importance could be his wife's trivial troubles with the servants?

These were the thoughts in my mind when we finished our contract and returned in the fall of 1969 to the University of Michigan in Ann Arbor. I was surprised to find that many other women were also questioning the expectations that they had grown up with. In the spring of 1970, a women's conference was announced. I hired a babysitter and attended, but I returned home more troubled than ever. Now that I knew housework was worth only a dollar a day, I couldn't take it seriously, but I wasn't angry in the same way these women were. Their militancy frightened me. Since I wasn't ready for a revolution, I decided I would have my own feminist movement. I would study the English language and see what it could tell me about sexism. I started reading a desk dictionary and making notecards on every entry that seemed to tell something about male and female. I soon had a dog-eared dictionary, along with a collection of notecards filling two shoe boxes. 4

Ironically, I started reading the dictionary because I wanted to avoid getting involved in social issues, but what happened was 5 that my notecards brought me right back to looking at society. Language and society are as intertwined as a chicken and an egg. The language that a culture uses is telltale evidence of the values and beliefs of that culture. And because there is a lag in how fast a language changes—new words can easily be introduced, but it takes a long time for old words and usages to disappear—a careful look at English will reveal the attitudes that our ancestors held and that we as a culture are therefore predisposed to hold. My notecards revealed three main points. Friends have offered the opinion that I didn't need to read the dictionary to learn such obvious facts. Nevertheless, it was interesting to have linguistic evidence of sociological observations.

## Women Are Sexy; Men Are Successful

First, in American culture a woman is valued for the attractiveness and sexiness of her body, while a man is valued for his physical strength and accomplishments. A woman is sexy. A man is successful. 6

A persuasive piece of evidence supporting this view are the eponyms—words that have come from someone's name—found in English. I had a two-and-a-half-inch stack of cards taken from men's names, but less than a half-inch stack from women's names, and most of those came from Greek mythology. In the words that came into American English since we separated from Britain, there are many eponyms based on the names of famous American men: bartlett pear, boysenberry, diesel engine, franklin stove, ferris wheel, gattling gun, mason jar, sideburns, sousaphone, schick test, and winchester rifle. The only common eponyms taken from American women's names are *Alice blue* (after Alice Roosevelt Longworth), *bloomers* (after Amelia Jenks Bloomer), and *Mae West jacket* (after the buxom actress). Two out of the three feminine eponyms relate closely to a woman's physical anatomy, while the masculine eponyms (except for *sideburns* after General Burnsides) have nothing to do with the namesake's body, but instead honor the man for an accomplishment of some kind. 7

Although in Greek mythology women played a bigger role than they did in the biblical stories of the Judeo-Christian cultures and so the names of goddesses are accepted parts of the language in such place names as Pomona from the goddess of fruit and Athens from Athena and in such common words as *cereal* from Ceres, *psychology* from Psyche, and *arachnoid* from Arachne, the same tendency to think of women in relation to sexuality is seen in the eponyms *aphrodisiac* from Aphrodite, the Greek name for the goddess of love and beauty, and *venereal disease*, from Venus, the Roman name for Aphrodite. 8

Another interesting word from Greek mythology is *Amazon.* According to Greek folk etymology, the a means "without" as in *atypical*, or *amoral* while *mazon* comes from *mazos*, meaning *breast* as still seen in *mastectomy*. In the Greek legend, Amazon women cut off their right breasts so that they could better shoot their bows. Apparently, the storytellers had a feeling that for women to play the active, "masculine" role that the Amazons adopted for themselves, they had to trade in part of their femininity. 9

This preoccupation with women's breasts is not limited to ancient stories. As a volunteer for the University of Wisconsin's *Dictionary of American Regional English (DARE)*, I read a western trapper's diary from the 1830s. I was to make notes of any unusual usages or language patterns. My most interesting finding was that he referred to a range of mountains as *The Teats*, a metaphor based on the similarity between the shapes of the mountains and women's breasts. Because today we use the French wording, *The Grand Tetons*, the metaphor isn't as obvious, but I wrote to the map-makers and found the following listings: *Nippletop* and *Little Nipple Top* near Mt. Marcy in the Adirondacks, *Nipple Mountain* in Archuleta County, Colorado, *Nipple Peak* in Coke County, Texas, *Nipple Butte* in Pennington, South Dakota, *Squaw Peak* in Placer County, California (and many other locations), *Maiden's Peak* and *Squaw Tit* (they're the same mountain) in the Cascade Range in Oregon, *Mary's Nipple* near Salt Lake City, Utah, and *Jane Russell Peaks* near Stark, New Hampshire. 10

Except for the movie star Jane Russell, the women being referred to are anonymous—it's only a sexual part of their body that is mentioned. When topographical features are named after men, it's probably not going to be to draw attention to a sexual part of their bodies but instead to honor individuals for an accomplishment. For example, no one thinks of a part of the male body when hearing a reference to Pike's Peak, Colorado, or Jackson Hole, Wyoming. 11

Going back to what I learned from my dictionary cards, I was surprised to realize how many pairs of words we have in which the feminine word has acquired sexual connotations while the masculine word retains a serious businesslike aura. For example, a *callboy* is the person who calls actors when it is time for them to go on stage, but a *callgirl* is a prostitute. Compare *sir* and *madam*. *Sir* is a term of respect while *madam* has acquired the specialized meaning of a brothel manager. Something similar has happened to *master* and *mistress*. Would you rather have a painting by *an old master* or an *old mistress?* 12

It's because the word *woman* had sexual connotations, as in "She's his woman," that people began avoiding its use, hence such terminology as *ladies' room*, *lady of the house*, and *girls' school* or *school for young ladies*. Feminists, who ask that people use the term *woman* rather than *girl* or *lady*, are rejecting the idea that *woman* is primarily a sexual term. They have been at least partially successful in that today *woman* is commonly used to communicate gender without intending implications about sexuality. 13

I found two hundred pairs of words with masculine and feminine forms, e.g., *heir–heiress*, *hero–heroine*, *steward–stewardess*, *usher–usherette*, etc. In nearly all such pairs, the masculine word is considered the base with some kind of a feminine suffix being added. The masculine form is the one from which compounds are made, e.g., from *king–queen* comes *kingdom* but not *queendom*, from *sportsman–sportslady* comes *sportsmanship* but not *sportsladyship*. There is one—and only one—semantic area in which the masculine word is not the base or more powerful word. This is in the area dealing with sex and marriage. When someone refers to a *virgin*, a listener will probably think of a female unless the speaker 14 specifies *male* or uses a masculine pronoun. The same is true for *prostitute*.

In relation to marriage, there is much linguistic evidence showing that weddings are more important to women than to men. A woman cherishes the wedding and is considered a bride for a whole year, but a man is referred to as a groom only on the day of the wedding. The word bride appears in *bridal attendant*, *bridal gown*, *bridesmaid*, *bridal shower*, and even *bridegroom*. *Groom* comes from the Middle English *grom*, meaning "man," and in this sense is seldom used outside of a wedding. With most pairs of male/female words, people habitually put the masculine word first—*Mr. and Mrs.*, *his and hers*, *boys and girls*, *men and women*, *kings and queens*, *brothers and sisters*, *guys and dolls*, and *host and hostess*—but it is the *bride and groom* who are talked about, not the *groom and bride*. 15

The importance of marriage to a woman is also shown by the fact that when a marriage ends in death, the woman gets the title of *widow*. A man gets the derived title of *widower*. This term is not used in other phrases or contexts, but *widow* is seen in *widowhood*, *widow's peak*, and *widow's walk*. A *widow* in a card game is an extra hand of cards, while in typesetting it is an extra line of type. 16

How changing cultural ideas bring changes to language is clearly visible in this semantic area. The feminist movement has caused the differences between the sexes to be downplayed, and since I did my dictionary study two decades ago, the word *singles* has largely replaced such sex-specific and value-laden terms as *bachelor*, *old maid*, *spinster*, *divorcee*, *widow*, and *widower*. And in 1970 I wrote that when a man is called a *professional* he is thought to be a doctor or a lawyer, but when people hear a woman referred to as a *professional* they are likely to think of a prostitute. That's not as true today because so many women have become doctors and lawyers that it's no longer incongruous to think of women in those professional roles. 17

Another change that has taken place is in wedding announcements. They used to be sent out from the bride's parents and did not even give the name of the groom's parents. 18

Today, most couples choose to list either all or none of the parents' names. Also it is now much more likely that both the bride and groom's picture will be in the newspaper, while a decade ago only the bride's picture was published on the "Women's" or the "Society" page. Even the traditional wording of the wedding ceremony is being changed. Many officials now pronounce the couple "husband and wife" instead of the old "man and wife," and they ask the bride if she promises "to love, honor, and cherish," instead of "to love, honor, and obey."

## Women Are Passive; Men Are Active

The wording of the wedding ceremony also relates to the second point that my cards showed, which is that women are expected to play a passive or weak role while men play an active or strong role. In the traditional ceremony, the official asks, "Who gives the bride away?" and the father answers, "I do." Some fathers answer, "Her mother and I do," but that doesn't solve the problem inherent in the question. The idea that a bride is something to be handed over from one man to another bothers people because it goes back to the days when a man's servants, his children and his wife were all considered to be his property. They were known by his name because they belonged to him and he was responsible for their actions and their debts. 19

The grammar used in talking or writing about weddings as well as other sexual relationships shows the expectation of men playing the active role. Men *wed* women while women *become* brides of men. A man *possesses* a woman; he *deflowers* her; he *performs*; he *scores*; he *takes away* her virginity. Although a woman can *seduce* a man, she cannot offer him her virginity. When talking about virginity, the only way to make the woman the actor in the sentence is to say that "She lost her virginity," but people lose things by accident rather than by purposeful actions, and so she's only the grammatical, not the real-life, actor. 20

The reason that women tried to bring the term *Ms.* into the language to replace *Miss* and *Mrs.* relates to this point. Married women resented being identified only under their husband's 21 names. For example, when Susan Glascoe did something newsworthy, she would be identified in the newspaper only as Mrs. John Glascoe. The dictionary cards showed what appeared to be an attitude on the part of editors that it was almost indecent to let a respectable woman's name march unaccompanied across the pages of a dictionary. Women were listed with male names whether or not the male contributed to the woman's reason for being in the dictionary or in his own right was as famous as the woman. For example, Charlotte Brontë was identified as Mrs. Arthur B. Nicholls, Amelia Earhart as Mrs. George Palmer Putnam, Helen Hayes as Mrs. Charles MacArthur, Jenny Lind as Mme. Otto Goldschmit, Cornelia Otis Skinner as the daughter of Otis Skinner, Harriet Beecher Stowe as the sister of Henry Ward Beecher, and Edith Sitwell as the sister of Osbert and Sacheverell. A very small number of women got into the dictionary without the benefit of a masculine escort. They were rebels and crusaders: temperance leaders Frances Elizabeth Caroline Willard and Carry Nation, women's rights leaders Carrie Chapman Catt and Elizabeth Cady Stanton, birth control educator Margaret Sanger, religious leader Mary Baker Eddy, and slaves Harriet Tubman and Phyllis Wheatley.

Etiquette books used to teach that if a woman had *Mrs.* in 22
front of her name then the husband's name should follow because *Mrs.* is an abbreviated form of *Mistress* and a woman couldn't be a mistress of herself. As with many arguments about "correct" language usage, this isn't very logical because *Miss* is also an abbreviation of *Mistress*. Feminists hoped to simplify matters by introducing *Ms.* as an alternative to both *Mrs.* and *Miss*, but what happened is that *Ms.* largely replaced *Miss* to become a catch-all business title for women. Many married women still prefer the title *Mrs.*, and some resent being addressed with the term *Ms.* As one frustrated newspaper reporter complained, "Before I can write about a woman, I have to know not only her marital status but also her political philosophy." The result of such complications may contribute to the demise of titles which are already being ignored by many computer programmers who find it more efficient to simply use names; for example in a business letter: "Dear Joan

Garcia," instead of "Dear Mrs. Joan Garcia," "Dear Ms. Garcia," or "Dear Mrs. Louis Garcia."

The titles given to royalty provide an example of how males can be disadvantaged by the assumption that they are always to play the more powerful role. In British royalty, when a male holds a title, his wife is automatically given the feminine equivalent. But the reverse is not true. For example, a *count* is a high political officer with a *countess* being his wife. The same is true for a *duke* and a *duchess* and a king and a *queen*. But when a female holds the royal title, the man she marries does not automatically acquire the matching title. For example, Queen Elizabeth's husband has the title of *prince* rather than *king*, but if Prince Charles should become king while he is still married to Lady or Princess Diana, she will be known as the queen. The reasoning appears to be that since masculine words are stronger, they are reserved for true heirs and withheld from males coming into the royal family by marriage. If Prince Phillip were called *King Phillip*, it would be much easier for British subjects to forget where the true power lies. 23

The names that people give their children show the hopes and dreams they have for them, and when we look at the differences between male and female names in a culture we can see the cumulative expectations of that culture. In our culture girls often have names taken from small, aesthetically pleasing items, e.g., *Ruby, Jewel*, and *Pearl. Esther* and *Stella* mean "star." *Ada* means "ornament," and *Vanessa* means "butterfly." Boys are more likely to be given names with meanings of power and strength, e.g., *Neil* means "champion," *Martin* is from Mars, the god of war, *Raymond* means "wise protection," *Harold* means "chief of the army," *Ira* means "vigilant," *Rex* means "king," and *Richard* means "strong king." 24

We see similar differences in food metaphors. Food is a passive substance just sitting there waiting to be eaten. Many people have recognized this and so no longer feel comfortable describing women as "delectable morsels." However, when I was a teenager, it was considered a compliment to refer to a girl (we didn't call anyone a *woman* until she was middle-aged) as a *cute tomato, a* 25 *peach, a dish, a cookie, honey, sugar,* or *sweetie-pie.* When being affectionate, women will occasionally call a man *honey* or *sweetie*, but in general, food metaphors are used much less often with men than with women. If a man is called a *fruit*, his masculinity is being questioned. But it's perfectly acceptable to use a food metaphor if the food is heavier and more substantive than that used for women. For example, pinup pictures of women have long been known as *cheesecake*, but when Burt Reynolds posed for a nude centerfold, the picture was immediately dubbed *beefcake*, c.f. *a hunk of meat*. That such sexual references to men have come into the general language is another reflection of how society is beginning to lessen the differences between their attitudes toward men and women.

Something similar to the *fruit* metaphor happens with ref- 26
erences to plants. We insult a man by calling him *a pansy*, but it wasn't considered particularly insulting to talk about a girl being a *wallflower*, a *clinging vine*, or a *shrinking violet*, or to give girls such names as *Ivy, Rose, Lily, Iris, Daisy, Camellia, Heather*, and *Flora*. A plant metaphor can be used with a man if the plant is big and strong, for example Andrew Jackson's nickname of *Old Hickory*. Also, the phrases *blooming idiots* and *budding geniuses* can be used with either sex, but notice how they are based on the most active thing a plant can do which is to bloom or bud.

Animal metaphors also illustrate the different expectations 27
for males and females. Men are referred to as *studs, bucks,* and *wolves* while women are referred to with such metaphors as *kitten*, *bunny*, *beaver*, *bird*, *chick*, and *lamb*. In the 1950s we said that boys went *tomcatting*, but today it's just *catting around* and both boys and girls do it. When the term foxy, meaning that someone was sexy, first became popular, it was used only for girls, but now someone of either sex can be described as a fox. Some animal metaphors that are used predominantly with men have negative connotations based on the size and/or strength of the animals, e.g., *beast, bull-headed, jackass, rat, loanshark,* and *vulture*. Negative metaphors used with women are based on smaller animals, e.g., *social butterfly, mousy, catty,* and *vixen*. The

feminine terms connote action, but not the same kind of large-scale action as with the masculine terms.

## Women Are Connected with Negative Connotations, Men with Positive Connotations

The final point that my notecards illustrated was how many positive connotations are associated with the concept of masculine, while there are either trivial or negative connotations connected with the corresponding feminine concept. An example from the animal metaphors makes a good illustration. The word *shrew* taken from the name of a small but especially vicious animal was defined in my dictionary as "an ill-tempered scolding woman," but the word *shrewd* taken from the same root was defined as "marked by clever, discerning awareness" and was illustrated with the phrase "a shrewd businessman." 28

Early in life, children are conditioned to the superiority of the masculine role. As child psychologists point out, little girls have much more freedom to experiment with sex roles than do little boys. If a little girl acts like a *tomboy*, most parents have mixed feelings, being at least partially proud. But if their little boy acts like a *sissy* (derived from *sister*), they call a psychologist. It's perfectly acceptable for a little girl to sleep in the crib that was purchased for her brother, to wear his hand-me-down jeans and shirts, and to ride the bicycle that he has outgrown. But few parents would put a boy baby in a white and gold crib decorated with frills and lace, and virtually no parents would have their little boy wear his sister's hand-me-down dresses, nor would they have their son ride a girl's pink bicycle with a flower-bedecked basket. The proper names given to girls and boys show this same attitude. Girls can have "boy" names—*Cris, Craig, Jo, Kelly, Shawn, Teri, Toni,* and *Sam*—but it doesn't work the other way around. A couple of generations ago, *Beverley, Frances, Hazel, Marion,* and *Shirley* were common boys' names. As parents gave these names to more and more girls, they fell into disuse for males, and some older men who have these names prefer to go by their initials or by such abbreviated forms as *Haze* or *Shirl*. 29

When a little girl is told to *be a lady*, she is being told to sit with her knees together and to be quiet and dainty. But when a little boy is told to *be a man*, he is being told to be noble, strong, and virtuous—to have all the qualities that the speaker looks on as desirable. The concept of manliness has such positive connotations that it used to be a compliment to call someone a *he-man*, to say that he was doubly a man. Today many people are more ambivalent about this term and respond to it much as they do to the word macho. But calling someone a *manly man* or a *virile man* is nearly always meant as a compliment. *Virile* comes from the Indo-European vir meaning "man," which is also the basis of *virtuous*. Contrast the positive connotations of both *virile and virtuous* with the negative connotations of *hysterical*. The Greeks took this latter word from their name for uterus (as still seen in *hysterectomy*). They thought that women were the only ones who experienced uncontrolled emotional outbursts and so the condition must have something to do with a part of the body that only women have. 30

Differences between positive male and negative female connotations can be seen in several pairs of words which differ denotatively only in the matter of sex. *Bachelor* as compared to *spinster* or *old maid* has such positive connotations that women try to adopt them by using the term *bachelor-girl* or *bachelorette*. *Old maid* is so negative that it's the basis for metaphors: pretentious and fussy old men are called *old maids*, as are the leftover kernels of unpopped popcorn and the last card in a popular children's game. 31

*Patron* and *matron* (Middle English for *father* and *mother*) have such different levels of prestige that women try to borrow the more positive masculine connotations with the word *patroness*, literally "female father." Such a peculiar term came about because of the high prestige attached to *patron* in such phrases as a *patron of the arts* or a *patron saint*. *Matron* is more apt to be used in talking about a woman in charge of a jail or a public restroom. 32

When men are doing jobs that women often do, we apparently try to pay the men extra by giving them fancy titles; for example, a male cook is more likely to be called a *chef*, while a male seamstress will get the title of *tailor*. The armed forces have a 33 special problem in that they recruit under such slogans as "The Marine Corps Builds Men!" and "Join the Army! Become a Man." Once the recruits are enlisted, they find themselves doing much of the work that has been traditionally thought of as "woman's work." The solution to getting the work done and not insulting anyone's masculinity was to change the titles as shown below:

waitress ——————> orderly
nurse ——————> medic or corpsman
secretary ——————> clerk-typist
assistant ——————> adjutant
dishwasher or kitchen helper ——> KP (kitchen police)

Compare *brave* and *squaw*. Early settlers in America truly admired Indian men and hence named them with a word that carried connotations of youth, vigor, and courage. But they used the Algonquin's name for "woman," and over the years it developed almost opposite connotations to those of *brave*. *Wizard* and *witch* contrast almost as much. The masculine *wizard* implies skill and wisdom combined with magic, while the feminine *witch* implies evil intentions combined with magic. Part of the unattractiveness of both *witch* and *squaw* is that they have been used so often to refer to old women, something with which our culture is particularly uncomfortable, just as the Afghans were. Imagine my surprise when I ran across the phrases grandfatherly advice and *old wives' tales* and realized that the underlying implication is the same as the Afghan proverb about old men being worth listening to while old women talk only foolishness. 34

Other terms which show how negatively we view old women as compared to young women are *old nag* as compared to *filly, old crow* or *old bat* as compared to *bird*, and being *catty* as compared to being *kittenish*. There is no matching set of metaphors for men. The chicken metaphor tells the whole story of a woman's life. In her youth she is a *chick*. Then she marries and begins *feathering her nest*. Soon she begins feeling *cooped up*, so she goes to *hen parties* where she *cackles* with her friends. Then 35 she has her *brood*, begins to *henpeck* her husband, and finally turns into *an old biddy*.

I embarked on my study of the dictionary not with the intention of prescribing language change but simply to see what the language would tell me about sexism. Nevertheless I have been both surprised and pleased as I've watched the changes that have occurred over the past two decades. I'm one of those linguists who believes that new language customs will cause a new generation of speakers to grow up with different expectations. This is why I'm happy about people's efforts to use inclusive language, to say *he* or *she* or *they* when speaking about individuals whose names they do not know. I'm glad that leading publishers have developed guidelines to help writers use language that is fair to both sexes, and I'm glad that most newspapers and magazines list women by their own names instead of only by their husbands' names and that educated and thoughtful people no longer begin their business letters with "Dear Sir" or "Gentlemen," but instead use a memo form or begin with such salutations as "Dear Colleagues," "Dear Reader," or "Dear Committee Members." I'm also glad that such words as *poetess, authoress, conductress*, and *aviatrix* now sound quaint and old fashioned and that *chairman* is giving way to *chair* or *head*, *mailman* to *mail carrier*, *clergyman* to *clergy*, and *stewardess* to *flight attendant*. I was also pleased when the National Oceanic and Atmospheric Administration bowed to feminist complaints and in the late '70s began to alternate men's and women's names for hurricanes. However, I wasn't so pleased to discover that the change did not immediately erase sexist thoughts from everyone's mind as shown by a headline about Hurricane David in a 1979 New York tabloid, "David Rapes Virgin Islands." More recently a similar metaphor appeared in a headline in the *Arizona Republic* about Hurricane Charlie: "Charlie Quits Carolinas, Flirts with Virginia." 36

What these incidents show is that sexism is not something existing independently in American English or in the particular dictionary that I happened to read. Rather, it exists in people's minds. Language is like an x-ray in providing visible evidence of invisible thoughts. The best thing about people being interested in and 37 discussing sexist language is that as they make conscious decisions about what pronouns they will use, what jokes they will tell or laugh at, how they will write their names, or how they will begin their letters, they are forced to think about the underlying issue of sexism. This is good, because as a problem that begins in people's assumptions and expectations, it's a problem that will be solved only when a great many people have given it a great deal of thought.

---

## *Meaning and Purpose*

1. What is your first response to Nilsen's essay? Are you aware of sexist language? Explain.
2. An argument is a reason or reasons stated for or against something. What is the author arguing for? What is she arguing against? Find one sentence from the essay that shows each position.
3. Where does Nilsen state her purpose in this essay? What is her point in each of the three sections, and how are these points related to the thesis?
4. The first three paragraphs tell about Nilsen's experiences in another culture. Why are those experiences included in this essay?
5. Nilsen fills her essay with examples of words and phrases that support her assertions about language. As a reader, how do you react to her using so many examples? Do you feel overwhelmed with information, or does she need the many examples to make her meaning clear?

## *Strategy*

1. Does Nilsen use specific, typical, or hypothetical examples? How effective is her choice?
2. Paragraph 33 lists examples of the differences in job descriptions between the jobs women hold in civilian life and those men hold

in the armed services. What role do you believe Nilsen thinks the language of these examples has in people's attitudes toward the jobs?

3. How does Nilsen use her final paragraph in the structure of the essay?

## *Style*

1. How do you characterize this essayist's tone? Is she angry? Is she informative? Is she calm? Is the tone neutral? Show evidence of Nilsen's tone from the essay.
2. How does her use of many short examples affect the pace of the essay, or your way of reading it?
3. Why does Nilsen use subtitles and divide her essay into sections? How effective are the subtitles?

## *Writing Tasks*

1. Write a paper contrasting the portrayal of men or women (or both) on a current television sitcom with their portrayal on a sitcom from the past. The older the reruns you watch, the more likelihood that you will see differences. Do the differences support Nilsen's confidence that our gender-related language is changing and that the changes in language will bring about a change in roles?
2. In a few paragraphs for each person, draw two hypothetical examples—one male and one female—illustrating the abstractions of masculinity and femininity.

## ❦ Ellen Currie ❦

*A frequent contributor to magazines and newspapers, Ellen Currie has also published a novel,* Available Light *(1986).*

# *Two Varieties of Killers*

*The essay from* The New York Times *expresses Currie's concern about the changing nature of crime in our country and also about the manner in which law-abiding people react to sensational crimes.*

*As you read think about the recently reported violent crimes in your area. Would any of them fit Currie's definition of sociable?*

---

Henry James, like many decorous and respectable people, entertained a lively interest in murder. He was a fan of the Scottish solicitor William Roughead, who wrote about real life crime for the first 40 years of this century; James once told Mr. Roughead he was interested in crime because through it "manners and morals become clearly disclosed." He urged Mr. Roughead to write about "the dear old human and sociable murders and adulteries and forgeries in which we are so agreeably at home. And don't tell me, for charity's sake, that your supply runs short." 1

Contemporary supplies of murder, adultery, and forgery remain abundant. But crime seems to me less sociable these days, if I am right in taking "sociable" to mean human and comprehensible and even sympathetic. The crimes get bigger and more horrible, and yet we are not sufficiently horrified by them; we pay less and less attention to the manners and the morals they disclose. 2

Look at the difference, for example, between the crimes of Madeleine Smith, who stirred arsenic into her lover's cocoa in 1857, and the convicted killer Theodore R. Bundy, who has been linked with the murders of 36 women he didn't even know. 3

4 Madeleine Smith, whose case greatly interested Henry James (he called her a "portentous young person"), was the daughter of a Glasgow architect. In 1855, when she was 19, she crossed paths with a young Frenchman. He was handsome, Mr. Roughead wrote, but "socially impossible." They met in secret and wrote to each other constantly. When they became lovers Miss Smith's letters took on what Mr. Roughead described as "a tropical and abandoned tone." They were indelicate letters, naive and outspoken. Another scholar of crime has pointed out that in a day when sex was supposed to be no more than a woman's bounden duty, Madeleine Smith found it a pagan festival.

5 Her lover kept her letters, 198 of them. When she accepted an older, richer and more settled suitor, she asked for the letters' return. Wild with jealousy, her lover claimed he would return them only to her father. That prospect drove Miss Smith mad with shame and fear. She bought arsenic. Her lover soon died of arsenic poisoning. She was brought to trial and conducted herself with great dignity. The verdict: not proven.

6 These people are not admirable, but they are real. Their awful situation is comprehensible: a blown up, highly colored version of the kind of dilemma ordinary people face. Madeleine Smith's crime was personal. It was a crime of passion.

7 The case of Ted Bundy is different. To me, it is not "sociable," not comprehensible on any human scale. It is peculiarly impersonal. He didn't even know his victims; they represented an abstraction—women. His are crimes not of passion but pathology. Our reaction to them seems to me to partake of pathology too.

8 According to the reports I have read, some law enforcement officials say Mr. Bundy may have killed more than 36 young women in sexual crimes across the country. (Like Madeleine Smith, Ted Bundy says he is innocent of any crime.) He has been convicted of battering to death, early on Super Bowl Sunday 1978 in the Chi Omega sorority house at Florida State University, two young women. He hideously beat two more young women in the same house and, blocks away, savaged another young woman. He didn't know any of them. Captured

and charged, Mr. Bundy was also indicted in the kidnapping and murder of a 12-year-old girl. He didn't know her, either. He was convicted of all charges. His execution, scheduled for July 3, was indefinitely postponed to give his lawyers time to frame an appeal.

The young women Ted Bundy has been convicted of killing, and is suspected of killing, resemble, an investigator said, "everyone's daughter." Their photographs show the sweet faces of their youth, the long hair of the period. Except for those who loved them, their identities overlap now, and blur. These women are not vivid and defined because they did nothing to bring about their deaths. They were not Ted Bundy's angry and discarded lovers. They did not refuse to return his disastrous, impassioned letters. They didn't know him. 9

At first all these deaths of pretty young women attracted wide public notice. But once Mr. Bundy was apprehended, the attention was all on his antics and not on the innocent dead. Bundy is a 20th century phenomenon. He is mediagenic. He is handsome, usually described as a former law student and witty, brilliant, charming, and polished. Oddly, these latter qualities do not come through in any of the several books about him. Mr. Bundy was once active in Republican politics; there are those who profess to believe that he might ultimately have been elected to high public office had he stayed the course. He has twice made dramatic escapes from custody. He has acted as his own counsel in sensational televised trials. He has been the subject of a television movie. Ted Bundy T-shirts, for, against, and smart aleck ("Ted Bundy is a one-night stand"), have enjoyed popularity. So have jingles: "Let's salute the mighty Bundy / Here on Friday, gone on Monday / All his roads lead out of town / It's hard to keep a good man down." Bundy Burgers and a Bundy cocktail had some play in a Colorado bar. Groupies have gathered at his trials. He gets a lot of mail. 10

Theodore Bundy is said by psychiatrists to be an antisocial personality, a man without conscience. In a strange, third person meditation on killings, Mr. Bundy described the rapes and murders as "inappropriate acting out." 11

Perhaps Ted Bundy doesn't labor under a conscience. But how about the rest of us? Shouldn't we feel more revulsion, more grief for those young lives? Something vile has happened to our ideas of what is valuable and what is waste. Perhaps we have seen too much evil and on too grand a scale. We are glib and dismissive of the moral issues. We think Mr. Bundy is good for a laugh. We made him a celebrity. (Richard Schickel, in his book "Intimate Strangers," about the nature of celebrity in modern society, contends that multiple murderers have grasped the essentials of the celebrity system better than normal people.) 12

Crime does disclose on manners and on morals. If people must kill people, I have to put my dollar down on wicked Madeleine Smith. With her sexy letters, poisoned cocoa, and caddish lover, she dealt in death. But she is piercingly familiar. Ted Bundy's unspeakable crimes and our cheap reaction to them reveal us to ourselves in a strange and deathly light. 13

---

## *Meaning and Purpose*

1. What is "sociable" murder according to Currie? Why is Ted Bundy's crime not sociable?
2. Where does Currie state the thesis of her essay?
3. Does Currie have a purpose beyond simply contrasting Madeliene Smith and Ted Bundy? What does she want us to think about besides the differences in their crimes?
4. What explanation is given for Bundy's crimes?
5. Why is Bundy called a "20th century phenomenon"? Can you think of other criminal suspects who might also be called that?

## *Strategy*

1. Does Currie use a subject-by-subject or point-by-point approach to presenting her material? Why?

2. Currie devotes a larger portion of the essay to Ted Bundy than she does to Madeleine Smith. Why?

## *Style*

1. In paragraph 4, Madeleine Smith's letters are described as having "a tropical and abandoned tone." Explain what this phrase means.
2. Bundy is described in paragraph 10 as being "mediagenic." What, in your view, makes a person mediagenic?
3. Madeleine's young Frenchman is called "socially impossible" in paragraph 4. Explain what that phrase means in the context of his relationship with Madeleine?
4. If necessary look up the meanings of these words in a dictionary: *portentous, bounden, pagan* (4); *savaged* (8); *vile, glib* (12).

## *Writing Tasks*

1. Using Currie's definition of "sociable" crime or developing a definition of your own, write a paper contrasting sociable and nonsociable crimes. Use a subject-by-subject development method. Use specific, typical and/or hypothetical examples to illustrate your general statements.
2. Write a comparison/contrast paper using a point-by-point method of development. Choose a subject relating to your personal experience at work, at school, or at home.

## ❦ Henry David Thoreau ❦

*When he was twenty-eight years old, Henry David Thoreau built a cabin in the woods by Walden Pond, Massachusetts, and lived there alone for two years. His best-known book,* Walden *(1854), is about that experience. Born in nearby Concord, Massachusetts, in 1817, Thoreau was educated at Harvard University and was influenced by the American essayist, poet, and philosopher Ralph Waldo Emerson, who was also a close friend. Thoreau believed in the citizens' duty to act on their conscience and once spent a night in jail for refusing to pay a poll tax on the grounds that he objected to United States involvement in war with Mexico. In his famed essay, "Civil Disobedience" (1849), he outlines his philosophy of passive resistance and has often been cited in support of the American civil-rights movement.*

# *The Battle of the Ants*

*In this extended analogy from* Walden, *Thoreau compares a battle between red ants and black ants that he witnessed on his woodpile, to the wars men have waged all through history. While elevating the ants by comparing them to men, Thoreau diminishes the glory of human wars by comparing them to battles among insects.*

*By using an analogy that compares ant wars to human wars, Thoreau satirizes the brutality and ultimate futility of war. Take notice of all the various aspects of war making he satirizes.*

---

One day when I went out to my wood-pile, or rather my pile of stumps, I observed two large ants, the one red, the other much larger, nearly half an inch long, and black, fiercely contending with one another. Having once got hold they never let go, but struggled and wrestled and rolled on the chips incessantly. Looking farther, I was surprised to find that the chips were covered with such combatants, that it was not a *duellum*, but a *bellum*, a war between two races of ants, the red always pitted against the black, and frequently two red ants to one black. The legions of 1 these Myrmidons covered all the hills and vales in my wood-yard, and the ground was already strewn with the dead and dying, both red and black. It was the only battle which I have ever witnessed, the only battle-field I ever trod while the battle was raging; internecine war; the red republicans on the one hand, and the black imperialists on the other. On every side they were engaged in deadly combat, yet without any noise that I could hear, and human soldiers never fought so resolutely. I watched a couple that were fast locked in each other's embraces, in a little sunny valley amid the chips, now at noonday prepared to fight till the sun went down, or life went out. The smaller red champion had fastened himself like a vise to his adversary's front, and through all the tumblings on that field never for an instant ceased to gnaw at one of his feelers near the root, having already caused the other to go by the board; while the stronger black one dashed him from side to side, and, as I saw on looking nearer, had already divested him of several of his members. They fought with more pertinacity than bulldogs. Neither manifested the least disposition to retreat. It was evident that their battle-cry was "Conquer or die." In the meanwhile there came along a single red ant on the hillside of this valley, evidently full of excitement, who either had dispatched his foe, or had not yet taken part in the battle; probably the latter, for he had lost none of his limbs; whose mother had charged him to return with his shield or upon it. Or perchance he was some Achilles, who had nourished his wrath apart, and had now come to avenge or rescue his Patroclus. He saw this unequal combat from afar—for the blacks were nearly twice the size of the red—he drew near with rapid pace till he stood on his guard within half an inch of the combatants; then, watching his opportunity, he sprang upon the black warrior, and commenced his operations near the root of his right foreleg, leaving the foe to select among his own members; and so there were three united for life, as if a new kind of attraction had been invented which put all other locks and cements to shame. I should not have wondered by this time to find that they had their respective musical bands stationed on some eminent chip, and playing their national airs the while, to excite the slow and cheer the dying combatants. I was myself excited somewhat even as if they had been men. The more you think of it, the less the difference. And certainly there is not the fight recorded in Concord history, at least, if in the history of America, that will bear a moment's comparison with this, whether for the numbers engaged in it, or for the patriotism and heroism displayed. For numbers and for carnage it was an Austerlitz or Dresden. Concord Fight! Two killed on the patriots' side, and Luther Blanchard wounded! Why here every ant was a Buttrick—"Fire! for God's sake fire!"—and thousands shared the fate of Davis and Hosmer. There was not one hireling there. I have no doubt that it was a principle they fought for, as much as our ancestors, and not to avoid a three-penny tax on their tea; and the results of this battle will be as important and memorable to those whom it concerns as those of the battle of Bunker Hill, at least.

I took up the chip on which the three I have particularly described were struggling, carried it into my house, and placed it under a tumbler on my window-sill, in order to see the issue. Holding a microscope to the first-mentioned red ant, I saw that, though he was assiduously gnawing at the near foreleg of his enemy, having severed his remaining feeler, his own breast was all torn away, exposing what vitals he had there to the jaws of the black warrior, whose breastplate was apparently too thick for him to pierce; and the dark carbuncles of the sufferer's eyes shone with ferocity such as war only could excite. They struggled half an hour longer under the tumbler, and when I looked again the black soldier had severed the heads of his foes from their bodies, and the still living heads were hanging on either side of him like ghastly trophies at his saddle-bow, still apparently as firmly fastened as ever, and he was endeavoring with feeble struggles, being without feelers, and with only the remnant of a leg, and I know not how many other wounds, to divest himself of them, which at length, after half an hour more, he accomplished. I raised the glass, and he went off over the window-sill in that crippled state. Whether he finally survived that combat, and spent the remainder of his days in some Hôtel des Invalides, I do not know; but I thought that his industry would not be worth much thereafter. I never learned which party 2 was victorious, nor the cause of the war, but I felt for the rest of that day as if I had my feelings excited and harrowed by witnessing the struggle, the ferocity and carnage, of a human battle before my door.

Kirby and Spence tell us that the battles of ants have long been celebrated and the date of them recorded, though they say that Huber is the only modern author who appears to have witnessed them. "Aeneas Sylvius," say they, "after giving a very circumstantial account of one contested with great obstinacy by a great and small species on the trunk of a pear tree," adds that " 'this action was fought in the pontificate of Eugenius the Fourth, in the presence of Nicholas Pistoriensis, an eminent lawyer, who related the whole history of the battle with the greatest fidelity.' A similar engagement between great and small ants is recorded by Olaus Magnus, in which the small ones, being victorious, are said to have buried the bodies of their own soldiers, but left those of their giant enemies a prey to the birds. This event happened previous to the expulsion of the tyrant Christian the Second from Sweden." The battle which I witnessed took place in the Presidency of Polk, five years before the passage of Webster's Fugitive-Slave Bill. 3

---

## Meaning and Purpose

1. Have you ever stopped to observe and perhaps become fascinated by small things in nature? Explain. What in Thoreau's essay reminds you of your own experience?
2. What was Thoreau's opinion of war? Use evidence from the essay for your answer.
3. Can you find a statement or statements of Thoreau's main point, or thesis?
4. Thoreau mentions Greek heroes, great historical battles, a pope, and a president of the United States. What is his purpose in these widely different references?
5. Think of the time in which Thoreau lived. What audience do you think he is addressing?

6. Although the last paragraph in the essay seems to drift into other topics, in fact, it serves an important purpose. What is that purpose?

## *Strategy*

1. The body of this essay is an extended analogy that parallels some activities of ants and men. What are two qualities that ants and men share in this essay? Give examples from specific sentences.
2. Midway through the first paragraph, Thoreau says, "The more you think of it, the less the difference." What is he comparing? What "difference" is he talking about?
3. Toward the end of paragraph 2, Thoreau wonders whether a crippled ant survived to spend the rest of his days "in some Hôtel des Invalides." What is the analogy here?
4. Thoreau makes generous use of satire as a strategy in his analogy. What is satire and how is it effective here?
5. Overall, how effective do you judge Thoreau's extended analogy is in comparing human battles with those of ants? Without this analogy, how might Thoreau have talked about the folly of war, and do you think his message would have been as forceful?

## *Style*

1. Early in the essay, Thoreau says that he witnessed an "internecine war." Define that kind of war.
2. The first paragraph in the essay includes "Concord Fight!" and "Two killed on the patriots' side, and Luther Blanchard wounded!" Where do these kinds of exclamations often appear? Who might Luther Blanchard be?
3. The second paragraph in the essay includes this description: "the dark carbuncles of the sufferer's eyes shone with ferocity such as war only could excite." Is this description realistic, or is it factual? Support your answer with your own opinions.

4. Thoreau says that the soldier-ants "fought with more pertinacity than bulldogs." Look up pertinacity. The word has at least two meanings. Which meaning compares ants with men? Which meaning compares ants with bulldogs?

## *Writing Tasks*

1. In the essay, Thoreau says, "I have no doubt that it was a principle they fought for, as much as our ancestors . . ." Can you think of a principle many people believe in that you feel is not worth fighting or working for? Write an essay in which you use an analogy and compare that principle to something familiar to readers in order to show why it is not worth the struggle.
2. There are other analogies for war besides the battle of the ants. Finish the statement "War is like . . .," listing three things to compare war to. Write a few paragraphs of analogy for each comparison you choose.

## ❦ *Responding to Photographs* ❦

*Comparison and Contrast*

The New Warriors

For general purposes, think of photography as having two main uses: to record private experiences and to record public experiences. A photograph of private experience—a snapshot of a family outing, a portrait of a father, a candid photo of a child—is appreciated within a private context by those who have some direct connection with the recorded event or person.

A photograph that records public experience usually has nothing directly to do with us, its viewers, but nevertheless we bring meaning to it based on our experiences.

Both private and public photographs can evoke infinite associations from the viewer's own experience. But most public photographs have a second dimension. They create social or political associations that many people share. Often they suggest discontinuity in our common social experience. As an organizing principle, photographers create discontinuity through juxtaposition—that is, they oppose contrasting elements in their photographs.

Select one of the following writing assignments to explore the use of contrasting elements in photographs. Before you begin, reread "Comparison and Contrast: Presenting Similarities and Differences" at the beginning of this chapter to review strategies for developing contrasts.

1. "The New Warriors" is a public photograph that ironically explores the ideas on which the United States is predicated. By referring to details in "The New Warriors," examine its contrasting elements and determine what social or political message it embodies. Remember you must select details from the photograph to support your contention, presenting them to readers as if they have not seen the image.
2. Select a private photograph from your or your family's collection. Be sure to find one that embodies contrasting elements. In a brief essay, examine the contrasting elements in the photograph. Keep in mind that since your readers have not been part of your family history, you must supply background information to create a context for the photograph.

## ❦ *Additional Writing Tasks* ❦

*Comparison and Contrast*

1. Using comparison and contrast as the dominant pattern, write an essay on one of these tasks or one you compose for yourself. Keep in mind that you may modify any of the tasks to fit your interests.
   a. At the library find two advertisements for the same product, one published in the 1950s and one published within the last year. Write an essay presenting the similarities and differences in these advertisements.
   b. Select two fairy tales that have similar patterns and characters, such as children journeying into a forest, an encounter with death, the appearance of a mysterious creature, a magical transformation. Identify at least three significant elements the tales have in common and three significant elements that are different. Write an essay comparing and contrasting the similarities and differences in these two tales.
   c. Collect several advertisements for two brands of the same product type that direct their advertising campaigns toward men and women, such as Marlboro cigarettes (men) and Virginia Slims (women). After examining the advertisements, write an essay comparing and contrasting how these advertisements appeal to male consumers and how they appeal to female consumers.
   d. Accurately and fairly, compare and contrast the arguments on both sides of a controversial issue, such as abortion, capital punishment, pornography, or gun control.
   e. Most people hold important social or political beliefs that are opposed by people close to them. Select a belief you hold and in an essay contrast your attitude to the opposing attitude of one of your parents, a brother, a sister, or a close friend.
   f. Select two classes you have attended, two jobs you have held, or two vacations you have taken. Write a comparison-and-contrast essay discussing the similarities and differences of your subjects.

g. Compare and contrast a past experience with a current experience. You might compare how you once viewed a holiday, such as Thanksgiving, Christmas, or Chanukah, with your view of it today. Or you might compare how you once viewed a special place, such as a vacation site, a fun zone, or even your bedroom, with your current view.
h. Compare and contrast how two people from different cultures, economic situations, or age groups might perceive the same experience.
i. Select two public figures with opposing views on one controversial issue. After familiarizing yourself with their positions, write an essay contrasting their attitudes.
j. Select two campus groups that hold opposing social values. In an essay, compare and contrast their views and behavior.

2. Write an essay with comparison and contrast as the dominant pattern on one of these general subjects or on a subject of your own choice. By the end of your essay, the reader should know why you prefer one thing to the other.
   a. two people who embrace different life-styles
   b. a national news program and a local news program
   c. two methods for losing weight
   d. female and male consumers
   e. children's games yesterday and today
   f. two characters from film or fiction
   g. a film created from a novel
   h. watching a movie on television and watching it in the cinema
   i. coverage of a news event by television and by a newspaper
   j. two classic films: horror, western, mystery, or romance
3. Read this quotation from social critic Morton Hunt:

> The record of man's inhumanity to man is horrifying, when one compiles it—enslavement, castration, torture, rape, mass slaughter in war after war. But who has compiled the record of man's kindness to man—the trillions of acts of gentleness and goodness, the helping hands, smiles, shared meals, kisses, gifts, healings, rescues? If we were no more than murderous predators,

> with a freakish lack of inhibition against slaughtering our own species, we would have been at a terrible competitive disadvantage compared with other animals; if this were the central truth of our nature, we would scarcely have survived, multiplied and become the dominant species on earth. Man does have an aggressive instinct, but it is not naturally or inevitably directed to killing his own kind. He is a beast and perhaps at times the cruelest beast of all—but sometimes he is also the kindest beast of all. He is not all good and not perfectible, but he is not all bad and not wholly unchangeable or unimprovable. That is the only basis on which one can hope for him; but it is enough.

Hunt stresses humanity's dual nature. Write an essay with comparison and contrast as the dominant pattern that makes Hunt's general observation specific.

# 7

## *Cause and Effect*

### *Identifying Reasons and Results*

## *The Method*

When you explain why something happened or the consequences of that happening, you are engaged in an intellectual activity that seems to be at the core of human curiosity—that is, the search for **causes and effects**.

In their simplest form cause-and-effect relationships appear as a series of escalating events, one triggering another like a chain reaction. Consider the children's song in which a woman swallows a fly. The lively fly causes her to swallow a spider to catch the fly. She then swallows a bird to catch the spider; then a cat to catch the bird; then a dog to catch the cat; then a goat; then a cow; and finally, a horse. The effect? She dies, of course.

In a more complex form, cause and effect is often at work in thrillers and mysteries. A wealthy politician falls dead during a banquet. He had been in excellent health. There seems to be no clear cause of death. Could he have been murdered in some mysterious way? The question triggers the appearance of a supersleuth who begins the investigation. The detective discovers clues, each of which reveals a new suspect. After an exhaustive exploration of the many reasons suspects had for wanting the victim dead, the murderer is unmasked, the mysterious murder method explained, and the dark reasons for the murder revealed.

Of course, mystery fans aren't consciously seeking cause or effect patterns. They're probably trying to beat the writer at his or her own game by figuring out "Whodunit?" before the final scene. But that question is not much different from, What caused it?

If you think of causes as **reasons** and effects as **results**, you might better understand cause-and-effect patterns. Like a detective you can begin with questions: Why did something happen? What are the consequences of something's happening? When you answer the Why, you are giving reasons; that is, causes. When you answer the What, you are giving results; that is, effects. Professional writers observe this distinction when exploring the causes or effects behind any event. Generally, the distinction keeps them on the track.

Consider this question: "Why did the women's liberation movement bloom in the 1960s?" The question would lead a writer to seek reasons—that is, causes.

But the question, "What were the consequences of the women's liberation movement on college campuses during the 1970s?" would lead a writer to seek results—that is, effects.

And the compound question, "Why did the women's liberation movement falter in the 1980s, and what will be the consequences in the 1990s?" would lead a writer to explain the reasons and the results—that is, both causes and effects.

## *Strategies*

When you begin analyzing the cause or effect relationships in a complex subject, you may feel somewhat like a detective unraveling a mystery. You must be prepared for the false starts and deceptive clues that will send you down the wrong path, but don't lose heart: you can learn by studying professional writers, who often approach cause-and-effect analysis from several angles, depending on the characteristics of their subjects. First, they may narrow their effort by concentrating only on the causes. Second, they may concentrate only on the effects. And third, they may choose to concentrate on both causes and effects. If you understand cause-and-effect development patterns and apply your knowledge critically as you read, you'll soon master the technique of analyzing cause-and-effect relationships in your own writing.

### *Identifying Causes*

When effects are clear, writers will concentrate on causes. In 1948, Harry Truman upset Thomas Dewey, Governor of New York, for the presidency. Dewey was predicted to win by a landslide. In fact, one newspaper prematurely printed headlines announcing Dewey's victory. The political pundits were wrong: Truman won. A writer who asked, "Why did Truman win?" would not have to establish the result (Truman's victory), but he or she would concentrate on the reasons—that is, the causes—behind Truman's victory. Did his "underdog" image generate sympathy among voters? Did a last-minute whistlestop campaign through America's heartland swing the election his way? Was it a well-oiled Democratic machine that kept the party faithful in line? These and other causes would have to be explored in any analysis of the election.

In *Redoing America*, Robert Faltermayer discusses the interwoven character of American cities. In the following paragraph, Faltermayer concentrates on causes. He opens with the common assumption that the automobile has had a destructive effect on the "close-knit fabric" of cities. He then presents the reasons for this phenomenon:

> The close knit fabric was blown apart by the automobile, and by the postwar middle-class exodus to suburbia which the mass-ownership of automobiles made possible. The automobile itself was not to blame for this development, nor was the desire for suburban living, which is obviously a genuine aspiration of many Americans. The fault lay in our failure, right up to the present time, to fashion new policies to minimize the disruptive effects of the automobile revolution. We have failed not only to tame the automobile itself, but to overhaul a property-tax system that tends to foster automotive-age sprawl and to institute coordinated planning in the politically fragmented suburbs that have caught the brunt of the postwar building boom.

In the opening sentence Faltermayer establishes a relationship between automobiles and the changing character of cities and sprawling suburbs. In the next sentence he refines his focus by dismissing two possible causes, the automobile itself and the desire for suburban living. In the remainder of the paragraph he explains what he believes to be the true cause, the failure to fashion public policies that would have controlled the automobile and the building boom.

### *Identifying Effects*

When writers select subjects with very clear causes, they will then concentrate on effects. For instance, drug merchants are expanding their operations into rural communities. Crack houses are springing up in small towns where drugs had previously been scarce. This fact has been substantiated by law-enforcement agencies across the nation. A writer who asked, "What are the consequences of increased drug use in rural communities?" would spend very little time establishing the existence of increased drug activity in small-town America because it is widely known. He or she would, however, concentrate on the effects this trend might have on rural communities. What, for instance, are the consequences for families? What will be the effects on undertrained and underbudgeted law-enforcement agencies, on social services, and on schools?

In this paragraph from *Anatomy of an Illness*, Norman Cousins uses this pattern. He quickly establishes the cause, a hypothetical injury, and then concentrates on exploring effects of pain suppressants on injured professional athletes.

> Professional athletes are sometimes severely disadvantaged by trainers whose job it is to keep them in action. The more famous the athlete, the greater the risk that he or she may be subjected to extreme medical measures when injury strikes. The star baseball pitcher whose arm is sore because of a torn muscle or tissue damage may need sustained rest more than anything else. But this team is battling for a place in the World Series; so the trainer or team doctor, called upon to work his magic, reaches for a strong dose of butazolidine or other powerful pain suppressants. Presto, the pain disappears! The pitcher takes his place on the mound and does superbly. That could be the last game, however, in which he is able to throw the ball with full strength. The

> drugs didn't repair the torn muscle or cause the damaged tissue to heal. What they did was to mask the pain, enabling the pitcher to throw hard, further damaging the torn muscle. Little wonder that so many star athletes are cut down in their prime, more the victims of overzealous treatment of their injuries than of the injuries themselves.

Cousins opens by establishing the direction the paragraph will take. He then states the cause of the effects that will follow—a hypothetical injury to a star baseball pitcher's throwing arm. Next, he develops the effects of the injury—under pressure to win, a trainer or team doctor prescribes a pain killer; the pitcher plays as if he had no injury; and the ultimate effect, a career cut short, not by injury but by the mistreatment of injury.

### *Identifying Causes and Effects*

Writers are always cautious about assuming that readers know the causes or effects of an event, especially when exploring a complex subject that is not part of common knowledge. When such a subject is discussed, they usually explain both causes and effects. Often they will alternate causes and effects in one paragraph.

Victor C. Cline uses this pattern in a paragraph from "How TV Violence Damages Your Children."

> Much of the research that has led to the conclusion that TV and movie violence could cause aggressive behavior in some children has stemmed from the work in the area of imitative learning or modeling which, reduced to its simplest expression, might be termed "monkey see, monkey do." Research by Stanford psychologist Albert Bandura has shown that even brief exposure to novel aggressive behavior on a *one-time basis* can be repeated in free play by as high as 88 percent of the young children seeing it on TV. Dr. Bandura also demonstrated that even a single viewing of a novel aggressive act could be recalled and produced by children six months later, without any intervening exposure.

> Earlier studies have estimated that the average child between the ages of 5 and 15 will witness, during this 10-year period, the violent destruction of more than 13,400 fellow humans. This means that through several hours of TV-watching, a child may see more violence than the average adult experiences in a lifetime. Killing is as common as taking a walk, a gun more natural than an umbrella. Children are thus taught to take pride in force and violence and to feel ashamed of ordinary sympathy.

Cline's first sentence establishes that children learn aggressive behavior from television through modeling, or, as Cline phrases it, "monkey see, monkey do." In the second sentence he presents his first cause and first effect—even *brief exposure* to aggressive behavior (cause) can lead to children's repeating it in free play (effect). In the third sentence, he presents the second cause and its effect—a *single viewing* of an aggressive act (cause) can be recalled by children six months later (effect). The next three sentences detail the violence a typical child might see over ten years, thus establishing a very dramatic cause. In his final sentence, Cline states the ultimate effect: television teaches children to take pride in violence and to be ashamed of sympathy.

Rather than alternate causes and effects in individual paragraphs, writers will sometimes divide them into separate paragraphs. The following two paragraphs are from Frank Trippett's humorous essay, "The Great American Cooling Machine." In the first paragraph, Trippett establishes that air conditioning has been overlooked as a major cause for change in American society. In the second paragraph he presents three effects of air conditioning on society.

> Neither scholars nor pop sociologists have really got around to charting and diagnosing all the changes brought about by air conditioning. Professional observers have for years been preoccupied with the social implications of the automobile and television. Mere glancing analysis suggests that the car and TV, in their most decisive influences on

American habits, have been powerfully aided and abetted by air conditioning. The car may have created all those shopping centers in the boondocks, but only air conditioning has made them attractive to mass clienteles. Similarly, the artificial cooling of the living room undoubtedly helped turn the typical American into a year-round TV addict. Without air conditioning, how many viewers would endure reruns (or even Johnny Carson) on one of those pestilential summer nights that used to send people out to collapse on the lawn or to sleep on the roof?

Many of the side effects of air conditioning are far from being fully pinned down. It is a reasonable suspicion, though, that controlled climate, by inducing Congress to stay in Washington longer than it used to during the swelter season, thus presumably passing more laws, has contributed to bloated government. One can only speculate that the advent of the supercooled bedroom may be linked to the carnal adventurism associated with the mid-century sexual revolution. Surely it is a fact—if restaurant complaints about raised thermostats are to be believed—that air conditioning induces at least expense-account diners to eat and drink more; if so, it must be credited with adding to the national fat problem.

### *Identifying Immediate and Ultimate Causes*

Careful writers usually distinguish between immediate and ultimate causes; that is, those which are most apparent and those which underlie them. In the example above, Trippett, in his humorous way, presents the ultimate effects of air conditioning: bloated government, the sexual revolution, and the national fat problem. The depth to which a writer analyzes causes or effects depends upon the subject and the purpose. Exploring the ultimate causes or effects requires more effort than getting to the immediate ones because a writer must establish a foundation for the analysis.

In *The Seasons of a Man's Life*, Daniel J. Levenson studies the psychological development of men. In these two paragraphs, after establishing a solid foundation for his conclusions, he presents the ultimate effects of middle age on a man's relationships with young adults.

> At around 40 a man is deeply involved in the Young/Old polarity. This developmental process has a powerful effect upon his relationships with his offspring and with young adults generally. When his own aging weighs heavily upon him, their exuberant vitality is more likely to arouse his envy and resentment than his delight and forbearance. He may be preoccupied with grievances against his own parents for damage, real or imagined, that they have inflicted upon him at different ages. These preoccupations make him less appreciative of the (often similar) grievances his offspring direct toward him.
>
> If he feels he has lost or betrayed his own early Dream, he may find it hard to give his wholehearted support and blessing to the Dreams of young adults. When his offspring show signs of failure or confusion in pursuing their adult goals, he is afraid that their lives will turn out as badly as his own. Yet, when they do well, he may resent their success. Anxiety and guilt may undermine his efforts to be helpful and lead him instead to be nagging and vindictive.

Levenson's analysis probes deeply into the nagging relationship some middle-aged men might have with young adults. He exposes the ultimate cause and its effects—anxiety over aging, failure, and competition.

In this paragraph from *The Faces of the Enemy*, Sam Keen explores the ultimate cause of war, not the politicians who start wars or the generals who carry them out, but the "good people" who allow their leaders to act out community neuroses by waging war.

> The major responsibility for war lies not with villains and evil men but with reasonably good citizens. Any depth understanding of the social function of war leads to the conclusion that it was the "good" Germans who created the social ecology that nurtured the Nazis. Lincoln said, "War is much too important to be left to the generals." But

> the psychological truth is much more disturbing. The generals are the (largely unconscious) agents of a (largely unconscious) civilian population. The good people send out armies as symbolic representatives to act out their repressed shadows, denied hostilities, unspoken cruelties, unacceptable greed, unimagined lust for revenge against punitive parents and authorities, uncivil sexual sadism, denied animality, in a purifying blood ritual that confirms their claim to goodness before the approving eyes of history or God. Warfare is the political equivalent of the individual process of seeking "vindictive triumph," which Karen Horney described as the essence of neurosis.

Writers keep two cautions in mind when exploring cause-and-effect relationships; be aware of them. First, writers avoid confusing process patterns with cause-and-effect patterns. The analysis of a process usually stems from a question of How? not Why? or What? *How* did Ronald Reagan get elected to the presidency? sends a writer into process analysis. *Why* was Ronald Reagan elected to the presidency? sends a writer into an examination of the causes—that is, the reasons. *What* were the consequences of Ronald Reagan's presidency? sends a writer to examine the effects—that is, the results.

Second, they avoid the *post hoc, ergo propter hoc* fallacy; that is, "after this, therefore because of this" or "false-cause," fallacy. Writers commit this fallacy (argument from a false inference) by jumping to conclusions based on insufficient information. That former president Ronald Reagan was elected when the electorate's average life expectancy was increasing does not mean an older voting population will elect older presidents.

In a variation of the false-cause fallacy, an event is identified as triggering a series of events in a cause-and-effect chain reaction, or *causal chain*. This kind of reasoning was at work in the arguments of politicians who supported the United States military action in Vietnam during the 1960s and 1970s. They maintained that if North Vietnam was successful in its efforts to take over South Vietnam, then the nearby Southeast Asian countries would soon be taken over by Communist regimes one at a time, like a file of falling dominoes triggered by the first domino toppling into the second. History, of course, has shown that these events did not happen. But keep in mind that causes of complicated events are seldom simple or obvious, and that predicting the future with cause-and-effect reasoning is a chancy business.

## *Cause and Effect in College Writing*

Essays exploring cause-and-effect relationships are common in classrooms across campus. In History you might be asked to discuss the causes of racial discrimination following the Civil War. In Economics you might be asked to explain the international effects of the massive United States budget deficit. In Psychology you might be asked to discuss the causes of clinical depression and its effects, or simply causes *or* effects.

### *Guidelines For Writing a Cause and Effect Essay*

1. Select a subject that lends itself to the analysis of cause-and-effect relationships. Use prewriting techniques to develop a list of causes, effects, or both.
2. Group the causes and effects identified in your prewritten material. If appropriate, separate immediate causes from ultimate causes.
3. Decide on your approach to the subject—that is, if the causes are clear, then concentrate on the effects; if the effects are clear, then concentrate on the causes; or concentrate on both the causes and effects. Be sure to emphasize the most important causes or effects to avoid becoming distracted by the obvious or trivial. Determine which causes or effects should be developed in a single paragraph and which should be developed in two paragraphs.
4. With the general purpose of the essay in mind, write a tentative thesis that signals whether you will mainly

emphasize causes, effects, or causes and effects. Write the first draft.

5. Revise your essay, avoiding the *post hoc, ergo propter hoc* fallacy.

## *A Student Essay Developed by Cause and Effect*

For a media studies course, Nancy Pringle responded to the following writing assignment:

> Discuss what you perceive to be the effects of modern communications technology on populations living under totalitarian governments. Concentrate on countries discussed in class, that is primarily countries in Eastern Europe and in Asia.

The class had just completed a unit on the uses of technology in revolutionary movements in Eastern Europe and the Middle East. Pringle decided to write about former Soviet-bloc countries. She knew the role televised news and video cameras played in recent liberation movements and could use this knowledge. But she felt any discussion of contemporary technology would have to include a discussion of the potential impact of the Internet.

### Tools of Freedom, Tools of Oppression

*Pringle's introduction establishes a common ground with readers by referring to the opinions of well-known writers who are concerned with the same subject. She closes the introduction with the thesis, which sharply contrasts with the view of the two writers.*

George Orwell's *1984* and Aldous Huxley's *Brave New World*, both anti-utopian novels, warn of the effect communication technology might have on society. Orwell warns that government might use it to control society by inflicting pain. Huxley warns that governments might use it to control society by stimulating pleasure. The ultimate effect would be the same: Dictators would stay in power by controlling history's most powerful medium—television. Recent events, however, seem to prove both authors wrong. The growth of television and related technology did not result in oppression; it resulted in liberation.

*The opening topic sentence establishes that the effects of television will be the subject of this paragraph.*

*Pringle develops this paragraph by giving two examples: entertainment programs and news broadcasts.*

*She ends the paragraph with a causal chain.*

In Europe's communist-bloc countries, television fueled the 1989 desire for liberty. Although Communist governments controlled their own broadcast systems, their citizens still had access to Western entertainment programs and films. These programs indirectly showed that West Europeans had more freedom and were more affluent than East Europeans, all of which generated discontent. Moreover, many oppressed Soviet-bloc countries saw news broadcasts that spilled over from neighboring countries. Oppressed East Berliners would watch West German news broadcasts. Communist-controlled Hungarians watched Austrian news broadcasts. People throughout the Soviet Union, East Germany, and Czechoslovakia watched liberalized Polish news broadcasts. Nightly news reports of political victories against Communist governments filled the airwaves. Soon a domino effect began: Polish victories inspired Hungarians; Hungarian victories inspired East Germans; and East German victories inspired the Czechoslovaks.

*The opening topic sentence announces that the effects of video cameras and VCRs will be the subject.*

*Pringle develops this paragraph with two examples: one from Poland and one from Czechoslovakia.*

Inexpensive video cameras and playback systems also dramatically affected liberation politics. In Poland Solidarity, the workers union that spearheaded the early Polish revolution, spread its message with crude "home movies" reproduced by the thousands and played in homes throughout Poland. The message was quite simple—there is an alternative to Communist-party rule—and had the effect of keeping the freedom movement alive. In Czechoslovakia, when the government-controlled television stations suppressed reports of uprisings, students used video cameras to film the events, copied the cassettes, and distributed them throughout the country, thus revealing to an entire nation the secret actions of its repressive government.

*This topic sentence announces that there is a major shift in the essay's direction—from past communication technologies to future technology—the Internet. What will be its future effects? she asks. Her prediction is a surprise—it will have little effect, she maintains; economic security will determine whether or not democratic values will survive.*

If television, video cameras, and VCRs helped fuel liberation movements throughout Eastern Europe, what will be the effect of today's information highway, that is, the global Internet? Each day brings more information into homes throughout the West. This information is not designed by governments to indoctrinate its citizens. Since information posted in "networld" has no regard for national boundaries or ideologies, it presents a variety of viewpoints to stimulate dialog among diverse populations. But only the most devout optimists believe that information alone will keep the democratic movement alive. In many newly liberated countries economic chaos will set in, and as the old demagogues tumble, new ones will rise, perhaps with different faces but with the same results. Information may fuel the spirit, but economics fuels the stomach. Unless today's liberation movements can satisfy a population's desire for economic stability, the result will be to reinstitute what's known—the state-run economy, which will ultimately lead to the new dictator who will smile benevolently at the desire for free access to information while keeping a tight grip on production and distribution.

*She concludes with the observation that Orwell and Huxley may yet prove to be right.*

Electronic media at first glance seems to prove both George Orwell and Aldous Huxley wrong. As never before more people have taken to the streets in the name of freedom to overthrow their oppressive governments. But this is merely act two of a dramatic confrontation between dictatorship and democracy. In act three we may find that Orwell and Huxley serve as the chorus that has predicted the reversal of events.

### *Comments*

Pringle had a head start on this assignment because she had taken extensive notes during the unit that concentrated on communication technology's effect on revolutionary movements. But after closely analyzing the subject, she realized she should also include her observations regarding the Internet, perhaps the most dramatic technological advancement since the revolutions in Eastern Europe. The Internet section is brief, only one paragraph, but well developed and effective. In it she reaches a conclusion that seems to contradict her earlier position. It doesn't. It merely extends her observations into the future.

Pringle concentrates on the effects of technology, both immediate effects as they manifested themselves in the revolutions and ultimate effects as she predicts the outcome of broadened access to the Internet in postrevolutionary Eastern Europe.

Development Strategy. Pringle immediately establishes a common ground with the reader by referring to two well-known authors, George Orwell and Aldous Huxley, who see media being used in different ways but with the same effect—oppressive dictatorship. In contrast, she states her position in a thesis statement: *The growth of television and related technology did not result in oppression; it resulted in liberation.*

In the second paragraph, Pringle begins the discussion section of her essay by presenting the effects of television, the most familiar communication technology. She explains how it affected the thinking of Eastern-bloc populations and ends with a causal chain of events that helped topple some oppressive governments.

In the third paragraph, Pringle discusses the effect of video cameras and playback systems on oppressed populations. She gives two examples: Polish revolutionaries, who used crude videos to spread information, and Czech revolutionaries who used videos to overcome suppressed reports of uprisings throughout the country. The result, of course, was more access to information that led to more uprisings.

In the fourth paragraph, Pringle extends the discussion to the

Internet. She raises the question: What will be the long-term effect of this new worldwide source for uncensored information? Her answer is brief—very little. She maintains that if economic stability does not return to Eastern Europe, then state-controlled economies will return no matter how much access to uncensored information citizens have.

In the conclusion Pringle returns to Orwell and Huxley. She points out that the confrontation between dictatorship and democracy isn't over. The ultimate result may prove the two authors right.

**Revision.** In an early draft Pringle tended to overstate her case and to pack too much information into her sentences. Readers, therefore, had trouble following her discussion. For the next draft, she revised these sentences for clarity by modifying her overly general observations, breaking the sentences into smaller units, and adding clarifying details and phrases. For example, study paragraph three along with her revisions:

's Communistic bloc-Countries, television
In Europe ~~television caused the 1989 revolutions.~~
fueled the 1989 desire for liberty.
Although Communist governments ~~totally~~ controlled ~~all~~ their
own broadcast systems, their citizens still had access to
These programs
Western entertainment programs and films. ~~which~~ indirectly
showed that West Europeans had more freedom and were
all of
more affluent than East Europeans, which generated discon-
moreover, many oppressed Soviet-bloc
tent. ~~News program broadcasts spilled~~ over from neighboring
Countries saw news broadcasts that spilled
countries. ~~which were more liberalized and showed reports of~~
Oppressed East Berliners would watch
~~political victories against Communist governments. Soon vic-~~
West German news broadcasts. Communistic
~~tories in one country inspired victories in others.~~
controlled Hungarians watched Austrian news

broadcasts. People throughout the Soviet Union, East Germany and Czechoslovakia watched liberalized Polish news broadcasts. Nightly news reports of political victories against Communist governments filled the airwaves. Soon a domino effect began: Polish victories inspired Hungarians; Hungarian victories inspired East Germans; and East German victories inspired the Czechoslovaks.

Now compare the revised draft of these paragraph with the final draft.

In Europe's communist-bloc countries, television fueled the 1989 desire for liberty. Although Communist governments controlled their own broadcast systems, their citizens still had access to Western entertainment programs and films. These programs indirectly showed that West Europeans had more freedom and were more affluent than East Europeans, all of which generated discontent. Moreover, many oppressed Soviet-bloc countries saw news broadcasts that spilled over from neighboring countries. Oppressed East Berliners would watch West German news broadcasts. Communist-controlled Hungarians watched Austrian news broadcasts. People throughout the Soviet Union, East Germany, and Czechoslovakia watched liberalized Polish news broadcasts. Nightly news reports of political victories against Communist governments filled the airwaves. Soon a domino effect began: Polish victories inspired Hungarians; Hungarian victories inspired East Germans; and East German victories inspired the Czechoslovaks.

As you will see while reading the essays that follow, professional writers frequently mix example and comparison and con-

## *Peer Review*

You may be asked to write an essay about one of the readings that follow. Before you meet with your writing group, review this introduction. As your read the papers of your group members, use these general writing principles about cause and effect to help guide your comments.

1. The paper should not belabor the obvious; it should not present causes or effects that are already well-known to most readers.
2. The causes that are discussed should clearly lead to the effects, and the effects discussed should clearly result from the causes.
3. The cause-and-effect relations should be based on sufficient information and logical reasoning.

trast patterns into essays dominated by cause and effect. Study these professionals for their craft. Examine how they construct their discussions. Separate the causes from the effects. And separate the immediate effects from the ultimate effects. Through this kind of critical reading, you will develop your own writing skills.

# ❦ E. M. Forster ❦

*Edward Morgan Forster was born in London in 1879 and attended King's College, Cambridge, where he studied classics and history and developed a strong interest in foreign cultures. From a family of bankers, he had no interest in business, and after finishing his education traveled to India, Greece, and Italy. He later settled in London to pursue a career as a writer. His travels in India (in 1912 and again in 1921) inspired his best-known novel,* A Passage to India *(1924). His other books include the novels,* A Room with a View *(1908) and* Howard's End *(1910), two collections of essays, and a collection of short stories. Forster died in 1970.*

## *My Wood*

*This selection is from Forster's* Abinger Harvest *(1936), a collection of essays. He opens with a reference to his novel* A Passage to India, *and uses his experience in buying a piece of land to examine the effects of property ownership. He distinguishes between the unavoidable materialism of "life on earth" and the problematic desire for ownership.*

*We usually associate wealth with freedom. In reading this essay, be alert to the ways Forster turns the common perception around to show how property ownership actually restricts freedom.*

---

A few years ago I wrote a book which dealt in part with the difficulties of the English in India. Feeling that they would have had no difficulties in India themselves, the Americans read the book freely. The more they read it the better it made them feel, and a cheque to the author was the result. I bought a wood with the cheque. It is not a large wood—it contains scarcely any trees, and it is intersected, blast it, by a public footpath. Still, it is the first property that I have owned, so it is right that other people should participate in my shame, and should ask 1 themselves, in accents that will vary in horror, this very important question: What is the effect of property upon the character? Don't let's touch economics; the effect of private ownership upon the community as a whole is another question—a more important question, perhaps, but another one. Let's keep to psychology. If you own things, what's their effect on you? What's the effect on me of my wood?

In the first place, it makes me feel heavy. Property does have this effect. Property produces men of weight, and it was a man of weight who failed to get into the Kingdom of Heaven. He was not wicked, that unfortunate millionaire in the parable, he was only stout; he stuck out in front, not to mention behind, and as he wedged himself this way and that in the crystalline entrance and bruised his well-fed flanks, he saw beneath him a comparatively slim camel passing through the eye of a needle and being woven into the robe of God. The Gospels all through couple stoutness and slowness. They point out what is perfectly obvious, yet seldom realized: that if you have a lot of things you cannot move about a lot, that furniture requires dusting, dusters require servants, servants require insurance stamps, and the whole tangle of them makes you think twice before you accept an invitation to dinner or go for a bathe in the Jordan. Sometimes the Gospels proceed further and say with Tolstoy that property is sinful; they approach the difficult ground of asceticism here, where I cannot follow them. But as to the immediate effects of property on people, they just show straightforward logic. It produces men of weight. Men of weight cannot, by definition, move like the lightning from the East unto the West, and the ascent of a fourteen-stone bishop into a pulpit is thus the exact antithesis of the coming of the Son of Man. My wood makes me feel heavy. 2

In the second place, it makes me feel it ought to be larger. 3

The other day I heard a twig snap in it. I was annoyed at first, for I thought that someone was blackberrying, and depreciating the value of the undergrowth. On coming nearer, I saw it was not a man who had trodden on the twig and snapped it, but a bird, and I felt pleased. My bird. The bird was not equally 4 pleased. Ignoring the relation between us, it took fright as soon as it saw the shape of my face, and flew straight over the boundary hedge into a field, the property of Mrs. Henessy, where it sat down with a loud squawk. It had become Mrs. Henessy's bird. Something seemed grossly amiss here, something that would not have occurred had the wood been larger. I could not afford to buy Mrs. Henessy out, I dared not murder her, and limitations of this sort beset me on every side. Ahab did not want that vineyard—he only needed it to round off his property, preparatory to plotting a new curve—and all the land around my wood has become necessary to me in order to round off the wood. A boundary protects. But—poor little thing—the boundary ought in its turn to be protected. Noises on the edge of it. Children throw stones. A little more, and then a little more, until we reach the sea. Happy Canute! Happier Alexander! And after all, why should even the world be the limit of possession? A rocket containing a Union Jack, will, it is hoped, be shortly fired at the moon. Mars. Sirius. Beyond which . . . But these immensities ended by saddening me. I could not suppose that my wood was the destined nucleus of universal dominion—it is so very small and contains no mineral wealth beyond the blackberries. Nor was I comforted when Mrs. Henessy's bird took alarm for the second time and flew clean away from us all, under the belief that it belonged to itself.

5 In the third place, property makes its owner feel that he ought to do something to it. Yet he isn't sure what. A restlessness comes over him, a vague sense that he has a personality to express—the same sense which, without any vagueness, leads the artist to an act of creation. Sometimes I think I will cut down such trees as remain in the wood, at other times I want to fill up the gaps between them with new trees. Both impulses are pretentious and empty. They are not honest movements towards money-making or beauty. They spring from a foolish desire to express myself and from an inability to enjoy what I have got. Creation, property, enjoyment form a sinister trinity in the human mind. Creation and enjoyment are both very, very good, yet they are often unattainable without a material basis, and at such moments property

pushes itself in as a substitute, saying, "Accept me instead—I'm good enough for all three." It is not enough. It is, as Shakespeare said of lust, "The expense of spirit in a waste of shame": it is "Before, a joy proposed; behind, a dream." Yet we don't know how to shun it. It is forced on us by our economic system as the alternative to starvation. It is also forced on us by an internal defect in the soul, by the feeling that in property may lie the germs of self-development and of exquisite or heroic deeds. Our life on earth is, and ought to be, material and carnal. But we have not yet learned to manage our materialism and carnality properly; they are still entangled with the desire for ownership, where (in the words of Dante) "Possession is one with loss."

And this brings us to our fourth and final point: the black- 6
berries.

Blackberries are not plentiful in this meagre grove, but they 7
are easily seen from the public footpath which traverses it, and all too easily gathered. Foxgloves, too—people will pull up the foxgloves, and ladies of an educational tendency even grub for toadstools to show them on the Monday in class. Other ladies, less educated, roll down the bracken in the arms of their gentlemen friends. There is paper, there are tins. Pray, does my wood belong to me or doesn't it? And, if it does, should I not own it best by allowing no one else to walk there? There is a wood near Lyme Regis, also cursed by a public footpath, where the owner has not hesitated on this point. He had built high stone walls each side of the path, and has spanned it by bridges, so that the public circulate like termites when he gorges on the blackberries unseen. He really does own his wood, this able chap. Dives in Hell did pretty well, but the gulf dividing him from Lazarus could be traversed by vision, and nothing traverses it here. And perhaps I shall come to this in time. I shall wall in and fence out until I really taste the sweets of property. Enormously stout, endlessly avaricious, pseudo-creative, intensely selfish, I shall weave upon my forehead the quadruple crown of possession until those nasty Bolshies come and take it off again and thrust me aside into the outer darkness.

## *Meaning and Purpose*

1. What is Forster's purpose in "My Wood," and where does he most clearly state it?
2. In paragraph 5, he says "property makes its owner feel that he ought to do something to it." What do you own that you have done something to, just because you owned it? A pair of shoes? a jacket? a car? Briefly describe the ways in which you changed it and your reasons for changing it.
3. An allusion often refers to a historical or literary figure, event, or object. Choose one allusion from this essay and learn more about it. If you chose "Canute," you might look it up in an unabridged dictionary, an encyclopedia, or other reference works. Select an allusion other than "Canute" and describe it briefly.
4. In paragraph 2, Forster says that owning many things restricts one's freedom. How does owning the wood restrict the author's freedom?
5. The first paragraph includes the words "blast it." Why does the author use that interjection?

## *Strategy*

1. Study the cause-and-effect structure of the essay. Does Forster alternate cause and effect in each paragraph, or develop them one at a time in separate paragraphs? Explain the effectiveness of the structure.
2. In the middle of paragraph 2 is the statement, "if you have a lot of things you cannot move about a lot, that furniture requires dusting, dusters require servants, servants require insurance stamps, and the whole tangle of them makes you think twice before you accept an invitation to dinner or go for a bathe in the Jordan." What is the cause-and-effect structure of this sentence called, and how is it used here?
3. The last paragraph in this essay says that the owner of a wood near Lyme Regis "really does own his wood." What caused that ownership? What is the effect of that kind of ownership?

4. In paragraph 6, he says that the fourth and final point in the essay is blackberries. But it is not. What is the fourth and final point, and why does the author tell us it is blackberries?

## Style

1. What is the occupation of the "ladies of an educational tendency," in paragraph 7, and why do you think the author describes them as he does?
2. In paragraph 4, the author says, "A little more, and then a little more, until we reach the sea." What is the author describing in this sentence?
3. Look at paragraphs 3 and 6. Why do you think each has only one sentence?

## Writing Tasks

1. The American writer Henry David Thoreau said, "A man is rich in proportion to the number of things which he can afford to let alone." E. M. Forster's essay "My Wood" has much in common with Thoreau's statement. In your paper, consider being rich a cause and discuss what you think are some of its effects. Develop each effect in a paragraph.
2. Here is a list of causes. Write about one effect of each. Develop at least one causal chain.
   Teenager watching MTV
   Landfill overflowing
   Apple trees blossoming
   Car breaking down in the fast lane during rush hour

## ❦ Stephen King ❦

*Stephen King was born in Portland, Maine, in 1947 and graduated from the University of Maine in 1970. Before finding enormous success with his writing, King worked in a knitting mill and as a janitor, laundry worker, and high school English teacher. Since then, he has become, arguably, the world's most successful writer of horror fiction. He has published short story collections, screenplays, and nearly thirty novels that have sold over 20 million copies. Many of those novels—including* Carrie *(1974),* The Shining *(1977), and* Pet Sematary *(1983)—have been made into movies. His short story "The Body," from the collection* Night Shift, *was produced as the film* Stand By Me. *His most recent novels include* Insomnia *(1994) and* Rose Madder *(1995). King also plays rhythm guitar for the Rock Bottom Remainders, a rock band composed entirely of professional writers. Amy Tan* *(see p.224–230)* *is a Remainderette—she sings backup vocals—with the same band.*

# *Why We Crave Horror Movies*

*In this essay, first published in Playboy magazine, Stephen King speculates on the reasons why horror films have been so enormously popular over the years. He concludes that they not only entertain in a ghoulish way, but also serve an important psychological and social purpose.*

*While you read, weigh the validity of King's conclusions against your own firsthand experience of horror films.*

---

I think that we're all mentally ill; those of us outside the asylums only hide it a little better—and maybe not all that much better, after all. We've all known people who talk to themselves, people who sometimes squinch their faces into horrible grimaces when they believe no one is watching, people who have some hysterical fear—of snakes, the dark, the tight place, the long drop . . . and, of course, those final worms and grubs that are waiting so patiently underground. 1

When we pay our four or five bucks and seat ourselves at tenth-row center in a theater showing a horror movie, we are daring the nightmare. 2

Why? Some of the reasons are simple and obvious. To show that we can, that we are not afraid, that we can ride this roller coaster. Which is not to say that a really good horror movie may not surprise a scream out of us at some point, the way we may scream when the roller coaster twists through a complete 360 or plows through a lake at the bottom of the drop. And horror movies, like roller coasters, have always been the special province of the young; by the time one turns 40 or 50, one's appetite for double twists or 360-degree loops may be considerably depleted. 3

We also go to re-establish our feelings of essential normality; the horror movie is innately conservative, even reactionary. Freda Jackson as the horrible melting woman in *Die, Monster, Die*! confirms for us that no matter how far we may be removed from the beauty of a Robert Redford or a Diana Ross, we are still light-years from true ugliness. 4

And we go to have fun. 5

Ah, but this is where the ground starts to slope away, isn't it? Because this is a very peculiar sort of fun, indeed. The fun comes from seeing others menaced—sometimes killed. One critic has suggested that if pro football has become the voyeur's version of combat, then the horror film has become the modern version of the public lynching. 6

It is true that the mythic, "fairy-tale" horror film intends to take away the shades of gray. . . . It urges us to put away our more civilized and adult penchant for analysis and to become children again, seeing things in pure blacks and whites. It may be that horror movies provide psychic relief on this level because this invitation to lapse into simplicity, irrationality and even outright madness is extended so rarely. We are told we may allow our emotions a free rein . . . or no rein at all. 7

If we are all insane, then sanity becomes a matter of degree. If your insanity leads you to carve up women like Jack the Ripper or the Cleveland Torso Murderer, we clap you away in the funny farm (but neither of those two amateur-night surgeons was ever 8 caught, heh-heh-heh); if, on the other hand, your insanity leads you only to talk to yourself when you're under stress or to pick your nose on your morning bus, then you are left alone to go about your business . . . though it is doubtful that you will ever be invited to the best parties.

The potential lyncher is in almost all of us (excluding saints, 9
past and present; but then, most saints have been crazy in their own ways), and every now and then, he has to be let loose to scream and roll around in the grass. Our emotions and our fears form their own body, and we recognize that it demands its own exercise to maintain proper muscle tone. Certain of these emotional muscles are accepted—even exalted—in civilized society; they are, of course, the emotions that tend to maintain the status quo of civilization itself. Love, friendship, loyalty, kindness—these are all the emotions that we applaud, emotions that have been immortalized in the couplets of Hallmark cards and in the verses (I don't dare call it poetry) of Leonard Nimoy.

When we exhibit these emotions, society showers us with 10
positive reinforcement; we learn this even before we get out of diapers. When, as children, we hug our rotten little puke of a sister and give her a kiss, all the aunts and uncles smile and twit and cry, "Isn't he the sweetest little thing?" Such coveted treats as chocolate-covered graham crackers often follow. But if we deliberately slam the rotten little puke of a sister's fingers in the door; sanctions follow—angry remonstrance from parents, aunts and uncles; instead of a chocolate-covered graham cracker, a spanking.

But anticivilization emotions don't go away, and they demand 11
periodic exercise. We have such "sick" jokes as, "What's the difference between a truckload of bowling balls and a truckload of dead babies? (You can't unload a truckload of bowling balls with a pitchfork . . . a joke, by the way, that I heard originally from a ten-year-old). Such a joke may surprise a laugh or a grin out of us even as we recoil, a possibility that confirms the thesis: If we share a brotherhood of man, then we also share an insanity of man. None of which is intended as a defense of either the sick joke or insanity but merely as an explanation of why the best horror films,

like the best fairy tales, manage to be reactionary, anarchistic, and revolutionary all at the same time.

The mythic horror movie, like the sick joke, has a dirty job to do. It deliberately appeals to all that is worst in us. It is morbidity unchained, our most base instincts let free, our nastiest fantasies realized . . . and it all happens, fittingly enough, in the dark. For those reasons, good liberals often shy away from horror films. For myself, I like to see the most aggressive of them—*Dawn of the Dead*, for instance—as lifting a trap door in the civilized forebrain and throwing a basket of raw meat to the hungry alligators swimming around in that subterranean river beneath. 12

Why bother? Because it keeps them from getting out, man. It keeps them down there and me up here. It was Lennon and McCartney who said that all you need is love, and I would agree with that. 13

As long as you keep the gators fed. 14

---

## *Meaning and Purpose*

1. What is King's thesis? Is it explicitly stated or is it implied?
2. Is King serious when he claims in the opening sentence that "we're all mentally ill"? What exactly does he mean by this? Explain.
3. In paragraph 4 King asserts horror movies are "innately conservative, even reactionary," and in paragraph 11 he claims them to be "reactionary, anarchistic, and revolutionary all at the same time." Explain what he means by these claims.
4. Why, according to King, are horror movies both a psychological and social good?

## *Strategy*

1. King grabs our attention with the opening sentence. Explain how the meaning of that sentence relates to the rest of the essay.

2. What does King claim are the immediate causes of the popularity of horror films? What is the ultimate cause? (See the introduction to this chapter, p. 328–344.)
3. Explain how King organizes his essay around the immediate and ultimate causes for the popularity of horror films. How much time and space does he spend on each? What effect does this organizational pattern have on the reader?
4. Why does King change from the first person singular (I) in the first sentence to the first person plural (we) in the second?
5. What evidence does King offer to support his claims about the reasons for the popularity of horror movies?

## *Style*

1. Reread the essay paying close attention to King's use of concrete language (Glossary, p. 683–708) and metaphor (Glossary p. 683–708). Point out passages where King uses these devices and comment on their effectiveness. Try translating at least two of these passages into more common usage. Which version is more lively?
2. What is King's tone in the essay (Glossary, p.683–708)? How does he establish that tone? Explain.
3. Closely examine the analogy King uses in paragraph 3 (Glossary, p. 683–708). What idea does it explain and how effectively does it clarify that idea?
4. If necessary, look the following words up in a dictionary: *grimaces, hysterical* (1); *province* (3); *voyeur* (6); *penchant, psychic* (7); *exalted* (9); *twit, sanctions, remonstrance* (10); *recoil, anarchistic* (11); *morbidity, subterranean* (13).

## *Writing Tasks*

1. Write an essay in which you explain the reasons (causes) that you attend horror films regularly, or attend them only occasionally, or never attend them at all. Use King's essay as a model, in

that you organize your essay so that you spend more time on ultimate causes and relatively less time on immediate causes.

2. Write an essay that examines the validity, or the invalidity, of King's claims in "Why We Crave Horror Movies." Make sure that you include as much supportive evidence as you can to prove your thesis.

## ❦ Gerald Early ❦

*A teacher of English and Afro-American studies at Washington University in St. Louis, Gerald Early began his career writing weekly columns for his college newspaper,* The Daily Pennsylvanian. *His work has appeared in* The Best American Essays *of 1988 and 1991. In the introduction to a collection of his essays,* Tuxedo Junction, Essays on American Culture *(1989), Early credits Amiri Baraka's (Le Roi Jones's)* Home: Social Essays *(1966) as the book that created his desire to be an essayist. Early's most recent book is* Daughters: On Family and Fatherhood *(1994).*

# *Baby, Take a Bow*

*In this selection from* Tuxedo Junction, *Gerald Early ponders the significance of the selection of Vanessa Williams as the first black Miss America and considers the role Miss America plays in our culture. He speculates on possible effects of Williams's selection on black people, white people, and the Miss America pageant itself.*

*Although the essay is a serious one, notice the gentle humor Early uses to establish a warm relationship with his readers.*

---

*Rich relations give crusts of bread and such.*

—Billie Holiday, "God Bless the Child"

*For the benefit of those who never knew*
*I'm a Miss America! How do you do!*
*I won a prize in '44 and of course all this is through with;*
*And I have a great big silver loving cup that I don't know what to do with.*

*I'm Miss America . . . so what?*
*They had me posing like I wouldn't*
*And they photographed me where they shouldn't,*

*But it's nice to be Miss America, it makes life so trés gai,*
*Now if I could only find a way to eat three times a day.*

—sung by Miss Venus Ramey, Miss America of 1944, in her nightclub act after her inauspicious reign

Dolgin's is the sort of store that reveals just what retailing will be like everywhere in America's future, a future that will show that expansion is reduction, after all; Dolgin's shelves tell the story of the slouch toward a cunning yet bland anonymity that has made the old style of crass salesmanship through the frenzied pitch outmoded. It is stores like Dolgin's that Sears wants to imitate, creating an ambience like an American consumer's fantasyland where customers buy items about which they know very little because through some sort of subliminal hearsay they were informed that the product was good or needed. American retailing nowadays does not seem condensed so much as it seems compressed; every huge retailing outlet must sell everything from blank tape cassettes to baby food, and the workers are no longer interested in selling anything; they merely "ring you out." One is left almost eerily to the mercies of one's own impulses. It was pleasant to think that at one time a store such as Dolgin's thought the customer needed the services of an informed, trained salesperson; but customers no longer have needs that must be accommodated, simply urges that must be appeased. Shopping, to a large extent, is a tawdry sort of therapy; one can push a cart up and down the aisles of any store now, not just supermarkets, and commune with the self while half believing that America is still a land of plenty. This mass shopping habit, so similar to the vision of retailing in Edward Bellamy's 1888 futuristic novel *Looking Backward*, is simply the intensified loneliness of the herd instinct of popular culture; the alienation we experience these days is not from the strange but from the familiar. 1

It was at Dolgin's that our new Miss America made her first—and probably only—appearance in St. Louis, giving away autographed snapshots of herself with anyone who cared to be in a picture with her. In fact, the event was advertised as "Have your photograph taken with Miss America." I suppose it was fitting that she should be appearing at Dolgin's; she was, in some sense, 2 another product that everyone should certainly be familiar with. There were no introductions made when she appeared before huge crowds waiting to see her and she said little or nothing to the people who came, one by one, to have their picture taken with her. Words were superfluous for someone who seemed to be more of an emanation from the Godhead than a human being. She smiled beautifully and constantly in a way that was completely expressionless. Her smile was not devoid of meaning; it resonated a rather genteel mocking quality that heightened its bored detachment. I especially liked how she stood on the ambiguous edge of being a tragic mulatto and a conjure woman, on the edge of absolute love and absolute power; for, at that moment, sitting in that store, she was the most loved and most suspect woman in America. She was loved as all Miss Americas are loved; she was, after all, no different from her predecessors: a sweet girl with ambition and a more than ardent belief that anyone in America can make it by working hard enough. She was the most suspect woman in America because she is black and, as such, is as inscrutable a symbol of American womanhood as one could hope to find. In other words, some blacks don't trust her motives and some whites don't trust her abilities. Yet she became, for those people in Dolgin's, America's version of a princess without a realm or, to put it more precisely, with a limitless realm since it was the entire fantasy of American popular culture. Doubtless, Dolgin's never had so many black folk pass through its portals or, at least, so many black folk pass through who had absolutely no intention of buying anything. There were young black men with fancy cameras, young black women with little sons and daughters dressed in their Sunday best, older black women who giggled with excitement every time they saw Miss America smile. It was as if they had all come to pay homage to some great person instead of merely having a picture taken with a young woman of twenty who had done nothing more notable than win a contest, which, I suppose, was more an act of chance than anything else. Yet these black people, who had come out in frightful rush-hour traffic in a tremendous autumnal rainstorm, must have felt that it was an act of destiny that this girl was crowned Miss America.

"This is history, man," said one young black man to another. "I would've come through a hurricane to meet *this* Miss America. They sure ain't gonna pick another black woman to be Miss America no time soon." 3

"That ain't no lie," replied the other. "White folks might be sorry they picked this one before the year is over." 4

"She sure is pretty," said a grandmotherly-looking black woman. "I never thought they'd pick a black girl to be Miss America during my lifetime." 5

"Hey, white folks gonna think we taking over," said another young black man. "First, we get a black mayor in Chicago, then we get the Martin Luther King holiday, and now we got Miss America. The man who run Dolgin's figure the only time he see this many niggers in his store is if he was giving away watermelons or Cadillacs." 6

People standing nearby laughed at the last remark. 7

"That's just it," said a young black woman. "They're not use to *black* people coming out to see Miss America." 8

And indeed that young woman spoke truer than she knew. In the past, I would imagine that the few black people who bothered to see Miss America when she made a public appearance were motivated only by the most disinterested sort of curiosity, a curiosity approaching the immaculate objectivity of the scientist: for, of course, a white woman as Miss America was merely an object for conversation, not veneration. For the first time, black people can now be motivated to see Miss America for the same reason that whites would crowd stores like Dolgin's to see her in the past: out of admiration, that sort of public love that, in the instance of black Americans, is so dammed up because they have so few public figures they can love so unconditionally and totally because nothing more is expected of them than that they look beautiful and act in some remotely "cultured," polished way. To be sure, a good many black people will seek excuses to hate our new Miss America, but a much greater number will love her obsessively. 9

There were many white folk standing and waiting as well, and while some probably came out of curiosity, most seemed to esteem truly and deeply our new Miss America. One blond woman, look- 10 ing as though she had just escaped a dull office and a duller job, was positively flushed with the electricity of the moment. A mother had her son rehearse these lines to say to Miss America when he would finally meet her: "I think you're very beautiful and I'm glad you're Miss America." Another woman had her young daughter, perhaps ten or twelve, wearing a blue dress, patent leather pumps, stockings, a tiara, and a banner draped across the shoulder that proclaimed "Miniature Miss." This youngster, possibly a future Miss America, certainly a future contestant in somebody's beauty contest, was the only person to curtsy before Miss America as if she were meeting the Queen of England. I heard a thirtyish white man speaking to a young black fellow: "I just had to come and get a picture of Miss America. I think this is wonderful. My wife won't believe that I saw Miss America unless I get a picture. I think this is wonderful. I can't believe it." I think that Miss America must have been gratified and grateful that so many whites were there, not so much because she sought their approval but because she sought their acceptance. Their presence might assure that her reign would not be a separate but equal one. The importance of this cannot be overstated, for she has probably unconsciously conceived her symbolic stature as a force to fuse, if only momentarily, our divided culture. Since her black skin, by virtue of the historic burden it carries, brings the element of "social relevance" to the dazzling idiocy of beauty contests, our new Miss America must be aware that she can do more with the title than any white woman ever could, that she can greatly enhance the symbolic yet antique meaning of young womanhood in this culture simply because she is black. She has effectively done two things: she has encouraged blacks to participate in this fairly sterile cultural rite of passage; she has revitalized white interest in the contest by forcing them to see the title in a new and probably more deeply appreciative light. For whites who relish the idea of a black woman as Miss America, she simply serves the artless assumption that America is truly a land without racism, a land of equal opportunity at last. After all, so goes the reasoning from these quarters, twenty-five years ago, if Dolgin's existed in St. Louis, blacks probably could not shop there; they certainly could not work there.

Now a young black woman as Miss America is signing autographs in such a store. Racial progress moves apace. Whites who detest the fact that a black woman is Miss America will simply campaign all the harder to make sure that such a lapse does not occur again. For more whites than one might care to imagine, the Miss America crown and the heavyweight title in prizefighting are the flimsy supports for the idea of racial superiority along sexual lines.

The last time a woman who was chosen Miss America was 11 even slightly enmeshed in a similar welter of social and cultural complexities was in 1945, when Bess Myerson, another Miss New York, became the first Jew to win the pageant. Admittedly, only *Life* magazine (of all the publications that ran stories on Myerson during her reign) briefly mentioned her religion; it was never an issue of public discussion because it was never an object of publicity. Yet with the ending of the Second World War—a war fought, in large part, against the absolute nihilism of pathological racism—and with the holocaust and the subject of war trials still fresh on everyone's mind, the selection of a Jew by the Miss America judges strikes one as being, at least, self-consciously but subtly profound or momentous; it was a contrived but important effort to legitimize the contest. Since the 1945 contest was the first in which scholarships were given away, it was essential that the winner also have some real talent. Myerson had already received her B.A. degree in music from Hunter College when she entered the pageant, and during the talent segment she played Gershwin on the flute and Grieg on the piano. There was little doubt that she was not only the most skilled contestant for *that* year, but probably the most gifted entrant in the entire history of the pageant. As *The New York Times* stated in an article printed the day after she won: "The only reason she entered the contest in the first place was . . . the lure of a $5,000 scholarship that would enable her to continue for another four years her twelve-year study of music." Myerson was not simply another pretty face; she changed the entire nature of the contest from being a gross flesh show to being, of all things, a scholarship competition. Vanessa Williams is seen by the people who run the Miss America contest as another possible legitimizing force. The selection of Myerson did not change the fundamental spirit or intention of the contest; nor did her winning enhance the general caliber of the average contestant who came after her. Myerson simply eased the way for the contest to return to its fantasy, pop-culture preoccupations and continue to select gentile mediocrities. Williams will most likely serve the same ends; the judges can, with a cleaner conscience, return to selecting white women almost exclusively. None of this is exactly sinister; it is, in fact, the bald, guileless stupidity and pointlessness of it all that galls one more than anything.

I stood in line for nearly an hour, along with my wife and two 12
small daughters, waiting to be photographed with Miss America. I might not have gone through all of this had my children been boys, but I knew I simply had to have my daughters in a photograph with the first black Miss America. They would, at least, find it amusing to see the picture when they were older and they might even think it "significant." The photograph turned out to be less than I hoped for. My four-year-old, who would have infinitely preferred having her photograph taken with Michael Jackson, was a bit confused by it all. My two-year-old was completely terrified of the crowd; she never even faced the camera when the picture was taken. So the picture shows a smiling, demure, quite lovely Miss America with a blue and black suit, light brown hair, and green eyes as bright and brilliant as slightly moistened, clear glass beads; a young father smiling slightly with his two children on his knees—one faintly nonplussed and greatly surprised, the other faintly annoyed and greatly distressed. I suppose I am the most humorous figure in the photograph, looking like nothing so much as a candidate for Father of the Year. Miss America probably felt a bit of sympathy for the valiant young father and his uncooperative children—but not half as much as I felt for her, traveling to all the stores like Dolgin's all over the country, signing autographs by the hundreds of thousands, surrounded by more guards than the president, seeing the worst of America as a grotesque phantasmagoria of shopping malls, hotels, and airports. As she sat there in Dolgin's, smiling benignly as each person stepped forward to have his or her picture taken, I could not help but think of her as a courtesan receiving her clients with graceful indifference. All of this was surely immaculate enough; no one was allowed to touch her. But that seems only to have intensified the perversity of the

service she was providing; for to maintain the purity of her presence, the public was, in some way, being reminded that it could only defile her, if it had its druthers. And perhaps we would have, since nothing brings out American bloodthirstiness more boldly than the victimization of the innocent.

We are secretly driven slightly mad by the fact that Miss America is sweet and wholesome because it reveals our tremendous preoccupation with our own vehemently stated innocence. Miss America is sweet and wholesome because she symbolizes our deep neurotic obsession with chastity (which is really the only quality that makes a young girl truly sweet and wholesome and *desirable* in our culture). Watching our new Miss America with her beautiful, overly made-up face and perfectly manicured hands, I thought of the direct counterpart to the question that was posed to James Baldwin, as he relates in his description of his conversion experience in *The Fire Next Time*: Whose little girl are you? And because Vanessa Williams's eyes answered dutifully to each person who came forward and silently posed the question: "Why, yours of course," it occurred to me that the ease with which the answer was given belied the sincerity of the response entirely. The Miss America role is tough work; one must have the beauty and charm of a princess, the elegant fortitude of a courtesan, and the cheap hustle of a tease. She is not America's dream girl, she is America's sick fantasy of girlhood and innocence. 13

As we were leaving the store with our photographs and our two rather relieved children, my wife turned to me and said, "Wouldn't it be something if one of our girls became Miss America twenty years from now? This photograph would be sought by all the papers: 'New Miss America photographed as child with first black Miss America.' " 14

"Yes," I said, "that would be something." 15

Although in one very obvious way it is very wonderful now that black mothers can tell their young daughters, "Yes, my darling, you too can become Miss America," one wonders what might be the larger psychic costs demanded by this bit of acculturation. Despite the fact that I do not wish my daughters to grow up desiring to be Miss America, I take a strange pleasure in knowing 16 that that contest can no longer terrorize them; and this pleasure is worth the psychic costs and dislocations, whatever they might be. After all, black folk knew for a long time before Henry James discovered the fact that it is a complex fate to be an American.

*Postscript*: In July 1984, shortly before this essay was published, Vanessa Williams became the first Miss America to be stripped of her crown, when *Penthouse* magazine published sexually provocative photos of Williams taken a few years before she became Miss America. Her replacement, Suzette Charles, Miss New Jersey, became the second black woman to become Miss America, which means that blacks are, on the whole, doing better than Jews in this business, as Bess Myerson remains the only Jew to have won the contest. Or perhaps blacks are doing worse, as some have perversely joked that it takes two light-skinned black women to equal the reign of one white woman. 17

---

## *Meaning and Purpose*

1. What is Early's thesis? Does he state it directly?
2. According to Early, what role does Miss America play in American culture?
3. What effect does the selection of a black Miss America have on black people?
4. What effect does the selection of a black Miss America have on white people?
5. In paragraph 13, Early discusses ultimate causes for the popularity of the Miss America contest. Do you agree? From your own familiarity with the contest, can you provide evidence to support or deny his assertion?

## *Strategy*

1. How does each of the two quotations that precede the essay relate to the essay as a whole?

2. Although the essay is about a personal appearance of the first black Miss America, Early begins with a long paragraph describing Dolgin's department store and American stores in general. How does this description tie in with the rest of the essay?
3. Why does Early include the conversation quotations in paragraphs 3–8?
4. Why does Early include the long paragraph (10) describing the behavior of the white people who have also come to see Miss America?
5. Early uses comparison when he relates the example of Bess Meyerson, the first Jewish Miss America. What does her example have to do with Vanessa Williams?

## Style

1. Early says, "American retailing nowadays does not seem condensed so much as it seems compressed." What is the difference between *condensed* and *compressed*?
2. This essay is obviously written by a well-educated, thoughtful person, and yet the tone is anything but "ivory tower." Examine paragraph 2 for examples of formal and informal phrasing. What effect does the combination of both have on your attitude as a reader?
3. How would you describe the tone of the essay's postscript? Does its tone have an effect on your perception of the meaning of the essay?
4. If necessary look up the following words in a dictionary: *ambience* (1); *emanation, inscrutable* (2); *veneration* (9); *gentile, guileless* (11); *nonplussed, phantasmagoria* (12); *acculturation* (16).

## Writing Tasks

1. Write a paper exploring the effects some popular entertainment celebrity has had on a portion of the American people. You might consider someone like Bart Simpson, Madonna, Oprah

Winfrey, Bruce Springsteen, Roseanne (Barr) Thomas, Eddie Murphy, Priscilla Presley, Tom Cruise, Paula Abdul.

2. People the world over are becoming increasingly concerned about environmental problems: the ozone layer, the greenhouse effect, pollution of waterways, the disappearing rain forest, and so on. Select one environmental problem and write an essay explaining why it has become a problem. Include both immediate and ultimate causes.

## ❦ Leonce Gaiter ❦

*Leonce Gaiter lives in Los Angeles and writes frequently about social issues.*

# *The Revolt of the Black Bourgeoisie*

*In this essay, first published in* The New York Times Magazine, *Leonce Gaiter describes how he and other African-Americans have been affected by the current stereotype of blacks in the media. He then traces how that stereotype has been enforced and perpetuated.*

*As you read, notice how Gaiter uses specific examples to support his contentions.*

---

1 At a television network where I once worked, one of my bosses told me I almost didn't get hired because his superior had "reservations" about me. The job had been offered under the network's Minority Advancement Program. I applied for the position because I knew I was exceptionally qualified. I would have applied for the position regardless of how it was advertised.

2 After my interview, the head of the department told my boss I wasn't really what he had in mind for a Minority Advancement Program job. To the department head, hiring a minority applicant meant hiring someone unqualified. He wanted to hire some semiliterate, hoop-shooting former prison inmate. That, in his view, was a "real" black person. That was someone worthy of the program.

3 I had previously been confronted by questions of black authenticity. At Harvard, where I graduated in 1980, a white classmate once said to me, "Oh, you're not really a black person." I asked her to explain. She could not. She had known few black people before college, but a lifetime of seeing black people depicted in the American media had taught her that real black people

talked a certain way and were raised in certain places. In her world, black people did not attend elite colleges. They could not stand as her intellectual equals or superiors. Any African-American who shared her knowledge of Austen and Balzac—while having to explain to her who Douglass and Du Bois were—had to be *willed* away for her to salvage her sense of superiority as a white person. Hence the accusation that I was "not really black."

But worse than the white majority harboring a one-dimensional vision of blackness are the many blacks who embrace this stereotype as our true nature. At the junior high school I attended in the mostly white Washington suburb of Silver Spring, Md., a black girl once stopped me in the hallway and asked belligerently, "How come you talk so proper?" Astonished, I could only reply, "It's proper*ly*," and walk on. This girl was asking why I spoke without the so-called black accent pervasive in the lower socioeconomic strata of black society, where exposure to mainstream society is limited. This girl was asking, Why wasn't I impoverished and alienated? In her world view, a black male like me couldn't exist. 4

Within the past year, however, there have been signs that blacks are openly beginning to acknowledge the complex nature of our culture. Cornel West, a professor of religion and the director of Afro-American Studies at Princeton University, discusses the growing gulf between the black underclass and the rest of black society in his book "Race Matters"; black voices have finally been raised against the violence, misogyny and vulgarity marketed to black youth in the form of gangsta rap; Ellis Cose's book "The Rage of a Privileged Class," which concentrates on the problems of middle- and upper-income blacks, was excerpted as part of a Newsweek magazine cover story; Bill Cosby has become a vocal crusader against the insulting depiction of African-Americans in "hip-hop generation" TV shows. 5

Yes, there are the beginnings of a new candor about our culture, but the question remains, How did one segment of the African-American community come to represent the whole? First, black society itself placed emphasis on that lower caste. This made 6 sense because historically that's where the vast majority of us were placed; it's where American society and its laws were designed to keep us. Yet although doors have opened to us over the past 20 years, it is still commonplace for black leaders to insist on our community's uniform need for social welfare programs, inner-city services, job skills training, etc. Through such calls, what has passed for a black political agenda has been furthered only superficially; while affirmative action measures have forced an otherwise unwilling majority to open some doors for the black middle class, social welfare and Great Society-style programs aimed at the black lower class have shown few positive results.

According to 1990 census figures, between 1970 and 1990 the number of black families with incomes under $15,000 rose from 34.6 percent of the black population to 37 percent, while the number of black families with incomes of $35,000 to $50,000 rose from 13.9 percent to 15 percent of the population, and those with incomes of more than $50,000 rose from 9.9 percent to 14.5 percent of the black population. 7

Another reason the myth of an all-encompassing black underclass survives—despite the higher number of upper-income black families—is that it fits with a prevalent form of white liberalism, which is just as informed by racism as white conservatism. Since the early 70's, good guilt-liberal journalists and others warmed to the picture of black downtrodden masses in need of their help. Through the agency of good white people, blacks would rise. This image of African-Americans maintained the lifeline of white superiority that whites in this culture cling to, and therefore this image of blacks stuck. A strange tango was begun. Blacks seeking advancement opportunities allied themselves with whites eager to "help" them. However, those whites continued to see blacks as inferiors, victims, cases, and not as equals, individuals or, heaven forbid, competitors. 8

It was hammered into the African-American psyche by media-appointed black leaders and the white media that it was essential to our political progress to stay or seem to stay economically and socially deprived. To be recognized and recognize oneself as middle or upper class was to threaten the political progress of black 9 people. That girl who asked why I spoke so "proper" was accusing me of political sins—of thwarting the progress of our race.

Despite progress toward a more balanced picture of black America, the image of black society as an underclass remains strong. Look at local news coverage of the trial of Damian Williams and Henry Watson, charged with beating the white truck driver Reginald Denny during the 1992 South-Central L.A. riots. The press showed us an African-print-wearing cadre of Williams and Watson supporters trailing Edi M. O. Faal, Williams's defense attorney, like a Greek chorus. This chorus made a point of standing in the camera's range. They presented themselves as the voice of South-Central L.A., the voice of the oppressed, the voice of the downtrodden, the voice of the city's black people. 10

To anyone watching TV coverage of the trial, all blacks agreed with Faal's contention that his clients were prosecuted so aggressively because they are black. Period. Reporters made no effort to show opposing black viewpoints. (In fact, the media portrait of the Los Angeles riot as blacks vs. whites and Koreans was a misrepresentation. According to the Rand Corporation, a research institute in Santa Monica, blacks made up 36 percent of those arrested during the riot; Latinos made up 51 percent.) The black bourgeoisie and intelligentsia remained largely silent. We had too long believed that to express disagreement with the "official line" was to be a traitor. 11

TV networks and cable companies gain media raves for programs like "Laurel Avenue," an HBO melodrama about a working-class black family lauded for its realism, a real black family complete with drug dealers, drug users, gun toters and basketball players. It is akin to the media presenting "Valley of the Dolls" as a realistic portrayal of the ways of white women. 12

The Fox network offers a differing but equally misleading portrait of black Americans, with "Martin." While blue humor has long been a staple of black audiences, it was relegated to clubs and records for *mature* black audiences. It was not peddled to kids or to the masses. 13

Now the blue humor tradition is piped to principally white audiences. If TV was as black as it is white—if there was a fair 14 share of black love stories, black dramas, black detective heroes—these blue humor images would not be a problem. Right now, however, they stand as images to which whites can condescend.

Imagine being told by your peers, the records you hear, the 15
programs you watch, the "leaders" you see on TV, classmates, prospective employers—imagine being told by virtually everyone that in order to be your true self you must be ignorant and poor, or at least seem so.

Blacks must now see to it that our children face no such bur- 16
den. We must see to it that the white majority, along with vocal minorities within the black community (generally those with a self-serving political agenda), do not perpetuate the notion that African-Americans are invariably doomed to the underclass.

African-Americans are moving toward seeing ourselves—and 17
demanding that others see us—as individuals, not as shards of a degraded monolith. The American ideal places primacy on the rights of the individual, yet historically African-Americans have been denied those rights. We blacks can effectively demand those rights, effectively demand justice only when each of us sees him or herself as an individual with the right to any of the opinions, idiosyncrasies and talents accorded any other American.

---

## *Meaning and Purpose*

1. In the first two paragraphs Gaiter describes applying for a job for which he was exceptionally qualified. Why was he nearly turned down?
2. Gaiter's "black authenticity" is questioned by a black girl in paragraph 4. Why?
3. What segments of American society, according to Gaiter, are guilty of stereotyping African-Americans?
4. What are the immediate causes of black stereotyping? The ultimate causes?
5. How do the TV programs Gaiter cites promote the black stereotype?

6. How, according to Gaiter, can African-Americans effectively demand that they be recognized as individuals?

## *Strategy*

1. What is the function of the first four paragraphs? What, precisely, is the point of the examples?
2. Describe the function of paragraph 5. How, specifically, does it carry the reader from one section of the essay to the next?
3. What point do the statistics in paragraph 7 support? How effective are these statistics?
4. Describe the function of paragraph 15.

## *Style*

1. What is "blue humor" (13)? What is the derivation of the term?
2. If necessary, look the following words up in a dictionary: *elite, salvage* (3); *pervasive, strata* (4); *misogyny, excerpted* (5); *candor* (6); *psyche, thwarting* (9); *cadre* (10); *bourgeoisie, intelligentsia* (11); *lauded* (12); *staple, relegated* (13); *condescend* (14); *peers, prospective* (15); *invariably* (16); *shards, degraded, monolith, primacy, idiosyncracies* (17).

## *Writing Tasks*

1. Construct an essay in which you either attack or defend Gaiter's contentions about the deleterious effects of media stereotyping. But don't feel confined to the stereotyping of African-Americans. Use the stereotype with which you are most familiar, and make sure to support your points with specifics.
2. Write an essay in which you defend Gaiter's contentions by citing further examples from the media that enforce his point of view. Or, attack his position by citing contrary examples. In either case, make sure you refer to the Gaiter essay in your argument.

# ❦ William Severini Kowinski ❦

*William Kowinski grew up in Pennsylvania and attended Knox College in Illinois. He spent one semester at the University of Iowa studying fiction and poetry writing. His writing career, however, has been in nonfiction. To research his book,* The Malling of America *(1985), Kowinski visited malls all over both the United States and Canada. He has been a writer and editor for the* Boston Phoenix *and for* Newsworks *of Washington, D.C., and his articles have appeared in* Esquire, The New York Times, *and the* New York Times Magazine.

## *Kids in the Mall:*
### *Growing Up Controlled*

*Many American children grow up almost entirely in the controlled environments of home, school, and "the mall." What are the effects, Kowinski asks, of "growing up controlled"? The essay is from his book,* The Malling of America: An Inside Look at the Great Consumer Paradise *(1985).*

*As you read Kowinski's essay, be alert to how he moves from causes to effects. Pay particular attention to how he passes judgments on some of his effects.*

---

Butch heaved himself up and loomed over the group. "Like it was different for me," he piped. "My folks used to drop me off at the shopping mall every morning and leave me all day. It was like a big free baby-sitter, you know? One night they never came back for me. Maybe they moved away. Maybe there's some kind of a Bureau of Missing Parents I could check with." 1

—Richard Peck
*Secrets of the Shopping Mall,*
a novel for teenagers

From his sister at Swarthmore, I'd heard about a kid in Florida whose mother picked him up after school every day, drove him straight to the mall, and left him there until it closed—all at his insistence. I'd heard about a boy in Washington who, when his family moved from one suburb to another, pedaled his bicycle five miles every day to get back to his old mall, where he once belonged. 2

These stories aren't unusual. The mall is a common experience for the majority of American youth; they have probably been going there all their lives. Some ran within their first large open space, saw their first fountain, bought their first toy, and read their first book in a mall. They may have smoked their first cigarette or first joint or turned them down, had their first kiss or lost their virginity in the mall parking lot. Teenagers in America now spend more time in the mall than anywhere else but home and school. Mostly it is their choice, but some of that mall time is put in as the result of two-paycheck and single-parent households, and the lack of other viable alternatives. But are these kids being harmed by the mall? 3

I wondered first of all what difference it makes for adolescents to experience so many important moments in the mall. They are, after all, at play in the fields of its little world and they learn its ways; they adapt to it and make it adapt to them. It's here that these kids get their street sense, only it's mall sense. They are learning the ways of a large-scale artificial environment: its subtleties and flexibilities, its particular pleasures and resonances, and the attitudes it fosters. 4

The presence of so many teenagers for so much time was not something mall developers planned on. In fact, it came as a big surprise. But kids became a fact of mall life very early, and the International Council of Shopping Centers found it necessary to commission a study, which they published along with a guide to mall managers on how to handle the teenage incursion. 5

The study found that "teenagers in suburban centers are bored and come to the shopping centers mainly as a place to go. Teenagers in suburban centers spent more time fighting, drinking, littering and walking than did their urban counterparts, but pre- 6 sented fewer overall problems." The report observed that "adolescents congregated in groups of two to four and predominantly at locations selected by them rather than management." This probably had something to do with the decision to install game arcades, which allow management to channel these restless adolescents into naturally contained areas away from major traffic points of adult shoppers.

The guide concluded that mall management should tolerate and even encourage the teenage presence because, in the words of the report, "The vast majority support the same set of values as does shopping center management." *The same set of values* means simply that mall kids are already preprogrammed to be consumers and that the mall can put the finishing touches to them as hard-core, lifelong shoppers just like everybody else. That, after all, is what the mall is about. So it shouldn't be surprising that in spending a lot of time there, adolescents find little that challenges the assumption that the goal of life is to make money and buy products, or that just about everything else in life is to be used to serve those ends. 7

Growing up in a high-consumption society already adds inestimable pressure to kids' lives. Clothes consciousness has invaded the grade schools, and popularity is linked with having the best, newest clothes in the currently acceptable styles. Even what they read has been affected. "Miss [Nancy] Drew wasn't obsessed with her wardrobe," noted *The Wall Street Journal*, "but today the mystery in teen fiction for girls is what outfit the heroine will wear next." Shopping has become a survival skill and there is certainly no better place to learn it than the mall, where its importance is powerfully reinforced and certainly never questioned. 8

The mall as a university of suburban materialism, where Valley Girls and Boys from coast to coast are educated in consumption, has its other lessons in this era of change in family life and sexual mores and their economic and social ramifications. The plethora of products in the mall, plus the pressure on teens to buy them, may contribute to the phenomenon that psychologist David Elkind calls "the hurried child": kids who are exposed to too much of the adult world too quickly, and must respond with 9 a sophistication that belies their still-tender emotional development. Certainly the adult products marketed for children—form-fitting designer jeans, sexy tops for preteen girls—add to the social pressure to look like an adult, along with the home-grown need to understand adult finances (why mothers must work) and adult emotions (when parents divorce).

10 Kids spend so much time at the mall partly because their parents allow it and even encourage it. The mall is safe, it doesn't seem to harbor any unsavory activities, and there is adult supervision; it is, after all, a controlled environment. So the temptation, especially for working parents, is to let the mall be their babysitter. At least the kids aren't watching TV. But the mall's role as a surrogate mother may be more extensive and more profound.

11 Karen Lansky, a writer living in Los Angeles, has looked into the subject and she told me some of her conclusions about the effects on its teenaged denizens of the mall's controlled and controlling environment. "Structure is the dominant idea, since true 'mall rats' lack just that in their home lives," she said, "and adolescents about to make the big leap into growing up crave more structure than our modern society cares to acknowledge." Karen pointed out some of the elements malls supply that kids used to get from their families, like warmth (Strawberry Shortcake dolls and similar cute and cuddly merchandise), old-fashioned mothering ("We do it all for you," the fast-food slogan), and even home cooking (the "homemade" treats at the food court).

12 The problem in all this, as Karen Lansky sees it, is that while families nurture children by encouraging growth through the assumption of responsibility and then by letting them rest in the bosom of the family from the rigors of growing up, the mall as a structural mother encourages passivity and consumption, as long as the kid doesn't make trouble. Therefore all they learn about becoming adults is how to act and how to consume.

13 Kids are in the mall not only in the passive role of shoppers—they also work there, especially as fast-food outlets infiltrate the mall's enclosure. There they learn how to hold a job and take responsibility, but still within the same value context. When *CBS*

*Reports* went to Oak Park Mall in suburban Kansas City, Kansas, to tape part of their hour-long consideration of malls, "After the Dream Comes True," they interviewed a teenaged girl who worked in a fast-food outlet there. In a sequence that didn't make the final program, she described the major goal of her present life, which was to perfect the curl on top of the ice-cream cones that were her store's specialty. If she could do that, she would be moved from the lowly soft-drink dispenser to the more prestigious ice-cream division, the curl on top of the status ladder at her restaurant. These are the achievements that are important at the mall.

Other benefits of such jobs may also be overrated, according to Laurence D. Steinberg of the University of California at Irvine's social ecology department, who did a study on teenage employment. Their jobs, he found, are generally simple, mindlessly repetitive and boring. They don't really learn anything, and the jobs don't head anywhere. Teenagers also work primarily with other teenagers; even their supervisors are often just a little older than they are. "Kids need to spend time with adults," Steinberg told me. "Although they get benefits from peer relationships, without parents and other adults it's a one-sided socialization. They hang out with each other, have age-segregated jobs, and watch TV." 14

Perhaps much of this is not so terrible or even so terribly different. Now that they have so much more to contend with in their lives, adolescents probably need more time to spend with other adolescents without adult impositions, just to sort things out. Though it is more concentrated in the mall (and therefore perhaps a clearer target), the value system there is really the dominant one of the whole society. Attitudes about curiosity, initiative, self-expression, empathy, and disinterested learning aren't necessarily made in the mall; they are mirrored there, perhaps a bit more intensely—as through a glass brightly. 15

Besides, the mall is not without its educational opportunities. There are bookstores, where there is at least a short shelf of classics at great prices, and other books from which it is possible to learn more than how to do sit-ups. There are tools, from hammers 16 to VCRs, and products, from clothes to records, that can help the young find and express themselves. There are older people with stories, and places to be alone or to talk one-on-one with a kindred spirit. And there is always the passing show.

The mall itself may very well be an education about the future. I was struck with the realization, as early as my first forays into Greengate, that the mall is only one of a number of enclosed and controlled environments that are part of the lives of today's young. The mall is just an extension, say, of those large suburban schools—only there's Karmelkorn instead of chem lab, the ice rink instead of the gym: It's high school without the impertinence of classes. 17

Growing up, moving from home to school to the mall—from enclosure to enclosure, transported in cars—is a curiously continuous process, without much in the way of contrast or contact with unenclosed reality. Places must tend to blur into one another. But whatever differences and dangers there are in this, the skills these adolescents are learning may turn out to be useful in their later lives. For we seem to be moving inexorably into an age of preplanned and regulated environments, and this is the world they will inherit. 18

Still, it might be better if they had more of a choice. One teenaged girl confessed to *CBS Reports* that she sometimes felt she was missing something by hanging out at the mall so much. "But I'm here," she said, "and this is what I have." 19

---

## *Meaning and Purpose*

1. What has been your experience in malls? What is your response to Kowinski's essay? Do you agree or disagree with him? Do you identify with the situations he describes?
2. What primary questions does the author attempt to answer in the essay? What is the thesis and where is it stated?
3. What negative effects does growing up in the mall have on children? Are there any positive effects?

4. Whom is Kowinski addressing in this essay? Who should hear his message?
5. Can a careful reading of the essay establish the author's values? What are they? Where are these attitudes evident?

## *Strategy*

1. Paragraphs 2–4 serve as the essay's introduction. How does each function independently? How do they fit together to form the larger unit?
2. Does Kowinski talk about immediate or ultimate causes and effects in paragraph 9? Explain.
3. Compare paragraphs 9 and 14. In paragraph 9, Kowinski describes "the hurried child syndrome," the negative effect on a child who is too quickly exposed to the adult world and must respond with a sophistication still beyond him or her. In paragraph 14, discussing how teenagers who work in malls work mostly with other teenagers, Kowinski cites an authority who claims kids need more time in their work with adults. Do you see a contradiction here?
4. A related cause-and-effect structure is visible in paragraphs 10–12. What is it and how does it work?
5. Study the structure of paragraph 18. How does it contribute to the essayist's main purpose of showing how stultifying and controlling malls are for teenagers?

## *Style*

1. Comment on the effects of the final sentence in paragraph 13 on the rest of the paragraph. What does it say about the mall experience as a whole?
2. What is Kowinski's attitude toward his subject? Where is this attitude manifest?
3. If necessary, look up the meanings of these words: *resonances* (4), *inclusion* (5), *plethora* (9), *denizens* (11), *impertinence* (17), *inexorably* (18).

## *Writing Tasks*

1. Kowinski takes a rather dim view of what happens to kids when they "grow up" in a mall. Write an essay in which you either show that mall experiences do not have such dire consequences, or agree with Kowinski. Either way, draw from your own experience or that of those you know. Be sure to discuss immediate and ultimate causes and effects, either alternately in the same paragraphs, or in separate paragraphs.
2. Think of a place, other than a mall, where you spent a lot of time during your teenage years—a hangout of some sort. What do you think some of the immediate and ultimate effects were and are from your having spent time there? Answer this question in a short essay. Be specific.

## ❦ *Responding to Photographs* ❦

*Cause and Effect*

A Woman

Noted author Sharon Curtin has criticized American attitudes toward those who are growing old. In the following quotation, she expresses her own feeling about aging and projects those feelings to others:

> I am afraid to grow old—we're all afraid. In fact, the fear of growing old is so great that every aged person is an insult and a threat to society. They remind us of our own death, that our body won't always remain smooth and responsive, but will someday betray us by aging, wrinkling, faltering, failing. The ideal way to age would be to grow slowly invisible, gradually disappearing, without causing worry or discomfort to the young. In some ways that does happen. Sitting in a small park across from a nursing home one day, I noticed that the young mothers and their children gathered on one side, and the old people from the home on the other. Whenever a youngster would run over to the "wrong" side, chasing a ball or just trying to cover

all the available space, the old people would lean forward and smile. But before any communication could be established, the mother would come over, murmuring embarrassed apologies, and take her child to the "young" side.

Curtin's reflections on aging find a haunting expression in "A Woman," which features an older woman with a photograph of herself when young. Drawing on Curtin's observations and elements in the photograph, compose an essay with cause and/or effect as the dominant development pattern. Before starting your project, review "Cause and Effect: Identifying Reasons and Results" at the beginning of the chapter; then select one of the following writing tasks as the basis for your essay.

1. Begin with the assertion that aging is the subject of "A Woman." Review Curtin's reflection on aging and also study the photograph, allowing its imagery to work on your imagination. Identify an emotion the photograph creates. Then relate the reasons the photograph has this effect.
2. Imagine you are a psychologist who shares Curtin's belief about growing old in our society. The young woman in "A Woman" is your client. She is beautiful, and because of her beauty, she has a deep fear of growing old. She asks you what you believe the physical and social effects of growing old will be for her. You decide to be blunt and state your feelings as directly as possible, but you decide to do so in writing. First you describe her current beauty and relate the effects of her beauty on others. Then you describe her as she will appear fifty years in the future and what will result from growing old. You then give her positive advice on how to deal with the aging process, and then you predict the effects the advice will have on her twilight years if she follows it.

## ❦ *Additional Writing Tasks* ❦

*Cause and Effect*

1. Using cause and effect (or one of the two alone) as the dominant development pattern, write an essay explaining something that interests you. These general questions are offered as ways to get you started. Revise them in any way that reflects your interests and then in a well-developed essay answer them, using the principles of cause and effect or one of the two.
   a. Why do works by some artists, filmmakers, poets, or novelists affect you?
   b. Why do people need "idols," such as singers, athletes, actors, and politicians?
   c. Why does a television series—police drama, situation comedy, talk show—succeed?
   d. What are the effects of music lyrics that some political activists believe are obscene and condone violence?
   e. What are the effects of stand-up comedians who deliver monologues that critics claim are racist and sexist?
   f. Why are stories that repeat familiar formulas successful?
   g. Is common sense an effective way to solve complex problems?
   h. Is routine the great deadener or do we need it to organize experience?
   i. Is homelessness a "real" problem in America?
   j. Can government solve the national-deficit problem by printing more money?
   k. Should children be seen and not heard?
   l. What results can you expect from an education?
   m. Is deceit self-destructive?
   n. Should children be made to feel guilty as a way of controlling teenage recklessness?
   o. Why should a dieter avoid eating foods high in fat?
   p. What causes stress and what are its temporary and lasting effects?
   q. What are the effects of a mental illness?
   r. Why does the destruction of symbols such as the American flag enrage some people?

s. What would happen if everyone were given the college degree of his or her choice without completing course work?

2. Discuss one of these subjects in an essay using cause and effect (or one of the two) as the dominant pattern.

a. Violence has always been a major element in action-oriented entertainment, from Flash Gordon to Indiana Jones. In recent years, however, action-oriented children's television cartoons, such as "G.I. Joe" and "Rambo," have become stripped of story line of any value and of characterization. The shows present unrelenting karate chopping and related mayhem and "us versus them" worlds with little or no complexity. Currently, some experts and a growing number of parents are beginning to worry about the possible harmful effects these shows might have upon children. In a cause-and-effect (or cause or effect alone) essay, explain the influence of action-oriented cartoons on children.

b. David A. Goslin, Ph.D., of the American Institute for Research in Washington, D.C., which conducts behavioral and social-science research, claims, "Choices do not make life easier; they make it more difficult, for all of us. As social scientists, we know that with an increase in choices, people tend to become more anxious."

In your experience, is Dr. Goslin's comment valid? Write a cause-and-effect (or cause or effect alone) essay discussing his point of view. You might keep in mind that Americans can choose from more than 25,000 items shelved in their supermarkets. They can tune in more than fifty television channels. They can buy more than 11,000 magazines or periodicals. They are solicited by tens of thousands of special-interest groups. Some call this opportunity "freedom of choice," but social critics and experts are beginning to believe that the marketplace may have outsmarted itself by creating all these choices.

c. In *The Tyranny of Malice*, Joseph H. Berke explains that "Envy is a state of exquisite tension, torment, and ill will provoked by an overwhelming sense of inferiority, impotence, and worthlessness. It begins in the eye of the beholder and is so painful to the mind that the envious person will go to almost any lengths to diminish, if not destroy, whatever or whoever may have aroused it." Basing a cause-and-effect (or cause or effect alone) essay on personal observation, discuss the sources of envy and how it might affect behavior.

d. "Think globally, act locally" was the rallying cry of environmental activism in the 1960s. This advice is as appropriate now as it was then. Just as the Greenpeace movement started more than two decades ago not with governments but at the grass roots, so today it is individuals who must occupy the front lines in protecting the environment. In a cause-and-effect (or cause or effect alone) essay discuss individual or local-government actions that have resulted from environmental activism.

e. In "The Slaughterer," a short story by Isaac Bashevis Singer, Yoineh Meir wanted to be a rabbi. Instead, the religious authorities in his community made him the ritual slaughterer. Obediently, Meir learned the laws of slaughter as found in religious texts and followed the command of authority.

"Barely three months had passed since Yoineh Meir had become a slaughterer," Singer wrote, "but the time seemed to stretch endlessly. He felt as though he were immersed in blood and lymph. His ears were beset by the squawking of hens, the crowing of roosters, the gobbling of geese, the lowing of oxen, the mooing and bleating of calves and goats; wings fluttered, claws tapped on the floor. The bodies refused to know any justification or excuse—every body resisted in its own fashion, tried to escape, and seemed to argue with the Creator to its last breath."

Yoineh Meir's life ended in madness: "The killing of every beast, great or small, caused him as much pain as though he were cutting his own throat. Of all the punishments that could have been visited upon him, slaughtering was the worst."

Although Yoineh Meir is an extreme example, many people are forced to follow the dictates of authority against their better judgment. In an essay describe a situation in which authority has been used to pressure an individual into action that seems contrary to his or her nature and discuss the related causes and effects.

# 8

# *Process Analysis*

## *Explaining Step by Step*

## *The Method*

Are you, like many readers, fascinated by how things work? Are you attracted to writing that explains how to organize your life and time? You might want to understand how the stock market works or how Colombian drug producers smuggle cocaine into the United States. Perhaps your interests have to do with the mind—you might want to learn how psychotherapy works. Authors of essays or books explaining how things work use **process analysis**: they help us to better understand something by breaking it down into its components.

In some ways process analysis comes close to narration and cause-and-effect analysis by attending to a sequence of related events. Narration, however, is meant to tell a story, and cause-and-effect analysis deals with the reasons for and results of an event or experience. In process analysis a writer examines the way in which something works. In short, narration concentrates on *what* happened; cause and effect, on *why* it happened; and process analysis, on *how* it happened.

## *Strategies*

Careful writers distinguish between two kinds of process analysis: **directive** and **informative**. Directive process analysis explains *how to* do something. Directive process analysis is usually a practical kind of writing based on the assumption that someone will follow the directions to complete a task. Informative process analysis emphasizes *how* something works rather than *how to* do something. Informative process analysis might explain how the brain functions, how gravity holds human beings to the face of the earth, or how food is grown, processed, and merchandised, but an informative process analysis will not offer directions for completing a task.

### *Directive Process Analysis*

Directive process analysis can range from brief instructions on a soup-can label to a complicated plan for putting an astronaut on another planet. Keep in mind that directive process analysis has one clear purpose: to guide a reader to a predetermined goal by breaking down the steps required to get there. Consider this paragraph from Tom Cuthbertson's *Anybody's Bike Book*, setting out simple directions for checking bike tire pressure.

> There's a great *curb-edge test* you can do to make sure your tires are inflated just right. Rest the wheel on the edge of a curb or stair so the bike sticks out into the street or path, perpendicular to the curb or stair edge. Get the wheel so you can push down on it at about a 45 degree angle from above the bike. Push hard on the handlebars or seat, depending on which wheel you're testing. The curb should flare the tire a bit but shouldn't push right through the tire and clunk against the rim. You want the tire to have a little give when you ride over chuckholes and rocks, in other words, but you don't want it so soft that you bottom out. If you are a hotshot who wants tires so hard that they don't have any give, you'll have to stick to riding on cleanswept Velodrome tracks, or watch very carefully for little sharp objects on the road. Or you'll have to get used to that sudden riding-on-the-rim feeling that follows the blowout of an overblown tire.

Cuthbertson's paragraph illustrates several characteristics of directive process analysis. First, he clearly establishes his purpose: to explain how to test bike tires for proper inflation. Second, he breaks the process down into simple steps and explains the final result: "The curb should flare the tire. . . ." Third, Cuthbertson addresses his reader directly by using the second person pronoun *you*, a practice that many writers adopt in directive process analysis: "There's a great curb-edge test *you* can do to make sure *your* tires are inflated just right." A fourth frequent characteristic of directive process analysis alerts the reader to possible mistakes and their consequences. Notice that Cuthbertson states the consequences of overinflated bike tires.

Now consider this passage from *The New York Times Complete Manual of Home Repair*. Bernard Gladstone gives directions for building a fire. Notice that Gladstone's passage embodies most of the common characteristics of process analysis, but he chooses not to address the reader as "you." Instead he writes in the more impersonal passive voice, which seems to create a distance between the reader and the subject.

> Though "experts" differ as to the best technique to follow when building a fire, one generally accepted method consists of first laying a generous amount of crumpled newspaper on the hearth between the andirons. Kindling wood is then spread generously over this layer of newspaper and one of the thickest logs is placed across the back of the andirons. This should be as close to the back of the fireplace as possible, but not quite touching it. A second log is then placed an inch or so in front of this, and a few additional sticks of kindling are laid across these two. A third log is then placed on top to form a sort of pyramid with air space between all logs so that flames can lick freely up between them.
>
> A mistake frequently made is in building the fire too far forward so that the rear wall of the fireplace does not get properly heated. A heated back wall helps increase the draft and tends to suck smoke and flames rearward with less chance of sparks or smoke spurting out into the room.
>
> Another common mistake often made by the inexperienced firetender is to try to build a fire with only one or two logs, instead of using at least three. A single log is difficult to ignite properly, and even two logs do not provide an efficient bed with adequate fuel-burning capacity.
>
> Use of too many logs, on the other hand, is also a common fault and can prove hazardous. Building too big a fire can create more smoke and draft than the chimney can safely handle, increasing the possibility of sparks or smoke being thrown out into the room. For best results, the homeowner should start with three medium-size logs as described above,

> then add additional logs as needed if the fire is to be kept burning.

Like Cuthbertson, Gladstone opens by clearly stating his purpose; that is, to explain the steps necessary to build a fire in a fireplace. He then follows with a series of steps—six in all—that are clearly written and easy to follow. After devoting a paragraph to directions for building a fire, he presents three common mistakes people make when building a fire, and their consequences, with one brief paragraph devoted to each mistake. Although Gladstone's directions for building a fire are longer than Cuthbertson's for testing air pressure in a bike tire, both follow the same general pattern. They begin with a clear statement of purpose, then present the steps necessary to complete the process, and, as is often done in directive process analysis, they identify the common mistakes people make when following the procedure.

### *Informative Process Analysis*

Instead of guiding a reader through a series of directions to complete a task as directive process analysis does, informative process analysis explains how something happens or how it works. In this paragraph from Caroline Sutton's *How Do They Do That?* she explains how stripes are put into striped toothpaste.

> Although it's intriguing to imagine the peppermint stripes neatly wound inside the tube, actually stripes don't go into the paste until it's on its way out. A small hollow tube, with slots running lengthwise, extends from the neck of the toothpaste tube back into the interior a short distance. When the toothpaste tube is filled, red paste—the striping material—is inserted first, thus filling the conical area around the hollow tube at the front. (It must not, however, reach beyond the point to which the hollow tube extends into the toothpaste tube.) The remainder of the dispenser is filled with the familiar white stuff. When you squeeze the toothpaste tube, pressure is applied to the white paste,

which in turn presses on the red paste at the head of the tube. The red then passes through the slots and onto the white, which is moving through the inserted tube—and which emerges with five red stripes.

Sutton doesn't expect any of her readers to make a tube of striped toothpaste, but she does answer a common question, one that might have aroused your curiosity, too, "How do they get the stripes into the tube?"

An informative process analysis is usually arranged in chronological order and makes careful use of transitional techniques to guide a reader through the process. Sometimes the procedure is quite simple and easily organized in a step-by-step sequence. Often, however, the process is complex, such as a chemical reaction or human digestion, and challenges a writer's organizational skills, especially when the writer wishes to interrupt the explanation to add additional information or description.

For example, John McPhee in *Oranges* devotes a paragraph to describing the process oranges undergo when made into concentrated juice. As you read McPhee's paragraph, notice that he interrupts to bring in related information—first, to explain that oranges culled from the crop were once dumped in fields and eaten by cattle, thus accounting for the orangeade flavor of Florida milk; and second, to describe two kinds of juicing machines. Even though McPhee interrupts the process, he still guides the reader's attention with clear transitional techniques, especially phrases that create a sense of movement, such as, "As the fruit starts to move . . .," "Moving up a conveyor belt . . .," "When an orange tumbles in . . .," and, finally, "As the jaws crush the outside. . . ."

As the fruit starts to move along a concentrate plant's assembly line, it is first culled. In what some citrus people remember as "the old fresh-fruit days," before the Second World War, about forty per cent of all oranges grown in Florida were eliminated at packinghouses and dumped in fields. Florida milk tasted like orangeade. Now, with the exception of the split and rotten fruit, all of Florida's orange

> crop is used. Moving up a conveyor belt, oranges are scrubbed with detergent before they roll on into juicing machines. There are several kinds of juicing machines, and they are something to see. One is called the Brown Seven Hundred. Seven hundred oranges a minute go into it and are split and reamed on the same kind of rosettes that are in the centers of ordinary kitchen reamers. The rinds that come pelting out the bottom are integral halves, just like the rinds of oranges squeezed in a kitchen. Another machine is the Food Machinery Corporation's FMC In-line Extractor. It has a shining row of aluminum jaws, upper and lower, with shining aluminum teeth. When an orange tumbles in, the upper jaw comes crunching down on it while at the same time the orange is penetrated from below by a perforated steel tube. As the jaws crush the outside, the juice goes through the perforations in the tube and down into the plumbing of the concentrate plant. All in a second, the juice has been removed and the rind has been crushed and shredded beyond recognition.

Some processes defy chronological explanation because they take place simultaneously. Here a writer must present the material in parallel stages, as McPhee does in the last three sentences of his paragraph when he describes juicing, clearly indicating with transitional markings that two or more interlocked events are taking place at once.

In a paragraph from in "The Spider and the Wasp," zoologist Alexander Petrunkevitch presents the procedure a female *Pepsis* wasp follows when paralyzing a tarantula before burying it with a wasp egg attached to its belly. The challenge Petrunkevitch faced was to show both the wasp's and the spider's simultaneous behavior.

> When the grave is finished, the wasp returns to the tarantula to complete her ghastly enterprise. First, she feels it all over once more with her antennae. Then her behavior becomes more aggressive. She bends her abdomen, protruding her sting, and searches for the soft membrane at the point

where the spider's legs join its body—the only spot where she can penetrate the horny skeleton. From time to time, as the exasperated spider slowly shifts ground, the wasp turns on her back and slides along with the aid of her wings, trying to get under the tarantula for a shot at the vital spot. During all this maneuvering, which can last for several minutes, the tarantula makes no move to save itself. Finally the wasp corners it against some obstruction and grasps one of its legs in her powerful jaws. Now at last the harassed spider tries a desperate but vain defense. The two contestants roll over and over on the ground. It is a terrifying sight and the outcome is always the same. The wasp finally manages to thrust her sting into the soft spot and holds it there for a few seconds while she pumps in the poison. Almost immediately the tarantula falls paralyzed on its back. Its legs stop twitching; its heart stops beating. Yet it is not dead, as is shown by the fact that if taken from the wasp it can be restored to some sensitivity by being kept in a moist chamber for several months.

Often the success of a process-analysis essay rests on clear information about the reader. The writer must estimate how much knowledge about the process the reader may already have and how much additional information must be included in the essay. If the writer's guess is wildly inaccurate, then he or she will include either too much information, which may send the reader into a fit of yawning, or too little, which may send the reader into an intellectual fog bank.

## *Process Analysis in College Writing*

In the sciences and social sciences, process analysis is an important development pattern. In laboratory sciences you will often use directive process analysis to write reports that communicate the procedure in an experiment or research project. In courses such as geology, biology, cultural anthropology, and social psychology you will often use informative process analysis to describe such subjects as the formation of mountains, photosynthesis, initiation ceremonies, and socialization.

### *Guidelines for Writing Process Analysis*

1. Select a subject that lends itself to either directive or informative process analysis. Be sure your subject is fresh—that is, avoid such common subjects as how to cook anything, how to put together anything, or how to find any place. Instead, look for the unusual, something from your own experience or research.
2. Decide if your analysis will be primarily directive, informative, or a little of each. Develop a list of steps necessary to complete the process or develop a list of key elements necessary to explain the process.
3. Use prewriting techniques to generate information necessary to understand and follow each element of the analysis. Then arrange your information in the proper order: for directive analysis, sequentially; for informative, chronologically.
4. Write your analysis. Carefully work in related information necessary to understand each step. *Remember*: A reader will be expected to follow the procedure in directive analysis, but only understand the process in informative analysis.
5. Revise your analysis. Pay particular attention to the transitions. Be sure they accurately guide the reader and be sure they clearly show the connection to related information and delineate simultaneous events.

In Introduction to Psychology, John Barton responded to the following writing task.

> In 550 to 600 words write an overview of a supplemental analytic practice that attempts to show family relationships. Your essay should give a clear impression of what is

involved in the process and how it proceeds. Select one of the following:

a. Transactional Analysis
b. Photoanalysis
c. Encounter Sessions
d. Psychodrama
e. Hypnotherapy
f. Cognitive Therapy

Barton selected item "b," photoanalysis, a subject his lecturer covered only briefly. He immediately knew he would write an informative analysis, since there are no specific steps therapists follow, no matter what the therapy. His main problem was to provide a reader who was unfamiliar with photoanalysis with enough information to understand it and to give a sense of how it might unfold in a therapeutic process.

Friendly Smile, Clenched Fist

*In the first two sentences, Barton establishes "photoanalysis" as the subject.*

*He gives an example of how photoanalysis can help in theraputic situations.*

*By the end of the introduction, a reader knows Barton will be describing the process of photoanalysis.*

Although many critics of psychotherapy claim that the field is slow to change, some new techniques are developing. One is photoanalysis. No doubt you have heard that "A photograph is worth a thousand words." Well, photoanalysists would agree, but with a slight revision, "A *family photo album* is worth a thousand words." For example, a person might be aware that he has difficulty showing affection and expressing himself. After a session with a photoanalyst, usually a certified psychiatrist or psychologist, he could become aware that the difficulty is rooted in his family history. Instead of spending hours verbally exploring his family relationships, a client working with a photoanalyst would examine a family photo album where the patterns of restraint might be documented in photographs.

Besides being trained as a therapist, a photoanalyst should also be sensitive to vi-

*In this paragraph Barton indicates what photographs are appropriate for analysis.*

sual images and the nonverbal expression they embody. But analyzing photographs to uncover family themes is not simple. The analyst should use group photographs taken over a number of years. A single photograph may whet curiosity but is no more helpful in unearthing patterns of family relationships than a crystal ball.

*Barton begins to describe the process. Notice how he works in related information*

Most analysts begin by spreading the photographs on a table. Then the analyst will study the faces to determine the general "tone" of the relationships. Are the subjects looking at each other or at the camera? Are their expressions happy? Or severe? Or angry? Often a child's first impression of the world comes from parents. Their expressions, captured in a series of photographs, may reveal their general perceptions.

*Barton uses a clear transition, "next," to indicate he has moved onto another phase of the process.*

Next, the analyst will study the body language of family members. Do they seem to interact with each other or do they seem emotionally isolated from each other? Are they touching? Perhaps one has an arm around another's shoulder or a hand on another's leg. Is the hand open or clenched?

*In the final phase, Barton gives plenty of related information to show the kinds of questions photoanalysis might raise. His tactic here is to raise questions and give possible answers.*

Finally, the analyst will also examine family members' proximity to each other. If they are close enough to rub elbows, they probably enjoy a warm relationship. If they put distance between themselves to avoid touching, they may shun intimacy with each other. What if males and females are clearly separated? Does this distance suggest that men and women play traditional roles within the family? An analyst will notice who takes the dominant place in the photographs. Mother? Father? A grandparent? Perhaps the children. Whoever takes a dominant place in a series of photographs probably takes the dominant role at home as well. A parent who consistently gravitates toward one child in photographs might play favorites in family relationships. A person who always chooses to stand at the outside of the group might feel like an outsider.

*In the conclusion, Barton cautions the reader about relying merely on an interpretation of photographs. They are supplemental to the patient's observations.*

Throughout a photoanalysis session, the analyst should avoid narrow interpretations of the photographs, but should offer observations for the client's response. After all, the client is the one with the direct experience and therefore should have the last word in interpreting any photograph. The photoanalyst must, however, point out that a friendly smile might be masking the tension revealed by a clenched fist half hidden in a lap.

### *Comments*

For such a brief essay, Barton gives a great deal of information. He certainly meets the writing task's requirements. In less than 600 words, he shows what is involved in photoanalysis and how a therapist might proceed in the process. He uses specific examples and details as opposed to abstract theory, which would have taken him away from his task.

Development Strategy. Because this writing task calls for a relatively brief response, Barton launches directly into his subject with an introduction that presents the subject and establishes, though indirectly, the purpose. He involves the reader by using an example that illustrates how photoanalysis might save time in uncovering personality problems.

Next he specifies the training a photoanalyst should have and the materials necessary to conduct a photoanalysis session—mainly, family photographs taken over a long period.

The third paragraph begins the description of the steps involved in the process. Since this is an informative process, the steps reflect the chronological unfolding of the process. The fourth and fifth paragraphs conclude the steps. Throughout this section, Barton gives the reader related information, raising questions and supplying possible answers. Barton concludes the essay by informing the reader about mistakes photoanalysts might make.

Barton's strategy is to be direct and to the point. He doesn't waste time presenting the theory underlying photoanalysis. He sticks to the task at hand. He arranges the information simply and presents it in plain, direct language.

**Revision.** In the first draft, Barton's introduction did not mention his specific subject—photoanalysis—until the final sentence. As a consequence, his essay was too long for the assignment. After rereading the essay, he realized his mistake and how to correct it: His second paragraph could serve as his introduction with a little modification. First, examine the introduction from the first draft of his essay:

> ~~Besides the major psychological therapies, such as psychoanalysis, analytical analysis, behaviorism, gestalt therapy, there are several supplemental practices therapists use that are effective in exploring certain aspects of character. For example, transactional analysis analyses psychological game playing, encounter sessions pits group members against each other and lets them confront one another. Psychodrama allows patients to act out their personal difficulties, and hypnotherapy uses hypnotism to reveal a patient's concerns. A new supplemental therapy is currently proving to be very effective: photoanalysis, which follows a few simple procedures.~~

Next examine the introduction in the final draft. Basically, Barton deleted his first draft's introduction—that is, he took a pencil and scratched it out, as indicated above. He then reworked the first draft's second paragraph to function as the new introduction. The result is effective, especially since the first draft's introduction was excessively wordy and withheld the purpose unnecessarily. Now reread the new introduction as it appeared in Barton's final draft.

> Although many critics of psychotherapy claim that the field is slow to change, some new techniques are developing. One is photoanalysis. No doubt you have heard that "A photograph is worth a thousand words." Well, photoanalysts would agree, but with a slight revision, "A *family photo album* is worth a thousand words." For example, a person might be aware that he has difficulty showing affection and expressing himself. After a session with a photoanalyst, usually a certified psychiatrist or psychologist, he could become aware that the difficulty is rooted in his family history. Instead of spending hours verbally exploring his family relationships, a client working with a photoanalyst would examine a family photo album where the patterns of restraint might be documented in photographs.

No matter what development pattern you use, it is a good practice to begin with your immediate subject. Don't back up to a more general subject and work to the immediate subject, as Barton does in his first draft, unless you have very strong reasons to do so.

In the professional examples that follow, you will find a variety of process analysis essays to study. Each is written for a different purpose. Yet each makes use of the fundamental strategies behind directive or informative process analysis. Study them with care to learn how professionals apply these strategies.

## *Peer Review*

You may be asked to write an essay about one of the readings that follow. Before you meet with your writing group, review this introduction. As you read the papers of your group, use these general principles of process analysis to help guide your comments.

1. The paper's complexity and vocabulary should be appropriate for the intended audience.
2. A process analysis paper should proceed in clearly defined steps. In a directive paper, readers should be warned of possible missteps at appropriate places. In an informative paper, readers should be told of actions that take place simultaneously.
3. A reader's understanding of the process can be enhanced with careful use of transitional words and phrases.

## ❦ Joan Gould ❦

*Joan Gould was born in 1927 in New York City and attended Bryn Mawr College. She has written a juvenile novel and the "Hers" column in* The New York Times, *and has contributed to major magazines such as* Esquire, Life, Sports Illustrated, *and* McCall's. *Many of her essays are very personal explorations of the experience of being a wife, a mother, a mother-in-law, and an adult daughter of an aging mother. Her book* Spirals: A Woman's Journey Through Family Life *(1988) is a collection of those essays.*

# *Binding Decisions*

*This essay was first printed in* Memories *magazine in 1989. The author describes an event from her past, the ritual of getting ready for a blind date in 1950, which she uses to reveal social attitudes about women and men, marriage, and relationships at that time. The essay invites us to wonder how much attitudes like these have changed since then.*

*This process comprises a set of steps, with a description of each step. As you read, separate the steps from their descriptions to find out exactly how many steps Joan Gould took to get ready for her date.*

---

I'm out of the bathtub. I'm ready to get dressed for my date 1 tonight, which is a blind date, serious business in this year of 1950 for any girl who's over 20 and still single. I'm 22. No matter how much money I may earn in my job, I'll never be allowed to have an apartment of my own; I'll never pay an electric bill or buy a bedspread or spend a night away from home without my parents; in fact, I'll never be a grown-up so long as I remain single.

How shall I dress? I want to look sexy enough to attract this 2 unknown man, so that he'll call and ask me for another date next week. (Needless to say, I won't call him, even if my life depends on it.) On the other hand, I don't want to hide the fact that I'm what's known as a Nice Girl, addicted to Peter Pan collars and velvet hats and white gloves, which means that I'm good wife material, and also makes it clear that he'll get nothing more than a goodnight kiss from me tonight.

3 And so I dress carefully. Every single item that I put on not only is complicated in itself but carries an even more complicated message.

4 My girdle comes first. Here's the badge, the bind, the bondage of womanhood. Here's the itch of it. This is the garment that tells me I'm not a little girl anymore, who wears only underpants, but neither am I middle-aged like my mother, who wears a real corset with bones that dig into her diaphragm and leave cruel sores there. I can get away with either a panty girdle or a two-way stretch, both of which are made of Lastex with a panel of stiff satin over the abdomen. The basic difference is that a panty girdle, unlike a two-way stretch, covers the crotch, which was considered a shocking—indeed obscene—idea when first introduced. Victorian women were obliged to wear half a dozen petticoats at a time to be respectable, but never, never would they put on anything that slipped between their thighs, like a pair of pants.

5 But why should I be bothering with this sausage casing when I weigh a grand total of a hundred and two pounds?

6 I bother because being thin has nothing to do with it. A girdle is a symbolic garment, and unless I want to be regarded as a child or a slut I have to put it on. When I go out with girlfriends in the daytime I may choose to be more comfortable in only a garter belt, a device with four long, wiggly elastics that dangle down my thighs like hungry snakes lunging at my stockings. When I'm with a boy, however, it would be unthinkable—it would be downright indecent—to let him see my rear end jiggle or let him notice that it has two halves. (All males are called "boys," no matter what their age, so long as they're single.) My backside is supposed to be molded in a rigid piece that divides into two legs, like a walking clothespin.

7 Besides, if I don't wear a girdle every day, the older girls warn me, I'm going to "spread." Spreading is somehow related to letting my flesh hang loose, which is in turn related to the idea of the

"loose" woman, and none of us wants to be considered loose. A man doesn't buy a cow if he can get milk for free, our mothers tell us in dire tones. We don't point out that we're not cows, and we don't fight against girdles, which apparently do a good job of discouraging wandering hands, since most of the single girls I know are virgins.

But which girdle should I wear? If I pick the panty girdle, I'll need 10 minutes' advance notice before going to the toilet. If I wear the two-way stretch, it will ride up and form a sausage around my waist. Either way, my flesh will be marked with welts and stripes when, at that delirious moment in my bedroom, I can strip off my clothes and scratch and scratch. 8

I pick the two-way stretch but, born compromiser that I am, put underpants over it. 9

Next comes the bra. I don't dare look at myself in the mirror as I put it on. This is the era of the pinup girl, the heyday of Lana Turner and Betty Grable, when breasts bubble and froth over the rims of C-cups and a flat chest is considered about as exciting as flat champagne. Not until Twiggy appears on the scene in the 1960's will thinness become acceptable in a girl, much less desirable—but how am I supposed to survive until then? The answer is the garment I've just put on, the confession of my disgrace—a padded bra. If I wear a strapless gown, I pin foam-rubber bust pads, which are known as "falsies," in place. Occasionally one of these breaks loose during a particularly ardent conga or mambo and rises above my dress like the rim of the sun peering over a hilltop. 10

At least the bra won't show under my silk slip. Silk is expensive, of course, and no male will see my underwear unless he marries me or I'm carried off to a hospital emergency room—but then, as all the mothers warn us, accidents do happen. 11

Stockings next. During World War II, just as I became old enough to wear them, our wonderful new nylons were snatched away from us in order to make parachutes for what was known as the "war effort." What were we girls supposed to do—go out on a date in socks, like little children? If there weren't any stockings around, we'd have to create them. And so we bought bottles of makeup base and painted stockings on our legs and drew seams 12 up the back with eyebrow pencils, which was undoubtedly the last time my seams were ever straight.

My dress, oddly enough, is easy to choose. For a woman of my years, a skirt-and-sweater is out of the question on a date. The dress mustn't be too high-style or expensive, however, or else the young man will think that I'm spoiled, a fatal defect in a girl who might otherwise qualify as good wife material. Never mind that I earned the money to buy my own clothes; I still have to show that it won't cost much to support me once we marry and I quit my job. For the same reason, wherever we go—which is always at his expense, of course—I'll insist that we travel by bus or subway, never by taxi. If he invites me out to dinner (which doesn't happen often, because of cost, and never on a first date), I'll eat a sandwich at home before I leave, to make sure I won't be tempted to order an appetizer or dessert in the restaurant. 13

Shoes. I'd like to wear my fashionable new ones, with their ankle straps crisscrossing in back and fastening above the ankle bone, but they have 3 $1/2$-inch heels, and I have no idea if I'll tower over this unknown man. If I choose low heels, on the other hand, he may think that I'm condescending. I pick the high heels but hide a low-heeled pair in the hall closet, just in case. Blind dates have their special hazards. 14

I still have to put on my makeup, which includes lots of lipstick, loose face power and an eyebrow pencil to extend my brow line, but no eye shadow, much less liner. I also have to do my hair, which is set with heavy lotion and rollers in the beauty parlor every week. (At night I sleep in a cotton mesh hairnet that I tie around my head, in order to preserve the set for at least a week.) 15

Speeding up the pace, I rush to equip my pocketbook with a monogrammed handkerchief and some "mad money," including several nickels for phone calls or a bus, obligatory for a blind date. I run to my glove drawer and hunt up a pair in white kid, since he's invited me to a concert. I won't need a hat. He'll wear one, of course. 16

The doorbell rings. I dab Shalimar on a tuft of cotton, which I tuck inside my bra; I check my stocking seams and move toward the door. For an instant, my hand rests on the knob, while 17

I wonder what sort of person is breathing out there, only inches away from me but still unrevealed, unexplored. And then I open the door, and I see his face and hear his voice, because he's already in mid-sentence. As a matter of fact, he's in mid-story, as if it's inconceivable that anyone could be less than fascinated with what he's saying, which happens to be true, or as if he's my husband already and has waited all day, or maybe all his life, to tell me about what happened to him that afternoon.

A box of Kleenex is tucked under his arm, because he has a 18
cold, and he lays the box down on the hall table with the assurance of the rightful prince stepping into his kingdom at last. This one I'll marry or I'll marry no one, I say to myself an hour later.

Three dates—which means three weeks—later, he proposes. 19
"Wait. I have to tell you something first," I declare in distress. He waits. I'm in turmoil. I'm risking everything on candor, and candor isn't a virtue in which I've had much practice. I've never said anything like this out loud before. "You have a right to know," I announced. "I wear a padded bra."

He says he imagines he can handle that. 20

We were married three months later. I wonder, if he hadn't 21
proposed so promptly, how much longer it would have been before he discovered my secret for himself.

---

## *Meaning and Purpose*

1. What significance does the title have for you after you read the essay?
2. In paragraph 6, Gould says that the girdle is a "symbolic garment." We still have symbolic garments. What is one of them? How is it symbolic?
3. The author makes sure that she "won't be tempted to order an appetizer or dessert" if she is invited by a date to eat in a restaurant (13). Why?
4. What is Gould's purpose in writing about the procedure of getting ready for a blind date in 1950? From what perspective is she writing?

5. In paragraph 10, she talks about what could happen during "an ardent conga or mambo." To what do *conga* and *mambo* refer? Why is *ardent* an appropriately descriptive word?

## *Strategy*

1. The process is this essay can be broken into specific steps. What are three of those steps?
2. Gould often interrupts the chronology of her process of dressing for a date to give explanations and related information. Where is one example of this strategy, and how does it work in the essay?
3. From the kind and detail of information in this essay, what decision would you say Gould has made about the knowledge her audience has of her subject?
4. The blind date is in "mid-story" as the author opens the door. What does this strategy of description tell you about the mental attitude of the blind date?

## *Style*

1. The process described in this essay was carried out forty or so years ago. Why is the essay written in the present tense?
2. What is Gould's attitude toward the procedure she must go through for a date? Point out specific language that illustrates her attitude.
3. Why is the word *delirious* so appropriate, as it is used in paragraph 8?
4. How does the word *candor* in paragraph 19 serve as an ironic comment on the entire process of dressing for a blind date in the 1950s?

## *Writing Tasks*

1. The title is quite important to this essay. The expression "binding decisions" means at least two things. Using the material in this

essay, write a paper exploring two meanings of "binding decisions": as the expression describes the process in this essay, and as the expression defines the reason the author carries out that process.

2. How do you dress for a date, or for some other occasion? Write a brief essay chronicling the steps in the process. If it is relevant, give background information that places your process in a larger social context.

## ❦ Richard Strozzi Heckler ❦

*Richard Strozzi Heckler not only holds a Ph.D. in psychology but also holds a fourth-degree black belt in Aikido, defined by its founder, Morihei Ueshiba, as "the activity of being taught by God about the echoes of the soul* (tamashii) *of the Universal Design* (shikumi)*." Dr. Heckler edited the anthology* Aikido and the New Warrior *(North Atlantic Books, 1985), from which the above definition comes. Currently living in the San Francisco Bay area, he is a practicing psychotherapist and consultant. He has written several articles for the* Whole Earth Review, *which first published this essay.*

# *Commanded by Love*

*In this essay, Richard Strozzi Heckler shows how it is possible to train a horse by using techniques that many readers find, ironically, to be applicable to "training" people. In fact, as you read this essay, you see that Heckler himself treats his horse humanly, even to the extent of carrying on conversations with the animal. And as a psychologist, Heckler applies his discipline's methods to his training sessions, to the point of using psychological jargon to describe parts of his and the horse's efforts to understand one another. As you read this essay, note the stages in the careful process that Heckler uses to establish the bond between him and the horse.*

---

This morning it took ten minutes to get Rios' attention and another twenty before he was really listening to me. First he distracted himself with two crows bickering in the cypress trees and then it was the flies that rose with the heat and dust of the day. Mostly I could feel he just wasn't with me. Perhaps he didn't feel my commitment; I was tired from a late night and not fully present when we began. When I finally got irritated, he perked up and we started to get some work done. It's been a week since we opened this new conversation and I feel we're just now beginning to listen to each other. 1

Rios is a young, green quarterhorse who is saddle-broke but has never been formally schooled. In the human world of sports he would be a pulling guard in football: he's muscular, quick, aggressive in turning a corner, and belligerent when he feels he's being forced or manipulated. He's not a mean or tricky horse, a juvenile delinquent maybe, but in fact he's patient in ways that allow my year-and-a-half-old daughter to walk safely around his legs. In any case he demands that I be present with him; if I'm not he'll go on his merry way—bolting out of riding rings, trying to peel me off on low-hanging limbs, turning unexpectedly in the opposite direction. In short, he's capable of anything. 2

In this stage of his training I'm asking Rios to bring his head down. When a horse brings his head to a vertical line he is more able to organize around his center of gravity; this increases his potential for moving in a balanced, effortless, coherent, and powerful way. A number of techniques and aids are commonly used to affect this behavior (and that's what it is, behavior modification)—side reins, dropped nosebands, bit-tying—but at a deeper level Rios and I are having a conversation about the nature of our relationship. This conversation tells a story—a table perhaps—about a horse and a man who are exploring a definition of power. It brings to mind Wittgenstein's observation, "To imagine a language is to imagine a form of life." The grammar of our discourse is conveyed through skin, muscles, legs, mouth, hands, voice; the syntax is the intention, trust, respect, and authenticity communicated between our energy fields. 3

What makes this conversation particularly challenging with Rios is that he has a different, already-in-place story about power. His previous owner, in asking him to respond to the same lessons that I am, was inordinately harsh with his mouth and bewildered him with mixed messages. Rios embodies this story by holding his head up and by constantly reacting to the bit in anticipation of being yanked around. His story about power revolves around dominance and fear and goes something like this: *The human with his whip, bit, spurs, and calculating mind will dominate me with pain and confusion, so I'll fear him enough to* 4 *obey his commands*. What happens in this kind of story, as it did with Rios, is that it makes a horse, or a person, neurotic and even psychotic. A crazy horse, like a crazy person, can never really be counted on to listen and respond with an open mind and heart. A story like this also confuses power, which has everything to do with enhancing one's capacity to love and be loved, with coercion. Love cannot be commanded, but we must be commanded by love.

At the beginning of our story I tell Rios that I want a relation- 5
ship with him. He's interested; the fraternal history of horse and man lives in his marbled flesh and surging neck. "But don't expect that your riding tack has any true authority," he adds. "It's only an emblem of power. You must earn the right to ride and command me. To start with, what are your assumptions about horse and rider?" he asks.

"I've never met a horse, nor a human, in which there is no 6
love that longs to emerge."

We proceed, one lesson at a time, always with the same ques- 7
tion Who are you? "How do you respond when I demand something from you?" I ask.

"How do you react when I refuse?" he counters. 8

"Why would a 1,300-pound animal let me ride him in the 9
first place?" I wonder.

Curiosity is a terrifyingly open force that moves us toward 10
some unknown understanding in the future. We struggle with trust and respect. Here the story is about the opportunity to fail, consequences, and redemption. Rios has a noble heart and, like most people, takes pride in overcoming obstacles and doing something difficult well.

Despite his attitude on any given ride—pissy, aloof, commit- 11
ted—I can always sense the dark pounding blood of his line; an incontestable dignity and robust spirit. If I say I want to ride him, and then act condescendingly—as in, "If I love and coddle you enough maybe you'll do what I ask"—he won't respect me. He'll think that my soul is flabby, that my love has no teeth. "Show me your commitment, show me that you really mean what you say,

give me a moral reason to want to do this with you," he asks moment to moment.

"Pay attention to my seat and legs. Quit fussing on the bit and come down here and listen to what I have to say," I demand. 12

"Are you there?" we constantly whisper back and forth, and the question itself shapes us into the moment, or not. 13

"You were hurt once," I recognize, "but I want you to trust that it is your radiance that inspires me. There is a great beauty within you that I can help summon." 14

"How can you know what I want?" 15

"I don't know," I confess, "but I do know that it is really me who is being commanded. It is the beauty within you that commands me. We are both, once and at the same time, leader and follower. The beauty in you commands me, my love of your beauty commands you." 16

Then there are the moments when he brings his head down, collects his power under him, and we become one. There are no more questions, no wondering, only wonder. The roles coalesce into a single mind. "This feeling is power," I say. "This is a powerful feeling," he replies. This power has no ownership, yet we both feel touched by its luminosity and splendor. It is still, yet immensely capable and alive. Then my hat blows off and I momentarily look back. Rios immediately changes gait and direction. "Does he think I have fallen out of love?" I question, "Have I?" 17

Rios thinks, "He demands so much of me and then leaves. He must love his hat also." Days later, leaving the ring after another session, he suddenly turns and walks over to my hat, fallen much earlier and forgotten. His taking command at that moment is an act of generosity and love. 18

As our story unfolds, we learn that power is not a thing, or something to be personally accumulated, or having someone obey us, but a capacity to surrender to something greater than either of us. Power is a reservoir of which we can partake, and to which each can lead the other. Psychology can define this power; technique and skill can take us to its threshold; but it is in a set of practices, within a living discipline of spirit and heart, that we 19 come to the realization: it is the surrendering itself that is empowering.

There are two other characters in our story. One is the land- 20
scape—the bronze hills, the lacquer-blue sky, dust, the trees faithful in their watching, the inevitable wind. The other is the great arc of time. Our story is not finished. What we learn takes time, and it links the tedious with the dramatic and the mundane with the transcendent. Rios and I, as in human relationships, are empowered only when we are available for it, moment by moment, in our continuing, forever-changing story of who we are together.

---

## *Meaning and Purpose*

1. In the first paragraph of this essay, the author says, "It's been a week since we opened this new conversation. . . ." What "new conversation" does he mean?
2. The author remarks in the last line of paragraph 2 that Rios is "capable of anything." No one or no animal is "capable of anything." What does the author mean by that phrase?
3. In paragraph 4, the author says that Rios already has his own "story of power." In your words, describe Rios' "story of power" as it is described in this paragraph.
4. In paragraph 11 is the clause ". . . my love has no teeth." Love is not usually thought of as having teeth in the first place. Why does the author use teeth as a reference for love?
5. What is the importance of the author's hat in this essay?

## *Strategy*

1. In classical rhetoric, the Latin term *significatio* ("sign") describes a phrase, passage, or statement that implies more than it says. In

paragraph 2, the phrase "juvenile delinquent" is an example of *significatio*. What does that phrase imply in that paragraph?
2. Why does the author refer to his year-and-a-half-old daughter in paragraph 2?
3. Paragraph 5 mentions "the fraternal history of horse and man." How is that "history" important to that paragraph?
4. What evidence does the reader have for saying that the author of this essay is an experienced horse trainer?
5. What is the purpose of having simulated conversations between the rider and the horse in this essay?

## *Style*

1. Why does the author begin the essay with "This morning," when obviously it is not now "This morning," the same morning as in the essay?
2. In paragraph 3, what is meant by the phrase "energy fields"?
3. One long sentence in paragraph 4 is cast in italics. Why did the author cast that sentence in italics?
4. Why is the word *coalesce*, as used in paragraph 17, important to understanding this essay?
5. Why, in your opinion, is time referred to as being an "arc" in the last paragraph of this essay?

## *Writing Tasks*

1. Each of us has had a kinship with an animal or with an inanimate object, such as a car, a book, or a piece of sports equipment. We have all had our pets and our properties. Write an essay in which you tell about the process of caring for your pet or your property and how that process served to connect you even more closely with that pet or property.
2. Using data from "Commanded by Love," write an essay that shows the sequential steps taken by the author to change Rios' at-

titude towards his surroundings. Point out which steps you believe are the most important and which steps are the least important.

## ❦ Matthew Maranz ❦

*Matthew Maranz wrote this essay while a student at the Columbia School of Journalism.*

# *Guns "Я" Us*

*In this essay, Maranz shows how easily one can purchase a firearm that was designed for no purpose except to kill people. While walking the reader through the purchasing process, Maranz maintains the calm and clarity of a food-recipe writer. He resists moralizing; instead, he approaches his subject as if it contains information that all of us eagerly await. While reading this essay, ask yourself where, particularly, Maranz "maintains his cool" while writing about especially grim aspects of how easy it is to purchase an automatic weapon. Additionally, note the occasional macabre humor in the essay.*

---

I am over 21 years of age. I am a citizen of the United States. 1
I have not been convicted of a felony. And I have not been treated or confined for drug addiction, drunkenness, or mental illness. According to the National Firearms Act of 1934, I thus qualify to purchase a fully automatic machine gun capable of firing hundreds of bullets with a single squeeze of the trigger. A few months ago, I decided to try.

As far as the federal government is concerned, private citi- 2
zens have always had the right to purchase machine guns—at a price. The Firearms Act, passed by Congress to curb mob warfare, added a $500 manufacturers' tax and $200 transfer tax to the cost. And in May 1986, Congress effectively doubled the price by banning the future manufacture of machine guns for private sale, making them an increasingly scarce commodity. Also, prospective machine-gun buyers must go through a lengthy (one to three months) licensing process, including fingerprinting, that helps the FBI do a background check. But provided I pass

muster on the federal (and state) level, a MAC-10 or Uzi can be mine.

In order to apply for a machine-gun permit, I have to specify exactly what make of machine gun I want. So I walked down to my local newsstand to consult the machine-gunners equivalent of *Consumer Reports. Assault Rifles* carried the definitive work on the .223 controversy—"Can it Measure up to the 7.62 on the Battlefield?" (rest easy, it can). *Firepower* ran a full-page color ad for "Rock n' Roll #3: Sexy Girls and Sexy Guns," a mail-order home video. It starred Dottie/Uzi, Tani Jo/MAC-10, Rosie/MP-5, and Lillian/MP-K and sold for $59.95 plus $3 shipping. Then I came upon an article referring to the Ingram M-11 LISP. The M-11 is a tiny machine pistol that fires 1,200 rounds per minute and fits neatly in a single hand. The CIA used to favor it as a weapon for operations behind enemy lines. That sounded like the gun for me. 3

Taking names from the advertisers' index, I started calling some of the nation's 3,530 licensed machine-gun dealers. My first call reached an answering machine: "Hello. This is SWD Incorporated. Our offices are closed for the holidays. M-11-9 semi-auto pistols and carbines are in stock. M-11-9, M-11-380, and M-10-45 submachine-guns are also in stock in limited quantities. All SMG [submachine-gun] orders must be prepaid to ensure you receive yours. We will ship semi-autos on a c.o.d. basis. Have a joyous holiday season." 4

The first dealer I actually contacted told me that federal law requires machine-gun purchases to be in-state transactions. He suggested I locate a local machine-gun shop. If it didn't have the gun I wanted, an out-of-state dealer would then sell the M-11 to the in-state dealer, who would sell it to me. Turning to "Guns" in the Yellow Pages, I found a local machine-gun salesman. I called and asked about the M-11. 5

"I won't sell it to you," he insisted. 6

I understood. Surely the Second Amendment wasn't meant to cover weapons used to mow down hundreds of innocent bystanders in the streets of our inner cities. 7

"It's a piece of junk," he continued. "Try the MAC-10." 8

The MAC-10 is capable of firing 900 rounds every 60 seconds. The .45 version is a mere $10\frac{1}{2}$ inches long and weighs 6.25 pounds. With telescope and silencer, it grows to 22 inches. Critics frown on its unreliability past 30 yards, but the MAC-10 remains an immensely popular weapon. One reason is that buyers don't just get a gun; they get a piece of history. The MAC-10 was one of the ancestors of the Uzi, arguably today's hippest machine gun. The CIA, FBI, DEA, and Special Forces endorse the MAC-10. So do the Crips and Bloods of Los Angeles gang war fame. And so did Tani Jo in "Rock n' Roll #3: Sexy Girls and Sexy Guns." Good enough for Tani Jo, good enough for me. I became a MAC-10 convert. 9

Now I was ready to apply for a state and federal machine-gun permit. How difficult that is depends on where you live. Some 14 states prohibit private ownership of machine guns; others like Texas, Virginia, and Ohio are notorious for their loose gun laws. In Massachusetts, gun laws are tight. Before going through the cumbersome federal process, I had to think of a subtle way to ask a boss and a friend to provide letters of reference certifying my ability to be a responsible owner of a machine gun. I had to obtain three 1.5" by 1.5" pictures of myself to attach to the handgun application that's required for a machine-gun license. I also had to deal with a police sergeant manning the licensing table who was understandably hostile to civilians seeking machine guns. I persevered. 10

But the eternally curious federal bureaucracy almost stopped me in my tracks. They sent me a slew of white Form 4's and yellow Form 7's required by the Bureau of Alcohol, Tobacco, and Firearms, which keeps track of the number of machine guns in private circulation (191,857 as of December 1988). No one, not the National Rifle Association, the local gun dealer, my friends at work, my mother, even the people I called at the Bureau of Alcohol, Tobacco, and Firearms, could decipher them. Paperwork is America's tightest means of gun control. 11

There had to be an easier, yet legal, way to evade the bureaucracy. I went back to my magazines and found Automatic Weaponry of Brentwood, Tennessee, "America's Foremost Supplier of Title II Firearms [machine guns and silencers]." 12

The man at Automatic Weaponry said they specialized in simplifying the federal licensing process. I give Automatic Weaponry basic biographical information over the phone. I send them a 50 percent deposit that's refundable except for a $100 processing fee. They mail me an order form, the already completed white Form 4 and two FBI Fingerprint Applicant Cards. I sign the forms, affix a recent 2" by 2" photograph, and declare a purpose for purchasing a machine gun ("don't put down 'to kill human beings,' " he suggested). I take them to my local chief law enforcement officer, who fingerprints me and verifies my identity and age. He also conducts a National Crime Information Center search for felony convictions (misdemeanors OK). He signs the forms. I mail the paperwork back to Automatic Weaponry. I pay the balance. (Automatic Weaponry accepts personal and business checks, and all major credit cards.) They ship the weapon to an in-state gun dealer via United Parcel Service. Seventy to 90 days after I first contact Automatic Weaponry, I pick up my machine gun. A MAC-10 .45 caliber in mint condition costs $1,295 plus the $200 federal machine-gun transfer tax (Tani Jo not included). 13

For those with less time, money, and respect for the law, there's an easier way. A semi-automatic MAC-10 retails for as little as $350 and is sold under the same federal regulatory guidelines as a rifle—no fingerprinting or background check required, just proof that you are a U.S. citizen over 18, are not a convicted felon, and have never been confined or incarcerated for drunkenness, drug addiction, or mental illness. In some states I could walk into a gun shop, fill out a few forms, plunk down some cash, and leave with gun in hand. True, like all semi-automatics it would fire only one bullet with each squeeze of the trigger. But if I wanted to risk a 20-year jail term and $20,000 fine, I could convert my semi- into a fully-automatic 900-round-a-minute weapon. A matchstick is all that's needed to convert some guns. The MAC-10 is more sophisticated: one gun dealer I spoke with said he's used a nickel. A guy at the NRA boasted it would take him 15 minutes. But what about someone like me, with zero mechanical ability? He asked if I could change a sparkplug. Probably, I replied. Don't worry, he said, you could do it in an hour. 14

---

## Meaning and Purpose

1. What is interesting about the title of this essay? What does the title imply?
2. The primary question being answered in this essay is, How does one purchase a machine gun in this country? What is unusual about how this question is answered?
3. What is the author's opinion of the gun laws he discusses? Provide evidence to support your answer.
4. Several lines in this essay are humorous. Note one of these lines and tell how you believe it adds to the view or views expressed in the paragraph containing the line.

## Strategy

1. Why did the author combine girls' names with guns' names in paragraph 3?
2. What probable "holiday season" is mentioned in paragraph 4? How does the author's mentioning that season lend irony to that paragraph? (See Glossary for a definition of *irony*.)
3. In paragraph 8, what does the salesman call "a piece of junk"? What is his reason for voicing that opinion?
4. In paragraph 14, we see that one can use a "matchstick" to convert some guns to fully automatic operation. But any gunsmith knows that you can use a paper clip, a small piece of wood, or even the plastic tip on a shoestring. Why would the author use "matchstick" to make his point?

## Style

1. In paragraph 11, to whom does the phrase "police sergeant" refer? Why, in your opinion, did the author use that particular phrase?
2. Why is the word *nickel* used in a sentence in paragraph 14? Why do many readers see that part of the sentence as humorous?

3. In paragraph 11, what does the word *subtle* mean?
4. In paragraph 9, what does the word *hippest* mean? What does the meaning of that word suggest to you, when it is used to describe a machine gun?

## *Writing Tasks*

1. In a well-constructed essay, describe the steps that a person your age and gender should take to get ready for a formal evening. In the essay you just read, the author tells his readers how to purchase a gun—by purchasing a gun. Show your reader how to get ready for a formal evening by telling that reader how you yourself would get ready.
2. By reading this essay, you have a fair idea of the steps one must take to buy a certain kind of gun. Now it's your turn: Imagine that four quality television shows come on at the same time, but on four different channels. Develop a process for determining which show a person of your age and gender should watch, and then write an essay containing the steps in your process and at least one reason for taking each of the steps.

# ❦ Joan Didion ❦

*A Californian by birth, educated at the University of California at Berkeley, descended from pioneers, Joan Didion has written extensively about contemporary life in the western United States. From 1956 to 1963 she was an associate feature editor at* Vogue *magazine, and during that time published widely in prominent national magazines. Her first book of essays,* Slouching Towards Bethlehem *(1968), compiles many of these early essays and focuses on America in the 1960s, particularly San Francisco. She has written four novels, including* Play It as It Lays *(1970) and* Book of Common Prayer *(1977), and collaborated with her husband on several screenplays. Her most recent works are* After Henry *(1992) and* Salvador *(1994). She is known for her incisive reflections and unique vision of American lifestyles.*

## *On Keeping a Notebook*

*In this essay from* Slouching Towards Bethlehem, *Joan Didion explains the purpose and importance, for her, of keeping a notebook. Though her analysis is primarily informational, it might also be considered directional for readers who are inclined to keep notebooks. She offers the process as a way for the writer to "keep in touch" with the people he or she "used to be."*

*As you read this essay, look for ways that Didion distinguishes between the factual steps and the psychological steps involved in keeping a diary.*

---

" 'That woman Estelle,' " the note reads, " 'is partly the reason why George Sharp and I are separated today.' *Dirty crêpe-de-Chine wrapper, hotel bar, Wilmington RR, 9:45* A.M. *August Monday morning.*" 1

Since the note is in my notebook, it presumably has some meaning to me. I study it for a long while. At first I have only the most general notion of what I was doing on an August Monday morning in the bar of the hotel across from the Pennsylvania 2

Railroad station in Wilmington, Delaware (waiting for a train? missing one? 1960? 1961? why Wilmington?), but I do remember being there. The woman in the dirty crêpre-de-Chine wrapper had come down from her room for a beer, and the bartender had heard before the reason why George Sharp and she were separated today. "Sure," he said, and went on mopping the floor. "You told me." At the other end of the bar is a girl. She is talking, pointedly, not to the man beside her but to a cat lying in the triangle of sunlight cast through the open door. She is wearing a plaid silk dress from Peck & Peck, and the hem is coming down.

Here is what it is: the girl has been on the Eastern Shore, and now she is going back to the city, leaving the man beside her, and all she can see ahead are the viscous summer sidewalks and the 3 A.M. long-distance calls that will make her lie awake and then sleep drugged through all the steaming mornings left in August (1960? 1961?). Because she must go directly from the train to lunch in New York, she wishes that she had a safety pin for the hem of the plaid silk dress, and she also wishes that she could forget about the hem and the lunch and stay in the cool bar that smells of disinfectant and malt and make friends with the woman in the crêpe-de-Chine wrapper. She is afflicted by a little self-pity, and she wants to compare Estelles. That is what that was all about. 3

Why did I write it down? In order to remember, of course, but exactly what was it I wanted to remember? How much of it actually happened? Did any of it? Why do I keep a notebook at all? It is easy to deceive oneself on all those scores. The impulse to write things down is a peculiarly compulsive one, inexplicable to those who do not share it, useful only accidentally, only secondarily, in the way that any compulsion tries to justify itself. I suppose that it begins or does not begin in the cradle. Although I have felt compelled to write things down since I was five years old, I doubt that my daughter ever will, for she is a singularly blessed and accepting child, delighted with life exactly as life presents itself to her, unafraid to go to sleep and unafraid to wake up. Keepers of private notebooks are a different breed altogether, lonely and resistant rearrangers of things, anxious malcontents, children afflicted apparently at birth with some presentiment of loss. 4

My first notebook was a Big Five tablet, given to me by my 5
mother with the sensible suggestion that I stop whining and learn to amuse myself by writing down my thoughts. She returned the tablet to me a few years ago; the first entry is an account of a woman who believed herself to be freezing to death in the Arctic night, only to find, when day broke, that she had stumbled onto the Sahara Desert, where she would die of the heat before lunch. I have no idea what turn of a five-year-old's mind could have prompted so insistently "ironic" and exotic a story, but it does reveal a certain predilection for the extreme which has dogged me into adult life; perhaps if I were analytically inclined I would find it a truer story than any I might have told about Donald Johnson's birthday party or the day my cousin Brenda put Kitty Litter in the aquarium.

So the point of my keeping a notebook has never been, nor is 6
it now, to have an accurate factual record of what I have been doing or thinking. That would be a different impulse entirely, an instinct for reality which I sometimes envy but do not possess. At no point have I ever been able successfully to keep a diary; my approach to daily life ranges from the grossly negligent to the merely absent, and on those few occasions when I have tried dutifully to record a day's events, boredom has so overcome me that the results are mysterious at best. What is this business about "shopping, typing piece, dinner with E, depressed"? Shopping for what? Type what piece? Who is E? Was this "E" depressed, or was I depressed? Who cares?

In fact I have abandoned altogether that kind of pointless en- 7
try; instead I tell what some would call lies. "That's simply not true," the members of my family frequently tell me when they come up against my memory of a shared event. "The party was not for you, the spider was *not* a black widow, *it wasn't that way at all*." Very likely they are right, for not only have I always had trouble distinguishing between what happened and what merely might have happened, but I remain unconvinced that the distinction, for my purposes, matters. The cracked crab that I recall having for lunch the day my father came home from Detroit in 1945 must

certainly be embroidery, worked into the day's pattern to lend verisimilitude; I was ten years old and would not now remember the cracked crab. The day's events did not turn on cracked crab. And yet it is precisely that fictitious crab that makes me see the afternoon all over again, a home movie run all too often, the father bearing gifts, the child weeping, an exercise in family love and guilt. Or that is what it was to me. Similarly, perhaps it never did snow that August in Vermont; perhaps there never were flurries in the night wind, and maybe no one else felt the ground hardening and summer already dead even as we pretended to bask in it, but that was how it felt to me; and it might as well have snowed, could have snowed, did snow.

*How it felt to me*: that is getting closer to the truth about a note- 8
book. I sometimes delude myself about why I keep a notebook, imagine that some thrifty virtue derives from preserving everything observed. See enough and write it down, I tell myself and then some morning when the world seems drained of wonder, some day when I am only going through the motions of doing what I am supposed to do, which is write—on that bankrupt morning I will simply open my notebook and there it will be, a forgotten account with accumulated interest, paid passage back to the world out there: dialogue overheard in hotels and elevators and at the hatcheck counter in Pavillon (one middle-aged man shows his hat check to another and says, "That's my old football number"); impressions of Bettina Aptheker and Benjamin Sonnenberg and Teddy ("Mr. Acapulco") Stauffer; careful *aperçus* about tennis bums and failed fashion models and Greek shipping heiresses, one of whom taught me a significant lesson (a lesson I could have learned from F. Scott Fitzgerald, but perhaps we all must meet the very rich for ourselves) by asking, when I arrived to interview her in her orchid-filled sitting room on the second day of a paralyzing New York blizzard, whether it was snowing outside.

I imagine, in other words, that the notebook is about other 9
people. But of course it is not. I have no real business with what one stranger said to another at the hatcheck counter in Pavillon; in fact I suspect that the line "That's my old football number" touched not my own imagination at all, but merely some memory

of something once read, probably "The Eighty-Yard Run." Nor is my concern with a woman in a dirty crêpe-de-Chine wrapper in a Wilmington bar. My stake is always, of course, in the unmentioned girl in the plaid silk dress. *Remember what it was to be me*: that is always the point.

It is a difficult point to admit. We are brought up in the ethic that others, any others, all others, are by definition more interesting than ourselves; taught to be diffident, just this side of self-effacing. ("You're the least important person in the room and don't forget it," Jessica Mitford's governess would hiss in her ear on the advent of any social occasion; I copied that into my notebook because it is only recently that I have been able to enter a room without hearing some such phrase in my inner ear.) Only the very young and the very old may recount their dreams at breakfast, dwell upon self, interrupt with memories of beach picnics and favorite Liberty lawn dresses and the rainbow trout in a creek near Colorado Springs. The rest of us are expected, rightly, to affect absorption in other people's favorite dresses, other people's trout. 10

And so we do. But our notebooks give us away, for however dutifully we record what we see around us, the common denominator of all we see is always, transparently, shamelessly, the implacable "I". We are not talking here about the kind of notebook that is patently for public consumption, a structural conceit for binding together a series of graceful *pensées*; we are talking about something private, about bits of the mind's string too short to use, an indiscriminate and erratic assemblage with meaning only for its maker. 11

And sometimes even the maker has difficulty with the meaning. There does not seem to be, for example, any point in my knowing for the rest of my life that, during 1964, 720 tons of soot fell on every square mile of New York City, yet there it is in my notebook, labeled "FACT." Nor do I really need to remember that Ambrose Bierce liked to spell Leland Stanford's name "£eland $tanford" or that "smart women almost always wear black in Cuba," a fashion hint without much potential for practical application. And does not the relevance of these notes seem marginal at best?: 12

In the basement of the Inyo County Courthouse in Independence, California, sign pinned to a mandarin coat: "This MANDARIN COAT was often worn by Mrs. Minnie S. Brooks when giving lectures on her TEAPOT COLLECTION."

Redhead getting out of car in front of Beverly Wilshire Hotel, chinchilla stole, Vuitton bags with tags reading:

MRS LOU FOX
HOTEL SAHARA
VEGAS

Well, perhaps not entirely marginal. As a matter of fact, Mrs. Minnie S. Brooks and her MANDARIN COAT pull me back into my own childhood, for although I never knew Mrs. Brooks and did not visit Inyo County until I was thirty, I grew up in just such a world, in houses cluttered with Indian relics and bits of gold ore and ambergris and the souvenirs my Aunt Mercy Farnsworth brought back from the Orient. It is a long way from that world to Mrs. Lou Fox's world where we all live now, and is it not just as well to remember that? Might not Mrs. Minnie S. Brooks help me to remember what I am? Might not Mrs. Lou Fox help me to remember what I am not?

But sometimes the point is harder to discern. What exactly 13
did I have in mind when I noted down that it cost the father of someone I know $650 a month to light the place on the Hudson in which he lived before the Crash? What use was I planning to make of this line by Jimmy Hoffa: "I may have my faults, but being wrong ain't one of them"? And although I think it interesting to know where the girls who travel with the Syndicate have their hair done when they find themselves on the West Coast, will I ever make suitable use of it? Might I not be better off just passing it on to John O'Hara? What is a recipe for sauerkraut doing in my notebook? What kind of magpie keeps this notebook? "*He was born the night the* Titanic *went down.*" That seems a nice enough line, and I even recall who

said it, but is it not really a better line in life than it could ever be in fiction?

But of course that is exactly it: not that I should ever use the line, but that I should remember the woman who said it and the afternoon I heard it. We were on her terrace by the sea, and we were finishing the wine left from lunch, trying to get what sun there was, a California winter sun. The woman whose husband was born the night the *Titanic* went down wanted to rent her house, wanted to go back to her children in Paris. I remember wishing that I could afford the house, which cost $1,000 a month. "Someday you will," she said lazily. "Someday it all comes." There in the sun on her terrace it seemed easy to believe in someday but later I had a low-grade afternoon hangover and ran over a black snake on the way to the supermarket and was flooded with inexplicable fear when I heard the checkout clerk explaining to the man ahead of me why she was finally divorcing her husband. "He left me no choice," she said over and over as she punched the register. "He has a little seven-month-old baby by her, he left me no choice." I would like to believe that my dread then was for the human condition, but of course it was for me, because I wanted a baby and did not then have one and because I wanted to own the house that cost $1,000 a month to rent and because I had a hangover. 14

It all comes back. Perhaps it is difficult to see the value in having one's self back in that kind of mood, but I do see it; I think we are well advised to keep on nodding terms with the people we used to be, whether we find them attractive company or not. Otherwise they turn up unannounced and surprise us, come hammering on the mind's door at 4 A.M. of a bad night and demand to know who deserted them, who betrayed them, who is going to make amends. We forget all too soon the things we thought we could never forget. We forget the loves and the betrayals alike, forget what we whispered and what we screamed, forget who we were. I have already lost touch with a couple of people I used to be; one of them, a seventeen-year-old, presents little threat, although it would be of some interest to me to know again what it feels like to sit on a river levee drinking vodka-and-orange-juice 15 and listening to Les Paul and Mary Ford and their echoes sing "How High the Moon" on the car radio. (You see I still have the scenes, but I no longer perceive myself among those present, no longer could even improvise the dialogue.) The other one, a twenty-three-year-old, bothers me more. She was always a good deal of trouble, and I suspect she will reappear when I least want to see her, skirts too long, shy to the point of aggravation, always the injured party, full of recriminations and little hurts and stories I do not want to hear again, at once saddening me and angering me with her vulnerability and ignorance, an apparition all the more insistent for being so long banished.

It is a good idea, then, to keep in touch and I suppose that 16
keeping in touch is what notebooks are all about. And we are all on our own when it comes to keeping those lines open to ourselves: your notebooks will never help me, nor mine you. "*So what's new in the whiskey business?*" What could that possibly mean to you? To me it means a blonde in a Pucci bathing suit sitting with a couple of fat men by the pool at the Beverly Hills Hotel. Another man approaches, and they all regard one another in silence for a while. "So what's new in the whiskey business?" one of the fat men finally says by way of welcome, and the blonde stands up, arches one foot and dips it in the pool, looking all the while at the cabana where Baby Pignatari is talking on the telephone. That is all there is to that, except that several years later I saw the blonde coming out of Saks Fifth Avenue in New York with her California complexion and a voluminous mink coat. In the harsh wind that day she looked old and irrevocably tired to me, and even the skins in the mink coat were not worked the way they were doing them that year, not the way she would have wanted them done, and there is the point of the story. For a while after that I did not like to look in the mirror, and my eyes would skim the newspapers and pick out only the deaths, the cancer victims, the premature coronaries, the suicides, and I stopped riding the Lexington Avenue IRT because I noticed for the first time that all the strangers I had seen for years—the man with the seeing-eye dog, the spinster who read the classified pages every day, the fat girl who always got off with me at Grand Central—looked older than they once had.

It all comes back. Even that recipe for sauerkraut: even that brings it back. I was on Fire Island when I first made sauerkraut, and it was raining, and we drank a lot of bourbon and ate the sauerkraut and went to bed at ten, and I listened to the rain and the Atlantic and felt safe. I made the sauerkraut again last night and it did not make me feel any safer, but that is, as they say, another story. 17

---

## *Meaning and Purpose*

1. After reading this essay, you know that a diary and a notebook differ. What is one big difference?
2. Do you keep a notebook or journal? If so, how does your method of writing in it, and the use you make of it, compare to Didion's?
3. What is one process the author discusses, and why does any writer need to become familiar with it?
4. In a line in paragraph 11, Didion says, "Our notebooks give us away." To whom do they give us away?
5. Several statements in the essay could be taken as versions of Didion's main point. What are some of them, and how are they related to one another?

## *Strategy*

1. The essay begins in the middle of an action—Didion is reading a note she wrote in her notebook. Then, before she gives a context for the note, she talks about it and embellishes it. Why do you think she begins in this way?
2. In the structure of her essay, how does Didion make use of the little stories behind the brief notes she has written in her notebook?
3. Didion ends her essay with the story of the recipe for sauerkraut, another note expanded into an anecdote. Is she ending

in the middle again, as she began? Discuss the effectiveness of the ending.

## Style

1. What is Didion's tone in this essay—her attitude toward her subject?
2. In paragraph 3, the writer says she "wants to compare Estelles," using the noun metaphorically. What is an "Estelle"?
3. "California complexion," in paragraph 16, is an example of stereotyping. In your opinion, what is "California complexion"?
4. In paragraph 5, Didion mentions that she has a "predilection for the extreme." Explain this phrase.

## Writing Tasks

1. Describe one of your dreams and discuss what it reveals about you, just as Didion discusses what her notebook reveals about her.
2. Didion describes a process linked to the creative imagination. Her notes themselves are not so important as what those notes suggest to her, imaginatively. Using a similar procedure, choose three related personal items. Write an informative process analysis in which you describe these items briefly, and then discuss what they mean emotionally to you.

## ❦ Donald M. Murray ❦

*Donald M. Murray was born in 1924 in Boston. He has had a long and distinguished career as a writer and teacher. Murray has published fiction, nonfiction, and poetry, served as an editor of* Time magazine, *and won the Pulitzer Prize for editorial writing in 1959. Currently he is a professor of English at the University of New Hampshire, Durham. His teaching career and the textbooks he has published on how to write—*A Writer Teaches Writing, Write to Learn, *and* Read to Write*—have established him as one of America's most influential teachers of writing. He sees the writing teacher as a coach and is convinced that a student must want to learn and be willing to exert much effort in order to write well.*

# *The Maker's Eye:*

## *Revising Your Own Manuscripts*

*Originally published in* The Writer, *this essay demonstrates the process professional writers go through to revise their manuscripts. Murray distinguishes the differences in attitudes that student writers and professional writers take to the revising process and cites other professional writers to argue for the essential importance of meticulous revision.*

*As you read, note any differences between the methods you use to revise a paper and the methods the professional writer uses. Jot down advice you might find helpful in improving your own writing.*

---

1 When students complete a first draft, they consider the job of writing done—and their teachers too often agree. When professional writers complete a first draft, they usually feel that they are at the start of the writing process. When a draft is completed, the job of writing can begin.

2 That difference in attitude is the difference between amateur and professional, inexperience and experience, journeyman and craftsman. Peter F. Drucker, the prolific business writer, calls his first draft "the zero draft"—after that he can start counting. Most

writers share the feeling that the first draft, and all of those which follow, are opportunities to discover what they have to say and how best they can say it.

To produce a progression of drafts, each of which says more and says it more clearly, the writer has to develop a special kind of reading skill. In school we are taught to decode what appears on the page as finished writing. Writers, however, face a different category of possibility and responsibility when they read their own drafts. To them the words on the page are never finished. Each can be changed and rearranged, can set off a chain reaction of confusion or clarified meaning. This is a different kind of reading, which is possibly more difficult and certainly more exciting. 3

Writers must learn to be their own best enemy. They must accept the criticism of others and be suspicious of it; they must accept the praise of others and be even more suspicious of it. Writers cannot depend on others. They must detach themselves from their own pages so that they can apply both their caring and their craft to their own work. 4

Such detachment is not easy. Science fiction writer Ray Bradbury supposedly puts each manuscript away for a year to the day and then rereads it as a stranger. Not many writers have the discipline or the time to do this. We must read when our judgment may be at its worst, when we are close to the euphoric moment of creation. 5

Then the writer, counsels novelist Nancy Hale, "should be critical of everything that seems to him most delightful in his style. He should excise what he most admires, because he wouldn't thus admire it if he weren't . . . in a sense protecting it from criticism." John Ciardi, the poet, adds, "The last act of the writing must be to become one's own reader. It is, I suppose, a schizophrenic process, to begin passionately and to end critically, to begin hot and to end cold; and, more important, to be passion-hot and critic-cold at the same time." 6

Most people think that the principal problem is that writers are too proud of what they have written. Actually, a greater problem for most professional writers is one shared by the majority of students. They are overly critical, think everything is 7 dreadful, tear up page after page, never complete a draft, see the task as hopeless.

The writer must learn to read critically but constructively, to cut what is bad, to reveal what is good. Eleanor Estes, the children's book author, explains: "The writer must survey his work critically, coolly, as though he were a stranger to it. He must be willing to prune, expertly and hard-heartedly. At the end of each revision, a manuscript may look . . . worked over, torn apart, pinned together, added to, deleted from, words changed and words changed back. Yet the book must maintain its original freshness and spontaneity." 8

Most readers underestimate the amount of rewriting it usually takes to produce spontaneous reading. This is a great disadvantage to the student writer, who sees only a finished product and never watches the craftsman who takes the necessary step back, studies the work carefully, returns to the task, steps back, returns, steps back, again and again. Anthony Burgess, one of the most prolific writers in the English-speaking world, admits, "I might revise a page twenty times." Ronald Dahl, the popular children's writer, states, "By the time I'm nearing the end of a story, the first part will have been reread and altered and corrected at least 150 times . . . . Good writing is essentially rewriting. I am positive of this." 9

Rewriting isn't virtuous. It isn't something that ought to be done. It is simply something that most writers find they have to do to discover what they have to say and how to say it. It is a condition of the writer's life. 10

There are, however, a few writers who do little formal rewriting, primarily because they have the capacity and experience to create and review a large number of invisible drafts in their minds before they approach the page. And some writers slowly produce finished pages, performing all the tasks of revision simultaneously, page by page, rather than draft by draft. But it is still possible to see the sequence followed by most writers most of the time in rereading their own work. 11

Most writers scan their drafts first, reading as quickly as possible to catch the larger problems of subject and form, then move in closer and closer as they read and write, reread and rewrite. 12

The first thing writers look for in their drafts is *information*. They know that a good piece of writing is built from specific, accurate, and interesting information. The writer must have an abundance of information from which to construct a readable piece of writing. 13

Next writers look for *meaning* in the information. The specifics must build a pattern of significance. Each piece of specific information must carry the reader toward meaning. 14

Writers reading their own drafts are aware of *audience*. They put themselves in the reader's situation and make sure that they deliver information which a reader wants to know or needs to know in a manner which is easily digested. Writers try to be sure that they anticipate and answer the questions a critical reader will ask when reading the piece of writing. 15

Writers make sure that the *form* is appropriate to the subject and the audience. Form, or genre, is the vehicle which carries meaning to the reader, but form cannot be selected until the writer has adequate information to discover its significance and an audience which needs or wants that meaning. 16

Once writers are sure the form is appropriate, they must then look at the *structure*, the order of what they have written. Good writing is built on a solid framework of logic, argument, narrative, or motivation which runs through the entire piece of writing and holds it together. This is the time when many writers find it most effective to outline as a way of visualizing the hidden spine by which the piece of writing is supported. 17

The element on which writers may spend a majority of their time is *development*. Each section of a piece of writing must be adequately developed. It must give readers enough information so that they are satisfied. How much information is enough? That's as difficult as asking how much garlic belongs in a salad. It must be done to taste, but most beginning writers underdevelop, underestimating the reader's hunger for information. 18

As writers solve development problems, they often have to consider questions of *dimension*. There must be a pleasing and effective proportion among all the parts of the piece of writing. There is a continual process of subtracting and adding to keep the piece of writing in balance. 19

Finally, writers have to listen to their own voices. *Voice* is the force which drives a piece of writing forward. It is an expression of the writer's authority and concern. It is what is between the words on the page, what glues the piece of writing together. A good piece of writing is always marked by a consistent, individual voice. 20

As writers read and reread, write and rewrite, they move closer and closer to the page until they are doing line-by-line editing. Writers read their own pages with infinite care. Each sentence, each line, each clause, each phrase, each word, each mark of punctuation, each section of white space between the type has to contribute to the clarification of meaning. 21

Slowly the writer moves from word to word, looking through language to see the subject. As a word is changed, cut, or added, as a construction is rearranged, all the words used before that moment and all those that follow that moment must be considered and reconsidered. 22

Writers often read aloud at this stage of the editing process, muttering or whispering to themselves, calling on the ear's experience with language. Does this sound right—or that? Writers edit, shifting back and forth from eye to page to ear to page. I find I must do this careful editing in short runs, no more than fifteen or twenty minutes at a stretch, or I become too kind with myself. I begin to see what I hope is on the page, not what actually is on the page. 23

This sounds tedious if you haven't done it, but actually it is fun. Making something right is immensely satisfying, for writers begin to learn what they are writing about by writing. Language leads them to meaning, and there is the joy of discovery, of understanding, of making meaning clear as the writer employs the technical skills of language. 24

Words have double meanings, even triple and quadruple meanings. Each word has its own potential for connotation and denotation. And when writers rub one word against the other, they are often rewarded with a sudden insight, an unexpected clarification. 25

The maker's eye moves back and forth from word to phrase to sentence to paragraph to sentence to phrase to word. The maker's 26 eye sees the need for variety and balance, for a firmer structure, for a more appropriate form. It peers into the interior of the paragraph, looking for coherence, unity, and emphasis, which make meaning clear.

I learned something about this process when my first bifocals were prescribed. I had ordered a larger section of the reading portion of the glass because of my work, but even so, I could not contain my eyes within this new limit of vision. And I still find myself taking off my glasses and bending my nose towards the page, for my eyes unconsciously flick back and forth across the page, back to another page, forward to still another, as I try to see each evolving line in relation to every other line. 27

When does this process end? Most writers agree with the great Russian writer Tolstoy, who said, "I scarcely ever reread my published writings, if by chance I come across a page, it always strikes me: all this must be rewritten; this is how I should have written it." 28

The maker's eye is never satisfied, for each word has the potential to ignite new meaning. This article has been twice written all the way through the writing process, and it was published four years ago. Now it is to be republished in a book. The editors make a few small suggestions, and then I read it with my maker's eye. Now it has been re-edited, re-revised, re-read, re-re-edited, for each piece of writing to the writer is full of potential and alternatives. 29

A piece of writing is never finished. It is delivered to a deadline, torn out of the typewriter on demand, sent off with a sense of accomplishment and shame and pride and frustration. If only there were a couple more days, time for just another run at it, perhaps then . . . 30

---

## *Meaning and Purpose*

1. According to Murray, what are the differences in the ways that professional writers and student writers view their first drafts?

Do his observations ring true? Do both types of writers share any common problems?

2. What two kinds of reading skills does the author distinguish? How does the writer's reading skill differ from that of the normal reader's?
3. What does Murray mean when he says, "Writers must learn to be their own best enemy"? Explain.
4. In paragraphs 13–30, Murray takes the reader chronologically through each of the elements that a writer must consider to revise a manuscript. Describe the ways a writer must consider each of these elements.
5. Murray distinguishes between "information" and "meaning." Explain the difference between the two.
6. Explain Murray's contention that "A piece of writing is never finished" (30).

## Strategy

1. What is the essay's thesis? Where is it stated?
2. Is the essay an example of directive or informative process analysis (see pp.390–396)? Explain.
3. Murray cites other writers in his description of the revision process. Why?
4. Explain the author's seemingly odd statement that " . . . most writers share the feeling that the first draft, and all of those which follow, are opportunities to discover what they have to say . . ." (2).
5. Murray doesn't actually begin a description of the professional writer's revision process until paragraph 12. What is the purpose of such a long introduction?

## Style

1. Murray changes from the third person ("writer," "writers," "the maker") to the first person ("I") in paragraphs 23, 27, and 29. What effect does he create by this change of person?

2. Why does Murray end the essay in mid-sentence?
3. If necessary, use a dictionary to determine the meanings of these words: *journeyman, prolific* (2); *euphoric* (5); *schizophrenic* (6); *connotation, denotation* (25).

## *Writing Tasks*

1. Write an essay in which you detail the way you revise an essay. Explain, in the process, why this method may work for you better than the method explained by Murray.
2. If you use a computer to write, explain the advantages of revising on a computer.
3. Write an essay in which you explain to the reader a process that you do regularly and well. Without being moralistic, demonstrate how this might actually benefit the reader.

## ❦ *Responding to Photographs* ❦

*Process Analysis*

Untitled

For some writers the act of writing can be so painful they go to remarkable lengths to postpone the labor. They travel to the farthest stationery store for the "right" pencil, the one with the exact texture of lead that works best with the amount of pressure they apply to the paper. When they return, they may discover that they are short of the right kind of paper—you know, the yellow pads with the blue lines. Again back to the stationery store. Home once again, all those new pencils must be sharpened to a fine, a very, very fine, point.

What's the solution to this kind of procrastination?

There probably isn't one, for writing is a deeply personal process, one that is full of mystery. Probably no two people go about it exactly the same way. We all use devices to get ourselves started and to keep ourselves at the task. Nevertheless, something must get written. We must get the images and thoughts out of our heads, translate them to words, and put them on paper. Then, of course, a new process begins—the revision process.

Clearly, the untitled photograph here captures a moment in the writing process. For this essay, you are to explore the writing process by completing one of the following writing tasks. Before beginning the task reread "Process Analysis: Explaining Step by Step" at the beginning of the chapter, to remind yourself of process analysis strategies.

1. Create an appropriate title for the untitled photograph. Then describe its content as capturing part of the writing process In your essay, account for all the elements in the photograph that relate to the writing process—manuscript, pencils, coffee, calendar, stapler, glasses, desk or table, even the writer's posture.
2. Document your own writing process with photographs of its various stages. Then use the photographs to compose a "photo-essay" that concentrates on your own writing process. Use at least five photographs, each one capturing a stage in the process, and explain to your readers what the photographs signify. Keep in mind that writing is a highly personal process, so be sure your photographs and essay embody your personal writing quirks.

## ❦ *Additional Writing Tasks* ❦

*Process Analysis*

1. Develop one of these subjects (or one you create for yourself) through *directive process analysis*. Explain the process one step at a time and be sure to provide your reader with enough detail to make each step clear.
   a. how to prepare a vegetable garden
   b. how to live without an automobile
   c. how to domesticate a wild creature, such as a falcon or rabbit
   d. how to get rid of pests without using poisons
   e. how to prepare for an acting role
   f. how to prepare a canvas for paint
   g. how to show appreciation to others
   h. how to toss a Frisbee, football, baseball, and so on
   i. how to skateboard, roller blade, roller skate
   j. how to bluff at poker
   k. how to survive Muzak
   l. how to complain effectively
   m. how to overcome shyness
   n. how to write an effective essay
   o. how to take effective notes
   p. how to outsmart a video game
   q. how to survive a natural disaster, such as an earthquake or tornado
   r. how to meditate in a crowded setting
   s. how to ride a roller coaster
   t. how to attend a concert
   u. how to run for local elected office
   v. how to win others to your point of view
   w. how to buy a used motorcycle or car
2. Develop one of these subjects (or one you create for yourself) through *informative process analysis*. Remember that this technique does not explain "how to" do something; it explains how something happens—it informs, often using narrative and descriptive techniques.

a. how psychoanalysis works
b. how secret codes are broken
c. how to read detective, espionage, or suspense fiction
d. how to learn from past experience
e. how a stroke damages the brain
f. how Alzheimer's disease develops
g. how dreams work
h. how intuition works
i. how to taste wine
j. how to create a frightening film scene
k. how to create suspense
l. how to collect art, rare books, or something else
m. how to detect lies
n. how to overcome guilt
o. how to change community thinking
p. how to live as an outsider
q. how to become an insider
r. how an idea becomes accepted
s. how voodoo works

# 9

# *Classification and Division*

## *Establishing Categories*

## *The Method*

Have you ever played Twenty Questions, a parlor game in which one participant selects a person, place, or thing and the other participants try to guess it? The participants have twenty yes-or-no questions to find the answer. To discover that answer is a difficult task—unless you understand the principles of **classification**.

The game usually begins with a series of questions that divide the world into three roughly drawn categories: animal, vegetable, or mineral. Once the correct category is determined—"animal," for our purposes—the interrogation begins, the participants moving logically from category to category.

"Does it live in water?" a questioner might ask. A sensible question, for the earth is easily divided into land and water.

"No," the person with the secret responds. But "No" means the animal lives on land, keeping in mind that birds may fly but may also nest on land. The process of elimination continues.

"Does it have two legs?" Another logical question, because animals can be classified by locomotion.

"No."

"Four legs?" The pace of questions quickens.

"No."

Aha! the questioner has it, "Is this creature an insect?"

"Nope!" Oops . . . must be a snake, right? But what snake? The only two large categories are venomous and nonvenomous. If the answer is venomous, the questions will take one direction, "Does it have rattles?" If the answer is nonvenomous, the questions will move in another direction, "Does it kill by coiling around and crushing its prey?" And so on, until the secret is revealed or twenty questions are exhausted.

To classify is to divide a large subject into components and sort them into categories with common characteristics, a principle that clearly guides the search in any round of Twenty Questions. Classification is so pervasive that it must be fundamental to the human way of perceiving and understanding experience. Few things, no matter how significant or insignificant, seem to escape classification. Think how chaotic your campus library would be without a clear classification system. Your supermarket trips are probably organized by the manager's way of classifying products—first the vegetables, on to dairy products, rush to meats, march to canned goods, stalled at the register. Television shows, books, actors, restaurants, fun-zone rides—the possibilities for classification are endless because of our desire to understand and organize experience.

Keep in mind, too, that most subjects can be classified in a number of ways, depending on the purpose and who's doing the classifying. Consider the subject *college students*. For statistical purposes, a registrar might classify college students by age, sex, major, grade-point average, or region. An art teacher might classify students by their talent: painters, sculptors, ceramicists, illustrators, and print makers. A political-science teacher might classify the same students by their politics: reactionary, conservative, liberal, or radical. Much of this kind of classification is done informally, but in writing, a classification system should be complete and follow consistent principles.

Writers using classification as a pattern of development begin by carefully analyzing their subject—that is, by breaking it into components. They look for qualities that some components share and that others don't share. Using the qualities they've identified, they create categories. They then sort through the various components to group them in the appropriate category. They are careful to be logical, sorting and grouping the parts in a consistent manner. They also keep in mind that their categories must be complete. It would not be complete if they divided voters into Republicans and Democrats, because some voters are registered in the Peace and Freedom and Libertarian parties, among others. But if a writer's subject is limited to elected senators, then the categories might indeed be Republicans and Democrats, because no other party is represented in the Senate. Writers also make sure their categories do not overlap. To classify a group of congresswomen as Republicans, Democrats, and politicians would not make much sense because all are politicians.

Professional writers distinguish between the terms *division* and *classification*, yet these categories are intellectual companions in the classification procedure. Writers begin by first *dividing* a subject into manageable categories. They then *classify* the components of the subject according to the shared qualities. Consider the subject *movies*, which can be broken down into such categories as mystery, romance, horror, musical, comedy, western, and war. This step is division. Once the categories are established, a writer might evaluate several films, and sort them according to the qualities of each category. This step is classification. Remember, division breaks one subject into categories; classification groups the parts of the subject into the categories. Although this distinction may be important for understanding the intellectual procedure of classification, it is less important in reaching the result, a system that shows the relationship among parts of a subject.

The simplest form of classification is **two-part**, often called **binary**, classification. This pattern divides a subject in two, usually into positive and negative categories, such as vegetarians and nonvegetarians; smokers and nonsmokers; television viewers and non–television viewers; deaf people and hearing people; or runners and nonrunners. But two-part classification is usually inexact and skirts the edge of comparison and contrast. Most classification systems, therefore, have at least three categories.

## *Strategies*

Careful writers arrange their classifications in a straightforward division, usually in blocks and according to the order that seems most appropriate. Each block is a subclass and will usually be identified by a name or phrase to keep the reader on track. In the following paragraph, anthropologist Ruth Benedict divides the ceremonial societies of the Zuni. She clearly identifies each society—the priestly societies, the masked-god societies, and the medicine societies—before describing them.

This ceremonial life that preoccupies Zuni attention is organized like a series of interlocking wheels. The priesthoods have their sacred objects, their retreats, their dances, their prayers; and their year-long program is annually initiated by the great winter solstice ceremony that makes use of all the different groups and sacred things and focuses all their functions. The tribal masked-god society has similar possessions and calendric observances, and these culminate in the great winter tribal masked god ceremony, the Shalkado. In like fashion the medicine societies, with their special relation to curing, function throughout the year and have their annual culminating ceremony for tribal health. These three major cults of Zuni ceremonial life are not mutually exclusive. A man may be, and often is, for the greater part of his life, a member of all three. They each give him sacred possessions "to live by" and demand of him exacting ceremonial knowledge.

Writers use one of two strategies to identify their categories. They either use ready-made categories or they create their own. In the next classification passage, from *Blood and Money*, Thomas Thompson uses subclasses to present his view of the personal characteristics that describe surgeons.

Among those who train students to become doctors, it is said that surgeons find their niche in accordance with their personal characteristics. The orthopedic surgeon is medicine's carpenter—up to his elbows in plaster of Paris—and tradition holds that he is a gruff, slapdash sort of man whose labor is in a very physical area of healing. Away from the hospital, the orthopedists are often hunters, boaters, outdoorsmen.

The neurosurgeon, classically, does not get too involved with his patients. Or, for that matter, with anybody. They are cool men, blunted, rarely gregarious.

Heart surgeons are thundering egotists, star performers in a dazzling operating theater packed with assistants, nurses, paramedics, and a battery of futuristic equipment

> which could seemingly lift the room into outer space. These are men who relish drama, who live life on the edge of the precipice.
>
> And the plastic surgeon? He is, by nature, a man of art, and temperament, and sensitivity. "We are the artists who deal in beauty lost, or beauty that never was," said one plastic man at a national convention. "Our stitches are hidden, and so are our emotions."

Because Thompson is working with established categories, part of his task is to make his material fresh. Most readers know the professional qualities of surgeons, and so Thompson creates a sense of the person holding the scalpel by including descriptive details of each type's dominant personality trait.

In the next paragraph, Larry McMurtry uses established categories in a slightly different way. He classifies beer bars in the city of Houston according to their location: East side, West side, and North side.

> The poor have beer-bars, hundreds of them, seldom fancy but reliably dim and cool. Most of them are equipped with jukeboxes, shuffleboards, jars of pig's feet and talkative drunks. There are lots of bar burlesques, where from 3 p.m. on girls gyrate at one's elbow with varying degrees of grace. On the East side there are a fair number of open-air bars—those who like to watch the traffic can sit, drink Pearl, observe the wrecks, and listen to "Hello, Vietnam" on the juke box. Louisiana is just down the road, and a lot of the men wear Cajun sideburns and leave their shirttails out. On the West side cowboys are common. Members of the cross-continental hitch-hiking set congregate on Franklin Street, at places like The Breaking Point Lounge. Symbolic latinos slip over to the Last Concert on the North side; or, if they are especially bold, go all the way to McCarty Street, where one can view the most extraordinary example of Mexican saloon-and-whorehouse architecture north of the border.

McMurtry opens with a general description of Houston beer bars: They are dim and cool with jukeboxes, shuffleboards, jars of pig's feet, and drunks—a watering hole for blue-collar men. After rendering the general qualities of these bars, McMurtry presents the geographic categories, each with a brief description that characterizes it.

Writers often classify a subject that has no ready-made categories. They must, therefore, create their own categories and the labels that identify them. In this paragraph from "Here Is New York," E. B. White divides the population of New York into three categories according to a person's relation to the city.

> There are roughly three New Yorks. There is, first, the New York of the man or woman who was born here, who takes the city for granted and accepts its size and its turbulence as natural and inevitable. Second, there is the New York of the commuter—the city that is devoured by locusts each day and spat out each night. Third, there is the New York of the quest of something. Of these three trembling cities the greatest is the last—the city of final destination, the city that is a goal. It is this third city that accounts for New York's high-strung disposition, its poetical deportment, its dedication to the arts, and its incomparable achievements. Commuters give the city its tidal restlessness; natives give it solidarity and continuity; but the settlers give it passion. And whether it is a farmer arriving from Italy to set up a small grocery store in a slum, or a young girl arriving from a small town in Mississippi to escape the indignity of being observed by her neighbors, or a boy arriving from the Corn Belt with a manuscript in his suitcase and a pain in his heart, it makes no difference: each embraces New York with the intense excitement of first love, each absorbs New York with the fresh eyes of an adventurer, each generates heat and light to dwarf the Consolidated Edison Company.

Commuters, natives, and settlers, these are White's three categories. He uses each category to present characteristics of New York City. The commuter gives the city a sense of restlessness; the native gives it solidarity; and the settler, the category he stresses, gives it passion.

## Classification in College Writing

The physical sciences, social sciences, and humanities all use classification, which some writers believe is the hardest rhetorical pattern to master. Whether the pattern is difficult or not, you can expect to use it across the academic curriculum.

### Guidelines for Classification

1. Select a subject that can be divided into at least three components. Identify the chief characteristics of each component. Use the characteristics to sort and group the components into categories.
2. Examine the categories with two questions in mind: Are they complete—that is, can all the components of your subject be grouped within them? Are the categories consistent—that is, can any of your component parts be classified in more than one category? If your categories are incomplete or inconsistent, then restructure them or move on to another subject.
3. Compose a thesis that clearly indicates you will be classifying your subject. If you use ready-made categories or name your categories, include the names as part of the thesis. Naming your categories early will prepare your readers for the shift from one category to another in the discussion.
4. Decide on how to arrange your categories effectively saving the most dramatic for last.
5. Revise your essay, making sure that each category is clearly distinguished and adequately developed.

### A Student Essay Developed by Classification

In a Cultural Anthropology class Mark Freeman used classification to write an essay on the general topic of people who collect artifacts from popular culture:

> From your own experience and observation, write a 500–600 word essay that concentrates on people who col-

> lect popular culture artifacts, such as baseball cards, garage sale paintings, bottles, magazines, movie posters, bottle caps, teaspoons, tourist novelties.

Freeman interpreted "magazines" to include comic books. Since he was once an avid comic book collector, he had plenty of material to work with.

In Search of the Comic

*Freeman opens with a sentence that immediately identifies his subject—comic-book collectors. He follows with a generalized physical description of collectors.*

*Freeman's thesis statement identifies the four categories of comic-book collectors to keep his readers on track as he shifts from one category to another in the discussion.*

*The discussion is divided into four paragraphs, one paragraph devoted to each category and beginning with an opening that names the category and identifies the collector's outstanding characteristic—the one that separates him from other collectors.*

Comic book collectors represent every economic strata and often fit the stereotype of the computer nerd, that is, whether young or old, they tend to be disheveled males, be pale, wear glasses, and speak a language the uninitiated seldom understand. They can be found rummaging through pile after pile of unsorted, secondhand comics in magazine marts across the country. These collectors, the serious ones, can be classified into four major groups: Antiquarians, Mercenaries, Idolaters, and Compulsive Completers.

The Antiquarian searches for classic comics only, subject matter is of no concern. He is looking for a 1933 Funnies on Parade or Famous Funnies, the first recognizable comic books and initially used as give-aways in advertising promotions. The Antiquarian, driven by a desire to connect with the past, will travel the country's backroads to find 1933 editions of The Spider, which was reintroduced as the Spiderman series in 1962.

The Mercenary searches for value. Certain numbers and titles ring a bell in his cash-register brain and start him checking through a half-dozen price sheets. A pristine first edition of Action Comics (value $12,000) would suit him just fine. He would also hunt down early editions of Marvel Comics, especially the first publications fea-

*Freeman also uses a key word "searches" in each opening, which suggests a quality they all share and unifies the discussion paragraphs.*

*Notice how Freeman includes details throughout the discussion that separate one group of collectors from the others, thus impressing upon the reader their distinguishing behavior.*

turing early superheroes, such as Captain America, the Punisher, and the Human Torch. The Mercenary would, no doubt, love to have first editions of Batman and Superman, but, being a realist, knows they are locked in vaults.

The Idolater has little interest in age or value. He searches for favorites: a Sheena, a Flash Gordon, or an Incredible Hulk. With little money to spend, the Idolater will usually be hiding in the corner of a comic mart, reading the comic books he cannot afford to buy. He will freely announce his dream of creating his own hero figure and is always eager to display his sketches to anyone willing to listen to his heroic tales and future visions. The Idolater will be the last one out of the mart at night and the first one back in the morning.

The most frustrated of the group is the Compulsive Completer. This obsessed collector will examine and reject thousands of comics in a search for a badly needed Felix the Cat to complete a year's set. The Completer is usually a specialist, perhaps concentrating on comic books featuring animals, such as Mighty Mouse, a pint-sized superhero who became famous when featured in cartoons shown between movies in theaters across America, or Super Rabbit, a long-eared protector of the innocent who became known during W. W. II for fighting Nazis in the pages of Marvel Comics. Compulsive Completers often become so desperate to acquire every issue published in one year they will seek bank loans to cover their costs.

*The conclusion is brief but effectively ends the essay. Freeman renames the categories and a characteristic that serves as an underlying theme and unites them—the thrill of the hunt.*

Although driven by different motivations, the Antiquarian, Mercenary, Idolater, and Compulsive Completer share a common trait: They love the thrill of the hunt.

### *Comments*

Since none existed, Mark Freeman created titles for each category of comic book collector—Antiquarian, Mercenary, Idolater, and Compulsive Completer. At times, however, it seems that collectors might spill from one category into another, thus creating the problem of inconsistency. For instance, why couldn't those who collect for investment reasons (Mercenaries) also pursue their favorites (Idolaters). They could, but Freeman classifies his collectors according to one dominant characteristic and then identifies specific behavior that results. Are his categories complete? What about another category, such as Explorers, the kids who buy comics on impulse, read them once, and then toss them aside or pass them on to friends? When asked this question, Freeman said, "They're not collectors, they're browsers. But," he conceded, "browsing is the first step toward collecting."

Development Strategy. Freeman's development strategy is straightforward. In the introductory paragraph he announces his general subject—comic book collectors—in the opening sentences. He creates a stereotypical portrait of them—male, nerdish, and speaking a private language—and indicates where they hang out. He closes the introduction by making it clear that he is going to classify comic book collectors and names the four categories he will group them into.

In the discussion paragraphs, Freeman keeps his readers on track by beginning with topic sentences that name the categories and identify each group's distinguishing characteristic. He also uses a key word, "searches" or "search," to unify the discussion paragraphs. He presents the most dramatic category last—the Compulsive Completer, who is willing to plunge himself into debt to complete a comic book series.

Freeman finishes with a brief conclusion, only one sentence, that renames the categories and identifies a powerful motivation they all share, no matter which group they belong to—the thrill of the hunt. Freeman's strategy here is quite simple. Since this essay is short, he decided to conclude it quickly, rather than tire readers with a restatement of his main points.

**Revision.** When rereading an early draft, Freeman decided the essay had two weaknesses: overwritten topic sentences and few references to specific comics or comic book characters. For example, in an early draft, the fifth paragraph's topic sentence read as follows:

> The Mercenary is a collector who wants full value for his money and will examine price sheets to be sure he gets it.

He felt the Mercenary's key characteristic was lost in the loose language. As a result, the sentence might misdirect his readers. He decided to revise the topic sentence so it would be as direct as he could make it.

> The Mercenary searches for value.

Now the sentence is clear and to the point. He revised each of his topic sentences to reflect it. But he then found that four topic sentences written this way became too mechanical, so he revised them again. For example, he revised the topic sentence of paragraph four to read as follows:

> The Idolater searches for favorites.

Then for the third time Freeman recast it—this time into two sentences. The first serves as a transition into the paragraph by referring to the preceding categories; the second identifies the Idolater's chief characteristic, and addresses another weakness, that is, the lack of specific references to comic book characters.

> The Idolater has little interest in age or value. He is looking for favorites: a Sheena, a Flash Gordon, or an Incredible Hulk.

For the last phase of the revision, Freeman began to insert more references to specific comics and characters, which he felt would give the noncollecting reader a sense of the comic book world. For example, study the edited draft of paragraph three:

The Mercenary searches for value. Certain numbers and
in his cash-register brain
titles ring a bell and start him checking through a half-dozen
of Action Comics
price sheets. A pristine first edition (value $12,000) would
He would also hunt down early
suit him just fine. ~~These might be first~~ editions of Marvel
especially the first publications such as Captain
Comics, ~~often~~ featuring early super heroes, ~~Being a realist,~~
America, the Punisher, and the Human Torch.
~~however,~~ the Mercenary would ~~realize that the early pub-~~
T
~~lished exploits of popular heroes are now already owned.~~
no doubt, love to have a first edition
of Batman and Superman, but being
a realist, he knows they are
locked in vaults.

Once Freeman finished editing the paragraph, he retyped the new version, polishing it as he went. Study the differences. Note how the added specific detail enlivens it.

The Mercenary searches for value. Certain numbers and titles ring a bell in his cash-register brain and start him checking through a half-dozen price sheets. A pristine first edition of Action Comics (value $12,000) would suit him just fine. He would also hunt down early editions of Marvel Comics, especially the first publications featuring early super heroes, such as Captain America, the Punisher, and the Human Torch. The Mercenary would, no doubt, love to have first editions of Batman and Superman, but, being a realist, he knows they are locked in vaults.

The essays that follow will show the variety of ways writers divide and classify subjects. Study them closely. Note the categories each

## *Peer Review*

You may be asked to write an essay about one of the readings that follow. Before you meet with your writing group, review this introduction. As you read the group papers, use these general principles of classification and division to help guide your comments.

1. A classification system should have at least three categories to distinguish it from comparison and contrast.
2. A classification paper should give a reader a fresh way of looking at a subject. Even if the categories used are already established and well-known, the content describing each category should be fresh.
3. The categories chosen should not overlap and allow a component to be assigned to more than one class.
4. The categories should be complete, covering the entire subject.

writer establishes. Ask yourself if the categories are complete and consistent, two important tests to determine if a classification essay is successful.

## ❦ Alison Lurie ❦

*Born in Chicago in 1926, Alison Lurie graduated from Radcliffe College. As a fiction writer, she has often been compared to Jane Austen, both for her style and for her subject matter, which has often been a particular segment of American society—that of the wealthy and educated. Since publication of her first novel,* Love and Friendship, *in 1962, she has published seven more, the latest of which is* The Truth about Lorin Jones *(1988). She received a Pulitzer Prize for her novel* Foreign Affairs *(1984). She has also published three children's books and a non-fiction book on the social history of clothes.*

# *American Regional Costume*

*In this excerpt from her book* The Language of Clothes *(1981), Lurie classifies American styles of dress by region, and the people of those regions by the clothes they wear. She traces the historical influences of climate, landscape, economy, and life-style on various regional "costumes."*

*While reading this essay, pay careful attention to the ways that Lurie carefully describes each regional costume so that the classifications of dress do not overlap.*

---

Even today, when the American landscape is becoming more and more homogeneous, there is really no such thing as an all-American style of dress. A shopping center in Maine may superficially resemble one in Georgia or California, but the shoppers in it will look different, because the diverse histories of these states have left their mark on costume. 1

Regional dress in the United States, as in Britain, can best be observed at large national meetings where factors such as occupation and income are held relatively constant. At these meetings regional differences stand out clearly, and can be checked by looking at the name tags Americans conventionally wear to conventions. Five distinct styles can be distinguished: (1) Old New 2

England, (2) Deep South, (3) Middle American, (4) Wild West and (5) Far West or Californian. In border areas, outfits usually combine regional styles.

Americans who do not travel much within their own country often misinterpret the styles of other regions. Natives of the Eastern states, for instance, may misread Far Western clothing as indicating greater casualness—or greater sexual availability—than is actually present. The laid-back-looking Los Angeles executive in his open-chested sport shirt and sandals may have his eye on the main chance to an extent that will shock his Eastern colleague. The reverse error can also occur: a Southern Californian may discover with surprise that the sober-hued, buttoned-up New Englander he or she has just met is bored with business and longing to get drunk or hop into bed. 3

## Northeast and Southeast: Puritans and Planters

The drab, severe costumes of the Puritan settlers of New England, and their suspicion of color and ornament as snares of the devil, have left their mark on the present-day clothes of New Englanders. At any large meeting people from this part of the country will be dressed in darker hues—notably black, gray and navy—often with touches of white that recall the starched collars and cuffs of Puritan costume. Fabrics will be plainer (though heavier and sometimes more expensive) and styles simpler, with less waste of material: skirts and lapels and trimmings will be narrower. More of the men will also wear suits and shoes made in England (or designed to look as if they had been made in England). The law of camouflage also operates in New England, where gray skies and dark rectangular urban landscapes are not unknown. 4

The distinctive dress of the Deep South is based on a climate that did not demand heavy clothing and an economy that for years exempted middle- and upper-class whites from all manual labor and made washing and ironing cheap. Today the planter's white suits and fondness for fine linen and his wife's and daughters' elaborate and fragile gowns survive in modern form. At our imaginary 5 national meeting the male southerners will wear lighter-colored suits—pale grays and beiges—and a certain dandyism will be apparent, expressing itself in French cuffs, more expensive ties, silkier materials and wider pin stripes. The women's clothes will be more flowery, with a tendency toward bows, ruffles, lace and embroidery. If they are white, they will probably be as white as possible; a pale complexion is still the sign of a Southern lady, and female sun tans are unfashionable except on tourists.

## Midwest and Wild West: Pioneers and Cowboys

The American Midwest and Great Plains states were settled by men and women who had to do their own work and prided themselves on it. They chose sturdy, practical clothes that did not show the dirt, washed and wore well and needed little ironing, made of gingham and linsey-woolsey and canvas. From these clothes descends the contemporary costume of Middle Americans. This style is visible to everyone on national television, where it is worn by most news announcers, politicians, talk-show hosts and actors in commercials for kitchen products. A slightly dowdier version appears in the Sears and Montgomery Ward catalogues. But even when expensive, Middle American fashion is apt to lag behind fashion as it is currently understood back East; it is also usually more sporty and casual. The pioneer regard for physical activity and exercise is still strong in this part of the country, and as a result the Midwesterners at our convention will look healthier and more athletic—and also somewhat beefier—than their colleagues from the cold, damp Northeast and the hot, humid South. Their suits will tend toward the tans and browns of plowed cornfields rather than the grays of Eastern skies. More of them will wear white or white-on-white shirts, and their striped or foulard ties will be brighter and patterned on a larger scale than those purchased in sober New York and Boston. 6

The traditional Western costume, of course, was that of the cowboy on the range. Perhaps because of the isolation of those wide-open spaces, this is the style which has been least influenced by those of other regions. At any national convention the Wild 7

Westerners will be the easiest to identify. For one thing, they are apt to be taller—either genetically or with the help of boots. Some may appear in full Western costume, the sartorial equivalent of a "he-went-thataway" drawl; but even the more conservative will betray, or rather proclaim, their regional loyalty through their dress, just as in conversation they will from time to time use a ranching metaphor, or call you "pal" or "pardner." A man in otherwise conventional business uniform will wear what look like cowboy boots, or a hat with an enlarged brim and crown. Women, too, are apt to wear boots, and their jackets and skirts may have a Western cut, especially when viewed from the rear. Some may wear red or navy-blue bandanna-print shirts or dresses, or an actual cotton-print bandanna knotted round their necks.

### The Far West: Adventurers and Beach Boys

The men and women who settled the Far West were a mixed and rather raffish lot. Restlessness, the wish for excitement, the hope of a fortune in gold and sometimes a need to escape the law led them to undertake the long and dangerous journey over mountains and deserts, or by sea round Cape Horn. In more than one sense they were adventurers, and often desperadoes—desperate people. California was a territory where no one would ask about your past, where unconventionality of character and behavior was easily accepted. Even today when, as the country song puts it, "all the gold in California is in a bank in the middle of Beverly Hills in somebody else's name," the place has the reputation of an El Dorado. Men and women willing to risk everything on long odds in the hope of a big hit, or eager to put legal, financial and personal foul-ups behind them, often go west. 8

Present-day California styles are still in many ways those of adventurers and eccentrics. Whatever the current fashion, the California version will be more extreme, more various and—possibly because of the influence of the large Spanish-American population—much more colorful. Clothes tend to fit more tightly than is considered proper elsewhere, and to expose more flesh: an inability to button the shirt above the diaphragm is common in 9 both sexes. Virtuous working-class housewives may wear outfits that in any other part of the country would identify them as medium-priced whores; reputable business and professional men may dress in a manner which would lose them most of their clients back east and attract the attention of the Bureau of Internal Revenue if not of the police.

Southern Californians, and many other natives of what is now called the Sun Belt (an imaginary strip of land stretching across the bottom of the United States from Florida to Santa Barbara, but excluding most of the Old South), can also be identified by their year-round sun tans, which by middle age have often given the skin the look of old if expensive and well-oiled leather. The men may also wear the getup known as Sun Belt Cool: a pale beige suit, open-collared shirt (often in a darker shade than the suit), cream-colored loafers and aviator sunglasses. The female version of the look is similar, except that the shoes will be high-heeled sandals. 10

## Regional Disguise: Sunbelt Puritans and Urban Cowboys

Some long-time inhabitants of California and the other sartorially distinct regions of the United States refuse to wear the styles characteristic of that area. In this case the message is clear: they are unhappy in that locale and/or do not want anyone to attribute to them the traits associated with it. Such persons, if depressed, may adopt a vague and anonymous mode of dress; if in good spirits they may wear the costume of some other region in order to proclaim their sympathy with it. In terms of speech, what we have then is not a regional accent, but the conscious adoption of a dialect by an outsider. 11

In the urban centers of the West and Far West bankers and financial experts of both sexes sometimes adopt an Eastern manner of speech and a Wall Street appearance in order to suggest reliability and tradition. And today in Southern California there are professors who speak with Bostonian accents, spend their days in the library stacks, avoid the beach and dress in clothes that would occasion no comment in Harvard Yard. New arrivals to the area sometimes take these men and women for visiting Eastern lecturers, and are surprised to learn that they have lived 12 in Southern California for thirty or forty years, or have even been born there.

The popularity of the various regional styles of American costume, like that of the various national styles, is also related to economic and political factors. Some years ago modes often originated in the Far West and the word "California" on a garment was thought to be an allurement. Today, with power and population growth shifting to the Southwestern oil-producing states, Wild West styles—particularly those of Texas—are in vogue. This fashion, of course, is not new. For many years men who have never been nearer to a cow than the local steakhouse have worn Western costume to signify that they are independent, tough and reliable. In a story by Flannery O'Connor, for instance, the sinister traveling salesman is described as wearing "a broad-brimmed stiff gray hat of the kind used by businessmen who would like to look like cowboys"—but, it is implied, seldom succeed in doing so. 13

The current popularity of Western costume has been increased by the turn away from foreign modes that has accompanied the recent right-wing shift in United States politics. In all countries periods of isolationism and a belligerently ostrichlike stance toward the rest of the world have usually been reflected in a rejection of international modes in favor of national styles, often those of the past. Today in America the cowboy look is high fashion, and even in New York City the streets are full of a variety of Wild West types. Some are dressed in old-fashioned, well-worn Western gear; others in the newer, brighter and sleeker outfits of modern ranchers, while a few wear spangled, neon-hued Electric Cowboy and Cowgirl costumes of the type most often seen on Texas country-rock musicians. 14

---

## *Meaning and Purpose*

1. If you were to classify American regional dress, would you choose Lurie's categories? Why or why not? If not, what would your categories be?

2. Why does Lurie claim that large, national meetings are best for observing regional dress?
3. What is Lurie's main point, and where does she state it?
4. Why is it possible to misinterpret the dress styles of different regions?
5. How does Lurie explain the differences in dress from region to region?
6. How does Lurie account for the current popularity of western costume? Do you agree with her?

## *Strategy*

1. What scheme does Lurie use to organize her categories?
2. In paragraph 2, Lurie lists five categories of style of dress, but only three subheadings cover those five categories. Why do you suppose she puts the first two and the second two together, and gives the Far West its own subheading?
3. Lurie adds to classification and division other rhetorical strategies to support her categories. Look again at paragraphs 4 and 5, and paragraph 8 and paragraph 9. What strategies does she use in these places?
4. Lurie quotes a country song in paragraph 8 and the short-story writer and novelist Flannery O'Connor in paragraph 13. What is the purpose of these quotations?

## *Style*

1. Lurie often juxtaposes formal sociological and anthropological language with the language of casual conversation and slang. What are some examples of this mixture? What is the effect of such juxtapositions?
2. In her categories and descriptions, is Lurie making any judgments about regional dress, or is she neutral? Support your answer with language from the essay.
3. If necessary, check a dictionary for the meanings of these expressions: *homogeneous, superficially* (1); *Puritan* (4); *dandyism* (5);

*gingham, linsey-woolsey, dowdier, foulard* (6); *sartorial* (7); *raffish* (8); *allurement* (13); *isolationism, belligerently* (14).

## *Writing Tasks*

1. Analyze the styles of dress popular on your campus. Create four or five style categories and use as many specific examples as you can. In a classification-and-division essay, establish clearly the basis for your classifications.
2. Examine the ways in which popular entertainment—movies, television, rock music, and rock-music stars—affects dress, speech, or hair style. Write a classification essay in which you show how these influences have produced the styles you describe.

# ❦ John Holt ❦

*John Holt is the author of, among other famous books,* How Children Fail *(1964) and* How Children Learn *(1967). He was born in 1923 and studied at Yale University His fourteen years of experience in elementary and high-school teaching led him to some radical and controversial conclusions about the ineffectiveness of the American educational system. In many of his books he addresses this problem and offers alternative methods for helping children learn. He was a visiting lecturer at Harvard University and the University of California at Berkeley. After 1969 he devoted himself primarily to writing, lecturing, social activism, and playing the cello, which he took up at age forty. He founded, edited, and published* Growing Without Schooling, *a magazine by and for families who choose to teach their children at home. He died in 1985.*

## *Three Kinds of Discipline*

*This tightly organized short essay offers a general prescription for the use of discipline by classifying into three categories. Here and in the book where this passage first appeared,* Freedom and Beyond *(1972), Holt argues that, in order to learn, children need to be left alone as much as they need to be disciplined.*

*As you read Holt's essay, think of your own childhood and compare the ways that you were disciplined with how Holt would like to see children disciplined.*

---

A child, in growing up, may meet and learn from three different kinds of disciplines. The first and most important is what we might call the Discipline of Nature or of Reality. When he is trying to do something real, if he does the wrong thing or doesn't do the right one, he doesn't get the result he wants. If he doesn't pile one block right on top of another, or tries to build on a slanting surface, his tower falls down. If he hits the wrong key, he hears the wrong note. If he doesn't hit the nail squarely on the head, it bends, and he has to pull it out and start with another. If he 1 doesn't measure properly what he is trying to build, it won't open, close, fit, stand up, fly, float, whistle, or do whatever he wants it to do. If he closes his eyes when he swings, he doesn't hit the ball. A child meets this kind of discipline every time he tries to *do* something, which is why it is so important in school to give children more chances to do things, instead of just reading or listening to someone talk (or pretending to). This discipline is a good teacher. The learner never has to wait long for his answer; it usually comes quickly, often instantly. Also it is clear, and very often points toward the needed correction; from what happened he can not only see that what he did was wrong, but also why, and what he needs to do instead. Finally, and most important, the giver of the answer, call it Nature, is impersonal, impartial, and indifferent. She does not give opinions, or make judgments: she cannot be wheedled, bullied, or fooled; she does not get angry or disappointed; she does not praise or blame; she does not remember past failures or hold grudges; with her one always gets a fresh start, this time is the one that counts.

The next discipline we might call the Discipline of Culture, of Society, of What People Really Do. Man is a social, a cultural animal. Children sense around them this culture, this network of agreements, customs, habits, and rules binding the adults together. They want to understand it and be a part of it. They watch very carefully what people around them are doing and want to do the same. They want to do right, unless they become convinced they can't do right. Thus children rarely misbehave seriously in church, but sit as quietly as they can. The example of all those grownups is contagious. Some mysterious ritual is going on, and children, who like rituals, want to be part of it. In the same way, the little children that I see at concerts or operas, though they may fidget a little, or perhaps take a nap now and then, rarely make any disturbance. With all those grownups sitting there, neither moving nor talking, it is the most natural thing in the world to imitate them. Children who live among adults who are habitually courteous to each other, and to them, will soon learn to be courteous. Children who live surrounded by people who speak a certain way will speak that way, 2 however much we may try to tell them that speaking that way is bad or wrong.

The third discipline is the one most people mean when they speak of discipline—the Discipline of Superior Force, of sergeant to private, of "You do what I tell you or I'll make you wish you had." There is bound to be some of this in a child's life. Living as we do surrounded by things that can hurt children, or that children can hurt, we cannot avoid it. We can't afford to let a small child find out from experience the danger of playing in a busy street, or of fooling with the pots on the top of a stove, or of eating up the pills in the medicine cabinet. So, along with other precautions, we say to him, "Don't play in the street, or touch things on the stove, or go into the medicine cabinet, or I'll punish you." Between him and the danger too great for him to imagine we put a lesser danger, but one he can imagine and maybe therefore wants to avoid. He can have no idea of what it would be like to be hit by a car, but he can imagine being shouted at, or spanked, or sent to his room. He avoids these substitutes for the greater danger until he can understand it and avoid it for its own sake. But we ought to use this discipline only when it is necessary to protect the life, health, safety, or well-being of people or other living creatures, or to prevent destruction of things that people care about. We ought not to assume too long, as we usually do, that a child cannot understand the real nature of the danger from which we want to protect him. The sooner he avoids the danger, not to escape our punishment, but as a matter of good sense, the better. He can learn that faster than we think. In Mexico, for example, where people drive their cars with a good deal of spirit, I saw many children no older than five or four walking unattended on the streets. They understood about cars, they knew what to do. A child whose life is full of the threat and fear of punishment is locked into babyhood. There is no way for him to grow up, to learn to take responsibility for his life and acts. Most important of all, we should not assume that having to yield to the threat of our superior force is good for the child's character. It is never good for *anyone's* character. To bow to superior force makes us feel impotent and cowardly for not having had the strength or courage to resist. Worse, 3 it makes us resentful and vengeful. We can hardly wait to make someone pay for our humiliation, yield to us as we were once made to yield. No, if we cannot always avoid using the discipline of Superior Force, we should at least use it as seldom as we can.

There are places where all three disciplines overlap. Any very demanding human activity combines in it the disciplines of Superior Force, of Culture, and of Nature. The novice will be told, "Do it this way, never mind asking why, just do it that way, that is the way we always do it." But it probably *is* just the way they always do it, and usually for the very good reason that it is a way that has been found to work. Think, for example, of ballet training. The student in a class is told to do this exercise, or that; to stand so; to do this or that with his head, arms, shoulders, abdomen, hips, legs, feet. He is constantly corrected. There is no argument. But behind these seemingly autocratic demands by the teacher lie many decades of custom and tradition, and behind that, the necessities of dancing itself. You cannot make the moves of classical ballet unless over many years you have acquired, and renewed every day, the needed strength and suppleness in scores of muscles and joints. Nor can you do the difficult motions, making them look easy, unless you have learned hundreds of easier ones first. Dance teachers may not always agree on all the details of teaching these strengths and skills. But no novice could learn them all by himself. You could not go for a night or two to watch the ballet and then, without any other knowledge at all, teach yourself how to do it. In the same way, you would be unlikely to learn any complicated and difficult human activity without drawing heavily on the experience of those who know it better. But the point is that the authority of these experts or teachers stems from, grows out of their greater competence and experience, the fact that what they do *works*, not the fact that they happen to be the teacher and as such have the power to kick a student out of the class. And the further point is that children are always and everywhere attracted to that competence, and ready and eager to submit themselves to a discipline that grows out of it. We hear constantly that children will never do anything unless compelled to by bribes or threats. But in their private lives, or in extracurricular activities in school, in sports, music, drama, art, running a newspaper, and so on, they 4 often submit themselves willingly and wholeheartedly to very intense disciplines, simply because they want to learn to do a given thing well. Our Little-Napoleon football coaches, of whom we have too many and hear far too much, blind us to the fact that millions of children work hard every year getting better at sports and games without coaches barking and yelling at them.

---

## *Meaning and Purpose*

1. What does Holt set out to say in this essay?
2. What methods of discipline have you seen in practice, and how effective do you think they are?
3. Do you agree with the statement, "Thus children rarely misbehave seriously in church, but sit as quietly as they can" (2). Does Holt make a good case for the truth of the statement? Why or why not?
4. What is Holt's attitude toward children? Where is this attitude evident in the essay?

## *Strategy*

1. Holt divides discipline into three kinds. What is the basis for this division, and why does he identify only three kinds?
2. Does paragraph 4 describe a fourth kind of discipline? If so, does this category cause an imbalance in the essay's structure (Holt announces only three categories in the beginning)? Why or why not?
3. How does Holt make use of examples in this essay?

## *Style*

1. Why do you think Holt capitalizes the names of the kinds of discipline he classifies?

2. What is Holt's attitude toward his subject? Is he neutral about it or is he advocating something? How do you know?
3. If necessary, look up the meaning of these words: *wheedled* (1); *contagious*, *fidget* (2); *impotent* (3); *novice*, *autocratic*, *suppleness* (4).

## Writing Tasks

1. Write an essay in which you classify parents according to the kinds of discipline they use with their children. Speak from first-hand knowledge, and take Holt as a model for using specific examples.
2. Write an essay in which you classify students. You might want to use elementary, high-school, or college students, or you might show how each kind of student behaves at each of the three levels of education. Make sure you use typical examples and then demonstrate them in real life with specific examples.

## ❦ Desmond Morris ❦

*Born in England in 1928, Desmond Morris studied at Birmingham University and Oxford University. After receiving his doctorate from Oxford, he was a researcher in the zoology department there for a short time. He later worked for several years at the Zoological Society of London, first as curator of mammals and later as director of the society's television and film department. He has also been director of London's Institute of Contemporary Arts, and in 1950 had a one-man show in which he exhibited his own paintings. He is best known, however, as writer of popular—if sometimes controversial—books on human behavior, including* The Naked Ape *(1967) and* The Human Zoo *(1969).*

# *Territorial Behavior*

*This essay is from Morris's book* Manwatching *(1974), another of his works on human behavior. He supports his premise that human beings are "remarkably territorial animals" by classifying and describing three kinds of human territory, each of which induces its own form of territorial behavior.*

*As you read this essay, pay close attention to how Morris uses metaphors and similes to help the reader understand each classification.*

---

A territory is a defended space. In the broadest sense, there are three kinds of human territory: tribal, family and personal. 1

It is rare for people to be driven to physical fighting in defense of these "owned" spaces, but fight they will, if pushed to the limit. The invading army encroaching on national territory, the gang moving into a rival district, the trespasser climbing into an orchard, the burglar breaking into a house, the bully pushing to the front of a queue, the driver trying to steal a parking space, all of these intruders are liable to be met with resistance varying from the vigorous to the savagely violent. Even if the law is on the side of the intruder, the urge to protect a territory may be so strong that otherwise peaceful citizens abandon all their usual controls 2 and inhibitions. Attempts to evict families from their homes, no matter how socially valid the reasons, can lead to siege conditions reminiscent of the defense of a medieval fortress.

The fact that these upheavals are so rare is a measure of the success of Territorial Signals as a system of dispute prevention. It is sometimes cynically stated that "all property is theft," but in reality it is the opposite. Property, as owned space which is *displayed* as owned space, is a special kind of sharing system which reduces fighting much more than it causes it. Man is a cooperative species, but he is also competitive, and his struggle for dominance has to be structured in some way if chaos is to be avoided. The establishment of territorial rights is one such structure. It limits dominance geographically. I am dominant in my territory and you are dominant in yours. In other words, dominance is shared out spatially, and we all have some. Even if I am weak and unintelligent and you can dominate me when we meet on neutral ground, I can still enjoy a thoroughly dominant role as soon as I retreat to my private base. Be it ever so humble, there is no place like a home territory. 3

Of course, I can still be intimidated by a particularly dominant individual who enters my home base, but his encroachment will be dangerous for him and he will think twice about it, because he will know that here my urge to resist will be dramatically magnified and my usual subservience banished. Insulted at the heart of my own territory, I may easily explode into battle—either symbolic or real—with a result that may be damaging to both of us. 4

In order for this to work, each territory has to be plainly advertised as such. Just as a dog cocks its leg to deposit its personal scent on the trees in its locality, so the human animal cocks its leg symbolically all over his home base. But because we are predominantly visual animals we employ mostly visual signals, and it is worth asking how we do this at the three levels: tribal, family and personal. 5

First: the Tribal Territory. We evolved as tribal animals, living in comparatively small groups, probably of less than a hundred, and we existed like that for millions of years. It is our basic social unit, a group in which everyone knows everyone else. Essentially, the tribal territory consisted of a home base surrounded by 6 extended hunting grounds. Any neighbouring tribe intruding on our social space would be repelled and driven away. As these early tribes swelled into agricultural super-tribes, and eventually into industrial nations, their territorial defence systems became increasingly elaborate. The tiny, ancient home base of the hunting tribe became the great capital city, the primitive war-paint became the flags, emblems, uniforms and regalia of the specialized military, and the war-chants became national anthems, marching songs and bugle calls. Territorial boundary-lines hardened into fixed borders, often conspicuously patrolled and punctuated with defensive structures—forts and lookout posts, check-points and great walls, and, today, customs barriers.

Today each nation flies its own flag, a symbolic embodiment 7
of its territorial status. But patriotism is not enough. The ancient tribal hunter lurking inside each citizen finds himself unsatisfied by membership of such a vast conglomeration of individuals, most of whom are totally unknown to him personally. He does his best to feel that he shares a common territorial defence with them all, but the scale of the operation has become inhuman. It is hard to feel a sense of belonging with a tribe of fifty million or more. His answer is to form sub-groups, nearer to his ancient pattern, smaller and more personally known to him—the local club, the teenage gang, the union, the specialist society, the sports association, the political party, the college fraternity, the social clique, the protest group, and the rest. Rare indeed is the individual who does not belong to at least one of these splinter groups, and take from it a sense of tribal allegiance and brotherhood. Typical of all these groups is the development of Territorial Signals—badges, costumes, headquarters, banners, slogans, and all the other displays of group identity. This is where the action is, in terms of tribal territorialism, and only when a major war breaks out does the emphasis shift upwards to the higher group level of the nation.

Each of these modern pseudo-tribes sets up its own special 8
kind of home base. In extreme cases non-members are totally excluded, in others they are allowed in as visitors with limited rights and under a control system of special rules. In many ways they are like miniature nations, with their own flags and emblems and

their own border guards. The exclusive club has its own "customs barrier": the doorman who checks your "passport" (your membership card) and prevents strangers from passing in unchallenged. There is a government: the club committee; and often special displays of the tribal elders: the photographs or portraits of previous officials on the walls. At the heart of the specialized territories there is a powerful feeling of security and importance, a sense of shared defence against the outside world. Much of the club chatter, both serious and joking, directs itself against the rottenness of everything outside the club boundaries—in that "other world" beyond the protected portals.

In social organizations which embody a strong class system, 9
such as military units and large business concerns, there are many territorial rules, often unspoken, which interfere with the official hierarchy. High-status individuals, such as officers or managers, could in theory enter any of the regions occupied by the lower levels in the peck order, but they limit this power in a striking way. An officer seldom enters a sergeant's mess or a barrack room unless it is for a formal inspection. He respects those regions as alien territories even though he has the power to go there by virtue of his dominant role. And in businesses, part of the appeal of unions, over and above their obvious functions, is that with their officials, headquarters and meetings they add a sense of territorial power for the staff workers. It is almost as if each military organization and business concern consists of two warring tribes: the officers versus the other ranks, and the management versus the workers. Each has its special home base within the system, and the territorial defence pattern thrusts itself into what, on the surface, is a pure social hierarchy. Negotiations between managements and unions are tribal battles fought out over the neutral ground of a boardroom table, and are as much concerned with territorial display as they are with resolving problems of wages and conditions. Indeed, if one side gives in too quickly and accepts the other's demands, the victors feel strangely cheated and deeply suspicious that it may be a trick. What they are missing is the protracted sequence of ritual and counter-ritual that keeps alive their group territorial identity.

Likewise, many of the hostile displays of sports fans and teenage gangs are primarily concerned with displaying their group image to rival fan-clubs and gangs. Except in rare cases, they do not attack one another's headquarters, drive out the occupants, and reduce them to a submissive, subordinate condition. It is enough to have scuffles on the borderlands between the two rival territories. This is particularly clear at football matches, where the fan-club headquarters becomes temporarily shifted from the clubhouse to a section of the stands, and where minor fighting breaks out at the unofficial boundary line between the massed groups of rival supporters. Newspaper reports play up the few accidents and injuries which do occur on such occasions, but when these are studied in relation to the total numbers of displaying fans involved it is clear that the serious incidents represent only a tiny fraction of the overall group behaviour. For every actual punch or kick there are a thousand war-cries, war-dances, chants and gestures. 10

Second: the Family Territory. Essentially, the family is a breeding unit and the family territory is a breeding ground. At the centre of this space, there is the nest—the bedroom—where, tucked up in bed, we feel at our most territorially secure. In a typical house the bedroom is upstairs, where a safe nest should be. This puts it farther away from the entrance hall, the area where contact is made, intermittently, with the outside world. The less private reception rooms, where intruders are allowed access, are the next line of defence. Beyond them, outside the walls of the building, there is often a symbolic remnant of the ancient feeding grounds—a garden. Its symbolism often extends to the plants and animals it contains, which cease to be nutritional and become merely decorative—flowers and pets. But like a true territorial space it has a conspicuously displayed boundary-line, the garden fence, wall, or railings. Often no more than a token barrier, this is the outer territorial demarcation, separating the private world of the family from the public world beyond. To cross it puts any visitor or intruder at an immediate disadvantage. As he crosses the threshold, his dominance wanes, slightly but unmistakably. He is entering an area where he senses that he must ask permission to do simple things that he would consider a right elsewhere. With- 11 out lifting a finger, the territorial owners exert their dominance. This is done by all the hundreds of small ownership "markers" they have deposited on their family territory: the ornaments, the "possessed" objects positioned in the rooms and on the walls; the furnishings, the furniture, the colours, the patterns, all owner-chosen and all making this particular home base unique to them.

It is one of the tragedies of modern architecture that there has 12
been a standardization of these vital territorial living-units. One of the most important aspects of a home is that it should be similar to other homes only in a general way, and that in detail it should have many differences, making it a *particular* home. Unfortunately, it is cheaper to build a row of houses, or a block of flats, so that all the family living-units are identical, but the territorial urge rebels against this trend and house-owners struggle as best they can to make their mark on their mass-produced properties. They do this with garden-design, with front-door colours, with curtain patterns, with wallpaper and all the other decorative elements that together create a unique and different family environment. Only when they have completed this nest-building do they feel truly "at home" and secure.

When they venture forth as a family unit they repeat the 13
process in a minor way. On a day-trip to the seaside, they load the car with personal belongings and it becomes their temporary, portable territory. Arriving at the beach they stake out a small territorial claim, marking it with rugs, towels, baskets and other belongings to which they can return from their seaboard wanderings. Even if they all leave it at once to bathe, it retains a characteristic territorial quality and other family groups arriving will recognize this by setting up their own "home" bases at a respectful distance. Only when the whole beach has filled up with these marked spaces will newcomers start to position themselves in such a way that the inter-base distance becomes reduced. Forced to pitch between several existing beach territories they will feel a momentary sensation of intrusion, and the established "owners" will feel a similar sensation of invasion, even though they are not being directly inconvenienced.

The same territorial scene is being played out in parks and 14
fields and on riverbanks, wherever family groups gather in their

clustered units. But if rivalry for spaces creates mild feelings of hostility, it is true to say that, without the territorial system of sharing and space-limited dominance, there would be chaotic disorder.

Third: the Personal Space. If a man enters a waiting-room and 15
sits at one end of a long row of empty chairs, it is possible to predict where the next man to enter will seat himself. He will not sit next to the first man, nor will he sit at the far end, right away from him. He will choose a position about halfway between these two points. The next man to enter will take the largest gap left, and sit roughly in the middle of that, and so on, until eventually the latest newcomer will be forced to select a seat that places him right next to one of the already seated men. Similar patterns can be observed in cinemas, public urinals, aeroplanes, trains and buses. This is a reflection of the fact that we all carry with us, everywhere we go, a portable territory called a Personal Space. If people move inside this space, we feel threatened. If they keep too far outside it, we feel rejected. The result is a subtle series of spatial adjustments, usually operating quite unconsciously and producing ideal compromises as far as this is possible. If a situation becomes too crowded, then we adjust our reactions accordingly and allow our personal space to shrink. Jammed into an elevator, a rush-hour compartment, or a packed room, we give up altogether and allow body-to-body contact, but when we relinquish our Personal Space in this way, we adopt certain special techniques. In essence, what we do is to convert these other bodies into "nonpersons." We studiously ignore them, and they us. We try not to face them if we can possibly avoid it. We wipe all expressiveness from our faces, letting them go blank. We may look up at the ceiling or down at the floor, and we reduce body movements to a minimum. Packed together like sardines in a tin, we stand dumbly still, sending out as few social signals as possible.

Even if the crowding is less severe, we still tend to cut down 16
our social interactions in the presence of large numbers. Careful observations of children in play groups revealed that if they are high density groupings there is less social interaction between the individual children, even though there is theoretically more opportunity for such contacts. At the same time, the high-density groups show a higher frequency of aggressive and destructive

behaviour patterns in their play. Personal Space—"elbow room"—is a vital commodity for the human animal, and one that cannot be ignored without risking serious trouble.

Of course, we all enjoy the excitement of being in a crowd, and this reaction cannot be ignored. But there are crowds and crowds. It is pleasant enough to be in a "spectator crowd," but not so appealing to find yourself in the middle of a rush-hour crush. The difference between the two is that the spectator crowd is all facing in the same direction and concentrating on a distant point of interest. Attending a theatre, there are twinges of rising hostility towards the stranger who sits down immediately in front of you or the one who squeezes into the seat next to you. The shared armrest can become a polite, but distinct, territorial boundary-dispute region. However, as soon as the show begins, these invasions of Personal Space are forgotten and the attention is focused beyond the small space where the crowding is taking place. Now, each member of the audience feels himself spatially related, not to his cramped neighbours, but to the actor on the stage, and this distance is, if anything, too great. In the rush-hour crowd, by contrast, each member of the pushing throng is competing with his neighbours all the time. There is no escape to a spacial relation with a distant actor, only the pushing, shoving bodies all around. 17

Those of us who have to spend a great deal of time in crowded conditions become gradually better able to adjust, but no one can ever become completely immune to invasions of Personal Space. This is because they remain forever associated with either powerful hostile or equally powerful loving feelings. All through our childhood we have been held to be loved and held to be hurt, and anyone who invades our Personal Space when we are adults is, in effect, threatening to extend his behaviour into one of these two highly charged areas of human interaction. Even if his motives are clearly neither hostile nor sexual, we still find it hard to suppress our reactions to his close approach. Unfortunately, different countries have different ideas about exactly how close is close. It is easy enough to test your own "space reaction": when you are talking to someone in the street or in any open space, reach out with your arm and see where the nearest point on his body comes. If you 18 hail from western Europe, you will find that he is at roughly fingertip distance from you. In other words, as you reach out, your fingertips will just about make contact with his shoulder. If you come from eastern Europe you will find you are standing at "wrist distance." If you come from the Mediterranean region you will find that you are much closer to your companion, at little more than "elbow distance."

Trouble begins when a member of one of these cultures meets 19
and talks to one from another. Say a British diplomat meets an Italian or an Arab diplomat at an embassy function. They start talking in a friendly way, but soon the fingertips man begins to feel uneasy. Without knowing quite why, he starts to back away gently from his companion. The companion edges forward again. Each tries in this way to set up a Personal Space relationship that suits his own background. But it is impossible to do. Every time the Mediterranean diplomat advances to a distance that feels comfortable for him, the British diplomat feels threatened. Every time the Briton moves back, the other feels rejected. Attempts to adjust this situation often lead to a talking pair shifting slowly across a room, and many an embassy reception is dotted with western-European fingertip-distance men pinned against the walls by eager elbow-distance men. Until such differences are fully understood, and allowances made, these minor differences in "body territories" will continue to act as an alienation factor which may interfere in a subtle way with diplomatic harmony and other forms of international transaction.

If there are distance problems when engaged in conversation, 20
then there are clearly going to be even bigger difficulties where people must work privately in a shared space. Close proximity of others, pressing against the invisible boundaries of our personal body-territory, makes it difficult to concentrate on non-social matters. Flatmates, students sharing a study, sailors in the cramped quarters of a ship, and office staff in crowded workplaces, all have to face this problem. They solve it by "cocooning." They use a variety of devices to shut themselves off from the others present. The best possible cocoon, of course, is a small private room—a den, a private office, a study or a studio—which physi-

cally obscures the presence of other nearby territory-owners. This is the ideal situation for non-social work, but the space-sharers cannot enjoy this luxury. Their cocooning must be symbolic. They may, in certain cases, be able to erect small physical barriers, such as screens and partitions, which give substance to their invisible Personal Space boundaries, but when this cannot be done, other means must be sought. One of these is the "favoured object." Each space-sharer develops a preference, repeatedly expressed until it becomes a fixed pattern, for a particular chair, or table, or alcove. Others come to respect this, and friction is reduced. This system is often formally arranged (this is my desk, that is yours), but even where it is not, favoured places soon develop. Professor Smith has a favourite chair in the library. It is not formally his, but he always uses it and others avoid it. Seats around a mess-room table, or a board-room table, become almost personal property for specific individuals. Even in the home, father has his favourite chair for reading the newspaper or watching television. Another device is the blinkers-posture. Just as a horse that overreacts to other horses and the distractions of the noisy racecourse is given a pair of blinkers to shield its eyes, so people studying privately in a public place put on pseudo-blinkers in the form of shielding hands. Resting their elbows on the table, they sit with their hands screening their eyes from the scene on either side.

A third method of reinforcing the body-territory is to use per- 21
sonal markers. Books, papers and other personal belongings are scattered around the favoured site to render it more privately owned in the eyes of companions. Spreading out one's belongings is a well-known trick in public-transport situations, where a traveller tries to give the impression that seats next to him are taken. In many contexts carefully arranged personal markers can act as an effective territorial display, even in the absence of the territory owner. Experiments in a library revealed that placing a pile of magazines on the table in one seating position successfully reserved that place for an average of 77 minutes. If a sports-jacket was added, draped over the chair, then the "reservation effect" lasted for over two hours.

In these ways, we strengthen the defences of our Personal 22
Spaces, keeping out intruders with the minimum of open hostil-

ity. As with all territorial behaviour, the object is to defend space with signals rather than with fists and at all three levels—the tribal, the family and the personal—it is a remarkably efficient system of space-sharing. It does not always seem so, because newspapers and newscasts inevitably magnify the exceptions and dwell on those cases where the signals have failed and wars have broken out, gangs have fought, neighbouring families have feuded, or colleagues have clashed, but for every territorial signal that has failed, there are millions of others that have not. They do not rate a mention in the news, but they nevertheless constitute a dominant feature of human society—the society of a remarkably territorial animal.

---

## *Meaning and Purpose*

1. What is the main point Morris makes in this essay? Does it have a thesis statement?
2. Can you tell from the title what kind of essay this will be?
3. In paragraph 11, the author says, "we feel at our most territorially secure" in our bedroom. Does this statement apply to you? Where is another place in which you feel quite "territorially secure"?
4. What does Morris say we do in our large tribal territory to feel a sense of belonging?
5. Why is it "one of the tragedies of modern architecture" that so many new homes look alike?
6. In paragraph 11, Morris calls the family and its territory a "breeding unit" and "breeding ground." What does he mean by these expressions? Is he being sarcastic or judgmental?

## *Strategy*

1. Morris begins his categories of territories in paragraph 6. How does he use the first five paragraphs?

2. What strategy does Morris use to develop the classification of "Tribal Territory"?
3. In the personal-space category, Morris has some subcategories. What are they, and how do they work in the structure of this category?
4. In paragraph 4, Morris mentions a "home base." If Morris had wanted, he could have classified several kinds of home bases. In your opinion, what are two kinds of home bases?

## *Style*

1. How would you describe the tone of this essay? Where is the tone evident?
2. What is a "pseudo-tribe"?
3. Judging from the tone and style of this essay, whom do you think Morris has in mind for his audience?

## *Writing Tasks*

1. Classify your "tribe's territory." How does your neighborhood, town, city, parish, county, or other easily identifiable political territory differ from others in its display? How do its looks make it different? How do its people make it different? How does its economy make it different? In what other ways does classifying your territory show that it is different from other territories in the same class?
2. Personal space is becoming more and more difficult to enjoy. What is your own definition of "personal space"? How do you separate and protect your space? How do you handle intruders into your space? How would you instruct elementary-school children who tell you they would like to learn how to have more personal space?

# ❦ Paul Fussell ❦

*Paul Fussell, born in 1924, earned his Ph.D. at Harvard and taught English at Connecticut College and at Rutgers. An infantry officer in World War II, he received the Bronze Star for bravery and was wounded twice. He is well known for his studies in eighteenth-century British literature and for his* Poetic Meter and Poetic Form *(1965; rev. 1979). His book* The Great War and Modern Memory, *a study of World War I and its literature, won the National Book Award. A contributing editor for* Harper's *and* The New Republic, *he is the Donald T. Regan Professor of English at the University of Pennsylvania.*

# *Notes on Class*

*This essay deals with a subject rarely discussed but often acknowledged: the classification of American society into distinct and recognizable segments. Fussell bases his analysis on such factors as income, actions, and appearances—but most of all on his personal perceptions.*

*As you read this essay, you might enjoy trying to place your friends, acquaintances, and relatives into one or more of the essay's social classes.*

---

If the dirty little secret used to be sex, now it is the facts about social class. No subject today is more likely to offend. Over thirty years ago Dr. Kinsey generated considerable alarm by disclosing that despite appearances one-quarter of the male population had enjoyed at least one homosexual orgasm. A similar alarm can be occasioned today by asserting that despite the much-discussed mechanism of "social mobility" and the constant redistribution of income in this country, it is virtually impossible to break out of the social class in which one has been nurtured. Bad news for the ambitious as well as the bogus, but there it is. 1

Defining class is difficult, as sociologists and anthropologists have learned. The more data we feed into the machines, the less likely it is that significant formulations will emerge. What follows here is based not on interviews, questionnaires, or any kind of 2 quantitative technique but on perhaps a more trustworthy method—perception. Theory may inform us that there are three classes in America, high, middle, and low. Perception will tell us that there are at least nine, which I would designate and arrange like this:

Top Out-of-Sight
Upper
Upper Middle

---

Middle
High-Proletarian
Mid-Proletarian
Low-Proletarian

---

Destitute
BottomOut-of-Sight

In addition, there is a floating, class with no permanent location in this hierarchy. We can call it Class X. It consists of well-to-do hippies, "artist," "writers" (who write nothing), floating bohemians, politicians out of office, disgraced athletic coaches, residers abroad, rock stars, "celebrities," and the shrewder sort of spies.

The quasi-official division of the population into three economic classes called high-, middle-, and low-income groups rather misses the point, because as a class indicator the amount of money is not as important as the source. Important distinctions at both the top and bottom of the class scale arise less from degree of affluence than from the people or institutions to whom one is beholden for support. For example, the main thing distinguishing the top three classes from each other is the amount of money inherited in relation to the amount currently earned. The Top Out-of-Sight Class (Rockefellers, du Ponts, Melons, Fords, Whitneys) lives on inherited capital entirely. Its money is like the hats of the Boston ladies who, asked where they got them, answer, "Oh, we *have* our hats." No one whose money, no matter how ample, comes from his own work, like film stars, can be a member of the Top Out-of-Sights, even if the size of his income and the extravagance of his expenditure permit him temporary social access to it. 3

Since we expect extremes to meet, we are not surprised to find 4 the very lowest class, Bottom Out-of-Sight, similar to the highest in one crucial respect: It is given its money and kept sort of afloat not by its own efforts but by the welfare machinery or the prison system. Members of the Top Out-of-Sight Class sometimes earn some money, as directors or board members of philanthropic or even profitable enterprises, but the amount earned is laughable in relation to the amount already possessed. Membership in the Top Out-of-Sight Class depends on the ability to flourish without working at all, and it is this that suggests a curious brotherhood between those at the top and the bottom of the scale.

It is this also that distinguishes the Upper Class from its betters. It lives on both inherited money and a salary from attractive, if usually slight, work, without which, even if it could survive and even flourish, it would feel bored and a little ashamed. The next class down, the Upper Middle, may possess virtually as much as the two above it. The difference is that it has earned most of it, in law, medicine, oil, real-estate, or even the more honorific forms of trade. The Upper Middles are afflicted with a bourgeois sense of shame, a conviction that to live on the earnings of others, even forebears, is not entirely nice. 5

The Out-of-Sight Classes at top and bottom have something else in common: They are literally all but invisible (hence their name). The facades of Top Out-of-Sight houses are never seen from the street, and such residences (like Rockefeller's upstate New York premises) are often hidden away deep in the hills, safe from envy and its ultimate attendants, confiscatory taxation and finally expropriation. The Bottom Out-of-Sight Class is equally invisible. When not hidden away in institutions or claustrated in monasteries, lamaseries, or communes, it is hiding from creditors, deceived bail-bondsmen, and merchants intent on repossessing cars and furniture. (This class is visible briefly in one place, in the spring on the streets of New York City, but after this ritual yearly show of itself it disappears again.) When you pass a house with a would-be impressive façade addressing the street, you know it is occupied by a mere member of the Upper or Upper Middle Class. The White House is an example. Its residents, even on those occasions when they are Kennedys, can never be classified as Top Out-of-Sight but only Upper Class. The house is simply too con- 6 spicuous, and temporary residence there usually constitutes a come-down for most of its occupants. It is a hopelessly Upper- or Upper-Middle-Class place.

Another feature of both Top and Bottom Out-of-Sight Classes is their anxiety to keep their names out of the papers, and this too suggests that socially the President is always rather vulgar. All the classes in between Top and Bottom Out-of-Sight slaver for personal publicity (monograms on shirts, inscribing one's name on lawn-mowers and power tools, etc.), and it is this lust to be known almost as much as income that distinguishes them from their Top and Bottom neighbors. The High- and Mid-Prole Classes can be recognized immediately by their pride in advertising their physical presence, a way of saying, "Look! We pay our bills and have a known place in the community, and you can find us there any time." Thus hypertrophied house numbers on the front, or house numbers written "Two Hundred Five" ("Two Hundred and Five" is worse) instead of 205, or flamboyant house or family names blazoned on façades, like "The Willows" or "The Polnickis." 7

(If you go behind the façade into the house itself, you will find a fairly trustworthy class indicator in the kind of wood visible there. The top three classes invariably go in for hardwoods for doors and panelling; the Middle and High-Prole Classes, pine, either plain or "knotty." The knotty-pine "den" is an absolute stigma of the Middle Class, one never to be overcome or disguised by temporarily affected higher usages. Below knotty pine there is plywood.) 8

Façade study is a badly neglected anthropological field. As we work down from the (largely white-painted) bank-like façades of the Upper and Upper Middle Classes, we encounter such Middle and Prole conventions as these, which I rank in order of social status: 9

*Middle*

1. A potted tree on either side of the front door, and the more pointy and symmetrical the better.
2. A large rectangular picture-window in a split-level "ranch" house, displaying a

table-lamp between two side curtains. The cellophane on the lampshade must be visibly inviolate.

3. Two chairs, usually metal with pipe arms, disposed on the front porch as a "conversation group," in stubborn defiance of the traffic thundering past.

*High-Prole* 4. Religious shrines in the garden, which if small and understated, are slightly higher class than

*Mid-Prole* 5. Plaster gnomes and flamingoes, and blue or lavender shiny spheres supported by fluted cast-concrete pedestals.

*Low-Prole* 6. Defunct truck tires painted white and enclosing flower beds. (Auto tires are a grade higher.)

7. Flower-bed designs worked in dead light bulbs or the butts of disused beer bottles.

The Destitute have no façades to decorate, and of course the Bottom Out-of-Sights, being invisible, have none either, although both these classes can occasionally help others decorate theirs—painting tires white on an hourly basis, for example, or even watering and fertilizing the potted trees of the Middle Class. Class X also does not decorate its façades, hoping to stay loose and unidentifiable, ready to re-locate and shape-change the moment it sees that its cover has been penetrated.

In this list of façade conventions an important principle 10
emerges. Organic materials have higher status than metal or plastic. We should take warning from Sophie Portnoy's aluminum venetian blinds, which are also lower than wood because the slats are curved, as if "improved," instead of classically flat. The same principle applies, as *The Preppy Handbook* has shown so effectively, to clothing fabrics, which must be cotton or wool, never Dacron or anything of that prole kind. In the same way, yachts with wood hulls, because they must be repaired or replaced (at high cost)

more often, are classier than yachts with fiberglass hulls, no matter how shrewdly merchandised. Plastic hulls are cheaper and more practical, which is precisely why they lack class.

As we move down the scale, income of course decreases, but income is less important to class than other seldom-invoked measurements: for example, the degree to which one's work is supervised by an omnipresent immediate superior. The more free from supervision, the higher the class, which is why a dentist ranks higher than a mechanic working under a foreman in a large auto shop, even if he makes considerably more money than the dentist. The two trades may be thought equally dirty: It is the dentist's freedom from supervision that helps confer class upon him. Likewise, a high-school teacher obliged to file weekly "lesson plans" with a principal or "curriculum co-ordinator" thereby occupies a class position lower than a tenured professor, who reports to no one, even though the high-school teacher may be richer, smarter, and nicer. (Supervisors and Inspectors are titles that go with public schools, post offices, and police departments: The student of class will need to know no more.) It is largely because they must report that even the highest members of the naval and military services lack social status: They all have designated supervisors—even the Chairman of the Joint Chiefs of Staff has to report to the President. 11

Class is thus defined less by bare income than by constraints and insecurities. It is defined also by habits and attitudes. Take television watching. The Top Out-of-Sight Class doesn't watch at all. It owns the companies and pays others to monitor the thing. It is also entirely devoid of intellectual or even emotional curiosity: It *has* its ideas the way it has its money. The Upper Class does look at television but it prefers Camp offerings, like the films of Jean Harlow or Jon Hall. The Upper Middle Class regards TV as vulgar except for the highminded emissions of National Educational Television, which it watches avidly, especially when, like the Shakespeare series, they are the most incompetently directed and boring. Upper Middles make a point of forbidding children to watch more than an hour a day and worry a lot about violence in society and sugar in cereal. The Middle-Class watches, preferring the more "beautiful" kinds of non-body-contact sports like tennis 12 or gymnastics or figure-skating (the music is a redeeming feature here). With High-, Mid-, and Low-Proles we find heavy viewing of the soaps in the daytime and rugged body-contact sports (football, hockey, boxing) in the evening. The lower one is located in the Prole classes the more likely one is to watch "Bowling for Dollars" and "Wonder Woman" and "The Hulk" and when choosing a game show to prefer "Joker's Wild" to "The Family Feud," whose jokes are sometimes incomprehensible. Destitutes and Bottom Out-of-Sights have in common a problem involving choice. Destitutes usually "own" about three color sets, and the problem is which three programs to run at once. Bottom Out-of-Sights exercise no choice at all, the decisions being made for them by correctional or institutional personnel.

The time when the evening meal is consumed defines class 13
better than, say, the presence or absence on the table of ketchup bottles and ashtrays shaped like little toilets enjoining the diners to "Put Your Butts Here." Destitutes and Bottom Out-of-Sights eat dinner at 5:30, for the Prole staff on which they depend must clean up and be out roller-skating or bowling early in the evening. Thus Proles eat at 6:00 or 6:30. The Middles eat at 7:00, the Upper Middles at 7:30 or, if very ambitious, at 8:00. The Uppers and Top Out-of-Sights dine at 8:30 or 9:00 or even later, after nightly protracted "cocktail" sessions lasting usually around two hours. Sometimes they forget to eat at all.

Similarly, the physical appearance of the various classes de- 14
fines them fairly accurately. Among the top four classes thin is good, and the bottom two classes appear to ape this usage, although down there thin is seldom a matter of choice. It is the three Prole classes that tend to fat, partly as a result of their use of convenience foods and plenty of beer. These are the classes too where anxiety about slipping down a rung causes nervous overeating, resulting in fat that can be rationalized as advertising the security of steady wages and the ability to "eat out" often. Even "Going Out for Breakfast" is not unthinkable for Proles, if we are to believe that they respond to the McDonald's TV ads as they're supposed to. A recent magazine ad for a diet book aimed at Proles stigmatizes a number of erroneous assumptions about body weight, proclaiming with some inelegance that "They're all a crock." Among such

vulgar errors is the proposition that "All Social Classes Are Equally Overweight." This the ad rejects by noting quite accurately.

> Your weight is an advertisement of your social standing. A century ago, corpulence was a sign of success. But no more. Today it is the badge of the lower-middle-class, where obesity is *four times* more prevalent than it is among the upper-middle and middle classes.

It is not just four times more prevalent. It is at least four times more visible, as any observer can testify who has witnessed Prole women perambulating shopping malls in their bright, very tight jersey trousers. Not just obesity but the flaunting of obesity is the Prole sign, as if the object were to give maximum aesthetic offense to the higher classes and thus achieve a form of revenge.

Another physical feature with powerful class meaning is the wearing of plaster casts on legs and ankles by members of the top three classes. These casts, a sort of white badge of honor, betoken stylish mishaps with frivolous but costly toys like horses, skis, snowmobiles, and mopeds. They signify a high level of conspicuous waste in a social world where questions of unpayable medical bills or missed working days do not apply. But in the matter of clothes, the Top Out-of-Sight is different from both Upper and Upper Middle Classes. It prefers to appear in new clothes, whereas the class just below it prefers old clothes. Likewise, all three Prole classes make much of new garments, with the highest possible polyester content. The question does not arise in the same form with Destitutes and Bottom Out-of-Sights. They wear used clothes, the thrift shop and prison supply room serving as their Bonwit's and Korvette's. 15

This American class system is very hard for foreigners to master, partly because most foreigners imagine that since America was founded by the British it must retain something of British institutions. But our class system is more subtle than the British, more a matter of gradations than of blunt divisions, like the binary distinction between a gentleman and a cad. This seems to lack plausibility here. One seldom encounters in the United States the sort of absolute prohibitions which (half-com- 16 ically, to be sure) one is asked to believe define the gentleman in England. Like these:

*A gentleman never wears brown shoes in the city, or*
*A gentleman never wears a green suit, or*
*A gentleman never has soup at lunch, or*
*A gentleman never uses a comb, or*
*A gentleman never smells of anything but tar, or*
*"No gentleman can fail to admire Bellini."*

W. H. Auden

In America it seems to matter much less the way you present yourself—green, brown, neat, sloppy, scented—than what your backing is—that is, where your money comes from. What the upper orders display here is no special uniform but the kind of psychological security they derive from knowing that others recognize their freedom from petty anxieties and trivial prohibitions.

---

## *Meaning and Purpose*

1. In the first paragraph, Fussell says, "it is virtually impossible to break out of the social class in which one has been nurtured," yet we call ours a "mobile society." Do you agree with Fussell's statement? If so, why? If not, why not?
2. What do the Bottom Out-of-Sight and the Top Out-of-Sight Classes have in common?
3. In paragraph 9, Fussell makes the statement, "Façade study is a badly neglected anthropological field," yet anthropologists do not have a field called "façade study." Why do you suppose Fussell makes that statement?
4. In paragraph 15, why are plaster casts called "a sort of white badge of honor"?
5. The last paragraph of this essay says that the "upper orders" are free from "petty anxieties and trivial problems." In your opinion, what are some of those petty anxieties and trivial problems?

## Strategy

1. Why does Fussell make the unusually strong statement in the first paragraph that "No subject today is more likely to offend" than facts about social class?
2. Why does Fussell call one of the classes "Class X"? Why not name the class, as he did with the other classes?
3. Paragraph 11 says that a mechanic and a dentist engage in trades that are "equally dirty." Why does Fussell choose that particular phrase?
4. Paragraph 12 makes the point that certain classes watch certain television shows. What do the names of some of the television shows suggest to you?
5. Why does the essay include the six lines of poetry in paragraph 16?

## Style

1. "Oh, we *have* our hats," say the Boston ladies in paragraph 3. What attitude or tone are the ladies conveying in that comment?
2. In paragraph 6, what do *claustrated* and *lamaseries* mean?
3. In paragraph 14, Fussell makes an ironic comment about being thin. What is that comment?
4. Look up the word *vulgar* in a college-level dictionary. Why do you suppose Fussell says in paragraph 7 that "the President is always rather vulgar"?
5. In paragraph 8, why is the word *den* set off in quotation marks?

## Writing Tasks

1. Classify several of your friends using a light, humorous tone. Invent and label your own categories, and make sure that your categories do not overlap.
2. Choose one of Fussell's classes, and show why or why not the class is a legitimate one, based on your perceptions of how people should be classified.

## ❦ Richard Daniel Altick ❦

*Born in 1915 in Lancaster, Pennsylvania, Richard Altick is a literary historian and biographer. He has had a long and distinguished career as a professor of English at Ohio State University. He began his teaching there as an assistant professor in 1945, and since 1982 has been Regent's Professor emeritus. His scholarly writing has been prolific and includes such works as* The Scholar Adventures *(1959),* Victorian People and Ideas *(1973), and* The Art of Literary Research *(1992). The following selection is excerpted from his* Preface to Critical Thinking *(1969).*

# *Obstacles to Clear Thinking*

*In this article, Altick identifies, explains, and gives examples of logical flaws that we encounter on a daily basis and that are used to convince us in political campaigns and media advertising.*

*Because these "abuses of logic" are so commonplace, we tend to overlook them and so never recognize them as logical fallacies. As you read, make sure you fully understand each point before you move on to the next.*

---

In addition to the many pitfalls awaiting the unwary in formal inductive and deductive thinking, there are a number of common errors which perhaps can be called "abuses of logic" only by courtesy; some of them, at least, may best be described as sheer avoidances of logic. 1

1. Among them, an important class involves the *introduction of irrelevant and irrational evidence*. There they were termed "name-calling" and "glittering generalities." Here we shall give them the labels they have in the books on clear thinking. But it is far less important to remember their names than it is to be able to recognize instances of them when we meet them—and to react to them as intelligent readers should react. 2

a. The *argumentum ad hominem*. Here the writer or speaker departs from his task of proving the point at issue to prejudice his audience against his opponent. In American politics, this argument (which is too dignified a word for it!) is called "mud slinging." If, for example, in attacking his opponent's position on the reduction of the national debt, a candidate refers to Mr. X's intimate connection with certain well-known gamblers, he ceases to argue his case on its objective merits and casts doubt upon his opponent's personal character. His object is not primarily to hurt Mr. X's feelings, but to arouse bias against Mr. X in his hearer's mind. Every critical reader or listener must train himself to detect and reject these irrelevant aspersions. It may be, indeed, that Mr. X *has* shady connections with the underworld. But that has nothing to do with the abstract rights or wrongs of his position on a national issue. Although, as the history of American politics shows, it is a hard thing to do, issues should be discussed apart from character and motives. The latter are also important, since obviously they bear upon a candidate's fitness for public office, but they call for a separate discussion. 3

b. The *argumentum ad populum*. This too involves an appeal to the feelings, passions, and prejudices, rather than the reason, of the group addressed; but whereas the preceding argument is directed specifically against one's opponent, the *ad populum* argument has a wider range. The writer uses emotionally weighted words to bias his audience in favor of or against a person (not necessarily his opponent), an idea, a political party, a class, a nation. The monotonously repeated phrases of Communist propaganda against Americans—"Wall Street monopolists," "rich gangsters," "capitalistic warmongers"—are the most familiar recent examples of the negative, or name-calling, aspect of this argument. But just as common is the other aspect—that of the glittering generality, by which a writer attempts to sway his readers to enthusiasm for something or someone. The twin language-devices of the *argumentum ad populum*, then, are the stenchbomb and the perfume atomizer. The constant task of the critical reader is to ignore the odor with which an idea has been sprayed and to concentrate on the idea itself. 4

The "transfer" device is a particular favorite of those who find 5
it to their advantage to use the *argumentum ad populum*. Like the use of name-calling and the glittering generality, it depends for its effectiveness upon the reader's or hearer's willingness to associate one idea with another, even though the two are not logically connected. Essentially, it represents an attempt to clothe one's pet policy or principle in borrowed raiment which will lend it a strength and dignity it does not possess by itself.

A common example of transfer is the habit which political 6
orators have of working into their speeches quotations from Scripture or from the secular "sacred writings" (the Declaration of Independence, the Preamble to the Constitution, the Gettysburg Address). Such quotations are depended upon to arouse favorable emotions in the breasts of the auditors, emotions which are then transferred to the orator's pet policy. Much of William Jennings Bryan's success as a public figure was due to the way in which he transformed an ordinary political campaign into a quasi-religious crusade by his "Cross of Gold" speech: "You shall not press down upon the brow of labor this crown of thorns; you shall not crucify mankind upon a cross of gold!" Actually, although the underlying idea, that the national monetary policy at the end of the nineteenth century worked to the serious disadvantage of the "common man," was entirely valid, the metaphor in which it was expressed was not. There is no connection between economics and the passion and crucifixion of Jesus. But the metaphor succeeded admirably in rallying to Bryan's ranks millions of Americans to whom Biblical quotation and allusion had the most powerful of connotations. It is noteworthy that as the influence of the Bible upon men's emotional habits declines, knowing politicians make less use of Biblical references; but such standard emotion-rousers as mention of Valley Forge, the Founding Fathers, and Abraham Lincoln are still found sprinkled through much propaganda. Whether they have any logical connection with the issues discussed is, to the speaker and (he hopes) to his audience, irrelevant; what they do is shed their own emotional effulgence upon ideas and pleas which might not otherwise be so acceptable.

The advertiser employs the transfer device just as commonly. Perhaps the most familiar instance of it is the use of the picture of a beautiful girl, not merely to attract attention to the advertisement but also to place the reader in a receptive frame of mind. Whether the girl has anything to do with the subject of the advertisement does not matter—so long as the reader is pleasantly affected. At certain periods when patriotic sentiment runs high, as during a war, commercial advertisers use the emotional symbols of patriotism for their own needs. Not only do they use the national colors and pictures of, or references to, the fighting men; their text often is designed to arouse fervent patriotic emotions which can then be transferred to a particular product. The following advertisement, dominated by a large drawing of the eagle on the United States seal, once appeared in eastern newspapers: 7

**Pride in the American Way**

> The way of life that is American, that expounds democracy, is a proud way of life. It is a manner of living so fine, so high in ideals and purpose that it stands over and above all others. The Grabosky Family, makers of Royalist cigars, are proud to be members of The American Family, proud to present a cigar so fine in quality that it stands above all others. Over 50 years of superb cigar-making experience lies behind Royalist . . . a proud name in a proud America.

c. The *argumentum ad verecundiam*. This is a special instance of the more general "transfer" device. Here it is not a matter of borrowing prestige from one institution, such as religion or a nation, to adorn something else; instead, the prestige is specifically that of a great name, an "authority," which is expected to have weight with the public. On the general matter of authority we shall have more to say in a little while. At this point, we need only stress the importance of critically analyzing any appeal which uses quotations from men and women who have achieved fame in one field or another. One crucial question is: Is the quotation appropriate here? Does it have real relevance to the point at issue? It is 8 all very well to quote Jefferson or Lincoln or Franklin Roosevelt in support of one's political stand—but it must be remembered that circumstances have changed immensely since these quotations were first uttered, and their applicability to a new situation is open to question. The implication is, This man, who we all agree *was* great and wise, said certain things which prove the justice of my own stand; therefore it behooves you to believe I am right. But to have a valid argument, the writer must prove that the word of the authorities whom he cites has a logical bearing on the present issue. If that is true, then he is borrowing not so much their popular prestige as their wisdom—which is perfectly permissible.

In essence, what the writer who invokes august authority for his point of view does is to imply that if the great men of the past were living today, they would write testimonials in behalf of his position. The familiar testimonials of present-day advertising are another instance of the transfer device. In some cases, the authority who testifies has some connection with the type of product advertised. The problem to settle here is, when we decide which brand of cigarette is best, how much weight may we reasonably attach to the enthusiastic statements of tobacco buyers, warehousemen, and auctioneers? In other cases, the testifying authority may have no formal, professional connection with the product advertised. An actor, who may very well be a master of his particular art, praises a whiskey, an after-shaving lotion, or a new convertible. He likes it, he says: but, we may ask, does the fact that he is a successful actor make him any better qualified than anyone who is *not* an actor to judge a whiskey, a lotion, or a car? Competence in one field does not necessarily imply competence in another. 9

Furthermore, in recent times it has been increasingly the custom for advertisers to borrow the prestige of science and medicine to enhance the reputation of their products. The American people have come to feel for the laboratory scientist and the physician an awe once reserved for bishops and statesmen. The alleged approval of such men thus carries great weight when it is a question of selling something, or (which is the same thing) inducing someone to believe something. Phrases such as "leading medical authorities say . . ." or "independent laboratory 10 tests show . . ." are designed simply to transfer the prestige of science, which presumably is incapable of either error or corruption, to a toothpaste or a cereal. Seldom if ever are the precise "medical authorities" or "independent laboratories" named. But the mere phrases have vast weight with the uncritical. Similarly too the honorific "Dr." or "professor" implies that the person quoted speaks with all the authority of which learned men are capable—when as a matter of fact "doctorates" can be bought from mail-order colleges. Whenever, therefore, an attempt is made to convince by appeal to the prestige that surrounds the learned, the reader should demand full credentials. Just *what* medical authorities say this? Can they be trusted? *What* independent laboratories made the test—and what, actually, did the test reveal? Who is this man that speaks as a qualified educator or psychologist or economist? Regardless of the fact that he is called "doctor," does he know what he is talking about?

In all cases where the persuasive power of reputation and au- 11
thority is invoked in behalf of a policy or a product, it is profitable to remember that before he can testify in a court of law, a man about to provide specialized evidence, which may have an important bearing on the jury's decision, must establish his competence in his field. A pathologist, a psychiatrist, an engineer, is asked briefly to outline the nature of his special training and experience. It would not hurt if, when we encounter the appeal to authority in any type of persuasive writing, we adopted the strategy of the opposing lawyer and probed more deeply into the witness' genuine competence to speak on the particular issue that is before us. A few pages later on, we shall suggest some pertinent questions in this respect.

2. *Begging the question.* Here the statement which is ostensibly 12
offered as a proposition to be proved actually assumes the proposition as already proven. "This ordinance will certainly reduce juvenile delinquency, because it provides for steps which will prevent crimes on the part of teenagers." In other words, A is good because A is good. "The reason why Sally is so mischievous is that she has just a little of the devil in her." "I would trust him with any of my personal affairs because he is certainly a reliable lawyer."

Every instance of name-calling or of the glittering generality involves question-begging. When a writer or speaker brands someone a "dangerous radical" or acclaims a policy as "the only way to escape national disaster" he is using words the truth of which he never questions—nor expects his audience to question. Yet all such words and phrases, weighted as they are with emotion and charged with controversy, stand very much in need of proof. And even if, when stripped of their irrelevant emotional wording, the ideas can be established as true, the argument remains sterile. Since its premise is identical with its conclusion, nobody who does not already accept the conclusion will accept the premise, and hence it convinces nobody. 13

3. *False analogy*. This fallacy consists of presenting a situation which is acknowledged to be true, and then, on the basis of it, commenting on another situation which is said to be similar. It is usually employed in an attempt to simplify and make more vivid a complex issue. Newspaper political cartoons are often nothing more than pictorial analogies. Often, of course, such analogies serve admirably to point up, dramatically and colorfully, the crux of a problem. The analogy of a governmental agency in the role of the legendary Dutch boy, trying desperately to stop a leak in the dike ("national economy") while the waves of the sea ("inflation") are already spilling over the top of the dike, is plainly very useful. But the ever-present danger is that the analogy will assume a vital resemblance between the two objects of comparison, where none really exists. "Don't change horses in the middle of a stream" is a familiar cry in political campaigns when, pleading a national emergency, the partisans of the incumbent in office declare he cannot be superseded without grave danger to the country. There is, of course, a superficial similarity between the two situations: changing horses in the middle of a swift stream is dangerous, and so too may be changing public officials at certain junctures in national affairs. But riding horseback is not much like being president of the United States, and while there may be only one or two reasons why one should or should not change horses, there may be very many reasons, none of them having anything to do with horseback riding, why one man should be elected president and 14

not another. Equally dangerous is any attempt to prove a point which is based on the fancy that the nations of the world are like school children, and that when one nation does not have its way it goes into a corner and sulks; or that two opponents, labor and capital, for example, may be likened to two prizefighters squaring off in the ring, with some government official or agency as referee. Such analogies are, we repeat, useful in dramatizing a situation; but it is always perilous to maintain that because two situations are "alike" in one or two respects, what is true of one is necessarily true of the other.

4. *Oversimplification*. False analogy may well be considered a 15
particular type of oversimplification. When we discussed the method of reasoning by hypothesis, we stressed the fact that no hypothesis can be considered sound unless we have taken into account all the factors that are related to it. Unfortunately, with our natural human indolence, to say nothing of our intellectual limitations, we are always eager to view questions in their simplest terms and to make our decisions on the basis of only a few of the many aspects which the problem involves. If that is true of problems of a practical nature, such as those we used to illustrate the use of the hypothesis, how much more true it is of those involving a problem of human conduct, or a grave decision facing the voters or the statesmen of a nation! Few of the decisions which we are called upon to make are so simple that we can say with confidence that one choice is completely right and the other is completely wrong. The problem of the so-called minority groups in America, for instance, is not simply one of abstract justice, as many would like to think it; it involves deeply complex questions of economics, sociology, and politics. Nor can we say with easy assurance: "The federal government should guarantee every farmer a decent income, even if the money comes from the pocketbooks of the citizens who are the father's own customers"—or "It is the obligation of every educational institution to purge its faculty of everyone who holds leftist sympathies." Perhaps each of these propositions is sound, perhaps neither is; but before he adopts it as a settled conviction, the intelligent man or woman must canvass its full im-

plications, just as he should do with any hypothesis. After the implications have been explored, it may be found that there is more evidence telling against the proposition than there is supporting it; in which case it should be abandoned. In any event, no one can call himself a conscientious citizen who fails to explore, so far as he is humanly able, the honest pros and cons of any issue he is called upon to help decide—and then to adopt the position he feels is best justified by the evidence he has surveyed.

Countless false generalizations concerning parties, races, religions, and nations—to say nothing of individuals—are the result of the deep-seated human desire to reduce a complex idea to its simplest terms. Democrats tend naturally to think all Republicans as progress-obstructing conservatives, when in fact many Republicans are more "liberal" than many Democrats. Many Protestants regard Catholics as bigoted and superstitious, even though the views they regard as "bigoted" and the practices they regard as "superstitious" may have their roots deep in the philosophical grounds of the Catholic religion. Similarly many Catholics regard Protestants as infidels or atheists, although there may be as much philosophical justification for Protestant doctrine as there is for Catholic. It is easier to condemn than to understand. But every man and woman has a pressing moral, as well as intellectual obligation to examine the basis of every judgment he or she makes: "Am I examining every aspect of the issue that needs to be examined—do I understand the pros and cons of the problem sufficiently to be able to make a fair decision—or am I taking the easiest way out?" 16

5. The innate intellectual laziness of human beings invites one further, crowning device of deception: the *distortion or the actual suppression of the truth.* If men will not actively demand the truth, why should persuaders provide them with it, when doing so would hurt their chances of success? And so it is usual in all forms of persuasion to prevent considerations which would damage the cause from reaching the minds of those who are to be persuaded. 17

a. One such device—there are many—is *card stacking* (also called "smoke screen"), which is used by a group, a political party 18 for instance, to divert attention from certain issues which it does not care to have discussed. Card stacking consists of laying heavy and insistent emphasis upon certain selected topics, discussion of which can probably do the party no harm. The party then hopes that the public, its attention centered on these topics, will not bother about the less attractive side of the party's record or program. A state administration, running for re-election, may devote all its propaganda to boasting about the reduction in taxes which it has effected in an "economy program"—and it will assiduously fail to mention the way in which state services have deteriorated as a result of the "slashed budget." This same practice is evident in virtually every advertisement one reads. The attractive points of a product are dwelt upon unceasingly; the less attractive ones, never. An automobile may be streamlined and easy-riding, it may have fast pickup in traffic, it may have a wealth of gadgets—these facts will be proclaimed from every newspaper, magazine, and billboard; but that the car eats up gasoline and oil, has a poorly made engine block, and costs $200 more than other cars in the same priceclass—these facts are religiously suppressed. But, as you will no doubt agree, they are worth knowing about.

b. Another closely related means by which attention is drawn 19
from the whole truth is one dear to every practical politician: the *red herring*. The red herring is an irrelevant issue which is drawn across the path of an argument when one side or the other is becoming embarrassed and wishes to change the subject. In a campaign for the mayoralty of a large city, for example, Party A (which is in office) may find itself in serious trouble because Party B has successfully given evidence of its waste of public funds. Four days before the election, therefore, Party A suddenly "discovers" that Party B's candidate has been seen in night clubs with a lady who is not his wife. Party A hopes that the injection into the contest of another, more appealing, topic of discussion will allow the public to forget the serious accusations that have been leveled against it. Whether or not Party A is able to prove that the B candidate's private frailties (if they do exist) disqualify him from holding public office, the red herring will have served its purpose if it ends the embarrassing talk about Party A's own shortcomings.

c. A third such device is that of *wrenching from context.* A sentence or a phrase can easily mean one thing when it is quoted alone, and a quite different thing if it is read against the background of the whole discussion to which it belongs. An extreme example is a sentence from a newspaper review of a new movie: "For about five minutes 'Fruits of Desire' is a topnotch show, brilliantly acted and magnificently photographed. After that it degenerates into a dismal spectacle of Hollywood hokum." It would not be surprising to see the subsequent advertisements of the movie flaunting this headline: "'A top-notch show, brilliantly acted and magnificently photographed . . . a spectacle'—Smith, *Daily News.*" The familiar "avoid foreign entanglements" advice in Washington's farewell address, when read in full context, means something very different from what it means when quoted separately. And probably no public figure whose statements are quoted in the newspapers or on the radio has ever escaped the chagrin that comes from seeing prominence given to one or two paragraphs of his latest speech which, thus isolated, completely distort his total argument. Such quotations must always be read with the greatest caution. The only way to be sure that they fairly represent the author's viewpoint is to read the complete text as printed in, for instance, *The New York Times.* 20

---

## *Meaning and Purpose*

1. To what in us do fallacies appeal?
2. Altick says that some logical errors are abuses of logic and others sheer avoidance of logic (1). Of the fallacies he describes, which seem to avoid logic altogether? Which twist logic to their own purposes? Be specific.
3. Sex and patriotism (7) are two examples of the *transfer* device (5) used by advertisers to sell their products. What other appeals do advertisers make that are examples of *transfer*?

4. Why is it so easy to deceive the public by distorting or suppressing the truth (17)?
5. What are some of the dangers of oversimplification (15–16)?

## *Strategy*

1. Altick uses division and classification as the main organizational pattern of his essay. What is his primary strategy in paragraph development? Give examples.
2. Why does Altick choose politics and advertising to demonstrate the fallacies he describes?

## *Style*

1. Is Altick's language purely descriptive of his subject, or is it sometimes judgmental?
2. If necessary look up the following words in a dictionary: *unwary, inductive, deductive* (1); *connotation* (2); *aspersions* (3); *raiment* (5); *auditors, effulgence* (6); *fervent* (7); *august* (9); *inducing* (10); *invoked, pertinent* (11); *ostensibly* (12); *crux, superseded, junctures, sulks* (14); *hypothesis, indolence, purge, canvass* (15); *innate* (17); *exigencies* (17); *assiduously* (18); *chagrin, prominence* (20).

## *Writing Tasks*

1. Write an essay in which you classify TV ads according to the kinds of fallacies they use. Use several ads for each category and analyze each ad in some depth.
2. Write an essay in which you classify political ads according to the kinds of fallacies they use. Follow the same admonitions as in the task above.

# ❦ *Responding to Photographs* ❦

*Classification and Division*

Veterans Day

Humans are social beings. We form groups and subgroups for a variety of purposes—social, economic, vocational, political.

Some of these groups are informal and temporary: a study group for the final exam, a tour group to a vacation spot, an ad hoc committee to support a municipal bond issue. Others are more formal and longer lasting, binding together the common interests of large numbers of people across geographic and generational lines. Why do we join groups? What do we expect our membership in the group to accomplish for us or for others? Do groups provide us with a sense of identity? Of self-worth? Undoubtedly the reasons vary from one individual to another.

The picture, "Veterans Day," shows two members of a veterans' group posing in uniform with an American flag unobtrusively in the background. Their stance, legs apart and feet planted firmly, gives a solidity to their figures, which is tempered by the warmth of their smiles. They look content, happy, proud. Clearly, each has found some satisfaction in belonging to this organization.

We might wonder, though, if the satisfaction of membership, or the reason for joining this organization, is the same for the woman as for the man. Wearing their uniforms and standing in the noonday sun, they represent the values of the veterans' organization. But as individuals their motivations for being here are personal, a product of their own backgrounds and experiences.

After reviewing "Classification and Division: Establishing Categories" at the beginning of the chapter, complete one of the following writing tasks.

1. Write a division paper that considers the woman and the man in the photograph separately. Describe the physical appearance of each. For each, determine what you believe are possible motivations for joining the armed services and, later, a veterans' organization. What do you imagine the service experience of each was like? What would the veterans' organization represent to each? What satisfactions would each receive from membership? One caution: Since there are only the two figures prominent in the picture, this will be a binary division. Don't slip into comparison and contrast, but profile the woman and the man separately.
2. Write a classification paper that presents categories of people of similar age: children, youth, young adults, older adults, seniors. Find at least five photographs of people of one age group in social situations. Describe the people in each photograph as representatives of a category of their age group. Discuss the characteristics of each category. Include the pictures when submitting your final draft.

## ❦ *Additional Writing Tasks* ❦

*Classification and Division*

1. Choose one of the following subjects and write an essay using division as the dominant pattern. Describe each component in some detail, distinguishing it from the other components. Keep your readers in mind by guiding them carefully from component to component.
    a. A musical performance
    b. A board game, like chess, Monopoly, Risk, or Clue
    c. The human mind
    d. A ceremonial event, such as a wedding, funeral, campaign rally, banquet, religious service
    e. A week at a teenage vacation spot
    f. A novel
    g. A police drama, situation comedy, or national news broadcast
    h. Your monthly income
    i. Bargaining in a foreign marketplace
    j. A meal in an expensive restaurant
2. Write an essay using classification as the dominant development method. Sort one of the following subjects into categories. Be sure the basis for your classification is clear. To direct your readers' attention, make up names for each category.
    a. The books, records, and/or video tapes you own
    b. Unusual sports, such as "earth games" or other sports seldom televised or reported in newspapers
    c. Talk-show hosts
    d. War toys, family-oriented toys, or intellectual toys
    e. People who like to hunt game
    f. Lies
    g. Ways to read a novel or poem
    h. Ways to watch a horror movie
    i. Kinds of photography
    j. Attitudes revealed by bumper stickers
    k. Trends in dating, marriage, or divorce
    l. Kinds of terror

m. Responses to a dramatic national or international event
n. New ways to learn
o. Kinds of good luck
p. Kinds of bad luck

# 10

# *Definition*

## *Limiting Meaning*

## *The Method*

Think of how many words you hear in a day. Tens of thousands? Hundreds of thousands? Millions? Spoken words are plentiful. They are easy to produce: just open your mouth, activate your larynx, wag your tongue, and words will take flight. Of course, spoken words are often strung together thoughtlessly. If you have any doubts about this description, just turn your television dial to a talk show and listen to the relentless babble.

But written words are different. They require work. Serious writers select them with care. Some words are so technical that only technically trained readers understand them. Some words are so rarely used that few readers know what they mean. Some have meanings so ambiguous that readers understand them differently. That is why definition is indispensable in writing.

## *Strategies*

Professional writers approach definition in three ways: etymological, or lexical, definition; stipulative definition; and extended definition.

### *Etymological Definition*

An etymological definition is a dictionary definition. It defines a word in a narrow way by specifying its class and its distinguishing characteristics. Consider the word "thriller." A good college dictionary tells you that a thriller is a suspenseful work of fiction—a novel, play, or film—that deals with crime or detection. Sometimes an etymological definition includes synonyms: a "thriller" might be referred to as a "whodunit."

Rather than use a ready-made dictionary definition, writers often expand dictionary information to fit the interests of their audience and requirements that suit their purposes. Consider the dictionary definition of *bird*: "a warm-blooded, two-legged, egg-laying vertebrate with a wishbone, feathers, and wings." Now imagine that a writer wishes to define *bird* for a ten-year-old reader. The definition might read something like this:

> A bird is an animal. It has a backbone, is warm-blooded, and walks on two legs, but a human being does, too. It flies, but insects and bats do, too. It lays eggs, but salamanders, some snakes, and turtles do the same.
>
> What then makes birds different from all other animals? Only birds have feathers and a wishbone.

### *Stipulative Definition*

Sometimes a writer uses a common word extensively in a special or limited way. The writer then usually stipulates the meaning of the word—that is, the writer explains how the word is to be understood as it appears throughout the essay. This explanation creates the *stipulative definition*. In this paragraph from *Amusing Ourselves to Death*, educator and communications critic Neil Postman stipulates the meaning of "conversation."

> I use the word "conversation" metaphorically to refer not only to speech but to all techniques and technologies that permit people of a particular culture to exchange messages. In this sense, all culture is a conversation or, more precisely, a corporation of conversations, conducted in a variety of symbolic modes. Our attention here is on how forms of public discourse regulate and even dictate what kind of content can issue from such forms.

And social critic Don Pierstorff stipulates a meaning for "suits" when examining Michael Levine's *Deep Cover*, an exposé of the Drug Enforcement Administration (DEA).

> Who are the "suits"? They are the men and women who crowd the corridors and sit behind the desks of the Drug Enforcement Administration. They are government bureaucrats and managers. According to Michael Levine, they are

> the people who have no first-hand experience of the drug war and are unwilling to listen to agents who do. They spend their days shuffling reports and briefing politicians.

Postman's paragraph stipulates the meaning of "conversation" by enlarging it to mean all the methods culture uses to communicate. Pierstorff's paragraph defines the commonly understood word "suits" by presenting its uncommon slang definition, the way in which DEA agents use it. Both authors anticipate that their readers will need to know these special definitions to understand what they are writing about.

### *Extended Definitions*

Etymological and stipulative definitions usually are concisely written for the sole purpose of clarification. Extended definitions are much more detailed and usually employ various patterns of development to fully explain a word or concept. In this paragraph from *Hog on Ice*, C. E. Funk defines "white elephant." He uses examples to establish its class and a brief narration about the word's origin to differentiate it from others.

> That large portrait of your wealthy Aunt Jane, given by her and which you loathe but do not dare to take down from your wall; that large bookcase, too costly to discard, but which you hope will be more in keeping with your future home; these, and a thousand other like items, are "white elephants"—costly but useless possessions. The allusion takes us to Siam. In that country it was the traditional custom for many centuries that a rare albino elephant was, upon capture, the property of the emperor—who even today bears the title Lord of the White Elephant—and was thereafter sacred to him. He alone might ride or use such an animal, and none might be destroyed without his consent. Because of that latter royal prerogative, it is said that whenever it pleased his gracious majesty to bring about the ruin of a courtier who had displeased him, he would present the poor fellow with an elephant from his stables. The cost of feeding

and caring for the huge animal that he might neither use nor destroy—a veritable white elephant—gave the term its present meaning.

In this two-paragraph passage from *Alligators in Sewers and Other Urban Legends*, Jan Harold Brunvand defines "urban legend." Brunvand first establishes the class to which "urban legend" belongs and then distinguishes it from other members of the class. His definition goes beyond the etymological category because he develops the expression in greater detail, primarily with brief comparison and contrast and examples.

Urban legends are realistic stories that are said to have happened recently. Like old legends of lost mines, buried treasure, and ghosts, they usually have an ironic or supernatural twist. They belong to a subclass of folk narratives that (unlike fairy tales) are set in the recent past, involving ordinary human beings rather than extraordinary gods and demigods.

Unlike rumors, which are generally fragmentary or vague reports, legends have a specific narrative quality and tend to attach themselves to different local settings. Although they may explain or incorporate current rumors, legends tend to have a longer life and wider acceptance; rumors flourish and then die out rather quickly. Urban legends circulate by word of mouth, among the "folk" of modern society, but the mass media frequently help to disseminate and validate them. While they vary in particular details from one telling to another, they preserve a central core of traditional themes. In some instances these seemingly fresh stories are merely updatings of classic folklore plots, while other urban legends spring directly from recent conditions and then develop their own traditional patterns in repeated retellings. For example, "The Vanishing Hitchhiker," which describes the disappearance of a rider picked up on a highway, has evolved from a 19th-century horse-and-buggy legend into modern variants incorporating freeway travel. A story called "Alligators in the Sewers," on the other hand, goes back no further than

> the 1930s and seems to be a New York City invention. Often, it begins with people who bring pet baby alligators back from Florida and eventually flush them down the drain.

Both Funk's definition of "white elephant" and Brunvand's definition of "urban legend" involve much more than merely looking up the established meanings; nevertheless, they do make use of a common pattern of definition by placing a term in a class and distinguishing it from other members of the class. Funk and Brunvand can use this pattern because the words they define have been in common use for some time. But the strength of an extended definition is to introduce new terms to readers, or, more accurately, to introduce concepts represented by those terms. This kind of extended definition may be highly personal, embodying a writer's values and independent observation.

In this three-paragraph passage from *Zen and the Art of Motorcycle Maintenance*, Robert M. Pirsig defines "mechanic's feel." Clearly, his definition is based on close observation during personal experience.

> The mechanic's feel comes from a deep inner kinesthetic feeling for the elasticity of materials. Some materials, like ceramics, have very little, so that when you thread a porcelain fitting you're very careful not to apply great pressures. Other materials, like steel, have tremendous elasticity, more than rubber, but in a range in which, unless you're working with large mechanical forces, the elasticity isn't apparent.
>
> With nuts and bolts you're in the range of large mechanical forces and you should understand that within these ranges metals are elastic. When you take up a nut there's a point called "fingertight" where there's contact but no takeup of elasticity. Then there's "snug," in which the easy surface elasticity is taken up. Then there's the range called "tight," in which all the elasticity is taken up. The force required to reach these three points is different for each size of nut and bolt, and different for lubricated bolts and for locknuts. The forces are different for steel and cast iron and brass

and aluminum and plastics and ceramics. But a person with mechanic's feel knows when something's tight and stops. A person without it goes right on past and strips the threads or breaks the assembly.

A "mechanic's feel" implies not only an understanding for the elasticity of metal but for its softness. The insides of a motorcycle contain surfaces that are precise in some cases to as little as one ten-thousandth of an inch. If you drop them or get dirt on them or scratch them or bang them with a hammer, they'll lose that precision. It's important to understand that the metal *behind* the surfaces can normally take a great shock and stress but that the surfaces themselves cannot. When handling precision parts that are stuck or difficult to manipulate, a person with mechanic's feel will avoid damaging the surfaces and work with his tools on the nonprecision surfaces of the same part whenever possible. If he must work on the surfaces themselves, he'll always use softer surfaces to work them with. Brass hammers, plastic hammers, wood hammers, rubber hammers and lead hammers are all available for this work. Use them. Vise jaws can be fitted with plastic and copper and lead faces. Use these too. Handle precision parts gently. You'll never be sorry. If you have a tendency to bang things around, take more time and try to develop a little more respect for the accomplishment that a precision part represents.

Pirsig's definition of "mechanic's feel" is unique. Readers have no resource to consult for a commonly accepted definition of an expression like that. Primarily relying on descriptive techniques, Pirsig carefully delineates the qualities of "mechanic's feel," right down to naming the degrees to which someone might tighten down a bolt: "fingertight," "snug," and "tight." Pirsig points out that metal has elasticity, and that someone with "mechanic's feel" must sense that quality or face the consequences—a broken assembly. Pirsig creates a sense of the soft, delicate surfaces of metal and names the tools someone should use when working on them—hammers of many materials varying in softness, as well as vise jaws fitted with soft faces. Someone with mechanic's feel is precise; in fact, the need for precision seems to be the message beneath the detail.

## *Definition in College Writing*

You will write definitions to clarify important terms or concepts, especially in the social sciences, history, and philosophy. Usually these will be stipulative definitions that are one or two paragraphs long and serve as part of an essay with another dominant development pattern. But sometimes an entire essay will be devoted to an extended definition. When you write an essay-length extended definition, the basic essay structure does not change: Begin with an introduction that ends with a clear statement of purpose or thesis. Write a discussion that develops the definition in several paragraphs. Write a conclusion that recalls the key points of the definition and restates the central purpose. Usually a definition will include examples that illustrate the term or concept and comparisons to show the meaning in relation to similar terms or concepts.

### *Guidelines for Writing a Definition Essay*

1. Select a term, or concept, that is currently being used in a new way or for which there is no clear etymological definition, such as a slang term or a new term from technology.
2. Develop a rough working explanation of what you will be defining. Then use prewriting techniques to generate examples and comparisons to illustrate it for your reader. If you are writing to define a special term, generate information that explains how to use it effectively and how it is misused.
3. Evaluate your prewritten material to see what you can and can't use effectively. Develop a clear purpose for your essay, one that clearly shows you will be writing a definition. Then shape the purpose into a thesis.

4. Write your essay. Organize it by moving from the general to the particular; that is, first create a broad sense of your term or concept then present particular examples, comparisons, and information to clarify it in more detail.
5. Revise your definition. Be sure your definition is clear, including everything in its category and excluding everything that isn't. Check your examples and comparisons to see that they are integrated effectively into the definition. Polish the entire definition for clarity.

### *A Student Essay Developed by Definition*

For Freshman Composition, Chris Schneider responded to the following writing task:

> Use definition to develop any of the following topics in 500 to 600 words. You may use any number of paragraph development patterns, such as description, example, and comparison, to develop your thought.
>
> a. commonsense
> b. code
> c. myth
> d. symbol
> e. sign
> f. saga
> g. tale
> h. legend

Schneider selected item "c." "Myth" had taken on new significance. He had encountered the new usage in culture studies.

*Schneider uses a catalogue of questions to present common social myths.*

*The thesis statement implies that perceptions are influenced by common "myths." "Myths" is the term to be defined.*

Myth Redefined

Do you believe childhood is a time of innocence separated from the emotions and cares of the adult world? Do you count on science to solve the dangers of fossil-fuel shortage, ozone depletion, and toxic pollution? Do you feel that men are rational, and women are intuitive? Men are active; women, passive? Men are ambitious; women, nurturing? If you do, then you have been influenced by common American "myths," as a group of contemporary scholars and social critics known as semiologists would claim.

*The topic sentence establishes "semiologists" as this paragraph's subject. Schneider uses the explanation of semiologist to begin to show what myth means. This paragraph contrasts semiologists with semanticists to clarify what semiologists do.*

Semiologists are interested in the study of meaning. They don't limit themselves to the meaning of words. This territory belongs to semanticists, that is, to those scholars who concentrate on linguistic significance. Semiologists may examine words, but they will also explore the ways that advertisements, television programs, films, clothes, toys, and other such things embody meaning, a kind of cultural meaning that semiologists sometimes refer to as "myth."

*The opening sentence leads into a discussion of the general category "myth" falls into. Schneider shows how myth is similar to and different from other terms in the category—legend and fable. Notice how the last sentence leads into the next paragraph.*

To most of us, the term "myth" might call to mind marvelous Greek stories of disguised gods cavorting with humans. We might think of heroes wielding swords against dragons or of magicians mesmerizing entire armies. We might recall the story of Johnny Appleseed planting apple trees across the American landscape or of Rip Van Winkle sleeping for twenty years or of John Henry racing against a steam-powered spike driver. These myths are different from legends because they lack historical background and shade into the supernatural. They are also different from fables because they lack an overt moral intent. Like legends and fables they are stories, imaginative stories, that, according to one popular view, embody cultural patterns. Now semiologists are using the term "myth" in a different way.

*The topic sentence signals Schneider will explain the new use of "myth."*

To semiologists "myth" refers to deeply rooted cultural beliefs not to ancient stories. These beliefs are held by most members of any given society. Despite whatever evidence there might be to contradict the validity of a myth, semiologists do not judge it as right or wrong. They merely recognize its existence and analyze its social influence. Whether valid or invalid, a myth, therefore, is a psychological and social fact projected onto experience. We never clearly see things as they really are; we only see their reflections in our cultural beliefs.

*The first two sentences serve as the topic sentence.*

*Schneider offers both typical and specific examples to show how cultural myths are used for manipulative purposes.*

Cultural myths are often used for manipulative purposes. For instance, one myth embedded in cultural conscious is the myth of the rugged individual. Usually a man, the rugged individual is one who can survive on his own in environments that would be hostile to all of us acculturated folks. Advertisers especially associate their products with the image of the rugged individual to manipulate consumers. For example, consider the Marlboro man, the lone cowboy who leads a rugged life herding steers on the open range. He calls to mind the rugged individuals cowboy actors John Wayne and Clint Eastwood play in western films, tough hombres who ride the range alone. Well, not quite alone; he has his cigarette. Of course, not everyone will respond to this myth. That's why advertisers employ many different kinds of cultural myths to sell their products.

*Schneider ends by showing that we are not the absolute prisoners of myth.*

*New perceptions allow us to see experiences differently.*

Myths, as semiologists use the term, pervade every aspect of our cultural experience. Sometimes these belief systems are unrecognized and have a powerful influence on how we view experience. Other times, we become aware of them and through that awareness, change our perception of the world. Remember this myth: The husband is the breadwinner; the wife is the homemaker. The world has changed dramatically since that perception dominated American thinking.

### *Comments*

Chris Schneider had a hard time limiting her essay to 600 words, the maximum length for this writing task. She had to delete a series illustrating common myths. She also deleted several more examples of myth at work in advertisements. Of all these examples she decided to keep the references to the "rugged individual" and the Marlboro man because she felt her readers could easily recognize them since they had been published in magazines for years.

**Development Strategy.** Schneider opens with a series of questions to help establish the concept of cultural myth. She ends with a thesis statement that clearly indicates she will define "myth" and that myths affect perception.

After writing an early draft, she realized she needed to explain what semiologists do. She developed the second paragraph through a brief contrast between semiologists and semanticists, two commonly confused scholars. This contrast helped her generally explain the difference. She didn't want to get sidetracked here, keeping in mind her dominant purpose was to define "myth," not "semiologist."

In the third paragraph, Schneider uses a common tactic in definition. She places the term in a general category, than shows how it is different then and similar to other category members. The fourth paragraph works with the third. In it she makes a direct statement about "myth." But rather than define "myth" in strict terms, which might be impossible, she continues to create an "impression" of myth. She is also moving from the general to the specific, each paragraph revealing her subject in more detail.

The fifth paragraph is the most detailed. Schneider uses some general references and a specific example to illustrate her point. One danger here: The subject is so large that she really needs more than one specific example. But because space was limited and she had created a broad impression of myth in the earlier paragraph, she felt one easily recognizable example would clarify her point.

Finally, Schneider offers a brief conclusion that makes effective use of a commonly believed myth that has been "exposed." This tactic illustrates that perception can be changed through awareness.

**Revision.** In the first draft, Schneider's introduction presented common myths in declarative sentences. Her group pointed out that to rephrase them as questions would involve a reader more directly. They also pointed out that she needed to include more specific detail, especially when referring to science and men and women. Finally, they recommended that she create a sense of who semiologists are. In revision, she tried to integrate their suggestions:

Do you

~~Some people~~ believe ~~that~~ childhood is a time of innocence

separated from the emotions and cares of the adult world?

Do you count on to the dangers of fossil

~~Some people believe that~~ science ~~will~~ solve fuel shortage,

ozone depletion and toxic pollution? Do you feel that

~~and environmental destrction.~~ ~~Some people believe~~ men ~~and~~

are rational and women are intuitive? Men are active;

~~women embody a set of opposing psychological and soc~~ial

women, passive? Men are ambitious; women, nurturing?

~~characteristics~~.

If you do, then you

~~The perceptions of these people~~ have been influenced by

Contemporary

common American "myths," as a group of ~~semiologists~~

scholars and social critics known as

~~would claim.~~

semiologists would claim.

Now read the final draft again with the changes integrated.

Do you believe childhood is a time of innocence separated from the emotions and cares of the adult world? Do you count on science to solve the dangers of fossil-fuel shortage, ozone

## Peer Review

You may be asked to write an essay about one of the readings that follow. Before you meet with your writing group, review this introduction. As you read the papers of your group, use these general principles of definition to help guide your comments.

1. A definition paper should go beyond a dictionary definition to give the reader a fuller understanding of the term being defined.
2. A definition paper should have a clear purpose. The reader should be told why the term is important and how it relates to some larger picture.

depletion, and toxic pollution? Do you feel that men are rational and women are intuitive? Men are active; women, passive? Men are ambitious; women, nurturing? If you do, you have been influenced by common American "myths," as a group of contemporary scholars and social critics known as semiologists would claim.

The additional specific detail helps clarify Schneider's thought. And, indeed, shaping the declarative statements into questions helps her to quickly involve the reader.

The essays that follow are developed with definition as their main purpose. Study them. Make note of each writer's strategy. Apply what you learn to your own writing.

## ❦ Judy Brady ❦

*Judy Brady was born in San Francisco in 1937. She studied painting at the University of Iowa, married and had children, and later worked as a secretary in San Francisco, having been discouraged by her male university professors from becoming a teacher. She later became very active in the feminist movement and has written numerous articles on women's roles in society and related subjects. In 1973 she went to Cuba to study social class relationships, having developed an interest in how societies change from her feminist political work.*

# *I Want a Wife*

*This essay was published in the first issue of* Ms *magazine in 1971 and has been widely reprinted since. This biting description of the "ideal" wife has become a classic of feminist satire. Brady first classifies herself as a wife, then proceeds to define "wife" by explaining why she wants a wife of her own.*

---

I belong to that classification of people known as wives. I am A Wife. And, not altogether incidentally, I am a mother. 1

Not too long ago a male friend of mine appeared on the scene fresh from a recent divorce. He had one child, who is, of course, with his ex-wife. He is looking for another wife. As I thought about him while I was ironing one evening, it suddenly occurred to me that I, too, would like to have a wife. Why do I want a wife? 2

I would like to go back to school so that I can become economically independent, support myself, and, if need be, support those dependent upon me. I want a wife who will work and send me to school. And while I am going to school I want a wife to take care of my children. I want a wife to keep track of the children's doctor and dentist appointments. And to keep track of mine, too. I want a wife to make sure my children eat properly and are kept clean. I want a wife who will wash the children's clothes and keep 3 them mended. I want a wife who is a good nurturant attendant to my children, who arranges for their schooling, makes sure that they have an adequate social life with their peers, takes them to the park, the zoo, etc. I want a wife who takes care of the children when they are sick, a wife who arranges to be around when the children need special care, because, of course, I cannot miss classes at school. My wife must arrange to lose time at work and not lose the job. It may mean a small cut in my wife's income from time to time, but I guess I can tolerate that. Needless to say, my wife will arrange and pay for the care of the children while my wife is working.

I want a wife who will take care of *my* physical needs. I want a wife who will keep my house clean. A wife who will pick up after my children, a wife who will pick up after me. I want a wife who will keep my clothes clean, ironed, mended, replaced when need be, and who will see to it that my personal things are kept in their proper place so that I can find what I need the minute I need it. I want a wife who cooks the meals, a wife who is a *good* cook. I want a wife who will plan the menus, do the necessary grocery shopping, prepare the meals, serve them pleasantly, and then do the cleaning up while I do my studying. I want a wife who will care for me when I am sick and sympathize with my pain and loss of time from school. I want a wife to go along when our family takes a vacation so that someone can continue to care for me and my children when I need a rest and change of scene. 4

I want a wife who will not bother me with rambling complaints about a wife's duties. But I want a wife who will listen to me when I feel the need to explain a rather difficult point I have come across in my course of studies. And I want a wife who will type my papers for me when I have written them. 5

I want a wife who will take care of the details of my social life. When my wife and I are invited out by my friends, I want a wife who will take care of the babysitting arrangements. When I meet people at school that I like and want to entertain, I want a wife who will have the house clean, will prepare a special meal, serve it to me and my friends, and not interrupt when I talk about things that interest me and my friends. I want a wife who will have 6 arranged that the children are fed and ready for bed before my guests arrive so that the children do not bother us. I want a wife who takes care of the needs of my guests so that they feel comfortable, who makes sure that they have an ashtray, that they are passed the hors d'oeuvres, that they are offered a second helping of the food, that their wine glasses are replenished when necessary, that their coffee is served to them as they like it. And I want a wife who knows that sometimes I need a night out by myself.

I want a wife who is sensitive to my sexual needs, a wife who makes love passionately and eagerly when I feel like it, a wife who makes sure that I am satisfied. And, of course, I want a wife who will not demand sexual attention when I am not in the mood for it. I want a wife who assumes the complete responsibility for birth control, because I do not want more children. I want a wife who will remain sexually faithful to me so that I do not have to clutter up my intellectual life with jealousies. And I want a wife who understands that *my* sexual needs may entail more than strict adherence to monogamy. I must, after all, be able to relate to people as fully as possible. 7

If, by chance, I find another person more suitable as a wife than the wife I already have, I want the liberty to replace my present wife with another one. Naturally, I will expect a fresh, new life; my wife will take the children and be solely responsible for them so that I am left free. 8

When I am through with school and have a job, I want my wife to quit working and remain at home so that my wife can more fully and completely take care of a wife's duties. 9

My God, who *wouldn't* want a wife? 10

---

## *Meaning and Purpose*

1. What are your ideas about what a wife is and does, and where do your ideas come from? How do they compare to what Brady says she wants her "wife" to be and do?
2. Brady repeats "I want a wife" many times throughout this essay. What is the purpose of that repetition?

3. Why does Brady use "of course" in paragraph 2?
4. Can you find a thesis statement in the essay? What is Brady's main point?
5. In listing a wife's duties, Brady also lists a husband's needs. What are some of these needs, and do you think Brady is fair to husbands in this essay?

## *Strategy*

1. Do you think the first paragraph is effective as an opening? How does it serve Brady's purpose?
2. Brady defines "wife" by listing the duties she would expect her wife to perform. She arranges these duties in clusters of similar items. For each of paragraphs 3–7, label the cluster and tell what human characteristics Brady describes.
3. Classify this essay by labeling it with a name such as "informative," "political," "sarcastic," or "optimistic." Try to think of your own name—use one of those above if you must—and explain your reasons for labeling it as you have.

## *Style*

1. Why is "A Wife" capitalized in the first paragraph?
2. What important attitude of Brady toward her "wife" does the word "replace" in paragraph 8 suggest?
3. Paragraph 4 says that the wife will not go on vacation with the author. Instead, she will go "along" on vacation. What is the difference in meaning between "going" and "going along" on vacation?
4. Why does Brady end her essay with a question? How is the question effective?

## *Writing Tasks*

1. Brady's "wife" is an ideal one described from an exaggerated selfish male viewpoint. Who is your ideal person in some classifica-

tion of people, such as parent, boy- or girlfriend, sister or brother, teacher, athlete, food server, or salesperson? Write a definition essay in which you define by describing this ideal's behavior in various circumstances.

2. Give a man's counterpoint to Brady's essay: "I Want a Husband." Write from a first-person male point of view and decide which categories to use. Try to imitate Brady's sarcastic and exaggerated tone.

## ❦ George Gilder ❦

*George Gilder is a sociologist. His works include* Men and Marriage *(1986),* Life After Television *(1994), and* Visible Man: A True Story of Post-Racist America *(1995).*

# *Why Men Marry*

*This excerpt from* Men and Marriage *recognizes the difficulty of defining the word "love" in a simple declarative sentence and makes no attempt to do so. Instead Gilder focuses on the psychological and biological needs that lead a man to replace the hunter love of youth with the procreative love of maturity.*

*As you read, notice how Gilder uses catalogs of images to convey pictures of various aspects of love, particularly in paragraphs 1, 4 and 6.*

---

Men marry for love. But what does this mean beyond what they got in their lives as single men: the flash of a new face, new flesh across a room. The glimpse of breasts shifting softly in a silken blouse. The open sesame of a missing ring. The excited pursuit, the misunderstood meanings, the charged meetings. The telling touch of hands. The eyes welling open to the gaze. The scent of surrender. The pillowed splash of unbound hair. The ecstatic slipping between new sheets. The race. The winning. The chase and the conquest . . . and back on the road. Definitely back on the road. Free again. Strong again. For new women, new pursuit. What more is there in life—in love—than this? 1

Marriage means giving it all up. Giving up love? That is how it seems to the single man, and that is why he fears it. He must give up his hunter's heart, forgo the getaway Honda growl, shear off his shaggy hair, restrict his random eye, hang up his handgun, bow down and enter the cage. At bottom, what he is is hunter. No way he will be hubby. 2

And yet, he will. For years he lunges at women's surfaces, but as time passes he learns of a deeper promise. For years he may not know the reasons or believe them or care. The heart, it is said, has its reasons. They spring from the primal predicament of man throughout the history of the race: the need to choose a particular woman and stay by her and provide for her if he is to know his children and they are to love him and call him father. 3

In procreative love, both partners consciously or unconsciously glimpse a future infant—precarious in the womb, vulnerable in the world, and in need of nurture and protection. In the swelter of their bodies together, in the shape and softnesses of the woman, in the protective support of the man, the couple senses the outlines of a realm that can endure and perpetuate their union: a pattern of differences and complements that goes beyond the momentary pleasures of reciprocal sex. 4

Marriage asks men to give up their essential sexuality only as part of a clear scheme for replacing it with new, far more important, and ultimately far more sexual roles: husband and father. Without these roles, a woman can bear a child, but the man is able only to screw. He can do it a lot, but after his first years it will only get him unthreaded, and in the end he is disconnected and alone. In his shallow heats and frustrations, he all too often becomes a menace to himself and his community. 5

There are millions of single men, unlinked to any promising reality, dissipating their lives by the years, moving from job to job, woman to woman, illusion to embitterment. Yet they are not hopeless. Many more millions have passed through the same sloughs, incurred the same boozy dreams, marijuana highs, cocaine crashes, sex diseases, job vapors, legal scrapes, wanderings. They follow the entire syndrome and then break out of it. Normally they do not escape through psychiatrists' offices, sex-education courses, VISTA or Peace Corps programs, reformatories, or guidance-counseling uplift. What happens, most of the time—the only effective thing that happens, the only process that reaches the sources of motivation and character—is falling in love. 6

Love is effective because it works at a deeper, more instinctual level than the other modes of education and change. Love does not teach or persuade. It possesses and transforms. . . . 7

It is not just an intelligent appraisal of his circumstances that transforms the single man. It is not merely a desire for companionship or "growth." It is a deeper alchemy of change, flowing from a primal source. It seeps slowly into the flesh, the memory, the spirit; it rises through a life, until it can ignite. It is a perilous process, full of chances for misfire and mistake—or for an ever more mildewed middle age. It is not entirely understood. But we have seen it work, and so have we seen love. Love infuses reason and experience with the power to change a man caught in a morbid present into a man passionately engaged with the future. 8

The change that leads to love often comes slowly. Many of the girls a man finds will not help. They tend to go along with him and affirm his single life. But one morning he turns to the stranger sleeping next to him, who came to him as easily as a whiskey too many, and left him as heavy-headed, and decides he must seek a better way to live. One day he looks across the room over a pile of dirty dishes and cigarette butts and beer cans and sex magazines and bills and filthy laundry, and he does not see the evidence of happy carousing and bachelor freedom; he sees a trap closing in upon him more grimly than any marriage. One day while joking with friends about the latest of his acquaintances to be caught and caged, he silently wonders, for a moment, whether he really wishes it were he. 9

Suddenly he has a new glimpse of himself. His body is beginning to decline, grow weaker and slower, even if he keeps it fit. His body, which once measured out his few advantages over females, is beginning to intimate its terrible plan to become as weak as an older woman's. His aggressiveness, which burst in fitful storms throughout his young life but never seemed to cleanse him—his aggression for which he could so rarely find the adequate battle, the harmonious chase—is souring now. His job, so below his measure as a man, so out of tune with his 10 body and his inspiration, now stretches ahead without joy or relief.

His sex, the force that drove the flower of his youth, drives still, drives again and again the same hard bargain—for which there are fewer and fewer takers, in a sexual arena with no final achievement for the single man, in which sex itself becomes work that is never done. 11

The single man is caught on a reef and the tide is running out. He is being biologically stranded and he has a hopeless dream. Studs Terkel's book *Working* registers again and again men's desire to be remembered. Yet who in this world is much remembered for his job? 12

Stuck with what he may sense as a choice between being trapped and being stranded, he still may respond by trying one more fling. The biological predicament can be warded off for a time, like Hemingway's hyena. Death often appears in the guise of eternal youth, at the ever-infatuating fountains: alcohol, drugs, hallucinogenic sex. For a while he may believe in the disguise. But the hyena returns and there is mortality in the air—diseases, accidents, concealed suicides, the whole range of the single man's aggression, turned at last against himself. 13

But where there is death, there is hope. For the man who is in touch with his mortality, but not in the grips of it, is also in touch with the sources of his love. He is in contact with the elements—the natural fires and storms so often used as metaphors for his passions. He is a man who can be deeply and effectively changed. He can find his age, his relation to the world, his maturity, his future. He can burn his signature into the covenant of a specific life. 14

The man has found a vital energy and a possibility of durable change. It has assumed the shape of a woman. It is the same form that has caught his eye and roiled his body all these years. But now there will be depths below the pleasing surfaces, meanings beyond the momentary ruttings. There will be a sense that this vessel contains the secrets of new life, that the womb and breasts bear a message of immortality. There will be a knowledge that to 15 treat this treasure as an object—mere flesh like his own, a mere matrix of his pleasure—is to defile life itself. It is this recognition that she offers a higher possibility—it is this consciousness that he has to struggle to be worthy of her—that finally issues the spark. And then arises the fire that purges and changes him as it consumes his own death. His children . . . they will remember. It is the only hope.

The man's love begins in a knowledge of inferiority, but it offers a promise of dignity and purpose. For he then has to create, by dint of his own effort, and without the miracle of a womb, a life that a woman could choose. Thus are released and formed the energies of civilized society. He provides, and he does it for a lifetime, for a life. 16

---

## *Meaning and Purpose*

1. Who do you think is the primary audience for this essay? What does Gilder hope to communicate to this audience?
2. According to Gilder, what is life like for men who do not marry? Be specific in your answer.
3. According to Gilder, what leads a man to give up the hunter life and seek procreative love?
4. Why, according to this essay are a man's children more important than his work?

## *Strategy*

1. We have included this essay as an example of extended definition, but Gilder also uses other development strategies that you have studied in earlier chapters of this text. What other strategies can you find and where are they located?
2. Gilder's essay is not a typical straightforward definition. You might say it defines more by implication than explication. How effective do you think his approach is? Support your answer with reasons.

## *Style*

1. In writing, the word *catalog* denotes a list composed of sentences, phrases, or words used to suggest the fullness of an idea. Most of paragraph 1, beginning with "the flash of . . ." is an example of a catalog. In what other places does Gilder use catalogs to convey his meaning? How effective is this technique?
2. Explain in your own words why Gilder says "the womb and breasts bear a message of immortality." (Paragraph 15)
3. In the last paragraph, Gilder says, "man's love begins in a knowledge of inferiority." What do you think this statement means. Is it valid in the context of this essay?
4. If necessary, check a dictionary for the meanings of these words: *ecstatic* (1); *primal* (3); *procreative* (4); *sloughs*, *vapors* (6); *alchemy*, *morbid* (8); *covenant*, *ruttings*, *purges* (15).

## *Writing Tasks*

1. For his essay, Gilder narrows the word "love" to "procreative love." Write a definition of an abstract word such as loyalty, courage, patriotism, conservative, or liberal. In your essay do a similar thing; that is, limit your word to something more manageable. For example, "courage" might be limited to "physical courage" or "moral courage."
2. Choose a group you believe is underprivileged, discriminated against, or misunderstood, such as illiterate adults, paraplegics, or gay parents. Define what it is to be a member of the group and the reality of what the person's life is like.

## ❦ Michael Harrington ❦

*Michael Harrington, a leading intellect on the American left, was a political scientist who has written and lectured widely, advocating democratic socialism. He was born in St. Louis in 1928 and studied at the Yale Law School and the University of Chicago. He has been an active and outspoken member of the Socialist Party since the 1950s and more recently served as cochair of the Democratic Socialists of America. His book* The Other America: Poverty in the United States *(1962), was instrumental in developing the War on Poverty, a government movement initiated by President Lyndon Johnson in 1964. Harrington has published more than a dozen books, including* The Vast Majority: A Journey to the World's Poor *(1977), which won the National Book Award, and* The New American Poverty *(1984), in which he assesses the War on Poverty. Just recently he died of cancer.*

# *A Definition of Poverty*

*Harrington's definition of poverty, excerpted from his very influential The Other America, is a response to more abstract definitions that avoid the reality of "here and now." As social and economic standards and conditions change through history, the definition of poverty must change accordingly, he claims. Harrington ends by delineating how poverty should be defined.*

*Notice how Harrington moves historically, from an older definition, to reasons for arguing against such a definition, and finally to reasons for his contemporary definition of poverty.*

---

In the nineteenth century, conservatives in England used to argue against reform on the grounds that the British worker of the time had a longer life expectancy than a medieval nobleman. 1

This is to say that a definition of poverty is, to a considerable extent, a historically conditioned matter. Indeed, if one wanted to play with figures, it would be possible to prove that there are no poor people in the United States, or at least only a few whose 2 plight is as desperate as that of masses in Hong Kong. There is starvation in American society, but it is not a pervasive social problem as it is in some of the newly independent nations. There are still Americans who literally die in the streets, but their numbers are comparatively small.

This abstract approach toward poverty in which one compares different centuries or societies has very real consequences. 3
For the nineteenth-century British conservative, it was a way of ignoring the plight of workers who were living under the most inhuman conditions. The twentieth-century conservative would be shocked and appalled in an advanced society if there were widespread conditions like those of the English cities a hundred years ago. Our standards of decency, of what a truly human life requires, change, and they should.

There are two main aspects of this change. First, there are new 4
definitions of what man can achieve, of what a human standard of life should be. In recent times this has been particularly true since technology has consistently broadened man's potential: it has made a longer, healthier, better life possible. Thus, in terms of what is technically possible, we have higher aspirations. Those who suffer levels of life well below those that are possible, even though they live better than medieval knights or Asian peasants, are poor.

Related to this technological advance is the social definition of 5
poverty. The American poor are not poor in Hong Kong or in the sixteenth century: they are poor here and now, in the United States. They are dispossessed in terms of what the rest of the nation enjoys, in terms of what the society could provide if it had the will. They live on the fringe, the margin. They watch the movies and read the magazines of affluent America, and these tell them that they are internal exiles.

To some, this description of the feelings of the poor might 6
seem to be out of place in discussing a definition of poverty. Yet if this book indicates anything about the other America, it is that this sense of exclusion is the source of a pessimism, a defeatism that intensifies the exclusion. To have one bowl of rice in a society where all other people have half a bowl may well be a sign of

achievement and intelligence; it may spur a person to act and to fulfill his human potential. To have five bowls of rice in a society where the majority have a decent, balanced diet is a tragedy.

This point can be put another way in defining poverty. One of the consequences of our new technology is that we have created new needs. There are more people who live longer. Therefore they need more. In short, if there is technological advance without social advance, there is, almost automatically, an increase in human misery, in impoverishment. 7

And finally, in defining poverty one must also compute the social cost of progress. One of the reasons that the income figures show fewer people today with low incomes than twenty years ago is that more wives are working now, and family income has risen as a result. In 1940, 15 percent of wives were in the labor force; in 1957 the figure was 30 percent. This means that there was more money and, presumably, less poverty. 8

Yet a tremendous growth in the number of working wives is an expensive way to increase income. It will be paid for in terms of the impoverishment of home life, of children who receive less care, love, and supervision. This one fact, for instance, might well play a significant role in the problems of the young in America. It could mean that the next generation, or a part of it, will have to pay the bill for the extra money that was gained. It could mean that we have made an improvement in income statistics at the cost of hurting thousands and hundreds of thousands of children. If a person has more money but achieves this through mortgaging the future, who is to say that he or she is no longer poor? 9

It is difficult to take all these imponderables together and to fashion them into a simple definition of poverty in the United States. Yet this analysis should make clear some of the assumptions that underlie the assertions in this book: 10

Poverty should be defined in terms of those who are denied the minimal levels of health, housing, food, and education that our present stage of scientific knowledge specifies as necessary for life as it is now lived in the United States. 11

Poverty should be defined psychologically in terms of those whose place in the society is such that they are internal exiles 12 who, almost inevitably, develop attitudes of defeat and pessimism and who are therefore excluded from taking advantage of new opportunities.

Poverty should be defined absolutely, in terms of what man and society could be. As long as America is less than its potential, the nation as a whole is impoverished by that fact. As long as there is the other America, we are, all of us, poorer because of it. 13

---

## *Meaning and Purpose*

1. Find Harrington's main points about poverty.
2. Harrington claims that "a definition of poverty is, to a considerable extent, a historically conditioned matter" (2). Explain what he means.
3. Harrington says that to compare the poverty of one time to that of another is an "abstract approach toward poverty" (3). Why does he find this approach objectionable?
4. What does Harrington mean in paragraph 8 when he says that "in defining poverty one must also compute the social cost of progress"?
5. In paragraphs 8 and 9, Harrington seems to suggest if women weren't in the work force in such numbers as they are, America's children would have fewer problems. What solutions can you think of for the "impoverishment of home life" other than women's staying at home?
6. Considering all that Harrington said before, explain what he means in the last sentence.

## *Strategy*

1. How does Harrington's argument in the first three paragraphs lead to his definitions of poverty?
2. How would you categorize Harrington's definitions—lexical, stipulative, or extended—and why?

3. What transitions does Harrington use to connect paragraphs 1–10?

## *Style*

1. Analyze the tone of the essay by looking closely at the language and word choices.
2. How does Harrington use the phrase "internal exiles" in paragraph 5?
3. Define these words: *pervasive* (1); *dispossessed*, *affluent* (5); *imponderables* (10).

## *Writing Tasks*

1. In an essay, develop a definition, or definitions, of wealth. Take social and economic factors into account. Consider offering solutions to the problems of the wealthy.
2. Choose one word, such as "student" or "happiness," and write three kinds of definitions for it—lexical, stipulative, and extended.

# ❦ Shari Miller Sims ❦

*Born in New York in 1956, Shari Sims, soon after graduating from Kenyon College, joined the staff at* McCall's *magazine, where she was an associate editor. She then spent six years as a staff writer and editor for* Vogue. *She began working for* Self *magazine in 1987 and is executive editor of Health and Beauty there. She is coauthor, with Lia Schorr, of two beauty books:* Lia Schorr's Skin Care Guide for Men *(1985) and* Seasonal Skin Care *(1988). She has also contributed to* Working Woman *magazine.*

## *Violent Reactions*

*Domestic violence, reports Sims in an essay from the March 1989 issue of* Self, *appears increasingly to be considered an "acceptable" form of communication within families and couples. In her essay she probes the changes in sex roles for possible causes, seeking a new definition for "violence."*

*Sims uses psychological and sociological observations to support her definition. As you read this essay, note how she uses the opinions of experts to strengthen her own statements.*

---

A thirty-year-old man moved out of a New York City apartment it had taken him months to find. Nothing unusual, except for the reason: the couple, just about his age, who lived next door. Their fights were getting progressively louder, more intense, and what he'd heard was more than words. The shouting seemed to have escalated into all-out warfare, and lately additional noises—breaking glass, the crash of objects being thrown echoed into his apartment. What was even more disturbing to him was their source: He was convinced it was the woman who was starting the fights, who was screaming the words of abuse and hurling things across the apartment—all aimed at the man. 1

A reporter recently asked a karate champion how she happened to choose her sport. "I tried running and I tried cycling. Then," she paused, "I tried karate. And I discovered how good it felt to hit someone." 2

When most American women hear the word "violence," they think of criminals armed with knives or guns, or tragic tales of cruelty, psychiatric troubles, alcohol and drug use that lead to headline-making cases of wife or child abuse. But those who study America's social landscape also recognize a more hidden—perhaps even more frightening—side: the emergence of violence as a socially acceptable means of communication, a way of grabbing, or holding on to, power, a way of speaking up for oneself. 3

In its narrowest sense, violence is defined as an act carried out with the intention of causing physical pain or injury to another. But in real life, severe physical violence is only one extreme of a whole spectrum of aggressive behavior that ranges from "verbal violence"—screaming, shouting, saying vicious, spiteful things—to banging one's fist on the table and slamming doors to actually pushing, hitting, kicking, throwing things at or beating another person. 4

Wherever one looks—in newspapers, on television, in social- and psychological-science journals—there is evidence that America in the late 1980s is a decidedly aggressive society. What's also showing up in the statistics, but is missing from the headlines: Women, contrary to most of our wishes and stereotypes, may not only be as aggressive as men, they may also, in certain situations, be just as violent. And this violence cuts across barriers of education, race and economic class. 5

## The Urge Toward Anger

At the most basic level, violence is an effort to subdue another person, the most extreme sort of control. In the animal kingdom, there is rarely, if ever, random violence; when violence does occur, it's generally in response to a threat, actual or implied, to an animal's family or home. Among people, aggressive impulses also arise in response to threats—to one's power, position, to the pos- 6 sibility that someone else may not follow orders. Women, traditionally, have been thought of as the less aggressive (even nonaggressive) sex. They have also been out of the seats of power and been trained, in a male-dominated society, to deny, rather than express, anger.

"Young girls are given the message, incredibly early in life, that it's 'not nice' to get angry," says Jay Lefer, M.D., associate professor of psychiatry at New York Medical College. "Studies in which tape recorders were put in families' homes revealed that as soon as a little girl sounded angry, her parents—and most often the father—would tell her to stop. Ironically, anger that is not expressed, that's bottled up, may be most dangerous, to oneself and to society." 7

Traditional psychological theory has it that men hit out in anger, women hit in. Depression, or melancholia as Freud called it, is thus thought to be the inward turning of aggression—and, again not coincidentally, is also thought to be primarily a woman's problem. Modern psychoanalysts, while acknowledging that some depressed patients do have a great deal of anger, see other possibilities. "A young girl who is taught to deny her feelings, who takes this lesson to heart, can eventually become so good at denial that she becomes alexithymic—which means not being able to put words to one's feelings, to a point at which one stops feeling," says Dr. Lefer. "This is the type of person who can say 'I'm furious' without the slightest hint of heat—or fury—in her voice." 8

Suppressing one's emotions, most of us are taught, is the "civilized" way to behave. Expressions such as "keeping a stiff upper lip" or "keeping one's cool" epitomize polite society. But human beings are a passionate species. And in the case of an emotion like anger, suppression may only intensify a feeling. Many mental-health experts believe that a significant amount of violence erupts from pent-up hostility, from anger so tightly bound up that it intensifies to a point at which it bursts out, literally beyond control. 9

"Anger may be the starting point for violence," says Dr. Lefer, "but true physical violence is usually an expression of anger at a much deeper level, of a truly helpless kind of rage. That point at which a person feels helpless is usually when violence occurs— 10 when there's a sense of no longer being able to master a situation. Just about everyone has fantasies of violence—of punching out the guy at the motor vehicle bureau who sends you to the end of yet another line after a two-hour wait, or of hurling your briefcase at the ninth person who tells you 'It's not my job'—but we normally don't act on these fantasies. The norms of civilized behavior just don't allow it."

## Verbal Violence: Women as Expert?

The norms of proper behavior do allow women to express 11 their feelings in words—and the angry barb, the rapier-sharp put-down have long been considered women's special province. It also sheds light on how much of what we assume to be natural differences between the sexes often starts with society's molding and controlling of our impulses.

"Most human behavior results from a combination of bio- 12 logical and societal factors," explains Estelle Ramey, M.D., who is professor emeritus of physiology at Georgetown University School of Medicine in Washington, D.C. "In a historical sense, women, being smaller in structure and musculature than the male of the species, would be more vulnerable to retaliation after physical expressions of anger. So it would be more to a woman's advantage to choose verbal weaponry, an area in which she would safely be on equal footing with a man, over physical force.

"Women have become, in one sense, masters of verbal vio- 13 lence. It's no accident that women are often portrayed in literature as nagging, whining or screaming, or that the expression 'sharp-tongued' is usually applied to a female."

What of the much-touted "testosterone factor" in male ag- 14 gression? Biological determinism, in this case, has been given far too much credence, argues Dr. Ramey. "It is true that testosterone, when given in abnormally high amounts, can induce aggressive behavior," she says. "A normal, healthy man, though, is not a victim of his hormones, any more than a woman is. Males and females, in fact, both respond to physical threats in the same way, with the release of adrenaline, corticosteroids and other stress hormones. While it's true that a woman's hormonal system may need a slightly greater stimulus to elicit the same biochemical level of response, as a practical matter this isn't a big difference. The vast majority of men in civilized cultures don't use physical violence—and women, on the other hand, can be trained to be incredibly ruthless soldiers. The biggest differences come in what boys and girls are taught: Women are sometimes so socialized not to express negative emotions that they are even afraid to hit back when faced with someone else instigating violence."

This socialization is confirmed by ground-breaking research into aggressive behavior. In an exhaustive review of fifty psychological studies conducted during the past twenty years, researchers Alice H. Eagly, Ph.D., and Valerie Steffen, Ph.D., concluded that the biggest deterrent to physical aggression for a woman was her concern about the consequences of her actions. 15

"Research supports the conclusion that women worried about the harm they could cause another person, the guilt or anxiety they would feel themselves, or the danger they would put themselves in by their actions. Interestingly, the studies that conclude that males are much more aggressive than females really apply primarily to children; by the time we're adults, the differences are smaller," notes Dr. Eagly, who is professor of psychology at Purdue University in Indiana. 16

## Power and Physicality

The social roles ascribed to men—the military, sports, the competition of the business world—as well as the superior status of men over women may all help to explain the positive way most men view aggressive behavior. These are spheres, Drs. Eagly and Steffen note, in which the "masculine values" of strength and controlled aggression are especially valued. 17

These are also spheres into which women have made highly visible, much publicized and encouraged moves within the last two decades. While in the past, women's traditional roles— 18 homemaker, mother, wife—emphasized nurturance and passivity, feminists have put a high value on assertiveness and on challenging the long-held view of women as "the weaker sex." Adopting masculine roles, sociologists have observed, also has meant for many women endorsing masculine values. "This is a highly charged topic, politically," acknowledges Jackie Macaulay, Ph.D., a former researcher at the University of Wisconsin in Madison who is now a lawyer. "There is just no scientific evidence that women are innately more peaceful than men. If women's nonviolence is a learned behavior, then we have to recognize the possibility that, as we change that learning, we may change women's behavior in ways that aren't all for the better. That's a message feminists don't want to hear."

It's also a message that is showing up in subtle and not so sub- 19
tle ways every day. As women have sought power in the workplace, in relationships and in society at large, they have also sought to claim physical power through fitness and sports. Women in exercise classes, says one observer, rarely seem happier than when doing the punching movements in aerobic dance routines. Fitness marketers seem to have noticed; they're appealing to women with a much more hard-edged approach. In an ad for Nike shoes, triathlete Joanne Ernst talks as tough as the guys: "Just do it," she snaps, staring down her audience.

Female wrestlers are now featured weekly on TV, while *People* 20
magazine trumpets the fact that the motorcycle magazine *Harley Women* now has nine thousand female readers. Even radio psychotherapists, normally empathetic, are said to be getting meaner—in a *New York Times* column, West Coast writer Anne Taylor Fleming says they now deliver "karate chops to the soul . . . over the airwaves."

And women are delivering more than figurative karate 21
chops. Enrollment in martial-arts classes is way up among women all across the country, as are the numbers of women taking boxing classes at once-all-male bastions like Gleason's Gym in New York City. While self-defense is a motive for some, many more are there for the physical challenge. In 1983, when dancer/choreographer Twyla Tharp took lessons at Gleason's in

preparation for the ballet *Fait Accompli*, she was an anomaly; today, Gleason's has nearly two hundred women regularly jabbing and feinting and "working out on the bags"—up from two women regulars just five years ago.

Few people would argue that gaining a sense of power in oneself—physically as well as emotionally—isn't a good thing. Or that women's testing themselves against male standards hasn't led to very real benefits for society as a whole. But there may be a fine line between relishing physical power and using it for not so positive ends—and it's a line that, the latest studies suggest, many women in America may be dangerously close to crossing. Recent statistics, for example, suggest that twelve million women in the U.S. own guns—a number that increased 50 percent in the last decade. Even more disturbingly, at a time when the study of family violence is shattering many of our illusions about the sanctity of our homes, research is revealing that on the home front, women's physical aggressiveness may not be the rarity it's assumed to be. 22

## Love and Violence

The popular notion of violence is something that happens "out there"—a random shooting in the street, an explosion from afar—but the reality is that "all intimate relationships have a higher propensity to violence than do encounters among strangers or even acquaintances. The sad fact is that the family is the most violent social institution, with the single exception of the army in times of war," says Murray A. Straus, Ph.D., professor of sociology and director, Family Research Laboratory, University of New Hampshire. 23

Perhaps the most controversial finding of all, says Dr. Straus, is that when it comes to violence against one's spouse, women participate in equal numbers to men. And while three fourths of the violence committed by women against their husbands is in acts of self-defense, one fourth is not. And it is that one fourth that Dr. Straus finds especially worrisome: "It's important to understand that men's greater size and strength means that a man's 24 punch will usually produce more injury and pain than a woman's. But that doesn't mean that violence by women should be hidden or overlooked. It is part of the hidden violence of American family life."

One reason the data on women's violence hasn't been publicized: fears of misinterpretation of the facts. In 1976, when Dr. Straus announced the results of the first National Survey on Family Violence, the statistics on women's aggression toward their husbands were seized by antifeminist groups in efforts to argue against the need for shelters for battered women. Their claims were that if women were violent, then they didn't need protection against men's violence. Other reports raised false alarms via greatly inflated estimates of the number of battered husbands. In 1985, when the survey was repeated, the number of women aggressors within couples actually increased slightly. But there was no rush to publicize the finding. Experts hesitated to discuss the statistics lest they be used against women. 25

In the last ten years, however, a growing number of studies have come to the same conclusion: An average of one third of unmarried men and women—whether dating, engaged or living together—have been involved in physical aggression with the opposite sex. In studies of couples living together before marriage, Patricia A. Gwaitney-Gibbs, Ph.D., associate professor of sociology at the University of Oregon, found that women were even slightly more likely than men to have thrown something, pushed, grabbed, shoved, slapped, kicked, beaten or punched their living-together partners. "Only in the truly severe areas of assault—beating up, threatening with a knife or gun or actually using a knife or gun—were the men more likely to have inflicted these acts on women," said Dr. Gwaitney-Gibbs. 26

These conclusions are echoed by other researchers. When psychologist K. Daniel O'Leary, Ph.D., of the State University of New York at Stony Brook, and his colleagues studied over two hundred fifty couples during their engagement periods and the first two years of marriage, they found that 44 percent of the women and 31 percent of the men reported pushing, slapping or shoving their partner at least once during the year before mar- 27 riage—and that, eighteen months later, the number who pushed, slapped or shoved their spouses were still "at a rate that warrants very serious concern.

"In contrast to cases of serious physical abuse, in which the aim is to truly inflict hurt," says Dr. O'Leary, "much of this violence is seen almost as a means of communication. These couples seem to view physical aggression as a permissible means of expression—a fact our society needs to be very concerned about." 28

In fact, that acceptance of aggressive behavior in general may be the real cause for concern, say experts in the field. While it is true that couples who are younger, poorer and have less education do seem to experience more violence as a group than those who are older, wealthier and more educated, violent relationships exist at all levels of society. It is the observation of violence as a child—along with social class, educational background and being a victim of violence oneself—that is the strongest predictor of becoming a violent adult, claim Dr. Straus and his coauthor, Richard J. Gelles, Ph.D., professor of anthropology and sociology at the University of Rhode Island, in their new book, *Intimate Violence*. The learning experience of being physically punished is most significant, they note, but seeing your mother and father strike one another also teaches a child three lessons: that those we love are those who hit us or are people we can hit; that it is morally right to hit those we love; and that if other means of getting one's way, dealing with stress or expressing oneself don't work, violence is permissible. 29

## Thresholds of Aggression

This sanctioning of violence can go on not only within the family but in society as well. And for women especially, there seems to have been an explosion of hyperaggressive role models in the seventies and eighties. "On television and in the movies, women certainly seem to be hitting out more," says New York City psychologist Loretta Walder, Ph.D. "In fifties shows like *The Honeymooners*, when Ralph got angry, he yelled, 'Bam! 30

Zoom!' but what did Alice do? She just stood there with her hands on her hips and said 'Ralph.' In the seventies, we started seeing women in gun-toting cop roles, as in *Police Woman* or *Charlie's Angels*, but the level of violence and danger was nothing like the eighties' *Cagney & Lacey*. There are also other messages now, as in *Moonlighting*. Maddie slams her door, David slams his—the door-slamming is one of the show's trademarks, and Maddie and David's means of communication. In the movie *Fatal Attraction*, a clearly psychotic woman tries to kill her lover and the entire American population seemingly can't get enough of the story."

While most experts emphasize that there is no proof that the portrayal or even glorification of violence in the media can actually incite similar actions in the public, many experts do worry that, as with the observation of violence in the family, it can raise a person's "comfort-zone" of physical aggression. 31

Seeing Sigourney Weaver wield a flame-thrower in *Aliens* can't make a woman run out of the movie theater and do something violent. "Human beings are clearly more intelligent than that. But it does add to society's message that violence is appropriate," says Jan Stets, Ph.D., assistant professor of sociology, Washington State University. "There is an attitude toward violence that's built up over time, out of observation and experience, that can increase a person's chances of using violent behavior in a moment of heightened emotion. Just as social learning goes on from one generation to the next within a family, there are messages that are passed on within a culture as well." In some studies, for example, dating couples who were verbally abusive toward each other were more likely to become physically aggressive later on; it was as if their threshold of aggression shifted upward. 32

If, in fact, women are being given the message by society that they need to be more and more assertive, to seize control, to be in charge, our society needs to examine where that will take us. Research into violence by men reinforces the notion of physical aggression as a means of control, of getting the other person to do what they wouldn't otherwise do. It also confirms that the most 33 egalitarian of relationships—in society and within a family—are also the least violent. It shouldn't come as a total surprise, then, that women struggling with unresolved issues of intimate relationships and control may be most vulnerable to the powerful and often irrational emotions that can so quickly make verbal violence turn physical.

---

## *Meaning and Purpose*

1. Seeing a word can cause you to picture elements of its definition. What elements in its definition do you think of when you see the word "violence"?
2. Sims says in paragraph 5 that "Wherever one looks . . . there is evidence that America in the late 1980s is a decidedly aggressive society." In your opinion, what is one current piece of evidence that shows America is a decidedly aggressive society, so far, in the 1990s?
3. What does Sims mean by "seats of power," in paragraph 6?
4. Why have women become, in one sense, "masters of verbal violence"?
5. In your own words, define "concern about the consequences of her actions," in paragraph 15, based on the comments in paragraph 16.

## *Strategy*

1. What kind of definition of violence does Sims give in paragraph 4? Why?
2. How does Sims structure her definition of violence, and why? What aspects of the meaning of the word does she include in her definition?
3. In your opinion, what are the differences in the definitions of the expression "civilized behavior," in paragraph 10, and the expression "proper behavior," in paragraph 11?

4. Several examples are included in paragraphs 20 and 21. What do these examples help the author illustrate?

## *Style*

1. Why do you think Sims begins her essay with two journalistic anecdotes?
2. What gives Sims authority to talk about women and violence? Where do you see this authority in the essay?
3. In paragraph 31, Sims says, "it can raise a person's 'comfort zone' of physical aggression." What does the pronoun *it* refer to in that clause?

## *Writing Tasks*

1. A "working definition" is one that defines a word or a phrase simply, for a specific occasion. Your car may have an "automatic drive," which is the "working definition" for a torque-conversion unit that converts and transfers power from the engine to the drive wheels.

   Select a recent issue of a newsmagazine such as *Time, Newsweek, Insight, U.S. News & World Report*, or *The Economist.* Leaf through the issue, listing all references to violence. Then write a "working definition" of the word *violence*, followed by examples of violence from the newsmagazine that illustrate your definition.
2. Based on the readings in this chapter, write a short essay in which you define a "definition essay." Use the readings as examples, and organize your essay according to what you see as the range of elements in a definition essay.

## ❦ Lewis H. Lapham ❦

*Born in San Francisco in 1935, Lewis Lapham was educated at Yale University and at Cambridge University in England. He has had a long career as a journalist, starting as a reporter for the* San Francisco Examiner. *He has also been a reporter for the* New York Herald Tribune *and a writer for the* Saturday Evening Post *and* Life. *He is currently the editor of* Harper's Magazine.

# *Who and What Is American?*

*Lapham takes the unusual approach of letting his definition grow implicitly out of a discussion of "false constructions of the American purpose and identity" used by groups and individuals for political purposes. Using the 1992 presidential election as his backdrop, he charges that these false constructions provide those seeking office with much of their rhetoric and ends by urging us to reject these erroneous descriptions of who we are, to "speak plainly about our differences," and to "value what we have in common."*

*Lapham's essay is presented with great vigor, and it may be too easy to become caught up in the whirlpool of his examples and arguments. As you read his discussion of the false constructions, note the sentences in each section that most clearly present the contradictory view—these constitute his definition of "American."*

---

There may not be an American character, but there is the emotion of being American. It has many resemblances to the emotion of being Russian—that feeling of nostalgia for some undetermined future when man will have improved himself beyond recognition and when all will be well.

—V. S. Pritchett

Were I to believe what I read in the papers, I would find it easy to think that I no longer can identify myself simply as an American. The noun apparently means nothing unless it is 1 dressed up with at least one modifying adjective. As a plain American I have neither voice nor authentic proofs of existence. I acquire a presence only as an old American, a female American, a white American, a rich American, a black American, a gay American, a poor American, a native American, a dead American. The subordination of the noun to the adjectives makes a mockery of both the American premise and the democratic spirit, but it serves the purposes of the politicians as well as the news media, and throughout the rest of this election year I expect the political campaigns to pitch their tents and slogans on the frontiers of race and class. For every benign us, the candidates will find a malignant them; for every neighboring we (no matter how eccentric or small in number), a distant and devouring they. The strategies of division sell newspapers and summon votes, and to the man who would be king (or president or governor) the popular hatred of government matters less than the atmosphere of resentment in which the people fear and distrust one another.

Democratic politics trades in only two markets—the market 2
in expectation and the market in blame. A collapse in the former engenders a boom in the latter. Something goes wrong in the news—a bank swindle of genuinely spectacular size, a series of killings in Milwaukee, another disastrous assessment of the nation's schools—and suddenly the air is loud with questions about the paradox of the American character or the Puritan subtexts of the American soul. The questions arise from every quarter of the political compass—from English professors and political consultants as well as from actors, corporate vice presidents, and advertising salesmen—and the conversation is seldom polite. Too many of the people present no longer can pay the bills, and a stray remark about acid rain or a third-grade textbook can escalate within a matter of minutes into an exchange of insults. Somebody calls Jesse Helms a racist, and somebody else says that he is sick and tired of paying ransom money to a lot of welfare criminals. People drink too much and stay too late, their voices choked with anecdote and rage, their lexicons of historical reference so passionately confused that both Jefferson and Lincoln find themselves doing thirty-second

commercials for racial quotas, a capital gains tax, and the Persian Gulf War.

The failures in the nation's economy have marked up the prices for obvious villains, and if I had a talent for merchandising I would go into the business of making dolls (black dolls, white dolls, red-necked dolls, feminist dolls, congressional dolls) that each of the candidates could distribute at fundraising events with a supply of color-coordinated pins. Trying out their invective in the pre-season campaigns, the politicians as early as last October were attributing the cause of all our sorrows to any faction, interest, or minority that could excite in its audiences the passions of a beloved prejudice. David Duke in Louisiana denounced the subsidized beggars (i.e., black people) who had robbed the state of its birthright. At a partisan theatrical staged by the Democratic Party in New Hampshire, Senator Tom Harkin reviled the conspiracy of Republican money. President Bush went to Houston, Texas, to point a trembling and petulant finger at the United States Congress. If the country's domestic affairs had been left to him, the President said, everybody would be as prosperous and smug as Senator Phil Gramm, but the liberals in Congress (blind as mollusks and selfish as eels) had wrecked the voyage of boundless opportunity. 3

The politicians follow the trends, and apparently they have been told by their handlers to practice the arts of the demagogue. Certainly I cannot remember an election year in which the political discourse—among newspaper editorialists and the single-issue lobbies as well as the candidates—relied so unashamedly on pitting rich against poor, black against white, male against female, city against suburb, young against old. Every public event in New York City—whether academic appointment, traffic delay, or homicide—lends itself to both a black and a white interpretation of the news. The arguments in the arenas of cultural opinion echo the same bitter refrain. The ceaseless quarrels about the canon of preferred texts (about Columbus the Bad and Columbus the Good, about the chosen company of the politically correct, about the ice people and the sun people) pick at the scab of the same questions. Who and what is an American? How and where do we 4 find an identity that is something other than a fright mask? When using the collective national pronoun ("we the people" "we happy few," etc.) whom do we invite into the club of the we?

Maybe the confusion is a corollary to the end of the Cold War. The image of the Soviet Union as monolithic evil held in place the image of the United States as monolithic virtue. Break the circuit of energy transferred between negative and positive poles, and the two empires dissolve into the waving of sectional or nationalist flags. Lacking the reassurance of a foreign demon, we search our own neighborhoods for fiends of convincing malevolence and size. 5

The search is a boon for the bearers of false witness and the builders of prisons. Because it's so easy to dwell on our differences, even a child of nine can write a Sunday newspaper sermon about the centrifugal forces that drive the society apart. The more difficult and urgent questions have to do with the centripetal forces that bind us together. What traits of character or temperament do we hold in common? Why is it that I can meet a black man in a street or a Hispanic woman on a train and imagine that he and I, or she and I, share an allied hope and a joint purpose? That last question is as American as it is rhetorical, and a Belgian would think it the work of a dreaming imbecile. 6

What we share is a unified field of emotion, but if we mistake the sources of our energy and courage (i.e., if we think that our uniqueness as Americans rests with the adjectives instead of the noun) then we can be rounded up in categories and sold the slogan of the week for the fear of the month. Political campaigns deal in the commodity of votes, and from now until November I expect that all of them will divide the American promise into its lesser but more marketable properties. For reasons of their own convenience, the sponsors of political campaigns (Democratic, environmental, racial, Republican, sexual, or military-industrial) promote more or less the same false constructions of the American purpose and identity. As follows: 7

> That the American achieves visible and specific meaning only by reason of his or her association with the political guilds of race, gender, age, ancestry, or social class. 8

The assumption is as elitist as the view that only a woman endowed with an income of $1 million a year can truly appreciate the beauty of money and the music of Cole Porter. Comparable theories of grace encourage the belief that only black people can know or teach black history, that no white man can play jazz piano, that blonds have a better time, and that Jews can't play basketball. 9

America was founded on precisely the opposite premise. We were always about becoming, not being; about the prospects for the future, not about the inheritance of the past. The man who rests his case on his color, like the woman who defines herself as a bright cloud of sensibility beyond the understanding of merely mortal men, makes a claim to special privilege not unlike the divine right of kings. The pretensions might buttress the cathedrals of our self-esteem, but they run counter to the lessons of our history. 10

We are a nation of parvenus, all bound to the hopes of tomorrow, or next week, or next year. John Quincy Adams put it plainly in a letter to a German correspondent in the 1820s who had written on behalf of several prospective émigrés to ask about the requirements for their success in the New World. "They must cast off the European skin, never to resume it," Adams said. "They must look forward to their posterity rather than backward to their ancestors." 11

We were always a mixed and piebald company, even on the seventeenth-century colonial seaboard, and we accepted our racial or cultural differences as the odds that we were obliged to overcome or correct. When John Charles Frémont (a.k.a. The Pathfinder) first descended into California from the East in 1843, he remarked on the polyglot character of the expedition accompanying him south into the San Joaquin Valley: 12

"Our cavalcade made a strange and grotesque appearance, and it was impossible to avoid reflecting upon our position and composition in this remote solitude . . . still forced on south by a desert on one hand a mountain range on the other; guided by a civilized Indian, attended by two wild ones from the Sierra; a Chinook from the Columbia; and our own mixture of American, French, German—all armed; four or five languages heard at once; 13

above a hundred horses and mules, half-wild; American, Spanish and Indian dresses and equipments intermingled—such was our composition."

The theme of metamorphosis recurs throughout the whole chronicle of American biography. Men and women start out in one place and end up in another, never quite knowing how they got there, perpetually expecting the unexpected, drifting across the ocean or the plains until they lodge against a marriage, a land deal, a public office, or a jail. Speaking to the improvised character of the American experience, Daniel Boorstin, the historian and former Librarian of Congress, also summed up the case against the arithmetic of the political pollsters' zip codes: "No prudent man dared to be too certain of exactly who he was or what he was about; everyone had to be prepared to become someone else. To be ready for such perilous transmigrations was to become an American." 14

That the American people aspire to become more nearly alike. 15

The hope is that of the ad salesman and the prison warden, but it has become depressingly familiar among the managers of political campaigns. Apparently they think that no matter how different the native songs and dances in different parts of the country, all the tribes and factions want the same beads, the same trinkets, the same prizes. As I listen to operatives from Washington talk about their prospects in the Iowa or New Hampshire primary, I understand that they have in mind the figure of a perfect or ideal American whom everybody in the country would wish to resemble if only everybody could afford to dress like the dummies in the windows of Bloomingdale's or Saks Fifth Avenue. The public opinion polls frame questions in the alphabet of name recognitions and standard brands. The simplicity of the results supports the belief that the American citizen or the American family can be construed as a product, and that with only a little more time and little more money for research and development all of us will conform to the preferred images seen in a commercial for Miller beer. 16

17 The apologists for the theory of the uniform American success sometimes present the example of Abraham Lincoln, and as I listen to their sentimental after-dinner speeches about the poor country grown to greatness, I often wonder what they would say if they had met the man instead of the statute. Throughout most of his life Lincoln displayed the character of a man destined for failure—a man who drank too much and told too many jokes (most of them in bad taste), who was habitually late for meetings and always borrowing money, who never seized a business opportunity and missed his own wedding.

18 The spirit of liberty is never far from anarchy, and the ur-American is apt to look a good deal more like one of the contestants on *Let's Make a Deal* (i.e., somebody dressed like Madonna, or Wyatt Earp, or a giant iguana) than any of the yachtsmen standing around on the dock at Kennebunkport. If America is about nothing else, it is about the invention of the self. Because we have little use for history, and because we refuse the comforts of a society established on the blueprint of class privilege, we find ourselves set adrift at birth in an existential void, inheriting nothing except the obligation to construct a plausible self, to build a raft of identity on which (with a few grains of luck and a cheap bank loan) maybe we can float south to Memphis or the imaginary islands of the blessed. We set ourselves the tasks of making and remaking our destinies with whatever lumber we happen to find lying around on the banks of the Snake or Pecos River.

19 Who else is the American hero if not a wandering pilgrim who goes forth on a perpetual quest? Melville sent Ahab across the world's oceans in search of a fabulous beast; and Thoreau followed the unicorn of his conscience into the silence of the Maine woods. Between them they marked out the trail of American literature as well as the lines of speculation in American real estate. To a greater or a lesser extent, we are all confidence men, actors playing the characters of our own invention and hoping that the audience—fortunately consisting of impostors as fanciful or synthetic as ourselves—will accept the performance at par value and suspend the judgments or ridicule.

The settled peoples of the earth seldom recognize the American as both a chronic revolutionary and a born pilgrim. The American is always on the way to someplace else (i.e., toward some undetermined future in which all will be well), and when he meets a stranger on the road he begins at once to recite the summary of the story so far—his youth and early sorrows, the sequence of his exits and entrances, his last divorce and his next marriage, the point of his financial departure and the estimated time of his spiritual arrival, the bad news noted and accounted for, the good news still to come. Invariably it is a pilgrim's tale, and the narrator, being American, assumes that he is addressing a fellow pilgrim. He means to exchange notes and compare maps. His newfound companion might be bound toward a completely different dream of Eden (a boat marina in Naples, Florida, instead of a garden in Vermont; a career as a Broadway dancer as opposed to the vice presidency of the Wells Fargo bank), but the destination doesn't matter as much as the common hope of coming safely home to the land of the heart's desire. For the time being, and until something better turns up, we find ourselves embarked on the same voyage, gazing west into the same blue distance. 20

> That the American people share a common code of moral behavior and subscribe to identical theories of the true, the good, and the beautiful. 21

Senator Jesse Helms would like to think so, and so would the enforcers of ideological discipline on the vocabulary of the doctrinaire left. The country swarms with people making rules about what we can say or read or study or smoke, and they imagine that we should be grateful for the moral guidelines (market-tested and government-inspected) imposed (for our own good) by a centralized bureau of temporal health and spiritual safety. The would-be reformers of the national character confuse the American sense of equality with the rule of conformity that governs a police state. It isn't that we believe that every American is as perceptive or as accomplished as any other, but we insist on the preservation of a decent and mutual respect across the lines of age, race, gender, and 22 social class. No citizen is allowed to use another citizen as if he or she were a means to an end; no master can treat his servant as if he or she were only a servant; no government can deal with the governed as if they were nothing more than a mob of votes. The American loathing for the arrogant or self-important man follows from the belief that all present have bet their fortunes (some of them bigger than others, and some of them counterfeit or stolen) on the same hypothesis.

The American premise is an existential one, and our moral code is political, its object being to allow for the widest horizons of sight and the broadest range of expression. We protect the other person's liberty in the interest of protecting our own, and our virtues conform to the terms and conditions of an arduous and speculative journey. If we look into even so coarse a mirror as the one held up to us by the situation comedies on prime-time television, we see that we value the companionable virtues—helpfulness, forgiveness, kindliness, and, above all, tolerance. 23

The passenger standing next to me at the rail might be balancing a parrot on his head, but that doesn't mean that he has invented a theory of the self any less implausible than the one I ordered from a department-store catalogue or assembled with the tag lines of a two-year college course on the great books of Western civilization. If the traveler at the port rail can balance a parrot on his head, then I can continue my discussion with Madame Bovary and Mr. Pickwick, and the two gentlemen standing aft of the rum barrels can get on with the business of rigging the price of rifles or barbed wire. The American equation rests on the habit of holding our fellow citizens in thoughtful regard not because they are exceptional (or famous, or beautiful, or rich) but simply because they are our fellow citizens. If we abandon the sense of mutual respect, we abandon the premise as well as the machinery of the American enterprise. 24

That the triumph of America corresponds to its prowess as a nation-state. 25

The pretension serves the purposes of the people who talk about "the national security" and "the vital interest of the American people" when what they mean is the power and privilege of government. The oligarchy resident in Washington assumes that all Americans own the same property instead of taking part in the same idea, that we share a joint geopolitical program instead of a common temperament and habit of mind. Even so faithful a servant of the monied interests as Daniel Webster understood the distinction: "The public happiness is to be the aggregate of individuals. Our system begins with the individual man." 26

The Constitution was made for the uses of the individual (an implement on the order of a plow, an ax, or a surveyor's plumb line), and the institutions of American government were meant to support the liberties of the people, not the ambitions of the state. Given any ambiguity about the order of priority or precedence, it was the law that had to give way to the citizen's freedom of thought and action, not the citizen's freedom of thought and action that had to give way to the law. The Bill of Rights stresses the distinction in the two final amendments, the ninth ("The enumeration in the Constitution, of certain rights, shall not be construed to deny or disparage others retained by the people") and the tenth ("The powers not delegated to the United States by the Constitution, nor prohibited by it to the States, are reserved to the States, respectively, or to the people"). 27

What joins the Americans one to another is not a common nationality, language, race, or ancestry (all of which testify to the burdens of the past) but rather their complicity in a shared work of the imagination. My love of country follows from my love of its freedoms, not from my pride in its fleets or its armies or its gross national product. Construed as a means and not an end, the Constitution stands as the premise for a narrative rather than a plan for an invasion or a monument. The narrative was always plural. Not one story but many stories. 28

That it is easy to be an American. 29

I can understand why the politicians like to pretend that America is mostly about going shopping, but I never know why 30 anybody believes the ad copy. Grant the existential terms and conditions of the American enterprise (i.e., that we are all bound to invent ourselves), and the position is both solitary and probably lost. I know a good many people who would rather be British or Nigerian or Swiss.

Lately I've been reading the accounts of the nineteenth-century adventurers and pioneers who traveled west from Missouri under circumstances almost always adverse. Most of them didn't find whatever it was they expected to find behind the next range of mountains or around the next bend in the river. They were looking for a garden in a country that was mostly desert, and the record of their passage is largely one of sorrow and failure. Travelers making their way across the Great Plains in the 1850s reported great numbers of dead horses and abandoned wagons on the trail, the echo of the hopes that so recently preceded them lingering in an empty chair or in the scent of flowers on a new grave. 31

Reading the diaries and letters, especially those of the women in the caravans, I think of the would-be settlers lost in an immense wilderness, looking into the mirrors of their loneliness and measuring their capacity for self-knowledge against the vastness of the wide and indifferent sky. 32

Too often we forget the proofs of our courage. If we wish to live in the state of freedom that allows us to make and think and build, then we must accustom ourselves to the shadows on the walls and the wind in trees. The climate of anxiety is the cost of doing business. Just as a monarchy places far fewer burdens on its subjects than a democracy places on its citizens, so also bigotry is easier than tolerance. When something goes wrong with the currency or the schools, it's always comforting to know that the faults can be easily found in something as obvious as a color, or a number, or the sound of a strange language. The multiple adjectives qualifying the American noun enrich the vocabulary of blame, and if the election year continues as it has begun I expect that by next summer we will discover that it is not only middle-aged Protestant males who have been making a wreck of the culture but also (operating secretly and sometimes in disguise) adolescent, sallow, Buddhist females. 33

Among all the American political virtues, candor is probably the one most necessary to the success of our mutual enterprise. Unless we try to tell each other the truth about what we know and think and see (i.e., the story so far as it appears to the travelers on the voyage out) we might as well amuse ourselves (for as long as somebody else allows us to do so) with fairy tales. The vitality of the American democracy always has rested on the capacity of its citizens to speak and think without cant. As long ago as 1838, addressing the topic of *The American Democrat*, James Fenimore Cooper argued that the word "American" was synonymous with the habit of telling the truth: "By candor we are not to understand trifling and uncalled for expositions of truth; but a sentiment that proves a conviction of the necessity of speaking truth, when speaking at all; a contempt for all designing evasions of our real opinions. 34

"In all the general concerns, the public has a right to be treated with candor. Without this manly and truly republican quality . . . the institutions are converted into a stupendous fraud." 35

If we indulge ourselves with evasions and the pleasure of telling lies, we speak to our fears and our weaknesses instead of to our courage and our strength. We can speak plainly about our differences only if we know and value what we hold in common. Like the weather and third-rate journalism, bigotry in all its declensions is likely to be with us for a long time (certainly as long as the next hundred years), but unless we can draw distinctions and make jokes about our racial or cultural baggage, the work of our shared imagination must vanish in the mist of lies. The lies might win elections (or sell newspapers and economic theories) but they bind us to the theaters of wish and dream. If I must like or admire a fellow citizen for his or her costume of modifying adjectives (because he or she is black or gay or rich), then I might as well believe that the lost continent of Atlantis will rise next summer from the sea and that the Japanese will continue to make the payments—now and forever, world without end—on all our mortgages and battleships. 36

Among all the nations of the earth, America is the one that has come most triumphantly to terms with the mixtures of blood and 37 caste, and maybe it is another of history's ironic jokes that we should wish to repudiate our talent for assimilation at precisely the moment in time when so many other nations in the world (in Africa and Western Europe as well as the Soviet Union) look to the promise of the American example. The jumble of confused or mistaken identities that was the story of nineteenth-century America has become the story of a late-twentieth-century world defined by a vast migration of peoples across seven continents and as many oceans. Why, then, do we lose confidence in ourselves and grow fearful of our mongrel freedoms?

The politician who would lift us to a more courageous understanding of ourselves might begin by saying that we are all, each and every one of us, as much at fault as anybody else, that no matter whom we blame for our troubles (whether George Bush, or Al Sharpton, or David Duke) or how pleasant the invective (racist, sexist, imperialist pig), we still have to rebuild our cities and revise our laws. We can do the work together, or we can stand around making strong statements about each other's clothes. 38

---

## *Meaning and Purpose*

1. Lapham's definition of "American" emerges from his refutations of each of what he calls "false constructions of the American purpose and identity." In each of his refutations he makes counterassertions about what Americans or American ideals really are. Find one or more sentences in each of his four refutations that best express his counterassertions.
2. Using the ideas expressed in the sentences you selected for question 1, fashion a definition of "American" that you believe reflects Lapham's view. You may have to change some phrasing and combine some ideas. Try to cover as many of Lapham's ideas as possible.
3. In Lapham's view, who is responsible for promoting these false constructions?

4. What does Lapham suggest are the means of overcoming the effect of these "false constructions"?
5. What is Lapham's attitude toward a culturally diverse society?

## Strategy

1. What structure does Lapham use to develop his counterarguments to each of the "false constructions"?
2. Lapham presents a lengthy introduction to the four assumptions he attacks. What is he establishing in these introductory paragraphs?
3. What does Lapham achieve by naming so many people and giving so many examples?
4. How successful is Lapham in defining *American* by refuting the assumptions instead of using a more straightforward technique?

## Style

1. What does the term *ur-American* in paragraph 18 mean?
2. Explain the difference between "centrifugal forces" and "centripetal forces" in paragraph 6.
3. If necessary look up the following words in a dictionary: *petulant* (3); *demagogue* (4); *parvenus* (11); *piebald* (12); *candor, cant* (34).

## Writing Tasks

1. Reread paragraphs 25–28 of Lapham's essay. Do you think Lapham's position here is patriotic or nonpatriotic? Explain your answer in an essay that offers an extended definition of the word *patriotic* or *patriotism* and then measures Lapham's paragraphs against the definition.

2. Select a group that has perhaps been misjudged by others: athletes, feminists, gays, teachers, motorcycle riders, gang members, lawyers, politicians, and so on. Write an essay defining the group's values, beliefs, or behaviors using Lapham's approach of stating the misjudgments first, then refuting them.

## Responding to Photographs

*Definition*

Touching a Snake

Symbols are visible objects or actions that communicate significance beyond their literal meaning. For example, the American flag might stir our patriotic feelings. A superstitious person might grow anxious if he breaks a mirror, predicting a streak of bad luck for himself. The flag, breaking a mirror—each is a symbol.

Often symbols have conventional meanings; for example, a heart sent on St. Valentine's Day is an emblem of affection. A wedding ring is an emblem of eternal commitment to another person. A Christian cross is an emblem of devotion. Many objects or actions do not have conventional meanings, but create significance form their context. For example, imagine you observe the following scene. You see a woman in black standing next to a tombstone, which reads:

Harold Ross
1930–1993
May He Rest in Peace

Next to the woman, with their heads bowed, stand three young children. From a few yards away you watch the scene, believing that this is a widow and her children in mourning. After all, the grave, the tombstone, the black dress, the bowed heads all suggest this interpretation. But then the woman turns from the grave and you see her face. She's smiling, joyfully smiling. The children begin to skip and sing, "Who's afraid of the big bad wolf/the big bad wolf/the big bad wolf? Who's afraid. . . ." Suddenly the significance of this symbolic scene has changed. To what? Well, that's open to interpretation, which is characteristic of symbolic experience.

Frequently, a symbolic dimension is at work in photographs. Photographers carefully compose the elements of their images so we sense a symbolic dimension in a photograph. "Touching a Snake" is such a photograph. With definition as the dominant development pattern, complete one of the following writing tasks. Before beginning the task, reread "Definition: Limiting Meaning" at the beginning of the chapter to review the conventions involved in writing a definition.

1. Begin by looking up the definition of *symbol* in an unabridged dictionary or other resource material in the library. From the information you gather and from information you glean from the introductory comments to this assignment, develop a full definition of symbol, using examples from your experience and reading. Next, interpret the symbolic significance of "Touching a Snake." Consider several elements: the snake itself, which has a rich conventional symbolic history; the teddy bear; the fact of the generational difference between the man and the boy; the image on the man's T-shirt. In the process of developing your material, you might decide that there are several ways to interpret the photograph. Try to accommodate them in your essay.

2. Research the symbolic significance of "snake" as it has appeared throughout history and in different cultures. Integrating the various symbolic meanings your research has uncovered, define "snake" as a multidimensional symbol, integrating its various interpretations. Finally, using one or more views of the symbolic snake, interpret the meaning of "Touching a Snake."

## Additional Writing Tasks

### *Definition*

1. Write an essay that defines one of the following terms. Explore the subject beyond its dictionary meaning, using a variety of methods to develop your definition. As part of this or any extended definition, you can state what the subject *excludes* as a way to clarify your definition.
   a. humanity
   b. education
   c. Armageddon
   d. terror
   e. leadership
   f. honesty
   g. fad
   h. evil
   i. female liberation
   j. male liberation
   k. corruption
   l. intuition
   m. liberation theology
   n. social responsibility
   o. obsession
   p. team player
   q. sociopath
   r. maverick
   s. imagination
   t. tragedy
   u. confidence
   v. luck
   w. glamour
   x. scorched earth
   y. genocide
   z. blindsided
2. From the following list of seldom-used slang terms, select one and define it in several paragraphs. After you explain the term, create a situation in which it might apply, using the term in

several sample sentences as a speaker might. Also include current slang that has a similar meaning.

a. hoodwink
b. greenhorn
c. whoopee
d. scam
e. boob
f. folknik
g. bamboozled
h. boodle
i. macho
j. bonehead

3. As a representative of a student rights organization, you have accepted the responsibility to convince a campus grievance committee composed of students, faculty, and administrators that a sexual harassment policy should be adopted as official college policy. Your first task is to define "sexual harassment" and to illustrate at least three different ways it manifests itself in behavior.
4. a. You are an environmentalist living in a major metropolitan area. You have formed an action group committed to protect all the natural landscapes that still exist in your city, even to the point of taking militant action against developers. You have used the phrase "urban environmentalist" to describe people who think and act as you do. In an essay, define "urban environmentalists" and describe what developers can expect from them.
   b. A group of self-designated "urban environmentalists" are disrupting development in the city. They see themselves as saviors of natural settings that exist within the urban landscape, but you regard them as "environmental terrorists." In an essay, define "environmental terrorists" and predict what city officials can expect from them.
5. Look up the medical explanation of a debilitating ailment such as Alzheimer's disease, Down's syndrome, or Hodgkin's disease. Once you understand the medical terminology, write a definition essay that explains the disease to someone who has no background in medicine. Create a case study of a person who has the disease to further explain its debilitating effects.

# 11

# *Persuasion and Argument*

*Convincing a Reader*

## *The Method*

An argumentative essay is an attempt to change or reinforce someone's opinion or to move someone to take action. On the one hand, the essay may be emotionally charged, appealing to a reader's feelings with emotional detail and biased language. The writing is then called *persuasion* or *persuasive argument*. On the other hand, an argumentative essay may be highly rational, appealing to a reader's intellect with logical explanation. This writing is called *argument* or *logical argument*. Political writing relies heavily on persuasion, and scientific writing on argument. Rarely, however, does an argumentative essay appeal only to emotion or only to reason. Usually, writers appeal to both, striving to convince their readers that their position is valid.

Imagine that you want to convince your readers of the merits of a vegetarian diet. You might begin by appealing to reason. First, you might contrast the high cost of meat with the low cost of grains that provide comparable protein. Second, you might point out that the grains grown for animal feed would be better used to feed the world's hungry. You might continue by presenting the danger highly marbled meat poses to health. You might then shift the appeal to emotion. You might construct an emotional description of animals being raised in pens, relating examples of force feeding and chemical injections, and describing slaughterhouse procedures. While composing the essay, you would keep an eye on your readers, anticipating their responses to your appeals by asking yourself if you are being too emotional or even too rational.

Throughout an argumentative essay a writer must carefully balance reason and emotion. A writer whose essay is so self-righteous that it ignores reason or so rational that it ignores feelings will alienate most readers. A general rule to follow is that an argumentative essay should be primarily rational or it may fail to convince critical readers. Consequently, writers of effective arguments usually present their opinions persuasively but develop ample and strong evidence throughout their essays. This practice will impress upon readers that the writer is *ethical*; that is, a well-informed, reasonable person committed to his or her position—and, therefore, worthy of being believed.

### Assertions and Evidence

An argumentative essay is predicated on an *assertion;* that is, the opinion you want a reader to accept or an action you want your reader to take. When stated in a sentence the assertion is referred to as a *proposition* or *thesis:* "The high-fashion fur industry should be curtailed"; "The state should resume capital punishment"; "Magazines featuring nudity, such as *Playboy, Penthouse,* and *Playgirl,* should be banned from community magazine stands." The writer then supports the proposition with evidence.

It is the quality of evidence that persuades the reader to agree with an assertion and reject an opposing assertion. Keep in mind that the evidence writers use in an argumentative essay is the same as that any of us uses in oral arguments: personal experience, the experience of others, and authoritative sources.

First, personal experience can be used to support a proposition. Suppose you wanted to develop the argument that police are harassing college-age drivers. You, yourself, have had first-hand experience. Several times a patrol car has pulled you over while you were driving near campus. Each time an officer initiated a search of your car. Once one even required you to take a field sobriety test, which you passed. At none of these times did any officer issue a traffic citation. These personal experiences could serve as legitimate evidence to support your opinion.

Second, the experience of others can also be used as evidence to support an argument. You might narrate a story of a friend who had a similar experience. You might also include observations by a passenger or bystander to corroborate your friend's experience. When using the experience of others, do all you can to be sure that the information is accurate. You know how accurate a description of your experience is because you lived it, but when you use the experience of others, you are, in effect, vouching for its veracity. It is wise, therefore, to include more than one account of the same event.

Finally, authoritative sources can also be used to support an opinion. An argument gains its strength from the quality of authoritative evidence a writer can marshal. You can develop some authoritative information yourself. Once again consider the argument supporting the proposition that police are harassing college-age drivers. To support your opinion even more thoroughly, you might research police records. If the research revealed that police stopped and searched a significantly larger number of college-age drivers than older drivers, then you would use the information as evidence.

Sometimes, however, you must rely on other authoritative sources, such as encyclopedias, dictionaries, handbooks, digests, journals, and scientific research as well as people who are recognized as having extensive knowledge about a subject. When citing knowledgeable people to support an argument, be sure their expertise is in the subject you are discussing. It will not do your argument much good to quote a well-known nuclear physicist's opinion on gun control; your reader won't accept that specialist's word as authoritative.

Facts and statistics from authoritative sources can lend a great deal of credibility to any argument. Facts are irrefutable. No matter what the source, a fact is a fact: The Earth revolves around the sun. John F. Kennedy, the thirty-fifth president of the United States, was assassinated on November 22, 1963. When facts are corroborated by statistics, they exert a powerful influence on a reader. The United States has more homicides each year than Japan, Taiwan, and the combined countries of Western Europe. But what does this statistical fact mean? Should the government execute all convicted murderers? Do we need stricter handgun laws? Should every citizen arm for self-protection? Answering these questions involves interpretations of fact based on personal feelings and beliefs—that is, it involves opinions.

## Strategies

Writers of argumentative essays will use any rhetorical method that is appropriate to their presentations: narration, description, examples, comparison and contrast, cause and effect, process analysis, and definition. Generally, however, effective argumentative essays do have five elements:

1. A clear statement of the writer's assertion;
2. An orderly presentation of the evidence;
3. A clear connection between the evidence and the argument;
4. A reasonable refutation of evidence that is counter to the writer's assertion;
5. A conclusion that emphasizes the assertion.

No doubt the most important of these elements is clear presentation of the evidence. To be convincing, evidence in an argumentative essay must be arranged in logical sequence or readers will reject the writer's conclusion. When composing an argument, writers reason from evidence to a conclusion through one of two processes: induction or deduction.

### *Inductive Reasoning*

Through *inductive reasoning* writers accumulate enough specific evidence to justify a *general conclusion*. In other words, inductive reasoning moves from the *specific* to the *general*. While growing up we all learned to use induction. A child may bite into a hard green apple and discover that it tastes bitter. When the child tastes a hard green pear, he finds that it, too, is bitter. At another time the child bites into a hard green plum and an apricot. Both are bitter. By induction, he draws the general conclusion that hard green fruit is bitter and should not be eaten.

Argumentative essays written with inductive reasoning follow a similar pattern but with one difference: they usually begin with a *hypothesis* or question that embodies the conclusion the writer wants the reader to accept as valid. To argue that a city named Glenwood is environmentally responsible, a writer will have to present evidence that leads directly to that conclusion.

Hypothesis: Glenwood is an environmentally responsible city. (or: Is Glenwood an environmentally responsible city?)

Evidence: Glenwood has instituted these environmental programs:
Curbside recycling for glass, newspaper, aluminum, and plastics;
Disposal of household toxic waste;
Law prohibiting release of ozone-depleting chlorofluorocarbons from air conditioners;
Refuse landfill designed to protect ground water from toxic pollution and to generate methane gas;
A wetlands bird habitat preserved as open space.

Conclusion: Glenwood is environmentally responsible.

Conclusions drawn from the inductive reasoning procedure are usually referred to as *probable conclusions*, or *inferences*, for they are reached with incomplete evidence. The reader's acceptance of a conclusion that follows from inductive reasoning is often referred to as the *inductive leap*. To establish a clear connection between the evidence and the conclusion, you must be sure that the evidence you present is *relevant, sufficient*, and *representative*.

To be relevant, the evidence must support the hypothesis and contribute directly to the conclusion. To be sufficient, the evidence must amply support the conclusion. And to be representative, the evidence must represent the full range of information related to the hypothesis, not just one side or the other. By following these criteria, a writer increases the probability that the conclusion is valid, thus bridging the distance from evidence to conclusion and making the reader's intellectual passage easier.

### *Deductive Reasoning*

Deductive reasoning is the opposite of inductive reasoning. Deductive reasoning moves from general assumptions, called *premises*, to a specific conclusion that follows from the general premises. In formal logic, this deductive pattern is called a *syllogism*, a form of organization that includes a *major premise,* a *minor premise* and a *necessary conclusion*, one that is the logical result of the two premises. The classic example of syllogistic form comes down to us from Aristotle:

| | |
|---|---|
| Major premise: | All humans are mortal. |
| Minor premise: | Socrates is human. |
| Conclusion: | Therefore, Socrates is mortal. |

The conclusion of a syllogism is always drawn from the major and minor premises, both of which must be accurate for the conclusion to be accurate. If the premises are drawn from relevant, sufficient, and representative evidence—the same criteria used to draw sound conclusions in inductive reasoning—the conclusion of a syllogism will probably be accurate. But syllogisms can be illogical. An inaccurate major premise may make the syllogism illogical:

| | |
|---|---|
| Major premise: | Professional gamblers carry large quantities of cash and drive expensive cars. |
| Minor premise: | John Murphy is a professional gambler. |
| Conclusion: | Therefore, John Murphy must carry large quantities of cash and drive an expensive car. |

The major premise is inaccurate. Ask yourself, Are all professional gamblers successful enough to have large quantities of cash on their person and drive expensive cars? Because the major premise is inaccurate the conclusion is inaccurate.

Sometimes the language of a syllogism is deceptive. Consider the use of "good American," "accept," and "change" in this flawed syllogism.

| | |
|---|---|
| Major premise: | Every good American accepts the United States Constitution. |
| Minor premise: | Martin Luther King did not accept the United States Constitution because he worked to change it. |
| Conclusion: | Therefore, Martin Luther King was not a good American. |

The phrase "good American" is vague, too vague to describe a class of people accurately. What do "accept" and "change" mean in this context? The United States Constitution has provisions for change. In fact, it has been amended many times. Anyone who accepts the Constitution accepts the possibility of changing it. Because language is used deceptively in the premises, the conclusion is meaningless.

Sometimes a syllogism is illogical because it is constructed improperly. First, examine this properly constructed syllogism:

Major premise: All artists rely on intuition.

In a properly constructed syllogism, the subject of the major premise, in this example "artists," must appear in the minor premise and be narrowed.

Minor premise: John is an artist.

The conclusion then follows necessarily from the major and minor premises.

Conclusion: Therefore, John relies on intuition.

This syllogism is properly constructed and is valid. Now examine this invalid syllogism:

| | |
|---|---|
| Major premise: | All artists rely on intuition. |
| Minor premise: | All psychics rely on intuition. |
| Conclusion: | Therefore, all psychics are artists. |

This syllogism is improperly constructed because the minor premise does not repeat the subject of the major premise. The conclusion, therefore, is invalid.

Like inductive reasoning, deductive reasoning can help organize an argument. But using deduction is never quite as simple as the skeletal form of syllogisms used to illustrate it.

Imagine that the Sierra Club has established a *representative sample* of environmentally responsible cities. By extensive inductive reasoning, the Sierra Club finds several cities, including Glenwood, from our previous example, operating effective environmental programs. Based on its analysis of these programs, the Sierra Club defines the environmentally responsible city. A syllogism showing that a city is environmentally responsible might be constructed in this sequence:

| | |
|---|---|
| Major premise: | Cities with ecologically beneficial programs for disposal of waste, conservation of energy, and preservation of open space are environmentally responsible. |
| Minor premise: | San Lorenzo has ecologically beneficial programs for disposal of waste, conservation of energy, and preservation of open space. |
| Conclusion: | Therefore, San Lorenzo is environmentally responsible. |

In an argumentative essay, a syllogism seldom appears in such clear form, but often its deductive structure is embedded in the text. If a writer wanted to argue that San Lorenzo is environmentally responsible, he or she might first construct a syllogism such as the one above, analyze the evidence needed to support the proposition, and then arrange the argument, incorporating syllogistic reasoning in the structure.

In the first section of the essay, the writer would address the questions raised in the major premise.

1. What is an ecologically beneficial program for disposing of waste?
2. What is an ecologically beneficial program for conserving energy?
3. What is an ecologically beneficial program for preserving open space?

To answer these questions would take several paragraphs, and the writer would have to rely on the authority of the Sierra Club's definition. An ecologically beneficial program for disposing of waste would probably require recycling usable trash, disposing of toxic waste, and stringent restrictions on use of landfills. An ecologically beneficial program for conserving energy would probably mean reducing use of automobiles to save fuel and increasing use of solar energy to save electricity. An ecologically beneficial program for preserving open space would probably include protection for unique land formations and wildlife habitats. This discussion would be rather broad because the definition is based on a representative sample of many cities that may vary dramatically in size and geographic location.

To develop the second section of the essay, the writer would address the questions raised by the minor premise:

1. What specific actions has San Lorenzo taken to implement an ecologically beneficial waste-disposal program?
2. What specific actions has San Lorenzo taken to implement ecologically beneficial programs for conserving energy?
3. What specific actions has San Lorenzo taken to implement an ecologically beneficial program for preserving open space?

The purpose of this section is to present evidence that San Lorenzo does indeed meet the definition of environmentally responsible cities. In this section, which would also require several paragraphs to fully develop, the writer would present as evidence the specific environmental programs San Lorenzo has implemented, thus demonstrating the validity of the syllogism's minor premise.

In the last section of the essay, by far the shortest, the writer would conclude that San Lorenzo is an environmentally responsible city. The writer might choose to summarize the key points of the argument, but here the force of deductive reasoning would be irresistible, making it unnecessary to rearticulate the argument in abbreviated form. But whether to develop a conclusion fully or to leave it implied is the decision of the writer, who is responsible for the argument's coherence and consistency. Risks lie in both strategies.

## *Logical Fallacies in Writing*

*Logical fallacies* are common mistakes in reasoning, and an argument tainted by them is ineffective. The word fallacy means "deception," or "a fault in reasoning." Fallacies deceive by distorting the truth and making logical conclusions unattainable. Using fallacies consciously signifies dishonesty; using them inadvertently demonstrates muddled thinking.

Study this list of eight most common fallacies. Remember that writers must scrutinize their arguments to avoid slipping into fallacious reasoning.

**Overgeneralization.** Writers overgeneralize when they draw a conclusion from insufficient or unrepresentative evidence.

> During the last year, three of five award-winning films concentrated on family violence. An examination of family violence was just broadcast on national television. No doubt these events indicate that family violence is on the rise.

A handful of films and a television program do not constitute a trend. The conclusion that family violence is rising could be substantiated with statistics and reports from authorities such as psychologists, sociologists, and law-enforcement officers.

**Oversimplification.** To oversimplify is to ignore essential information from which a conclusion is drawn. Be careful to avoid this fallacy when writing about complicated subjects. You might become too eager to offer a simple explanation to a complicated problem.

> The problems of air pollution, ozone depletion, and global warming are not really problems at all. They are merely manifestations of our educational system. We have too many scientists working in universities with nothing to do but study our environment.

**Faulty Either/Or Reasoning.** The either/or fallacy is a type of oversimplification in which a writer assumes only two alternatives, black or white, when there are others, including gray. The slogan, "America, love it or leave it," implies that love of country must be unqualified, which has the effect of excluding constructive criticism.

> Everyone would agree that America is being severely damaged by the sale and use of illegal drugs. The only two courses of action are these: the country's leaders can ignore the problem, or they can enforce the law to its maximum limits.

Of course, other actions are possible—initiate public education, fund rehabilitation for former drug users, develop agreements with other countries to curtail manufacturing of drugs, and even legalize use of drugs. The choice is not between doing nothing or joining a law-and-order crusade.

***Post Hoc* Argument.** The complete Latin phrase is *post hoc, ergo propter hoc*, which means "after this, therefore because of this." The assumption in this fallacious argument is that one event causes another event simply because the second follows the first in time.

> For more than a year, I have been meditating nightly for one hour. Although I usually have the flu at least once each year, I didn't have it last year. No doubt the meditation prevented me from catching the flu.

As stated, the only relationship between meditation and catching the flu is that one followed the other. Other explanations could be found: perhaps that year had no flu epidemic, or perhaps the person was lucky enough to avoid a deadly sneeze. Time sequence alone cannot prove that a cause-and-effect relationship applies.

*Non Sequitur.* In Latin, *non sequitur* means "it does not follow." A *non sequitur* is a conclusion that does not logically follow from its premises.

> The city in this county that has the most crime also has the highest-paid police force. The city with the least crime has the lowest-paid police force. It does not make sense for our city to pay higher salaries to our police when doing so will not reduce crime.

The reasons for high crime rates are many, a high incidence of poverty being one of them. But we doubt that high police salaries contribute to a rising crime rate. In fact, dangerous working conditions could lead to higher wages for police.

False Analogy. Someone using a false analogy assumes that if two things are similar in one or more characteristics, then they are similar in other characteristics.

> We should not forget the lessons of Grenada and Panama, when our leaders tried to negotiate settlements and failed. Once we sent in the Marines, peace and a working relationship were restored. The best way to deal with renegade countries who act against our interests is to invade them to show other hostile governments we will not be bullied.

We are not living in the same world we lived in even five years ago. The break-up of communist-bloc countries, the danger of renegade terrorist action, the proliferation of nuclear weapons, all make the international scene too complex for rash action based on a false analogy.

***Ad Hominem* Argument.** When a writer attacks a person associated with an issue rather than the argument supporting the issue, then the writer is committing an *ad hominem* fallacy, which in Latin means "to the man."

> Councilman Hunt has made a strong argument against raising the gasoline tax for revenue to build more roads. Why shouldn't he? He takes the bus to work each day, and he has the money to fly to any part of the country where he might want to vacation.

This statement ignores the argument for a tax increase and concentrates instead on the person making the argument.

**Association Fallacy.** To commit the association fallacy is to claim that an act or belief is worthy or unworthy simply because of the people associated with it.

> Congressman Will is supported by some of Hollywood's leading figures. Because actors, directors, and producers know talent when they see it, you should support Congressman Will too.

Do Hollywood figures know any more about the qualities necessary to serve as an effective congressman than most other voters?

## *Argument in College Writing*

Whether presenting examples, comparing two subjects, explaining a process, or classifying components into distinctive categories, you must think clearly and write logically. One development method, however, holds writers to the highest standard of clear thinking and logical writing—argumentation. At some point in the term, most instructors, especially those in the humanities and social sciences, will require you to take a position in relation to a particular opinion or controversial subject—that is, they will require you to write an argument.

### *Guidelines for Writing Argument*

1. Once you select a controversial subject and decide on your position, marshal two kinds of evidence: that which supports your position and, if appropriate, that which opposes it.
2. Develop a plan that arranges the evidence in a logical progression. Use inductive arrangement if the presentation of your evidence would best be organized by arguing from specifics to a general conclusion; use deductive arrangement if the presentation of your evidence is best organized by arguing from a general conclusion to the specifics.
3. Determine who your readers are. If you perceive your readers to be committed to your position, then you will not have to establish your credibility nor will you have to write an argument dense with facts, examples, and statistics. Your goal: To reinforce their support.

   If you perceive your readers to be uncommitted, then you must establish yourself to be a reliable source and offer a detailed presentation of the evidence, one that not only informs them but also stirs their emotion. Your goal: To win their support.

   If you perceive your readers to be hostile, then you must establish your authority, present compelling evidence—that is, indisputable facts and carefully reasoned arguments—and avoid emotional appeals, which they might perceive as an emotional attack on their beliefs. Your goal: To encourage them to question their position.

4. Write the essay. If the arrangement is inductive, begin with a stated or implied hypothesis and lead your reader through the evidence to a reasonable conclusion.

   If the arrangement is deductive, begin with an introduction that states your position and ends with a thesis that clearly indicates an argument will follow. Develop the evidence, which should address questions your thesis raises, in an orderly, step-by-step fashion. Note, where appropriate, the position that opposes yours. Conclude by restating your thesis and reviewing the evidence to show the reader that your position is valid and should be accepted.
5. Review the essay to catch and correct any errors in reasoning you find. Look for logical fallacies, such as overgeneralization, oversimplification, faulty either/or reasoning, and flawed syllogistic reasoning embedded in your discussion.

In a Mass Communications course, Rhonda Burris responded to the following assignment:

> Take a position for or against what some social critics perceive to be a detriment to the public welfare that is perpetuated in popular culture.

Burris decided to convince her readers that films that feature characters who smoke should carry a warning much like the one the law requires cigarette companies to place in magazine advertisements. She uses an inductive structure—that is, she leads her readers from a specific observation through the evidence to a logical conclusion.

*Burris begins indirectly. She uses Bogart's cult status to show the romantic image of smoking and the realistic results.*

Argument in College Writing

Among college students Humphrey Bogart is a cult figure. Films he starred in, such as The <u>Maltese Falcon</u>, <u>The Harder They Fall</u>, and <u>To Have and Have Not</u> are

*Is her conclusion that Bogart's lung cancer was caused by smoking a non sequitur? Based on overwhelming evidence linking smoking to lung cancer, she decided her conclusion is valid.*

still shown on college campuses across America. Just last Saturday the campus Classic Film Society sponsored a Bogart film retrospective. Probably for the fifteenth time I watched Casablanca, a film that could be classified as a cult favorite. It becomes more romantic each time I view it, capturing an exotic place and time, featuring mysterious supporting characters, and concentrating on the dilemma the beautiful heroine faces when trying to decide between two men who love her, a political idealist and a world-weary cynic whom Bogart plays. Bogart is suave, his style dominating the film, but during this viewing I saw something I had not noticed before: No actor could handle a cigarette better than Bogart. Hanging from the corner of his mouth as he talks or held between two fingers as he drinks, the burning cigarette is part of the eternally suave image Bogart projects to the viewer. Bogart the actual man, however, was not eternal. He died, at the relatively young age of fifty-eight, of lung cancer brought on by heavy smoking. Toward the end of the film, I asked myself how many film aficionados smoke because they admired Bogart's suave handling of a cigarette? If even one filmgoer was influenced to smoke, shouldn't films that feature characters who smoke carry a warning about the dangers of smoking?

*Burris casts her hypothesis in question form, "shouldn't films that feature characters who smoke carry a warning about the dangers of smoking?" This hypothesis embodies the conclusion she wants you to reach—yes, these films should carry warnings.*

Apparently the power of association to influence someone's decision to smoke has not been lost on cigarette manufacturers. In an effort to sell more of its products, the Phillip Morris Company, the people who sell such popular brands as Benson and Hedges ("For people who love to smoke") Virginia Slims ("You've come a long way, Baby"), and Merit ("For those who want marital bliss") once paid $350,000 to have secret

*Burris builds her argument on an assumption: If cigarette manufacturers (the Philip Morris Company in particular) are willing to pay film producers*

*to prominently display their products, then doing so must influence moviegoers to smoke. Simple—but is this assumption valid?*

*She uses specific examples to develop her argument, first describing an attempt to influence young men and then describing an attempt to influence young women.*

*Throughout the discussion, she emphasizes that the attempt is made indirectly, that is, through association. It is important that she include strong specific examples to avoid overgeneralizing the issue.*

agent 007 James Bond smoke Lark Cigarettes in License to Kill. Why? Many young men, Phillip Morris seems to believe, are too immature to make the obvious connection between smoking and death, so they make the ridiculous connection between smoking and the adventurous life James Bond leads, even though that life is only a movie life, not a real one.

A couple of years before License to Kill was released the Phillip Morris Company paid a substantial amount to have Lois Lane smoke Marlboro cigarettes in Superman II. The payment went unnoticed until one movie critic raised the question that if characterization of Lois Lane required that she smoke, why feature a brand of cigarette so prominently? Now the answer is clear. Phillip Morris must have been counting on the power of association even then. Will every immature young woman who saw Superman II come to believe that if she smokes Marlboro cigarettes, sooner or later her own Man of Steel will arrive? Probably not consciously, but the subconscious might associate smoking and sex appeal. What more could a cigarette advertiser expect?

Movies are rated according to who should be allowed to see them. The National Coalition on Television Violence discovered that cigarette smoking appears in 100 percent of PG-13 films, which are approved for people over thirteen who have parental permission to view them. Clearly, young people who attend films (what young people do not?) are exposed to actors from various stations in life smoking in various situations. Even if they come from families who do not smoke, they are exposed to powerful images that show smoking as accepted an behavior among popular entertainment figures they admire. But where is the warning that smoking is a health hazard?

Cigarette advertisements have been banned from television and radio. When they appear in magazines, cigarette advertisements must by law include the Surgeon General's warning that smoking can result in cancer, heart disease, or fetal injury in pregnant women. This requirement is a sensible public-health policy, but where does such a warning appear in films that feature characters who smoke? Clearly one cigarette manufacturer believes that by associating its cigarettes with appealing characters it will influence a person's decision to smoke. Why else would Phillip Morris pay movie producers to feature its products?

*Burris is depending on logical reasoning, not hard evidence, to win her argument. If moviegoers are warned about violence in films because it might promote destructive behavior, then doesn't it follow that they should be warned about films that feature characters who smoke because such films promote a health hazard? Burris is developing an argument by analogy. Is it valid? This is a question that plagued her while writing the essay.*

The practice of featuring characters who smoke in films is disturbing enough, but when cigarette manufacturers actually pay to have their brands featured in a film, the practice goes beyond being disturbing to being criminal. It is time government put a stop to this kind of indirect advertising or at the very least, require that films featuring characters who smoke announce the dangers of smoking before the plot begins. Then the next time someone watches Humphrey Bogart raise a glass, squint through a cloud of cigarette smoke at Ingrid Bergman, and say, "Here's looking at you, Kid," the viewer will not concentrate on the romantic image but on the excruciating pain Bogart must have felt while dying of lung cancer.

### *Comments*

Burris's argument seems to be directed to readers who are already opposed to smoking. She presents a logical argument that is hard to resist (even a hostile audience generally would not support a clandistine attempt to promote smoking, especially one directed at young people). Her goal, then, is to offer a new perspective for antismoking advocates to consider, one that does not call for a ban on smoking in films, but one that asserts that films should be treated like advertisements. This position seems reasonable. After all, as she points out, the precedent has already been established. This is a form of arguing from analogy, but one that seemed valid to her reading group.

**Development Strategy.** Burris has carefully mixed emotion and logical argument to support her position. She begins her argument indirectly by discussing Humphrey Bogart. She refers to *Casablanca*, one of Bogart's most popular movies, and creates an impression of the suave Bogart style. In the closing sentences she sets up her hypothesis by revealing that Bogart, usually portrayed with a cigarette in hand, died of lung cancer. She maintains that films that feature appealing actors smoking may influence viewers by leading them to smoke.

In paragraphs 2 and 3, Burris develops her argument with examples of the Phillip Morris Company actually paying to have its cigarettes prominently displayed in films: The goal, she argues, is to associate its products with appealing characters, hoping that the association will benefit sales. In paragraph 4, Burris presents an interesting observation: movies are evaluated for the violence they display, but nothing is done to warn viewers that smoking, a clear hazard to health, is displayed in appealing ways. At the end of the paragraph she raises a question that echoes her conclusion: "Where is the warning that smoking is hazardous to health?"

In paragraph 5, Burris points out something we all know: cigarette advertisements in magazines must carry the Surgeon General's warning, a sensible public-health policy. Burris's reasoning clearly leads us to one conclusion. In the final paragraph, Burris completes the inductive sequence and states her thesis: "It's time the government put a stop to this kind of indirect advertising, or at the very least, require that films featuring characters who smoke announce the dangers of smoking before the plot begins."

She closes with an emotional reference to *Casablanca* and Bogart's painful death from lung cancer.

**Revision.** In a rough draft Burris found herself making "loaded" statements when describing cigarette makers and their behavior, such as "greedy manufacturers," "legalized murder," "perpetuating a health holocaust." When rereading to polish the final draft, she decided to delete these emotion-stirring references and rewrite the passages with less emotion while leading readers to accept her position. For example, study how she revised her closing paragraph to eliminate the loaded references while still appealing to reader emotion.

The practice of featuring characters who smoke in films is
disturbing enough, but when ~~greedy~~ cigarette manufacturers
the practice goes beyond being disturbing
actually pay to have their brands featured in a film, ~~they are~~
to being criminal.
~~financing a health holocaust and should be seen as criminals.~~
this kind of indirect
It is time government put a stop to advertising ~~that sells~~
~~death~~ or at the very least, require that films featuring characters who smoke announce the ~~mortal~~ dangers of smoking before the plot begins. Then the next time someone watches Humphrey Bogart raise a glass, squint through a cloud of cigarette smoke at Ingrid Bergman, and say, "Here's looking at you, Kid," the viewer will not concentrate on the romantic im-
the excruciating pain
age but on Bogart ~~as a victim of legalized murder.~~
must have felt while dying of lung cancer.

Now, study Burris's final draft. She has deleated all but one emotionally loaded word—"criminal." Instead of trying to fire reader emotion, she lets the emotionally charged details—an icon dying a painful death because of smoking—carry the argument.

> The practice of featuring characters who smoke in films is disturbing enough, but when cigarette manufacturers actually pay to have their brands featured in a film, the practice goes beyond being disturbing to being criminal. It is time government put a stop to this kind of indirect advertising or at the very least, require that films featuring characters who smoke announce the dangers of smoking before the plot begins. Then the next time someone watches Humphrey Bogart raise a glass, squint through a cloud of cigarette smoke at Ingrid Bergman, and say, "Here's looking at you, Kid," the viewer will not concentrate on the romantic image but on the excruciating pain Bogart must have felt while dying of lung cancer.

In the following essays, you will see argument at work. Study them; analyze the different ways professional writers attempt to win over their readers.

## *Peer Review*

You may be asked to write an essay about one of the readings that follow. Before you meet with your writing group, review this introduction. As you read the group papers, use these general principles of persuasion and argument to help guide your comments.

1. As stated on page 577, an argumentation paper should have the following:

   a. a clear statement of the writer's assertion;
   b. an orderly presentation of the evidence;
   c. a clear connection between the evidence and the argument;
   d. a reasonable refutation of evidence that is counter to the writer's assertion;
   e. a conclusion that emphasizes the assertion.

2. An argumentative essay should have an appropriate balance between reason and emotion.
3. An argumentative essay should avoid logical fallacies. See pages 583–586.

## ❦ Joy Williams ❦

*Joy Williams, born in Massachusetts in 1944, was educated at Marietta College in Ohio and at the University of Iowa. She has written three novels,* State of Grace *(1973),* The Changeling *(1978), and* Breaking and Entering *(1988), and two collections of short stories,* Taking Care *(1982) and* Escapes *(1991). She has also contributed nonfiction pieces to a number of magazines including* Esquire, *where the following essay was first published. She lives in Key West, Florida, and has written a history and guidebook about the Florida Keys.*

# *The Killing Game*

*Williams's essay, presented here in a shorter version than the original in Esquire, argues passionately against hunting. She examines the traditional reasons advanced by hunters to explain the attraction of hunting and the arguments used to justify it, rejecting each in turn. Then she advances her personal interpretation of why humans hunt. Whichever side of the argument you are on, Williams's skillful use of language is sure to hold your interest and probably elicit a strong response.*

*As you read the essay, be aware of your response to each paragraph. Which of her arguments do you accept and which do you reject?*

---

Death and suffering are a big part of hunting. A big part. 1
Not that you'd ever know it by hearing hunters talk. They tend to downplay the killing part. To kill is to put to death, extinguish, nullify, cancel, destroy. But from the hunter's point of view, it's just a tiny part of the experience. *The kill is the least important part of the hunt,* they often say, or, *Killing involves only a split second of the innumerable hours we spend surrounded by and observing nature . . .* For the animal, of course, the killing part is of considerably more importance. José Ortega y Gasset, in *Meditations on Hunting,* wrote, *Death is a sign of reality in hunting. One does not hunt in order to kill; on the contrary, one kills in*

*order to have hunted.* This is the sort of intellectual blather that the "thinking" hunter holds dear. The conservation editor of *Field & Stream*, George Reiger, recently paraphrased this sentiment by saying, *We kill to hunt, and not the other way around,* thereby making it truly fatuous. A hunter in West Virginia, one Mr. Bill Neal, blazed through this philosophical fog by explaining why he blows the toes off tree raccoons so that they will fall down and be torn apart by his dogs. *That's the best part of it. It's not any fun just shooting them.*

Instead of monitoring animals—many animals in managed areas are tagged, tattooed, and wear radio transmitters—wildlife managers should start hanging telemetry gear around hunters' necks to study their attitudes and listen to their conversations. It would be grisly listening, but it would tune out for good the *suffering as sacrament* and *spiritual experience* blather that some hunting apologists employ. *The unease with which the good hunter inflicts death is an unease not merely with his conscience but with affirming his animality in the midst of his struggles toward humanity and clarity,* Holmes Rolston III drones on in his book *Environmental Ethics.* 2

There is a formula to this in literature—someone the protagonist loves has just died, so he goes out and kills an animal. This makes him feel better. But it's kind of a sad feeling-better. He gets to relate to Death and Nature in this way. Somewhat. But not really. Death is still a mystery. Well, it's hard to explain. It's sort of a semireligious thing . . . Killing and affirming, affirming and killing, it's just the cross the "good" hunter must bear. The bad hunter just has to deal with postkill letdown. 3

Many are the hunter's specious arguments. Less semireligious but a long-standing favorite with them is the vegetarian approach: you eat meat, don't you? If you say no, they feel they've got you—you're just a vegetarian attempting to impose your weird views on others. If you say yes, they accuse you of being hypocritical, of allowing your genial A&P butcher to stand between you and reality. The fact is, the chief attraction of hunting is the pursuit and murder of animals—the meat-eating aspect of it is trivial. If the hunter chooses to be ethical about it, he might cook his kill, but the meat 4 of most animals is discarded. Dead bear can even be dangerous! A bear's heavy hide must be skinned at once to prevent meat spoilage. With effort, a hunter can make okay chili, *something to keep in mind,* a sports rag says, *if you take two skinny spring bears.*

As for subsistence hunting, please . . . Granted that there 5
might be one "good" hunter out there who conducts the kill as spiritual exercise and two others who are atavistic enough to want to supplement their Chicken McNuggets with venison, most hunters hunt for the hell of it.

For hunters, hunting is fun. Recreation is play. Hunting is 6
recreation. Hunters kill for play, for entertainment. They kill for the thrill of it, to make an animal "theirs." (The Gandhian doctrine of nonpossession has never been a bit hit with hunters.) The animal becomes the property of the hunter by its death. Alive, the beast belongs only to itself. This is unacceptable to the hunter. *He's yours . . . He's mine . . . I decided to . . . I decided not to . . . I debated shooting it, then I decided to let it live . . .* Hunters like beautiful creatures. A "beautiful" deer, elk, bear, cougar, bighorn sheep. A "beautiful" goose or mallard. Of course, they don't stay "beautiful" for long, particularly the birds. Many birds become rags in the air, shredded, blown to bits. *Keep shooting till they drop!* Hunters get a thrill out of seeing a plummeting bird, out of seeing it crumple and fall. *The big pheasant folded in classic fashion.* They get a kick out of "collecting" new species. *Why not add a unique harlequin duck to your collection?* Swan hunting is satisfying. *I let loose a three-inch Magnum. The large bird only flinched with my first shot and began to gain altitude. I frantically ejected the round, chambered another, and dropped the swan with my second shot. After retrieving the bird I was amazed by its size. The swan's six-foot wingspan, huge body, and long neck made it an impressive trophy.* Hunters like big animals, trophy animals. A "trophy" usually means that the hunter doesn't deign to eat it. Maybe he skins it or mounts it. Maybe he takes a picture. *We took pictures, we took pictures.* Maybe he just looks at it for a while. The disposition of the "experience" is up to the hunter. He's entitled to do whatever he wishes with the damn thing. It's dead.

Hunters like categories they can tailor to their needs. There are the "good" animals—deer, elk, bear, moose—which are allowed to exist for the hunter's pleasure. Then there are the "bad" animals, the vermin, varmints, and "nuisance" animals, the rabbits and raccoons and coyotes and beavers and badgers, which are disencouraged to exist. The hunter can have fun killing them, but the pleasure is diminished because the animals aren't "magnificent." 7

Then there are the predators. These can be killed any time, because, hunters argue, they're predators, for godssakes. 8

Many people in South Dakota want to exterminate the red fox because it preys upon some of the ducks and pheasant they want to hunt and kill each year. They found that after they killed the wolves and coyotes, they had more foxes than they wanted. The ring-necked pheasant is South Dakota's state bird. No matter that it was imported from Asia specifically to be "harvested" for sport, it's South Dakota's state bird and they're proud of it. A group called Pheasants Unlimited gave some tips on how to hunt foxes. *Place a small amount of larvicide* [a grain fumigant] *on a rag and chuck it down the hole . . . The first pup generally comes out in fifteen minutes . . . Use a .22 to dispatch him . . . Remove each pup shot from the hole. Following gassing, set traps for the old fox who will return later in the evening . . .* Poisoning, shooting, trapping—they make up a sort of sportsman's triathlon. . . . 9

Large predators—including grizzlies, cougars, and wolves—are often the most "beautiful," the smartest and wildest animals of all. The gray wolf is both a supreme predator and an endangered species, and since the Supreme Court recently affirmed that ranchers have no constitutional right to kill endangered predators—apparently some God-given rights are not constitutional ones—this makes the wolf a more or less lucky dog. But not for long. A small population of gray wolves has recently established itself in northwestern Montana, primarily in Glacier National Park, and there is a plan, long a dream of conservatists, to "reintroduce" the wolf to Yellowstone. But to please ranchers and hunters, part of the plan would involve immediately removing the wolf from the endangered-species list. Beyond the 10 park's boundaries, he could be hunted as a "game animal" or exterminated as a "pest." (Hunters kill to hunt, remember, except when they're hunting to kill.) The area of Yellowstone where the wolf would be restored is the same mountain and high-plateau country that is abandoned in winter by most animals, including the aforementioned luckless bison. Part of the plan, too, is compensation to ranchers if any of their far-ranging livestock is killed by a wolf. It's a real industry out there, apparently, killing and controlling and getting compensated for losing something under the Big Sky.

Wolves gotta eat—a fact that disturbs hunters. Jack Atcheson, an outfitter in Butte, said, *Some wolves are fine if there is control. But there never will be control. The wolf-control plan provided by the Fish and Wildlife Service speaks only of protecting domestic livestock. There is no plan to protect wildlife . . . There are no surplus deer or elk in Montana . . . Their numbers are carefully managed. With uncontrolled wolf populations, a lot of people will have to give up hunting just to feed wolves. Will you give up your elk permit for a wolf?* 11

It won't be long before hunters start demanding compensation for animals they aren't able to shoot. . . . 12

Hunters' self-serving arguments and lies are becoming more preposterous as nonhunters awake from their long, albeit troubled, sleep. Sport hunting is immoral; it should be made illegal. Hunters are persecutors of nature who should be prosecuted. They wield a disruptive power out of all proportion to their numbers, and pandering to their interests—the special interests of a group that just wants to kill things—is mad. It's preposterous that every year less than 7 percent of the population turns the skies into shooting galleries and the woods and fields into abattoirs. It's time to stop actively supporting and passively allowing hunting, and time to stigmatize it. It's time to stop being conned and cowed by hunters, time to stop pampering and coddling them, time to get them off the government's duck-and-deer dole, time to stop thinking of wild animals as "resources" and "game," and start thinking of them as sentient beings that deserve our wonder and respect, time to stop 13 allowing hunting to be creditable by calling it "sport" and "recreation." Hunters make wildlife *dead, dead, dead*. It's time to wake up to this indisputable fact. As for the hunters, it's long past check-out time.

---

## *Meaning and Purpose*

1. Is Williams's essay designed to change or reinforce a reader's opinion, to move someone to action, or both? Who is the intended audience? Support your answer with evidence from the essay.
2. According to the essay, what reasons do hunters use to explain why they hunt?
3. What are the real reasons hunters hunt according to Williams?
4. What information about hunting that you were previously unaware of has this essay given you? List specific items.
5. Do you find this essay convincing? Why or why not?
6. Underlying Williams's essay, though not directly stated, is an assumption about life and nature. What is that assumption?

## *Strategy*

1. Williams frequently quotes the apparent words of hunters. What effect does she achieve by doing this? Point to at least one such quotation and explain why you think she included it.
2. On page 574 we say, "Throughout an argumentative essay a writer must carefully balance reason and emotion." Has Williams, in your opinion, achieved that balance? Support your answer by references to specific portions of the essay.
3. Where does Williams directly state her assertion (thesis)? Why do you think she delays a direct statement for so long?
4. Williams devotes a considerable portion of her essay to the words and arguments of hunters. Why do you suppose she gives

them so much space when she wants her readers to reject those ideas?

## *Style*

1. How would you describe the tone of the essay? Point out specific examples that contribute significantly to that tone.
2. Point out examples of irony, sarcasm, and the use of emotional words and phrases.
3. What is the effect of the series of words for death in sentence 5 of the first paragraph and the three-word series in the third-to-last sentence of the essay? How do they work together?
4. If necessary look up these words in a dictionary: *fatuous* (1); *specious* (4); *atavistic* (5); *vermin and varmints* (7); *abattoir, sentient* (13).

## *Writing Tasks*

1. Write an argumentative essay defending hunting. Refer to Williams's arguments as appropriate and/or quote her directly and answer her charges.
2. Write an essay calling for the abolishment of something. For example, the sale of handguns, the presidential primaries, a particular kind of tax, or athletic scholarships. Balance emotion and logic in your arguments.

## ❦ Vicki Hearne ❦

*A Yale University professor and an active professional dog trainer, Vicki Hearne is the author of three volumes of poetry,* Nervous Horses *(1980),* In the Absence of Horses *(1983), and* The Parts of Light: Poems *(1994); and two books of essays,* Adam's Task: Calling Animals by Name *(1986) and* Bandit: Dossier of a Dangerous Dog *(1992). Her collection of prose,* Animal Happiness, *was published in 1994. Originally appearing in* Harper's Magazine *(1991), "What's Wrong with Animal Rights" was selected by Susan Sontag for* The Best American Essays 1992.

# What's Wrong with Animal Rights

*Vicki Hearne wrote this essay to explore the meanings and other qualities of terms such as "rights," "happiness," "philosophy," "ownership," and other related signifiers as they are used, often thoughtlessly and mostly by those in the "animal-rights movement" who have adopted, if not taken over, the moral high ground labeled "animal rights."*

*While reading this essay, see if you can relate to Professor Hearne's comments about the worth of animals. Especially if you have a pet, try to determine whether you agree strongly with the author's comments about how we should treat animals. As soon as you can after reading the essay, contemplate the author's attitudes toward animals in terms of your own attitudes toward animals. See, if only for the moment, whether the essay has caused you to reconsider any of your previous thinking about animals and their place in the world.*

---

Not all happy animals are alike. A Doberman going over a hurdle after a small wooden dumbbell is sleek, all arcs of harmonious power. A basset hound cheerfully performing the same exercise exhibits harmonies of a more lugubrious nature. There are chimpanzees who love precision the way musicians or fanatical housekeepers or accomplished hypochondriacs do; others for whom happiness is a matter of invention and variation—chimp 1 vaudevillians. There is a rhinoceros whose happiness, as near as I can make out, is in needing to be trained every morning, all over again, or else he "forgets" his circus routine, and in this you find a clue to the slow, deep, quiet chuckle of his happiness and to the glory of the beast. Happiness for Secretariat is in his ebullient bound, that joyful length of stride. For the draft horse or the weight-pull dog, happiness is of a different shape, more awesome and less obviously intelligent. When the pulling horse is at its most intense, the animal goes into himself, allocating all of the educated power that organizes his desire to dwell in fierce and delicate intimacy with that power, leans into the harness, and MAKES THAT SUCKER MOVE.

If we are speaking of human beings and use the phrase "animal happiness," we tend to mean something like "creature comforts." The emblems of this are the golden retriever rolling in the grass, the horse with his nose deep in the oats, the kitty by the fire. Creature comforts are important to animals—"Grub first, then ethics" is a motto that would describe many a wise Labrador retriever, and I have a pit bull named Annie whose continual quest for the perfect pillow inspires her to awesome feats. But there is something more to animals, a capacity for satisfactions that come from work in the fullest sense—what is known in philosophy and in this country's Declaration of Independence as "happiness." This is a sense of personal achievement, like the satisfaction felt by a good wood-carver or a dancer or a poet or an accomplished dressage horse. It is a happiness that, like the artist's, must come from something within the animal, something trainers call "talent." Hence, it cannot be imposed on the animal. But it is also something that does not come *ex nihilo*. If it had not been a fairly ordinary thing, in one part of the world, to teach young children to play the pianoforte, it is doubtful that Mozart's music would exist. 2

Happiness is often misunderstood as a synonym for pleasure or as an antonym for suffering. But Aristotle associated happiness with ethics—codes of behavior that urge us toward the sensation of getting it right, a kind of work that yields the "click" of satisfaction upon solving a problem or surmounting an obstacle. In his 3

*Ethics,* Aristotle wrote, "If happiness is activity in accordance with excellence, it is reasonable that it should be in accordance with the highest excellence." Thomas Jefferson identified the capacity for happiness as one of the three fundamental rights on which all others are based: "life, liberty, and the pursuit of happiness."

I bring up this idea of happiness as a form of work because I am an animal trainer, and work is the foundation of the happiness a trainer and an animal discover together. I bring up these words also because they cannot be found in the lexicon of the animal-rights movement. This absence accounts for the uneasiness toward the movement of most people, who sense that rights advocates have a point but take it too far when they liberate snails or charge that goldfish at the county fair are suffering. But the problem with the animal-rights advocates is not that they take it too far; it's that they've got it all wrong. 4

Animal rights are built upon a misconceived premise that rights were created to prevent us from unnecessary suffering. You can't find an animal-rights book, video, pamphlet, or rock concert in which someone doesn't mention the Great Sentence, written by Jeremy Bentham in 1789. Arguing in favor of such rights, Bentham wrote: "The question is not, Can they *reason*? nor, can they *talk*? but, can they suffer?" 5

The logic of the animal-rights movement places suffering at the iconographic center of a skewed value system. The thinking of its proponents—given eerie expression in a virtually sadopornographic sculpture of a tortured monkey that won a prize for its compassionate vision—has collapsed into a perverse conundrum. Today the loudest voices calling for—demanding—the destruction of animals are the humane organizations. This is an inevitable consequence of the apotheosis of the drive to relieve suffering: death is the ultimate release. To compensate for their contradictions, the humane movement has demonized, in this century and the last, those who made animal happiness their business: veterinarians, trainers, and the like. We think of Louis Pasteur as the man whose work saved you and me and your dog and cat from rabies, but antivivisectionists of the time claimed that rabies increased in areas where there were Pasteur Institutes. 6

An anti-rabies public relations campaign mounted in England in the 1880s by the Royal Society for the Prevention of Cruelty to Animals and other organizations led to orders being issued to club any dog found not wearing a muzzle. England still has her cruel and unnecessary law that requires an animal to spend six months in quarantine before being allowed loose in the country. Most of the recent propaganda about pit bulls—the crazy claim that they "take hold with their front teeth while they chew away with their rear teeth" (which would imply, incorrectly, that they have double jaws)—can be traced to literature published by the Humane Society of the United States during the fall of 1987 and earlier. If your neighbors want your dog or horse impounded and destroyed because he is a nuisance—say the dog barks, or the horse attracts flies—it will be the local Humane Society to whom your neighbors turn for action. 7

In a way, everyone has the opportunity to know that the history of the humane movement is largely a history of miseries, arrests, prosecutions, and death. The Humane Society is the pound, the place with the decompression chamber or the lethal injections. You occasionally find worried letters about this in Ann Landers's column. 8

Animal-rights publications are illustrated largely with photographs of two kinds of animals—"Helpless Fluff" and "Agonized Fluff," the two conditions in which some people seem to prefer their animals, because any other version of an animal is too complicated for propaganda. In the introduction to his book *Animal Liberation,* Peter Singer says somewhat smugly that he and his wife have no animals and, in fact, don't much care for them. This is offered as evidence of his objectivity and ethical probity. But it strikes me as an odd, perhaps obscene underpinning for an ethical project that encourages university and high school students to cherish their ignorance of, say, great bird dogs as proof of their devotion to animals. 9

I would like to leave these philosophers behind, for they are inept connoisseurs of suffering who might revere my Airedale for his capacity to scream when subjected to a blowtorch but 10 not for his wit and courage, not for his natural good manners that are a gentle rebuke to ours. I want to celebrate the moment not long ago when, at his first dog show, my Airedale, Drummer, learned that there can be a public place where his work is respected. I want to celebrate his meticulousness, his happiness upon realizing at the dog show that no one would swoop down upon him and swamp him with the goo-goo excesses known as the "teddy-bear complex" but that people actually got out of his way, gave him room to work. I want to say, "There can be a six-and-a-half-month-old puppy who can care about accuracy, who can be fastidious, and whose fastidiousness will be a foundation for courage later." I want to say, "Leave my puppy alone!"

I want to leave the philosophers behind, but I cannot, in part because the philosophical problems that plague academicians of the animal-rights movement are illuminating. They wonder, do animals have rights or do they have interests? Or, if these rightists lead particularly unexamined lives, they dismiss that question as obvious (yes, of course animals have rights, prima facie) and proceed to enumerate them, James Madison style. This leads to the issuance of bills of rights—the right to an environment, the right not to be used in medical experiments—and other forms of trivialization. 11

The calculus of suffering can be turned against the philosophers of festering flesh, even in the case of food animals, or exotic animals who perform in movies and circuses. It is true that it hurts to be slaughtered by man, but it doesn't hurt nearly as much as some of the cunningly cruel arrangements meted out by "Mother Nature." In Africa, 75 percent of the lions cubbed do not survive to the age of two. For those who make it to two, the average age at death is ten years. Asali, the movie and TV lioness, was still working at age twenty-one. There are fates worse than death, but twenty-one years of a close working relationship with Hubert Wells, Asali's trainer, is not one of them. Dorset sheep and polled Herefords would not exist at all were they not in a symbiotic relationship with human beings. 12

A human being living in the "wild"—somewhere, say, without the benefits of medicine and advanced social organization— 13 would probably have a life expectancy of from thirty to thirty-five years. A human being living in "captivity"—in, say, a middle-class neighborhood of what the Centers for Disease Control call a Metropolitan Statistical Area—has a life expectancy of seventy or more years. For orangutans in the wild in Borneo and Malaysia, the life expectancy is thirty-five years; in captivity, fifty years. The wild is not a suffering-free zone or all that frolicsome a location.

The questions asked by animal-rights activists are flawed, because they are built on the concept that the origin of rights is in the avoidance of suffering rather than in the pursuit of happiness. The question that needs to be asked—and that will put us in closer proximity to the truth—is not, do they have rights? or, what are those rights? but rather, what is a right? 14

Rights originate in committed relationships and can be found, both intact and violated, wherever one finds such relationships—in social compacts, within families, between animals, and between people and nonhuman animals. This is as true when the nonhuman animals in question are lions or parakeets as when they are dogs. It is my Airedale whose excellencies have my attention at the moment, so it is with reference to him that I will consider the question, what is a right? 15

When I imagine situations in which it naturally arises that A defends or honors or respects B's rights, I imagine situations in which the relationship between A and B can be indicated with a possessive pronoun. I might say, "Leave her alone, she's my daughter" or "That's what she wants, and she is my daughter. I think I am bound to honor her wants." Similarly, "Leave her alone, she's my mother." I am more tender of the happiness of my mother, my father, my child, than I am of other people's family members; more tender of my friends' happinesses than your friends' happinesses, unless you and I have a mutual friend. 16

Possession of a being by another has come into more and more disrepute, so that the common understanding of one person possessing another is slavery. But the important detail about the kind of possessive pronoun that I have in mind is reciprocity: if I have a friend, she has a friend. If I have a daughter, she has a mother. The possessive does not bind one of us while freeing the other; it can- 17 not do that. Moreover, should the mother reject the daughter, the word that applies is "disown." The form of disowning that most often appears in the news is domestic violence. Parents abuse children; husbands batter wives.

Some cases of reciprocal possessives have built-in limitations, such as "my patient/my doctor" or "my student/my teacher" or "my agent/my client." Other possessive relations are extremely limited but still remarkably binding: "my neighbor" and "my country" and "my president." 18

The responsibilities and the ties signaled by reciprocal possession typically are hard to dissolve. It can be as difficult to give up an enemy as to give up a friend, and often the one becomes the other, as though the logic of the possessive pronoun outlasts the forms it chanced to take at a given moment, as though we were stuck with one another. In these bindings, nearly inextricable, are found the origin of our rights. They imply a possessiveness but also recognize an acknowledgment by each side of the other's existence. 19

The idea of democracy is dependent on the citizens' having knowledge of the government; that is, realizing that the government exists and knowing how to claim rights against it. I know this much because I get mail from the government and see its "representatives" running about in uniforms. Whether I actually have any rights in relationship to the government is less clear, but the idea that I do is symbolized by the right to vote. I obey the government, and, in theory, it obeys me, by counting my ballot, reading the *Miranda* warning to me, agreeing to be bound by the Constitution. My friend obeys me as I obey her; the government "obeys" me to some extent, and, to a different extent, I obey it. 20

What kind of thing can my Airedale, Drummer, have knowledge of? He can know that I exist and through that knowledge can claim his happinesses, with varying degrees of success, both with me and against me. Drummer can also know about larger human or dog communities than the one that consists only of him and me. There is my household—the other dogs, the cats, my husband. I have had enough dogs on campuses to know that he can learn that Yale exists as a neighborhood or village. My older dog, 21

Annie, not only knows that Yale exists but can tell Yalies from townies, as I learned while teaching there during labor troubles.

Dogs can have elaborate conceptions of human social structures, and even of something like their rights and responsibilities within them, but these conceptions are never elaborate enough to construct a rights relationship between a dog and the state, or a dog and the Humane Society. Both of these are concepts that depend on writing and memoranda, officers in uniform, plaques and seals of authority. All of these are literary constructs, and all of them are beyond a dog's ken, which is why the mail carrier who doesn't also happen to be a dog's friend is forever an intruder—this is why dogs bark at mailmen. 22

It is clear enough that natural rights relations can arise between people and animals. Drummer, for example, can insist, "Hey, let's go outside and do something!" if I have been at my computer several days on end. He can both refuse to accept various of my suggestions and tell me when he fears for his life—such as the time when the huge, white flapping flag appeared out of nowhere, as it seemed to him, on the town green one evening when we were working. I can (and do) say to him either, "Oh, you don't have to worry about that" or, "Uh oh, you're right, Drum, that guy looks dangerous." Just as the government and I—two different species of organism—have developed improvised ways of communicating, such as the vote, so Drummer and I have worked out a number of ways to make our expressions known. Largely through obedience, I have taught him a fair amount about how to get responses from me. Obedience is reciprocal; you cannot get responses from a dog to whom you do not respond accurately. I have enfranchised him in a relationship to me by educating him, creating the conditions by which he can achieve a certain happiness specific to a dog, maybe even specific to an Airedale, inasmuch as this same relationship has allowed me to plumb the happiness of being a trainer and writing this article. 23

Instructions in this happiness are given terms that are alien to a culture in which liver treats, fluffy windup toys, and miniature sweaters are confused with respect and work. Jack Knox, a sheepdog trainer originally from Scotland, will shake his crook at a novice handler who makes a promiscuous move to praise a dog, 24 and will call out in his Scottish accent, "Eh! Eh! Get back, get BACK! Ye'll no be abusin' the dogs like that in my clinic." America is a nation of abused animals, Knox says, because we are always swooping at them with praise, "no gi'ing them their freedom." I am reminded of Rainer Maria Rilke's account in which the Prodigal Son leaves—has to leave—because everyone loves him, even the dogs love him, and he has no path to the delicate and fierce truth of himself. Unconditional praise and love, in Rilke's story, disenfranchise us, distract us from what truly excites our interest.

In the minds of some trainers and handlers, praise is dishonesty. Paradoxically, it is a kind of contempt for animals that masquerades as a reverence for helplessness and suffering. The idea of freedom means that you do not, at least not while Jack Knox is nearby, helpfully guide your dog through the motions of, say, herding over and over—what one trainer calls "explainy-wainy." This is rote learning. It works tolerably well on some handlers, because people have vast unconscious minds and can store complex preprogrammed behaviors. Dogs, on the other hand, have almost no unconscious minds, so they can learn only by thinking. Many children are like this until educated out of it. 25

If I tell my Airedale to sit and stay on the town green, and someone comes up and burbles, "What a pretty thing you are," he may break his stay to go for a caress. I pull him back and correct him for breaking. Now he holds his stay because I have blocked his way to movement but not because I have punished him. (A correction blocks one path as it opens another for desire to work; punishment blocks desire and opens nothing.) He holds his stay now, and—because the stay opens this possibility of work, new to a heedless young dog—he watches. If the person goes on talking, and isn't going to gush with praise, I may heel Drummer out of his stay and give him an "Okay" to make friends. Sometimes something about the person makes Drummer feel that reserve is in order. He responds to an insincere approach by sitting still, going down into himself, and thinking, "This person has no business pawing me. I'll sit very still, and he will go away." If the person doesn't take the hint from Drummer, I'll give the pup a little backup by saying, "Please don't pet him, he's working," even though he was not under any command. 26

The pup reads this, and there is a flicker of a working trust now stirring in the dog. Is the pup grateful? When the stranger leaves, does he lick my hand, full of submissive blandishments? This one doesn't. This one says nothing at all, and I say nothing much to him. This is a working trust we are developing, not a mutual congratulation society. My backup is praise enough for him; the use he makes of my support is praise enough for me. 27

Listening to a dog is often praise enough. Suppose it is just after dark and we are outside. Suddenly there is a shout from the house. The pup and I both look toward the shout and then toward each other: "What do you think?" I don't so much as cock my head, because Drummer is growing up, and I want to know what he thinks. He takes a few steps toward the house, and I follow. He listens again and comprehends that it's just Holly, who at fourteen is much given to alarming cries and shouts. He shrugs at me and goes about his business. I say nothing. To praise him for this performance would make about as much sense as praising a human being for the same thing. Thus: 28

A. What's that?
B. I don't know. [Listens] Oh, it's just Holly.
A. What a gooooood human being!
B. Huh?

This is one small moment in a series of like moments that will culminate in an Airedale who on a Friday will have the discrimination and confidence required to take down a man who is attacking me with a knife and on Saturday clown and play with the children at the annual Orange Empire Dog Club Christmas party. 29

People who claim to speak for animal rights are increasingly devoted to the idea that the very keeping of a dog or a horse or a gerbil or a lion is in and of itself an offense. The more loudly they speak, the less likely they are to be in a rights relation to any given animal, because they are spending so much time in airplanes or transmitting fax announcements of the latest Sylvester Stallone anti-fur rally. In a 1988 *Harper's* forum, for example, Ingrid 30

Newkirk, the national director of People for the Ethical Treatment of Animals, urged that domestic pets be spayed and neutered and ultimately phased out. She prefers, it appears, wolves—and wolves someplace else—to Airedales and, by a logic whose interior structure is both emotionally and intellectually forever closed to Drummer, claims thereby to be speaking for "animal rights."

She is wrong. I am the only one who can own up to my Airedale's inalienable rights. Whether or not I do it perfectly at any given moment is no more refutation of this point than whether I am perfectly my husband's mate at any given moment refutes the fact of marriage. Only people who know Drummer, and whom he can know, are capable of this relationship. PETA and the Humane Society and the ASPCA and the Congress and NOW—as institutions—do have the power to affect my ability to grant rights to Drummer but are otherwise incapable of creating conditions or laws or rights that would increase his happiness. Only Drummer's owner has the power to obey him—to obey who he is and what he is capable of—deeply enough to grant him his rights and open up the possibility of happiness. 31

---

## *Meaning and Purpose*

1. How does the author distinguish between people and animals in this essay?
2. Why does the author refer to the Declaration of Independence in paragraph 2?
3. What is the overall importance to this essay of Jeremy Bentham's "Great Sentence," in paragraph 5?
4. Why does the author mention her husband in this essay?

## *Strategy*

1. What point does the author make by using the information contained in paragraphs 12 and 13?

2. Why does the author want to leave philosophers behind, as she maintains in paragraph 10? Why can't she?
3. In your own words, tell how "Obedience is reciprocal," as the author maintains in paragraph 23. Do you agree with this concept? Why or why not?
4. Why does the author use *being* in paragraph 17? Why doesn't she use a word like man, woman, or person, for example?

## *Style*

1. What does the word *calculus* mean, as it is used in paragraph 12?
2. Many people have noticed that in this essay, the author treats dogs in at least one respect the same way that most people treat other people. In what way or ways does the author treat dogs like people?
3. What does the author mean by "Helpless Fluff" and "Agonized Fluff" in paragraph 9?
4. Why does the author describe the government and herself as "two species of organism," in paragraph 23?

## *Writing Tasks*

1. Write an essay in which you agree with Hearne's position on animal "rights." Strengthen your essay by using your personal examples and other outside examples of how animals are far better off than certain groups would have you believe.
2. Argue against Hearne's position on animal "rights." Strengthen your essay by using your personal examples and other outside examples of how animals suffer at the hands of people and therefore should be freed or allowed to have rights.

# ❦ Jonathan Swift ❦

*Born in Ireland in 1667 to English parents, Swift attended Trinity College in Dublin and Oxford University in England and was ordained an Anglican priest in 1694. While in England he was active in both religion and politics and worked as a pamphlet writer for the Tory party. Frustrated for many years in his attempts to gain advancement in the church, however, Swift returned to Ireland in 1713 as Dean of St. Patrick's Cathedral in Dublin. Increasingly he devoted himself to writing satire that exposed England's injustices against the Irish. His* Drapier Letters *(1724), in which he openly attacked the English for their abuses, made him a national hero in Ireland. The satirical allegory,* Gulliver's Travels *(1726), is his most famous work. When he died in 1745, three years after being declared of unsound mind, his estate went to found a hospital for the insane.*

# *A Modest Proposal*

*The barbaric conditions of English rule over Ireland in the 1720s and England's blatant refusal to help the Irish poor is the subject of this biting satire, first published anonymously in 1729. Logic, hard facts, tone, and emotional appeal all contribute to the power of this argument.*

*Before you read this essay, read the definitions of irony and persona in the Glossary. Look for examples of irony in the essay and try to imagine what sort of person (persona) would write this essay.*

---

1 It is a melancholy object to those who walk through this great town or travel in the country, when they see the streets, the roads, and cabin doors, crowded with beggars of the female sex, followed by three, four, or six children, all in rags and importuning every passenger for an alms. These mothers, instead of being able to work for their honest livelihood, are forced to employ all their time in strolling to beg sustenance for their helpless infants, who, as they grow up, either turn thieves for want of work, or leave

their dear native country to fight for the Pretender in Spain, or sell themselves to the Barbados.

I think it is agreed by all parties that this prodigious number of children in the arms, or on the backs, or at the heels of their mothers, and frequently of their fathers, is in the present deplorable state of the kingdom a very great additional grievance; and therefore whoever could find out a fair, cheap, and easy method of making these children sound, useful members of the commonwealth would deserve so well of the public as to have his statue set up for a preserver of the nation. 2

But my intention is very far from being confined to provide only for the children of professed beggars; it is of a much greater extent, and shall take in the whole number of infants at a certain age who are born of parents in effect as little able to support them as those who demand our charity in the streets. 3

As to my own part, having turned my thoughts for many years upon this important subject, and maturely weighed the several schemes of other projectors, I have always found them grossly mistaken in their computation. It is true, a child just dropped from its dam may be supported by her milk for a solar year, with little other nourishment; at most not above the value of two shillings, which the mother may certainly get, or the value in scraps, by her lawful occupation of begging; and it is exactly at one year old that I propose to provide for them in such a manner as instead of being a charge upon their parents or the parish, or wanting food and raiment for the rest of their lives, they shall on the contrary contribute to the feeding, and partly to the clothing, of many thousands. 4

There is likewise another great advantage in my scheme, that it will prevent those voluntary abortions, and that horrid practice of women murdering their bastard children, alas, too frequent among us, sacrificing the poor innocent babes, I doubt, more to avoid the expense than the shame, which would move tears and pity in the most savage and inhuman breast. 5

The number of souls in this kingdom being usually reckoned one million and a half, of these I calculate there may be about two hundred thousand couples whose wives are breeders; from which number I subtract thirty thousand couples who are able to main- 6 tain their own children, although I apprehend there cannot be so many under the present distress of the kingdom; but this being granted, there will remain an hundred and seventy thousand breeders. I again subtract fifty thousand for those women who miscarry, or whose children die by accident or disease within the year. There only remain an hundred and twenty thousand children of poor parents annually born. The question therefore is, how this number shall be reared and provided for, which, as I have already said, under the present situation of affairs, is utterly impossible by all the methods hitherto proposed. For we can neither employ them in handicraft nor agriculture; we neither build houses (I mean in the country) nor cultivate land. They can very seldom pick up a livelihood by stealing till they arrive at six years old, except where they are of towardly parts; although I confess they learn the rudiments much earlier, during which time they can however be looked upon only as probationers, as I have been informed by a principal gentleman in the county of Cavan, who protested to me that he never knew above one or two instances under the age of six, even in a part of the kingdom so renowned for the quickest proficiency in that art.

I am assured by our merchants that a boy or a girl before 7
twelve years old is no salable commodity; and even when they come to this age, they will not yield above three pounds, or three pounds and half a crown at most on the Exchange; which cannot turn to account either to the parents or the kingdom, the charge of nutriment and rags having been at least four times that value.

I shall now therefore humbly propose my own thoughts, 8
which I hope will not be liable to the least objection.

I have been assured by a very knowing American of my ac- 9
quaintance in London, that a young healthy child well nursed is at a year old a most delicious, nourishing, and wholesome food, whether stewed, roasted, baked, or boiled; and I make no doubt that it will equally serve in a fricassee or a ragout.

I do therefore humbly offer it to public consideration that of 10
the hundred and twenty thousand children, already computed, twenty thousand may be reserved for breed, whereof only one fourth part to be males, which is more than we allow to sheep, black cattle, or swine; and my reason is that these children are sel-

dom the fruits of marriage, a circumstance not much regarded by our savages, therefore one male will be sufficient to serve four females. That the remaining hundred thousand may at a year old be offered in sale to the persons of quality and fortune through the kingdom, always advising the mother to let them suck plentifully in the last month, so as to render them plump and fat for a good table. A child will make two dishes at an entertainment for friends; and when the family dines alone, the fore or hind quarter will make a reasonable dish, and seasoned with a little pepper or salt will be very good boiled on the fourth day, especially in winter.

I have reckoned upon a medium that a child just born will 11
weigh twelve pounds, and in a solar year if tolerably nursed increaseth to twenty-eight pounds.

I grant this food will be somewhat dear, and therefore very 12
proper for landlords, who, as they have already devoured most of the parents, seem to have the best title to the children.

Infant's flesh will be in season throughout the year, but more 13
plentiful in March, and a little before and after. For we are told by a grave author, an eminent French physician, that fish being a prolific diet, there are more children born in Roman Catholic countries about nine months after Lent, than at any other season; therefore, reckoning a year after Lent, the markets will be more glutted than usual, because the number of popish infants is at least three to one in this kingdom; and therefore it will have one other collateral advantage, by lessening the number of Papists among us.

I have already computed the charge of nursing a beggar's child 14
(in which list I reckon all cottagers, laborers, and four fifths of the farmers) to be about two shillings per annum, rags included; and I believe no gentleman would repine to give ten shillings for the carcass of a good fat child, which, as I have said, will make four dishes of excellent nutritive meat, when he hath only some particular friend or his own family to dine with him. Thus the squire will learn to be a good landlord, and grow popular among the tenants; the mother will have eight shillings net profit, and be fit for work till she produces another child.

Those who are more thrifty (as I must confess the times re- 15
quire) may flay the carcass; the skin of which artificially dressed

will make admirable gloves for ladies, and summer boots for fine gentlemen.

As to our city of Dublin, shambles may be appointed for this purpose in the most convenient parts of it, and butchers we may be assured will not be wanting; although I rather recommend buying the children alive, and dressing them hot from the knife as we do roasting pigs. 16

A very worthy person, a true lover of his country, and whose virtues I highly esteem, was lately pleased in discoursing on this matter to offer a refinement upon my scheme. He said that many gentlemen of his kingdom, having of late destroyed their deer, he conceived that the want of venison might be well supplied by the bodies of young lads and maidens, not exceeding fourteen years of age nor under twelve, so great a number of both sexes in every country being now ready to starve for want of work and service; and these to be disposed of by their parents, if alive, or otherwise by their nearest relations. But with due deference to so excellent a friend and so deserving a patriot, I cannot be altogether in his sentiments; for as to the males, my American acquaintance assured me from frequent experience that their flesh was generally tough and lean, like that of our schoolboys, by continual exercise, and their taste disagreeable; and to fatten them would not answer the charge. Then as to the females, it would, I think with humble submission, be a loss to the public, because they soon would become breeders themselves; and besides, it is not improbable that some scrupulous people might be apt to censure such a practice (although indeed very unjustly) as a little bordering upon cruelty; which, I confess, hath always been with me the strongest objection against any project, how well soever intended. 17

But in order to justify my friend, he confessed that this expedient was put into his head by the famous Psalmanazar, a native of the island Formosa, who came from thence to London above twenty years ago, and in conversation told my friend that in his country when any young person happened to be put to death, the executioner sold the carcass to the persons of quality as a prime dainty; and that in his time the body of a plump girl of fifteen, who was crucified for an attempt to poison the emperor, was sold 18 to his Imperial Majesty's prime minister of state, and other great mandarins of the court, in joints from the gibbet, at four hundred crowns. Neither indeed can I deny that if the same use were made of several plump young girls in this town, who without one single groat to their fortunes cannot stir abroad without a chair, and appear at the playhouse and assemblies in foreign fineries which they never will pay for, the kingdom would not be the worse.

Some persons of a desponding spirit are in great concern 19
about that vast number of poor people who are aged, diseased, or maimed, and I have been desired to employ my thoughts what course may be taken to ease the nation of so grievous an encumbrance. But I am not in the least pain upon that matter, because it is very well known that they are every day dying and rotting by cold and famine, and filth and vermin, as fast as can be reasonably expected. And as to the younger laborers, they are now in almost as hopeful a condition. They cannot get work, and consequently pine away for want of nourishment to a degree that if any time they are accidentally hired to common labor, they have not strength to perform it; and thus the country and themselves are happily delivered from the evils to come.

I have too long digressed, and therefore shall return to my 20
subject. I think the advantages by the proposal which I have made are obvious and many, as well as of the highest importance.

For first, as I have already observed, it would greatly lessen 21
the number of Papists, with whom we are yearly overrun, being the principal breeders of the nation as well as our most dangerous enemies; and who stay at home on purpose to deliver the kingdom to the Pretender, hoping to take their advantage by the absence of so many good Protestants, who have chosen rather to leave their country than to stay at home and pay tithes against their conscience to an Episcopal curate.

Secondly, the poorer tenants will have something valuable of 22
their own, which by law may be made liable to distress, and help to pay their landlord's rent, their corn and cattle being already seized and money a thing unknown.

Thirdly, whereas the maintenance of an hundred thousand 23
children, from two years old and upwards, cannot be computed at

less than ten shillings a piece per annum, the nation's stock will be thereby increased fifty thousand pounds per annum, besides the profit of a new dish introduced to the tables of all gentlemen of fortune in the kingdom who have any refinement in taste. And the money will circulate among ourselves, the goods being entirely of our own growth and manufacture.

Fourthly, the constant breeders, besides the gain of eight shillings sterling per annum by the sale of their children, will be rid of the charge for maintaining them after the first year. 24

Fifthly, this food would likewise bring great custom to taverns, where the vintners will certainly be so prudent as to procure the best receipts for dressing it to perfection, and consequently have their houses frequented by all the fine gentlemen, who justly value themselves upon their knowledge in good eating; and a skillful cook, who understands how to oblige his guests, will contrive to make it as expensive as they please. 25

Sixthly, this would be a great inducement to marriage, which all wise nations have either encouraged by rewards or enforced by laws and penalties. It would increase the care and tenderness of mothers toward their children, when they were sure of a settlement for life to the poor babes, provided in some sort by the public, to their annual profit instead of expense. We should see an honest emulation among the married women, which of them could bring the fattest child to the market. Men would become as fond of their wives during the time of their pregnancy as they are now of their mares in foal, their cows in calf, or sows when they are ready to farrow; nor offer to beat or kick them (as is too frequent a practice) for fear of a miscarriage. 26

Many other advantages might be enumerated. For instance, the addition of some thousand carcasses in our exportation of barreled beef, the propagation of swine's flesh, and improvements in the art of making good bacon, so much wanted among us by the great destruction of pigs, too frequent at our tables, which are no way comparable in taste or magnificence to a well-grown, fat, yearling child, which roasted whole will make a considerable figure at a lord mayor's feast or any other public entertainment. But this and many others I omit, being studious of brevity. 27

Supposing that one thousand families in this city would be constant customers for infants' flesh, besides others who might have it at merry meetings, particularly weddings and christenings, I compute that Dublin would take off annually about twenty thousand carcasses, and the rest of the kingdom (where probably they will be sold somewhat cheaper) the remaining eighty thousand. 28

I can think of no one objection that will possibly be raised against this proposal, unless it should be urged that the number of people will be thereby much lessened in the kingdom. This I freely own, and it was indeed one principal design in offering it to the world. I desire the reader will observe, that I calculate my remedy for this one individual kingdom of Ireland and for no other that ever was, is, or I think ever can be upon earth. Therefore, let no man talk to me of other expedients: of taxing our absentees at five shillings a pound: of using neither clothes nor household furniture except what is of our own growth and manufacture: of utterly rejecting the materials and instruments that promote foreign luxury: of curing the expensiveness of pride, vanity, idleness, and gaming in our women: of introducing a vein of parsimony, prudence, and temperance: of learning to love our country, in the want of which we differ even from Laplanders and the inhabitants of Topinamboo: of quitting our animosities and factions, nor acting any longer like the Jews, who were murdering one another at the very moment their city was taken: of being a little cautious not to sell our country and conscience for nothing: of teaching landlords to have at least one degree of mercy toward their tenants: lastly, of putting a spirit of honesty, industry, and skill into our shopkeepers; who, if a resolution could now be taken to buy only our native goods, would immediately unite to cheat and exact upon us in the price, the measure, and the goodness, nor could ever yet be brought to make one fair proposal of just dealing, though often and earnestly invited to it. 29

Therefore, I repeat, let no man talk to me of these and the like expedients, till he hath at least some glimpse of hope that there will ever be some hearty and sincere attempt to put them in practice. 30

But as to myself, having been wearied out for many years with offering vain, idle, visionary thoughts, and at length utterly despairing of success, I fortunately fell upon this proposal, which, as it is wholly new, so it hath something solid and real, of no expense and little trouble, full in our own power, and whereby we can incur no danger in disobliging England. For this kind of commodity will not bear exportation, the flesh being of too tender a consistence to admit a long continuance in salt, although perhaps I could name a country which would be glad to eat up our whole nation without it. 31

After all, I am not so violently bent upon my own opinion as to reject any offer proposed by wise men, which shall be found equally innocent, cheap, easy, and effectual. But before something of that kind shall be advanced in contradiction to my scheme, and offering a better, I desire the author or authors will be pleased maturely to consider two points. First, as things now stand, how they will be able to find food and raiment for an hundred thousand useless mouths and backs. And secondly, there being a round million of creatures in human figure throughout this kingdom, whose sole subsistence put into a common stock would leave them in debt two millions of pounds sterling, adding those who are beggars by profession to the bulk of farmers, cottagers, and laborers, with their wives and children who are beggars in effect; I desire those politicians who dislike my overture, and may perhaps be so bold to attempt an answer, that they will first ask the parents of these mortals whether they would not at this day think it a great happiness to have been sold for food at a year old in this manner I prescribe, and thereby have avoided such a perpetual scene of misfortunes as they have since gone through by the oppression of landlords, the impossibility of paying rent without money or trade, the want of common sustenance, with neither house nor clothes to cover them from the inclemencies of the weather, and the most inevitable prospect of entailing the like or greater miseries upon their breed forever. 32

I profess, in the sincerity of my heart, that I have not the least personal interest in endeavoring to promote this necessary work, 33 having no other motive than the public good of my country, by advancing our trade, providing for infants, relieving the poor, and giving some pleasure to the rich. I have no children by which I can propose to get a single penny; the youngest being nine years old, and my wife past childbearing.

---

## *Meaning and Purpose*

1. Swift uses the persona of a "projector," a person who suggests plans for social and economic change (see paragraph 4) to put forth a "modest proposal." Describe the character of this projector. How do his views differ from those of Swift? Where do you find Swift's voice and beliefs coming to the surface?
2. Exactly what is Swift's "modest proposal"? What problems is it designed to solve? In what ways would it solve those problems?
3. What, primarily, does Swift condemn in the essay?
4. Underneath all the irony, what is Swift arguing for?
5. What objections to Swift's proposal can you think of?

## *Strategy*

1. What does Swift do in paragraph 1 to set the reader up for the text that follows?
2. What means does Swift use to establish the narrator as reasonable, ethical, and trustworthy?
3. Where does Swift first give the reader a clue that his plan is horrible, not modest?
4. What purpose does the final paragraph serve?

## *Style*

1. How does Swift's choice of words enforce the barbarity of his proposal? Pay particular attention to his referring to Ireland's poor in language usually reserved for livestock, such as

"breeders" (6) and "fore or hind quarter" (10). Find other such expressions or sentences.

2. How would you describe Swift's writing style? Support your opinion by giving examples. Do his style and diction inhibit your understanding and appreciation of the essay? Why or why not?
3. If necessary, check the meanings of these words in a dictionary: *importuning* (1); *prodigious* (2); *rudiments* (6); *fricassee, ragout* (9); *prolific, papists* (13); *repine* (14); *deference* (17); *mandarins, gibbet* (18); *desponding* (19); *tithes* (21); *vintners* (25); *farrow* (26); *parsimony, animosities* (29); *disobliging* (31); *inclemencies, entailing* (32).

## *Writing Tasks*

1. Think of a personal, social, or economic problem that you have an opinion about, and write an outrageous solution to it in a rational and responsible voice. Share your essay with other students to see if you have made your point effectively with irony.
2. Take the same problem you discussed in task 1 and propose a real, not an outrageous, solution to it. Consider your audience and whether to appeal to emotion or reason.

# ❦Martin Luther King, Jr.❦

*Born in Atlanta, Georgia, King was the son of a Baptist minister. At age eighteen he was an ordained minister himself. He went on to study at Morehouse College, Crozer Theological Seminary, and Boston University, where he earned a Ph.D. Until his assassination in Memphis, Tennessee, in 1968, he was the acknowledged leader of the American civil-rights movement, having gained national recognition in 1955 by organizing a successful boycott of the segregated busing system of Montgomery, Alabama. He was arrested and jailed more than a dozen times as a civil-rights leader, once for eight days, during which time he wrote the now-famous letter reprinted here. He founded and acted as president of the Southern Christian Leadership Conference, through which he promoted a philosophy of nonviolent resistance to racial discrimination that has often been compared to Gandhi's. In 1964 he was awarded the Nobel prize for peace.*

## *Letter from Birmingham Jail*

*King's letter is written in response to a public statement by Birmingham clergymen who opposed the demonstrations King was leading to protest against the city's segregated transportation system. The argument is backed by examples from history, philosophy, theology, and literature, but the power of the writing lies equally in King's rich rhetorical style.*

*One of the strengths of King's style is that it is highly coherent, in the sense that the content in each paragraph flows into the content of the next paragraph. As you read this essay, notice the extraordinarily strong transitions from paragraph to paragraph.*

---

MY DEAR FELLOW CLERGYMEN:

While confined here in the Birmingham city jail, I came across 1
your recent statement calling my present activities "unwise and untimely." Seldom do I pause to answer criticism of my work and ideas. If I sought to answer all the criticisms that cross my desk, my secretaries would have little time for anything other than such

correspondence in the course of the day, and I would have no time for constructive work. But since I feel that you are men of genuine good will and that your criticisms are sincerely set forth, I want to try to answer your statement in what I hope will be patient and reasonable terms.

I think I should indicate why I am here in Birmingham, since you have been influenced by the view which argues against "outsiders coming in." I have the honor of serving as president of the Southern Christian Leadership Conference, an organization operating in every southern state, with headquarters in Atlanta, Georgia. We have some eighty-five affiliated organizations across the South, and one of them is the Alabama Christian Movement for Human Rights. Frequently we share staff, educational, and financial resources with our affiliates. Several months ago the affiliate here in Birmingham asked us to be on call to engage in a nonviolent direct-action program if such were deemed necessary. We readily consented, and when the hour came, we lived up to our promise. So I, along with several members of my staff, am here because I was invited here. I am here because I have organizational ties here. 2

But more basically, I am in Birmingham because injustice is here. Just as the prophets of the eighth century B.C. left their villages and carried their "thus saith the Lord" far beyond the boundaries of their home towns, and just as the Apostle Paul left his village of Tarsus and carried the gospel of Jesus Christ to the far corners of the Greco-Roman world, so am I compelled to carry the gospel of freedom beyond my own home town. Like Paul, I must constantly respond to the Macedonian call for aid. 3

Moreover, I am cognizant of the interrelatedness of all communities and states. I cannot sit idly by in Atlanta and not be concerned about what happens in Birmingham. Injustice anywhere is a threat to justice everywhere. We are caught in an inescapable network of mutuality, tied in a single garment of destiny. Whatever affects one directly, affects all indirectly. Never again can we afford to live with the narrow, provincial "outside agitator" idea. Anyone who lives inside the United States can never be considered an outsider anywhere within its bounds. 4

You deplore the demonstrations taking place in Birmingham. But your statement, I am sorry to say, fails to express a similar concern for the conditions that brought about the demonstrations. I am sure that none of you would want to rest content with the superficial kind of social analysis that deals merely with effects and does not grapple with underlying causes. It is unfortunate that demonstrations are taking place in Birmingham, but it is even more unfortunate that the city's white power structure left the Negro community with no alternative. 5

In any nonviolent campaign there are four basic steps: collection of the facts to determine whether injustices exist; negotiation; self-purification; and direct action. We have gone through all these steps in Birmingham. There can be no gainsaying the fact that racial injustice engulfs this community. Birmingham is probably the most thoroughly segregated city in the United States. Its ugly record of brutality is widely known. Negroes have experienced grossly unjust treatment in the courts. There have been more unsolved bombings of Negro homes and churches in Birmingham than in any other city in the nation. These are the hard, brutal facts of the case. On the basis of these conditions, Negro leaders sought to negotiate with the city fathers. But the latter consistently refused to engage in good-faith negotiation. 6

Then, last September, came the opportunity to talk with leaders of Birmingham's economic community. In the course of the negotiations, certain promises were made by the merchants—for example, to remove the stores' humiliating racial signs. On the basis of these promises, the Reverend Fred Shuttlesworth and the leaders of the Alabama Christian Movement for Human Rights agreed to a moratorium on all demonstrations. As the weeks and months went by, we realized that we were the victims of a broken promise. A few signs, briefly removed, returned; the others remained. 7

As in so many past experiences, our hopes had been blasted, and the shadow of deep disappointment settled upon us. We had no alternative except to prepare for direct action, whereby we would present our very bodies as a means of laying our case before the conscience of the local and the national community. Mindful 8 of the difficulties involved, we decided to undertake a process of self-purification. We began a series of workshops on nonviolence, and we repeatedly asked ourselves: "Are you able to accept blows without retaliating?" "Are you able to endure the ordeal of jail?" We decided to schedule our direct-action program for the Easter season, realizing that except for Christmas, this is the main shopping period of the year. Knowing that a strong economic-withdrawal program would be the by product of direct action, we felt that this would be the best time to bring pressure to bear on the merchants for the needed change.

Then it occurred to us that Birmingham's mayoral election 9
was coming up in March, and we speedily decided to postpone action until after election day. When we discovered that the Commissioner of Public Safety, Eugene "Bull" Connor, had piled up enough votes to be in the run-off, we decided again to postpone action until the day after the run-off so that the demonstrations could not be used to cloud the issues. Like many others, we waited to see Mr. Connor defeated, and to this end we endured postponement after postponement. Having aided in this community need, we felt that our direct-action program could be delayed no longer.

You may well ask, "Why direct action? Why sit-ins, marches, 10
and so forth? Isn't negotiation a better path?" You are quite right in calling for negotiation. Indeed, this is the very purpose of direct action. Nonviolent direct action seeks to create such a crisis and foster such a tension that a community which has constantly refused to negotiate is forced to confront the issue. It seeks so to dramatize the issue that it can no longer be ignored. My citing the creation of tension as part of the work of the nonviolent-resister may sound rather shocking. But I must confess that I am not afraid of the word "tension." I have earnestly opposed violent tension, but there is a type of constructive, nonviolent tension which is necessary for growth. Just as Socrates felt that it was necessary to create a tension in the mind so that individuals could rise from the bondage of myths and half-truths to the unfettered realm of creative analysis and objective appraisal, so must we see the need for nonviolent gadflies to create the kind of tension in society that

will help men rise from the dark depths of prejudice and racism to the majestic heights of understanding and brotherhood.

The purpose of our direct-action program is to create a situation so crisis-packed that it will inevitably open the door to negotiation. I therefore concur with you in your call for negotiation. Too long has our beloved Southland been bogged down in a tragic effort to live in monologue rather than dialogue. 11

One of the basic points in your statement is that the action that I and my associates have taken in Birmingham is untimely. Some have asked: "Why didn't you give the new city administration time to act?" The only answer that I can give to this query is that the new Birmingham administration must be prodded about as much as the outgoing one, before it will act. We are sadly mistaken if we feel that the election of Albert Boutwell as mayor will bring the millennium to Birmingham. While Mr. Boutwell is a much more gentle person than Mr. Connor, they are both segregationists, dedicated to maintenance of the status quo. I have hoped that Mr. Boutwell will be reasonable enough to see the futility of massive resistance to desegregation. But he will not see this without pressure from devotees of civil rights. My friends, I must say to you that we have not made a single gain in civil rights without determined legal and nonviolent pressure. Lamentably, it is an historical fact that privileged groups seldom give up their privileges voluntarily. Individuals may see the moral light and voluntarily give up their unjust posture; but, as Reinhold Niebuhr has reminded us, groups tend to be more immoral than individuals. 12

We know through painful experience that freedom is never voluntarily given by the oppressor; it must be demanded by the oppressed. Frankly, I have yet to engage in a direct-action campaign that was "well timed" in the view of those who have not suffered unduly from the disease of segregation. For years now I have heard the word "Wait!" It rings in the ear of every Negro with piercing familiarity. This "Wait" has almost always meant "Never." We must come to see, with one of our distinguished jurists, that "justice too long delayed is justice denied." 13

We have waited for more than 340 years for our constitutional and God-given rights. The nations of Asia and Africa are 14 moving with jetlike speed toward gaining political independence, but we still creep at horse-and-buggy pace toward gaining a cup of coffee at a lunch counter. Perhaps it is easy for those who have never felt the stinging darts of segregation to say, "Wait." But when you have seen vicious mobs lynch your mothers and fathers at will and drown your sisters and brothers at whim; when you have seen hate-filled policemen curse, kick, and even kill your black brothers and sisters; when you see the vast majority of your twenty million Negro brothers smothering in an airtight cage of poverty in the midst of an affluent society; when you suddenly find your tongue twisted and your speech stammering as you seek to explain to your six-year-old daughter why she can't go to the public amusement park that has just been advertised on television, and see tears welling up in her eyes when she is told that Funtown is closed to colored children, and see ominous clouds of inferiority beginning to form in her little mental sky, and see her beginning to distort her personality by developing an unconscious bitterness toward white people; when you have to concoct an answer for a five-year-old son who is asking, "Daddy, why do white people treat colored people so mean?"; when you take a cross-country drive and find it necessary to sleep night after night in the uncomfortable corners of your automobile because no motel will accept you; when you are humiliated day in and day out by nagging signs reading "white" and "colored"; when your first name becomes "nigger," your middle name becomes "boy" (however old you are) and your last name becomes "John," and your wife and mother are never given the respected title "Mrs."; when you are harried by day and haunted by night by the fact that you are a Negro, living constantly at tiptoe stance, never quite knowing what to expect next, and are plagued with inner fears and outer resentments; when you are forever fighting a degenerating sense of "nobodiness"—then you will understand why we find it difficult to wait. There comes a time when the cup of endurance runs over, and men are no longer willing to be plunged into the abyss of despair. I hope, sirs, you can understand our legitimate and unavoidable impatience.

You express a great deal of anxiety over our willingness to break laws. This is certainly a legitimate concern. Since we so diligently urge people to obey the Supreme Court's decision of 1954 outlawing segregation in the public schools, at first glance it may seem rather paradoxical for us consciously to break laws. One may well ask: "How can you advocate breaking some laws and obeying others?" The answer lies in the fact that there are two types of laws: just and unjust. I would be the first to advocate obeying just laws. One has not only a legal but a moral responsibility to obey just laws. Conversely, one has a moral responsibility to disobey unjust laws. I would agree with St. Augustine that "an unjust law is no law at all." 15

Now, what is the difference between the two? How does one determine whether a law is just or unjust? A just law is a man-made code that squares with the moral law or the law of God. An unjust law is a code that is out of harmony with the moral law. To put it in the terms of St. Thomas Aquinas: An unjust law is a human law that is not rooted in eternal law and natural law. Any law that uplifts human personality is just. Any law that degrades human personality is unjust. All segregation statutes are unjust because segregation distorts the soul and damages the personality. It gives the segregator a false sense of superiority and the segregated a false sense of inferiority. Segregation, to use the terminology of the Jewish philosopher Martin Buber, substitutes an "I-it" relationship for an "I-thou" relationship and ends up relegating persons to the status of things. Hence segregation is not only politically, economically, and sociologically unsound, it is morally wrong and sinful. Paul Tillich has said that sin is separation. Is not segregation an existential expression of man's tragic separation, his awful estrangement, his terrible sinfulness? Thus it is that I can urge men to obey the 1954 decision of the Supreme Court, for it is morally right; and I can urge them to disobey segregation ordinances, for they are morally wrong. 16

Let us consider a more concrete example of just and unjust laws. An unjust law is a code that a numerical or power majority group compels a minority group to obey but does not make binding on itself. This is *difference* made legal. By the same 17 token, a just law is a code that a majority compels a minority to follow and that it is willing to follow itself. This is *sameness* made legal.

Let me give another explanation. A law is unjust if it is inflicted on a minority that, as a result of being denied the right to vote, had no part in enacting or devising the law. Who can say that the legislature of Alabama which set up that state's segregation laws was democratically elected? Throughout Alabama all sorts of devious methods are used to prevent Negroes from becoming registered voters, and there are some counties in which, even though Negroes constitute a majority of the population, not a single Negro is registered. Can any law enacted under such circumstances be considered democratically structured? 18

Sometimes a law is just on its face and unjust in its application. For instance, I have been arrested on a charge of parading without a permit. Now, there is nothing wrong in having an ordinance which requires a permit for a parade. But such an ordinance becomes unjust when it is used to maintain segregation and to deny citizens the First-Amendment privilege of peaceful assembly and protest. 19

I hope you are able to see the distinction I am trying to point out. In no sense do I advocate evading or defying the law, as would the rabid segregationist. That would lead to anarchy. One who breaks an unjust law must do so openly, lovingly, and with a willingness to accept the penalty. I submit that an individual who breaks a law that conscience tells him is unjust, and who willingly accepts the penalty of imprisonment in order to arouse the conscience of the community over its injustice, is in reality expressing the highest respect for law. 20

Of course, there is nothing new about this kind of civil disobedience. It was evidenced sublimely in the refusal of Shadrach, Meshach, and Abednego to obey the laws of Nebuchadnezzar, on the ground that a higher moral law was at stake. It was practiced superbly by the early Christians, who were willing to face hungry lions and the excruciating pain of chopping blocks rather than submit to certain unjust laws of the Roman Empire. To a degree, academic freedom is a reality today because Socrates practiced 21 civil disobedience. In our own nation, the Boston Tea Party represented a massive act of civil disobedience.

We should never forget that everything Adolf Hitler did in Germany was "legal" and everything the Hungarian freedom fighters did in Hungary was "illegal." It was "illegal" to aid and comfort a Jew in Hitler's Germany. Even so, I am sure that, had I lived in Germany at the time, I would have aided and comforted my Jewish brothers. If today I lived in a Communist country where certain principles dear to the Christian faith are suppressed, I would openly advocate disobeying that country's anti-religious laws. 22

I must make two honest confessions to you, my Christian and Jewish brothers. First, I must confess that over the past few years I have been gravely disappointed with the white moderate. I have almost reached the regrettable conclusion that the Negro's great stumbling block in his stride toward freedom is not the White Citizen's Counciler or the Ku Klux Klanner, but the white moderate, who is more devoted to "order" than to justice; who prefers a negative peace which is the absence of tension to a positive peace which is the presence of justice; who constantly says, "I agree with you in the goal you seek, but I cannot agree with your methods of direct action"; who paternalistically believes he can set the timetable for another man's freedom; who lives by a mythical concept of time and who constantly advises the Negro to wait for a "more convenient season." Shallow understanding from people of good will is more frustrating than absolute misunderstanding from people of ill will. Lukewarm acceptance is much more bewildering than outright rejection. 23

I had hoped that the white moderate would understand that law and order exist for the purpose of establishing justice and that when they fail in this purpose they become the dangerously structured dams that block the flow of social progress. I had hoped that the white moderate would understand that the present tension in the South is a necessary phase of the transition from an obnoxious negative peace, in which the Negro passively accepted his unjust plight, to a substantive and positive peace, in which all men will respect the dignity and worth of human 24 personality. Actually, we who engage in nonviolent direct action are not the creators of tension. We merely bring to the surface the hidden tension that is already alive. We bring it out in the open, where it can be seen and dealt with. Like a boil that can never be cured so long as it is covered up but must be opened with all its ugliness to the natural medicines of air and light, injustice must be exposed, with all the tension its exposure creates, to the light of human conscience and the air of national opinion, before it can be cured.

In your statement you assert that our actions, even though peaceful, must be condemned because they precipitate violence. 25
But is this a logical assertion? Isn't this like condemning a robbed man because his possession of money precipitated the evil act of robbery? Isn't this like condemning Socrates because his unswerving commitment to truth and his philosophical inquiries precipitated the act by the misguided populace in which they made him drink hemlock? Isn't this like condemning Jesus because his unique God-consciousness and never-ceasing devotion to God's will precipitated the evil act of crucifixion? We must come to see that, as the federal courts have consistently affirmed, it is wrong to urge an individual to cease his efforts to gain his basic constitutional rights because the quest may precipitate violence. Society must protect the robbed and punish the robber.

I had also hoped that the white moderate would reject the 26
myth concerning time in relation to the struggle for freedom. I have just received a letter from a white brother in Texas. He writes: "All Christians know that the colored people will receive equal rights eventually, but it is possible that you are in too great a religious hurry. It has taken Christianity almost two thousand years to accomplish what it has. The teachings of Christ take time to come to earth." Such an attitude stems from a tragic misconception of time, from the strangely irrational notion that there is something in the very flow of time that will inevitably cure all ills. Actually, time itself is neutral; it can be used either destructively or constructively. More and more I feel that the people of ill will have used time much more effectively than have the people of good will. We will have to repent in this generation not merely for

the hateful words and actions of the bad people, but for the appalling silence of the good people. Human progress never rolls in on wheels of inevitability; it comes through the tireless efforts of men willing to be co-workers with God, and without this hard work, time itself becomes an ally of the forces of social stagnation. We must use time creatively, in the knowledge that the time is always ripe to do right. Now is the time to make real the promise of democracy and transform our pending national elegy into a creative psalm of brotherhood. Now is the time to lift our national policy from the quicksand of racial injustice to the solid rock of human dignity.

You speak of our activity in Birmingham as extreme. At first I 27
was rather disappointed that fellow clergymen would see my nonviolent efforts as those of an extremist. I began thinking about the fact that I stand in the middle of two opposing forces in the Negro community. One is a force of complacency, made up in part of Negroes who, as a result of long years of oppression, are so drained of self-respect and a sense of "somebodiness" that they have adjusted to segregation; and in part of a few middle-class Negroes who, because of a degree of academic and economic security and because in some ways they profit by segregation, have become insensitive to the problems of the masses. The other force is one of bitterness and hatred, and it comes perilously close to advocating violence. It is expressed in the various black nationalist groups that are springing up across the nation, the largest and best-known being Elijah Muhammad's Muslim movement. Nourished by the Negro's frustration over the continued existence of racial discrimination, this movement is made up of people who have lost faith in America, who have absolutely repudiated Christianity, and who have concluded that the white man is an incorrigible "devil."

I have tried to stand between these two forces, saying that we 28
need emulate neither the "do-nothingism" of the complacent nor the hatred and despair of the black nationalist. For there is the more excellent way of love and nonviolent protest. I am grateful to God that, through the influence of the Negro church, the way of nonviolence became an integral part of our struggle.

If this philosophy had not emerged, by now many streets of the South would, I am convinced, be flowing with blood. And I am further convinced that if our white brothers dismiss as "rabble-rousers" and "outside agitators" those of us who employ nonviolent direct action, and if they refuse to support our nonviolent efforts, millions of Negroes will, out of frustration and despair, seek solace and security in black-nationalist ideologies—a development that would inevitably lead to a frightening racial nightmare. 29

Oppressed people cannot remain oppressed forever. The yearning for freedom eventually manifests itself, and that is what has happened to the American Negro. Something within has reminded him of his birthright of freedom, and something without has reminded him that it can be gained. Consciously or unconsciously, he has been caught up by the *Zeitgeist*, and with his black brothers of Africa and his brown and yellow brothers of Asia, South America, and the Caribbean, the United States Negro is moving with a sense of great urgency toward the promised land of racial justice. If one recognizes this vital urge that has engulfed the Negro community, one should readily understand why public demonstrations are taking place. The Negro has many pent-up resentments and latent frustrations, and he must release them. So let him march; let him make prayer pilgrimages to the city hall; let him go on freedom rides—and try to understand why he must do so. If his repressed emotions are not released in nonviolent ways, they will seek expression through violence; this is not a threat but a fact of history. So I have not said to my people, "Get rid of your discontent." Rather, I have tried to say that this normal and healthy discontent can be channeled into the creative outlet of nonviolent direct action. And now this approach is being termed extremist. 30

But though I was initially disappointed at being categorized as an extremist, as I continued to think about the matter I gradually gained a measure of satisfaction from the label. Was not Jesus an extremist for love: "Love your enemies, bless them that curse you, do good to them that hate you, and pray for them which despitefully use you, and persecute you." Was not Amos 31 an extremist for justice: "Let justice roll down like waters and righteousness like an ever-flowing stream." Was not Paul an extremist for the Christian gospel: "I bear in my body the marks of the Lord Jesus." Was not Martin Luther an extremist: "Here I stand; I cannot do otherwise, so help me God." And John Bunyan: "I will stay in jail to the end of my days before I make a butchery of my conscience." And Abraham Lincoln: "This nation cannot survive half slave and half free." And Thomas Jefferson: "We hold these truths to be self-evident, that all men are created equal. . . ." So the question is not whether we will be extremists, but what kind of extremists we will be. Will we be extremists for hate or for love? Will we be extremists for the preservation of injustice or for the extension of justice? In that dramatic scene on Calvary's hill three men were crucified. We must never forget that all three were crucified for the same crime—the crime of extremism. Two were extremists for immorality, and thus fell below their environment. The other, Jesus Christ, was an extremist for love, truth, and goodness, and thereby rose above his environment. Perhaps the South, the nation, and the world are in dire need of creative extremists.

I had hoped that the white moderate would see this need. 32
Perhaps I was too optimistic; perhaps I expected too much. I suppose I should have realized that few members of the oppressor race can understand the deep groans and passionate yearnings of the oppressed race, and still fewer have the vision to see that injustice must be rooted out by strong, persistent, and determined action. I am thankful, however, that some of our white brothers in the South have grasped the meaning of this social revolution and committed themselves to it. They are still all too few in quantity, but they are big in quality. Some—such as Ralph McGill, Lillian Smith, Harry Golden, James McBride Dabbs, Anne Braden, and Sarah Patton Boyle—have written about our struggle in eloquent and prophetic terms. Others have marched with us down nameless streets of the South. They have languished in filthy, roach-infested jails, suffering the abuse and brutality of policemen who view them as "dirty nigger-lovers." Unlike so many of their moderate brothers and sisters, they have recognized the urgency of the

moment and sensed the need for powerful "action" antidotes to combat the disease of segregation.

Let me take note of my other major disappointment. I have been so greatly disappointed with the white church and its leadership. Of course, there are some notable exceptions. I am not unmindful of the fact that each of you has taken some significant stands on this issue. I commend you, Reverend Stallings, for your Christian stand on this past Sunday, in welcoming Negroes to your worship service on a nonsegregated basis. I commend the Catholic leaders of this state for integrating Spring Hill College several years ago. 33

But despite these notable exceptions, I must honestly reiterate that I have been disappointed with the church. I do not say this as one of those negative critics who can always find something wrong with the church. I say this as a minister of the gospel, who loves the church; who was nurtured in its bosom; who has been sustained by its spiritual blessings and who will remain true to it as long as the cord of life shall lengthen. 34

When I was suddenly catapulted into the leadership of the bus protest in Montgomery, Alabama, a few years ago, I felt we would be supported by the white church. I felt that the white ministers, priests, and rabbis of the South would be among our strongest allies. Instead, some have been outright opponents, refusing to understand the freedom movement and misrepresenting its leaders; all too many others have been more cautious than courageous and have remained silent behind the anesthetizing security of stained glass windows. 35

In spite of my shattered dreams, I came to Birmingham with the hope that the white religious leadership of this community would see the justice of our cause and, with deep moral concern, would serve as the channel through which our just grievances could reach the power structure. I had hoped that each of you would understand. But again I have been disappointed. 36

I have heard numerous southern religious leaders admonish their worshipers to comply with a desegregation decision because it is the law, but I have longed to hear white ministers declare: "Follow this decree because integration is morally right and be- 37 cause the Negro is your brother." In the midst of blatant injustices inflicted upon the Negro, I have watched white churchmen stand on the sideline and mouth pious irrelevancies and sanctimonious trivialities. In the midst of a mighty struggle to rid our nation of racial and economic injustice I have heard many ministers say: "Those are social issues, with which the gospel has no real concern." And I have watched many churches commit themselves to a completely otherworldly religion which makes a strange, unBiblical distinction between body and soul, between the sacred and the secular.

I have traveled the length and breadth of Alabama, 38
Mississippi, and all the other southern states. On sweltering summer days and crisp autumn mornings I have looked at the South's beautiful churches with their lofty spires pointing heavenward. I have beheld the impressive outlines of her massive religious-education buildings. Over and over I have found myself asking: "What kind of people worship here? Who is their God? Where were their voices when the lips of Governor Barnett dripped with words of interposition and nullification? Where were they when Governor Wallace gave a clarion call for defiance and hatred? Where were their voices of support when bruised and weary Negro men and women decided to rise from the dark dungeons of complacency to the bright hills of creative protest?"

Yes, these questions are still in my mind. In deep disappoint- 39
ment I have wept over the laxity of the church. But be assured that my tears have been tears of love. There can be no deep disappointment where there is not deep love. Yes, I love the church. How could I do otherwise? I am in the rather unique position of being the son, the grandson, and the great-grandson of preachers. Yes, I see the church as the body of Christ. But, oh! How we have blemished and scarred that body through social neglect and through fear of being nonconformists.

There was a time when the church was very powerful—in the 40
time when the early Christians rejoiced at being deemed worthy to suffer for what they believed. In those days the church was not merely a thermometer that recorded the ideas and principles of popular opinion; it was a thermostat that transformed the mores

of society. Whenever the early Christians entered a town, the people in power became disturbed and immediately sought to convict the Christians for being "disturbers of the peace" and "outside agitators." But the Christians pressed on, in the conviction that they were "a colony of heaven," called to obey God rather than man. Small in number, they were big in commitment. They were too God-intoxicated to be "astronomically intimidated." By their effort and example they brought an end to such ancient evils as infanticide and gladiatorial contests.

Things are different now. So often the contemporary church is 41 a weak, ineffectual voice with an uncertain sound. So often it is an archdefender of the status quo. Far from being disturbed by the presence of the church, the power structure of the average community is consoled by the church's silent—and often even vocal—sanction of things as they are.

But the judgment of God is upon the church as never before. 42 If today's church does not recapture the sacrificial spirit of the early church, it will lose its authenticity, forfeit the loyalty of millions, and be dismissed as an irrelevant social club with no meaning for the twentieth century. Every day I meet young people whose disappointment with the church has turned into outright disgust.

Perhaps I have once again been too optimistic. Is organized 43 religion too inextricably bound to the status quo to save our nation and the world? Perhaps I must turn my faith to the inner spiritual church, the church within the church, as the true *ekklesia* and the hope of the world. But again I am thankful to God that some noble souls from the ranks of organized religion have broken loose from the paralyzing chains of conformity and joined us as active partners in the struggle for freedom. They have left their secure congregations and walked the streets of Albany, Georgia, with us. They have gone down the highways of the South on tortuous rides for freedom. Yes, they have gone to jail with us. Some have been dismissed from their churches, have lost the support of their bishops and fellow ministers. But they have acted in the faith that right defeated is stronger than evil triumphant. Their witness has been the spiritual salt that has preserved the true meaning of the gospel in these troubled times. They have carved a tunnel of hope through the dark mountain of disappointment.

I hope the church as a whole will meet the challenge of this decisive hour. But even if the church does not come to the aid of justice, I have no despair about the future. I have no fear about the outcome of our struggle in Birmingham, even if our motives are at present misunderstood. We will reach the goal of freedom in Birmingham and all over the nation, because the goal of America is freedom. Abused and scorned though we may be, our destiny is tied up with America's destiny. Before the pilgrims landed at Plymouth, we were here. Before the pen of Jefferson etched the majestic words of the Declaration of Independence across the pages of history, we were here. For more than two centuries our forebears labored in this country without wages; they made cotton king; they built the homes of their masters while suffering gross injustice and shameful humiliation—and yet out of a bottomless vitality they continued to thrive and develop. If the inexpressible cruelties of slavery could not stop us, the opposition we now face will surely fail. We will win our freedom because the sacred heritage of our nation and the eternal will of God are embodied in our echoing demands. 44

Before closing I feel impelled to mention one other point in your statement that has troubled me profoundly. You warmly commended the Birmingham police force for keeping "order" and "preventing violence." I doubt that you would have so warmly commended the police force if you had seen its dogs sinking their teeth into unarmed, nonviolent Negroes. I doubt that you would so quickly commend the policemen if you were to observe their ugly and inhumane treatment of Negroes here in the city jail; if you were to watch them push and curse old Negro women and young Negro girls; if you were to see them slap and kick old Negro men and young boys; if you were to observe them, as they did on two occasions, refuse to give us food because we wanted to sing our grace together. I cannot join you in your praise of the Birmingham police department. 45

It is true that the police have exercised a degree of discipline in handling the demonstrators. In this sense they have conducted 46 themselves rather "nonviolently" in public. But for what purpose? To preserve the evil system of segregation. Over the past few years I have consistently preached that nonviolence demands that the means we use must be as pure as the ends we seek. I have tried to make clear that it is wrong to use immoral means to attain moral ends. But now I must affirm that it is just as wrong, or perhaps even more so, to use moral means to preserve immoral ends. Perhaps Mr. Connor and his policemen have been rather nonviolent in public, as was Chief Pritchett in Albany, Georgia, but they have used the moral means of nonviolence to maintain the immoral end of racial injustice. As T. S. Eliot has said, "The last temptation is the greatest treason: To do the right deed for the wrong reason."

I wish you had commended the Negro sit-inners and 47
demonstrators of Birmingham for their sublime courage, their willingness to suffer, and their amazing discipline in the midst of great provocation. One day the South will recognize its real heroes. They will be the James Merediths, with the noble sense of purpose that enables them to face jeering and hostile mobs, and with the agonizing loneliness that characterizes the life of the pioneer. They will be old, oppressed, battered Negro women, symbolized in a seventy-two-year-old woman in Montgomery, Alabama, who rose up with a sense of dignity and with her people decided not to ride segregated buses, and who responded with ungrammatical profundity to one who inquired about her weariness: "My feets is tired, but my soul is at rest." They will be the young high school and college students, the young ministers of the gospel and a host of their elders, courageously and nonviolently sitting in at lunch counters and willingly going to jail for conscience' sake. One day the South will know that when these disinherited children of God sat down at lunch counters, they were in reality standing up for what is best in the American dream and for the most sacred values in our Judaeo-Christian heritage, thereby bringing our nation back to those great wells of democracy which were dug deep by the founding fathers in their formulation of the Constitution and the Declaration of Independence.

Never before have I written so long a letter. I'm afraid it is much too long to take your precious time. I can assure you that it would have been shorter if I had been writing from a comfortable desk, but what else can one do when he is alone in a narrow jail cell, other than write long letters, think long thoughts, and pray long prayers? 48

If I have said anything in this letter that overstates the truth and indicates an unreasonable impatience, I beg you to forgive me. If I have said anything that understates the truth and indicates my having a patience that allows me to settle for anything less than brotherhood, I beg God to forgive me. 49

I hope this letter finds you strong in faith. I also hope that circumstances will soon make it possible for me to meet each of you, not as an integrationist or a civil-rights leader but as a fellow clergyman and a Christian brother. Let us all hope that the dark clouds of racial prejudice will soon pass away and the deep fog of misunderstanding will be lifted from our fear-drenched communities, and in some not too distant tomorrow the radiant stars of love and brotherhood will shine over our great nation with all their scintillating beauty. 50

Yours for the cause of Peace and Brotherhood,
MARTIN LUTHER KING, JR.

## *Meaning and Purpose*

1. Of what significance is it that King writes his letter from jail?
2. In paragraph 1, King says that he seldom pauses "to answer criticism." Why does he do so here?
3. How does King justify the demonstrations? Why does he claim that the time for negotiation is past?
4. How does King respond to the admonition that the time for racial equality is not now, that he should "wait" until the time is right?
5. Describe King's distinction between just and unjust laws. What justifications does he use to advocate breaking unjust laws?

6. How does King turn the accusation of being an extremist from a criticism to praise?

## *Strategy*

1. In paragraph 1, King clearly establishes the setting in which he is writing the letter and addresses his intended readers as "men of genuine good will." Why?
2. Where does King address the clergymen's objections to his activities in Birmingham? How does he refute them? How do his refutations figure in the construction of his own essay?
3. Does King appeal to reason or emotion in his argument? Explain the effectiveness of his appeal, and give examples from the essay.
4. The last three paragraphs don't further King's argument. What do they do?

## *Style*

1. Reread paragraph 14. The sentence beginning "But when you have seen" is more than 300 words long. Discuss its effectiveness and its emotional effect. What does King do to keep such a long sentence clear?
2. Find some metaphors in King's letter and explain how he uses them.
3. If necessary, check a dictionary for the meanings of these words: *provincial* (4); *gainsaying* (6); *gadflies* (10); *millennium*, *lamentably* (12); *abyss* (14); *anarchy* (20); *elegy* (26); *incorrigible* (27); *sanctimonious* (37); *interposition*, *clarion* (38); *laxity* (39); *mores* (40); *inextricably* (43); *scintillating* (50).

## *Writing Tasks*

1 Write a persuasive essay illustrating King's statement in paragraph 4: "Injustice anywhere is a threat to justice everywhere."

Think of an example of injustice and argue that it has implications beyond that case.

2. Think of a situation in which you feel that some person or group is being unjustly opposed, such as freshman students not being allowed some privilege that upperclassmen are allowed. In a brief essay, argue for a course of action that resolves the injustice. Who is your audience? What kind of appeal will you choose, and with what kind of evidence will you support your argument?

## ❦ Andrew Klavan ❦

*Andrew Klavan, born in 1954, is a two-time Edgar Award-winner who writes under three names. As Keith Peterson and Margaret Tracy he writes detective novels, mysteries, and thrillers. Some of these include the highly acclaimed John Wells mysteries:* The Trapdoor, There Fell a Shadow, The Rain, *and* Rough Justice. *As Andrew Klavan, he is a well-known screenwriter and journalist. His most recent novel is* True Crime *(1994). A former resident of New York City, Klavan now lives in Great Britain with his wife and family.*

# *The Shrieking of the Lambs*

*This essay, first published in the June–September 1994 issue of the* Boston Review, *contends that fictional violence, now under constant attack by would-be censors, must not be defended. Rather, fictional violence must be celebrated.*

*Klavan's point of view is, if anything, unconventional. Read his essay critically to determine how convincing the points of his argument are.*

---

I love the sound of people screaming. Women screaming—with their clothes torn—as they run down endless hallways with some bogeyman in hot pursuit. Men, in their priapic cars, screaming as the road ends, as the fender plummets towards fiery oblivion under their wild eyes. Children? I'm a little squeamish about children, but okay, sure. I'll take screaming children too. And I get off on gunshots—machine gun shots goading a corpse into a posthumous jitterbug; and the coital jerk and plunge of a butcher knife; and axes; even claws, if you happen to have them. 1

Yes, yes, yes, only in stories. Of course; in fictions only: novels, TV shows, films. I've loved the scary, gooey stuff since I was a child. I've loved monsters, shootouts, bluddy murther; Women In Jeopardy (as they say in Hollywood); the slasher in the closet; the intruder's shadow that spreads up the bedroom wall like a stain. 2

And now, having grown to man's estate, I make a very good living writing these things: thriller novels like *Don't Say A Word*, which begins with a nice old lady getting dusted and ends with an assault on a child, and *The Animal Hour* which features a woman's head being severed and stuffed into a commode.

Is it vicious? Disgusting? Sexist? Sick? Tough luck, it's my imagination—sometimes it is—and it's my readers' too—always, for all I know. And when they and I get together, when we dodge down that electric alleyway of the human skull where only murder is delight—well then, my friend, it's showtime. 3

But enough about me, let's talk about death. Cruel death, sexy death, exciting death: death, that is, on the page and on the screen. Because this is not a defense of violence in fiction, it's a celebration of it. And not a moment too soon either. 4

Hard as it is for a sane man to believe, fictional violence is under attack. Again. Floundering in a mean street America where bigots and enablers dither while the malicious play catch with live ammo, where one interest group calls a machine gun a hunting weapon and another calls a kitchen knife a form of feminist expression, where children are stolen from their houses and killed and tourists are executed for the crime of getting lost on their way to Disneyworld, the folks back home have understandably panicked, and the unerring eye of political opportunism has once more found its scapegoat: those good people who make up scary stories to help you pass the time. This year's list of would-be censors trying to shoulder their way to the trough of celebrity is hardly worth enumerating: their 15 minutes might be up by the time I'm done. Film critic Michael Medved says cinematic violence is part of a pop culture "war on traditional values"; Congressman Edward Markey says television violence should be reduced or regulated; some of our less thoughtful feminists tried to quash the novel *American Psycho* because of its descriptions of violence toward women and even some more thoughtful, like Catherine MacKinnon, have fought for censorship in law, claiming that written descriptions of "penises slamming into vaginas" deprive actual human beings of their civil rights. 5

It's nonsense mostly, but it has the appeal of glamour, of flash. The "issue" of fictional violence lifts crime out of the impoverished, muddy-minded, rage-filled milieus in which it usually occurs, and superimposes it on the gaudy images manufactured in Hollywood and Manhattan. Instead of trying to understand the sad, banal, ignorant souls who generally pull the trigger in our society, we get to discuss Hannibal Lecter, Ice-T, penises, vaginas. It makes for good sound bytes, anyway—the all-American diet of 15 second thoughts. 6

But Britain—where I've come to live because I loathe real guns and political correctness—is far from exempt. Indeed, perhaps nowhere has there been a more telling or emblematic attack on fictional violence than is going on here right now. It is a textbook example of how easily pundits and politicians can channel honest grief and rage at a true crime into a senseless assault on the innocent tellers of tales. 7

It began here this time with the killing of a child by two other children. On 12 February, Jamie Bulger, a two-year-old toddler, was led out of a Merseyside shopping mall by two ten-year-olds—two little boys. The boys prodded and carried and tugged the increasingly distraught baby past dozens of witnesses who did not understand what they were seeing. When they reached a deserted railroad embankment, the two boys tortured, mutilated, and finally killed their captive for no reasons that anyone has been able to explain. 8

The explicit testimony at the trial last November verged on the unbearable. Even the more restrained newspapers could not be read without nausea and tears. And looking at the photographs of the killers—two sweetly mischievous Just William faces, Lords of the Flies in their Sunday best—there arose, in me, in everyone I spoke to, the desperate urge to understand, to grasp, to know: *What? What is it? What rough beast, its hour come round at last?* 9

At first, the pundits did their best to answer but the answers seemed miserably inadequate. Psychiatrists noted the fierce sibling rivalry felt by one of the killers; sociologists noted the broken homes, the poverty, the family violence; columnists talked about 10 the breakdown of society; one gay writer blamed everything on the pressures of heterosexual manhood; even the usually brilliant Martin Amis weighed in with a rather sleepy piece on the dissipation of moral energy in the west. And it wasn't just the media flailing about. At dinner parties, we daringly ventured to talk about Evil, and then let our voices trail off to nothing. At home, we tried to be nicer to our children—until the little pests caught on and began to run riot. And in almost any pub, you could hear it explained how the murderers were demon freaks of nature—an opinion that seemed a lot less ridiculous and a lot more comforting than by any rights it should've done.

But the nation's search for an answer, its grief and disgust, its 11
sense of social despair, did not resolve themselves upon a single issue until the trial judge pronounced sentence. "It is not for me to pass judgment on their upbringing," Mr. Justice Morland said of the boys as he sentenced them to be detained at Her Majesty's pleasure. "But I suspect exposure to violent video films may in part be an explanation."

No one knew why he said such a thing. There had been spec- 12
ulation in some of the papers that *Child's Play 3*, which had been rented by one of the killers' fathers, had given the son ideas. But there was no testimony at the trial, no evidence presented showing that the boy had seen it or that it had had a contributing effect. Detective Superintendent Albert Kirby, who headed the investigation into the murder, said "the area of videos was one we looked very closely at" but that no link had been established by the police at all.

It didn't matter. As far as journalists were concerned, as far as 13
public debate was concerned, "video nasties," as they are called here, became the central issue of the case. Forget the subconscious, the broken home, the poverty, the family cruelty, the breakdown of western society, even the trials of masculinity and the moral energy stuff. For the next few days, the newspapers were splattered with stories about *Child's Play 3* as writers combed the film for tenuous connections between the rampages of the movie's devil doll Chucky and the savage attack perpetrated by the Merseyside rails. In the aftermath, the British opening of the film *The Good Son*, starring Macauley Culkin as an evil child, was

canceled. The video release of *Reservoir Dogs* was indefinitely postponed. Twenty-five doctors and academics who had previously dismissed the effects of screen violence made front page news with a mea culpa report saying their liberal ideals had made them naive. Action was called for, and Liberal Democrat MP David Alton answered the call on the run. With the backing of rebel Tories, Alton nearly pushed through a proposal that even the country's chief censor said would prevent the video release of "half the films made in the last quarter century and some of the greatest films ever made." The Alton bill was only tabled when Home Secretary Michael Howard reluctantly agreed to implement some Draconian restrictions of his own. From hereon in, if you rent *My Cousin Vinny* to an 11-year-old, you're looking at jail time, mate.

And why not? Now, thanks to Mr. Justice Morland and an eager press, we finally know what we are seeing when we look upon the rampaging fire of violence in our society: we are seeing the effects of fiction on us. Got it? Our leaders are either mindless ideologues or soulless bureaucrats. Our cultural heritage is under attack by morons who stand on the shoulders of giants and think that they can fly. Our moral verities are crumbling by the hour. Our families are shattering. Our gods are dead. The best lack all conviction while the worst are full of passionate intensity. 14

And it's all Chucky's fault. 15

The instinct to censor is the tragic flaw of utopian minds. "Our first job," said Plato in his classic attack on the democratic system, "is to oversee the work of the story-writers, and to accept any good stories they write, but reject the others." Because the perfectibility of human society is a fiction itself, it comes under threat from other, more believable fictions, especially those fictions which document and employ the cruel, the chaotic, the Dionysian for their thrills. It's a form of homeopathic magic really. (A point once made by the magician Teller of Penn and Teller in an op-ed piece in *The New York Times*.) The chants and rituals of that old witchcraft are gone, but the template of belief remains in the censor's mind: if you erase the image, he tells us, you will magically erase the thing itself. 16

And this superstitious fallacy plays into some prevailing fallacies of academic and political theory: the idea that language is the way we understand the world, that metaphor generates consciousness and imagery fashions our feelings and choices, that a work, an author, a reader are wholly constructed of the influences they wreak upon each other. Under such theories, literature becomes an action taken with potentially harmful or beneficial effects on the society and politics of the age (rather than, say, a sight to be seen like a sunset or a mountain range). Again, with their isomorphic links between image and reality, such theories can lead to a sort of homeopathic magic in materialist guise. 17

Yet one can understand the appeal of these intricate alchemies. With their emphasis on interpretation, they allow critics to sublimate their frustration at not being artists. With their urgent dashes for control of the shaping culture, they allow artists to feel they are engaged in struggles of great pith and moment. In general, they allow all of us who sit in lonesome rooms fiddling with language to feel a little bit more like Vaclav Havel and a little bit less like Bobo the Juggling Clown. Very tempting stuff, especially in a nation which largely refuses to make martyrs of its literati and so deprives them of political heroism; leaves them instead to splash about like trained seals in the shallow waters of commercial failure and success. 18

Fortunately for our purposes, however, a seal's life is exactly the life for me. I'm just a simple barefoot spinner of yarns plying my wares from town to town. I don't know nothing about birthing a perfect society. For me to engage the latterday Platos on their own materialist, political terms would be to be sucked in to a form of dialogue that does not reflect the reality I know—and know I know. Because personally, I understand the world not through language but through an unfathomable spirit and an infinite mind. I sit down through an urge and with a talent as basic to my personality as inborn personality itself. With language as a rude tool I try to convey a shadow of the world my imagination makes of the world at large. I do this for money and pleasure and to win the admiration of women. And when, in an uncertain hour, I crave the palliative of meaning, I remind myself that people's souls 19 run opposite to their bodies and grow more childlike as they mature—and so I have built, in my work, little places where those souls can go to play.

The proper response to anyone who would shut these playgrounds down for any reason—to anyone who confuses these playgrounds with the real world—is not the specious language of theory or logic or even the law. It's the language of the spirit, of celebration and screed, of jeremiad and hallelujah. Of this. 20

Now I would not say that my fictions—any fictions—have no effect on real life. Or that books, movies and TV are mere regurgitations of what's going on in the society around them. These arguments, frequently advanced by violence-meisters such as *Death Wish* director Michael Winner, strike me as disingenuous and self-defeating. Rather, the relationship between fiction and humanity's unconscious is so complex, so resonant, and even stichomythic that it is impossible to isolate one from the other in terms of cause and effect. The gentle family man enjoys a day at the beach with *Red Dragon*, the assassin cuddles up with *Catcher In The Rye*. Writers in Ceausescu's murderous Roumania weren't allowed to admit that homegrown murder even existed while the civilized and liberalizing high Victorians made a bestseller out of *Dracula*, in which babies are devoured by women and women are devoured by wolves. (Interestingly, Bram Stoker made virtually the same argument in favor of censoring pornography as has Catherine MacKinnon. He feared it would incite the susceptible sex to crime: "Women are the worst offenders in this form of breach of moral law," said Bram.) 21

Perhaps it is true that children, sociopaths, and American academics should be protected, in their emotional immaturity, from the more vicious and explicit imagery of fiction. I know I wouldn't want any of them reading my books, and would support sane and limited measures to keep them out of their hands. But for the rest of us, who can honestly say why a film like *Psycho* inspires a sort of moral mourning in me, whereas the Bible inspires David Koresh to be, well, David Koresh? The studies are always suspect and seem to change with the political winds. Last week, a new 22 study here purported to show a relation between child violence and video nasties. This week, a new study claimed to show that criminals watched the same things as everyone else. It all depends on how you slice it, as it were.

So fiction and reality do interact, but we don't know how, not at all. And since we don't understand the effect of one upon the other—or, that is, the effect seems to be so individualistic, to depend so much upon the specific work and person at the moment they connect—whence arises this magical certainty that violence in fiction begets violence in real life like one of those old 3D films that promised to "leap off the screen?" 23

The answer seems to come straight out of the pages of Sigmund Freud. Or St. Paul if you prefer: "Wherein thou judgest another, thou condemnest thyself." It's *Psychology 1A*, but that doesn't negate the truth of it: that pleasure which is unknowingly repressed is outwardly condemned. The censor always attacks the images that secretly appeal to him or her the most. The assault on violent fiction is not really an attempt to root out the causes of violence—no one can seriously believe that. The attempt to censor fictional violence is a guilt-ridden slap at ourselves, in the guise of a mythical *them*, for taking such pleasure in make-believe acts that, in real life, would be reprehensible. How—we seem to be asking ourselves—how, in a world in which Jamie Bulger dies so young, can we kick back with a beer at night and enjoy a couple of hours of *Child's Play 3*? How can a man who has to fear so for his wife or daughter read *American Psycho* with such a goofy simper? How can a woman who tries to teach her children to negotiate the world in peace cheer like a maniac for the marauding cruelties of *Thelma and Louise*? 24

How can we enjoy this stuff so much? So very much. 25

Not all of us perhaps. I'm forever being told that there are people who'd rather not take violence with their fiction—although I wonder how many would say so if you included the delicate violence of an Agatha Christie or the "literary" violence of, say, Hemingway and Faulkner. But even if we accept the exceptions, even if we limit the field to real gore, it does seem to me that the numbers are incredible, the attraction truly profound. 26

For instance, in the years when we could not afford to go to the movies, my wife and I would read aloud to each other: a mutual entertainment that could be stretched over several days. Once, I picked out what looked like a cheap horror novel by an author I'd never heard of. We began reading it right after dinner. Around nine o'clock, we hit the scene where a little boy was sacrificed and gutted by the factotum of a vampire. It was about four a.m. before we reached the part where a priest was forced to guzzle the spurting blood from the vampire's chest. Long after dawn, hoarse and wide-eyed, we reached the novel's apocalyptic conclusion. Even my wife—who generally does avoid this sort of thing—agreed that it was one of the most wonderfully ugly and frightening things we'd ever read. 27

For months afterward, I asked every reader I knew if they had ever heard of the book, *Salem's Lot*, or its author, Stephen King. None of them had. It had been nicely published but largely unpublicized. Later, the movie *Carrie* helped launch what has to be one of the most successful novelistic careers since Dickens. But even before that, all over the country, all over the world eventually, readers like me and my wife were steadily discovering the nausea and mayhem and terror of the man's vision. 28

The moral, I mean, is this: To construct a bloodsoaked nightmare of unrelenting horror is not an easy thing. But if you build it, they will come. 29

And so the maker of violent fiction—ho, ho—he walks among us in Nietzschean glee. He has bottled the Dionysian whirlwind and is selling it as a soft drink. Like the *hausfrau* who charmed her babes with descriptions of the dismembered brides in *The Robber Baron*, like deep-browed Homer, when he told of a spear protruding from a man's head with an eyeball fixed to the point, the violent storyteller knows that that gape of disgust on your respectable mug is really the look of love. You may denounce him, you may even censor him. You may just wrinkle your nose and walk away. But sooner or later, in one form or another, he knows you'll show up to see and listen to him—and if you don't, your children will, in droves. 30

Nothing can be more cruelly risible than watching experts debate a piece of fictional violence on American television, always pretending that they are above and exempt from the sweet glee that fiction provides. Is *American Psycho* an eroticized attack on womankind or an exploration of modern madness? Is *Falling Down* an incitement to murder minorities or a warning against the promptings of urban rage? The idea seems to be that whoever can impose a meaning on the fiction—a meaning which will support his cause or career—wins. 31

But fiction, like life, is not about its meanings. Like life, any good story can support any number of interpretations, many of them mutually exclusive, and many of them at odds with the author's purposes and peccadilloes. This is precisely why fiction causes single-minded political thinkers to stomp and gnash so much. Fiction lives or dies, not on its messages, but on the depth and power of the emotional experience it provides. And from the *gravitas* of the Aristotelian notion of catharsis to the pseudoscientific palaver of modern literary theory, an enormous amount of intellectual energy seems to have been expended in a failed attempt to suppress the central, disturbing and irreducible fact of this experience: it's fun. Like sex: it's lots of fun. We watch fictional people love and die and screw and suffer and weep for our pleasure. It gives us joy. 32

And we watch them kill too. And this seems to give us as much joy as anything. 33

All right, I suppose you can talk about the catharsis of terror, or the harmless release of our violent impulses. Those are plausible excuses, I guess. It doesn't take a genius to notice how often—practically always—it's the villain of a successful piece of violent art who becomes its icon. Hannibal Lecter and Leatherface, Freddy Kreuger and Dracula—these are the posters that go up on the wall, the characters that we remember. Several commentators have been disturbed by the fact that modern thrillers seem more and more to take the point of view of the bad guy rather than the hero, but perhaps that's just our increasing honesty about the nature of what's repressed. Plenty of kids have built plastic models of 34

Frankenstein's monster, but I don't know a single one who's ever built a model of a Tyrolean peasant with a torch.

So I suppose, if you must, you could say these creatures rep- 35
resent our buried feelings. Whether it's Medea or Jason (from *Friday The 13th*), the character who commits acts of savage violence always has the appeal of a Caliban: that thing of darkness that must be acknowledged as our own. Not that people are essentially violent, but that they are violent among other things and the violence has to be repressed. After all, if I could shoot my kids every time they were snotty and beat my wife every time she was right, I'd probably be St. Francis of Assisi in my spare time. But if you want to have a civilization, you've got to roll with the discontents. Some emotions must be repressed and repressed emotions return via the imagination in distorted and inflated forms: that's the law of benevolent hypocrisy, the law of civilized life. It is an unstated underpinning of utopian thought—what Nietzsche keenly called Socratic thought—that the repressed can be eliminated completely or denied or happily freed or remolded with the proper education. It can't. Forget about it. Cross it off your list of things to do. The monsters are always there in their cages. As Stephen King says, with engaging simplicity, his job is to take them out for a walk every now and then.

But again, this business of violent fiction as therapy—this 36
modern-jargon version of Aristotle—it's a defense, isn't it, as if these stories needed a reason for being. In order to celebrate violent fiction—I mean, *celebrate* it—it's the joy you've got to talk about. The joy of cruelty, the thrill of terror, the adrenaline of the hunter, the heartbeat of the deer—all reproduced in the safe playground of art. A joy indeed.

Americans don't seem to like that word much: joy. Every day, 37
some newspaper seems to publish some doctor's or sociologist's reasons why we should or shouldn't take our pleasure. It deadens our brain cells, it cleans our heart, it makes us live longer, it kills us. We need to know that smoke or drink or sport, sex or entertainment, is somehow medicinal before we allow it to take the edge off the miseries of existence. Even more, Americans, cultur-

ally puritanical and yet committed to the ideal of tolerance, like to tie themselves in knots trying to show that your pleasures are not good for *them*, that is, the society at large. As a culture, we seem unable to accept the words of our great philosopher, Dr. Seuss, who said—though admittedly in a wholly other context—"These things are fun, and fun is good."

When it comes to our messier, our somehow unseemly, plea- 38
sures, like fictional gore, we are downright embarrassed by our delight. But delight is certainly what it is. Nubile teens caught out *in flagrante* by a nutcase in a hockey mask? You bet it's erotic. Whole families tortured to death by a madman who's traced them through their vacation photos. Ee-yewwww. Goblins who jump out of the toilet to devour you ass first. Delightful stuff.

I remember when *The Exorcist* (still unavailable on video in 39
the UK) first came out over 20 years ago. The hype was extensive. The film's dramatization of a neurotic Catholic view of menarche was genuinely disgusting. Excitement in the seats ran high. Toward the climax of the picture, it all got to be too much. The fellow sitting next to me suddenly started to hyperventilate and I had to carry him out into the lobby. It was like a battlefield out there: girls sobbing, guys with their heads in their hands—a funny little mustachioed theater manager hopping from victim to victim with a stick of smelling salts. The lines to get in to the next show went around the block. I mean, we were having a *good* time now.

And we've always been that way. The myths of our ancient 40
gods, the lives of our medieval saints, the entertainments of our most civilized cultures have always included healthy doses of rape, cannibalism, evisceration, and general mayhem. Critics like Michael Medved complain that never before has it all been quite so graphic, especially on screen. We are becoming "desensitized" to bloodshed, he claims, and require more and more gore to excite our feelings. But when have human beings ever been particularly "sensitized" to fictional violence? The technology to create the illusion of bloodshed has certainly improved, but read *Titus Andronicus* with its wonderful stage direction. "Enter a messenger with two heads and a hand," read the orgasmic staking of Lucy in *Dracula*, read de Sade, for crying out loud. There were always

some pretty good indications of which way we'd go once we got our hands on the machinery.

Because we love it. It makes us do a little inner dance of excitement, tension, and release. What pains we go to to disguise that. With a "serious" violent work, like *Time's Arrow* or *Goodfellas*, we tell ourselves it's important, we say we thought it was good but we didn't really enjoy it—whatever that means. When we read the accounts of the Jamie Bulger case, when we watch the latest victims being dragged in pieces from the marketplace of Sarajevo, when we follow the next installment of the Menendez trial or the Amy Fisher case, we say we're out for information, a spur to political action, an insight into life—it's the *news* after all; it's really happening. 41

But violent fiction with its graver purposes, if any, concealed—fiction unadorned with overt messages or historical significance—rubs our noses in the fact that narratives of horror, murder, and gore are a blast, a gas. When Freddy Krueger disembowels someone in a geyser of blood, when Hannibal Lecter washes down his victim with a nice Chianti, even when the vicar merely shoots the colonel in the drawing room—the only possible reason for this non-real, non-meaningful event to occur is that it's going to afford us pleasure. Which leaves that pleasure obvious, exposed. It's the exposure, not the thrill, the censors want to get rid of. Again: celebration is the only defense. 42

And yet—I know—while I celebrate, the new, not-very much-improved Rome is burning. 43

Last year sometime, I had a conversation with a highly intelligent Scottish filmmaker who had just returned from New York. Both of us had recently seen Sylvester Stallone's mountaineering action picture *Cliffhanger*. I'd seen it in the placid upper class neighborhood of South Kensington, he'd seen it in a theater in Times Square. I had been thrilled by the movie's special effects and found the hilariously dopey script sweetly reminiscent of the comic books I'd read as a child. My friend had found the picture grimly disturbing. The Times Square theater had been filled with rowdy youths. Every time the bad guys killed someone, the 44 youths cheered—and when a woman was murdered, they howled with delight.

I freely confess that I would have been unable to enjoy the movie under those circumstances. Too damned noisy for one thing. And, all right, yes, as a repression fan I could only get off on the cruelty of the villains insofar as it fired my anticipation of the moment when Sly would cut those suckers down. Another audience could just as easily have been cheering the murders of Jews in *Schindler's List* or of blacks in *Mississippi Burning*. I understand that, and it would be upsetting and frightening to be surrounded by a crowd which seemed to have abandoned the non-negotiable values. 45

Michael Medved believes—not that one film produces one vicious act—but that a ceaseless barrage of anti-religion, anti-family, slap-happy gore films and fictions has contributed to the erosion of values so evident on 42nd Street. I don't know whether this is true or not—neither does he—but, as with the judge's remarks in the Bulger case, it strikes me as a very suspicious place to start. The postwar generation, in which these values went openly to the wall, was raised, after all, not on the films and books that are available now, but on the value-bloated pabulum of the 1950s. And Medved's old-fashioned values, to go by the interviews he gives, have not been noticeably eroded, though he's in the business of watching these things. Surely, the Scotsman's story illustrates that the problem lies not on the screen but in the seats, in the lives that have produced that audience. Fiction cannot make of people what life has not, good or evil. "Nothing ever becomes real till it is experienced," said Keats. "Even a proverb is no proverb to you till your Life has illustrated it." 46

But more to the point: though the Times Square crowd's reaction was scary—rude too—it was not necessarily harmful in itself, either to them or me. For all I know, it was a beneficial release of energy and hostility, good for the mental health. And in any case, it took place in the context of their experience of a fiction and so (outside of the unmannerly noise they made) was beyond my right to judge, approve, or condemn. Nobody has to explain his private pleasures to me. 47

Because fiction and reality are different. It seems appalling that anyone should have to say it, but it does need to be said. Fiction is not subject to the same moral restrictions as real life. It should remain absolutely free because, at whatever level, it is, like sex, a deeply personal experience engaged in by consent in the hope of anything from momentary release to satori. Like sex, it is available to fools and creeps and monsters, and that's life; that's tough. Because fiction is, like sex, at the core of our individual humanity. Stories are the basic building blocks of spiritual maturity. No one has any business messing with them. No one at all. 48

Reality, on the other hand, needs its limits, maintained by force if necessary, for the simple reason that there are actions that directly harm the safety and liberty of other people. They don't merely offend them; they don't just threaten their delicate sense of themselves; they *hurt* them—really painfully, a lot. Again, it seems wildly improbable that this should be forgotten, but Americans' current cultural discussions show every evidence that it has been. Just as fictions are being discussed as if they were actions (as when MacKinnon recently made the loony tune claim that she had been effectively raped in print), actual crimes and atrocities are being discussed as if they were cultural events, subject to aesthetic considerations. Trial lawyers won a lesser conviction for lady-killer Robert Chambers by claiming his victim was promiscuous; columnists defended dick-chopper Lorena Bobbit, saying it might be all right to mutilate a man in his sleep, provided he was a really nasty guy. The fellows who savaged Reginald Denny during the L.A. riots claim they were just part of the psychology of the mob. And the Menendez brothers based much of their defense on a portrayal of themselves as victims, a portrayal of their victims as abusers. These are all arguments appropriate to fiction only. Only in fiction are crimes mitigated by symbolism and individuals judged not for what they've done but because of what they represent. We can allow our sympathies with fictional characters to be excited more easily by illustrative circumstances because our sympathies depend upon the fact that *no one has really gotten hurt.* 49

Our thrills depend upon that as well. The woman who cheers when Louise (or is it Thelma?) shoots a would-be rapist who has 50 already put his hands up and his penis down is not the same as the columnist who supports such an act in real life, where it would be cold-blooded murder. The man who sports a hard-on after reading Bret Ellis's meticulous eviscerations is not the same as the guy who says "she asked for it," when hearing of an actual rape. To say that the reaction to fiction and the reaction to reality are on a continuum is moral nonsense. Every thought is on a continuum with every other. Reasonable distinctions along the continuum are the only moral game in town.

And fiction and real life must be distinguished from one another. The radical presumption of fiction is play, the radical presumption of real life is what Martin Amis called "the gentleness of human flesh." If we have lost the will to defend that gentleness, then God help us, because consigning Chucky to the flames is not going to bring it back. 51

One of the very best works of violent fiction to come along in the last few years is Thomas Harris's novel, *The Silence of the Lambs*. The story, inspired, like *Psycho*, by the real-life case of murderer Ed Gein, concerns the hunt for the serial killer Jame Gumb, a failed transsexual, who strips his female victims' flesh in order to create a woman costume in which he can clothe himself. Expertly worked as an entertainment, the novel brings us face to face with the necessary corollaries to the century's materialist, non-spiritual approach to the human body. Gumb, in his obsession with the outline of his own body, treats other people as outlines as well, as shapes, things, that he can use and transform at his will. But more than that, the book calls up our own materialist reactions to the flesh. All the ugliest violence in the book is committed against women who are already dead. Our disgust is excited not by the taking of human life, but only by the butchery of flesh that used to be human life. Even the victims themselves only balk at obeying the killer's commands when they realize what's going to happen after they're gone. And yet, what moral difference does it make what Gumb does to people once he's shot them? The horror of it is nightmarish, but its moral value is nil. Our reactions seem almost to confirm Gumb in his attitudes, and underscore 52 our flirtation with the rationalist cannibal Hannibal Lecter, the ultimate believer in humanity as meat.

When Harris introduces the killer's next victim—Catherine Martin—he presents us with a character whom we aren't meant to like very much. Rich, spoiled, arrogant, dissolute, Catherine is admirable only for the desperate cleverness she shows in her battle to stay alive. But for the rest of the novel—the attempt to rescue Catherine before it's too late—Harris depends on our fear for her, our identification with her, our deep desire to see her get out of this in one piece. The killer refers to Catherine as "It." But Harris has the artistic intelligence to know that we, the reader, will care and worry for her; if we don't, the story simply won't be any fun. 53

Harris allows us the forbidden kick of our identification with the *übermensch* Lecter whose intelligence, wit, and appreciation of fine music in no way prevent him from killing and feeding on the human race. At the same time, he relies on our irrational—spiritual—conviction that Catherine, irritating though she may be, must not be killed because . . . for no good reason: because she Must Not. Harris knowingly taps in to the purely emotional imperative we share with the book's heroine, Clarice Starling: like her, we won't be able to sleep until the screaming of innocent lambs is stopped. Harris makes pretty well sure of it. 54

At the end, in the only injection of auctorial opinion in the book, Harris wryly notes that the scholarly journals which include articles on the Gumb case never use the words *crazy* or *evil* in their discussions of the killer. The intellectual world is uncomfortable with the inherent Must-Not, the instinctive absolute, and the individual responsibility those words ultimately suggest. In short, though not killers themselves, these materialist thinkers share the moral blindness of their brilliant colleague Lecter, who really, in the end, has logic on his side. Harris, I think, is trying to argue that if we don't trust our mindless belief in the sanctity of human life, we produce monsters that the sleep of reason never dreamed of. *The Silence of the Lambs*, as the title suggests, is a dramatization of a world in which the spirit has lost its power to speak. 55

We live in that world, no question. "Destitute of faith, and terrified at skepticism": Carlyle's phrase still applies. With our cul- 56 ture atomizing, we think we can make up enough rules, impose enough restrictions, inject enough emptiness into our language to replace the shared moral conviction that's plainly gone. I think all stories—along with being fun—have the potential to humanize precisely because the richest fun of them is dependent on our identification with their characters; in order to have a really good time, we have to stretch the muscles of the I-and-Thou. But stories can't do for us what experience hasn't. They're just not that powerful. No murderous sexual psychopath is going to walk out of *The Piano* with a new-found respect for womankind; no decent bloke is going to close *The Silence of the Lambs* and start digging an oubliette—it doesn't matter how many times these experiences are repeated: the lives of the audience will out. And if some people are living lives in our society that make them unfit for even the most shallow thrills of fiction, you can't solve that problem by eliminating the fiction; it doesn't even begin to make sense. By allowing politicians and pundits to turn our attention to "the problem of fictional violence," we are really allowing them to make us turn our backs on the problems of reality. We know it too, down deep, where we're in despair. After a crime like the Jamie Bulger murder, we should be asking ourselves a million questions: about our abandonment of family life, about our approach to poverty and unemployment, about the failures of our educational systems—about who and what we are and the ways we treat each other, the things we do and omit to do. These are hard, sometimes boring questions. But when instead we let our discussions devolve, as they have, into this glamour-rotten debate on whether people should be able to enjoy whatever fiction they please, then we make meaningless the taking of an individual's life. And that's no fun at all. And it's no fun to sit back and watch it happen.

---

## *Meaning and Purpose*

1. According to Klavan, those who claim that fictional violence contributes to real violence really make the situation worse, not better. How? Why?

2. Klavan uses a work of fiction (The Silence of the Lambs) to support his contentions about how critics of fictional violence blur the distinctions between fiction and reality. Describe how this is so. What irony is created by this blurring?
3. Klavan claims that current attempts to censor media violence is "nonsense mostly" (6), yet these attempts have popular appeal. Why?
4. What points of Klavan's argument does the story of the Jamie Bulger murder support?
5. Klavan, on one level, seems to accept the argument that fictional violence is psychologically healthy (34–35). On another level, he dismisses that argument. Explain.
6. Klavan claims that no one can seriously believe that attempts to censor fictional violence are attempts to "root out the causes of violence" (24). How does he explain these attempts at censorship?
7. What final reason does Klavan give for antisocial behavior? Where must we look for the real causes and cures?

## *Strategy*

1. What attitude does Klavan strike against those with opposing viewpoints? How is this attitude designed to impress readers?
2. What opposing arguments does Klavan recognize? How does he dispose of them?
3. Explain Klavan's comparison of media violence to sex.
4. Paragraphs 15, 25, 33, and 43 are extremely short and undeveloped. What are their functions?
5. What evidence does Klavan cite to show that fictional violence has an honorable history and is, in fact, often respectable?

## *Style*

1. In paragraph 42 Klavan calls the scene in *Silence of the Lambs* when Hannibal Lecter eats his victim and washes him down with wine a "nonreal, nonmeaningful event." Explain.

2. What is the tone of the essay? Does the tone of the language change in the essay? To what purpose?
3. What is the connotation (see *Connotation* in the Glossary) of the phrase "trough of celebrity" (5)? How does that connotation affect the phrase's meaning in context?
4. If necessary look up the following words in a dictionary: *priapic, plummets, oblivious, squeamish, goading, posthumous, jitterbug, coital* (1); *jeopardy, estate, dusted, commode* (2); *quash* (5); *banal, milieus* (6); *emblematic, pundits* (7); *distraught, mutilated* (8); *tenuous, mea culpa, Draconian* (13); *rampaging, verities* (14); *utopian* (16 and 35); *Dionysean* (16 and 30); *homeopathic, template* (16); *fallacy, isomorphic* (17); *alchemies, sublimate, pith, literati* (18); *unfathomable, palliative* (19); *specious, screed, jeremiad, hallelujah* (20); *resonant, stichomythic* (21); *sociopaths* (22); *guise* (24); *factotum* (27); *mayhem* (28); *hausfrau, denounce* (30); *risible* (31); *peccadilloes, gravitas, catharsis, palaver, expended* (32); *icon* (34); *benevolent* (35); *nubile, in flagrante, goblins* (38); *menarche* (39); *evisceration* (40); *disembowels, geyser* (42); *placid* (44); *satori* (48); *atrocities, aesthetic, promiscuous, mitigated* (49); *consigning* (51); *corollaries* (52); *ubermensch* (54); *auctorial* (55); *atomizing, humanize, bloke, oubliette, devolve* (56).

## Writing Tasks

1. Write an essay that argues against Klavan's contention that fictional violence has no real negative effect on real life. In order to do that you will have to effectively dispose of Klavan's argument. You will also have to cite evidence that convincingly shows the relationship of fictional and real violence.
2. Write an essay defending Klavan's point of view. In doing so, dispose of Michael Medved's argument in "Denial Behavior" (pages 667–676) in more detail than Klavan did. Make sure you use specific examples in the development of your thesis.

# ❦ Michael Medved ❦

*Michael Medved graduated with honors from Yale University and is a film critic for the* New York Post *and the Public Broadcasting System. He has written several nonfiction books including* What Really Happened to the Class of '65 *(co-authored with David Wallechinsky),* Hospital: The Hidden Lives of a Medical Center Staff, *and* Hollywood vs. America.

# *Denial Behavior*

*In this selection, taken from* Hollywood vs. America, *Medved is critical of the film and television industries for denying that the content of their films and programs influence the behavior of their audiences.*

*As you read, take particular note of what Medved is claiming and what he is not claiming in regard to the media's influence on us.*

---

## A Cultural Nuthouse

In the wake of the horrifying riots in Los Angeles, thoughtful observers of every political persuasion began taking a fresh look at the connection between media messages and antisocial behavior. 1

"Now we live in a cultural nuthouse, a mad world of blood, torture and murder that surrounds us in the movies and follows us home when we turn on T.V. 'entertainment,' " editorialized A. M. Rosenthal in *The New York Times* (May 5, 1992). ". . . Violence made fashionable in the cause of a buck is unworthy of people of talent. Aren't those who do that becoming ashamed of themselves? Haven't they discovered that ketchup can become blood?" 2

In their most recent responses to such charges, leaders of the entertainment industry frankly acknowledge the appalling elements in the "cultural nuthouse" they have built, but they refuse to accept the idea that this ominous structure has significantly influenced society. 3

Instead of defending the content of their work, they simply deny its impact. . . . 4

The industry apologists insist that popular entertainment is by its very nature inconsequential, and that no one is seriously damaged by the fleeting images or subtle themes in a movie, TV show, or popular song. As the Hollywood establishment never tires of pointing out, several decades of research by social scientists have failed to produce conclusive, irrefutable proof that brutality and promiscuity in a product of the mass media can *cause* destructive behavior in the real world. . . . 5

## Hollywood 4, Straw Men 0

In March 1992, I took part in a well-publicized panel discussion on the global impact of popular culture sponsored by the American Enterprise Institute in Washington. Seated to my immediate right at the long table of participants was Mr. Jack Valenti, the unfailingly articulate and courtly president of the Motion Picture Association of America, and the most prominent spokesman for the Hollywood establishment. In the course of an occasionally heated exchange of views. Mr. Valenti made an emphatic statement that neatly summed up the industry's first line of defense in all discussions of its impact on society. "I have examined the archives of people who write on socological things in this country and sociologists, and I've found that social scientists are like psychiatrists in a murder trial," Valenti declared. "The prosecution has one . . . and the defense has one. . . . *But I haven't found anybody who has said that movies cause anybody to do anything.*" 6

Along similar lines, Mike Medavoy, chairman of TriStar Pictures and one of the most thoughtful and respected of all motion picture executives, told a 1991 meeting of Hollywood political activists that even though he personally disliked watching violence on screen, "to make a claim that films are *responsible* for violence in society is ludicrous." 7

In January 1992, *Los Angeles Times* columnist Robert A. Jones offered a more detailed explanation of film's allegedly limited abil- 8 ity to influence its audience. "The truth is this: the power of a movie tends to last only as long as the lights are down and the screen flickers," he wrote. "While you're watching, it owns you. But as soon as you walk out of the theater and the cold air hits your face, the movie starts to evaporate, almost like it's leaking through your skin. By the time you reach the parking lot, it's mostly gone."

This reassuring notion turns up time and again in the industry's efforts to confound its critics. An especially eloquent and effective attack on those of us who try to draw a connection between media violence and its real-world counterpart came from Teller, one half of the celebrated Penn and Teller magic-and-comedy duo, who wrote an Op-Ed piece for *The New York Times* in January 1992. In it, he derided those 9

> who seem to think that if we stop showing rape in movies people will stop committing it in real life. Anthropologists call this "magical thinking." It's the same impulse that makes people stick pins in voodoo dolls, hoping to cripple an enemy. It feels logical, but it does not take into account that rape predates home video by thousands of years.
>
> Zealots have long tried to prove that "evil" fiction causes wickedness in the real world. But the facts fail to cooperate. . . . Those who want us to give up our freedom disagree. They claim people are not smart enough to tell make-believe from reality. Give us a break! When one pays seven dollars to go into a theater to see big pictures moving on a wall, one does not have to be a mental giant to realize you are watching a movie. It makes you wonder how they explain the millions of people who saw Psycho without stealing bankrolls or bumping off blondes.

With this elegant flourish, the magician brought off a rhetorical sleight of hand, imputing to his ideological opponents opinions that they do not hold and demolishing positions that they had never advanced. 10

To the best of my knowledge, none of the prominent participants in the current national debate on media values has ever sug- 11 gested that "if we stop showing rape in movies people will stop committing it in real life"; nor has anyone seriously suggested that "people are not smart enough to tell make-believe from reality."

Instead of confronting the substantive concerns of those who question Hollywood's excesses, what Teller and the other commentators quoted above have done is to set up convenient and highly vulnerable straw men. Naturally, their self-contained debate against these phantoms allows them to achieve a magnificent victory, with a final score reading Hollywood 4, Straw Men 0. 12

## Essential Distinctions

In an attempt to avoid the application of such deceptive tactics to the arguments advanced in this book, I want to leave no room for confusion about what I *am* saying—and what I am *not* saying—about the popular culture's impact on society. 13

All future disputants in this controversy, please take note: 14

- I do not claim that media messages *cause* destructive behavior, but I do contend that they *encourage* it. I have never suggested that Hollywood is single-handedly responsible for America's social problems, but I do believe that the entertainment industry exacerbates them and that it has become an important contributing factor in many of our current difficulties. 15
- At the same time, I never stress the pernicious power of *one* movie, or one TV show, or one hit song; what concerns me is the accumulated impact of irresponsible messages that are repeated hour after hour, year after year. The most significant problems of the popular culture stem from the pervasive presence of antisocial material, not from a few isolated examples of offensiveness. 16

With these essential distinctions in mind, I believe that some of the most outspoken critics of Hollywood's values make a serious mistake when they try to indict the industry by emphasizing a handful of shocking episodes in which unbalanced individuals 17 injured themselves or others by imitating behavior they saw on screen.

We have all read lurid press accounts of such cases, describing the tragic toll of twenty-six people who killed themselves in games of Russian roulette shortly after *The Deer Hunter* aired on national TV; or the fourteen-year-old girl who meticulously copied the murders she saw in the movie *Heathers* (1990) by organizing a game of croquet and a picnic in which she poisoned two of her best friends: or the two sixteen-year-olds who put bullets through their heads while listening again and again to Ozzy Osbourne's "Suicide Solution"; or the four Oklahoma high school dropouts who recently gang-raped and battered two of their classmates while repeatedly playing a tape of the rap song "Gangster of Love"—which specifically glorifies just such an assault. 18

These and many similar incidents are most certainly dramatic and disturbing, but the lawsuits and public controversy surrounding them only serve to distract attention from the more significant questions about Hollywood and society. 19

The most profound problem with the popular culture isn't its immediate impact on a few vulnerable and explosive individuals, but its long-term effect on all the rest of us. The deepest concerns about Hollywood go beyond the industry's role in provoking a handful of specific crimes and involve its contribution to a general climate of violence and self-indulgence. 20

## A Clear Consensus

The entertainment establishment responds to these concerns by supplementing its standard rhetorical tricks with a few laughably bald-faced lies. On May 18, 1992, Barbara Dixon, Jack Valenti's colleague as spokesperson for the Motion Picture Association of America, told the *Los Angeles Times:* "We have dealt with this issue for a long time and have looked at a number of studies. According to the First Amendment lawyers who have handled the issue for us, none of [the studies] say that motion picture violence affects the behavior of people." 21

If Ms. Dixon has accurately summarized the report she received from her lawyers, then she should immediately seek more competent legal representation: in fact, more than three thousand research projects and scientific studies between 1960 and 1992 have confirmed the connection between a steady diet of violent entertainment and aggressive and antisocial behavior. 22

In a comprehensive 1982 report, published along with five thick volumes of social science surveys, the Surgeon General of the United States concluded that "there is a clear consensus among most researchers that television violence leads to aggressive behavior." Or, as the American Psychological Association declared in a 1991 resolution following a five-year task-force investigation: "The conclusion drawn on the basis of twenty-five years of research . . . is that viewing televised violence may lead to increases in aggressive attitudes, values, and behavior, particularly in children." 23

## Corporate Arrogance

In a stunning display of corporate arrogance, the major entertainment conglomerates disregard the conclusions of all the leading researchers and continue to insist that their work has no harmful impact on society. 24

With almost ritualized regularity, their official representatives repeat the claim that scientific investigations show "mixed" results on the question of media influence. "There are so many yesses and nos in the literature that it's confusing," declared CBS vice president David Blank in one typical statement in 1978. In a striking demonstration of wishful thinking, he then added. "I'm not sure anyone will ever solve the problem." 25

Meanwhile, the entertainment industry greatly encourages the confusion described by Dr. Blank by spending literally millions of dollars to commission its own studies which—surprise!—usually demonstrate that the media exert no influence on anyone. CBS, ABC, and NBC have all sponsored such projects with great fanfare, and the resulting research is regularly dusted off and trotted out whenever the industry wants to 26 demonstrate divided opinion among the experts on the question of the pop culture's impact.

The fact that such studies are taken seriously at all is itself a scandal: the industry-originated surveys deserve no more respect or consideration than we grant to all the many research reports commissioned by the tobacco industry to prove that the Surgeon General is wrong and that cigarette smoking is actually good for you. 27

The claims that Hollywood's messages do nothing to shape attitudes and behavior are equally ludicrous, and on occasion the truth is so obvious that not even the generous expenditure of industry funds can guarantee the research results the moguls desire. In 1978, CBS invested $290,000 on a six-year study on the effect of television on teenage boys conducted by the Survey Research Centre of the London School of Economics. William Belson, who supervised the project, concluded from his examination that "the evidence is very strongly supportive of the hypothesis that long-term exposure to violence increases the degree to which boys engage in violence of a serious kind. The same goes for violence of the less serious kind, such as swearing and the use of bad language, aggressiveness in sport or play, threatening to use violence on another boy, writing slogans on walls, and breaking windows." 28

Predictably enough, when confronted with these unexpected and unwelcome results, CBS managed to keep its enthusiasm firmly under control. The network's embarrassed spokesman. David Blank, did his level best to downplay the value of the findings his own company had financed, announcing that "Belson's study was interesting, but has come along after a lot of other work has been done and adds nothing of consequence from our standpoint." 29

## The Height of Hypocrisy

As representatives of the television business continue to stonewall, insisting that their programming has no power whatever to influence the public, no one seems to have noticed that 30 this utterly implausible position contradicts the most basic assumptions of their industry.

In 1982, ABC released a commissioned study in which the 31
hired-gun experts declared that "the research does not support the conclusion that television significantly cultivates viewer attitudes and perceptions of social reality."

If the executives at ABC sincerely believe this nonsense and 32
agree that their broadcasts fail to "cultivate viewer attitudes," then the network should prepare to refund all the billions of dollars of advertising revenue that it has collected under false pretenses.

The mighty mechanism of commercial television is based en- 33
tirely on the premise that broadcast advertising can alter the buying behavior of a significant segment of the huge viewing audience. That is why hardheaded corporations will gladly invest millions of dollars in a few thirty-second commercials, secure in the knowledge that even this sort of fleeting exposure can make an important difference in the public's point of view.

It is the height of hypocrisy that the same network execu- 34
tives who accept—and demand—this lavish payment for the briefest moments of broadcast advertising simultaneously try to convince us that all their many hours of programming do nothing to change the attitudes of the audience. In short, they have adopted the outrageously illogical assumption that a sixty-second commercial makes a more significant impression than a sixty-minute sitcom.

On the one hand we're told that an hour of television pro- 35
gramming does nothing to shape the sentiments of the public, and on the other we're asked to believe that the brief spots that interrupt this program are powerful enough to change perceptions of anything from canned goods to candidates. The underlying idea appears to be the bizarre notion that the average viewer ignores or shrugs off the televised entertainment he has chosen to watch, while sitting up in his chair and paying close attention only when the commercials come on.

The industry simply cannot have it both ways: if it claims a 36
near magical ability to sell products or politics, planting lasting images in just a few quick seconds, then it must acknowledge the

long-term impact of its prime time programs, with their frequently violent and antisocial themes.

The motion picture business faces a similarly absurd internal contradiction in its refusal to acknowledge the influence of the movies it makes. 37

In recent years, what Hollywood calls "product placement" has played an increasingly prominent role in the production process, with corporate logos and brand names frequently displayed in the course of every major film. This process helps the producers defray the astronomical costs of filmmaking, as the advertiser provides props or sets or costumes, or agrees to help sell the film by mounting a tie-in promotional campaign at the time of its release. As the *Wall Street Journal* reports: "Friendly producers send scripts . . . weeks and even months before filming starts, and the company analyzes them scene by scene to see if it can place a product—or advertising material, a billboard perhaps—on, under, or behind the stars." 38

According to most estimates, these efforts result in several million dollars in benefits to the producers of a typical major studio film. Writing in the *Atlantic Monthly*, Mark Crispin Miller reports that the 1989 James Bond entry, *License to Kill*, featured a scene in which 007 ostentatiously smokes Larks—a magical moment for which Philip Morris paid $350,000. In the Michael Keaton comedy *Mr. Mom* (1983), Miller identified plugs for McDonald's, Domino's pizza, Terminix exterminators. Folger's coffee, Lite beer, Jack Daniel's, Van Camp's chili, Ban deodorant, Windex, Tide, Spray 'n Wash, Borax, Clorox 2, and Downy fabric softener. 39

Corporate marketing experts invest considerable effort and expense in these placements because their research indicates that they are highly effective. Even if the viewer registers the name of the product only in an unconscious manner, the association between a familiar brand and a glamorous star will make a measurable difference in future sales. 40

This is an established principle in the motion picture business—accepted without question when it comes to taking the money of eager advertisers. At the same time that everyone agrees that a two-second glimpse of a box of Tide can help the manufac- 41 turer, there is no acknowledgment that two hours of graphic gore can hurt the audience.

Imagine a forthcoming feature film with a torrid sex scene between two charismatic stars. On the night stand beside the bed is a subtle product placement—say a bottle of mouthwash, with its label turned toward the camera. The current logic of the motion picture business suggests that the typical member of the audience turns his eyes away from two naked, gorgeous bodies in transports of passion and instead focuses all attention on the bottle of mouthwash at the edge of the frame. How else can one explain the assumption that the mouthwash label will influence the viewers' future behavior, but the vivid sex scene will not? 42

In short, the industry's position is both flagrantly dishonest and lavishly illogical. 43

---

## *Meaning and Purpose*

1. What is Medved claiming about the impact of popular culture on society?
2. Some critics attack the entertainment industry by pointing to copy-cat crimes that imitate the action in certain movies. Does Medved agree?
3. According to Medved, do research studies show any connection between violent entertainment and aggressive and antisocial behavior?
4. How does Medved relate television advertising and product placement in movies to the entertainment industry's denial that their products influence human behavior.
5. What is the main point of this selection and where is it stated?

## *Strategy*

1. Why does Medved quote from Valenti, Medavoy, Jones, and Teller in the second section of this selection, "Hollywood 4, Strawmen 0"?

2. What is a strawman? Hoes does Medved use the concept of the strawman to his advantage?
3. Why does Medved place his argument about advertising and product placement at the end of this selection?
4. Where does Medved most concisely state the view of the entertainment industry as to the effect on society of violence in the media?
5. What argument does Medved present solely through reasoning? How effective is this argument?

## *Style*

1. Find at least five examples of Medved's use of emotional language to sway his audience.
2. If necessary, use a dictionary to look up the meaning of the following words: *zealots* (9); *exacerbates* (15); *pernicious* (16); *lurid* (18); *conglomerates* (24); *moguls* (28); *hypocrisy* (34); *charismatic* (42).

## *Writing Tasks*

1. Write an essay supporting or denying Medved's contention that "antisocial material" is pervasive in American culture. Base the paper on your personal knowledge of recent movies, television programs, books, and popular music.
2. Imagine that you are a spokesperson for the entertainment industry. Write an essay refuting Medved's essay. You may want to draw ideas from essays by King (pages 626–644) or Klavan (pages 647–664).

## ❦ *Responding to Photographs* ❦

### *Persuasion and Argument*

Saturday Morning—USA

What is the impact of television violence on children? Does television violence cause aggressive behavior? Research has not conclusively proven that it does or does not teach children to use force or violence in their relationships with other children. But most researchers agree that when children watch hours of television they participate in "imitative learning" or "modeling." In simple terms—watching television creates a "monkey-see, monkey-do" effect.

Research has even shown that onetime exposure to televised aggressive behavior can be repeated in children's play by as many as 88 percent of the children who have seen it. Moreover, a single experience viewing a dramatic aggressive act can be recalled and reenacted by children six months after the viewing. Earlier studies indicate that the average child between 5 and 15 will witness during this ten-year period the violent deaths of more than 13,400 humans. Surely the accumulated impact of television violence must influence monkey-see, monkey-do behavior. Or does it?

"Saturday Morning—USA" captures a moment when television generates "imitative learning." Drawing on details from the photograph and from the discussion here, compose an argument based on one of the following assignments. Before beginning your first draft, reread "Persuasion and Argument: Convincing a Reader" at the beginning of the chapter to review the conventions of a sound argument.

1. Compose an inductive or deductive argument which leads your reader to conclude that children should be curtailed from watching television violence. Here are a few suggestions to get you started. Include a description of "Saturday Morning—USA" which leads to the conclusion that television has a powerful modeling effect. You might also include some of your own observations of children modeling violent television behavior. You might then point out what research suggests about the effect of television violence on play, thus leading your reader to an obvious conclusion.
2. Compose an inductive or deductive essay that takes the opposing position called for in option 1; that is, the viewing of television violence should not be curtailed because it, like all television viewing, stimulates creative play. Here are a few suggestions to get you started. In this approach you will describe the contents of "Saturday Morning—USA" but interpret the photograph as an indication that television stimulates imaginative play, not actual violent behavior. You might also draw on your own experience modeling television violence during play, but point out that you and your friends are not criminals or violent people. You might state and agree with the research alluded to in the opening discussion of the writing task, but you would interpret it in a way that supports your point; that is, modeling is a powerful teacher, but children have the ability to separate television behavior from reality.

## ❦ *Additional Writing Tasks* ❦

### *Persuasion and Argument*

1. Write an argument in which you express one of your own deeply felt opinions. If the subject you select has undergone extensive public discussion, assume that your reader is familiar with the general elements of the debate and develop specific evidence based on your own observations, reading, and experience. Use the following list to stimulate your thinking, but do not feel bound by the subjects.

    a. Fraternities
    b. Sororities
    c. Hiring quotas
    d. Euthanasia
    e. Prayer in schools
    f. Giving birth control advice to teenagers
    g. Sex education
    h. Legalized drugs
    i. Capital punishment
    j. Smoking in public buildings
    k. Public profanity
    l. Disruptive behavior in public places
    m. Requiring people on public assistance to work for the city
    n. Animal rights
    o. Student code of conduct
    p. Violence on television
    q. Movie ratings
    r. Subliminal messages in music
    s. Emotional advertising in political campaigns
    t. Censorship

2. Plastic disposable diapers are becoming a significant problem. Each year Americans toss approximately eighteen billion diapers—containing an estimated 2.8 million tons of excrement and urine—in the trash. Every one of these disposable diapers takes

up to five hundred years to decompose. Aside from the solid waste issue, there are also growing concerns about infectious material seeping into our soil and ground water, wasted natural resources, the rising costs of diaper production, "disposal," and increasing risks of severe rashes and toxic shock syndrome in children.

Write an argument essay in opposition to disposable diapers. Direct your essay to new parents.

3. Many people find junk mail entertaining, something to thumb through during a leisure moment. You, however, believe junk mail is not only a nuisance but also a hazard. For example, all the junk mail you receive this year will have consumed the equivalent of one and a half trees. One year's junk mail sent in the United States amounts to a hundred million trees.

   Write an essay arguing against junk mail. Here are some commonly known facts you might want to use:

   a. Almost two million tons of junk mail are sent each year.
   b. Over 40 percent of all junk mail is never opened.
   c. Junk mail receives special postage rates—currently 10.1 cents per piece if arranged in presorted batches.
   d. The average American will spend eight months of his or her life just opening junk mail.
   e. The junk mail sent to a million people means the destruction of 1.5 million trees.

4. A radical counterculture has emerged in Germany's inner cities. They are the *autonomen*, a term that means the same as "autonomous" in English. The *autonomen*, who wear masks at demonstrations, are composed of squatters and street people. They see themselves as the last hope of revolutionary activism. The group refuses to participate in any political or social system, and its brand of activism is usually spontaneous, unorganized, and often violent.

   The *autonomen* have no counterpart on the American social scene, but some social psychologists predict our government's failure to solve the problems of homelessness, drug abuse, and street gangs will lead to the formation of groups like the *autonomen* to express the anger and alienation the inner-city underclass already feels.

Write an essay in which you argue that inner-city life must be improved or city governments will soon be dealing with groups like Germany's *autonomen*. You might begin by using the *Reader's Guide to Periodic Literature* to find background information on these groups.

# *Glossary*

**Abridgment** A shortened version of a work, but one in which the compiler attempts to include all pertinent parts of the longer work.

**Abstract** Abstract words or terms describe ideas, concepts, or qualities, as opposed to **concrete** entities. Sample abstract words and expressions are *philosophy, remorse, happiness, beauty, honor, peace, organizational climate, achievement motive*, and *burden of proof* (*see* **concrete**).

**Acronym** A word formed by combining the first letters or syllables of words, to form a new word. An example is BASIC, the word that names a computer language; it is an acronym meaning "Beginner's All-purpose Symbolic Instruction Code."

**Ad hominem argument** *See* **Logical fallacies**.

**Allusion** An allusion briefly and often casually refers to something the writer believes is common knowledge. If you write that your neighbor's fence "looks like the Berlin Wall," you allude to the state of the Berlin Wall, which is in ruins. "Future Schlock," the title of the Neil Postman essay in Chapter 5, is an allusion to Alvin Toffler's *Future Shock*, a book about what to expect in the future. A Robert Frost poem about the sudden death of a boy is titled, " 'Out, Out—,' " an allusion to lines from Shakespeare's *Macbeth*:

> Out, out, brief candle!
> Life's but a walking shadow, a poor player
> That struts and frets his hour upon the stage,
> And then is heard no more (V,v,23).

**Analogy** An analogy is an imaginative comparison between two things, one less familiar than the other, usually intended to clarify a description of the less familiar one. In his novel *The Red and* *the Black*, the French author Stendhal (Marie Henri Beyle) wrote, "A novel is a mirror that strolls along a highway. Now it reflects the blue of the skies, now the mud puddles underfoot," clarifying his concept of the novel by imaginatively comparing it to a common, familiar item.

**Analysis** In an analysis, a writer examines a piece of writing by paying special attention to its elements of thought. An analysis is based on the premise that some ideas or concepts are actually combinations formed of other ideas or concepts. An analysis of an idea or concept as incorporated in an extended piece of writing often shows that many smaller thoughts have been combined into larger thoughts. Analyzing the Pledge of Allegiance to the Flag shows that it includes a definition of an ideal republic, which has its roots in classical Greek philosophy.

**Anecdote** An anecdote is an incident, or **narration**, which reveals a facet of character, most often about a well-known person.

**Argument** An argument is meant to persuade an audience to accept the qualities of a proposition (a statement to be supported), so that the audience will be convinced of the proposition's truth or falsity. In his commentary on rhetoric, Aristotle spoke of "artistic proofs," so called because they are invented in the sense of being thought up or devised for the specific purpose of swaying an audience to an orator's point of view.

Aristotelian proofs as they are used when writing arguments appeal to the audience in one of three ways: rationally, emotionally, or ethically. A rational appeal (*logos*) appeals to the audience's reason: an emotional appeal (*pathos*) appeals to the audience's emotions or passions; an ethical appeal (*ethos*) appeals to the audience's confidence in the writer's character or credentials Today, an argument commonly includes more than one of these proofs, and may also embody such nonartistic proofs as statistics, results of polls, scientific data, and other scientifically verifiable statements.

**Association fallacy** *See* **Logical fallacies**.

**Audience** An audience is a reader or a class of readers whom writers keep in mind while they write and particularly while they revise their writing. Writers determine as much as they can about their audiences, including their expertise, their education, their biases, their political and cultural background, their assumptions, and their interests. Writers deal with many kinds of audiences, including those who already share the writer's convictions. Each audience affects the writer's way of casting the writing.

Knowing as much as they can about their audiences helps writers determine which **strategies** to use, such as sentence structure, reasoning, **definition**, **emphasis**, organization, and **style**.

Audiences also affect writers' **diction**. A writer aiming at an audience of experienced amateur sailors would use words like *pulpit* and *roach*, but for an audience knowing nothing of nautical terminology, the writer would use "the platform on the forward part of the ship from which sailors handle and change sails," instead of *pulpit*, and "the curved portion of a sail closest to the rear end of the ship," instead of *roach*.

**Body** The main part of a piece of writing is its body. Here, events are dramatized, dialogue is sustained, **conflicts** are developed, and other **strategies** are applied to sustain the reader's involvement.

**Categories** Classes or divisions in an organized **classification**. Under the classification *general education requirements*, a writer could list the categories humanities, foreign languages, and sciences. Further, the writer could subcategorize by listing *foreign languages* such as French, Latin, German, and Japanese.

**Cause and effect** A cause is that which came before an effect, the effect being the result of that cause. Combined, *cause and effect* is a useful way of analyzing reasons for actions and for the results of those actions. In the sentence, "Because Gwen did not study, she failed the calculus examination," one can see the immediate cause and the immediate effect. But what ultimate cause was behind Gwen's not studying? Not even Gwen can be absolutely sure, because most causes in our daily lives are probable, not certain. Aware of this uncertainty, writers use with caution the cause-and-effect strategy.

**Circumlocution** Circumlocution in writing fails to make a point clearly or evades a point because many words are used where fewer would have sufficed. The sentence, "What is the cause of the source of his pain cannot be other than his appendix, which seems to be less than healthy," illustrates circumlocution. The sentence could have been recast as, "His pain is probably caused by appendicitis."

**Claim** The philosopher and rhetorician Stephen Toulmin devised a model of reasoning similar to the **syllogism**. One of the Toulmin model's primary elements is *claim*, which is the conclusion. The other two elements are *data*, which form the evidence, and *warrant*, which is the supporting argument. This sentence briefly illustrates the Toulmin model: Jasmah is a physicist (*data*); therefore, Jasmah is intelligent (*claim*) because all physicists are intelligent (*warrant*).

**Classification** Classification is a system for sorting things into distinct categories, or classes. A music lover might want to organize her cassettes. After sorting them, she sees that she can classify them into these categories, according to types of music: jazz, classical, and country and western. Later, perhaps when she wants to write a paper about her jazz cassettes, she can classify them into categories according to the musical styles of the featured artists on her tapes, making sure that each category is described clearly so that it is distinct from other categories.

**Cliché** In French, the *cliché* is an outmoded system for making metal printing plates with which to print the same thing again and again. In English, the name describes words and phrases that have been used again and again so that they have become worn out, tired. Examples abound: A person can be "as old as the hills." A night can be "as black as coal." We can be "afraid of our own shadow." Someone can have "an ax to grind." A child can be "a chip off the old block," "here today; gone tomorrow," "a square peg in a round hole," "start from scratch," and so on. When revising, writers "keep an eye peeled" for clichés so that they can replace those with fresh, colorful expressions of their own **invention**.

**Climax** In a **narration** essay, the climax is the conclusion, the highest point of interest. In other kinds of writing the climax, or peak of interest, marks the turning point in the action.

**Coherence** Coherence clearly, consistently, and logically connects the parts in a piece of writing. It is the glue that holds together all vigorous, effective writing. Among other techniques, coherence invokes **transitions** to show introductory relationships among ideas, paragraphing to signal shifts in thought, sentences that follow reasonably from those which came before them, and **diction** appropriate to the **audience**.

**Colloquial expressions** Colloquial expressions, such as "Don't even try to psych out Professor Sherman," and "Ralph crammed all his stuff into his closet" characterize informal (and often playful) speaking and writing. Therefore, they have limited use in formal writing because their very casualness can distract readers.

**Comparison and contrast** A comparison involves similarities; a contrast, differences. Combining these two ways of judging qualities can lead to discoveries about two things formerly thought to be ordinarily alike or unalike. A writer who compares and contrasts an electric typewriter and a computer discovers that whatever an electric typewriter can do, a computer with a word-processing program and printer can do more efficiently (a comparison). The writer will also discover the many things that a computer, equipped with various programs, can do that a typewriter cannot possibly do, such as maintaining a continuous record of household expenditures (a contrast). On the other hand, the writer will discover that both machines can be used for writing brief informal notes, but a computer can also retain easily correctable copies of those notes on a disk (comparison and contrast).

**Conclusions** Conclusions are ways of ending essays. The way in which an essay is concluded depends in great part on the content of the essay itself. An essay arguing for or against gun control is likely to end by restating the reasons for taking one position or another. An essay explaining one of the complex relationships between human beings and nature might conclude by warning the reader that the relationship is endangered. An essay with several examples of how the world's economies are intertwined might end with one sterling example of an economy that is vitally connected to our own. An essayist offering information about an inexpensive medicine for a common disease might conclude by recommending that readers consult their personal physicians for more information.

Conclusions do not drift into other topics, nor do they shift an essay's emphasis away from its own topic. A writer would not end an essay taking a firm stand against showing pornographic movies on television by writing something like, "It all depends on each person's tastes."

So-called cute conclusions suggest to the audience that the writer was not deeply involved in thinking about the essay's content. They should be avoided.

Conclusions grow logically and sufficiently from the essay, and they should bring an essay to a satisfying close.

**Concrete** Concrete words or expressions refer to things experienced by the senses, as opposed to **abstractions**. These words and expressions are concrete: *chair, perfume, music, automobile, bitter, cardboard box, dictionary, window*, and *refrigerator*.

**Conflict** In writing, a conflict is a struggle that grows from two opposing beliefs, values, characters, and so on, which are developed in the **body** of the piece.

**Connotation** The word "connotation" describes the implied meanings that become attached to words, *Skinny* and *slender* both mean thin or slight, but the first has negative connotations (emaciation and perhaps ill health), and the latter implies grace, even elegance.

The descriptive phrase *cheap furniture* carries connotations of shoddy workmanship and poor quality. The phrase *inexpensive furniture*, however, implies only the furniture's low cost. Although *cheap* and *inexpensive* are dictionary synonyms, the meaning implied in *cheap* sets it apart from *inexpensive*. Careful writers keep in mind what words mean according to dictionaries and what those same words may imply beyond their dictionary definitions.

**Data** The proofs in Stephen Toulmin's model of reasoning are *data*. They are the evidence that supports the model's **claim**, or conclusion.

Data are also nonartistic proofs (see **argument**) used in other models of reasoning. These kinds of data come from scientific observations, record keeping, or statistics—facts or figures from which conclusions can be inferred, and information from credible, reliable sources.

**Deduction** A deduction is the result of reasoning from a general statement to a specific instance. If your college requires that all prospective students be tested in a foreign language before they are enrolled, then you can reason that Pat, who sits next to you in English class, has taken a test in a foreign language. Deductions are not always that clear-cut, though.

One might think that all small cars get good gas mileage and then buy a small car to save money on fuel, only to find that this car gets poor mileage. The original assumption, then, was false.

**Definition** A definition outlines, limits, or states the meaning of a word, term, phrase, or concept.

A formal definition puts a term into a class and then shows how it differs from other members of the same class. A trumpet (term) is a brass musical wind instrument (class) consisting of a tube in an oblong loop or loops, with a flared bell at one end, a curved mouthpiece at the other, and three valves for making tonal changes (difference).

An extended definition, a form of **exposition**, not only defines in the senses above but also explains issues by employing rhetorical strategies, such as **narration, description, example**, and **classification.**

**Denotation** The term *denotation* applies to the literal, lexical meaning of a word—that which is explained in a good dictionary.

**Description** The technique of making pictures with words is *description*. An effective description includes clear evidence that appeals to one or more of the senses—sight, touch, taste, smell, or hearing—as well as **explanation**. Henry David Thoreau's "The Battle of the Ants," in Chapter 6, demonstrates this combination of description and explanation. "his own breast was all torn away, exposing what vitals he had there to the jaws of the black warrior, whose breastplate was apparently too thick for him to pierce; and the dark carbuncles of the sufferer's eyes shone with ferocity such as only war could excite."

**Diction** Diction is deliberate choice of words. Writers conscientiously choose words and the ways in which they use them, being guided by their audience and their purpose. Writers make their selections from various levels of usage, including **standard English, slang**, conversational expressions, regionalisms (choosing among "spigot," "tap," and "faucet"), and scientific and technical **jargon**.

Consider these sentences:

1. "Christine resigned her position."
2. "Chris quit her job."
3. "Chris told him he could take his job and shove it!"

What determines which of these sentences is correct? The audience and the purpose.

Sentence 1 is appropriate for a formal audience and a formal purpose: perhaps the writer's audience was college-level readers and the purpose was to describe her best friend's employment difficulties.

Sentence 2 might have been for a semiformal audience and a semiformal purpose, such as writing an essay for the readers of a college alumnae newsletter to help graduates keep track of their classmates.

Sentence 3 might have been for an informal audience and purpose, such as writing an essay for other members of a composition class to explain how one of them had reacted to being treated poorly by the manager of a local pizza parlor.

Whoever the audience and whatever the purpose, writers are guided by their own sense of propriety and by dictionaries and a thesaurus. They rarely use a thesaurus, however, without also consulting a dictionary to be sure that the words they have chosen from the thesaurus are in fact appropriate for their audience and purpose.

**Directive process analysis** A directive process analysis tells how to do something. It is a sequence of directions to guide a reader who wants to complete a specific task. Such an analysis tells how to plant a tree, but *not* how a tree grows, the latter topic being an **informative process analysis**.

**Division** Division is a subclass of **classification**. Writers divide a classification into logical parts, usually for description or explanation. Let's say that a writer wanted to describe a personal computer. First, you would classify it, telling how it differs from mainframe computers, from large industrial computers, and from laptop computers. Then you would divide the home computer into its logical parts: the keyboard, the central processing unit, and the video monitor. After making that division, you would describe each of these components. By your division, you help the reader to see one component at a time, rather than try to imagine an entire home computer all at once.

**Dominant impression** The dominant impression is the main sensation or conception that the author strives to fix in the reader's mind, by carefully shaping the details of a **description**.

**Effect** It is part of **cause and effect**, the result or outcome of an occurrence or action, but the word *effect* also refers to the impression that writing—whether a word, sentence, paragraph, essay, or larger work—makes on its audience.

**Emphasis** With emphasis, writers emphasize or highlight the things they want their readers to see as most important in their writing. Writers use such **strategies** as **diction**, sentence structure, position, active voice, repetition, and mechanics to emphasize their main points.

*Diction:* A writer who wanted to emphasize a negative opinion of a newly opened restaurant could write, "This restaurant has food fit to eat only if you are starving."

*Sentence structure:* If you wanted to emphasize your opinion of the food itself, you could write a periodic sentence, which moves from supporting details to the main idea. "With lukewarm coffee, half-cooked cold chicken, salty mashed potatoes, and burned vegetables, my meal was barely edible." You could emphasize your description of the food by writing a loose sentence, in which the supporting details follow the main idea: "I had a barely edible meal of lukewarm coffee, half-cooked cold chicken, salty mashed potatoes, and burned vegetables."

*Position:* That which we read last, we remember longest, whether chapters in a book, groups of words in a sentence, or paragraphs in an essay. Commenting on an unsavory experience in a restaurant, you might begin a paper by describing how you had read about the restaurant in a respectable tourist guide, where it had been awarded three stars. Then you might devote a short paragraph to the small problem you had in finding the place because it was in a part of the city unfamiliar to the taxicab driver, who had been profusely apologetic. You then might describe the restaurant's décor, a delightful amalgam of French Provincial and Early American, and your waitress, a pleasant young lady dressed in a peasant frock, who was also attending law school at the nearby university. Finally, because you had been shocked at the poor quality of the food, in utter contrast to the treat you had been expecting, you might conclude the essay with a paragraph meant to shock your readers as well, thus emphasizing the most important point in your experience by putting it last.

*Active voice:* Verbs in active voice—"This restaurant serves poorly prepared food"—are more emphatic than those in passive voice: "Poorly prepared food is served by this restaurant."

*Repetition:* "I spent a valuable hour of my vacation sipping the lukewarm coffee at Harry's Restaurant, chewing Harry's half-cooked chicken, tasting the salty mashed potatoes at Harry's, and staring at the vegetables Harry burned. Never again will I eat in Harry's Restaurant."

*Mechanics:* Usually the least appropriate way to emphasize formal writing, mechanics include underlining, quotation marks, and exclamation points: "When I was served the 'food' I had ordered in this 'restaurant,' I was *shocked* to see how *poorly* it had been prepared!" Such devices must be used sparingly. Your emphasis will be more successfully communicated with diction, sentence structure, position, active voice, and repetition.

**Essay** The word *essay* is from the French *essai*, meaning "attempt" or "experiment." In English, an essay is a relatively short piece of nonfiction prose on a specified topic. It is an attempt by a writer to persuade, inform, explain, argue, describe, narrate, expose, or in some other way organize and develop a topic to interest an **audience**.

Essays are occasionally defined as informal or formal, although the definitions admittedly are vague. Generally, however, a formal essay includes **diction** appropriate to a serious audience, has a serious **tone**, and is focused on a serious topic. An informal essay, on the other hand, often has a light, perhaps humorous tone and informal language, and is focused on a personal, perhaps frivolous topic.

**Evaluation** An evaluation determines the worth or quality of a work. If you are revising your own work or reading someone else's, you try to evaluate it objectively, to see how well it fulfills its purpose. Usually, those who evaluate a work look to see how well its thesis is stated and supported, how strongly its proofs support its claims, how clearly it is organized, whether or not its language is clear, and whether or not it is appropriately written for its intended audience.

**Evidence** Evidence is support for a theory, claim, or **thesis**. The commonest kinds of evidence are obvious evidence, manifest evidence, and clear evidence. Obvious evidence, usually scientific, is readily perceived or easily inferred. If $6 + 2 + x = 9$, then the evidence is obvious that $x = 1$. Manifest evidence is immediately clear to the understanding, often by intuition. If you see water in its solid state, then you know almost without thinking that it is frozen. Clear evidence, the kind essayists use most often, supports and clarifies a reader's understanding of the writer's thesis. If the writer's thesis is that marriage vows are hopelessly outmoded, then you must offer clear evidence to support that thesis. You must examine and clarify the vows, compare them with the spousal responsibilities in modern marriages, illustrate how those vows conflict with reality, and so on.

**Examples** An example is an instance that follows and illustrates the assertion in a statement. Among the more usual are specific examples, typical examples, and hypothetical examples. Specific examples amplify one experience, event, incident, or fact. They clarify in detail your earlier statement. Typical examples illustrate many experiences, events, incidents, or facts. They clarify generally your earlier statement, so that they will be representative. Hypothetical examples are imagined or supposed representations. They clarify the probability of your earlier statement.

**Exposition** An exposition is a detailed explanation of the content of an idea, an object, an attitude, or a position. An exposition exposes, makes something accessible to a reader, by using any of a number of **strategies**, including examples, comparisons and contrasts, analogies, and classifications. Most essays in this book are expository, as are most essays written in college.

**False analogy** *See* **Logical fallacies**.

**Faulty either/or reasoning** *See* **Logical fallacies**.

**Figures of speech** Tropes, or figures of speech, make a clear style vivid by adding **connotations** to statements, which appeal to the reader's imagination. The most used figures of speech are metaphor, simile, personification, hyperbole (overstatement), litotes (understatement), synecdoche, metonymy, and paradox.

A *metaphor* is an implied comparison between two dissimilar things: "Jamie is the tiger on the team." Tigers are noted for their speed, intelligence, and strength—the attributes that this metaphor gives to Jamie.

A *simile* is an explicit comparison between two dissimilar things, using the word *as* or *like:* "Jamie is as southern as Georgia."

*Personification* gives human qualities to inanimate objects or abstract ideas: "Six tall, menacing pine trees guard our campus at night."

*Hyperbole* (overstatement) is deliberate exaggeration used for emphasis: "It was raining so hard that I almost drowned while driving to school."

*Litotes* (understatement) is deliberate understatement used for emphasis: "Getting a D on my history test was not my greatest birthday present."

*Synecdoche* substitutes part of something for the whole: "Two hands left the ship just before it sailed." In this example, *hands* substitutes for "sailors."

*Metonymy* substitutes the whole for a part of something: "The Pentagon said today that, except for Near Eastern flareups, fewer troops will be needed in the next decade." In this example, *The Pentagon* substitutes for "a spokesperson for the army."

A *paradox* appears to be contradictory, but in fact carries some truth: "The wealthier you are, the poorer you may be." Wealth is not always measured by money. It is also measured by wisdom, knowledge, morality, love, and other qualities.

**Focus** In photography, a subject that is in focus is sharply defined. That is also true in writing. Writers who focus on their subject bring it into sharp detail. They begin by thinking about a large unfocused topic, such as "crime in the streets." Then they may decide to focus on some part of crime in the streets—"street crime in our city." After they have found their focus, they may narrow it even more—to "street crime in my neighborhood." How sharply they focus on a subject often depends on their **audience** and **purpose**.

**General and specific** General words are names for broad classes of things, from which you can move to words that designate members of those classes. One broad class is *automobiles*. A term that designates a member of that class is *sports car*. A designation for a more specific member of the sports-car class is *Alfa Romeo*. Writers are guided by their **audience** and by their **purpose** when they choose among general and specific names.

**Generalization** A generalization is a broad statement that rests on personal observation or acquired information. The sentence "Children usually follow their parents' advice" suggests that its writer has experience with raising children and from that experience has written a generalization that includes all children.

Writers sometimes begin with generalizations and then move toward conclusions based on their generalizations. But to avoid hasty generalizations, they often use qualifiers in their conclusions: "She has a degree in English, and so she *probably* knows a lot about Shakespeare." Or, "She has a degree in English, and so she *might* know *something* about Shakespeare." *See also* **induction**.

**Hyperbole** *See* **Figures of speech**.

**Hypothetical examples** *See* **Examples**.

**Image** An image appeals to the imagination through the senses. It is a **strategy** many writers apply to help readers "see" what they are reading. The sentence, "Her ancient face was a sheaf of small etched road maps to nowhere," is an image that describes an old and wrinkled countenance. The sentence, "He sings the songs of an old man's childhood, the golden past that never was," describes a person who reminisces about former times, which seem far more attractive now ("the golden past") than they were then.

**Induction** An induction is the result of reasoning that interprets limited evidence to arrive at a general truth. A person who has owned three or four friendly and alert cocker spaniels over the years may reason that all cocker spaniels are friendly and alert.

Inductive reasoning is useful in writing because it is a powerful persuader. Writers who want to persuade readers of a general truth use enough sound evidence to make their claims reasonably acceptable. If you wanted to persuade readers of the benefits in jogging, you might offer as evidence all your healthy friends who jog, newspaper articles that endorse jogging as a healthy activity, well-known athletes who jog, your doctor's saying that jogging promotes health, and so on. The more sound evidence you present, the more apt the reader is to accept your persuasive **argument**.

**Informative process analysis** With an informative process analysis, you tell how something is done. You describe sequentially the steps in a natural procedure that does not involve intervention. An informative process analysis might tell how a tree grows, but *not* how to plant a tree, the latter topic being a **directive process analysis**.

**Introduction** An introduction begins a piece of writing. An effective introduction establishes the essay's topic, tone, and territory. It leads directly into the main idea or issue discussed in the **body** of the paper. Its purpose is to engender readers' interest. To achieve that purpose, writers include such **strategies** as **rhetorical questions**, unusual facts, **anecdotes**, and personal comments.

The length of an introduction depends on the essay's **purpose** and its intended **audience**.

**Invention** Writers use invention to develop their subjects. It includes planning the piece of writing, thinking of ways of organizing material, of presenting material, and of deciding how to handle questions that you anticipate readers will raise

**Irony** A difference between appearance and reality creates irony. When it compliments, it is ironically condemning. When it condemns, it is ironically complimenting. The sentence "What a magnificent car," when used to describe a rusting hulk sitting in a junkyard, is ironic. The sentence "It's not a bad paint job," when used to describe Michelangelo's Sistine Chapel ceiling, is ironic. When the irony is not subtle but is intended to cause deliberate harm, it is called **sarcasm**. If someone says, "Thank you. It's just what I've always wanted," when reacting to the ketchup stain you accidentally put on her new blouse, she is using sarcasm.

When they are contrary to our anticipation, situations can also be ironic. You might discover that you were not hired for a job because you failed a company's mandatory typing test, only to learn that the job for which you applied required no typing at all.

**Jargon** Jargon is technical vocabulary that is appropriate only among experts in a field. As a kind of shorthand, it saves time in their communication. Among themselves lawyers use such expressions as "caveat," "entrapment," "estoppel," "the M'Naghten Rule," and "mens rea," knowing that they all understand legal jargon. To a lay listener, however, the words mean little. For lay audiences, writers use jargon sparingly, and when they do use it, they include definitions.

Another kind of jargon, sometimes called bureaucratese, is nothing more than pompous **diction** used more to impress readers than to inform them. The sentence "Our consumer demand analysis precludes our implementation of the proposed planning stage"—which means, by the way, "We don't need to plan to produce something that no one wants to buy"—typifies the jargon of pomposity.

**Litotes** *See* **Figures of speech**.

**Logical fallacies** Mistakes in reasoning that lead to faulty conclusions are logical fallacies or fallacious reasoning.

An *ad hominem argument* attacks a person rather than the issue that is being considered.

The *association fallacy* suggests that an act or belief is worthy or unworthy merely because of the people who are associated with it.

A writer falls into *false analogy* by presuming that if two things are alike in one or more ways, then they must be alike in other ways as well.

The *either/or fallacy* is a type of oversimplification in which a writer assumes only two alternatives are possible when in fact many others should be considered.

A *non sequitur* is a conclusion that does not follow from the premise.

A writer making an *overgeneralization* draws a conclusion from insufficient or unrepresentative evidence.

With an *oversimplification*, we draw a conclusion while ignoring information essential to the subject.

Someone who accepts the *post hoc* argument assumes that if one event occurred before another, then the second event was caused by the first.

**Metaphor** *See* **Figures of speech**.

**Metonymy** *See* **Figures of speech**.

**Narration** A narration tells a story and often includes extensive **description**. Narrations, usually chronological, include among their purposes entertaining, informing, and instructing. Some narrations have a plot, a story line that moves toward an insight about the principal character in the narration.

**Narrative effect** The main **effect** from reading a **narration** is named the *narrative effect*. Each narration incorporates a reason for being. Writers decide the main effect that their narrative should have on their readers, and then form the narrative so as not to depart from their decision.

**Non sequitur** *See* **Logical fallacies**.

**Nonstandard English** Words and expressions that are often spoken but rarely written except when the writer has a clear reason for using them sometimes include nonstandard English. Some examples are *ain't, nohow, irregardless, theirselves, hisself, we'uns, could care less* (for "could not care less"), and *them* (instead of *those*), as in *Them people ain't got no smarts*, instead of "Those people do not seem intelligent."

**Objective and subjective** Objective writing is designed to be a distanced, factual account presented in language that is plain, direct, and free of value judgments. Pure objectivity is hard to achieve because people's perceptions are almost always colored by their experiences, their values, and their biases. But in writing such as scientific papers and technical reports, authors strive for objectivity. Subjective writing is more personal, more indicative of the writer's thoughts, feelings, and attitudes. The emphasis here is on the writer's relationship to the topic rather than the topic itself. Very few essays are exclusively objective or subjective. Most often, writings combine the two.

**Opening** An opening is the first part of a three-part narrative essay. The other two parts are the body and the climax. The beginning sentences usually capture the reader's attention without giving away the outcome. The opening may hint at the purpose of the story about to unfold, but may not actually reveal it.

**Order of ideas** Ideas can be arranged in various ways, but all are derived from the subject and the writer's purpose. The order may be spatial, moving from top to bottom, side to side, or background to foreground. Or the order may simply be chronological, as in a narrative. The writer may work from least important to most important. The sequence of ideas should always be well thought out, chosen for its greatest effect.

**Overgeneralization** *See* **Logical fallacies**.

**Oversimplification** *See* **Logical fallacies**.

**Paradox** *See* **Figures of speech**.

**Paragraph** The paragraph is the basic unit in an essay. It is composed of a group of closely related sentences that together develop one of the essay's main ideas. The main or unifying idea of a paragraph is usually stated in a topic sentence, often found at the beginning of the paragraph. All other sentences in the paragraph relate directly to the topic sentence, thus establishing unity and coherence. But occasionally a unified and coherent paragraph has no topic sentence. The paragraph then undoubtedly has a leading idea that is strongly implied in every sentence. Paragraphs also work visually in an essay, graphically demonstrating the progress of ideas and also providing visual relief to the reader.

**Parallel structure** The repetition of similar grammatical elements within or between sentences makes a parallel structure. Logic dictates that grammatical elements with equal value in a sentence be constructed in the same grammatical form. Thus, "I prefer running, jumping, and to swim" does not exhibit parallelism, but does have awkwardness. "I prefer running, jumping, and swimming" demonstrates parallelism and logic. Parallel structure is also a stylistic technique often used to create emphasis and drama. The long fourth sentence in paragraph 14 of Martin Luther King's "Letter from Birmingham Jail" (Chapter 11) is a particularly effective example of parallel structure.

**Paraphrase** A paraphrase is a restatement of another person's words in your own words. This technique is particularly necessary when writing any essay in which you use others' ideas or words as evidence supporting your own argument. Often, you paraphrase instead of using a direct quotation in order to more easily mold the idea to fit your argument. The sense of the original, as well as the tone and order of ideas, remains the same. In either a paraphrase or a direct quotation you must give credit to your source. In a more informal paper you incorporate the credit into your text: "According to Charles Neerland, being a Minneapolitan means being cold much of the year." In more formal writing, such as a research paper, footnoting is required.

**Person** The grammatical distinction between the speaker (first person: I, we); the person spoken to (second person: you, singular and plural); and the subject spoken about (third person: he, she, it, or they) is labeled *person*.

**Persona** A fictional speaker in an essay or the fictional narrator of a story is its persona. The character, attitudes, and ideas of the persona are often different from those of the author. In fact, it is often the persona's character, attitudes, and ideas that are held up for criticism. The persona of Swift's "A Modest Proposal" voices ideas that Swift obviously finds abhorrent.

**Personification** *See* **Figures of speech**.

**Persuasion or persuasive argument** Persuasive writing is an attempt to win readers to a point of view and, often, move them to action. It appeals primarily to the emotions, as opposed to *argument*, which is meant to win the reader by reason and logic. Most often, the two are used together.

**Plagiarism** Presenting someone else's words or ideas as if they were your own is plagiarism. It is a serious offense in the academic world and can lead to consequences such as failure and expulsion from school. Whenever you use someone else's words or ideas you must give that person credit in your own text or by citation (*see* **paraphrase**).

**Point-by-point and subject-by-subject development** These are the two basic methods for developing a comparison-and-contrast essay. Point-by-point development alternately presents each point being considered. Subject-by-subject development presents all the details about one side of the argument first and follows with all the details about the other side.

**Point of view** In an argumentative essay the point of view is the author's opinion or the thesis the writer hopes to advance. In expository essays it is the physical or mental vantage point from which the author views the subject. An essay on professional football told from a player's first-hand experience would be approached differently from that of the team's owner (whose interest may be exclusively financial) or from that of a newspaper reporter. Each would approach the subject with a different kind of authority. And that authority would mean a difference in vocabulary, style, and tone. The player might use first **person** to capture immediacy. The owner might want to involve the reader in experiencing her financial woes and so use second person. Or, to create a mood of objectivity, the reporter might use the third person. The point of view in an essay must remain consistent. An inconsistent point of view can leave the reader confused and disconcerted.

**Post hoc argument** *See* **Logical fallacies**.

**Premise** A deductive **syllogism** is composed of two premises and a conclusion. The first or major premise is an assumption and the second or minor premise is a fact or another assumption based on evidence: All mammals are animals (first premise is an assumption). Raccoons are mammals (second premise is a fact). Therefore, all raccoons are animals (conclusion is logically deduced from the two premises).

**Prewriting** All the activities a writer goes through before actually beginning to write are part of *prewriting*. These might consist of brainstorming for a subject, doing background reading, narrowing the subject, devising a thesis, planning the essay—everything, in other words, that leads to the actual writing.

**Probable conclusions** Conclusions arrived at by inductive reasoning and from incomplete evidence are *probable conclusions*. The reader's acceptance of a conclusion that follows from inductive reasoning is often referred to as the *inductive leap*. To establish a clear connection between the evidence and the conclusion, the writer must be sure to present **relevant evidence, sufficient evidence**, and **representative evidence**.

**Proposition or thesis** In argument, the proposition or thesis is a written assertion, the opinion the writer wants a reader to accept, or an action the writer wants a reader to take.

**Psychological time** Arranging events in a narrative so as to show how they are connected in memory, shifting back and forth in time while keeping a sense of forward movement, creates *psychological time*.

**Purpose** The goal the writer wants to achieve is the *purpose*. The clearer the writer's purpose, the more clarity, coherence, and unity the essay will have. If the writer's purpose is muddled, the essay too will be muddled. All kinds of purposes are possible: to entertain with an amusing story; to inform; to convince readers of a point of view and move them to action. These purposes can be achieved by using the rhetorical modes: narration, description, exposition, and argument. In an essay you may use them alone or in combination.

**Qualification** Tempering broad statements to make them more logically acceptable is the technique called *qualification*. In qualifying a statement the writer admits that exceptions to that assertion are possible or probable, thereby indicating that the statement is not oversimplified. In these days with much emphasis on physical fitness, the statement "Physical exercise is good" might, at first blush, seem valid. But exercise may, in fact, be detrimental to some people. Therefore the statement needs qualifying. "Exercise is good for most people" might be a more acceptable statement.

**Reason and result** Another way of saying **cause and effect**.

**Refutation** The attempt to counter an opposing argument by revealing its weaknesses is called *refutation*. You must refute the opposition's argument if it is obvious and is strong or logical enough to be a real alternative to your own. The refutation usually is done early in an argumentative essay to get it out of the way so that you can proceed with your own argument. The three most usual strategies are pointing our weaknesses in the opposition's evidence, questioning the argument's relevance, and pointing out errors in logic. Refutation indicates that the writer is aware the issue is complex and is willing to consider opposing opinions. To be effective, refutation must always be done in a moderate tone and must always be accurate in representing the opposing argument. To do otherwise is to risk being judged harshly by the reader for sounding intemperate and for treating the opposition unfairly.

**Relevant evidence** You can directly support the essay's thesis and contribute directly to its conclusion with relevant evidence (*see* **representative evidence** and **sufficient evidence**).

**Representative evidence** Representative evidence covers the full range of information related to an essay's thesis, not just one side or the other. An argument cannot be convincing unless evidence from every point of view is admitted (*see* **relevant evidence** and **sufficient evidence**).

**Representative sample** A representative sample is a typical example chosen from among examples that exhibit similar characteristics.

**Rhetoric** Rhetoric is the study and art of using prose effectively. The various methods of prose discourse described and exemplified in this textbook—narration, description, exposition, and argument—are rhetorical forms.

**Rhetorical question** A rhetorical question is posed for effect and no answer is expected. It is a question meant to provoke thought or to launch the writer into the subject to be discussed in the writing.

**Satire** The form of writing using wit, irony, and ridicule to attack foolish and vicious human behavior and the institutions and customs that promote such behavior is *satire*. Two main types of satire are at the writer's disposal: social satire, which is used to attack foolish, but not dangerous, behavior and does it by invoking laughter and sympathy; ethical satire, which is far sharper and points with anger and indignation at social corruption and evil (*see* Jonathan Swift's "A Modest Proposal" in Chapter 11).

**Sentimentality** Sentimental writing overemotionalizes its subject and thus becomes ineffective. Sentimentality is often emotion displayed for the sake of emotion, losing connection with the actuality of the thing that supposedly caused the emotion. Sentimental writers risk readers' ridicule because they don't fully acquaint the reader with the actuality and thus appear to overreact.

**Simile** *See* **Figures of speech**.

**Slang** Colorful and humorous expressions, mostly short-lived and often peculiar to a group of people, are called *slang*. Almost always informal, slang is unacceptable in formal writing except in quotations and for creating special effects.

**Specific examples** *See* **Examples**.

**Standard English** The English language in its most widely accepted form, written and spoken by educated people in both formal and informal contexts, and having universal currency though it incorporates regional differences, is *standard English*.

**Strategy** The means by which writers effectively accomplish their purpose is *strategy*, which involves evaluating the audience, narrowing the subject, choosing a dominant rhetorical pattern such as narration, description, examples, comparison and contrast, and definition, among others.

**Style** The distinctive way in which a writer writes creates an individual *style*. Choice of words, structure of sentences, use or nonuse of figurative language—all contribute to a writer's style. Two writers may write about the same subject, have the same attitude toward the subject (*see* **tone**), and yet "sound" distinctly different. Style is a writer's writing personality and can be developed with practice.

**Subject-by-subject development** *See* **Point-by-point development**.

**Sufficient evidence** In an argumentative paper you must supply ample evidence to convincingly support your conclusion (*see* **relevant evidence** and **representative evidence**).

**Summary** A summary is a comprehensive and usually brief recapitulation of previously stated facts or statements. Summarizing your main points is one way of concluding a paper.

**Suspense** The pleasurable uncertainty or excitement we feel when anticipating what will happen next as we read a story is *suspense*. This tactic is most evident in mystery or detective stories but is less dramatically present in much narration.

**Syllogism** A form of deductive reasoning composed of two premises and a conclusion is the *syllogism*. The first premise (major premise) is an assumption and the second (minor premise) is a fact or another assumption based on **evidence**.

The conclusion is logically deduced from the two premises: All human beings are animals (major premise is an assumption). Ephraim is a human (minor premise is a fact). Therefore, Ephraim is an animal (conclusion is logically deduced from the two premises).

**Symbol** A symbol is any concrete thing that means something beyond itself. Many symbols are, on the surface, clear-cut and readily acceptable. The flag, of course, represents country and elicits patriotic feeling. But ideas and attitudes differ about what constitutes patriotism and what things conjure patriotic feelings. Some people become proud when their country asserts itself militarily. Others find their patriotic values in freedom, tolerance, fairness, and compassion. The flag, a rather simple symbol as symbols go, therefore has a complex of powerful meanings beyond itself. Symbols are employed most in fiction and poetry, less in exposition and argument. But they can be used in the latter to express meaning concisely and palpably.

**Synecdoche** *See* **Figures of speech**.

**Thesis** The thesis is the main point in expository writing, an idea that all the other ideas and facts in an essay should point to and support. A thesis can be either clearly stated or implied. It is most commonly found at the end of an early paragraph. A thesis cannot be a statement of fact, because facts do not need proving. A thesis, therefore, must have an argumentative edge, a point of view that will be proven or demonstrated in some way somewhere in the paper.

**Tone** Diction, sentence variety, figurative language, and anything else that establishes the writer's attitude toward the subject forms the tone, which can vary extensively. A writer's tone can be amused, angry, exasperated, approving, surprised, sarcastic. It can, in other words, run the gamut of human emotions. But tone should be consistent, for it must inform the entire essay and lead the reader to the response the writer desires.

**Topic sentence** A topic sentence states the main idea of a paragraph. All other sentences in the paragraph support the topic sentence. Most often it appears at the beginning but can be placed anywhere in the paragraph.

**Transitions** Transitions are words, phrases, sentences, and paragraphs that link ideas. Because a reader cannot get into the writer's head, it is the writer's responsibility to make sure that the ideas are clearly stated and that relationships between the ideas are clear. The first way to ensure that clarity is to organize ideas so that they flow logically from one to another. But even sturdier bridges are needed to carry the reader from sentence to sentence and from paragraph to paragraph. For this continuity you will need to use transitional devices such as these:

1. In the first sentence of a paragraph repeat some words or phrases from the last sentences in the preceding paragraph.
2. Use pronouns to refer to nouns in the preceding paragraph. You must be careful here to make precisely clear which words the pronouns refer to.
3. Use transitional expressions to carry the reader.

   *Addition:* also, in addition, too, moreover, and besides, further, furthermore, equally important, next, then, finally.

   *Example:* for example, for instance, thus, as an illustration, namely, specifically.

   *Contrast:* but, yet, however, on the other hand, nevertheless, conversely, in contrast, on the contrary, still, at the same time.

   *Comparison:* similarly, likewise, in like manner, in the same way, in comparison.

   *Concession:* of course, to be sure, certainly, naturally, granted.

   *Result:* therefore, thus, consequently, so, accordingly.

   *Summary:* as a result, hence, in short, in brief, in summary, in conclusion, finally, on the whole.

   *Time sequence:* first, second, third, fourth, next, then, finally, afterward, before, soon, later, during, meanwhile, subsequently, immediately, at length, eventually, in the future, currently.

   *Place:* at the front, in the foreground, at the back, in

the background, at the side, adjacent, nearby, in the distance, here, there.

**Two-part classification** Often called *binary*, two-part classification is the simplest way of breaking a subject down. This pattern divides the subject in two, usually into positive and negative categories, such as vegetarians, nonvegetarians; smokers, nonsmokers; television viewers, nonviewers of television, and so on. But two-part classification is usually inexact and skirts the edge of comparison and contrast. Most classification systems, therefore, have at least three categories.

**Typical examples** *See* **Examples**.

**Understatement (Litotes)** *See* **Figures of speech**.

**Unity** In a paragraph, every idea and every sentence relates directly to and helps support the main idea, usually stated in the topic sentence. Likewise, in the essay as a whole, every unified paragraph points to and supports the essay's main idea expressed in the thesis.

**Warrant** Warrant is the supporting argument in Toulmin's model of reasoning (*see* **Claim**).

**Writing process** The various tasks a writer must perform to produce a piece of writing are called the writing process. **Prewriting** entails a series of activities that pave the way for the actual writing. Only after this stage can the writer make the first draft, revise it into a number of subsequent drafts, and then polish it to achieve the final product.

# *A Guide to Editing and Revising Sentences*

This guide will help you revise your sentences to make them more readable and interesting. Unfortunately, no one has invented a clear procedure to follow when editing and revising prose. Some writers revise as they carefully work their way through a first draft; others swoop through the first draft and then revise during a second or third draft. Each writer, it seems, devises his or her own approach.

Two preliminary steps in revision do seem to be adopted by all writers. First, they must learn what makes writing effective. We offer this guide as a source of suggestions you can use to gain that knowledge. Second, they must pick up a pencil and go to work on their sentences. We must now stand aside and wish you the best of luck.

### *Eliminate pretentious language.*

Pretentious writing draws attention to itself. The vocabulary is unnecessarily complex, perhaps because the writer has thumbed through a thesaurus replacing simple words with difficult words. Always try to select simple words over fancy ones. If you want to indicate that dogs make good pets, do not write, "Domesticated canines will contribute felicity to anyone's life."

The earthquake ~~struck with a malignant force that~~ killed ~~destroyed the lives of~~ more than than four thousand villagers.

Children ~~frolicking with their companions exhibit~~ playing with friends demonstrate these fears.

### Eliminate obsolete, archaic, and recently invented words.

Over the years some words and their meanings change or fall from common use. A good dictionary labels these words and meanings "obsolete" or "archaic." Obsolete words or meanings should not be used at all. "Yestereen," meaning last evening, is obsolete. Archaic words still occur in special contexts, especially in literary or religious works. "Thou" and "thee," "brethren," and "kine" appear in the King James version of the Bible and are identified as "archaic" in dictionaries. Unless you have a special reason for using archaic words, they too should be eliminated from your writing.

Recently invented words, or *neologisms*, are so new to the language that they may be unacceptable in college writing. Often neologisms, such as "teleplay," "floppy disk," and "aerobics" become part of our common vocabulary because they are the clearest way of referring to the things they stand for. But neologisms may quickly fall from use, as "usership," "time frame," and "palimony" may do any day. If a neologism is in common usage, then feel free to use it, but if it was created very recently, then use another word or phrase or risk confusing your reader.

### Eliminate sexist language.

Rid your sentences of sexual bias. Traditionally, the masculine pronouns "he," "him," and "his" have been used to refer to members of either sex when gender is indefinite. Today, such usage leads to gender stereotyping, and we have a number of simple ways of eliminating sexist language in writing. One option is to change "his" to "his or her."

*Faulty:* Every attorney must prepare *his* closing remarks with care.

*Revised:* Every attorney must prepare *his* or her closing remarks with care.

This solution may generate wordiness and become awkward if applied throughout a longer passage. An alternative solution is to revise the sentence with the plural "attorneys," which would call for the plural pronoun "their" and eliminate the suggestion of gender.

> *Revised:* Attorneys must prepare their closing remarks with care.

"Man" and "men" are used to refer to both men and women. With some thought you can change this practice in your writing. "Policeman" can be changed to "police officer"; "mailman" to "mail carrier"; "congressman" to "member of Congress"; "mankind" to "humanity," "people," or "human beings."

### *Eliminate slang and regional expressions.*

*Slang* can be the colorful vocabulary that arises from the experience of a group of people with common interests, such as teenagers, rock stars, jazz musicians, actors, baseball fans, street gangs, and truck drivers. Unfettered by dictionary definitions, slang changes rapidly, reflecting each group's perceptions. Most slang expressions, such as "awesome," "bummer," "downer," "sleezoid," "rad," "bro," and "stoked" appear, increase in use, and then either become trite or shift in meaning. When slang words such as "jazz" and "A-bomb" become part of the general vocabulary, you may use them freely. Generally in college writing, however, revise your sentences to eliminate slang because it is imprecise and may be confusing.

> unpredictable, depressed
> As a type, comedians are ~~trippy, bummed out~~ one moment
> elated
> and ~~flying~~ the next.

> criticized
> The reviewers ~~ragged on~~ Kaufmann's poetry collection for
> being sentimental.

*Regional expressions* are associated with a geographical area. A "soda pop" in one part of the country is a "tonic" in another. A "skillet" in one region is a "frying pan" in another. Generally, you should eliminate regional expressions from your college writing for the same reason as you should avoid slang: you may confuse the reader.

> The vice squad had been ~~fixing~~ preparing to arrest Hawkins for months.

### *Use technical language, or jargon, with care.*

When writing for a group of computer specialists, you may use such terminology as "hard disk," "modem," "user area," and "megabyte" with confidence that your readers will understand; these are technical terms, or jargon, which computer specialists use freely.

Most occupations and special activities have technical vocabularies. A person in advertising uses "story board," "outsert," "keyline," and "live tag" with ease. A ballet dancer feels equally at ease with "adagio," "barre," "sickle foot," and "pointe." Such language, however, is inappropriate for most readers.

Technical language is especially insidious when taken from its proper field and used in a broader context. Technical vocabulary from psychiatry is inappropriate when used to describe the behavior of any animals other than human beings.

> The whale seemed ~~traumatized~~ stunned as it floundered in the shallow surf, struggling to beach itself and ~~fulfill~~ die. ~~its unconscious death wish~~.

### *Consider the denotation and connotation of words.*

*Denotation* is a word's literal definition, found in a dictionary. *Connotation* describes the emotional colorings that surround the word and influence how a reader might respond to it.

According to one dictionary, the word "apple" denotes "a round, firm, fleshy, edible fruit with a green, yellow, or red skin and small seeds." For some of us the word "apple" also connotes health ("an apple a day keeps the doctor away") and knowledge (the apple is often referred to as the forbidden fruit in the Garden of Eden, and the apple is the gift left on the teacher's desk). No wonder the name "Apple" seemed appropriate for the country's first popular personal computer (the logo even features an apple with a bite taken from it, "a little bite (byte) of knowledge is healthy for you"). It became "the apple of the consumer's eye"!

As a writer you must consider both the denotation and connotation of the words you use. If you do not, you may create a meaning you did not intend, as the writer of the next sentence does in attempting to describe how the company president moved through a crowded room to sit down and start a meeting.

> *Faulty:* Robert Rice, the company president, maneuvered himself to the chair at the head of the table.

Inadvertently, the writer creates a feeling that Robert Rice manipulated his way into the presidency of the company.

> *Revised:* Robert Rice, the company president, sat in the chair at the head of the table.

When selecting one of several words that have nearly the same meaning, you must take special care. Consider the words "emulate," "copy," and "mimic." Their denotations are similar, but they differ in connotation.

> Beginning writer Jane West ~~mimics~~ *emulates* romance novelist Rosemary Rogers's style.

The connotation of "mimic" is too negative for the sense this writer wants to convey, which is that West strives to achieve quality equaling that of Rogers.

***Select concrete and specific words rather than abstract and general ones.***

Abstract words name qualities, ideas, and concepts we experience in our feelings and our thoughts: "freedom," "love," "hate," "hope," "democracy," "honesty," and so on. Concrete words label things we experience through our senses: "smack," "kiss," "laugh," "smoke," "dance," "shout," and so on.

General words cover relatively large groups of things: "food," "places," "people." Specific words name specific things, a more limited segment of a large group: "pizza," "Boston," "Tom Cruise." "General" and "specific" are relative words. Language becomes more specific as it moves from the general group to a unique example of the group, as from "athlete" to "professional athlete," to "baseball player," to "Babe Ruth."

| *General* | *Specific* | *More specific* |
|---|---|---|
| weapon | pistol | .45 automatic |
| fish | shark | hammerhead |
| food | pasta | linguini |
| music | popular music | rock and roll |
| Native Americans | Plains Indians | Sioux |

College writers are inclined to overuse abstract and general words. Their sentences, therefore, can be vague, leaving their writing drab and lifeless. As you revise your sentences, replace vague wording with more concrete and specific wording wherever you can.

The subway ~~was frightening.~~ smelled of fear.

A crowd ~~waited~~ restlessly milled in the square.

The night ~~was dark~~ turned black as clouds swept in from the north.

Envy ~~brings out the worst in people~~ makes people scheme, manipulate, and steal.

You should also replace *euphemisms* with specific language. A euphemism is a word or phrase substituted for another word that is harsh or blunt. The funeral industry substitutes "loved one" or "the deceased" for "corpse," "vault" for "coffin," and "final resting place" for "grave site."

Euphemisms often may be necessary for tactfulness. No doubt most of us prefer to ask a stranger to guide us to the restroom rather than the toilet. Euphemisms may, however, distract us from the realities in experiences such as poverty, unemployment, and war. We have become accustomed to the euphemism of "low income," "inner city," and "correctional facility" as substitutes for "poor," "slum" or "ghetto," and "jail." Euphemisms are pervasive in the language of "polite society" and so you must guard against their slipping into your finished papers. If you find euphemistic phrasing when revising your sentences, consider rewriting the phrase in more specific language.

decline
The ~~deteriotion of his ecomonic status~~ began when he ~~became~~
lost his job, car, and house.
~~unemployed~~.

lying
Military officials seem to believe that ~~misrepresenting the facts~~

is acceptable ~~behavior~~.

### *Use figurative language with care.*

*Figurative language* draws a comparison between two things that are essentially different but alike in some underlying and surprising way. The two commonest figures of speech are simile and metaphor.

A *simile* expresses a comparison directly by connecting two ideas with "like" or "as."

His face was like the sky, one minute overcast, the next minute bright.

—*Joseph Conrad*

The bowie knife is as American as the half-ton pickup truck.

—*Geoffrey Norman*

A metaphor expresses a comparison indirectly, with neither "like" nor "as."

Roads became black velvet ribbons with winking frost sequins.

—*Hal Borland*

A sleeping child gives me the impression of a traveler in a very far country.

—*Ralph Waldo Emerson*

To be effective, a simile or metaphor must create a verbal image or clarify a writer's thought by making it understandable in other words. When a simile or metaphor is trite or overblown, it must be revised.

When he leaned toward the audience and smiled, his gold tooth
reflected the light.
~~shined like a bright star~~.

*Mixed metaphors* create confusion by combining two or more incompatible comparisons.

circling
Thought is restless, soaring and diving before ~~coiling around~~ an idea.

"Soaring" and "diving" suggest a bird in flight. "Coiling" suggests a snake, leaving the metaphor mixed and in need of repair.

### Eliminate trite expressions.

*Trite expressions* are phrases that have become stale by overuse. They include clichés ("He ran around the neighborhood *like a chicken without a head*"), wedded adjectives and nouns ("They made a *lifelong commitment*"), and overused phrases ("We all know that *the rich get richer and the poor get poorer*"). Many trite phrases appear in early drafts of college papers, especially if the writing has been rushed. When revising, strike out trite expressions and reword them in a more direct way.

> undeniably
> He was ^ guilty ~~beyond a shadow of doubt.~~ ⊙
>
> almost bankrupt.
> The business was ^ ~~sinking in a sea of red ink.~~
>
> T
> ~~To make a long story short,~~ the widow married the banker.

To make you more aware of trite phrases, here are some of the most exhausted ones.

| | |
|---|---|
| a crying shame | in the final analysis |
| a thinking person | in the nick of time |
| after all is said and done | last but not least |
| at this point in time | method in his madness |
| depths of despair | never a dull moment |
| drop in the bucket | none the worse for wear |
| face the music | pay the piper |
| flat as a pancake | quick as a flash |
| in this day and age | sadder but wiser |

### Eliminate wordiness.

*Empty phrases* make your writing unnecessarily wordy. Often one word will do the work of an entire empty phrase.

> Barthes believes ~~is of the opinion~~ that culture can be understood by reading the "signs" it generates.
>
> ~~It is usually the case that~~ ~~d~~Diet books usually encourage the dieter's fantasies about being slim.

Study this list to become familiar with common empty phrases and substitutes for them.

| *Empty phrase* | *Substitute* |
|---|---|
| at all times | always |
| at this point in time | now |
| at any point in time | then |
| by means of | by |
| due to the fact that | because |
| for the purpose of | for |
| give consideration to | consider |
| give encouragement to | encourage |
| in order to | to |
| in the event that | if |
| in the final analysis | finally |
| make contact with | call |
| of the opinion that | that |
| regardless of the fact that | although |
| the fact that | that |
| until such time as | until or when |

Repetition of key words is often necessary for parallel structure or for emphasis, but needless repetition leads to boring, wordy sentences.

> The Pacific rattler ~~rattlesnake~~ is California's most dangerous snake.

I ~~continue to~~ still believe that government will not continue unless the Attorney General acts.

*Redundancy* is similar to needless repetition in that it conveys the same meaning twice, as in the phrases "visible to the eye" and "large in size." Like needless repetitions, redundancies make your sentences wordy and should be eliminated during revision. At times, an entire sentence or passage may need to be rewritten.

> If researchers probe the fac~~tual truth deeply~~ts, they will find the solution.
>
> Millions of ~~people who~~ voters support national health insurance.
>
> Though suffering from malaria, he continued ~~on~~ his journey to the Mayan temple.

These are some common redundancies.

- advance forward
- autobiography of her life
- basic fundamentals
- circle around
- close proximity
- combine together
- consensus of opinion
- continue to go on
- disappear from sight
- factual truth
- important essential
- refer back
- repeat again
- round in shape

***Eliminate unnecessary expletive constructions.***

The word "there" followed by a form of the plain verb "to be" is an *expletive*, a word used to fill out a sentence. An expletive signals that the subject of the sentence will follow the verb. This construction is unnecessarily wordy and lacks the vigor of subject-verb constructions.

> ~~There are~~ two horses trotting in the meadow.
>
> ~~There is no hope for~~ the rain forests, face destruction.

The pronoun "it" often functions as an expletive in similar constructions.

> ~~It is difficult to~~ analyze poetry, is difficult.

At times, however, "it" often is needed as an expletive, as in "It is raining."

***Revise passive sentences.***

*Voice* is the quality in verbs that shows whether a subject is the actor or is acted upon. "The arroyos were flooded by rain" is a passive sentence because the subject, "arroyos," is acted upon. In contrast, "Rain flooded the arroyos" is an active sentence because the subject, "rain," is the actor. Active constructions are more concise, direct, and forceful than passive constructions.

> The tornado left death
>
> ~~Death~~ and despair ~~was left by the tornado.~~
>
> T~~he western world's attention was captured by~~ Nelson Mandela's speeches, captured the western world's attention
>
> Scientists consider astrology
>
> ~~Astrology is considered by scientists~~ to be a mere superstition.

Although generally in revising you should eliminate unnecessary passive constructions, at times the passive may be necessary. Passive constructions are appropriate when the subject is ambiguous or when you wish to emphasize the receiver of an action.

> The mysterious rumor was received from New York.

In this example, the writer does not know who started the rumor.

> His self-esteem was damaged by years of severe criticism.

In this example, the writer wishes to emphasize the thing that received the action, "self-esteem."

### *Revise for proper coordination.*

Clauses that have equal importance in a sentence are *coordinate* and should be connected by a coordinating word or punctuation mark. To show the relationship between equal clauses you need to select the proper coordinator.

*Coordinating conjunctions*

and but for nor or so yet

*Correlative conjunctions*

both . . . and either . . . or neither . . . nor
not only . . . but also whether . . . or

*Conjunctive adverbs*

| | | | |
|---|---|---|---|
| consequently | furthermore | however | meanwhile |
| moreover | nevertheless | therefore | thus |

Different coordinators show different relations. The common kinds of relations are addition, contrast, choice, and result.

*Addition:* Reviewers criticized his paintings, and collectors stopped buying them.

*Contrast:* Once novels were the primary home entertainment, but today television predominates.

*Choice:* Either we human beings will stop polluting the earth, or we will perish amid our waste.

*Result:* Advertising campaigns sell products; therefore, manufacturers are willing to pay for them.

Writers sometimes use semicolons to give equal emphasis to main clauses when the main clauses they connect are closely related in meaning and structure.

In Irish folklore, spirits sometimes appear as men or women; at other times they appear as birds and beasts.

When revising a paper, correct faulty coordination that gives equal emphasis to unequal or unrelated clauses.

*Faulty:* John Fowles is the author of three bestsellers, and he lives in England.

The clause "he lives in England" has little connection to the clause "John Fowles is the author of three bestsellers." These two clauses therefore should not be coordinated. Still, the writer might want to include the information, even though it does not relate directly to the main idea.

*Revised:* John Fowles, who lives in England, is the author of three bestsellers.

*Revised:* John Fowles, an English writer, is the author of three bestsellers.

You should also revise to eliminate excessive coordination; that is, stringing main clauses together for no apparent purpose. This practice can become monotonous for the reader and fails to show the proper relation between clauses. A sentence with excessive coordination must be untangled and rewritten.

*Excessive:* Americans desire heroes, and they find them in films, sports, and politics, but sometimes the real-life behavior of hero figures is disappointing, and then they must find new ones.

*Revised:* Americans desire heroes, whom they find in films, sports, and politics, but sometimes the real-life behavior of hero figures is disappointing, which means they must find new ones.

*Revised:* Americans desire heroes, whom they find in films, sports, and politics. Sometimes the behavior of real-life hero figures is disappointing, which means they must find new ones.

### *Revise for proper subordination.*

Clauses deserving less emphasis in a sentence are dependent and should be introduced by a subordinating word. To establish the correct relation between a main clause and a dependent clause, you must use the proper subordinating word.

*Common subordinating conjunctions*

| | | | |
|---|---|---|---|
| after | although | as | as if |
| as soon as | because | before | if |
| in order that | since | so that | though |
| unless | until | unless | when |
| whenever | where | wherever | while |

*Relative pronouns*

| | | | | |
|---|---|---|---|---|
| that | what | whatever | which | whichever |
| who | whoever | whom | whomever | whose |

Choosing which clause to subordinate depends, of course, on your intention, but writers commonly subordinate a clause to show concession, identification, time, cause, condition, and purpose.

*Concession* ("as if," "though," "although")

*Although the evidence clearly called for a guilty verdict,* the jury found him innocent.

*Identification* ("that," "when," "who")

Medical researchers, *who came from around the world,* gathered in San Francisco for the convention.

*Time* ("before," "while," "as soon as")

The attacks continued *as soon as the troops withdrew.*

*Cause* ("because")

*Because historians know how events turned out,* they study the causes of those events.

*Condition* ("if," "unless," "provided")

*If bombastic masculinity hides fear of inferiority,* many police officers lack feelings of self-worth.

*Purpose* ("so that," "in order that")

Following a catastrophe, people must accept reality *so that healing can begin.*

When revising your sentences, check to see if you have faulty or excessive subordination. If so, rewrite the sentences.

reproductive

Professor Clark, ~~who is~~ noted for her work in

cell

~~the~~ chemistry, ~~of cells when they reproduce has~~

prestigious

received the Louis Pasteur Award, ~~which is~~

~~highly prestigious.~~

***Place modifiers with care.***

A writer can confuse a reader by misplacing a modifier in a sentence. When revising your sentences, be sure to place modifiers so that a reader will be certain which words they modify.

Revise sentences with a *dangling modifier,* a phrase or clause not clearly attached to any word in the sentence. To correct a dangling modifier, see that it clearly relates to the intended word.

> *As he ran*
> ~~Running~~ through the meadow, his breathing made steamy clouds.
>
> *a writer must keep*
> To complete a screen play, a daily schedule ~~must be kept.~~
>
> *he spent* *his*
> After six months in therapy, ~~the~~ psychiatrist pronounced him cured.
>
> *I was*
> When a student at Reed, Ken Kesey was the student body's favorite writer.

For clarity, revise sentences to place modifiers as close as possible to the words they modify.

> *in Hollywood restaurants*
> Many beginning actors wait on tables to support themselves ~~in Hollywood restaurants.~~
>
> An aging athlete who exercises occasionally hurts himself.

Be particularly aware of where you place limiting modifiers, such as "only," "hardly," "just," "nearly," "almost," and "ever." They can function in many positions in a sentence, but they modify the expression immediately following them. As these limiting modifiers change position in a sentence, the meaning of the sentence also changes.

> I will go *only* if he asks me. [Otherwise I will stay.]
> *Only* I will go if he asks me. [The others will stay.]
> I will go if *only* he asks me. [Please ask!]
> I will go if he asks *only* me. [If he asks others, I will stay.]

Revise sentences with lengthy modifiers placed between important sentence elements.

B

~~Inner city crime~~, because of the increase in drug

inner city crime

use and reduced law-enforcement budgets, is rising.

T

~~The winning candidates appeared~~, to the surprise

the winning candidate appeared

of his supporters, unprepared.

W

~~The rescue team has been~~ with the help of local

the rescue team has been

scouts, searching for the lost teenagers all night.

Revise sentences with modifiers that split infinitives awkwardly. An infinitive consists of "to" plus the simple form of a verb: "to dance," "to moan," "to study," and so on. Usually, a split infinitive can be revised effectively by placing the modifier more accurately.

When oil was discovered, even conservative bankers began

to frantically invest in land.

Sometimes a sentence with a split infinitive cannot be revised without creating a misreading. Rewrite the sentence.

| | |
|---|---|
| *Faulty:* | His inability to *clearly* explain the issues cost him the election. |
| *Faulty revision:* | His inability to explain the issues *clearly* cost him the election. |
| *Rewritten:* | His inability to explain the issues *in clear language* cost him the election. |

### *Eliminate faulty pronoun reference.*

*Pronoun reference* is the relation between a pronoun and its *antecedent*—that is, the word to which it refers. If a pronoun's reference is unclear, the sentence will confuse or misinform a reader. Revise sentences so that a pronoun refers clearly to one antecedent.

> After Duff had studied Shakespeare for a decade, he realized
> Shakespeare
> that ~~he~~ was a master psychologist.

Revise sentences that use "this," "that," or "it" to make a broad reference to an entire sentence.

> I ed
> While ^ watch~~ing~~ *Friday the 13th* on television, my cat howled
> which
> and sprang onto my lap, ^ ~~This~~ ^ frightened me.

Revise sentences that use "it," "they," and "you" without specific antecedents. In conversation these pronouns are often used to make vague reference to people and situations in general. In writing, this practice should be avoided.

> one reporter
> During the "Six O'Clock News," ~~it~~ ^ gave a special report on
> intelligence testing.
>
> School policy does
> ~~They do~~ not allow soliciting on campus.
>
> a police officer
> In law enforcement~~, you~~ ^ must stay alert to a community's
> changing values.

Using "you" to refer to "you the reader" is perfectly appropriate in all but the most formal writing.

If *you* major in accounting, then you should find a job easily.

Revise sentences with pronouns ending in "-self" and "-selves" in place of other personal pronouns.

> The philosophy professor tried to convince Robin and me ~~myself~~ that Albert Camus was fundamentally an optimist.

Pronouns ending in "-self" and "-selves" should refer to words within the sentence.

> To stay calm, *I* talked to *myself*.
> Nick Ufre is such a sly character, *he* tricked *himself*.

***Eliminate inconsistencies in sentences.***

Revise your sentences for faulty shifts that indicate your thinking is not clear. Often a faulty shift in consistency takes place in pronoun reference.

> If students properly prepare for their tests, they ~~you~~ will not fear failing.

> If you stretch your muscles before a workout, you ~~a runner~~ will not face injury.

Faulty shifts also afflict verb tenses, which can confuse time sequences.

> The dancer rehearsed for six months, but finally master~~s~~ed the movement and was ready to perform.

Sometimes shifts in the *mood* of a verb confuse a writer's intent.

> Study the causes of World War I, and then ~~you should~~ study World War II.

A common inconsistency befalls a writer who shifts from active to passive voice, thus dropping from the sentence someone or something performing the action.

> In the game of curling a player slides a heavy stone over the ice toward a target, and a teammate sweeps the ice in front of the stone ~~is swept~~ to influence its path.

You should also revise sentences with shifts between direct and indirect discourse. *Direct discourse* includes a direct quotation: "Dr. Jones said, 'Life, my friends, is boring.' " *Indirect discourse* rephrases a direct quotation and therefore does not require quotation marks: "Dr. Jones had indicated that life is boring."

| | |
|---|---|
| *Faulty shift:* | The judge said to pay the fine and "Never return to my court again." |
| *Revised:* | The judge said to pay the fine and never return to his court again. |
| *Revised:* | The judge said, "Pay the fine and never return to my court again." |

Finally, revise sentences with *faulty predication,* which occurs when the information that follows a linking verb does not rename or describe the subject of the verb. In the sentence, "Dr. Brown is a full professor," both "Dr. Brown" and "full professor" refer to the same person. And in the sentence, "Dr. Brown is short," "short" clearly describes "Dr. Brown." In both sentences the predication is logically consistent; that is, the information following the linking verb "is" clearly renames or describes the subject. When the sentence's predication is faulty, however, you must revise it.

*Faulty:* The issue of gun control is an easy solution to a complicated problem.

The predication is faulty because the subject "issue" is not a "solution," as the sentence indicates. The "issue," however, is "complicated."

*Revised:* The issue of gun control is complicated.

*Revised:* Gun control is an easy solution to a complicated problem.

Sometimes predication is faulty because "when" is misused; the word should be used to indicate time.

*Faulty:* Nepotism is when officials appoint their relatives to desirable positions.

*Revised:* Nepotism is the appointing of relatives to desirable positions.

*Revised:* Nepotism takes over when relatives are appointed to desirable positions.

***Complete your sentences.***

Some sentences are incomplete because they lack words a reader needs to understand them. Often comparisons are not complete. Revise your comparisons to make them clear and logical.

Dr. Casey treats students better/ than other professors.

Mystery novels are easier to read than romance novels/ are.

The silence of the streets was more frightening

a wail from

than ^ a siren.

In some sentence constructions writers omit words that are understood, and this practice is correct.

> *Correct:* Two people control the city government: one is the mayor; the other, the mayor's wife.

But if omitted words do not fit consistently into the structure, the omission is faulty and the sentence must be revised.

> In the woods I feel the peace of nature; now, [I feel] the violence of the city.
>
> Humans have a strong belief [in] and desire for love.

***Maintain parallelism.***

When you revise a paper, maintain *parallel structure* by keeping similar ideas in the same grammatical form. In a pair or a series, you must make items parallel to avoid awkward shifts in construction. A noun must be matched with a noun, a verb with a verb, a phrase with a phrase, and a clause with a clause. Revise your sentences to make coordinate ideas parallel.

> She loved reading Anne Tyler's novels and [Anne Sexton's] ~~the~~ poetry. ~~of Anne Sexton.~~
>
> His summer activities were [dancing] ~~the dances~~ at Hotspur's and sleeping until noon.

Words such as "by," "in," "to," "a," "the," and "that" should usually be repeated when they apply to both elements in a parallel construction.

> By not developing their land and [by] ignoring tax-reporting requirements, the family found itself bankrupt.

Revise your sentences to make compared and contrasted ideas parallel.

> Ms. Lauko would prefer ~~to~~ work on her physics project rather than playing chess.
>
> Zen masters are materially poor, but they are rich ~~in spirit~~.

Revise correlative constructions to make them parallel. The ideas joined by correlative conjunctions, such as "either . . . or," "rather . . . than," and "not only . . . but also," should be parallel.

> The law applies not only to people but also corporations.
>
> Cosmo is either dreaming about the future or ~~in a deep~~ examin~~ation o~~f the past.

***Provide variety in your sentences.***

One way to create varied sentences is to revise sentence beginnings. Most inexperienced writers start their sentences with a subject. Unyielding repetition of this pattern can become monotonous, but if you frequently vary your sentence beginnings, you can offset the monotony.

***Begin with an adverb.***

> The answer came unexpectedly in a dream.
>
> A low moan suddenly echoed through the empty mansion.

### *Begin with a prepositional phrase or verbal phrase.*

Victory for most politicians justifies any behavior.

A banker who wants to be successful must speak Japanese and "computerese."

Allen Bates rubbed his hands together and studied the photograph.

### *Begin with descriptive phrases.*

Violence, which was the only solution left, hung in the air like a heavy mist.

He picked up the pencil and felt his hand tremble.

The basics necessary for a secure childhood include food, shelter, and love.

You can also vary sentences by mixing their structures. In an early draft you might rely too heavily on one kind of structure. When you revise your paper, include varied structures.

Simple sentences have only one main clause and no dependent clauses, although they may have several modifiers and modifying phrases.

A crucial function in writing advertisements is manipulating clichés. They help involve consumers.

Compound sentences have two or more main clauses but no dependent clauses.

> Puns are said to be the lowest form of humor, but ad writers breathe new life into them.
>
> Consumers must analyze an ad writer's techniques, and ad writers must create new ones.

Complex sentences have one main clause and at least one dependent clause.

> When ad writers sit at their word processors, they must rely on their understanding of the popular imagination.
>
> Ad writers who work at major advertising firms are dramatically influencing public perceptions.

Compound-complex sentences have at least two main clauses and at least one dependent clause.

> If you are curious about commercial influences in society, examining advertisements critically will reveal the desires ad writers stimulate, but be careful because the examination may stimulate your desire for a new car, a trip to exotic islands, or merely time with "people who like beer."

You should also consider revising your sentences to vary their form. You might include an inverted sentence now and then, but not often. Inverted sentences reverse typical subject-verb structures by moving the verb ahead of the subject.

> At
> ~~The vault is at~~ the bottom of a winding staircase that leads into the cellar. is the vault

Occasionally use a question to create sentence variety.

What does the ? means "mask" and

~~The~~ word "persona" mean~~s~~ ~~mask.~~" It refers to a theatrical mask

that Greek actors wore on stage.

# *Acknowledgments*

"What You See Is the Real You" by Willard Gaylin, *The New York Times*, October 7, 1977, OP-ED. Copyright © 1977 The New York Times Company. Reprinted by permission.

"Photographs of My Parents" from *The Woman Warrior* by Maxine Hong Kingston. Copyright © 1975, 1976 by Maxine Hong Kingston. Reprinted by permission of Alfred A. Knopf, Inc.

"Meat" by Sallie Tisdale. Copyright © 1994 by the Antioch Review, Inc. First appeared in the *Antioch Review*, Vol. 52, No. 3 (Summer 1994). Reprinted by permission of the Editors.

"Once More to the Lake" from *Ones Man's Meat* by E.B. White. Copyright 1941 by E.B. White. Reprinted by permission of HarperCollins Publishers, Inc.

"The War Room at Bellevue" by George Simpson. Originally seen in *New York Magazine* Reprinted by permission of the author.

Excerpt from *Match to the Heart* by Gretel Ehrlich. Copyright © 1994 by Gretel Ehrlich. Reprinted by permission of Pantheon Books, division of Random House, Inc.

"Finishing School" from *I know Why the Caged Bird Sings* by Maya Angelou. Copyright © 1969 by Maya Angelou. Reprinted by permission of Random House, Inc.

"A Hanging" from *Shooting an Elephant and Other Essays* by George Orwell, copyright 1950 by Sonia Brownell Orwell and renewed 1978 by Sonia Pitt-Rivers, reprinted by permission of Harcourt Brace & Company.

"The Masked Marvel's Last Toehold" from *Confessions of a Knife* by Richard Selzer. Copyright © 1979 by David Goldman and Janet Selzer, Trustees. By permission of William Morrow and Company, Inc.

"Trapped in Another Life" by Art Harris, © 1990 The Washington Post. Reprinted with permission.

"Los Pobres," excerpt from *Hunger of Memory* by Richard Rodriguez, pp. 130-139. Reprinted by permission of David R. Godine, Publisher, Inc. Copyright © 1982 by Richard Rodriguez.

"On Natural Death," pp. 102–5, copyright © 1979 by Lewis Thomas, from *The Medusa and the Snail* by Lewis Thomas. Used by permission of Viking Penguin, a division of Penguin Books USA Inc.

"Mother Tongue" by Amy Tan. © Amy Tan. First published in *The Threepenny Review,* 1990. Reprinted by permission.

"Black Men and Public Space" by Brent Staples. Originally published in *The New York Times Book Review*. Reprinted by permission of the author Brent Staples, author of the memoir, "Parallel Time: Growing Up in Black & White."

"Tools of Torture" by Phillis Rose. Copyright © 1986 by Phyllis Rose. Reprinted by permission of Georges Borchardt, Inc. for the author.

Excerpt from "Future Shlock" from *Conscientious Objections* by Neil Postman. Copyright © 1988 by Neil Postman. Reprinted by permission of Alfred A. Knopf, Inc.

"Grant and Lee: A Study in Contrasts" by Bruce Catton. Copyright © U.S. Capitol Historical Society. Reprinted by permission.

"Los Otros, Mis Hermanos," excerpt from *Hunger of Memory* by Richard Rodriguez, pp. 12–18. Reprinted by permission of David R. Godine, Publisher, Inc. Copyright © 1982 by Richard Rodriguez.

"Sexism in English: A 1990s Update" by Alleen Pace Nilsen. Copyright © 1990 by Alleen Pace Nilsen. Reprinted by permission of the author.

"Hers; Two Varieties of Killers" by Ellen Currie, *The New York Times,* August 21, 1986. Copyright © 1986 by the New York Times Company. Reprinted by permission.

"My Wood" from *Abinger Harvest,* copyright 1936 and renewed 1964 by E.M. Forster, reprinted by permission of Harcourt Brace & Company.

"Why We Crave Horror Movies" by Stephen King. Reprinted with permission. © Stephen King. All rights reserved.

"Baby, Take a Bow" from "Waiting for Miss America" from *Tuxedo Junction: Essays in American Culture.* Copyright © 1989 by Gerald Early. First published by The Ecco Press in 1989. Reprinted by permission.

"The Revolt of the Black Bourgeoisie" by Leonce Gaiter, *The New York Times Magazine,* June 26, 1994. Copyright © 1994 The New York Times Company. Reprinted by permission.

"Kids in the Mall: Growing Up Controlled" from *The Malling of America* by William Severini Kowinski. Copyright © 1985 by William Severini Kowinski. By permission of William Morrow and Company, Inc.

"Binding Decisions" by Joan Gould. First published in *Memories* Magazine, February/March 1989. Reprinted by permission of Harold Ober Associates Incorporated. Copyright © 1989 by Joan Gould.

"Commanded by Love" by Richard Strozzi Heckler. Reprinted from *Whole Earth Review,* Fall 1993. Reprinted by permission of Richard Strozzi Heckler, author of *The Anatomy of Change* and the nationally acclaimed *In Search of the Warrior Spirit.*

"Guns R Us" by Matthew Maranz, *The New Republic,* January 23, 1989. Reprinted by permission of *The New Republic,* © 1989 The New Republic, Inc.

"On Keeping a Notebook" from *Slouching Towards Bethlehem* by Joan Didion. Copyright © 1968 by Joan Didion. Reprinted by permission of Farrar, Straus & Giroux, Inc.

"The Maker's Eye: Revising Your Own Manuscripts" by Donald M. Murray. From *The Writer,* October, 1973. Reprinted by permission of the author.

"American Regional Costume" from *The Language of Clothes* by Alison Lurie. Copyright © 1981 by Alison Lurie. Reprinted by permission of Melanie Jackson Agency.

"Three Kinds of Discipline," excerpted from *Freedom and Beyond* by John Holt. Reprinted by permission of Holt Associates (Boynton/Cook Publishers, A Subsidiary of Reed Elsevier Inc., Portsmouth, NH, 1995, 1972).

"Territorial Behavior," reprinted from *Manwatching* by Desmond Morris. Published in 1977 by Harry N. Abrams, Inc., New York. All rights reserved. Reprinted by permission.

Excerpt from "Notes on Class" from *The Boy Scout Handbook and Other Observations* by Paul Fussell. Copyright © 1982 by Paul Fussell. Reprinted by permission of Oxford University Press, Inc.

"Obstacles to Clear Thinking" by Richard D. Altick, excerpted from *Preface to Critical Reading*, Sixth Edition by Andrea A. Lunsford and Richard D. Altick, copyright © 1984 by Holt, Rinehart and Winston, Inc., reprinted by permission of the publisher.

"I Want a Wife" by Judy Brady, *Ms.* Magazine, December 1971. Reprinted by permission of the author.

Excerpt from "Why Men Marry" from *Men and Marriage*, by George Gilder, copyright © 1986 by George Gilder, used by permission of the publisher Pelican Publishing Company, Inc.

"A Definition of Poverty" is excerpted with the permission of Simon & Schuster from *The Other America* by Michael Harrington. Copyright © 1962, 1969, 1981 by Michael Harrington.

"Violent Reactions" by Shari Miller Sims, *Self* Magazine, March 1989. Courtesy *Self*. Copyright © 1989 by the Conde Nast Publications Inc. Reprinted by permission.

"Who and What is American?" by Lewis H. Lapham. Copyright © 1991 by *Harper's Magazine*. All rights reserved. Reproduced from the January, 1992 issue by special permission.

This is an excerpt from "The Killing Game" by Joy Williams which first appeared in *Esquire*. Copyright © 1990 by Joy Williams. Reprinted by permission of the author.

"What's Wrong with Animal Rights?" by Vicki Hearne. Copyright © 1991 by *Harper's Magazine*. All rights reserved. Reproduced from the September issue by special permission.

"Letter from Birmingham Jail" from *Why Can't We Wait* by Martin Luther King, Jr. Reprinted by arrangement with the Heirs to the Estate of Martin Luther King, Jr., c/o Joan Daves Agency as agent for the proprietor. Copyright © 1963 by Martin Luther King, Jr., copyright renewed 1991 by Coretta Scott King.

"The Shrieking of the Lambs" by Andrew Klavan. First appeared in *Boston Review*, June-September 1994. Copyright © 1994 by Andrew Klavan. Reprinted by permission of the Author.

"Denial Behavior" from *Hollywood vs. America* by Michael Medved. Copyright © 1992 by Michael Medved. Reprinted by permission HarperCollins Publishers, Inc.

**Photo Credits**

Chapter 1, © Michael McGovern/The Picture Cube; Chapter 2, © Walter S. Silver/The Picture Cube; Chapter 3, © Fredrik Bodin/Stock, Boston; Chapter 4, © Jerry Howard/Stock, Boston; Chapter 5, © Spencer Grant/The Picture Cube; Chapter 6, © Rick Smolan/Stock, Boston; Chapter 7, © Glen Korengold/Stock, Boston; Chapter 8, © Jerry Howard/Stock, Boston; Chapter 9, © Lionel Delevingne/Stock, Boston; Chapter 10, © Gale Zucker/Stock, Boston; Chapter 11, © Michael Weisbrot/Stock, Boston.

# *Instructor's Manual for The Longwood Reader*

*Instructor's Manual for*

# *The Longwood Reader*

*Third Edition*

Edward A. Dornan
Charles W. Dawe

*Orange Coast College*

Allyn and Bacon

Boston London Toronto Sydney Tokyo Singapore

A Viacom Company
160 Gould Street
Needham Heights, MA 02194



ISBN 0-205-26234-1

Printed in the United States of America

10 9 8 7 6 5 4 3 2 1     99 98 97 96

# Contents

## 6 / Comparison and Contrast IM-46



## 7 / Cause and Effect IM-60



## 8 / Process Analysis IM-75



## 9 / Classification and Divisionx IM-92

## 10 / Definition IM-107



## 11 / Persuasion and Argument IM-120

# *Preface to the Instructor's Manual*

On the following pages we have provided commentary on the essays in Chapters 3–11. For each essay we have included Teaching Suggestions, Notes, and Possible Answers.

Our suggestions for teaching are just that—merely suggestions. You will find that they often give some background information to help set the stage for class discussion and then refer to the essay itself.

Following each teaching suggestion, we have provided a series of notes arranged sequentially through the paragraphs of the essay. These notes are chock-full of observations on writing strategies, comments about allusions, information about references, and musings on culture. Their main purpose is to save you time.

Following the notes, we offer possible answers to the questions that follow each essay.

We have tried to be helpful. We hope you will find this material useful and interesting.

# 3 / Description

## *Photographs of My Parents*

### Maxine Hong Kingston

### Teaching Suggestions

Rarely will an author attempt to develop an essay by focusing readers' attention on description primarily, as Kingston does in "Photographs of My Parents." Ostensibly describing meager biographical artifacts, Kingston outlines her mother's life, from young adult to aged matriarch, obliquely including remnants of her own life.

Archeology scientifically studies ancient lives and cultures, in part by examining artifacts excavated at the sites of ancient civilizations. You might begin an "archeological exercise" by asking the class to discuss one famous person: a politician, a movie star, a world leader, or the like. Then ask them to imagine that thousands of years from now, archeologists discover the site where this famous person thrived. The question for discussion is this: "What five artifacts—any objects made by human beings—would best represent or symbolize this person's qualities?"

After such a discussion, students see that much can be learned about people by scrutinizing their possessions; they can create a carefully contrived descriptive essay by concentrating on the artifacts that go into the essay, rather than on characters, actions, or settings.

### Notes

**Paragraph 1**

"joy": The word joy is represented in "abstract" Chinese ideographs; that is, the classical ideographs themselves have been shaped into a form combining message and ornamentation.

During the Chinese Civil War (1945–1949) between the communist troops of Mao Tse-Tung and the nationalist troops of Chiang Kai-Shek, many Chinese fled China for Hong Kong.

"bat": In China, the bat is emblematic of happiness and long life.

"Canton, Hong Kong . . .": Kingston mentions four predominantly Chinese regions in the Far East, each having its distinct politics and customs; all are Chinese, nonetheless.

**Paragraph 2**

The National Republic of China, under Chiang Kai-Shek, was formally recognized by the United States in 1928.

"A stork and . . .": The stork-brings-the-baby myth can be traced to an Old Norse legend. To account for the mother's bed rest after giving birth, children were told that the stork bit the mother just before he departed. The stork has long been a symbol of filial devotion: The Romans enforced *Lex Ciconaria*, the "Stork's Law," compelling children to care for their aged parents.

"Ex-assistant etranger . . .": literally, "Former foreign teacher (ex-assistant) at the surgical and maternity clinic of the University of Lyons."

*Chop* is from Hindi *chap*, "impression, stamp." A chop is an official stamp or seal; also, a person's "signature stamp," used in many parts of Asia.

**Paragraph 3**

The small mystery about the mother's true age heightens interest in this descriptive passage.

**Paragraph 5**

The white chrysanthemum has a long and fabled history in both China and Japan. The famous haiku poet Basho wrote that the white chrysanthemum "remains immaculate," even under intense scrutiny.

"dartless": In tailoring, a dart is a short, stitched fold meant to make a garment fit closely while conforming to the natural shape of the body.

"My mother has eyes . . .": Earlier, Kingston's mother had "spacy eyes, as all people recently from Asia have." Now the eyes have become "accustomed" to America, and the description gives Kingston a chance to comment obliquely on her mother's life.

**Paragraph 6**

The beginning of a *flashback*, a device with which writers present a scene or incident that happened before some preceding scene or incident in the work.

Fred Astaire (1899–1987) starred in such musical comedies as *Top Hat* (1935) and *Shall We Dance?* (1937). His graceful and original tap dancing was famous.

**Paragraph 9**

The photographs are described as if they were ordinary identification or passport photos.

"sea bird": A sea bird painted on a ship's bow may be a traditional emblem of protection, but it is also interesting that a bird, according to Jungian theory, is a beneficent creature representing spirits or angels, supernatural aid, or thoughts and flights of fancy.

"Two quilts": Notice that Kingston's mother took one quilt for each of them.

## Possible Answers

*Meaning and Purpose*

1. Encourage students to discuss how they feel about old photographs. Ask them to describe some photographs in as much detail as Kingston does.
2. The Chinese in the photographs are nearly expressionless because "Chinese do not smile for photographs" (3), and Kingston "can't tell if [her mother] is happy" (4). The Chinese-Americans in the photographs are "always laughing" (6), and they pose as westerners do.
3. The seals and words over the photographs of Kingston's mother show that the photographs were official. They are not taken for pleasure, or to capture fun or happiness, as those of Kingston's father are.
4. Kingston's father is happy-go-lucky in some photographs. He works in a laundry, watches American movies, adapts an American custom about "stomping on straw hats" (6), and pursues a course of study. He seems to combine fun, work, and ambition.
5. The women were unaccustomed to decoration, and the dresses did not conform to the female figure. The flowers therefore seem out of place, and were pinned on awkwardly.
6. The bat is a symbol of happiness and long life in China.

*Strategy*

1. Kingston organizes her essay as the contents of the metal tube are organized: she describes the three scrolls as they appear, one inside another. The transitions from one section to the next are the second sentence in paragraph 2, and the first sentences in paragraphs 4 and 9.
2. Some examples of sensory details are: *smell*—"The smell of China flies out, a thousand-year old bat . . . brain" (1) (metaphor); *sight*—"Her naturally curly hair is parted on the left, one wavy wisp tendrilling off to the right" (3) (image); and "flowers that look like gears for a gold machine" (1) (simile). Examples of *impression* or *feeling* are: "Most of the graduates are girls whose faces have not yet formed . . . happy" (4), and "She wears a scholar's white gown and she is not thinking about her appearance" (3).
3. This is a subjective essay, told from the author's point of view.
4. Kingston describes the tube in careful details that evoke China: the "joy" ideographs, the flowers, and the stamps. The tube was damaged in the mail but still carries the smell of China. These details already suggest a contrast between East and West and prepare readers for the depth of detail that follows.

*Style*

1. Kingston is nostalgic about the China of her mother's younger life when she describes, in paragraph 1, the smell flying out of the tube, and in paragraph 9, "In China, there was time to complete feelings." She describes her mother with affectionate detail.
2. Kingston's mother embodies the essence of China, as the tube does. She is rigid and contained, and her Chinese customs are "damaged" by life in the West, like the tube.
3. *Ophthalmology*, specialty in eyes; *pediatrics*, specialty in children's medicine; *gynecology*, specialty in women's medicine; *dermatology*, specialty in the skin; *therapeutics*, specialty in remedies.

# *Sins of the Flesh*

## Sallie Tisdale

### Teaching Suggestions

A good way to start a discussion of Tisdale's essay is the obvious: Ask students whether they eat meat. This seemingly innocuous question generates a surprising combination of answers. Some students say that they eat meat, but only special cuts (T-bone steaks, liver, and hamburger, for example) and only for special reasons (to give them "strength," to get their iron supply for the day, to be social, and so forth). And, of course, many students these days have become informed vegetarians who will argue firmly against eating any meat. You will also have the "in-betweens," those who drink milk but consume no other animal-produced food and those who eat fish but nothing else that breathes. Your reason for asking this question, obviously, is to get to the core of that question: Why do students prefer their personal diets? Nowadays, with our focus on getting healthy and remaining so, this question naturally follows the first one. Then, you will find it stimulating to ask if anyone has had a reason similar to Tisdale's, for giving up eating meat. The point is to have your class discuss what they believe to be Tisdale's reason.

## Notes

**Paragraph 1**

Note the "clean skin" description. At this point, the butcher shop not only appeals to the sense of sight but also to the sense of smell.

**Paragraph 2**

The juxtaposition of parts of the author's body with parts of the butcher shop shows how intimate, in some sense, the author feels about her surroundings. She and the items in the butcher shop have, to her way of thinking, a strong relationship; its textures are her textures, when *textures* refers to "the qualities given, as to a musical or literary work, by the combinations of interrelations of parts or elements."

**Paragraph 3**

The basement is "lifeless," yet the author injects life into it with the "freezing queer fog" blowing into her face and her skin breathing again. And notice how disorderly/orderly this life/no-life microcosm is, with its carefully labeled meat sitting like a "haphazard pile of white rocks."

**Paragraph 4**

Here is the first strongly autobiographical commentary in the essay. Tisdale describes her family by the kinds of meat that it eats, how, and when. In the sense that it is used here, the word *purchase* means "to get a leverage on; to apply a lever, pulley, or other aid," in this case the carving knife.

**Paragraph 5**

"time seemed to stand still": Note the tense change following this clause. The author tells the reader, in past tense, about time's standing still. And then, by changing to the present tense, she causes time to stand still in the reader's mind. This strategy of playing with time, common in Tisdale's writings, reminds readers of the flow of the present into the past.

**Paragraph 7**

Again we have Tisdale's interesting strategy of changing from the past, introductory tense, to the present, on-going tense, which gives a sense of life to that which has already occurred again and again in the author's past.

**Paragraph 8**

"papillae" (plural): small protuberances, bulges, concerned with the sense of taste. Note that the tongue itself moves in metaphor from being "an enormous apostrophe of flesh" to being "as soft as angel cake."

**Paragraph 9**

Tisdale addresses the reader in the modern equivalent of *prosopopoeia*, which is the classical-rhetoric term used to describe "an imaginary or absent person speaking or acting." While she has all along addressed the implied reader, here the author directly talks to her. The paragraph itself is the turning point in the essay, moving as it does from Tisdale the innocent to Tisdale the informed: In the most "natural" way, she is told the origin of meat.

**Paragraph 11**

This "effect" paragraph shows how Tisdale changed her diet upon discovering where meat comes from; it moves from the immediate effect, that of going without meat altogether, to the on-and-off-again effect that has lasted until now.

"It's a heartfelt knowledge": Note that the words used in her description of that knowledge—"visceral," gut-level," and "organic"—are words that strongly imply meat itself.

**Paragraph 12**

Tisdale's condensed version of her growing up and then moving on with her life passes from adolescence to young maturity, ending with the most painful action, that of leaving her home. Note that she did not merely "leave"; she grew "wings like angel wings" and "flew away." As well as being linked to various religions, the angel symbolizes invisible forces, of powers that ascend and descend between life and afterlife.

**Paragraph 13**

"Butcher": The Old English *bucca* means "he-goat," equivalent to the Old French *bouchier*, "he-goat," which is the more direct ancestor of "butcher". (See e.g., *The Random House Dictionary of the English Language*, 2nd edition unabridged, revised 1987.) "*shehitah*": This Hebrew noun refers to the slaughtering of animals for food by a certified person, in the manner set forth by Jewish law. "*shochet*": Also spelled *shohet*, this word refers to the person certified by a rabbi or Jewish court of law to slaughter animals for food, as prescribed by Jewish law.

**Paragraph 15**

"you can't be cleansed": The causes of one's being "dirty" in this sense must be well known by a person before the ritual cleansing can be effective. The association between the ideas of sacrifice and salvation appear in many religions.

## Possible Answers

### *Meaning and Purpose*

1. The answer will probably deal in some way with juxtaposition, the act of placing close together for purposes of comparing and contrasting. Before the author realizes where meat comes from, she sees the shop as a clean, orderly, welcome place. She has no idea that such a place could be involved in the bloody forming of animals into meat. The description of the butcher shop symbolizes her innocence, thus preparing us for her later shock.
2. As described in paragraph 11, Tisdale eats no meat "for a long time after that." Later, as shown in the same paragraph, she moves back and forth from being a total vegetarian to being an almost crazed meat eater.
3. Answers vary but the gist of a satisfactory answer contains statements showing that the student knows the vocation itself has had a long and honorable history extending from the simple act of killing and cutting up animals to the religious acts embedded in, for example, Judaism.
4. The author quite honestly describes the fire in objectively descriptive prose for the most part; however, she does say that it was a "great fire." And her noting the "shriek of metal" suggests satisfaction if not outright happiness. In this same vein, "apocalypse," as used in the second sentence of this paragraph, refers to the forces of good triumphing over the forces of evil.

### *Strategy*

1. This strategy helps to reinforce the idea of sameness: The same activity occurs every time the author and her mother visit the butcher shop—again and again and again. Shifting to present tense makes the first sentence seem repetitious, which it should be because the act itself is repetitious.

2. This is an example of *personification*, giving animate characteristics to inanimate objects. Panting is how dogs perspire, and making the summer days "perspire" connects the description of the weather with the description of an animal, most appropriate in this essay for obvious reasons.
3. Answers vary, their quality depending on the student's supporting evidence. Paragraph 4 is most often chosen because of its catalog of the many kinds of meat that appear on the family dinner table and because of the description of how that meat is carved—with gusto.
4. In paragraph 8, the beef tongue is shown to be one of the "really special" treats that the butcher occasionally sells to the author's mother. In that same paragraph, the cooked tongue is compared to angel cake, its "delicious strips unlike anything else, melting, perfumed."

*Style*

1. The word *flaccid* refers to being soft, limp, not firm, and so forth. In this paragraph, the steaks look almost comfortable; lying in their "neat rows," they seem to be calmly awaiting their fate. The description contains no indication of the former strength of a live animal.
2. The word "pig's" is italicized to emphasize the author's shock at learning that what she had thought to be a "colorful metaphor" was in fact an accurate description.
3. Answers vary more than perhaps expected. Many students take this passage to mean that the author was ecstatic; others strongly argue that the author had no reason to be happy about leaving. After all, they point out, the family did nothing on purpose to cause the author grief.
4. The word *apocalypse* can refer to a cataclysm in which the forces of good triumph finally over the forces of evil. The word can also denote any widespread disaster. The author could well be using the word in both senses: The meat market's destruction represents a moral outcome for the author but a great loss for those who eat meat.
5. The word *turnouts* as it is used in paragraph 14 refers to the uniforms worn by the firefighters and to the fire-fighting equipment that they carry.

# *Once More to the Lake*

## E. B. White

### Teaching Suggestions

This evocative essay deals with time: its delightful past, its pleasant present, and its tragic future—when the author finally acknowledges its passing.

The subject intrigues students, mainly because it has not often been taken seriously: time is now, to many of us. Only as our days close do we realize that time is not constantly on the sidelines. It's here and we are its products. Hemingway said to Lillian Ross, "Time is the least thing we have of."

Instructors have energized a conversation on time by asking students, "How old is old?" Experience suggests that answers will vary, from "Five years older than I am right now," to "Forty." These answers will help to establish the chronological climate in which students approach this essay, which was written when White was about forty-one, about the age that is still considered a time for reflection.

After students have discussed age well enough to establish that no one has a definitive answer, instructors have asked, "How far back can you remember?" Again, answers range from five years to whenever, depending on how long students think about their answers.

The third and fourth questions lead in to White's essay: "How far back can you remember a pleasant experience that has meaning for you now?" followed quickly by "Has the meaning of the experience changed for you, over the years?" These two questions are not lightly answered, for they require much memory-searching, which one student calls "scratching the bottom of the database barrel."

When White visited the lake as a boy, the experience had no meaning for him except as a trigger: Lake = joy. No more. With age, however, his experience took on hitherto unsuspected meaning. Students often see that the past event, plus time, equals a new meaning for the event—after they have thought over their class discussion about time.

## Notes

**Paragraph 1**

Born in 1899, White would have been about five years old at the time of the earlier excursion.

*Nostalgia*, a longing for former happy times, is White's stimulus to return to the lake to "revisit old haunts," after almost forty years.

**Paragraph 2**

White combines light tension and reverie in this paragraph. First, he worries about how the lake might have been changed by encroaching civilization. Next, he recounts memories of his early days on the lake.

White reminds us that we can remember our calm moments of joy if we allow ourselves to pursue the mental paths of least resistance, letting one memory softly lead into another.

At the end of this paragraph, notice White's combining an image of nature (the lake) with a symbol of religion.

**Paragraph 3**

White gives us the larger picture of the lake, pointing out its general virtues, and then he mentions how those virtues appear through the eyes of a child—as "primeval"; that is, "of the earliest times or ages."

**Paragraph 4**

Throughout the essay, the boy is never clearly described; he is never identified beyond mere "boy." William Wordsworth's lines from *My Heart Leaps Up* (1807) are worth reviving here, as capturing the essence of White's "boy":

*The child is father of the man;*
*And I could wish my days to be*
*Bound each to each by natural piety.*

White approaches an almost instinctual, innate need to see himself as the boy.

**Paragraph 5**

The beginning of the adventure, the reliving of White's childhood. His years fall away, he becomes the boy again, and the water remains as when he had first seen it.

Water as symbol has a venerable history. Limitless and immortal in the eyes of the ancients, water is the beginning of all life. Homer, in book IV of *The Iliad*, speaks of "Ocean, who is the source of all." Modern psychology sees water as symbolizing the unconscious: the nonformal, dynamic, motivating, female side of the personality.

**Paragraph 6**

"enchanted sea": To enchant is "to cast a spell over," "to charm greatly," and more. An enchantment is a reduction to an inferior state, as in a person changing into an animal, for which see the story of Circe, as told in *The Odyssey*. White's "sea" enchants; that is, in mysterious ways the lake itself has its effect on White, causing him in a way to "be" his childhood self.

"This cultist": A cult is a system of ritual. White's passing comment is that some things never change. We will always have the pseudo-cultists of nature with us, who despoil nature by using it, this time to bathe with scum-producing soap.

**Paragraph 7**

White is no longer in 1904 or thereabout. Horse-drawn wagons produce three tracks, the middle one made by the horse. Now that the automobile has replaced the horse, the middle track has disappeared. For that matter, middle alternatives in people's lives also disappear with passing time, White suggests, but life itself goes on, "there having been no passage of time, only the illusion of it."

**Paragraph 8**

In ancient Greece, a paean was a hymn of thanksgiving to the gods, especially to Apollo, the god of music, poetry, prophecy, and medicine, represented as exemplifying manly youth and beauty. In this paragraph of unrestrained and timeless joy, White has written his own modern paean.

**Paragraph 9**

The less frequently we see something, the less likely we are to recognize it because of familiarity alone. In this paragraph, White dwells on the sheer excitement a boy feels (or felt) at the moment when the family arrived at the lake. These times were worth saving in the storehouse of his memory, from which other times have long since faded. (Nothing nowadays is as exciting as memories of past excitement.)

**Paragraph 10**

The paragraph begins with a complaint: the new outboard motors are too loud. Then it drifts into the past, when the older motors were comparatively silent and depended more on the operator. White as a boy had more control over machines; he could tinker with them, experiment, attain complete mastery. The man could control more of his life when he and machines were young.

**Paragraph 11**

As he does with the other paragraphs in this essay, White is playing with time. Halfway through this paragraph, he abruptly shifts from past to present, from "what it had felt like to think about girls then" to "After breakfast we (he and his boy) would go up to the store." This strategy reinforces his earlier claim that things remain the same, timeless in his eyes, a point that he makes clear in the last line of this paragraph, where the boy and he become indivisible.

**Paragraph 12**

"old melodrama": Typically, a melodrama ended happily, after the second-act *climax*, which describes the intensity of interest in the audience. White remains with the "timelessness motif," saying that "The whole thing was so familiar." The storm itself is indeed timeless: It is melodramatic, with its kettle, snare, and bass drums, and ancient Greece with its "gods grinning and licking their chops." It ends with the eternal comedian, who is out of place yet strangely appropriate—the two conditions of comedy.

**Paragraph 13**

The shock of recognition. White suddenly realizes that time in fact passes, and that he will pass with time as part of his life—his boy—goes on. No stores of imagination or memory can erase the knowledge that sooner or later one reaches the point of no return.

## Possible Answers

### *Meaning and Purpose*

1. Let students share experiences about places for which they feel nostalgia. Ask them how they look at the changes time has made in the place and in themselves, and how their feelings compare to White's.
2. White states that he wants to return to the lake to fish and "revisit old haunts" (1). He longs for "the placidity of a lake in the woods" (1), and to reconnect with his youth. This paragraph sets the scene for the return.
3. The title has a poetic ring that suits White's descriptions of nature. The words "Once More" are not final and suggest that this may not be White's last visit to the lake.
4. White understands that time at the lake has stood still because so many things are the same as when he was a boy—"The small waves were the same, chucking the rowboat under the chin as we fished at anchor, and the boat was the same boat, the same color green and the ribs broken in the same places . . ." (5). He even confuses his identity with his son's in paragraph 4. At the same time, White notices changes all around him—"The middle track was missing, the one with the marks of the hooves and the splotches of dried, flaky manure" (7)—and understands that change is inevitable.
5. White is suddenly confronted with his own death and the relentless march of time. Readers are prepared only in little ways as White records each change he sees.

### *Strategy*

1. In paragraph 12, White creates the impression of a storm as a natural drama played out. First it is oppressive, then percussive, then calm. White manipulates language to create impressions. "It was like the revival of an old melodrama"—a simile. The approach of the storm creates a "feeling of oppression," "a curious darkening of the sky," and a "lull in everything." Comparing the storm to the sound of drums is a metaphor. The language that describes the lake after the storm is quite different: "return of light and hope and spirits," "joy and relief," and "bright cries."
2. White uses many transitions to avoid confusion about time. In paragraph 2, thinking about returning to the lake with his son, he slips into a memory: "I guess I remembered clearest of all. . . ." In paragraph 5, he describes fishing with his son and says, "There had been no years between the ducking of this dragonfly and the other one—the one that was part of memory." Another shift to memory occurs in paragraph 9 with, "It seemed to me, as I kept

remembering all this, that those times and those summers had been infinitely precious and worth saving." Let students find other transitions between past and present.

3. The more specific the writing, the more nearly universal the meaning. Most students will have had some experience to help them identify with White's lake. But he goes beyond the specific, as in paragraph 8, when he talks about "summer without end" and "the American family at play," and also in paragraph 9, "There had been jollity and peace and goodness." White offers his lake as a symbol of natural goodness and American family values, the necessary retreat from the ills of the city.
4. White's "boy" becomes himself as White remembers his boyhood summers at the lake (5). If he had given the boy a more specific identity, it would have been harder for White to sustain the illusion that he becomes the boy.

*Style*

1. Some of the descriptive words about the lake are "Placidity" (1); in paragraph 2, "holy spot," "cool and motionless," "sweet outdoors," "the stillness of a cathedral." These words show the lake as a sacred place, undisturbed and natural, respected and held in awe, almost in a religious way. In paragraph 3, "remote and primeval" reinforces these impressions, as if to say the lake is prehistoric, without the imprint of people.
2. The essay is nostalgic and affectionate in tone, a little sad, and peaceful, like a reverie. White seems to need reconnecting with the lake before it's too late, before he, too, passes on. He delights in what he finds on his return: "I could tell it was going to be pretty much the same as it had been before" (4). And he feels sad and "jarred" by some changes (see sentences 2 and 3 of paragraph 10).
3. *Gunwale*, the upper edge of a ship's or boat's side; *primeval*, existing from the beginning; *transposition*, a changing of the normal order; *hellgrammite,* the dark brown aquatic larva of a fly, used as fish bait; *undulating*, moving in a wavy or flowing manner; *petulant*, rude, or capriciously ill-humored; *premonitory*, giving warning; *languidly*, sluggishly or listlessly. White expects his audience to be fairly well educated.

# *The War Room at Bellevue*

## George Simpson

### Teaching Suggestions

Reportorial description, the "see-it, write-it" detached yet energetic prose of the experienced observer, appeals to the reader's imagination because it displays little of the writer's own imaginative commentary, allowing readers to explore freely their own reactions. The fewer the writer's remarks about descriptions, the more readers can conjure their own remarks, a vital force behind all "appearance-versus-reality" prose.

Sometimes we look, but we do not see. Instructors can take advantage of this fact when introducing the article by asking students to look around, to see the classroom itself, often for the first time. How would the room seem to the outside observer?

Students often reply that the room is no more than "just a room." "Yes," you can reply, "and to medical personnel experienced in trauma, a battered woman is just a battered woman, a corpse is just a corpse, and a gunshot wound or a stabbing is just that. No more." To illustrate your point, you can then introduce this essay.

## Notes

**Paragraph 1**

Bellevue: The author lists the word's *connotations*, the implications or emotional surroundings that words in context carry, as distinguished from their denotative or lexical meanings. Simpson reinforces the connotations by quoting a nurse about Bellevue's rumored reputation.

**Paragraph 2**

Bedlam: In London, an old insane asylum, later a hospital for the mentally ill.

"Chance for survival": Bellevue has a world-class reputation for its trauma center.

**Paragraph 3**

A "typical" Friday night in Bellevue begins and all is routine, down to deciding who will go for coffee.

Simpson foreshadows events by showing the shock and seriousness of what has already happened.

"stiletto": A stiletto's blade is slender and tapering, designed for use as a weapon.

**Paragraph 4**

"Emergent!": In trauma-care jargon, *emergent* means "sudden, or unforeseen."

"Catheter": A catheter is a tube passed through the body for evacuating or injecting fluids from or into body cavities. This paragraph mirrors the standard operating procedure for trauma victims, which includes first aid for shock, test for blood type, and quick evaluation of internal organs.

**Paragraph 5**

Medically, shivers are slight tremors of the skin, as from cold or fear. To a nonmedical person like Simpson, perhaps it suggests shock, which is marked by paleness of skin.

The doctor tries to determine the depth of the wound and its nearness to bone, nerves, and other parts or systems of the human body. The yellow disinfectant probably is a tincture of iodine.

**Paragraph 6**

Juxtaposing the wounded man and the derelict suggests the spectrum of patients treated by Bellevue's staff.

**Paragraph 7**

Again, coupling examination of the Hispanic girl with that of the old white woman helps illustrate the kinds of patients who go to Bellevue. Notice that each woman is attended by a specialist.

**Paragraph 8**

"tetanus": Tetanus is an acute infectious disease that causes painful muscle spasms. Because its first sign is stiffness of the jaw, it is sometimes called "lockjaw." It is usually, but not always, fatal. Gamma globulin is a protein formed in the blood; it and other proteins, concentrated, resist infection.

**Paragraph 9**

"methadone": Methadone hydrochloride is a habit-forming, synthetic, analgesic drug with potency equal to that of morphine, but with weaker narcotic action. Under careful supervision, methadone hydrochloride is used to treat people who are dependent on drugs derived from opium, such as heroin.

**Paragraph 11**

The story of the suicide continues. Simpson shows that Bellevue becomes one setting for the drama of many people's lives.

**Paragraph 12**

Emergency room. Simpson's descriptions of people include a representative spectrum from military personnel to members of minority groups to children to battered women.

**Paragraph 13**

While preparing for a shift change, the conversations are normal. No one recounts a specific incident that happened during her shift. The implication is that no matter what happens, it is "normal" for Bellevue.

**Paragraph 14**

"triage": A triage nurse screens and classifies sick and injured people to determine the most efficient way of using medical and nursing personnel, equipment, and facilities. In emergency rooms, the triage nurse ranks patients in order of importance for treatment.

"IV's": Intravenous infusions. Solutions such as those containing saline, dextrose, or potassium chloride are injected into veins in an attempt to produce immediate results, when treating hemorrhage, shock, or collapse.

The casual comment at the end of this paragraph is not to be taken as a cold, unfeeling statement. People who work daily in trauma centers have learned to mask their feelings. The alternative is to destroy their careers by becoming psychologically involved with their work.

**Paragraph 15**

An appearance-versus-reality paragraph. The midnight episode quickly reminds other patients that their problems, in the harsh, comparative light of reality, may not be so serious after all.

**Paragraph 16**

Another appearance-versus-reality paragraph, this time comparing patients' view of the various emergencies with the Bellevue staffers' view of them.

**Paragraph 17**

Just as the drama of the suicide had a follow up paragraph earlier, the murder drama has its follow-up—Simpson's method of showing that life goes on, desperately or otherwise, despite the deaths at Bellevue.

**Paragraph 18**

"0 to 60": Simpson compares the quickness of the Bellevue trauma staff with that of an automobile that can accelerate from 0 to 60 miles an hour in five seconds, which is remarkably fast.

"Collapsed right lung": Although normal in a fetus, a collapsed lung in a mature adult is serious, often caused (though not in this case) by the rupture of a bleb (an "internal blister") on the pleural (membrane) surface of the lung, which then becomes airless or nearly so.

"As the nurses work . . .": Again, the nurses deal realistically with their lives while treating the lives of others. This healthy way of handling a job that could be emotionally painful distinguishes expert trauma center personnel from those who do not last long as employees there.

**Paragraph 19**

The last paragraph strongly reinforces what Simpson has been describing and commenting about all along: Although unnerving for lay visitors, emergencies are routine for the medical experts at a trauma center, particularly at Bellevue.

## Possible Answers

### *Meaning and Purpose*

1. Give students a chance to relate their own experiences in hospital emergency rooms and compare theirs to those Simpson describes.
2. Simpson's purpose is to expose a vital feature of Manhattan representing its people, violence, and trauma. He also wants to praise the emergency team by showing them in action.
3. At Bellevue injured people have a good chance for survival (2). Bellevue is a "monstrous complex" (2) like an "indoor war zone" (1). Some think it's only "for crazy people" (1). The emergency staff are highly trained and efficient. Simpson's details of the varied cases that come to them illustrate their expertise. "'This is nothing, about normal, I'd say,' concludes the head nurse. 'No big deal'" (19).
4. From the emergency ward Manhattan looks like a violent, harsh city with a wide racial and ethnic mixture. "A policeman . . . twisted his knee struggling with an 'alleged perpetrator.'" (10). "A Hispanic man complains of pains in his side." (12).
5. "Bedlam" is capitalized because it is a variant of "Bethlehem"—the Hospital of St. Mary of Bethlehem, an old insane asylum in London. Bedlam: a state of uproar and confusion, a wild and frantic condition.

### *Strategy*

1. Two introductory paragraphs set the scene and describe the hospital's reputation. Paragraphs 3–18 describe the typical activity of the emergency room from 9:00 P.M. Friday to 1:20 A.M. Saturday. The suicide story (8) has a follow-up in paragraph 11, and the gunshot victim (14–15) in paragraph 17. The final paragraph telescopes the activity till morning. This structure is clear and easy to follow. The sections by time suggest the methodical and orderly running of the emergency room.
2. Other stimulus-response patterns: the gunshot victim arrives (14), and the stab victim arrives (18).
3. Transitions indicating simultaneous action: "Meanwhile in the lobby" (6); "A Young Hispanic man interrupts" (7); "The pace continues to increase" (9); and "Meanwhile, patients arrive in the lobby" (12).
4. The present tense creates an immediacy that conveys the quick action and intensity of the emergency room.
5. A panoramic view of admitting desk, waiting room, and emergency room, where "one man sleeps fitfully" (3). A far-to-near arrangement shows when the ambulance arrives, the "glass doors burst open," and a man is put on the treatment table (4). Another visual sweep takes the eye from trauma room to examination rooms to hallway (8).

*Style*

1. The intense emergency-room activity shows in the depth of detail—"After a few seconds another doctor inserts his finger into the wound. It sinks in all the way to the knuckles" (5). Simpson is objective and detached; "Another woman breaks down in hysterics; everywhere young Hispanics are crying and comforting each other" (15), and "The young woman of the stairs is getting stitches in a small gash over her left eye" (18).
2. Words suggestive of battle are "war zone," "wounded and bleeding," "harried doctors," "rush from stretcher to stretcher," "crushing number of injured," "battlefield," and "survival."
3. The closing paragraph quickly surveys the time from 1:20 a.m. to "the morning hours." Simpson catalogues the cases even more dispassionately, not even specifying who has which injuries. This activity is routine. The tone conveys a less harried, less immediate, less alarming atmosphere. The narrator has pulled back from the situation.
4. The sound words are "whistle has blown," "mutter of voices," "sit quietly," "tiny bleep," and "nurses can hear." Paragraph 4 has mostly touch words, and paragraph 14, sound words.

# *Struck by Lightning*

## Gretel Ehrlich

### Teaching Suggestions

A successful gambit is to invite the students to talk about personal experiences to which they responded. You can open the discussion by noting that all of us have hundreds of small experiences daily; however, we remember only those to which we respond. For example, we might drive to school down a particular road, street, freeway, or expressway every day. We become so used to doing it that we rarely remember our drive to school. But one day, a car swerves directly into our path, we jam on the brakes, skid, and our car comes within inches of the other car's rear bumper. Our reaction to that experience will cause us to remember that experience for a long, long time.

Introduce this activity by telling the students that however else they describe their experiences, they should include as much of the "how, what, when, where, who, and why" details that they remember—in other words, be descriptive enough to help their listeners mentally recreate the experience. You should have quite a good time with this activity because many students have had rather touching experiences and some have had hilarious ones. After a few student examples of descriptive responses, go to the essay itself, to see how a master describer, Ehrlich, recounts a fantastic personal journey.

### Notes

**Paragraph 1**

"Deep in an ocean": Ehrlich begins her essay with reference to one of the oldest symbols in literature—water. Limitless and immortal, water in many religions and philosophies is the beginning and the end of all things on earth. Modern psychology has interpreted water as a symbol of the unconscious, that is, of the non-formal, dynamic, motivating, female side of the personality.

"liquid clouds of dust": This is an example of *synaeceosis*, a condensed paradox. Logically, either "liquid" or "dust" would be part of this phrase; ordinarily, we can't have it both ways. Compare Milton's "darkness visible," for example.

"the continent of the body": The word *microcosm* has several definitions, one being "human beings, humanity, or the like viewed as an epitome of the world." Ehrlich's phrase exemplifies that definition.

**Paragraph 2**

"Blue trickles in": Ehrlich refers to blood, which turns red when exposed.

**Paragraph 3**

"Blue water": Freud's *Introduction to Psycho-Analysis* points out that in dreams, birth is usually expressed through water imagery.

**Paragraph 4**

"My two beloved dogs": Dogs have long been emblems of faithfulness. In Christian symbolism, the dog is empowered with guarding and guiding the sheep, the flock.

**Paragraph 5**

Here the reader learns why the opening of this essay has been eerily mystical. Ehrlich has been struck by lightning; what has come before this paragraph describes in abundant physical and metaphysical detail her return to consciousness.

**Paragraph 6**

"its blue path": compare this "blue" with the *blue* in paragraphs 2 and 3, where the color is the product of the signs of blood and birth. The *blue* in this paragraph is the blue that attends the cause of the author's earlier statements containing that color.

"I had been walking": Here, the author takes the reader to the beginning of the events leading to her being struck by lightning. One might point out to students that this clause is a fine example of a "lead-in," a phrase or clause that helps the reader to try to predict what information will follow.

**Paragraph 7**

"you're okay as long as you're with me": The *irony*, the outcome of events contrary to what was expected, is that the dogs ultimately help Ehrlich to be "okay."

**Paragraph 8**

"I woke in a pool": The unpredictable shift from paragraph 7 to paragraph 8, without a transitional marker, mirrors the unpredictable shift from safety to disaster. One minute the author was "okay"; the next minute she "woke up in a pool of blood."

"dark pools in sand": The author begins and ends the paragraph with blood imagery, her rhetorical questions rendered into blood that turns the sand into "dark pools."

**Paragraph 10**

"Buddhist": The Buddha (566?–c.480), also called Siddhartha or Prince Siddhattha, founded Buddhism, which holds that life is filled with suffering caused by desire. The way to end the suffering is by enlightenment, which empowers one to halt the sequence of births and deaths to which one is otherwise subjected.

"sutra": *Sutra* refers to a Hindu collection of aphorisms on how to conduct one's life. In the Pali Hindi dialect, *sutta* refers to any of the sermons of Buddha.

"paradox": This term, from the Greek meaning "contrary to opinion or expectation," describes a seemingly self-contradictory statement that sometimes in a surprising way is true: "The night was dark until she smiled."

**Paragraph 11**

"the gate on the ranch": The ranch gate leading to nowhere mirrors the author's quizzical attitude towards her own fate.

**Paragraph 12**

"To be struck by lightning": Note the grim humor from juxtaposing *lightning* and *enlightened*.

"such terrible pain": In moments of terrible pain, the body feels as if it is disconnected from the mind; this is one of the feelings that denote shock.

**Paragraph 13**

"I loved those dogs": As noted in another context, the dog symbolizes faithfulness. In this sense, it appears often at the feet of women in the engravings on medieval tombs.

"until I faced east": The east, because it is where the sun rises, symbolizes spiritual illumination; to turn towards the east is to turn in spirit to the source of intellectual or spiritual enlightenment.

**Paragraph 14**

"I considered my options": The author is collecting her thoughts. She became again rational as she "calmly assessed what might be wrong" with her.

**Paragraph 15**

"To be struck again": Defying all odds, the author has actually been struck by lightning twice, at two different locations. She has a strong reason to wonder why.

**Paragraph 16**

"my brain was torn": Note that this image, often taken at face value by quick readers, actually refers to the author's state of mind.

**Paragraph 18**

"refulgence": that which shines radiantly. The intermediate description, linked as it is to the final clause, "I wondered when I would no longer be able to breathe," provides strong evidence that the author indeed believed that she was dying.

**Paragraph 20**

"tatami": From the Japanese: Thick, woven, straw mats, usually about three feet by six feet.

"EMT": Emergency Medical Technician, a person trained in techniques of administering emergency care.

**Paragraph 21**

"Sam and Yaki": Coincidentally, *Yaki* is Japanese for "broil," which suggests how the author sometimes seemed to feel—as if she had been broiled.

"IVs": In medical care, I.V. is jargon for any fluid being injected intravenously, within or into a vein.

**Paragraph 22**

"Cody": a town in Wyoming named after William Frederick ("Buffalo Bill") Cody.

**Paragraph 23**

"EKG": abbreviation for the German *elektrokardiogramm*. Here, the term refers to a device that records the electrical activity of the heart. The electrocardiogram gives important information concerning the spread of excitation to the different parts of the heart, which helps in diagnosing cases of abnormal cardiac rhythm, for example.

**Paragraph 24**

"ventricular fibrillation": a ventricle is a small cavity, in this case in the heart. A fibrillation is a quivering contraction of individual muscle fibers. Ventricular fibrillation, the quivering contractions of muscle fibers in a heart cavity, may be caused by mechanical injury to the heart; the common, loose definition of a heart attack.

"medullary": The medullary centers of the brain are the innermost portions, in contrast to the outer portion or cortex.

"comatose": In a condition of coma, an abnormal deep stupor occurring in illness, as a result of it, or due to an injury.

"apneic": From *apnea*, a temporary cessation of breathing.

"circulatory collapse": Shock occurring when the peripheral blood flow is inadequate to return sufficient blood to the heart for normal function.

**Paragraph 25**

"aura": In medical parlance, *aura* refers to a subjective sensation preceding a paroxysmal (sudden or periodic) attack.

"ER or ICU": *ER* is medical jargon for "emergency room" (and for "external resistance"); *ICU* is medical jargon for "intensive care unit."

"kerauno": This Greek prefix means lightning.

**Paragraph 26**

"hematocrit": A centrifuge for separating solids from plasma in the blood.

"osmolality": The characteristics of a solution determined by the ionic concentration of the dissolved substances per unit of solvent. (An ion is a particle containing an electrical charge.)

**Paragraph 27**

"gurney": A litter equipped with wheels, used in hospitals to transport patients.

**Paragraph 28**

"cool gold": From the Golden Fleece to the Holy Grail, world literature abounds with gold symbolizing hidden or elusive treasure of one kind or another; consequently, gold signifies all that is superior.

"dead face tipped backwards toward the moon": The symbolism of the moon, ancient and complex, often negatively alludes to error, arbitrary fantasy, or imaginative sensitivity.

**Paragraph 31**

"CAT scan": CAT is an acronym for "computerized axial tomography." A CAT scan is a non-invasive technique of showing detailed images of structures, in this case within the human body. It differs from an X-ray in that a CAT scan shows detailed images by blurring images in all other planes.

**Paragraph 32**

"arrhythmias": Irregularity or loss of rhythm, especially of the heartbeat.

**Paragraph 34**

"A rattlesnake": Throughout world literature, the snake has been imbued with energy. In India, cults of the snake are connected with the symbolism of the waters of the sea. Snakes also guard the springs of life and of immortality, from Adam and Eve to Jason and Medea, or vice versa.

**Paragraph 35**

"the dogs came back": In this final paragraph, the dogs clearly symbolize the best of defense in the name of faithfulness. Interestingly, in mythology the dog often appears as the companion of the dead on their final voyage.

## Possible Answers

### *Meaning and Purpose*

1. The casting of the answers will vary. Many students indicate one way or another that the first paragraph describes (or seems to describe) an embryo; this might be the beginning of a thorough description of how it feels to be a fetus. Others say that it could depict another kind of life beginning, perhaps at the bottom of the sea. The strength of the answers depends of course on their evidence.
2. The author, in fact, survived a kind of explosion. She attempts here to make some sense of it, and the first explosions she might remember are fictional ones, the mind's attempt to restore order from chaos. As quickly as she realizes what she is thinking, she wants to laugh.
3. Ample evidence shows that the reader has abiding interest in non-Western thought. Probably the strongest evidence is contained in paragraph 10, with its discussion of the "Buddhist instruction regarding dying." The author also has tatami in her house (paragraph 20), and one of her dogs has a Japanese name (*Yaki* = "broil").
4. Given their diction, sentence structure, and style, these paragraphs are obviously from a medical text. They might have been inserted by the author as an efficient way to inform her audience about the symptoms and treatment of lightning victims.

### *Strategy*

1. By putting those "heartbeat sentences" so far away from each other, the author is emphasizing just how slowly her heart was beating. In fact, as it says later in the essay, her body was slowly recovering from a heart attack at that time.
2. The dogs are both faithful and unquestionably loyal at a time when even nature seems chaotic and untrustworthy. They function as a steady foil to the disorder that permeates the essay, thus illustrating by contrast how much confusion existed.
3. Although the doctor "had never completed a residency and had been barred from ER or ICU work in the hospitals of Florida," the author was fortunate because he had had much experience dealing with patients who had been struck by lightning.
4. Paragraph 27, with its three-wheeled gurney slamming the patient into a wall, also notes that neither doctor nor nurse had cleaned the cuts in the patient's head. She was finally cleaned up by her friend Laura. Other evidence is in paragraph 28, where the author is said to be the only patient, and in paragraph 31, where "no one had bothered to find out why" the patient had lost consciousness, for example.

### *Style*

1. The author humorously links "lightning" and "enlightened," as if a cause-and-effect sequence obviously existed. However and clearly, *enlightened* refers to one who has received intellectual or spiritual knowledge, not a massive electrical shock.
2. Answers vary interestingly: Based on the definition in the textbook's glossary, many students say that the question is clearly rhetorical, citing the part of the

definition that says a rhetorical question is posed for effect, not to elicit an answer. Others, however, have argued that it must be something else because the question does not provoke thought in the reader. Instead, it is a question from the author to herself, posed in wonder. If that's the case, then the question is in the form of an *apostrophe*, a breaking off of discourse to address directly (in this instance) the author herself. How the student supports the answer usually determines its worth.

3. The author is describing how she is not fully in control of her faculties, to the extent that she can not even control her voice.
4. This phrase is a quick way to describe ten miles of the road. Those ten miles are not paved. This curt description might indicate her opinion of that part of the road, as well.

# 4 / *Narration*

## *Finishing School*

Maya Angelou

### Teaching Suggestions

One possible lead-in to assigning this selection is to briefly discuss how much personal names matter: How do we feel when people mispronounce or forget our names? Do some names suggest personality or character traits? Do our names influence our behavior? Do the names parents select for children suggest (at least to the parents) qualities the parents want their children to have? Why are names so important? Such a discussion should help prepare students for reading Maya Angelou's narrative.

After students have read the story, discussion might turn to structure. Have students notice the careful and thorough attention the narrator gives to presenting background information: first, about herself in paragraphs 1 and 2, and then about Mrs. Cullinan, her house, and her family in paragraphs 3 through 12. After setting up this background, the narrator presents three brief incidents: the speckled-faced woman's suggestion that "Margaret" be shortened to "Mary," Mrs. Cullinan's first use of the name "Mary," and the climactic incident of Marguerita's breaking the china. Have students discuss the purposes of each. Finally, have them discuss how effective the last two paragraphs are.

### Notes

**Paragraphs 1 and 2**

These paragraphs set the stage for the narration by contrasting early training of white girls with that of black girls.

"munching along": just getting by

"mid-Victorian values": values of middle-class respectability, which would include a high degree of class consciousness.

**Paragraph 3**

The physical description of Mrs. Cullinan, though brief, allows the reader to picture her quite accurately.

**Paragraph 4 and 5**

Students should notice the value attached to things and their names at Mrs. Cullinan's house, an ironic contrast to the way in which names of the servants are changed for convenience.

**Paragraph 8**

All mentions of Mr. Cullinan remark on his insignificance to the girl and even to Mrs. Cullinan.

**Paragraph 9**

The next few paragraphs establish the girl's consideration and loyalty until Mrs. Cullinan does the unforgivable.

**Paragraph 13**

The suggestion of a name change in this incident is the turning point in the girl's sympathy for Mrs. Cullinan.

**Paragraph 21**

This incident illustrates Mrs. Cullinan's thoughtfulness about her white neighbors and her casual disregard of her black servants.

**Paragraph 26**

This paragraph emphasizes how greatly names affect a sense of personal dignity.

**Paragraph 27**

Miss Glory's acceptance of her name change represents the older ways of accommodation. In contrast, the girl finds the name change intolerable and resolves to leave.

**Paragraph 32**

Two paragraphs of transition lead to the last incident.

**Paragraph 33**

The final incident, the result of a deliberate plan to get fired, once again reveals Mrs. Cullinan's values. It also illustrates Bailey's wise understanding of how vulnerable these values are.

**Paragraph 39 and 40**

The two short paragraphs close the narrative on a defiant and triumphant note.

## Possible Answers

### *Meaning and Purpose*

1. Give students time to explore their experiences of being angered or humiliated when treated unfairly. Did they feel powerless? Did they seek revenge? Be sure they compare their experiences with Angelou's.
2. Before Mrs. Cullinan calls her Mary, Marguerita is critical but cooperative, and even sympathetic, about her inability to have children ("For weeks after I arrived early, left late and tried very hard to make up for her barrenness" [12]). After Mrs. Cullinan calls her Mary, Marguerita is justifiably angry and deliberately breaks precious dishes to take revenge and get herself fired.

3. Angelou wants readers to feel as she feels about Mrs. Cullinan. Angelou also gives information about how a young black girl was expected to be trained and what she had to deal with in the world of privileged whites.
4. Angelou's audience could be people of all colors who want to hear about her experiences and perhaps be made to think about how blacks were—and are—treated. They are people who want to understand why Angelou writes what she writes. Her readers are educated and aware.
5. Angelou says the blacks "had a hellish horror" of not being called by their correct names because of the abusive names they have been called for centuries. Even in calling her Margaret, Mrs. Cullinan doesn't use Angelou's correct name.
6. Glory accepted and even preferred having her name changed by whites, just as most blacks then were docile and submissive. Marguerita rebelled against being called Mary and would not accept the role Glory accepted. The contrast between the two women emphasizes Angelou's point about names.

### *Strategy*

1. The payoff for the reader is the lesson in how prejudice affects one young black girl, and, by extension, all minorities. The moral is that prejudice is evil and should be rebelled against.
2. The introduction recounts for readers first how Angelou gets into the story she tells (a white woman asked Angelou about her hometown and then made the remark about a "debutante" [1]). Then Angelou gives general information about the differences between how white and black girls were trained in domestic arts. The second paragraph has some details about what black girls learned and then gets Angelou into the setting of her narrative. After reading these two paragraphs, readers know something about the larger context for the story that begins in paragraph 3.
3. Obviously Angelou is telling this story from the perspective of an adult looking back on herself at age ten. Her memory is perhaps fuzzy because the events happened a long time ago, and they happened fast. Her credibility is not in question because an adult is usually a more reliable narrator than a child. Rather, her saying she can't remember exactly what happened is honest, and true to her adult perspective.
4. Some transitional phrases are: "On our way home one evening" (9); "For weeks after" (12); "That evening I decided" (20); "Then Bailey solved my dilemma" (33). These and others keep the story flowing through its chronological order.
5. The last sentence emphasizes that Mrs. Cullinan is in fact not right in most things she says about her young black servant, including her correct name, which is not Margaret. Mrs. Cullinan does not understand her own actions and Marguerita's feelings. The one thing she finally does understand—that Marguerita's name is not going to be Mary—is a victory for Marguerita. This sentence reminds readers of the differences in training between white and black girls that Angelou talks about in her first two paragraphs.

### *Style*

1. Paragraph 30 is a good example of Angelou's telling us Marguerita's thoughts. They reveal that Marguerita understands, even at age ten, the abuse

and unfairness in Glory's not being called by her given name. And the thoughts show that Marguerita plans to get out of her job for good cause. Marguerita is shrewd and smarter than her employer.

2. a. The irony is that the white woman's kitchen could never teach anyone how to be a "debutante"; she also makes sure she is "finished" with this finishing school. b. Marguerita is expected to learn names that Mrs. Cullinan values, but Mrs. Cullinan doesn't bother to learn Marguerita's name. c. Mrs. Cullinan is melodramatic about her situation, and in fact is probably not lonely and in pain. Marguerita's sympathy is misdirected toward someone who cannot sympathize with her not wanting to be called Mary. d. Mrs. Cullinan doesn't get the point at all about the broken dishes. She is disturbed only about losing something she valued that Marguerita scorned.
3. In paragraph 9, "She was keeping herself embalmed" refers, in a humorous and sad way, to Mrs. Cullinan's drinking habit. Marguerita's explanation of the habit fits the perspective of a ten-year-old. Paragraph 11 is a humorous description of what Marguerita thinks Mr. Cullinan's daughters must look like—beautiful and with straight hair, unlike herself. That Marguerita says "Poor Mrs. Cullinan" shows her naiveté, and the reader gets the benefit of the humor.

# *A Hanging*

## George Orwell

### Teaching Suggestions

The simplicity and subject of this essay will appeal to most students. After they discuss the idea of the essay—what it says about executions and their effect on those involved—you can profitably turn to Orwell's style of presentation. Understated, matter of fact, but rich in descriptive detail—it is a good example of the power of words to create vivid images in our minds. Ask students to notice the ease with which each scene can be visualized, as if they were watching a movie.

### Notes

**Paragraph 1**

Like a movie camera moving from a long shot, to a medium shot, to a close-up, Orwell begins with the jail yard, moves to the row of cells, and finally comes to the description of a prisoner, the one to be executed today.

**Paragraph 3**

The bugle call and the superintendent's voice get the narration under way.

**Paragraph 4**

"Dravidian": a speaker of one of a family of languages used in southern India.

**Paragraph 6**

The dog's natural behavior contrasts sharply with the official military solemnity of the march to the gallows. His picking the prisoner for a special greeting links the man and the dog and reminds all of the prisoner's human worth.

"pariah": literally a drum beater; now a member of any oppressed social class, particularly in India. The dog is of mixed breed, probably unkempt, perhaps a stray.

**Paragraph 9**

The prisoner's natural movements and his side-stepping the puddle lead the narrator to thoughts on the wrongness of taking a human life.

**Paragraph 11**

Orwell returns to objective description following the meditative thoughts in the preceding paragraph.

**Paragraph 12**

"Ram": Rama, an incarnation of the Hindu god Vishnu, the Preserver.

**Paragraph 14**

"Chalo": Hindu; a command to let the prisoner drop through the gallows.

**Paragraph 17**

The execution completed, the men turn to other activities, with exaggerated alacrity to relieve the tension.

"lathis": wooden police sticks.

"pannikin": a metal cup or dish.

**Paragraph 18**

"boxwallah": a jewelry-box merchant.

**Paragraph 24**

The matter-of-fact last sentence is more effective than a moralistic caution against cruelty would be.

## Possible Answers

### *Meaning and Purpose*

1. The simple title is effective because it fits the solemn, matter-of-fact tone and the lack of emotion in the descriptions. The title implies no judgment, as the essayist makes no explicit judgment. "*The* Hanging" is specific, but "A Hanging" says this is one of many similar hangings—unremarkable. He wants readers to figure out his point themselves.
2. The leaping, barking dog is too painful and sharp a contrast to the subdued prisoner, and the somber observers, to be comfortable.
3. The narrator sees clearly that the prisoner has a life "in full tide" (10) when he avoids the puddle. The narrator feels a connection among all the men there, "together, seeing, hearing, feeling, understanding the same world." And the death of one would mean "one mind less, one world less." The narrator sees the condemned man as an individual and understands that taking his life will demean us all.
4. After the hanging, the men are relieved and even jubilant, chattering and laughing. They are suddenly past the burden of anticipating and carrying out the execution or of taking moral responsibility for it. They need to distance themselves emotionally from it.
5. Orwell questions the morality of capital punishment and the colonial rule that imposed it, as well as the small value placed on one Indian life. His specific story illustrates how Indians were oppressed under British rule and his sympathy for them.

### *Strategy*

1. Orwell uses first person and refers to the group of men he is with as "we." Because he and the others are spectators, the first-person voice has an

objective and detached sound. Orwell is participant and spectator at the same time. This voice understates the situation and makes it all the more stark.

2. Orwell uses chronological order, beginning with his "waiting outside the condemned cells" (1), right through the hanging, and having a drink afterward. In paragraph 10 Orwell briefly stops the forward movement to reflect on "what it means to destroy a healthy, conscious man."
3. The crime is unimportant because, under British rule, the Indians had little or no value as individuals. The hanged man is simply one example of an execution. That his identity and specific crime make no difference expresses Orwell's point about injustice.

*Style*

1. The tone is somber and solemn, even depressing. Words such as "sodden morning of the rains," "sickly light," and "brown, silent men" establish the mood. Later in the essay, "desolately thin" (3), and "The Indians had gone grey like bad coffee" (13) carry this tone through the hanging. Then the words change to describe the men's elation and laughter, beginning in paragraph 17. But the somber mood lurks under the gaiety. Orwell's emotionless descriptions maintain the original tone.
2. The sentence, "We set out for the gallows" in paragraph 6 is understatement because it carries no emotion, yet suggests a somber and horrible journey. And, "The superintendent reached out with his stick and poked the bare brown body; it oscillated slightly" in paragraph 16 is also understatement. Orwell shows the lack of feeling in this scene, and emphasizes the emotional and moral detachment.
3. The next-to-last sentence describes the men drinking together "amicably," "native and European alike," when the reality is that one group rules the other and considers them of little value as people. In fact, the British have just executed one of them, and yet they drink together. The last sentence heightens starkly the contrast between the execution and the moral detachment of the men that allows them to be jolly.

# *The Masked Marvel's Last Toehold*

## Richard Selzer

### Teaching Suggestions

Profitable areas of discussion for this selection might concentrate on Selzer's way of blending description and action and his tying the three sections of the essay together by repeating phrases and images. His skill as a writer is evident in both techniques. A third possibility is a discussion of figurative language and irony.

In some ways, this essay is a shocker. It allows us to see the same man at two stages in his life—once vigorous and successful and somewhat famous, at the end he is anonymous, diabetic, and facing amputation of his second leg. These are the changes that time has wrought. Students may not be old enough to have witnessed such changes in those they know, but perhaps they saw the equally shocking juxtaposition of pictures of Greta Garbo as a young actress and as she appeared months before her death. At any rate, Selzer's essay will work on their imaginations.

## Notes

**Paragragh 1**

The first paragraph establishes the setting and the series of questions establishes an empathy that the narrator maintains throughout the essay.

**Paragraph 4**

The conversation between doctor and patient reveals who the patient is (or has been) and, in effect, answers the questions in the first paragraph. Elihu has been thinking proudly about his past as a contrast to the present.

**Paragraph 23**

The essay's long middle section recaptures an evening of wrestling from the doctor's childhood. Seen through the boy's eyes, it is marvelous and full of excitement. The memories of that evening heighten Elihu's plight now as his identity is revealed.

**Paragraph 32**

"bosselated": characterized by lumps and protuberances.

**Paragraph 33**

Have students notice how some phrases in this section echo phrases in the first section. The same thing will occur in the third section closely binding the three though they take place years apart.

**Paragraph 34**

Selzer blends physical description and action to create an exciting narrative.

**Paragraph 43**

"carnal": of the natural as opposed to the spiritual world.

**Paragraph 47**

The short third section is especially full of echoes from the second section that heighten our perception of the irony in Elihu's fate.

## Possible Answers

### *Meaning and Purpose*

1. Without either leg, The Masked Marvel can't be held in a toehold. The title is made significant because the doctor breaks the last toehold by amputating the second leg. Elihu Koontz has lost his hold on what he was—a wrestler.
2. This essay is about loss and pain. Selzer relates a memory that connects him to a patient. He dramatizes, with narrative, who Elihu Koontz once was, and how the surgeon has come to appreciate his role in the former wrestler's life. If the memory of the Masked Marvel can be alive in the surgeon's mind, then Koontz will always be the wrestler the boy was in awe of. He won't really lose what he was.
3. This sentence describes the pain during the wrestling match: "The Masked Marvel does not hide his agony, but pounds and slaps the floor with his hand, now and then reaching up toward the Angel in an attitude of supplication" (35). As a patient, Elihu Koontz had "pain so great as to set him apart from all other men in a red-hot place where he had no kith or kin." (1). The wrestler's pain sounds fake compared to the pain of gangrene. The surgeon is keenly aware of how his patient suffers and was sensitive to the look of pain even as a boy.

4. Uncle Max gets so excited at the wrestling match, shouting for a leg, that he turns gray and has to take a pill. He chuckles at the boy's fear for The Masked Marvel. The boy, future doctor that he is, is solicitous of his uncle and tells him to take a pill. And the boy takes the wrestling match seriously and doesn't see it as a performance, as the uncle does. The contrast in their reactions shows the point of view of the adult looking back and emphasizes the irony in the essay.
5. The surgeon says, "I am masked" (47), "And I think that forty years later I am making the catch" (48), and "I step forward to break The Masked Marvel's last toehold" (49). These details put the surgeon in the wrestler's place and unify the essay by bringing readers back to the scene at the match, by recalling Koontz's identifying himself as The Masked Marvel, and by restating the title.

*Strategy*

1. The first section takes place two years before the last section, and the middle section takes place forty years before the first, when the narrator was a boy. Selzer makes the most of putting readers in a situation, going back in time to a memory that connects to that situation, then making the story both ironic and poignant in the end. Chronological order would diminish the effect of the irony, at least.
2. The repeated details in section two are about The Masked Marvel's breasts (33), and his "bed of pain" (46). In section three the repeated details are: "*I am masked*," "Elihu Koontz pinned," "beats feebly at the side of the operating table," "Tear off a leg. Throw it up here," "It's not fair," and "to break The Masked Marvel's last toehold." The repetition unifies the language and makes the essay rich in irony, especially in the last section, where the surgeon becomes like the wrestler who subdued The Masked Marvel.
3. In paragraph 22, Koontz is going through old photographs and clippings, and Selzer says, "and I remember." Then comes a space break, and he begins the memory, "It is almost forty years ago" (23). At the end of the second section, Selzer pulls us back to the first section with, "All this I remember as I stand at the bedside of Elihu Koontz" (46). Section three begins after a space break, "Once again I am in the operating room" (47), and it is two years after the opening scene. These transitions make the time order clear. The reader is always in the "present" of his narrator.
4. As a surgeon in the first section, the narrator is compassionate and patient: "I do not withdraw from this loving" (6), and "He *wants* me to remember" (16). As a boy he is sympathetic and aware of the wrestler's pain and his uncle's state of health: "I have never seen such suffering" (35); "'Sit down, Uncle Max,' I say, 'Take a pill please'" (38); and "'Stop him. Please, somebody, stop him'" (44). The last section shows the surgeon observant and aware of the painful irony: "It seems to me that I have never seen such misery" (47), and "It's not fair" (49).

*Style*

1. The dialogue makes scenes immediate and dramatic and puts readers in the scenes. Without dialogue, the essay would be full of exposition and probably dull. Selzer would be telling, not showing.
2. Each section is written in present tense, making the scenes vivid and real.

Because transitions to the different times are so clear, readers easily distinguish the times, even though each is in present tense.

3. In the final section, the surgeon is in the operating room and imagines it as an amphitheater. He hears Uncle Max yelling for a leg and realizes that he, the boy who was awed by The Masked Marvel, is now the surgeon who will literally tear a leg off.

# *Trapped in Another Life*

## Art Harris

### Teaching Suggestions

Students will find this story of Pamela Rodgers's two lives engrossing. Undoubtedly, they will have differing opinions about the proper disposition of the case. After discussing the content and the law-enforcement dilemma, you may wish to have students examine the way in which Harris uses different rhetorical patterns—comparison and contrast, cause and effect, description, and chronological narration—to tell Pamela's story. It is a good time to emphasize that essays are not usually written in one "pure" rhetorical pattern. In any one essay a writer may use many patterns as they become appropriate.

### Notes

**Paragraph 1**

Harris begins with a contrast between prison life and life outside and between Kay and her former self.

**Paragraph 4**

Beginning here, Harris goes to the more distant past, then relates her recent past in paragraphs 5–9.

**Paragraph 10**

Continuing the chronological sequence, Harris relates the most immediate past and describes her present situation.

**Paragraphs 16–19**

The next four paragraphs contrast two views about her possible pardon.

**Paragraph 20**

Returning to the chronological, Harris now goes to the far distant past, relating her background up to her committing criminal acts, using a cause-and-effect pattern.

**Paragraph 34**

The next six paragraphs continue the cause-and-effect pattern leading up to her jail sentence and her escape.

**Paragraph 50**

This next section, to paragraph 69, details the recent past and her new life.

**Paragraph 70**

Paragraphs 70–78 report the events leading to her arrest again.

**Paragraph 79**

The final section relates the present situation as she and her family await word of a possible parole.

## Possible Answers

### *Meaning and Purpose*

1. Crime doesn't pay, but neither is our justice system always fair. Even though Kay seemed to have left her criminal life behind, the law caught up with her. Harris's purpose is to show her struggle to live a decent life after her misguided early life and to question the justice of her returning to prison. Perhaps Harris hopes that telling Kay's story sympathetically in the newspaper will rally support for her release and pardon.
2. Though Kay changed her life when she married Ray, she "remained haunted by the past and present" (70). Back in prison, she says, "There wasn't any freedom for the last ten years, not for anyone with a conscience" (81). The two lives she had were starkly different, and her earlier life kept her trapped.
3. Harris draws a sympathetic portrait of Kay in the first fifteen paragraphs and so leads readers to favor Hassett's statement. Harris describes Kay's exemplary life and quotes a person who says how conscientious she was. Being taken back to prison seems wrenching and unfair after these descriptions.
4. Max Factor is a cosmetics company. The phrase refers to makeup and how little Kay wore. Harris equates her use of little makeup with her new life of decency and moral uprightness.
5. Each description sounds like fiction, a stereotype. They contrast sharply, and readers will feel disbelief that both could describe the same person, will feel intrigued, even skeptical, and will want to know more.

### *Strategy*

1. Paragraphs 1–3 describe a scene and place readers in it. Enough mystery hovers about the scene ("a devoted but baffled brood") to arouse interest. Not calling Kay by name till paragraph 3 delays this necessary information and gives Harris time to create an impression before readers know who she is. The contrasting descriptions of her in paragraph 3 have readers interested enough to read on.
2. This is a newspaper article and readers want information fast. A survey of Kay's life lets readers know the gist, then they can read on for details. If Harris had begun with her early life, readers would have a harder time sympathizing with her, and Harris's points would not be as effectively—and dramatically—made.
3. The essay is mostly a summary of events, giving highlights and leaving out a lot of details. The two sentences, "She remembers her father's belt, his guns, his whiskey, his temper" (20), and "With six or so months left to serve, in January, 1978, she hitched as far as Glen Burnie, Maryland, rented a room, took a job as a waitress in a Greek diner" (50) summarize events but do not dramatize them in a scene.
4. Harris is careful to put present events in the present tense, as in the opening scene in prison. He tells of her past life in past tense ("Somehow she managed to keep it together as she lived in fear and hid her past, even from her husband" [9]), but he again intersperses the present tense for her present life ("She wears a purple prison jumpsuit" [13] and "Family and friends have canvassed the community" [15]). The direct quotations are in present tense ("Kay says of her father" [23]).

*Style*

1. Harris sympathizes with Kay from the start when he paints a stark, lonely picture of her in prison. He highlights events that show her as victim, as in paragraph 28 when Danny slaps her, and in paragraph 31. When Harris describes her reformed life, he tells of good and generous things she did. The tipoff to her identity as a fugitive is inadvertently given by her son—she did nothing to draw the attention of the law. All these details arouse sympathy in readers and question the justice of putting Kay back in prison.
2. Though these words are fairly understandable in context, they are jargon, and Harris's audience might be readers unfamiliar with trucking. But any audience could understand this essay.
3. The language is concise and fast-paced, but Harris doesn't care about being objective. He portrays Kay as victimized in her young life, now trying to live a decent life, and recently yanked away from her family and thrust back into prison. Harris intends readers to see the irony when he reports that Kay "was classified by Maryland prison officials as a security risk" (14). Clearly, Harris thinks she should be released and pardoned, and his article is like a plea for this action.

# *Los Pobres*

## Richard Rodriguez

### Teaching Suggestions

This selection is a good example of narrative used as a springboard to serious thoughts. A summer job serves as a growth experience for the narrator because he is aware of his own thoughts and emotions. Have students notice how much self-examination Rodriguez includes in this piece. It begins in the first paragraph and continues throughout. But it is not self-absorption. He is always aware of the others and his relationship to them.

The narrative covers a long time (an unspecified number of years), but the heart of the experience is in a few awkward moments Rodriguez spent attempting to converse with a group of Mexican alien workers. The narrator carries those moments with him as he examines his life since that summer.

### Notes

**Paragraph 1**

The first paragraph introduces the narrator and his situation. The narrator pictures himself as a nontypical student in some characteristics: almost an outsider, not quite as sophisticated as his classmates.

**Paragraph 6**

This passage is required for the reader's understanding that it is not distaste for manual labor that separates the narrator from *los pobres*.

**Paragraph 7**

The brief incident recalled in paragraphs 7, 8, and 9 gives the narrator the insight that a summer job will not really admit him to the world of the laborer and prepares the reader for the larger insight that follows in paragraphs 20–24.

**Paragraph 10**

The narrator discovers the diversity among American workers and finds himself at ease in their company. The comfort contrasts with the coming description of his uneasiness in addressing the Mexican aliens.

**Paragraph 16**

The man's glance over the narrator's shoulder toward *el patrón* tells the narrator that he is seen only as a messenger from the boss and dashes his hopes for a bond between him and the Mexican workers.

**Paragraphs 18 and 19**

These paragraphs take us to a more recent past and confirm the narrator's acceptance of his membership in a privileged class.

**Paragraphs 20–24**

The final paragraphs sum up his understanding of what the earlier experience means. The fundamental distinction between the narrator and *los pobres* is an attitude that grows from different experiences.

Beginning the last two paragraphs with the same sentence emphasizes the Mexican workers' compliance and vulnerability and leaves us with wonder at the chasm between the classes.

## Possible Answers

*Meaning and Purpose*

1. Rodriguez is observant of his fellow students and believes they are wealthier and more privileged than he. He feels inferior, more kin to the Mexican-American janitors and gardeners, and he is sensitive about his dark skin. He doesn't think he is appealing physically: he "didn't linger in mirrors" (1).
2. Rodriguez had never done hard physical labor, as his father had. Wanting to rise above the working class, he was surprised when "desire uncoiled" (2) in him for the construction job. Challenged by physical labor, he didn't want his parents to think he'd taken a job beneath him, or that he had no ambition.
3. Rodriguez's main point is realizing what makes people *los pobres*. In paragraph 21 he says, "What made me different from them was an attitude of *mind,* my imagination of myself." He worked with white laborers who had college degrees and with Mexican laborers who were silent, compliant, and vulnerable (24). It was not occupation but his perception of himself, and the voice his education had given him, which would keep him from ever being one of *los pobres* (21).
4. The insight is that Rodriguez cannot "gain admission to the world of the laborer" (9) just by working at a summer construction job. He was not bound to the job and could savor the sensation of fatigue. The connection with "But I was not one of *los pobres*" (21) is that his body might be capable of physical labor and his hands as "tough as theirs" (21), but his "attitude of mind" (21) and his education keep him from being poor.
5. Being paid as a group eliminates their individuality as men. The contractor takes advantage of their alien status and their inability to bargain for themselves.

6. The Mexican workers are silent because they have no union, no grounds, no "public identity" (23). They depend on others' good will. Finally their silence brings Rodriguez "face to face with *los pobres*."

*Strategy*

1. The order is chronological, so that Rodriguez can show his early naiveté about class and life-style, then his later sophistication and ability to understand his summer.
2. The summer job, core of the narrative, requires details to make the point about Rodriguez's realizing what it means to be poor. Sections two and three compress time and summarize the life-style he later lived and now lives. These two sections don't describe just one event but show Rodriguez looking back through postcollege experiences that help him understand that summer.
3. Rodriguez uses both summary and scene. The summer job is presented more as scene, a drama acted out with characters and dialogue. (" 'Don't make your back do so much work,' he instructed. I stood patiently listening" [8]). But some of it is summarized: "I labored with excitement the first morning—and all the days after" (6). Section two is summary about his physical condition and the clothes he wears (18–19). And in section three, he also summarizes (20). The summary parts have little or no dialogue and no scenes are acted out.
4. Rodriguez uses first person to tell his own story, but he is looking back from his thirties on the summer job in college. With this point of view he can show how he came to understand what it is to be poor. Examples that show this effectiveness are: "The more I remember that summer, the more I realize that there was no single *type* of worker" (10); "And I can still hear the quiet, indistinct sounds of the Mexican, the oldest, who replied . . . " (17).

*Style*

1. In the last sentence of paragraph 10, *los pobres* is what the middle-class construction workers just described are not. A *bracero* (5) is "no longer afraid," but a strong worker. The *patrón* (13), or the contractor, gives orders to the Mexicans. *Gringo* (17) comes right after the description of how the contractor pays the Mexicans, and how "loudly confident" his voice is. *Gringo* is a disparaging name for whites.
2. Three fragments in the first two paragraphs are: "Less tortured perhaps"; "But still kin"; "Nothing too hard." These fragments create the informal, conversational tone of the opening, and they are emphatic in their brevity.
3. Rodriguez re-creates life, especially in describing the Mexican workers, who seem immediate and real, even in their anonymity.

# 5 / Examples

## *On Natural Death*

### Lewis Thomas

#### Teaching Suggestions

This brief essay can be used to illustrate the difference between deductive and inductive arrangement of material. Writers frequently use examples to illustrate a thesis already stated (deductive); Thomas inverts that sequence to present examples first and their meaning later (inductive). Class discussion might consider how this arrangement suits Thomas's purpose. He asks us to consider death from a somewhat different angle, and his inductive arrangement seemingly allows us to witness his thinking. His method leads to speculative conclusions rather than certain ones and creates a meditative tone attractive to most readers.

#### Notes

**Paragraph 1**

Students will probably see how ironically associating books on dying with how-to books sets up the subtle humor in the last sentence of the paragraph. His point in the essay is that dying is a "natural" phenomenon. His including sex manuals (designed to instruct us in another natural activity) in his list of how-to books helps sharpen the irony.

**Paragraph 2**

Thomas points out that we consider deaths of people to be "special" but deaths in nature "natural," part of a recycling. You might ask your students if nature has "special" deaths. Remind them that we have pet cemeteries, which suggest that we value some animals more than others.

**Paragraph 3**

A specific example. Thomas's elm tree was "taken" in two senses. "Taken" is a euphemism for "died," and in the literal sense the tree was "carted off." This might be a good time to ask students to think of other expressions we use to describe death, such as "passed away" and "moved on." Ask why we don't simply say "They died," when we talk about people we knew.

**Paragraph 5**

A typical example comparing the death of an animal to that of a tree. Because the mouse, unlike the tree, has pain receptors, it must feel pain before it dies (but maybe not just before it dies, as the author explains in paragraph 6). The death of an animal seems horrid, compared to that of a tree. This comparison prepares us for later discussion of human deaths.

**Paragraph 6**

Thomas uses clinical words to explain the mouse's absence of pain. He elevates (or reduces) the immediate pain before death to a scientific description. This cold, clinical analysis lacks emotional appeal. Then Thomas shifts abruptly to the mouse, who would "shrug" if he could, bringing us back to the warmth of emotion. Your students might want to give some thought to this question: If we knew absolutely that we were going to die, would we "shrug"?

**Paragraph 8**

Montaigne quotation: A specific example. Montaigne's view of death connects with the speculation about the final peacefulness of the mouse's death (6). Inspired by the Latin classics, especially Plutarch, Montaigne's essays reflect his skeptical spirit.

**Paragraph 9**

Thomas talks about "the early days of the invasion." Some students need to be told that Thomas refers to an action during World War II, and that "MPs" means "military police." This paragraph brings us to Thomas's personal credibility: he witnessed deaths that share the natural features of the mouse's death in paragraphs 4 and 5. In a sense, the MPs "shrugged."

**Paragraph 10**

In his conclusion, Thomas expresses admiration for nature's way of handling death. He no longer sees it as an abomination, as he mentions in paragraph 4, but as an "indispensable part of living," handled efficiently.

## Possible Answers

### *Meaning and Purpose*

1. The reader discovers the topic of the essay in sentence 1, paragraph 3, suddenly, as the elm dies almost overnight. This sudden shift leads the reader into the topic of "natural death," also mentioned in the title of the work.
2. Thomas describes the sophisticated—and rather beautiful—mechanism that shuts down pain; it sets in naturally when a creature is mortally injured. He therefore suggests that the natural process of death is not trivial but something to be admired, even to be in awe of.
3. He uses the specific examples of a tree stricken with blight, a mouse caught in a cat's jaws, and soldiers crushed in a jeep. These are all individual events or experiences. Thomas does say that he doesn't know if his "story" about the mouse's dying without pain is true. This story part of the example has hypothetical elements.
4. Students might respond by saying something about how important it is to know that dying is natural, even painless. Some may mention that they had never before thought about the actual experience of dying, but only about the prelude and the aftermath.
5. This quotation is important because the essayist deals with the knowledge that nature knows how to handle death. The mildly sarcastic statement quoted in the question says much the same thing.

### *Strategy*

1. Everyone sings to show that life itself goes on, oblivious to the natural death of an elm tree. It is "natural" to sing while one works. The dead elm tree is now a thing to be removed, a job.
2. Thomas begins with the lesser life form to emphasize his point that "natural"—and all the sophistication it implies—is not necessarily trivial. By the time we read about the soldiers' deaths, we can easily apply Thomas's thesis and see the connection death makes among all living things.

3. This light humor, mostly in the first paragraph and in the author's way of describing his relationship with the cat in paragraph 4, helps hold the reader's interest in a potentially morbid subject. This touch generates interest in a topic that readers often avoid.
4. In this personal essay that deals with a universal topic the author uses "I" throughout, comments personally on death, and concludes with another personal reference. Students might comment on his various uses of the first person.

*Style*

1. The word *amiable* suggests the connotative qualities that constitute friendliness. Cats are not by nature overly friendly, but they have natural "amiable" qualities that make people like them. The word *beheld* suggests the regal quality often associated with feline demeanor. *Spectacle* connotes drama, consistent with the many small dramas witnessed by the author.
2. "Had a hunch" and "close call" are trite phrases inappropriate to a formal sentence.
3. "End game" compares the finality of death to the end of a chess game.

# *Mother Tongue*

## Amy Tan

### Teaching Suggestions

One entrance into this essay is to have your students describe situations in which the subjects of their conversations and the language they use vary. That is, what do they talk about when they are with friends of the same sex? Friends of both sexes? What do they talk about when with people they don't know well? With their co-workers? With their parents? Does their language change with the subject matter? How? Point out to them that when they give examples, particularly examples that entail some narrative, they are following the format that Tan uses in her essay.

### Notes

**Paragraphs 1 and 2**

At the outset, Tan establishes that what follows will not be a scientific examination of language. Indeed, her evidence will be anecdotal and, therefore, inappropriate for scientific discourse. She does, however, establish her authority over her subject matter in the second paragraph since she is a professional writer and a lifelong lover of language.

**Paragraph 3**

Tan begins with a story that introduces us to one of her "Englishes," standard English.

**Paragraph 4**

She now tells another story to introduce us to her family language of intimacy that will be her primary focus.

**Paragraph 5**

Here Tan summarizes her mother's story that she will then quote verbatim in paragraph 6.

**Paragraph 8**

The body of the essay, which begins here, is an extended examination of her mother's "limited" English and the effects it has had on her, Tan.

**Paragraph 9**

The conclusion of paragraph 8 leads to Tan's consideration of the various ways her mother's language had limited both of them.

Tan uses general examples to demonstrate why her perceptions of her mother were limited.

**Paragraphs 10–13**

These paragraphs constitute a humorous extended anecdote that demonstrates her mother's recognition of her own language limitations.

**Paragraph 14**

Another anecdote, this time a more serious one, further illustrates her mother's acute awareness of her limitations.

CAT (computerized axial tomography) scan: a method for diagnosing disorders of the brain, lung, liver, spleen, and other soft tissue using a computerized combination of many X-ray photographs taken by a special instrument that displays computerized cross-sectional images of the body.

**Paragraph 15–17**

These paragraphs concentrate on the ways Tan herself was limited.

**Paragraph 18**

In the first paragraph of this concluding section, Tan considers the possibility that the personal limitations she described in the previous three paragraphs can be extended to other Asian-Americans.

**Paragraph 19**

Tan now contracts her focus to herself—how she became a writer and the writing of her first novel, *The Joy Luck Club*.

**Paragraph 21**

After concentrating on limitations, Tan ends with a near paean to her mother, a respect and love that has been implicit in all of her anecdotes.

**Paragraph 22**

Appropriately, Tan's mother becomes her most telling critic.

## Possible Answers

### *Meaning and Purpose*

1. Tan states her thesis in the last sentence of the second paragraph.
2. Tan's mother exhibits a keen understanding of language by reading *Forbes*, listening to *Wall Street Week*, conversing with her stockbroker, and reading Shirley MacLaine's books—the last a tongue-in-cheek example (7). She also understands how her own English limits her and has a firm grasp of the predicaments which that inability puts her in. Tan gives two examples of this understanding. The first is the humorous story about her stockbroker (10–13), the second a serious anecdote about the results of a CAT scan (14).
3. As a girl Tan was embarrassed by her mother's English, thinking her defective language reflected defective thinking. This embarrassment severely limited Tan's perception of her mother (9).
4. Tan believes that the language spoken by the family, especially insular immigrant families, shapes the language of the child more than sociologists and

linguists think. She thus was a higher achiever in math than she was in English (15) and conjectures this influence may account for the former paucity of Asian-American writers (18).

*Strategy*

1. A narrative essay usually has a single story line. Tan's anecdotes are individual stories that illustrate individual points.
2. Tan's examples are always specific, written in concrete language, and are often humorous, or poignant, or both.
3. Tan divides her essay into three parts. The first section (1–7) introduces the reader to the idea that she uses several "Englishes" and describes in detail her "family" English. The second section (8–17) is more reflective and examines the ways her mother's English have been limiting. The final section (18–21) describes why she became a writer and how she writes. The three sections serve as the essay's introduction, body, and conclusion.

*Style*

1. Most students will be able to decipher the gist of the story, and many may recognize it as colorful and perceptive. Tan's childhood assessment that this stumbling English reflected defective thinking was certainly faulty.
2. Tan's "Englishes" can be placed in two categories: the English she grew up with: "simple" English, "broken" English, "watered down" English; standard English that she " . . . had learned in school and through books . . .".
3. The line is awkward, the diction pretentious. As an exercise you might have your students translate the line into plain English. "That was the beginning of my uncertainty," is a possibility.
4. *Wrought*: worked; *nominalized*: to have converted another part of speech into a noun, as in changing the adjective *lowly* to *the lowly*, or to have converted an underlying clause into a noun phrase, as in changing he *drinks* to *his drinking*; *transcribed*: made a written copy; *belies*: shows to be false, contradicts; *empirical*: derived from or guided by experience; *guise*: general external appearance; *impeccable*: faultless; *benign*: not malignant; *insular*: detached, isolated; *semantic*: arising from the different meanings of words; *quandary*: a state of perplexity or uncertainty; *nascent*: beginning to exist or develop.

# *Black Men and Public Space*

## Brent Staples

### Teaching Suggestions

Staples' essay can be used effectively to demonstrate the necessity of using concrete examples to back-up generalizations, thereby giving those generalizations meaning and life. The essay is full of examples—general examples, specific examples, and anecdotes—that give concrete meaning and vivid life to Staples' points. Question 3 under *Strategy* is designed to get the students to do their own analyses of the essay's structure. But, whether or not you have the students do that question on their own, it might be a good idea to lead them through the essay paragraph-by-paragraph, discussing the number and kinds of examples Staples uses, as well as the skillful way he mixes them up to give the essay variety. You may or may not choose to use the answer to question 3 of *Strategy* in this manual as a guide.

The essay could also be used in conjunction with Leone Gaiter's "The Revolt of the Black Bourgeoisie" (pp. 368–373) to get at Staples' meaning and the social and psychological ramifications of his observations. While Staples states that he has merely "inherited" his ability "to alter public space," Gaiter conjectures some specific reasons why young, black men have inherited this dubious power. Using the two essays together might lead to a lively and thoughtful discussion.

## Notes

**Paragraph 8**

"perilous flavor": the first sentence of this paragraph serves as the topic sentence for the three anecdotes that follow. The three anecdotes lead to the general truth in the last sentence of paragraph 10, the conclusion to this three-paragraph section of the essay.

**Paragraph 12**

Beethoven: Ludwig von Beethoven (1770–1827) German composer. Beethoven began his career as a classical composer who used Haydn and Mozart as his models (Haydn was his teacher). His music became more powerfully emotional as he grew older, and he thus became the first and greatest of the romantic composers. One of the greatest geniuses in the history of western music, Beethoven was deaf for a good portion of his composing career.

Vivaldi: Antonio Vivaldi (c. 1675–1741) baroque Italian composer and violinist, known familiarly as *il prete rosso* (the red-haired priest). Vivaldi wrote more than four hundred concertos for various instruments and combinations of instruments, thirty-eight operas, and church music, of which the *Gloria* (c. 1726) is well known. The *Four Seasons* is his most popular and most recognizable secular piece.

## Possible Answers

*Meaning and Purpose*

1. Staples describes himself in the first paragraph as young, black, large, and male. Simply by being so, he causes fear in others, particularly women, and particularly at night. He claims this questionable power to be an "unwieldy inheritance" (2), something he has simply by being a young, black man. He gives a partial explanation for this when he observes that "Women are particularly vulnerable to street violence, and young black males are drastically overrepresented among the perpetrators of that violence" (5). But this observation certainly cannot account for the fear projected onto virtually all young, black males by non-blacks. (Leonce Gaiter gives one explanation for this disturbing phenomenon in "The Revolt of the Black Bourgeoisie," pp. 368–372.) So, implicitly underlying the entire essay is the specter of racism.
2. The first time Staples fully recognizes that he has "the ability to alter public space in ugly ways" (2) he feels "surprised, embarrassed, and dismayed all at once" (2), because he has been unjustifiably associated with "the muggers who occasionally seeped into the area" (2). He learns "the language of fear" (3) thoroughly, in two different ways, in fact. Because he is automatically feared in certain situations, he is himself placed in danger, and so knows fear from two sides. And because he is "ever the suspect, a fearsome entity with

whom pedestrians avoid making eye contact" (5), he becomes profoundly alienated. All of this results in a "rage [he] felt at so often being taken for a criminal" (11), a rage that he must smother so he can assume an attitude and demeanor that whites will find nonthreatening (11 and 12).

3. Staples offers no solutions. So while the essay ends on a relatively light and humorous note, that humor has a decidedly dark edge to it.
4. Staples speaks for all black males who have had to behave similarly. We know this because all of the examples he gives in the essay, both general and specific, can be applied to all young, black men.

*Strategy*

1. The first paragraph grabs the reader with the first sentence. Staples plays with stereotypes he's going to use later—a woman who is about to become the victim of a young, black man in an isolated park at night—to create an immediate tension. That tension gives the anecdote drama. Staples builds both the tension and, therefore, the drama by narrating the event in an ever-quickening pace. He further dramatizes the event by describing himself in the third person ("the youngish black man") so that we see him from the frightened woman's point of view, over her shoulder. Ironically, the anecdote ends anticlimactically with the woman running safely away from a man who offers her no danger. The anecdote, then, becomes emblematic of the sad, racial ironies Staples presents in the rest of the essay. A most skillful and effective beginning.
2. Staples tells us in the second paragraph that the incident he narrated in the first paragraph happened more than ten years before, when he was only twenty-two. Now, more mature, he is able to reflect on the incident, to recollect in tranquility, as it were, and consider its meaning, significance, and ramifications. The second paragraph, therefore, explains the first.
3. Staples develops his essay by using examples that make explicitly clear what he means by "the ability to alter public space." He opens with a personal anecdote. He then uses general examples in paragraphs 2, 3, 4, 5 and 7. He uses personal anecdotes in paragraphs 8 and 9, and an anecdote about another black man in paragraph 10. His conclusion, paragraphs 11 and 12, is replete with general examples. By varying the kinds of examples, Staples creates an interesting pattern instead of a repetitious laundry list.

*Style*

1. Staples' language is always controlled, tempered. The situations he describes are full of fear, alienation, rage, and potential violence. The discrepancy between the language and the situations the language describes creates a tension that effectively reflects the tension in the situations themselves.
2. The woman in the opening paragraph has nothing to fear from Staples, even though she perceives herself as his potential victim. In fact, it is Staples and all other law-abiding, black men who are victimized by a society that sees all black men as potentially violent and threatening.
3. The analogy is particularly apt because, in a single example, it captures the irony of the entire essay. As a young, black man, Staples is feared. Being feared, he is constantly placed in situations that are dangerous to him, not to the people who fear him. So, when he whistles a melody from Vivaldi, he

alleviates the fear in others that could actually threaten him, just as a hiker's bell mitigates the potential danger to the innocent hiker by frightening the bears away.

4. *Affluent*: having an abundance of wealth; *mean*: inferior in quality; *impoverished*: reduced to poverty; *discreet*: modest, unobtrusive; *unwieldy*: not easily handled or managed; *quarry*: any object of pursuit or attack; *dicey*: unpredictable, risky, uncertain; *foyer*: the entrance or lobby of a building; *taut*: tense; *warrenlike*: like a warren, an area containing many tenants in limited or crowded quarters; *bandolier*: a broad belt worn over the shoulder by soldiers and having a number of small loops or pockets for holding cartridges; *forge*: to move ahead slowly, steadily; *solace*: comfort in sorrow, misfortune or trouble; *bravado*: a pretentious, swaggering display of courage; *ad hoc*: for the special purpose or end presently under consideration; *labyrinthine*: complicated, torturous; *cursory*: hasty; *skittish*: uncertain, shy; *constitutionals*: walks taken for the benefit of one's health; *steely*: resembling steel in strength and hardness; *warbling*: singing or whistling with trills, quavers, or melodic embellishment.

# *Tools of Torture*

## Phyllis Rose

### Teaching Suggestions

A discussion of this essay might begin by considering the various kinds of torture Rose describes. Students can be asked to contribute their own examples from books they have read or movies they have seen. Then ask how they react to a discussion of torture methods. Why do such devices often fascinate us? Why are there exhibits of torture instruments like the one in Paris that Rose mentions?

From there a discussion might move to the assertions Rose makes about institutionalized torture and how people are led to accept torture as a reasonable tool in the service of a noble cause (6,7). Do Rose's explanations conform with the view of torture presented in modern books and films? If not, how do they differ? Why are we so seldom asked to be on the side of the torturer in current fiction and films? Are we ever asked to believe torture is natural and acceptable? Paragraph 8 can be examined in this context.

Finally, what do students think of Rose's suggestion that we "refuse to allow the nobly abstract to seduce us from the sweetness of the concrete" (9)?

### Notes

#### Paragraph 1

The first sentence of the paragraph serves as the topic sentence and emphasizes the idea that even without modern technology the human imagination has devised a horrendous variety of torture devices. Rose goes on to a lengthy series of grotesque examples.

The Inquisition was a Roman Catholic ecclesiastical tribunal instituted by Pope Innocent III in the thirteenth century to suppress heresy and punish heretics. The inquisitor's chair was one of the tortures devised to further this end, as were most of the other devices described in the essay. That is the reasoning behind the claim in paragraph 6 that human torture has been instituted, condoned, and "vetted" hand-in-hand by church and state.

**Paragraph 4**

The French colonized Algeria in 1830. The native Muslim Algerians, like all conquered peoples, continually smarted under foreign rule and finally rebelled, attaining independence in 1962. In the last convulsions of the revolution, the French tortured Algerians with electrodes and other devices to elicit information. Having ruled Algeria for so long, the French involved in the atrocities considered their acts both patriotic and necessary.

**Paragraph 6**

After explaining why so many instruments of torture are to be found, the author proposes to move to the even more important question of why they were invented in the first place.

**Paragraph 7**

Stanley Milgram: Milgram's experiments reinforce the idea that sadists are not responsible for institutionalized human cruelty. On the contrary, ordinary people can be convinced that the pain they inflict is for some higher cause, this time for scientific learning. Milgram also cites Hannah Arendt's 1963 book, *Eichmann in Jerusalem*. She contends that the prosecution's assertion that the Nazi Eichmann was a sadist monster, responsible for the murder of thousands of Jews, was wrong. Rather, she claims, he came closer to being a dull bureaucrat who simply sat at his desk and followed orders (Stanley Milgram, *Obedience to Authority*, 1974).

**Paragraph 8**

Benthamite: Jeremy Bentham (1748–1832) was an English philosopher who promoted utilitarianism, the ethical doctrine that asserted actions are right or good in proportion to their usefulness or as they tend to promote happiness. The doctrine claimed that the end and criterion of public action is the greatest happiness of the greatest number. Thus, human happiness becomes the one and only measure of right and wrong.

**Paragraph 9**

Marie Antoinette (1755–1793), queen of France, was the wife of Louis XVI, whom she married when she was fifteen. As daughter of Maria Theresa of Austria, she sought Austria's aid against French revolutionaries. In 1791 she counseled Louis to flee from France, an attempt that ended in their imprisonment. They were regarded as traitors and Marie Antoinette was guillotined on October 16, 1793. Her personal charm, her naive ignorance of practical life, her extravagance, and her frank and courageous honesty contributed to her unpopularity both at court and with the French masses. When she was told that a revolution was threatening because the people had no bread, she is said to have replied, "Let them eat cake."

## Possible Answers

### *Meaning and Purpose*

1. Paragraph 1, sentences 2–4.
2. Rose gluts her readers with names and descriptions of torture devices, much as her eyes may have been glutted with them in the exhibit she mentions. The list of examples also elaborates her topic immediately and leaves the reader under no illusion that she will deal with the topic gently. Students

may or may not think this opening a good one, depending on their responses to the topic.

3. When connected with food, the word "unthinkable" is positive, indicating imaginative power dedicated to gustatory pleasure. Connected with torture, however, the word's severe negative connotations come into play: when the power of the imagination is applied to evil, the results are too horrible.
4. Legal, social, and religious institutions working in unison create torture in order to perpetuate themselves (6). Feeling the need to belong, people become convinced that their actions against others, normally considered morally abhorrent, contribute to society's greater good. Torture thus becomes a patriotic duty (6). Rose cites the French torture of Algerians (4), the Nazis and the French again (8), and the Milgram experiments (7).
5. Because allegiance to abstract ideals leads people to torture, its precise opposite, the absolute pursuit of sensual pleasure, is torture's natural antidote (9).

*Strategy*

1. Electricity vastly expands the potential for human torture, but even without it the fertility of the human imagination applied to torture is impressive.
2. One specific example is Milgram's experiment (7). It supports the topic (first) sentence of paragraph 1 and is concrete: it actually happened. In one typical example, Rose describes how a person might have been tortured on the wheel (3). The example is effective because it suggest that this torture was used many times on nameless, and helpless, victims.
3. Paragraph 7 is focused on the Milgram experiments. Rose reminds us that cruelty was accepted before the enlightenment; thus, Milgram's experiments would have been meaningless at that time (8). Recent history suggests, however, that the enlightenment's ideals have not really taken hold. She considers the possibility that cruelty may have drifted to the margins of society, leading to her conclusion that radical hedonism may be the cure for abstract idealism (9).
4. Some readers might consider the graphic examples an assault on the senses. Rose does not back away from her topic and make torture seem less terrible than it is or was. This honest tone gives her argument strength and her voice as a writer credibility.

*Style*

1. Because one of Rose's themes is that the French have a unique talent for creating ways to give "loving attention to the body," it is appropriate to use the French rather than English word in order to capture the French flavor. *Parfumerie* means perfume store (the author gets her massage in one). *Soins esthétiques* means beauty care.
2. The final paragraph sums up Rose's belief that Paris can be considered the "capital of pleasure." She has already given specific examples (4, 5). Ending the essay with her thoughts on the pleasures of modern Paris is a neat connection to her having begun with thoughts on the opposite sensation (pain) in medieval Paris.
3. Because the puritans shunned the flesh, the idea that beauty radiates from the inner self must be puritanical. The French, according to the author, will have none of that thinking.

4. *benign*: showing or expressive of gentleness or kindness; *aesthetician*: a person who is versed in aesthetics, the branch of philosophy dealing with such notions as the beautiful, the ugly, the sublime, and the comic as applicable to the fine arts; *malevolent*: evil, harmful, injurious; *vetted*: to have appraised, verified, or checked for accuracy, authenticity, validity, and so on; *inalienable*: not transferable to another or capable of being repudiated; *transitory*: not lasting, enduring, permanent, or eternal; *touchstone*: a test or criterion for the quality of a thing.

# *Future Shlock*

## Neil Postman

### Teaching Suggestions

Postman is provocative, though easy to understand. His remarks about the show-business mentality in politics, religion, education, and news programs should elicit strong responses from students. Some will think he exaggerates. Others will be eager to provide additional examples. A good beginning is a discussion of student responses to the overall message.

Don't miss the opportunity to discuss the strategies Postman employs to keep the reader interested and to present his challenging views as reasonable.

### Notes

**Paragraph 1**

The first three sentences plunge us directly into the subject. If you assign this essay as outside reading, it might be useful to read these sentences aloud in class first and ask if students are inclined to agree or disagree at first thought.

The long example of Germany prior to World War II may need amplification, briefly identifying the men listed:

Albert Einstein (1879–1995). Physicist; theory of relativity. Nobel Prize, 1921. Became United States citizen in 1940.
Sigmund Freud (1856–1939). Founder of modern psychoanalysis.
Thomas Mann (1875–1955). Novelist and critic. Nobel Prize, 1929. Came to United States in 1937.
Stefan Zweig (1881–1942). Austrian dramatist, critic, novelist.
Konrad Lorenz (1903–1989). Ethologist. Nobel Prize, 1973.
Werner Heisenberg (1901–1976). Physicist. Nobel Prize, 1932.
Martin Heidegger (1889–1976). Philosopher and writer.
Gerhardt Hauptmann (1862–1946). Dramatist, novelist, poet. Nobel Prize, 1912.
Marcel Proust (1871–1922). French novelist.
André Gide (1869–1951). French novelist, poet, critic. Nobel Prize, 1947.
Emile Zola (1840–1902). French novelist.
Jack London (1876–1916). United States novelist and short-story writer
Upton Sinclair (1878–1968). United States novelist.

The paragraph ends with an emphatic clincher sentence. Postman often uses this device to drive a point home or to look ahead to the next paragraph. See paragraphs 2–4, 11, 14, 15, 18, and 22.

**Paragraph 2**

Having evoked the memory of pre-World War II Germany, an easy-to-accept example, Postman challenges his readers by saying that a similar erosion of intelligence could happen in the United States. This contrast between America's past and Postman's perception of its present condition gives his readers a measure of how much he feels has been lost.

**Paragraph 3**

Land-Grant Act: The Land Grant Act of 1862 was a federal government act that financed the establishment of state colleges.

Henry Steele Commager: (born 1902). United States historian and author.

"Shlock": Of inferior quality, cheap, junk (also spelled *schlock*).

**Paragraph 4**

The first sentence is a fairly direct statement of Postman's thesis. (A fuller statement is at the end of paragraph 11.)

For readers who are saying to themselves that the United States is different from Germany, Postman accepts the objection, but argues that similar methodology is not necessary. He picks up this contrast later in discussing Orwell's *1984* and Huxley's *Brave New World.*

Have students comment on the effectiveness of the three sentences that begin with "a culture" and the shock value of the word "stupidity" in the last sentence.

**Paragraphs 5 and 6**

Many students will be familiar with *The Gods Must Be Crazy* first shown in the United States in 1984 and frequently offered on cable. In paragraph 5, he presents the situation in the movie, and in paragraph 6, he explains the bottle's disrupting effect: "The people begin to love their bottle more than they love themselves."

**Paragraph 7**

Before moving to the second movie example, you may want to make sure that students understand Postman's point: A new technology should be examined carefully and rejected if necessary.

**Paragraph 8**

The second movie example illustrates a different point: We are in danger of so trivializing dignified, serious, and important aspects of life that they will become mere entertainment.

**Paragraph 12**

Aldous Huxley: (1894–1963). English novelist and critic

Big Brother, the television image in Orwell's *1984*, as well as "Ministries of Propaganda," "gulags," and "concentration camps" represent the tyranny of force.

The Coca-Cola bottle is used as a symbol of new technologies.

**Paragraph 13**

George Orwell [Eric Blair] (1903–1950) was an English novelist and essayist.

**Paragraph 14**

This paragraph marks the culmination of Postman's interpretation of the current situation. His examples thus far have pointed to the insufficiently examined power of show business (particularly, but not exclusively, television) to trivialize serious discourse.

**Paragraph 15**

Beginning with paragraph 15, Postman turns to examples of this trivialization in politics, religion, education, and news in the next four paragraphs.

**Paragraph 16**

Jonathan Edwards (1703–1758). Clergyman and theologian.
Charles Finney (1792–1875). Clergyman and educator.
George Whitefield (1714–1770). Methodist revivalist.
Jimmy Swaggart (born 1935). Television evangelist.
Jim Bakker (born 1948). Former television evangelist.
Jerry Falwell (born 1933). Television evangelist.

**Paragraph 18**

How do your students take to the accusation leveled against all of us at the end of this paragraph?

**Paragraph 19**

In three paragraphs (19,20,21), Postman tells us he is not blaming television alone, nor is he attacking the visual arts or entertainment in themselves.

**Paragraph 21**

This paragraph restates his belief that "entertainment" has permeated the serious aspects of our culture and reminds us, using the words "the gods must be crazy," about the message of that film: The effects of new technology must be examined carefully.

**Paragraph 22**

In the concluding paragraph he reminds us again that America seems to have chosen the Huxleyan rather than the Orwellian road.

Postman offers no specific way out of the situation he describes. In fact, paragraph 21 ends with a discouraging note: "there is no mountaintop from which we can return what is dangerous to us."

## Possible Answers

### *Meaning and Purpose*

1. Postman's purpose is to warn us about the "rapid erosion of our own intelligence" as a result of the trivialization of serious matters: politics, education, religion, and news. He simply informs us; he does not offer solutions. The last sentences in paragraphs 20–22 discourage hope. Students should be able to support their opinions about whether or not the purpose succeeds.
2. Paragraph 11 includes the statement that seems most nearly complete.
3. *The Gods Must Be Crazy* example shows that new technologies profoundly affect cultures, and they should be examined and discarded if necessary. *The Producers* example shows how serious matters can be trivialized.
4. Perhaps only a few students will agree with Postman completely. Some may feel he exaggerates; others will strongly resist his intensely critical message.

### *Strategy*

1. This sentence—"We will become, in a phrase, a people amused into stupidity"—summarizes the lengthy sentence preceding it and provides shock value with the word "stupidity" (11).

   "And that is how television brings ruin . . . ." The uncompromising harshness of "ruin" conveys the seriousness of his charge in the preceding sentence (14).

   "I would suggest that television has annihilated it." The word annihilated means total erasure of the line, thus conveying Postman's contention that politics has become entertainment (15).

"To be sure, we know *of* many things; but we know *about* very little." The parallelism used here to contrast *of* and *about* creates a memorable phrasing, reinforcing his point that television news is not really educating people (18).

"I agree." Coming after a long (sixty-word) sentence developed with parallel structure, the punchiness of this two-word sentence is emphatic (22).

2. Germany is, first, a notorious example of unexplained "madness." Therefore, it is easy for a reader to accept the example and the conclusion. When he moves in the next paragraph to the United States example, the reader has already, at least in part, accepted his credibility.
3. Postman appeals to an intelligent, aware audience that can understand many of his historical references, or know how to look them up. Yet he probably knows that some of his readers get most of their information from television, even though he criticizes this habit. He surely intends to be provocative and make readers think and perhaps reevaluate.
4. In the first half of the essay (through paragraph 13), he uses specific, extended examples: Germany, the United States, *The Gods Must Be Crazy*, *The Producers*, and *Brave New World*, as well as a brief mention of *1984*.

   In the second half of the essay the examples are brief and both specific and typical (see paragraph 18 for a good illustration).

*Style*

1. *Cathedral* may be loosely applied to any large church. The connotation here is of spiritual authority, suggesting dedication, piety, learning, reverence, love, aspiration—the best human qualities.

   A *cesspool* is a drainage hole for sewage. It brings to mind filth, foul smells, disease, and waste.

   *Barbarian* originally meant anyone who belonged to a group outside one's own culture, and *barbaric* denoted such a person's behavior, whatever it might be. Now the word commonly indicates lack of learning, lack of restraint, wild, uneducated, uncivilized, and uncultured—a person living without reasonable values and behaviors.

   The metaphor moves from the lofty to the debased and characterizes the change as a retreat to less than civilized behavior.
2. The Coca-Cola bottle is a metaphor for new technologies. The quotations, in turn, mean a new technology can become tyrannical, recall the bottle's effect on the tribe, connect television with the Coke bottle, and restate the original metaphor.
3. *Schlock*: shoddy; *nemeses* (plural of nemesis): a powerful rival, one who inflicts destruction; *rhetorical*: use of words for persuasion; *precipitous*: steep; *preemption*: acquisition or appropriation of something beforehand; *banal*: predictable, trite; *sacrality*: religious rites; *paradigm*: a model; *countenance*: appearance.

# 6 / Comparison and Contrast

## *Grant and Lee: A Study in Contrasts*

Bruce Catton

### Teaching Suggestions

You might want to start by discussing how some current civil conflicts (Lebanon, Northern Ireland, and Sierra Leone, perhaps) resemble our Civil War and how they differ. Outlining these similarities and differences can lead to discussion of the essay's structure: the first three paragraphs as introduction; paragraphs 4–6 describing the attributes of Robert E. Lee and the society he represented; paragraphs 7–9 describing Ulysses S. Grant and the values he represented; paragraphs 10 and 11 paired against each other; point-by-point contrast in paragraph 12; paragraph 13 a transition moving from contrast to comparison; and paragraphs 14, 15, and 16 showing the similarities of the two men, moving from the least important to the most important.

From there you might ask students to evaluate the contrary social ideals the two men represented.

### Notes

**Paragraph 1**

The contrast between the closing of "a great chapter in American history" taking place in "the parlor of a modest house" emphasizes the enormity of the occasion.

**Paragraph 2**

"poignant": After students have looked up this word, you might discuss why it is so fitting here, why it is better than *teary, sad*, or *touching*, for instance.

**Paragraph 3**

Not only does this sentence serve as the essay's thesis, but it also has a metaphor that emphasizes the strength of the two men's personalities and characters and the power of the two societies they represented; that is, they were "two conflicting currents" so powerful that when they met the "collision" was "final."

**Paragraph 4**

This sentence is a kind of mini-thesis that controls the essay's next section, paragraphs 5 and 6.

**Paragraph 5**

It was the Virginia tidewater where the very first permanent English settlers landed and founded Jamestown, well before the *Mayflower* (1620). Ironically, in fact, the *Mayflower* was headed there but veered off course and landed at Plymouth instead. These first settlers brought with them medieval English ideals (chivalry and all the aristocratic and ritualistic courtesies that went with it, including idealization of women) and a feudal social structure, described in the rest of the paragraph.

**Paragraph 6**

The implication here seems to be that as the war wore on to an end and it became more and more apparent that the Confederacy itself would fall, the Confederate soldier found it psychologically necessary to personify his ideals in a living man. Lee, thus ironically, became a symbol, an abstraction.

**Paragraph 7**

The first sentence, the topic sentence, immediately draws the distinctions between Lee and Grant. Grant, a product of the frontier rather than the settled and aristocratic East Coast, differed from Lee in everything. The rest of the paragraph lists some primary differences.

**Paragraph 11**

Whereas Lee's commitment to community was local and insular, Grant's was national and even expansionist.

**Paragraph 13**

This paragraph serves as a transition, carrying the reader from the differences between the two men to a comparison of their likenesses.

**Paragraph 14**

The topic sentence cites their first similarity and is followed by examples.

**Paragraph 16**

After citing the qualities that made them great warriors, Catton points out that their greatest virtue was their ability to be men of peace after the fighting was over.

Catton's phrasing of the last two sentences recalls that of the thesis sentence in paragraph 3, thus bringing the essay to a satisfying close.

## Possible Answers

### *Meaning and Purpose*

1. Recall some of the economic and social differences between the North and South that Catton cites as the cause of the United States Civil War. Lead students to discuss in detail the major differences between the Civil War and modern conflicts in other regions. Currently, civil strife exists in Bosnia and seems endless in the Middle East and Northern Ireland.
2. In paragraph 5, Catton describes a social system in which privilege was based on land ownership, inspiring a strong sense of obligation to the community. Lee, embodying "the noblest elements of this aristocratic ideal" (6), became a symbol of that ideal for the soldiers who had been willing to die to preserve it.
3. Throughout history, wars have been fought for emotional attachment to ideals rather than intellectual understanding of realities. Ask students for examples of this tendency (the Crusades, Vietnam). Even poor southerners saw Lee as a hero who could save the integrity of the southern way of life. The romance in backing such a cause was stronger, for many, than the fear of deprivation and death.
4. Grant represented a society with great hope for the future and disregard for the past. He stood for democracy, with privilege based on what a man did for himself, not on landed birthright (8).
5. Both Lee and Grant had virtues that made them great soldiers, such as "tenacity," "fidelity," and the "ability to think" (14,15). Greatest among these virtues was their ability to become men of peace after the war (16). Their pivotal difference was the kind of society each represented: Grant stood for a modern, expanding one; Lee an established, stagnant one.
6. The expression "tidewater Virginia" refers to the tidal flats, up to the Piedmont Plateau, where all the rivers met. Here grew the quintessential southern plantations where slavery began, and where the Virginia aristocracy was founded.

*Strategy*

1. The first three paragraphs form the introduction, which ends with the thesis (3); the next paragraph begins the body of the essay with a discussion of Lee. The rest of the essay is structured as a comparison and contrast; the introduction is not. In the introduction, Catton gives background facts about the meeting between the two generals at the close of the Civil War, and sets the basis for comparison.
2. The first and second sentences tell us that Lee and Grant, "these men" (the transition from the preceding paragraph), have brought the war to a virtual end, the key word being virtual. The third confirms that the war is essentially over, and the fourth, which concludes the paragraph, points forward to the body of the essay, the contrasts between the two men and the societies they represented.
3. Catton uses paragraph 13 as a transition from contrasting the differences between the two men to comparing their likenesses.
4. The first sentence in each paragraph uses a clear transition that tightly connects it with the preceding paragraph, thus giving the entire essay solid coherence.
5. Catton uses the subject-by-subject method in paragraphs 4 to 11. Paragraph 13 begins point-by-point comparison of similarities between the two men until the conclusion in paragraph 16. The subject-by-subject structure gives, uninterrupted, all the background on each man that Catton needs to make his point-by-point comparisons in the second half.

*Style*

1. The metaphor suggests that the unfolding history of the United States is a story—a narrative that could be written and read—and that the close of the Civil War is a natural ending to one chapter and beginning of another. The metaphor is effective because Catton goes on to tell the "story" of Lee and Grant.
2. Lee, as a knight in shining armor, may represent a lost cause and a social ideal that has been bypassed by history, but to interpret such a description satirically would miss the tone of the essay, which is entirely laudatory.
3. *Virtual*: being in effect, though not actually or expressly; *poignant*: keenly distressing to the feelings; *chivalry*: the medieval institution and principles of knighthood, the ideal qualities of which include courage, generosity, and courtesy; *legends*: nonhistorical or unverifiable stories handed down by tradition from earlier times and popularly accepted as historic; *myths*: stories or beliefs that are attempts to explain basic truths; *embodied*: given a concrete form; *deportment*: demeanor, conduct, behavior; *obeisance*: a movement of the body expressing deep respect or deferential courtesy, as before a superior; *static*: pertaining to or characterized by a fixed or stationary condition; *tenacity*: holding fast; *fidelity*: loyalty; *indomitable*: unable to be subdued or overcome.
4. Ending the essay in the same place as it began brings it full circle and reconnects the reader to the situation described in the first paragraph. This technique is structurally satisfying because in the body of the essay Catton has given background on and expanded the meaning of the scene in the Court House.

5. Though Lee and Grant represent two entirely different social ideals, Catton admires them both. Both were, in their own ways, admirable. Even when the author contrasts them, he always does so on positive terms. When comparing them, he speaks only of virtues: tenacity and faithfulness (14); daring, resourcefulness, and the ability to think quickly (15); and, ultimately, the capacity to be men of peace (16).

# *Los Otros, Mis Hermanos*

## Richard Rodriguez

### Teaching Suggestions

You might begin by asking your students for whom English is their second language, or who come from a bilingual household, to compare their experiences with language to those of Rodriguez. Ask native speakers to relate their experiences with languages other than English. Were there situations for both groups that made them feel discomfort or frustration? From that discussion you might lead the students to a consideration of some of the elements of the essay's construction: the point-by-point development of paragraphs 2 and 3, for instance, and the subject-by-subject development of 7 and 8. You might want to teach the essay in conjunction with the other Rodriguez essay, "Los Pobres," or with Maya Angelou's "Finishing School."

### Notes

**Paragraph 1**

All of the opening images set Rodriguez, his family, and his house apart from his neighbors: the size of the family, the color of the house, the animals.

**Paragraph 2**

In the opening two paragraphs Rodriguez uses both parallel structure and clear transitions to keep his contrasts clear. The phrases "In public" (sentence 1) and "At home" (sentence 3) are participial phrases that begin their respective sentences and clearly distinguish the subject of each. The opening prepositional phrase of the second paragraph's opening sentence connects the time of the paragraph with that in the opening paragraph and thus serves as a transition.

**Paragraph 3**

The compound sentence is balanced by the semicolon, with thesis (hearing) in the first part and antithesis (replying) in the second.

**Paragraph 4**

Paragraphs 4, 5, 6, and the first half of 7 concentrate on the child's lack of ability to speak and understand English.

**Paragraph 7**

"But" in the middle of the paragraph is an emphatic transition that brings the reader's attention from the child's language difficulties to his parents' and the consequent change of attitude he has.

**Paragraph 8**

The first half of the paragraph shows how his parents' language problems didn't really matter when he looks at the situation from an adult perspective. But after the transitional "And yet . . ." he shows how their language struggles meant something significant to him as a child.

**Paragraph 9**

Here Rodriguez uses a general example to illustrate how the power of English and his parents' difficulties in dealing with it caused him to lose confidence in them.

**Paragraph 10**

These next two paragraphs concentrate on the comforts he found in his family's language, *Español.* For him his family becomes extended to anyone who speaks Spanish. Paragraph 10 begins with the oppositional transition "But," and the two paragraphs contrast with the preceding three.

**Paragraph 13**

Because his private and public worlds remained so separate, Rodriguez believes his psychological development was retarded.

**Paragraph 16 and 17**

While the final two paragraphs are full of the comforting images of home, family, and native language, he makes the negative moral judgment that such extended separation of public and private language is not healthy (first sentence, paragraph 17).

## Possible Answers

*Meaning and Purpose*

1. Spanish, for the youthful Rodriguez, is the language of home and family. In all of the examples he gives, he associates Spanish with the comfort and protection of home, a safe oasis that protects him from the surrounding and alien world of *los gringos*. English, the language of the public world that surrounds him, he finds threatening. Both he and his parents struggle to understand and speak English, but they must do so just to function in the Anglo world in which they live. Even the sounds of English he finds alien and grating: "The accent of *los gringos* was never pleasing nor was it hard to hear" (6). So Spanish, the language of home and protection, becomes an escape from the frightening and alien public world of English. "It [Spanish] became the language of joyful return" (10).
2. As a child Rodriguez views his own insecurity and fear as natural. His security lies with his parents. So when he sees them stumble in their attempts to speak English in the public world, his insecurity is heightened and he is, in a sense, embarrassed. He recognizes the surety of the native English speakers, compared to his parents, in their voices' volume: "I'd notice, moreover, that my parents' voices were softer than those of *gringos* we'd meet" (7).
3. As an adult Rodriguez recognizes that his parents' English language insufficiencies made no practical difference in either his or their lives. They could handle the language well enough to manage everyday problems. But as a child his trust in their authority diminished because he perceived his own security was threatened by their English language deficiencies in the public world.
4. For the native English speaker, the language of family and the language of the other, "public" world are the same, so the two worlds become connected early. For the non-native speaker, like Rodriguez, his Spanish-speaking

home becomes a refuge from the ubiquitous English-speaking world outside of his home and the larger Spanish speaking community that he considers family. He therefore remains psychologically dependent on his family longer than would a native speaker.

## *Strategy*

1. The first paragraph introduces the reader to the general contrast between his home and family and the outside world represented by a salesman and his neighbors. He then focuses in on the differences in his perceptions of Spanish and English in the second paragraph with point-by-point development.
2. The illustration contrasts Rodriguez's attitudes toward English as an adult to when he was a child. Now, when he is abroad, English stands out because it is different from the language that predominates in the area, just as English stood out when he was a Spanish-speaking child in an English-speaking world. But he finds hearing English in such a context comforting now because English makes up his world. The entire paragraph, except for the transitional opening two sentences, contrasts with the preceding paragraph.
3. The example illustrates Rodriguez's last point in the preceding paragraph: When he heard his parents struggle with English, his ". . . trust in their protection and power weakened."
4. Rodriguez emphasizes the sentence by making it a separate paragraph. It dramatizes the boy's relief in returning home from the threatening world of *los gringos* with an emphatic affirmation.

## *Style*

1. The author uses point-by-point development to quickly emphasize the differences between his two childhood worlds. He uses subject-by-subject development in two different ways. In the first, he contrasts individual paragraphs. The stumbling and insecure English of his parents and himself described in paragraph 7, for instance, is contrasted against the confidence of native English speakers in paragraphs 3 and 4. He also uses subject-by-subject development within paragraphs, as when he contrasts the two different ways he felt about his parents' English insufficiencies (8).
2. The sense of the Spanish words, if not all of their precise meanings, should be clear to any reader. Almost all students will know the meaning of *los gringos*, though they may be unclear about the phrase's connotations. Rodriguez translates *inglés* for us in paragraph 3. They may not know the exact meaning of *los otros* (the others), but it is clearly associated with "my separateness" and "*los gringos*" that precedes and follows it (10). It is clear, too, in paragraph 17 that *mis hermanos* (my brothers) refers to his siblings.
3. *Gringo* means foreigner, especially one of U.S. or English descent, and is usually used disparagingly. But the pejorative connotation seems muted in this piece, since the boy views his surrounding world of *los gringos* as threatening rather than hostile.

# *Sexism in English: A 1990s Update*

## Alleen Pace Nilsen

### Teaching Suggestions

How we label the things around us determines how we view them. What of the school mascot? If it had been the Teddy bear, how would our athletic teams feel about themselves? What if automobiles had names like Plymouth Rock or Chrysler Banana or Cadillac El Desperfecto (which means "the flaw")?

Younger students in the 1990s occasionally do not realize how the feminist movement has affected their lives. For that matter, they sometimes are not aware that discrimination still pervades our culture. A lively discussion grows from the question, "Why is it that we have never had a woman president of the United States?" The usual quick answer is that no woman has applied for the job. But wait a minute: Why has no woman applied? Is it because she has no chance of winning? If she has no chance of winning, then why does she have no chance of winning? Do men completely control politics in this country, so that "women need not apply"?

The real question, though not so dramatic, runs deep: Have we, consciously or not, used language in such a way for so many years that women have been perceived as "the weaker sex," the "sexy" gender, the "passive" gender, the "second sex"—only because of our language usage and without reason or logic? Are we not aware that the language can operate against our notions of equality?

### Notes

**Paragraph 1**

Sometimes, people are fortunate enough to travel to other countries where they can better see the merits and demerits of their own country by objective comparison. Being in another country and not knowing its culture and customs, they see in a way that the natives do not see—by comparing their own ways with the way of the Afghans, in this example.

**Paragraph 2**

Nilsen compares the roles of Afghan women with those of American women, particularly those in Kabul. She gives examples of how women are treated in Kabul, which open her eyes to the ways in which women in general are treated.

**Paragraph 3**

Removed from their own culture, the American women in Kabul take up ways of life that are unusual for them. Nilsen gives examples of how the American women's activities in Kabul changed her way of thinking about women's roles in general.

"One woman's husband . . .": Notice the hint of imitation here. The American man seems to be imitating what he sees as a facet of Afghan culture. He takes "valuable" time out from his "important work"—an hour a week—to listen to his wife's complaints. The rhetorical question that concludes this paragraph is meant to reflect sarcastically the man's inflated view of his job.

**Paragraph 4**

Nilsen decides to take up academic involvement in the feminist movement, rather than an overtly political part. Not being ready for a revolution, she instead decides to study the ways in which language affects people's attitudes.

**Paragraph 5**

"The language that a culture uses . . .": Briefly, the "Whorfian hypothesis" (after Benjamin Lee Whorf) says that the language a culture uses determines its perceptions of the world. The popularity of this view has waned because we seem to have no way to prove that different groups of languages reflect different thought processes. Nilsen is not dealing with *language* linguistically defined, however; she is dealing with words and how those words can tell us something about ourselves, which is part of the semantic component of language.

**Paragraph 7**

The writer offers general arguments based on examination of the evidence, then moves from general arguments to particular examples that support those arguments. "A women is sexy" is a general argument, as is "A man is successful." Nilsen sets out to prove both general arguments by offering the wealth of examples that she found to support them.

**Paragraph 10**

Moving from examples in Greek mythology to examples in American regional English, Nilsen shows that our own language is stocked with examples to prove her argument that "Women are sexy."

**Paragraph 12**

Remind students that connotation refers to the meaning "surrounding" a term or word. They may have a friend who is "mildly obese" (a positive connotation) though someone they do not particularly like is "fat" (a negative connotation).

**Paragraph 13**

In this paragraph, she discusses some words historically, showing how they change (or are changed) in meaning as time passes. Students are interested to learn that the best source in which to study how words change meaning is the *Oxford English Dictionary*.

**Paragraph 15**

First cited from evidence in the twelfth century, Middle English *grom* means "young man" or "boy." The Middle English *guma*, "man," is the original suffix in "bridegroom." The "bride and groom" are talked about in that order, just as many people still begin speeches with "Ladies and Gentlemen."

**Paragraph 16**

The *widow's peak* is the point formed by hair that grows down in the middle of a forehead. At one time it was believed to signal early widowhood. A *widow's walk* is a roof platform built on some New England coastal homes, so that one could observe ships at sea.

**Paragraph 17**

In the relatively few years since Nilsen's first in-depth study of words and sexism, cultural ideas have helped to change the connotations of some words. Notice that every time Nilsen offers a general argument, she follows it with examples that show her argument's worth.

**Paragraph 18**

As words have changed, so also have customs and attitudes. Younger students often do not realize how many changes have occurred in such a short time, resulting in comparatively diminished sexist attitudes.

**Paragraph 19**

The transition from the preceding subtopic is structurally smooth, moving from the wedding-ceremony examples to roles in general, considered historically and currently.

**Paragraph 20**

"grammar": In some regions of the country, the verb form *to wed* has been replaced by the nonsexist verb form to *marry*. That is, a woman can "marry" a man, and a man can "marry" a woman.

**Paragraph 21**

*Ms.* first came into use in the 1950s as a title before a woman's surname when her marital status was unknown or irrelevant. In the early 1970s, the women's movement encouraged *Ms.*, reasoning that if *Mr.* does not indicate a man's marital status, then we have no reason to indicate a woman's marital status.

**Paragraph 22**

*Mrs.*, first recorded in the seventeenth century, was originally synonymous with *Miss.*; both were abbreviations for *mistress*.

**Paragraph 23**

Traced from its Germanic roots, *king* probably means in its basic sense "head of a kin" or "son of noble kin." The word *queen* comes from the Gothic *qens*, "woman." The husband of a queen who rules in her own right is the prince consort, to distinguish him from other princes of the royal family.

**Paragraph 25**

This paragraph illustrates inductive reasoning: The writer moves from a series of examples to her conclusion, that the gender line is dimming.

**Paragraph 29**

"The proper names given to girls . . .": We rarely examine masculine names, feminine names, and crossover names, all at the same time. The class might consider names other than those in this paragraph, such as Sydney, Jamie, Sandy, Wendy, and Merle, and nicknames, such as Curly, Red, Happy, Shorty, and Smiley. Which in the preceding list are absolutely masculine names, according to your class? Which are absolutely feminine names?

**Paragraph 30**

Students are interested to learn that the Latin *vir*, "man," is akin to the Old English *wer*, the "man" in *werewolf*.

**Paragraph 32**

The word *patron*, from Latin *patronus*, "legal protector or advocate," is derived from *pater*, "father." The word *matron* is from Latin *mater*, "mother."

**Paragraph 34**

"Wizard and witch . . .": Students are interested to learn that *warlock* refers to the male equivalent of *witch*. Also, some students have pointed out that colloquially, *wizard* can refer to anyone who does something quite well, as in the sentence, "Shirley is a math wizard."

"Just as the Afghans . . .": Nilsen comes full circle here, mentioning that the Afghan proverb and some English phrases share some features.

**Paragraph 35**

A filly is a young female horse. Interestingly, in horse-racing jargon, a "maiden" is any horse that has never won a race.

In some American-English dialects, "old dog" refers to an old man, and "young whelp," albeit redundant, refers to a young man.

A biddy is a chicken and, by extension, a fussy old woman.

**Paragraph 37**

Nilsen ends her essay positively, pointing out that our language is changing for the better, socially and politically. And she reminds us that our speaking and writing determine our way of viewing our world.

## Possible Answers

### *Meaning and Purpose*

1. Encourage students to examine their own experiences with sexism in language and compare those experiences with some of Nilsen's information.
2. The author argues for examining the words that we use to describe the genders so that we may see what we mean when we use them. She argues against using any words that demean people, especially women. Several sentences could be cited, including the "for" sentence, "I'm one of those linguists who believes that new language customs will cause a new generation of speakers to grow up with different expectations" (36); and the "against" sentence, the last in paragraph 28.
3. Nilsen's main point is stated in paragraph 5, when she says, "The language that a culture uses is telltale evidence of the values and beliefs of that culture." Each of the sections has a main point, or thesis, which is a more specific example of the main thesis. The first sentence in each section is the main point of that section.
4. These experiences are included because they pushed the author into awareness of how another culture treated its females, and made her question sexism in our own culture.
5. Some students will be overwhelmed with the examples. Others will say they are necessary to show the reader just what Nilsen means, and will not feel overwhelmed because each example is brief.

### *Strategy*

1. Nilsen's examples are specific—they are all words and their meanings and connotations. Her study requires specific examples to support her assertion about sexism in language.
2. Nilsen suggests that the language fools no one but is necessary for image. She refers to the military job titles as "fancy titles."
3. Nilsen ends with some examples of how language is changing to eliminate sexism. In her final paragraph she refines her thesis to say, "(Sexism) exists in people's minds. Language is like an x-ray in providing visible evidence of invisible thoughts." She uses this paragraph to express her opinion that people will begin thinking consciously about the language they use. This positive statement somewhat balances all the examples of sexism still in force that she has given in the essay.

### *Style*

1. Nilsen is calm and informative. She intends to expose sexism in language for what it is without being militantly feminist. One example of this tone is the sentence, "When topographical features are named after men, it's probably not going to be to draw attention to a sexual part of their bodies but instead to honor individuals for an accomplishment" (11).
2. The reading pace is fast because each example is short and gives way quickly to the next. Readers have one interesting bit of information to read after another.
3. The three sections set off the three large areas in which Nilsen found sexist language. These sections are necessary for clarity and readability in an essay that is so long and full of facts. They help guide the reading.

# *Two Varieties of Killers*

## Ellen Currie

### Teaching Suggestions

You might begin by asking the class if they remember the Ted Bundy case (he was executed by the State of Florida in 1989) or can recall any other cases where the accused was accorded similar attention. After listening to their examples, turn the discussion to, Why? Why do we give such cases this kind of attention? Why the jokes? Why the T-shirts? Why the not infrequent offers of support? Why the tendency to forget the victims? You may not arrive at definitive answers to these questions, but some examination of them may lead to a general awareness that such cases affect people in some important way. Some of our reactions may be attempts to distance us from the horror of the crimes. Some reactions may be motivated by desires to make connections with something, almost anything. From there the discussion might broaden into other aspects of popular culture: radio and television talk shows, tabloid newspapers and television programs, or new age spiritualism, all of which also seem to be ways to reassure us or shield us or give us something to attach our lives to.

### Notes

**Paragraph 1**

Henry James (1843–1916), an American born writer who later became a British subject. The author of numerous novels, short stories, sketches and critical essays. One of his recurring themes is the contrast between American and European character, which he explored in the novels *Wings of the Dove* (1902), *The Ambassadors* (1903) and *The Golden Bowl* (1904).

By quoting James about "manners and morals" and "human and sociable" crimes, Currie gives weight to her use of such terms in the discussion of Smith and Bundy.

**Paragraphs 2 and 3**

Here Currie tells us she will be contrasting crimes (2) and announces which specific crimes (3).

**Paragraphs 4, 5, and 6**

These paragraphs state the facts about Madeleine Smith's crime and describe it as a personal crime, one of passion, one of the kind Henry James liked.

**Paragraph 7**

This paragraph serves as a transition to Bundy by reversing the idea of paragraph 6: his crime was not personal, not a crime of passion.

**Paragraphs 8 and 9**

Currie describes Bundy's crimes, as she did for Smith in paragraphs 4 and 5.

**Paragraph 10**

Here Currie shifts to the public reaction to the trial.

**Paragraph 11 and 12**

These paragraphs explain Bundy's behavior (he is antisocial) and then question the reasons for the behavior of the rest of us.

**Paragraph 13**

The last paragraph sums it up: Smith's crime is not good, but it is understandable. Bundy's crimes are not understandable, nor is our reaction to him.

## Possible Answers

### *Meaning and Purpose*

1. Sociable crimes are "human and comprehensible and even sympathetic" (paragraph 2).
2. Her thesis is stated at the end of paragraph 2: "The crimes get bigger and more horrible, and yet we are not sufficiently horrified by them; we pay less and less attention to the manners and the morals they disclose."
3. Yes. She wants us to think primarily about our reaction to them. In her last paragraph she says, "Ted Bundy's unspeakable crimes and our cheap reaction to them reveal us to ourselves in a strange and deathly light."
4. Bundy is "an antisocial person, a man without conscience." (11)
5. Bundy is all image. He creates a picture of himself as charming, witty, handsome, articulate, polished, capable (he is his own attorney and twice escaped from custody). He is mediagenic and has been the subject of a television movie.

### *Strategy*

1. Currie uses a subject-by-subject organization. The contrast between Smith and Bundy is not complicated, so it's easy for a reader to keep Smith's case in mind as she reads about Bundy. The subject-by-subject method also emphasizes the dramatic difference between the two crimes.
2. Ted Bundy's crimes and our reaction to his case are Currie's main concerns. Smith's case is offered merely to show the difference between a "sociable murder" and the "20th century phenomenon."

### *Style*

1. "Tropical" means hot and humid, by association with the climate of the tropics; "abandoned" means freed from restraints; in this case, the restraints of properly modest feminine behavior.
2. A mediagenic person, at a minimum, would be physically attractive, articulate, more aggressive than passive, and have a story to tell, the more unusual the better.
3. Apparently "socially impossible" refers to class distinctions. Madeleine is the daughter of a Glasgow architect, presumably of some prominence in the community, and Madeleine is later betrothed to an "older, richer, and more settled suitor."
4. *Portentous*: significant; *bounden*: obligatory; *pagan*: hedonistic; *savaged*: assaulted; *vile*: highly offensive or objectionable; *glib*: superficially or insincerely fluent; unconstrained.

# *The Battle of the Ants*

## Henry David Thoreau

## Teaching Suggestions

This essay extends an analogy, like tentacles, into several allied topics, but the body of the analogy remains clear. Our modern battles are usually no more important, though just as exciting to an objective observer, as the battle of the ants. Students occasionally need reminding that each recent generation has had a war: World War II in the 1940s, the Korean War in the 1950s, the Vietnam War in the late 1960s and early 1970s. What about the 1990s? For openers, we have Desert Storm.

Thoreau's ants mirror the actions of two peoples at war. Thoreau's ants are fighting for a principle, the author remarks sarcastically. No war, at least according to propaganda, was ever fought except for a principle. But some of the principles are as trivial as that which caused the Trojan War, the kidnaping of one person.

Students like to brainstorm principles. List several words on the chalk board and then discuss whether those words in fact name principles. Truth? Honesty? Art? Ethics? The discussion invariably leads to analogies, for students will use analogies to explain their thinking about each "principle."

## Notes

### Paragraph 1

Thoreau, a legendary master of diction, using words precisely, did not "see" the ants; he "observed" them. The analogy between ants and soldiers becomes obvious in description in sentence 1: the ants are not "fighting"; they are "fiercely contending." This strategy of *personification*, writing about something as if it were human, permeates the essay.

"chips": The chips are left over from Thoreau's chopping wood. A *duellum* is a duel; a *bellum* is a war. The "races" of ants remind us that Thoreau's America was militantly divided over slavery, and Thoreau was strongly against it.

Myrmidons: The Myrmidons were ants, changed into warriors by Zeus, supreme deity of the ancient Greeks. They accompanied Achilles to the Trojan War.

"a couple": The soldier ants "fast locked in each other's embraces" remind students that lovers, not warriors, are usually so described. The next sentence heightens that ironic comparison by moving us from lovers' to warriors' language. The writer's almost microscopic view of ants in battle alludes to the notion that all wars are petty and that nature itself carries on benignly.

"Divested him of several of his members": Notice that Thoreau's euphemism here substitutes inoffensive words for some that could be distasteful ("tore off his legs"). This phrase also contributes to the mock heroic tone.

"Conquer or die": A Roman motto, *aut vincere aut mori*, literally "either to conquer or to die," was intended to inspire soldiers going into battle.

"In the meanwhile . . .": Have students notice the personification, the human qualities of the red ant.

"Whose mother . . .": The mothers of Sparta, an ancient Greek city state, told their sons, "Return with your shield or (carried) upon it," literally, "Win or die trying."

Achilles: a Greek hero in the Trojan Wars; Patroclus was his friend slain in those wars. From Homer's *Iliad*.

The movement from ant wars to human wars, reinforces the analogy.

Austerlitz, Dresden: two bloody battles won in the early 1800s by Napoleon's armies.

The Battle of Concord Bridge, 1775, involved few soldiers (including "Davis and Hosmer") but became famous in American history.

"Three-penny tax": A reference to the Boston Tea Party, December 16, 1773, when the colonists defied the English crown. The British won the battle of Bunker Hill, fought in June 1775, but suffered enormous casualties.

**Paragraph 2**

Notice the calm, objective curiosity here, contrasted with the furious life-and-death battle being studied. The description that follows depicts graphically and minutely the thirty-minute struggle.

*Hotel des Invalides*: a home for old soldiers, in Paris, and the actual tomb of Napoleon I, as well.

**Paragraph 3**

Kirby, Spence, and Huber were three leading specialists in the study of insects.

Eugenius the Fourth (1383–1447): Pope from 1431 to 1447.

Nicholas Pistoriensis (1490–1558): Swedish Roman Catholic ecclesiastic and historian who wrote a Swedish history that was long accepted in Europe as authoritative.

Olaus Magnus (1481–1559): called "The Cruel." King of Denmark and Norway, 1513–1523. Showed extreme cruelty against the Swedes massacring their nobility (1520). Imprisoned for life in 1532.

James Knox Polk (1795–1849) was eleventh president of the United States (1845–1849). Thoreau published his first book, *A Week on the Concord and Merrimac Rivers*, in 1849.

The Fugitive-Slave Bill required that slaves who escaped to the North be captured and returned to their owners in the South.

## Possible Answers

### *Meaning and Purpose*

1. Encourage students to explore first their personal responses to Thoreau's essay. Ask them to be specific in connecting their responses to statements or ideas in the essay.
2. Thoreau considered war a far from noble pursuit, beneath human dignity, to be fought by ants if fought at all. This extended analogy between ants and soldiers is evidence of this opinion, as are his numerous and satiric examples of wars fought throughout history.
3. Thoreau buries his thesis statements well into the first paragraph: "I was myself excited somewhat even as if they had been men. The more you think of it, the less the difference." The next sentence might also be considered part of his main point.
4. Thoreau's commentary is timeless. With mockery, he raises the battle of the ants to such "heights" as comparing it to an ancient Greek war and a patriotic American war. Of course, he is mocking our seeing wars as glorious, serving his purpose (satire), and extending his analogy.
5. Thoreau wrote mostly for an educated male readership. Most who could then read were well educated men, many holding authority in government or church. Thoreau used this essay to mock the very thing most learned men admired, and to point out to them the folly in their thinking.
6. Thoreau extends the analogy through history by showing that such battles have been noteworthy for centuries. With great mocking, Thoreau raises the battle of the ants to the level of recorded human history and compares it to other ant battles celebrated in writing. He ends the extended analogy by poking fun at academic historians, whose style he mocks here.

### *Strategy*

1. Ants and men in this essay share cruelty, tenacity, courage, bravery, and other qualities associated with combat.

2. The comparison is between soldiers and ants. He has been personifying ants and talking about them as if they were men. He realizes that he is as excited as if they were human and that the ant–human differences are less than he thought. Of course Thoreau is making fun here.
3. The analogy is between a wounded ant and a wounded soldier who spends his days in a home for old soldiers, trying to keep the glory of the war alive. Of course, the analogy is factually weak, but it is ironic.
4. Satire is a literary technique or style that combines humor and wit with a critical attitude for the purpose of improving human institutions or actions. The satirist pokes fun not so much to tear down as to inspire remodeling of the subject being satirized. Jonathan Swift's famous "A Modest Proposal" is a good example of satire to place alongside Thoreau's essay.
5. Students should evaluate Thoreau's use of satire on his subject. Without the analogy's mockery, Thoreau might have written a more formal, pedantic, or sermonlike treatise on war and principles and how thinly they disguise petty human squabbles. Such a hypothetical essay probably would have been boring by comparison, not as attention-getting, amusing, or successful in making his points.

*Style*

1. An internecine war is mutually destructive, full of slaughter, with enormous casualties on both sides. It is a "no-win" war.
2. These kinds of exclamations appear in newspaper headlines. Luther Blanchard, in the headline's context, is an American who fought at Concord.
3. This could have been a factual description of a man-soldier, but not an ant-soldier. Ants do not have the eyes described here, or the kind of body that permits a carbuncle. By analogy, however, it is a realistic description imaginatively comparing ant with man.
4. *Pertinacity* means "the quality of holding firmly to a belief or purpose," and "the quality of being hard to get rid of, physically." The first meaning compares ants with men, the second with bulldogs.

# 7 / *Cause and Effect*

## *My Wood*

E. M. Forster

### Teaching Suggestions

One way to introduce students to the ideas of this essay is to ask, "What responsibilities go with material wealth?" The answers will be mixed, many students saying that materially wealthy people should care for the homeless and the hungry, others saying that the affluent have few responsibilities beyond caring for themselves and their own families. The follow-up question is, "Does material wealth cause a restriction of one's freedom?" Usually, students reply, "No," almost in unison.

But wait! Many materially wealthy people must wear specific kinds of clothing; otherwise, they will risk being outcasts from their own society. How about cars? Don't materially wealthy people have to drive expected makes and models? What about friends? Can materially wealthy people afford to have poor friends? What about bodyguards? Security gates? Special places in which to live?

After students see that one effect of material wealth is lack of social freedom, they are better able to grasp the points made in Forster's essay.

## Notes

### Paragraph 1

The British have been in India since 1600. India became independent in 1947, after many years of strife. Forster's *A Passage to India* chronicles life among the British in India before its independence. Mention the British and American English differences: Many American dialects have "woods" for *wood*, and Americans spell *cheque* "check." Notice the simple cause-and-effect statement in the first paragraph. Forster's check allows him to buy the wood. The interjection "blast it" is Forster's momentary opinion of the public footpath in his wood. The paragraph's last sentence introduces the psychological cause-and-effect topic of the essay.

### Paragraph 2

"Kingdom of Heaven": See New Testament, Matthew 19:24: "It is easier for a camel to go through the eye of a needle, than for a rich man to enter into the kingdom of God." Forster follows that verse with a coupling of the religious and secular cause-and-effect possibilities. Leo Tolstoy (1828–1910), social and moral philosopher and Russian mystic, wrote *War and Peace* (1865–1869), among other great works. He emancipated his serfs in 1861. *Stone*: a unit of weight in Great Britain equal to 14 pounds. The stout bishop weighs 196 pounds.

The first and last lines of the paragraph end with the same four words, for effective emphasis: "makes me feel heavy." Forster, too, feels stout.

### Paragraph 3

"In the second place" is the clearest kind of transition, as the author moves from the psychological effect of weight, caused by owning his property, to that of size. The property Forster acquired has caused him to want more.

### Paragraph 4

"The other day" begins Forster's example displaying how the psychological effect of wanting more property has caused him to view his surroundings—greedily. King Ahab in the Old Testament, the seventh king of Israel (c. 875–853 B.C.), greatly expanded his territories, especially by marrying Jezebel, daughter of the king of Sidon. In Herman Melville's *Moby Dick*, Captain Ahab's obsession was to find and kill the white whale, at whatever cost. Forster discusses his growing obsession for getting more land. Canute II of Denmark (994?–1035), subject of many legends, conquered England and was chosen king in 1017 by the *witan*, the king's council of Anglo-Saxons. Alexander the Great (356–323 B.C.), said to have wept after he had no more worlds to conquer, directed enormously successful campaigns in Greece, Persia, northern India, Syria, and Egypt, among others. Sirius, the Dog Star, is the brightest star in the constellation Canis Major. Forster's imaginary domain is boundless, a cause of sadness when he compares it with his real, limited domain. The bird reminds us of nature's "definition" of property. We "own" only ourselves.

**Paragraph 5**

"In the third place . . .": Owning property causes us to want to change it, to make it clearly ours. This psychology of ownership—nothing really belongs to us until we change it, pseudo-creatively—deeply bothers Forster. We want to mold our property into an extension of our personality, but without a creative motive. Shakespeare's Sonnet 129 begins, "The expense of spirit in a waste of shame / Is lust in action. . . ." The "internal defect" is our inability to accept ourselves as we are, just as we are unable to accept our property for what it is. As Forster uses *carnal*, the word relates to the body as the seat of physical appetites, without intellectual or moral influence. Our life on earth should be carnal and material, yet managed by the intellect and morality. Ironically, however, our desire for ownership manages our intellect and morality. Dante Alighieri (1265–1321) wrote *The Divine Comedy*.

**Paragraph 6**

Forster's homely transition detaches us from his deeply philosophical paragraph.

**Paragraph 7**

The natural products of Forster's wood attract people. Foxgloves have long spikes of thimble like flowers. A medicine made from their leaves (digitalis) is used as a heart stimulant. Bracken are large, coarse, weedy ferns. All the public activity causes Forster to question the definition of ownership. Does the owner own the property, or does the property own the owner? For Dives, see the parable of the selfish rich man, Luke 16:19–31; Lazarus is the poor diseased man in the same parable.

"possession": To make his "quadruple crown of possession," Forster weaves together the four subtopics in this essay: worldly wealth, greed, false creativity and selfishness. "[N]asty Bolshies": Bolsheviks are Communists or, loosely used, any radicals.

## Possible Answers

*Meaning and Purpose*

1. Forster intends to explore the questions he poses in the first paragraph: "What is the effect of property upon the character?" and "What's the effect on me of my wood?" These two sentences are his thesis in question form; he is asserting that ownership does affect a person.
2. Encourage students to share their stories about things they have owned and done something to. Be sure they account for clear causes and effects, such as "I painted an American flag on my leather jacket because I want people to know that I am patriotic."
3. Students are free to select their own allusions. Occasionally reading and discussing the better papers in class is an exercise that helps students realize this essay's depth.
4. The author's freedom is restricted by his imagined obligations to himself and his possession, which stem from his owning the wood in the first place. Now that he has the wood, he feels obliged to enlarge it, improve it, and protect it.
5. The interjection "blast it" sums up his opinion of the wood's being publicly and easily accessible by the footpath. This is the first clue that Forster will feel possessive about his wood.

*Strategy*

1. Forster gives the cause in paragraph 1: the acquiring of money that enabled him to buy the wood. In subsequent paragraphs, he develops one effect at a

time. This structure is effective because it is clear and makes his reasoning easy to follow. Giving one long paragraph to each effect allows him to single it out and explore it in depth.

2. The statement quoted is an example of a causal chain, or a series of things, one triggering the next, in chronological order. This technique here exaggerates Forster's point that owning property is heavy or cumbersome. He imagines that ownership will cause slowness, having things "you cannot move about," until you'd better think twice before you "bathe in the Jordan." Forster is using humor to stress one danger of ownership.
3. The ownership was caused by the high stone walls that the owner built on both sides of the path. The effect is that those walls have imprisoned the owner.
4. The fourth and final point is selfishness. Forster means that blackberries lure people in until he is tempted to "wall in and fence out . . . property. [acts that are] Enormously . . . selfish" (7).

*Style*

1. The ladies are probably elementary school teachers, and the author thinks little of them for "grubbing" in his wood just to show the children toadstools.
2. Forster extends his need to enlarge the boundary of his wood all the way to the sea to keep out noise and children. This exaggeration stresses his point that once he is an owner, his greed will know no bounds.
3. These two paragraphs are transitions from discussion of one effect to the next. They are clear statements of Forster's chronology in presenting his points. And they are stylistically effective because they are short and rather abrupt between two long paragraphs. They catch attention and bring the reader back on track.

# *Why We Crave Horror Movies*

## Stephen King

### Teaching Suggestions

A lively discussion of King's essay might be initiated by inviting students to list their favorite horror films and the specific aspects of each film that made it particularly effective. What were the students' reactions to the film? Did those reactions correspond to King's speculations about why horror films have been, and are, so popular? From this discussion you might try to then focus attention on the essay's form: how King grabs our attention with the first sentence; how he dispenses rather quickly and amusingly with the first three reasons for the popularity of horror films in the first five paragraphs; and, finally, how he spends the entire rest of the essay exploring what is, in his opinion, the most important cause of the film genre's popularity. There's a lesson here on how effectively to proportion an essay, allotting the most space to the most important points.

We think King's use of metaphoric language is also worth noting, for it certainly lends vibrancy to his prose. Question 1 in *Style* deals with this.

In a longer project you might want to teach the essay in conjunction with Andrew Klavan's "In Praise of Gore", which argues the efficacy of film violence, and Michael Medved's "Denial Behavior", which argues against it.

## Notes

**Paragraph 4**

*Die, Monster, Die*: A 1965 film with Boris Karloff, Nick Adams, and Freda Jackson, based on a story by H.P. Lovecraft (1890–1937), an American writer of horror tales in the tradition of Poe. In the film, Karloff is a recluse who discovers a meteor which gives him strange powers. It was remade as *The Curse* in 1987.

**Paragraph 8**

Jack the Ripper: Name given to the unknown murderer of at least seven women, all prostitutes, in the East End of London, from August 7 to November 10, 1888. All but one of his victims were killed while soliciting customers on the street. In each instance the woman's throat was cut, and the body then mutilated in a way that indicated the murderer had a considerable knowledge of human anatomy. The Ripper was history's first recorded pattern killer and sexual psychopath. One of the most famous unsolved mysteries of English crime, the case has retained its hold on the popular imagination.

Cleveland Torso Murderer: One of the names given to an unknown murderer of at least twelve people in Cleveland, Ohio, from the fall of 1935 to the spring of 1942. Newspapers at the time also called him The Mad Butcher and The Headhunter. He preyed, for the most part, on obscure or anonymous people, many thought to have been residents of the hobo jungles of the Great Depression. The murderer beheaded and dismembered his victims with surgical precision. He was, arguably, America's first serial killer.

**Paragraph 9**

Leonard Nimoy: An American actor (b. 1931) in TV, films, and theater. He is best known as Paris in the TV series *Mission Impossible* and Dr. Spock in both the TV series and movie *Star Trek*. He has published two books of poetry self-illustrated with photographs, *You and I* (1973) and *Will I Think of You* (1974)—neither much appreciated, obviously, by King.

**Paragraph 12**

*Dawn of the Dead*: The 1978 sequel to *The Night of the Living Dead* (1968), which has been called the touchstone modern horror film. In it, seven people barricade themselves inside a farmhouse while an army of flesh-eating zombies roams the countryside. In the sequel, the zombie population has increased, and four people set up a quasi-Utopian existence in a barricaded shopping mall.

**Paragraph 13**

Lennon and McCartney: John Lennon (1940–1980) and Paul McCartney (1942– ), two of the four original Beatles, an English musical group that enjoyed worldwide adulation in the 1960's. Lennon wrote most of the lyrics to their songs while McCartney wrote most of the music.

## Possible Answers

*Meaning and Purpose*

1. King never explicitly states his thesis, but it is, nonetheless, implicitly clear: there are four reasons (causes) why "we crave horror movies," why they have been so popular over the years: to show "that we are not afraid" (3); "to re-establish our feelings of essential normality" (4); "to have fun" (5); to give vicarious release to our destructive, antisocial emotions (6–14).
2. King claims that all people have hostile, antisocial emotions, but, it is only those who act out those aggressive emotions in the most horrendous ways (Jack the

Ripper or the Cleveland Torso Murderer, paragraph 8) who must be institutionalized. The rest of us manifest those emotions in less drastic ways: talking to ourselves, picking our noses in public, (8), or getting back at our "pukey" sister simply for being "pukey" (10). It is in this sense that he is serious and reflects the self observation of the Roman playwright, Terence (c. 190–159 B.C.): "I am a man: nothing human is alien to me" (*The Self-Tormentor*).

3. Horror films are conservative or reactionary in that they "re-establish our feelings of essential normality (4). They are anarchistic or revolutionary in that they display antisocial—or, as King says, "anticivilization" (11)—emotions.
4. Horror movies serve as a safe outlet for our hostile emotions. King, in claiming that these emotions need such an outlet for both psychological and social health, reflects, among others, English poet William Blake (1757–1827) who wrote, "He who desires but acts not, breeds pestilence" and, "Sooner murder an infant in its cradle than nurse unacted desires" (*The Marriage of Heaven and Hell*) and Freud.

### *Strategy*

1. King's opening statement is indeed bold, and grabbing. He modifies the statement immediately, but if we accept his premise, however haltingly, we will be more open to his argument that we all need an acceptable outlet for our antisocial impulses, the ultimate reason for the popularity of horror films.
2. King offers four causes for the popularity of horror films. The first three are "simple and obvious" (3) and are the immediate causes: "to show we are not afraid" (3); "to re-establish our feelings of essential normality" (4); "to have fun" (5). The ultimate cause is the psychological and social need to face up to our dark sides.
3. King gets rid of the three immediate causes quickly, in five short paragraphs. The ultimate cause, and the focus of his argument, he spends the rest of the essay exploring. By eliminating the immediate causes so quickly, he reinforces his claim that they are "simple and obvious" (3). Conversely, he emphasizes the importance of the ultimate cause by using the bulk of the essay to explore it in detail.
4. King begins with the first person singular to establish the seemingly outlandish opening statement as a personal conviction. He immediately switches to the plural to group his readers with himself among those who aren't mentally ill enough to be institutionalized.
5. King offers no evidence, not even anecdotal evidence. He relies on the readers recognizing themselves in the group of the insane who "squinch their faces into horrible grimaces" (1), or who "talk [to themselves] when [they're] under stress" (8). For if they accept the premise that they are insane, at least to a degree, they can then easily accept his conclusions.

### *Style*

1. King's use of concrete and metaphoric language informs the entire essay, transforming what in less skillful hands could be dry and academic. Instead of saying, for instance, that the problem he poses begins to become difficult to fully understand, he says, instead, that "the ground starts to slope away" (6). Instead of fearing death, we fear "those final worms and grubs that are waiting so patiently underground" (1). And horror movies, instead of break-

ing through our conscious mind to satisfy the dark fears of our unconscious mind, are presented as "lifting a trap door in the civilized forebrain and throwing a basket of raw meat to the hungry alligators swimming around in that subterranean river beneath" (12).

2. King's tone, though informal, never becomes extremely slangy. Nor does he ever deviate into psychological jargon or the stylistic flourishes of formal prose. He calls two brutal murderers "amateur night surgeons" and even imitates a deranged cackle, "heh, heh, heh" (8) when he tells us they're still at large. He calls our little sisters (notice his assumption that his readers are male) "rotten little puke[s]" (10). But underneath this informal language, language appropriate for his *Playboy* audience, is a seriousness of intention. In his conclusion, for instance, when he tells us that horror movies solve our most aggressive, unconscious impulses, he skillfully uses the colloquial "man," a word that, in context, keeps his informal language consistent and emphasizes, as well, the seriousness of his message: "Because it [horror movies feeding our subterranean alligators] keeps them from getting out, man" (13).
3. King's rollercoaster analogy aptly objectifies the swirl of emotions a horror movie can elicit, emotions that include fear and fun at the same time.
4. *Grimaces*: facial expressions, often ugly or contorted, that indicate disapproval, pain, etc.; *hysterical*: uncontrollably emotional; *province*: a sphere of authority; *voyeur*: a person who gets sexual gratification by looking at sexual objects or acts, especially secretly; *penchant*: a strong inclination, taste, or liking for something; *psychic*: mental, as opposed to physical; *exalted*: raised or elevated, as in rank or character; *twit*: to taunt, tease, or ridicule; *sanctions*: penalties for disobedience; *remonstrance*: disapproval; *recoil*: to draw or shrink back, as in alarm, horror, or disgust; *anarchistic*: promoting disorder or revolt against any established order or rule; *morbidity*: the state of being unwholesomely gloomy, sensitive, or extreme; *subterranean*: existing or operating out of sight, hidden.

# *Baby, Take a Bow*

## Gerald Early

### Teaching Suggestions

A discussion of this essay could begin with general contributions from the class about their personal responses to the annual beauty contests that take place virtually everywhere in the world. How popular are these events among college students? Are they important or mere amusement? What do these contests offer us? What age groups find them most appealing and why? The discussion might then turn to Early's essay and investigate his thoughts about the importance, if any, of the first black Miss America.

### Notes

**Prologue**

The two quotations here serve as comments on part of what is to come: (1) the crowning of a black Miss America may be just a "crust of bread" given by whites, and (2) the title itself may be of no lasting importance anyway.

*trés gai*: especially happy.

**Paragraph 1**

Edward Bellamy: Edward Bellamy's (1850–1898) *Looking Backward* presented a method of economic organization, socialistic in nature, that would guarantee material equality for all citizens.

**Paragraph 2**

This paragraph may seem superfluous at first, but is really integral: Miss America is another "consumer item" and consumers fulfill individual needs through their contact with her.

"another product" ties this paragraph to the preceding one.

Two brief mentions of causes (reasons) for being "most loved" and "most suspect."

This paragraph examines the fantasy aspects of Miss America.

**Paragraphs 3–8**

These paragraphs illustrate the triumphant enthusiasm and humor of these black people who are also in the grip of the fantasy.

**Paragraph 10**

"separate but equal": an allusion to the phrase used to justify separate schools for black and white children prior to the Supreme Court decision in Brown vs. Board of Education (1954) in which Chief Justice Earl Warren wrote, "The doctrine of 'separate but equal' has no place. Separate educational facilities are inherently unequal." An earlier use of the phrase, from which it may have been borrowed by segregationists, occurs in the Declaration of Independence: "When . . . it becomes necessary for one people . . . to assume . . . separate and equal station. . . ."

"revitalized white interest": The presence of so many whites at the photo signing indicates another possible effect of her winning the crown.

"For whites who relish. . .": The effect on whites may be divided into two further effects (results) depending on a white's attitude toward race.

**Paragraph 11**

"The last time . . .": Early shifts to an earlier example of a Miss America from a minority group.

"The selection of Myerson . . .": Early speculates that just as the selection of the talented Myerson legitimized the contest and therefore allowed a return to the selection of mediocrities, the selection of the first black Miss America may allow a comfortable return to the selection of white contestants.

**Paragraph 13**

Early deepens the significance of the essay by presenting an ultimate cause of our fascination with Miss America.

**Paragraph 14**

He ends with a personal scene in his own family.

**Paragraph 17**

The humor of the postscript pulls us back to a more mundane perception of the whole Miss America phenomenon.

## Possible Answers

### *Meaning and Purpose*

1. Early's thesis is multifaceted and not stated directly at any one point. He is examining possibilities rather than defending a position. Among the conclu-

sions that might be drawn from his essay: (1) the selection of a black Miss America might broaden the meaning of the title or it might be just a temporary "crust of bread"; (2) Miss America is a product, like any other at Dolgin's; (3) Blacks no longer need to be "terrorized" by the contest, but there may be psychic costs; and (4) Miss America is our "sick fantasy of girlhood and innocence."

2. The winner serves as an object of public love (2) as well as a symbol of "our deep neurotic obsession with chastity" (13).
3. Though the author warns (9) that some blacks will hate her, at least for those at Dolgin's her selection brings a sense of triumph of winning something previously denied. This sense of triumph is most clearly revealed in the quoted conversations of paragraphs 3–8. Even the author, who has a more detached view throughout the essay, takes pleasure in the selection, though he is extremely cautious about its real significance (16).
4. For those at Dolgin's she is easily accepted and her selection is seen as a hope for the healing of racial tensions. This hope is best seen in the rehearsed lines of a small boy, ". . . and I'm glad you're Miss America" (10), a gesture of harmony his mother would probably not have had him recite to a white Miss America. Early reminds us, though, that some whites detest the selection (10) and others, he hints, will accept it as a momentary gesture allowing a return to the selection of white winners (11).
5. This question calls for personal responses and answers will vary.

*Strategy*

1. Both quotations relate to points Early makes later in the essay. "Crusts of bread" relates to his conjecture that having chosen a black Miss America, the judges can, in good conscience, return to many years of selecting white women (11). The song from Venus Ramey's nightclub act suggests that a Miss America's fame is brief and that she is used for some symbolic public purpose and then discarded. Ask students the name of the most recent Miss America or how many Miss Americas they can recall. See also paragraphs 2 and 13.
2. Phrases describing the store are echoed in the description of Miss America in paragraph 2 and beyond. For example: "bland anonymity" is echoed in "completely expressionless smile" and "no different from her predecessors"; "subliminal hearsay" sells products. "No introductions" are given Miss America and "words were superfluous." Students will doubtless find other examples here and in other paragraphs.
3. These bits of conversation reveal the good-natured enthusiasm of the black people who have come to see Miss America and reflect their sense of a victory in a never-ending contest with white people.
4. This paragraph shows she is accepted with equal enthusiasm by whites and allows Early to comment that some see this as "racial progress." He cautions at the end of the paragraph, though, that not all whites share this attitude.
5. Both Meyerson and Williams, while seeming to broaden and elevate the process of selecting a Miss America, may actually share a common fate—to be used as excuses to return to the selection of gentile mediocrities (in Meyerson's case) and to white women (in Williams's case).

*Style*

1. Although roughly synonymous in most contexts, here *condensed* means "reduced" and *compressed* means "forced into less space." As Early states, retail outlets tend to sell everything, adding merchandise even when unable to add space. Perhaps the only thing that has been reduced is the service.
2. Different readers may take different stands on the effect of this inclusion of formal and informal phrasing, but most will probably agree that it humanizes the writer and gives the essay a warmth that could be absent in an essay of similar content by a less skillful writer. Formal: "words were superfluous"; "an emanation from the Godhead"; "resonated a rather genteel mocking"; "as inscrutable a symbol." Informal: "snapshots"; "conjure woman"; "don't trust"; "black folk"; "giggled."
3. In the latter half of the postscript, the tone turns amusingly cynical, in effect ridiculing any too profound concern for the significance of having a black Miss America.
4. *ambience*: the atmosphere of a particular setting; *emanation*: to originate from a particular source; *inscrutable*: difficult to understand; enigmatic; *veneration*; to regard with great respect; *gentile*: non-Jewish; *guileless*: without deceit; *nonplussed*: perplexed; bewildered; *phantasmagoria*: a changing scene made up of many elements; dreamlike images; *acculturation*: adapting to a new culture or becoming used to new behaviors.

# *The Revolt of the Black Bourgeoisie*

## Leonce Gaiter

### Teaching Suggestions

A discussion of the perniciousness of social stereotyping might be initiated by asking your students to list other media sources of the stereotype of the underclass black who stands for all blacks. A rather lengthy list may result. Then ask them to list the characteristics that make up that stereotype and how the stereotype is represented on each item in the list. Then ask them to list TV programs that present middle class African-Americans, or black artists and intellectuals. The two lists may appear a bit unbalanced. This could lead to a discussion of the stereotyping of other racial groups in the media and how stereotyping, because it oversimplifies and plays to popular prejudices, demeans those it represents.

In an even larger project, you might teach the essay in conjunction with Maya Angelou's "Finishing School," Gerald Early's "Baby, Take a Bow," and Brent Staples' "Black Men and Public Space." Each deals with specific ways African-Americans cope in a racially divided society.

We think the structure of Gaiter's essay is also worth exploring: how paragraphs 1–3 give examples of how he has been affected by whites stereotyping blacks; how paragraph 4 shows how blacks have accepted the stereotype themselves; how he uses paragraph 5 as a transition from the effects of stereotyping to a discussion of the causes of the stereotype in paragraphs 6–14; how he rather quickly dispenses with the two immediate causes of black stereotyping in paragraphs 6–8; how he explores the ultimate cause extensively (9–14); and how he concludes the essay in three paragraphs by summarizing the effects of stereotyping (15), and by offering remedies (16–17).

## Notes

### Paragraph 3

Austen: Jane Austen (1775–1817), English novelist, regarded by many as the greatest of women novelists. Her world was rather narrow and parochial, but from that world she fashioned such great novels as *Sense and Sensibility*, *Pride and Prejudice*, *Mansfield Park*, *Emma*, *Northanger Abbey*, and *Persuasion*, all distinguished by their satirical wit and brilliant comedy, and their complex view of human nature. *Persuasion* and *Sense and Sensibility* have recently been made into popular films, and there are three versions of *Emma* currently being filmed. The plot of *Clueless*, a recent teenage film, is loosely based on *Emma*. The BBC made a six part serial of *Pride and Prejudice*, enormously popular in England, which then played on Cable TV's A&E in the U.S.

Balzac: Honore de Balzac (1799–1850), French novelist. He wrote more than ninety novels and tales, combining realistic details and ordinary situations with the flagrantly romantic qualities of melodramatic plots, violent passions, and rhetorical passages. His characters, too, are romantic in the extreme. Some of his finest novels include *Eugenie Grandet* and *Le Pere Goriot*. *La Comedie humaine*, an attempt to present a complete social history of France in a thorough and scientific manner, is generally considered his masterpiece.

Douglass: Frederick Douglass (1817?–1895), American abolitionist, orator, and journalist. The son of a slave and a white father, Douglass escaped to the North in 1838. He delivered a speech at an anti-slavery convention in Nantucket in 1841 that was so eloquent that he was soon in great demand as a speaker. He described being mobbed and beaten because of his views in his forthright autobiography, *Narrative of the Life of Frederick Douglass* (1845). He lived for two years in Great Britain where he earned enough money to buy his freedom in this country. He founded *The North Star*, a newspaper he published for seventeen years and in it advocated the use of black troops during the Civil War and civil rights for freed men. He held a number of public offices after the war.

Du Bois: W[illiam] E[dward] B[urghardt] Du Bois (1868–1963), American civil rights leader, writer, editor and teacher. The descendant of a French Huguenot and an African slave, he was trained as a sociologist, receiving his B.A., M.A., and Ph.D. degrees from Harvard. Among the first important leaders to advocate complete economic, political, and social equality for blacks, Du Bois cofounded in 1909 the National Negro Committee, which later became the NAACP. He taught history and economics at Atlanta University from 1897 to 1910 and again from 1932 to 1944. *The Souls of Black Folk* (1903), a collection of essays, is his best known work.

### Paragraph 12

*Valley of the Dolls*: a novel by Jacqueline Susann (1921–1974). A sensationalistic best seller in 1966, the novel is about three women: Anne starts as a theatrical attorney's secretary and later becomes a nationwide glamour figure selling cosmetics; Neely wins quick success as a singer, then alternates between stage glories and sanitariums; Jennifer, always seeking a true romance, gains fame in French-made nude movies and later commits suicide. The novel was made into a prodigiously inept film in 1967.

## Possible Answers

### *Meaning and Purpose*

1. Gaiter was almost denied a job for which he was "exceptionally qualified" (1) because he didn't fit the department head's idea of what a black man should be, his idea of a "real" black man a stereotype based on popular TV characters.
2. Ironically, many black people, just like white people, have accepted the stereotype of a black as illiterate and impoverished. Thus, a junior high girl questions Gaiter's black credentials.
3. Gaiter indicts all segments of society for racial stereotyping. He was accused by a white classmate in college of not being "really a black person" (3). He claims she had to have black people fit her stereotype so she could feel superior. White liberals, he says, are as racist as white conservatives, because, in trying to help disadvantaged blacks, they do so to bolster their own sense of superiority (8). And many blacks themselves either accept the racial stereotype out of ignorance, like the junior high girl already cited (4), or to advance their own political agendas (9–11).
4. Gaiter asserts two immediate causes for black stereotyping: black society placing emphasis on the lower class because that's where most were placed (6); white liberals seeing blacks as inferiors, not equals (8). The ultimate cause of racial stereotyping is the media, particularly TV programs, that Gaiter examines in the bulk of the essay (10–14).
5. Gaiter cites news programs that give a skewed view of black society (10–11), dramas that are praised for presenting the underbelly of black life (12), and a comedy that showcases risque humor (13–14). It's not that these representations are necessarily untrue; it's that they give only one view of a black society that is in reality far more diverse and complex.
6. African-Americans must, according to Gaiter, see to it that their children are not burdened with the idea that they are "invariably doomed to the underclass" (16) by seeing themselves, and demanding that others see them as well, as individuals (17).

### *Strategy*

1. As the essay's introduction, the first four paragraphs graphically illustrate the effects racial stereotyping have had on real people, both blacks and whites.
2. Paragraph 5 serves as a transition from the real effects racial stereotyping has had on real people to the question of how a stereotype of just one segment of black society has come to represent the whole (6), to an examination of the causes of that phenomenon (6–14). It does this by citing specific examples of the revolt of the "black bourgeoisie" against inaccurate stereotyping.
3. The statistics Gaiter cites are meant to support his final two points in paragraph 6: that affirmative action policies have opened "some doors for the black middle class," and that "social welfare and Great Society-style programs aimed at the black lower class have shown few positive results." Superficially, the statistics seem to bear out his contentions. The percentage of blacks with poverty level incomes has grown by 2.4 percent while the percentage of middle income blacks has grown an insignificant 1.1 percent. But he leaves unexplained the reasons for the 4.6 percent increase in the number

of upper income blacks. And because the income statistics are the only evidence Gaiter offers, he seems to imply that income is the only measure of the success of affirmative action or social welfare programs. Indeed, there may be other measures.

4. Paragraph 15 indignantly sums up how the stereotype of the underclass black is perpetuated (its causes) and its effects on African-Americans. In so doing, the paragraph is the first of a three paragraph conclusion.

*Style*

1. "Blue humor" is lewd, lascivious, somewhat obscene, erotic humor. The term had become a colloquialism by about 1900. Its derivation is obscure. *The Dictionary of American Slang* (1960), compiled and edited by Wentworth and Flexner, suggests the erotic association of the term may be because the color blue is associated with burning brimstone. Your students may have a difficult time finding the term, but its meaning is easily enough derived from its context in the essay.
2. *Elite*: the choice or best of anything considered collectively; *salvage*: the act of saving anything from danger; *pervasive*: spread out through all parts; *strata*: layers or levels; *misogyny*: hatred, dislike, or mistrust of women; *excerpted*: having taken a passage from; *candor*: frank, open, and sincere in speech and expression; *psyche*: the human soul, spirit, or mind; *thwarting*: successfully preventing or frustrating; *cadre*: a group of trained or otherwise qualified personnel capable of forming, training, or leading an expanded organization like a political or religious faction; *bourgeoisie*: the middle class; *intelligentsia*: intellectuals considered as a group or a class; *lauded*: praised or extolled; *staple*: a basic feature or part; *relegated*: sent or consigned to an inferior position or place; *condescend*: to behave as if one is conscious of descending from a superior position, rank, or dignity; *peers*: a person equal to another; *prospective*: potential; *invariably*: constantly; *shards*: fragments; *degraded*: lowered in dignity or estimation; *monolith*: something having a uniform, massive quality; *primacy*: being first in order, rank, importance; *idiosyncracies*: characteristics, mannerisms, habits, etc., that are peculiar to an individual.

# *Kids in the Mall: Growing Up Controlled*

## William Severini Kowinski

### Teaching Suggestions

Many, if not most, of your students will have had first-hand and extensive mall experience. They can testify to the validity of Kowinski's observations, therefore, from immediate, first-hand knowledge—not always from an unbiased or critical perspective, perhaps, but from an extensive background nonetheless. Starting off by asking students to respond to the first two paragraphs can serve several purposes in getting them to evaluate the essay critically. First, because they will have personal knowledge, they will, we're sure, be able to add examples to those that Kowinski gives in paragraphs 1 and 2. This examination could turn into a discussion of the author's strategy in the first three paragraphs to convince the reader of the importance of thinking about what spending so much time in the mall does to teenagers. Most students will probably agree with Kowinski's early observations. Many, no doubt, will object to his later, critical commentary. The question could then be asked: If his early factual observations seem on target, how does he go wrong in evaluating this behavior later on? No doubt some students will remain adamant in their uncritical acceptance of the behavior Kowinski describes. Others may start looking more objectively at his evaluation.

## Notes

**Paragraphs 1 and 2**

The examples the author gives are second-hand evidence, but this origin doesn't diminish their validity. On the contrary, they indicate that the author's observations are not isolated but widespread.

**Paragraph 3**

The first sentence serves as a transition and leads into the description of typical teenage mall activities. The examples are arranged chronologically to show typical stages in teenage development The question at the end of the paragraph tells us that a cause-and-effect discussion will follow.

**Paragraph 4**

"Street sense" connotes hard-won practical knowledge; "mall sense" connotes a knowledge that is somehow separated and protected from the real world.

**Paragraphs 5, 6, and 7**

These paragraphs show how mall developers were originally unprepared for the incursion by teenagers, how they then studied the phenomenon, and how, finally, the malls became finishing schools for kids who had already been indoctrinated into the consumer ethic.

**Paragraph 9**

Kowinski cites authority to demonstrate that the seemingly benevolent mall of the preceding paragraph can actually be psychologically damaging.

**Paragraph 12**

The real psychological growth that involves active acceptance of responsibility is contrasted with the mall's promotion of passive consumption. This passivity is further emphasized in the opening sentence of the next paragraph.

**Paragraph 14**

The meaninglessness of teenage mall employment in the preceding paragraph is assaulted a second time by citing academic authority.

**Paragraph 15**

"curiosity, initiative . . .": Because the author has already established that mall teenagers have been conditioned as consumers before they ever became mall denizens and have now completed their consumer higher education, the likelihood is slight that they will ever assimilate this list of deeper values.

**Paragraph 16**

A sad irony colors this entire paragraph. Though the mall has objects with educational value, they will never be bought or used by mall children. And though older people with stories are there—knowledge used to be handed down from the old to the young in stories—the stories will not be heard. Instead, teenagers will just watch the "passing show."

## Possible Answers

*Meaning and Purpose*

1. Most students will probably have experiences to relate about shopping malls. Encourage them to compare their experiences with the situations Kowinski talks about.
2. Kowinski asks, "Are these kids being harmed by the mall?" (3). His thesis is the last sentence in paragraph 4. The thesis does not completely answer the question because he has yet to explore the values of the mall environment and the extent of their effects on kids.
3. Kowinski points out all through the essay that mall life hones to a fine edge kids' already accepted false assumptions that life's primary goal is to buy and consume (7). Probably the most damaging effect the mall has on our kids is serving as a surrogate nurturing mother and family (10–12). All the mall's positive effects are described ironically.
4. Teenagers themselves would probably have their eyes opened by some of the facts Kowinski presents. But certainly the parents of mall teenagers would benefit most from reading this article. The information, the language, and the authorities cited suggest that adults are the target audience.
5. Kowinski's values can be determined by simply inverting the values he finds disconcerting—in his title, in his discussion of consumerism, and particularly in his description of the mall serving as a surrogate family (10–12). More explicitly, he lists attitudes he finds valuable that are not made in the mall: "curiosity, initiative self-expression, empathy, and disinterested learning" (15).

*Strategy*

1. Kowinski cites two specific examples, both tinged with dark humor, of kids who live at malls (2). He switches to typical examples to show how many children have gone through typical milestones of development at the mall (3). He speculates about all that important experience happening in an artificial environment and states his thesis in the final sentence (4).
2. The immediate cause is the "plethora of products in the mall, plus the pressure on teens to buy them." The effect from this cause is both immediate and ultimate—"the hurried child"—who must grow up too fast. This child learns how to shop in the short term, but in the longer term, he or she is pressured to look like an adult and to understand adult finances and emotions.
3. Superficially the two examples seem contradictory, but they are almost totally unlike. First, children are pressured to act in adult ways sexually and emotionally far beyond their own emotional development. Second, children just beginning to face responsibilities in the public work force need adult models on which to base their own behavior.
4. The cause of kids' spending time in the mall is that parents allow or encourage it (10). Kids' spending time at the mall becomes a cause of the mall's role of surrogate parent, which is the effect, but then this role itself becomes a cause (11) of structure being imposed on kids and elements of family life. Because kids crave structure and family life, they are drawn to cuddly merchandise and "home cooking." These elements in turn are causes, and their effects are that kids embrace passivity and consumerism. The whole progression is a causal chain.

5. Paragraph 18 is divided into two parts. The first two sentences describe how frighteningly insulated a child's mall existence is and how, therefore, every place becomes the same place. The next two sentences project that this is actually a good preparation for the future they face. In the first part, Kowinski looks back at the essay and encapsulates the experience he has just described, and in the second he looks forward to an ominous future.

*Style*

1. After describing how a teenage girl's major ambition was to learn how to put the perfect swirl on an ice-cream cone in order to gain a promotion in the company she worked for, and then to call that "achievement," makes a mockery of the emptiness and vapidity of the entire mall experience. Compare that to the achievement of "attitudes" (15).
2. Kowinski seems sympathetic toward his subject. He both acknowledges and understands the problem of teenagers in malls (first sentence in 4, 8, and 10). Still, he sees the dangers and hopes for a better choice for teenagers (7; first sentence, 19).
3. *Resonances*: the states or qualities of resounding or echoing; *incursion*: a hostile entrance into or invasion of a place or territory, especially a hostile one; *plethora*: overabundance, excess; *denizens*: inhabitants, residents; *impertinence*: unmannerly intrusion or presumption, insolence; *inexorably*: unyieldingly, unalterably.

# 8 / *Process Analysis*

## *Binding Decisions*

### Joan Gould

### Teaching Suggestions

To some members of the class, 1950 designates a time in the dark ages. To help students make historical connections between then and now, occasionally teachers mention a few facts about the 1950s: In 1950, World War II had been over for only five years. Harry S Truman was president of the United States. George VI was king of England. Josef Stalin was still heading Russia. The Korean War ("police action") was fought from 1950 to 1953. And the contraceptive pill was not developed until 1955. (By the end of 1961, 500,000 American women were on "the pill.")

A good way to engender discussion is to ask both male and female students how long the process of dressing for a date takes them. As a follow-up question, you might want to ask if the procedure takes longer for a blind date than for a date already known. For that matter, do we "dress for" a date now, or do we mostly dress for ourselves? One way to fire the discussion is to ask a question like this: Would you favor returning to the dress code of 1950? Why or why not?

## Notes

**Paragraph 1**

The author not only sets the stage, but she also comments on cultural affairs in 1950. A single woman over twenty should be worried about being unmarried. Being single means not being grown up. A woman cannot call a man for a date. She must signal that she is a "nice girl."

**Paragraph 2**

Culturally significant in 1950, each item of clothing carries its own signal, which she hopes will be received properly by the man.

**Paragraph 4**

The process begins: step 1. Notice that each step is descriptively, personally, and culturally explained. These paragraphs hold a wealth of information beyond the description of girdles. The cultural process described here reflects the lock-step 1950s thinking in Gould's element of society. Gould fits her process to the symbolism required by each social situation because such modifications are expected by her mother and her friends, who themselves are bound to the same symbol-laden process. Gould finally compromises, but not to the point of innovation. Betty Friedan says about the generation following Gould's in *The Feminine Mystique* (1963), "When she stopped conforming to the conventional picture of femininity, she finally began to enjoy being a woman" (chapter 14).

**Paragraph 10**

Lana Turner and Betty Grable, voluptuous American movie stars and pinup girls during World War II, predated Twiggy, the British model thin almost to emaciation, by more than twenty years. The padded bra was first advertised in nineteenth-century Paris. The first modern bra was designed and made by socialite Mary Phelps Jacobs, in 1913. Notice the mother's warning. Some things never change.

**Paragraph 12**

Nylon stockings were again available in 1950. Gould reminisces about "stockings" during World War II. The Du Pont chemical company had invented nylon in 1938 and sent spools of nylon to selected hosiery manufacturers in 1940. Chosen stores received nylon stockings only if they agreed not to sell them before May 15, 1940, "Nylon Day"; riots nearly broke out as women all over the United States rushed hosiery departments. By the end of 1940, 36 million pairs of nylons had been sold—only because no more could be had.

**Paragraph 13**

Notice how Gould embodies her times. Although the man is obliged socially to pay for everything on the date, Gould is obliged to do all that society expects from a woman who "needs" to marry.

**Paragraph 14**

Her process of dressing for the occasion is consciously based on 1950s social requirements for a date.

**Paragraph 15**

Tell the class about this 1770 legislation in the British Parliament: "That women of whatever age, rank, or profession, whether virgins, maids, or widows, who shall seduce or betray into matrimony, by scents, paints, cosmetic washes, artificial teeth, (or) false hair, shall incur the penalty of the law as against witchcraft, and that the marriage shall stand null and void." The bill was defeated.

**Paragraph 16**

Her process of getting ready for the date is almost complete. In this entire essay, Gould has mentioned only two requirements for her blind date: that he pay all expenses incurred on the date and that he wear a hat, as befits the occasion.

**Paragraph 17**

Shalimar: A popular scent by Guerlain, developed in 1925. Its name is from Sanskrit, meaning "temple of love." Notice that the process is completed with the opening of the door. Her blind date, oblivious to her careful preparations for the evening, concentrates on himself and his cold. She wears Shalimar; he carries Kleenex.

**Paragraph 19**

All the planning and process itself lead to the man's proposing, after the proper length of time has passed, of course. Before she gives him her answer, she injects candor, in a sense revealing part of the process.

**Paragraph 21**

The process works! Notice the element of small mystery in the last line.

## Possible Answers

*Meaning and Purpose*

1. Gould devotes several paragraphs to the subject of girdles (4–9). The "Binding" of the title relates first to what girdles do to the body (sentence 2, paragraph 4). A bra, which Gould describes choosing, is also binding. Dressing for a date in 1950 bound young women to a rigid set of behaviors and values. The word "Decisions" in the title is ironic because young women then were not free to choose not to follow the rules of dating, courtship, and marriage; they could make only decisions that were ultimately insignificant and superficial, such as which girdle to wear.
2. Students may choose any symbolic garment, including white wedding gown, veil, necktie, vest, and hat. Their reasoning provides the key to judging the answer to this question.
3. She might want to show that she is "naturally" frugal, or she might want to keep down her date's expenses. Either way, she will be more appealing as a wife.
4. We know from Gould's mention of Twiggy in the 1960s (10) that Gould is looking back from more than a decade in the future of 1950. Her article captures a particular social etiquette in a particular time and intimates the values of the whole decade. This period-piece article can be useful for comparison with any current dating preparations and social values.
5. The conga originated in Latin America; the mambo in Cuba; both are energetic dances quite popular in the 1950s. *Ardent* means "warm or intense in feeling; passionate." The author feared becoming too intense during either dance, and therefore forgetful.

*Strategy*

1. Three of the steps are: choosing a girdle (8); putting on a padded bra (10); and "Stockings next" (12).
2. In describing her choice of a girdle, Gould begins with "My girdle comes first" (4). From here through 7, she digresses about girdles that older women wear, girdles that Victorian women wore, the girdle as a symbolic garment

(6), and the consequences of not wearing a girdle (7). Gould then resumes the chronology of dressing (8).

3. Gould does not spare details about dressing for a date, or other relevant facts. She assumes her readers may be younger than herself, may not have first-hand experience with the procedure she describes, and may know little about dating and women's clothes in the 1950s. On the other hand, readers who were dating in the 1950s might be amused and carried back by her details. The information thus is not necessarily too much for an audience of Gould's peers.
4. The young man seems nervous, intent on talking to himself, and not attentive to his date.

*Style*

1. Written in present tense, the essay has a tone of immediacy, of excitement. The author is reliving her own past. This tone fits the essay's process—of dressing symbolically and appropriately, with anxiety, for a blind date who later becomes the author's husband.
2. Gould, even at the time of the date, is less than pleased with the rigmarole she has to go through. But her perspective from a future time also shows that she considered the ritual false and unnecessary, even humorous. Some language that illustrates her attitude: paragraph 4, "Here's the itch of it"; paragraph 5, "sausage casing"; paragraph 6, "like a walking clothespin"; and paragraph 10, "rises above my dress like the rim of the sun peering over a hilltop." Ask students for other examples.
3. The word *delirious* means, among other definitions, "wildly excited." The author is ecstatic because she can now "scratch and scratch," and be relieved of the binding girdle.
4. The word candor refers to "sharp honesty or frankness in expressing oneself." The author's candor serves as counterpoint to the masquerade imposed by society on her choice of clothing, here, the padded bra. Custom restricted her from using candor until now.

# *Commanded by Love*

## Richard Strozzi Heckler

### Teaching Suggestions

A good way to begin your discussion is by having the class consider the apparent inconsistency between the title's two main words, *commanded* and *love*. Ordinarily, the two are not considered partners: One either commands or one loves. So how can one "command" by "love"? This question elicits all sorts of responses, ranging from "My parents love me, yet they command me to do things," to "If a person shows love, then a command does not seem too harsh." "Nevertheless," you might prod, "a command is a command, and love is love, so how can the two concepts intertwine?" Also, one might add, is it possible to have a command-love relationship between two people? Or is this kind of relationship successful only when it is obvious that one actor, in the final analysis, is far more powerful than the other, yet chooses not to exercise that power? Questions such as these often lead to worthy discussions of how people do or do not exercise self-control and of whether self-control is part of a process that is linked to self-esteem.

## Notes

**Paragraph 1**

"Rios," the name of the horse, means "rivers" in Spanish. Note that this paragraph establishes the attitude of the author towards Rios. Noting that the horse is "distracted" and that he perhaps did not feel Heckler's "commitment," the author shows the close, almost entirely human relationship between the two. Also, by saying that "I feel we're just now beginning to listen to each other," the author further implies the close and kindly association between him and the horse.

**Paragraph 2**

A "quarterhorse" is one of a breed of strong saddle horses developed in the western United States, called a "quarterhorse" because it was originally trained to race up to a quarter of a mile.

"has never been formally schooled": Here we see again the tight focus that the author maintains for us to see clearly that his relationship with the horse resembles one's relationship with a child.

"trying to peel me off on low-hanging limbs": Rios occasionally treats his rider-trainer as if that rider-trainer were of no more consequence than a particularly bothersome scab.

**Paragraph 3**

"behavior modification": This phrase refers to the psychological concept of shaping behavior by manipulating reinforcements to obtain the desired behavior. Behavior therapy itself is based on the theory that hypothetical emotional factors and mental states are useless data in the study of psychopathology.

Wittgenstein: Meaning is studied in modern linguistics by making detailed analyses of how words and sentences are used in specific contexts. Scholars in other disciplines share this approach, one of the most notable being the Austrian philosopher Ludwig Wittgenstein (1889–1951).

"grammar": As well as referring to a systematic study of language, grammar can also refer to the basic principles of any area of knowledge.

"syntax": Though almost always associated with the study of language, this word has a more inclusive definition, the systematic arrangement of nearly anything. One can discuss the "syntax" of algebra or music as clearly as one can discuss the syntax of a language.

**Paragraph 4**

This paragraph describes the process by which Rios' previous owner attempted to teach him, by combining commands and dominance to produce obedience.

"neurotic": From the word *neurosis*, this loosely used term is applied to a variety of comparatively mild disorders.

"psychotic": From the word *psychosis*, this word denotes a mental disorder that interferes seriously with the usual functions of life.

**Paragraph 5**

This paragraph begins the staged dialogue between Rios and his rider. Notice the horse's personality here, as brought out by his "speech": He remains independent and leery of custom.

**Paragraphs 6,7,8, and 9**

In these short paragraphs, we have queries closely akin to *koans*, paradoxical or nonsensical questions originally from Zen philosophy, whose answers require stressing the kind of meditation that can bring forth philosophical illumination.

**Paragraph 10**

"like most people": Note the deliberate ambiguity in that sentence. The author combines Rios with people in terms of what motivates both.

**Paragraph 11**

"moral reason": Jean Piaget (1896–1980), the Swiss psychologist who studied the cognitive development of children, held that moral realism is the attitude characteristic of small children: Morality is inherent in an act as an objective fact and is observable to all. The moral reason that Rios requests in this paragraph resembles Piaget's moral realism.

**Paragraph 16**

At this point, we see the commingling of the commanded and that which commands. The reciprocity between beauty and love commands the rider and the horse to be both "at the same time, leader and follower."

**Paragraph 17**

After reinforcing the proposition in paragraph 16, that the leader and follower have become one, the author introduces the emblem of the hat and how it, too, has become integral to their relationship.

**Paragraph 18**

Here, the author uses an anecdote of the hat to show how much he and Rios have become commanded by one another.

**Paragraph 19**

We see in this paragraph what in classical rhetoric is called *diatyposis*, recommending useful precepts to someone else: Empowering and surrendering are by no means antonymous.

**Paragraph 20**

A reiteration of the precept contained in paragraph 19, this paragraph reminds the reader that time is measured in moments, each moment bringing an opportunity for conscious empowerment.

## Possible Answers

*Meaning and Purpose*

1. He means, of course, the "new conversation" between him and Rios, the horse. The thoughtful student might well write that the new conversation is between the author and himself, acting out the character of Rios. The point of the answer is to establish the fact that the author begins the essay on a highly personal note, as if the horse had human attributes.
2. This is an example of a *hyperbole*, a deliberate exaggeration used to emphasize the author's point. Again, students often detail the notion that while of course no one is "capable of anything," in fact, that is how we use the language when we want to clarify or reinforce a statement.
3. Answers vary, of course, but the core of the answer is that Rios has learned from experience with a previous owner who used raw power to attempt to train Rios; therefore, the horse's "story of power" is a story that includes being dominated and fearful.

4. In this context, teeth symbolize an almost prehistoric rawness, the brute force of the jungle, a metaphor for strength. The author combines *teeth* and *love* to produce a statement implying that love without strength to support it, is love without worth.
5. The author's hat blows from his head just as the author and Rios magnetize into a kinship of one, in paragraph 17. This incident breaks the mood of the moment. In paragraph 18, Rios associates the author's love for him with the author's love for his hat, which helps us to see that the author himself draws no distinctions between love for the animate and for the inanimate. Love is love. Finally, Rios shows that he understands his new relationship with his owner, in paragraph 18, by walking over to the fallen hat, which the author had by that time forgotten. As the author says in the last line of that paragraph, "His taking command at that moment is an act of generosity and love."

*Strategy*

1. The phrase "juvenile delinquent" implies a young person who exhibits antisocial or criminal behavior. The phrase implies that Rios himself has become a juvenile delinquent for some of the reasons that young people become juvenile delinquents, such as having a less-than-pleasant home life, a dysfunctional "parent," and, consequently, mixed messages about how he should act.
2. The author's having a year-and-a-half old daughter sends the message that the author can deal with younger "children." The daughter herself can walk around safely around Rios' legs, which shows that Rios can be patient when he realizes that he needs to be patient.
3. The word *fraternal* ordinarily refers to that which pertains to brothers. Horses and men have been combined for centuries in story and myth; in this essay, this horse and this man are brothers in the sense of being on equal levels of learning. The phrase is important in this paragraph because it shows that Rios is, partially, a historical product of his close relationship to man. The problems Rios faced earlier in his life were caused by one man's not honoring that fraternity and by Rios' not being able to feel that fraternity.
4. Answers vary according to the data the students retrieve from the essay. For example, many students use material taken mostly from paragraph 3, where the author discusses horse training in general terms, using jargon not commonly used by lay people, including "side reins," "dropped nosebands," "bittying." Other students note that the author starts the essay by talking about its being just another day, whereas a less experienced person would have talked about nervousness and anxiety.
5. By having this simulated conversations, Heckler reminds his readers early and often that to him, no communication boundaries exist between animals and people. What goes on in the mind of a person is just as apt to go on in the mind of an animal.

*Style*

1. The author establishes a sense of timelessness by beginning his essay "This morning." As the essay goes on to demonstrate, all days are the same; it is

what a person does during each day that is significant. Also, by beginning with "This morning," the author establishes a sense of immediacy, putting the reader into the action now.

2. In physics, a *field* is a region of space characterized by some physical property; *energy* is the work that a physical system can do in changing from its actual state to a specified reference state. The energy fields in the essay are the two psychic regions, the authoı's and the horse's, in which the author and the horse work to change their relationship with one another.
3. The author italicized this sentence to emphasize its great importance: It is the summation of Rios' autobiography before meeting the author, and shows why he behaves as he does early in his new relationship.
4. If it were possible to use only one word as a synonym-summary of the essay's style, it would be *coalesce*, which means, "to blend or come together." Using such strategies as personification, metaphor, simile, and hyperbole, Heckler brings himself and the horse to an equal realization that, as he says in paragraph 19, "it is the surrendering itself that is empowering." He and the horse have coalesced into a single psychic unit comprising commanding and loving.
5. Answers vary, depending on the student's perception of *arc*. For example, some see it geometrically, as any unbroken part of the circumference of a circle or other curved line, and reason from that definition to the idea that the word as it is used here suggests that time is timeless, that it can not be "broken." Other students see an arc as being bow-shaped, and reason from that perception that time resembles age in that we all are born, reach our heights, and then descend. Either way, students usually agree that time is a realistic character in the essay, and many of them have mentioned that until reading this essay, they had not thought of time's being a character in their own lives as well.

# *Guns Я Us*

## Matthew Maranz

### Teaching Suggestions

Like it or not, we have watched children play with toy guns for generations, particularly since World War II. One child shoots another child who recovers instantly, then shoots his adversary "dead." Students are interested to learn that many people view life as a some kind of game. Most games require accessories, and most game accessories are toys: No wonder Maranz imitated the name of a large toy retailer in his title.

Teachers of this essay often begin by asking their students how many "murders" they have witnessed that week, a figure students reach by adding up all the murders they have seen on television, in movies, and occasionally in a park or playground. Then, if you adopt this approach, you might ask how many of those who were "murdered" have reappeared elsewhere, in yet other television shows and movies. The point of this beginning exercise is to demonstrate that, consciously or not, we might view the crime of murder as temporary, for after all, don't most of the corpses return to life after a week or so? After having made the point that a human life is often devalued in fiction, ask your students if they would like to own a weapon especially designed to kill people. You might be surprised at their responses, but however they respond, now is the time for you to tell them that this essay outlines precisely what was needed for just such a purchase.

## Notes

**Paragraph 1**

Notice how quickly Maranz informs his audience of what is needed to purchase a machine gun. This "quick-write" strategy parallels the requirements for the purchase, which are themselves few and quick.

**Paragraph 2**

"to curb mob warfare": This sentence contains the kind of irony that expresses a meaning nearly the opposite of what was intended. Instead of going after the mob members, the government tried to tax their weapons, hoping that the tax would prevent gangsters from buying automatic weapons.

"MAC-10 or Uzi": The latter weapon is used primarily by the Israeli Defense Force. Both of these weapons and the other weapons mentioned in the essay have common features: They are small enough to be easily concealed, they fire rounds rapidly, and they are designed for use against people.

**Paragraph 3**

Notice the tense change from present to past. Maranz here gives the process feature in the present tense and carries out that part of the process in the past. The present-tense sentence is directed to its reader so that the reader herself can do what it tells her to do; the past tense sentences show how Maranz himself did it.

".223 controversy": This refers to the caliber (diameter) of a rifle round as measured in inches. The .223 rifle was designed primarily for shooting varmints; the 7.62 is the North Atlantic Treaty Organization (NATO) caliber of rifles carried by NATO troops. The designation 7.62 refers to the diameter of the rifle round as measured in millimeters. Notice the implied association of varmints with people in this "controversy."

"Dottie/Uzi": The association of "sexy girls and sexy guns" has been with us since the pinups so popular with combat troops in World War II.

**Paragraph 4**

"closed for the holidays": This phone message is grim in its juxtapositions, the placing of comments side by side: It opens by saying that the gun merchant is closed for the holidays, then lists its deadly merchandise, and then closes with "Have a joyous holiday season," presumably Christmas.

**Paragraphs 5 and 6**

"Yellow Pages": The author shows how easily one can acquire information about purchasing a machine gun. He then shows relief when told that a salesman won't sell him the "M-11." But the salesman goes on saying, "Try the MAC-10."

**Paragraph 7**

"the Second Amendment": This second amendment, in the Bill of Rights, is not usually quoted in its entirety, especially by those who favor the open ownership of any kind of gun. Here is the full text of the amendment: "A well *regulated Militia being necessary to the security of a free State*, the right of the people to keep and bear Arms shall not be infringed." That which is in italics above has become the source of great contention between those who believe all people should be able to buy and keep many kinds of firearms and those who believe that only under carefully defined circumstances should people be allowed to buy and keep certain kinds of guns.

**Paragraph 9**

"MAC 10": What follow are the specifications and histories of two particularly lethal weapons.

"today's hippest machine gun": Apparently, guns and clothes have at least one common feature; that is, some are more stylish, or "in," than others.

**Paragraph 11**

Compare in format with paragraph 3: When describing the process, the author uses the present tense; when describing how he carried out this part of the process, the author uses the past tense. The reason for this strategy is that the process itself can be used by anyone. A straight process, such as those contained in cookbooks, is of course in the present tense because it is straightforward, not anecdotal.

**Paragraph 12**

"means of gun control": In the last sentence of this paragraph, the author refers to the kind of gun control that might be successful, providing all people obeyed the law. Criminals, of course, have no need for such formalities as filling out paperwork.

"Automatic Weaponry": The paragraph gives the step-by-step process for easily buying an automatic weapon. The author makes it sound quite simple, and it is.

**Paragraph 13**

"Tami Jo": Note the dry humor ending this paragraph.

**Paragraph 14**

"In some states": The author obtained a MAC-10, as mentioned in paragraph 11, by conforming with federal laws. However, as he says here, some states have gun laws much more lenient than the federal ones that he used to purchase his weapon.

"a matchstick": In some states, it is possible to buy a semi-automatic weapon, one that fires a single round every time one pulls the trigger, by simply filling out a form and paying for the gun. But such guns can be easily converted to fully automatic weapons capable of firing hundreds of rounds per minute.

## Possible Answers

### *Meaning and Purpose*

1. The title of the essay purposely reminds readers of the nation-wide toy store chain, Toys Я Us, implying that guns in this country are often treated with the same seriousness that we treat toys.
2. What is unusual about the answer is that the author goes through the entire process personally, and in the process of answering the question for his readers, he ends up owning a machine gun.
3. Answers vary, depending what evidence students offer. Usually, however, students realize that the author's opinion is low. For example, paragraph 2 shows that the reasons for the laws in the first place were to prevent criminals from owning automatic weapons—as if the criminals would choose to obey this particular law.
4. Again, depending on the students' choices, answers vary. Often, for example, students believe that "Have a joyous holiday season," in paragraph 4, is humorous because it immediately follows "We will ship semi-autos on a c.o.d. basis."

*Strategy*

1. Students have all sorts of interesting answers to this question, most of them hinging on the notion that despite efforts to the contrary, sex still sells products. What is particularly bothersome to some is that women, often the symbol of motherhood, are here combined with weapons made for killing.
2. The probable holiday season is Christmas. The sentence "Have a joyous holiday season" is used for no other event. The irony is that the season commemorating the birth of Jesus Christ is closely associated in this paragraph with symbols of violent death.
3. This is a typical salesman ploy, demeaning one product and then praising its competitor.
4. Matchsticks, at least to the author of this essay, are easily available. They can be found in the street. They are free. And it also must be noted that matches cause fires, those fires sometimes causing casualties.

*Style*

1. Broadly defined, a "police sergeant" is any minor bureaucrat whose main occupation is to follow the rules—whatever the rules—unquestioningly. The author, most students agree, uses this term as one of derision.
2. Some guns can be converted with a matchstick to fully automatic weapons; others, which are more sophisticated, require a nickel. The level of sophistication is so low as to be ludicrous, which many readers find humorous.
3. *Subtle* refers to the author's trying to be cunning, wise, or crafty.
4. The slang term *hippest* refers to the latest style. When used to describe a machine gun, the term suggests that styles in guns, just as styles in clothing, come and go, again implying that our general attitude towards buying and using any kind of firearms is anything but serious.

# *On Keeping a Notebook*

## Joan Didion

### Teaching Suggestions

In this essay the writer imaginatively discovers the writing process, engaging it by using her notes as a source of invention (accumulating information). Then she moves to drafting and revising, which for her requires an active imagination and memory, including "what some would call lies." She leaves out mention of the edited version, trusting that the essay readers hold in their hands will show that such a thing is possible.

You might want to discuss briefly the writing process, focusing on poetic license as it is used when writing drafts, according to this essay. Some students who have heard the expression "poetic license" seem to believe that it means "to write in any way you want because it's *your* writing." "Poetic license" connotes departing from that which is acceptable as normal, but the departure must have its own defense. Didion uses "lies" in drafts of her essays, but her defense is that such a strategy gives her the creative latitude necessary to produce another kind of truth, universally interesting truth. Didion uses her notes to trigger her creative imagination.

You might want to have students bring to class and discuss an editorial or a story from the sports page of a newspaper, examining word choice. Do athletic teams "kill," "slaughter," "roll over," or "stomp" their opponents? Or do they merely "win"?

## Notes

**Paragraph 1**

The essay begins *in medias res*, "in the midst of things." Didion opens the story in the middle of an action and then adds information with flashbacks and other devices. *crêpe-de-Chine*: soft, crinkly fabric, usually silk.

**Paragraph 2**

The process of keeping a notebook has shaped Didion's life by helping her recollect general incidents. Her memory is jogged here, and the audience receives an anecdote replete with detail.

**Paragraph 3**

She develops the psychological details of the incident, expanding the note into a developing story. The 1960s New York stock character in the story represents Didion's imaginatively working out the details in her note.

**Paragraph 4**

The process is cyclic. The author reads one of her notes and then develops the note into a detailed fictional account. Then she moves to question herself about having written the note in the first place. Or about keeping a notebook, for that matter, which she justifies as being compulsive, growing from an impulse unique to some people.

**Paragraph 5**

The cyclic process moves autobiographically, giving the author a chance to remark that she did not progress gradually through life. Instead, she went through stages, a concept that permits Didion to examine her five-year-old self as if that person were now external.

**Paragraph 6**

Didion's notebook, not factually accurate, nevertheless provides a psychological record of her experiences. The process of keeping the notebook holds her life together, but not necessarily in the austere, orderly way that would come from her keeping a record of each day's events.

**Paragraph 7**

The author's cyclic process of keeping and using a notebook, her way of recording experiences and then remembering them, grows from her imagination. Unlike the newspaper journalist or the keeper of a diary, Didion does not simply record experiences. She filters her experiences however she wishes. But when she looks back at what she has done to those experiences—adding a fictitious cracked crab to a lunch, for example—she remembers the details of their reality.

**Paragraph 8**

Didion's notebook causes her to remember Didion, rather than the events around her. She sees events, she writes them down colored by her own reactions to them or their effects on her, and she later processes them, adding her own details. Life processes life.

The cyclic process is explained here. The ostensible reason for her keeping a notebook is to have detailed descriptions of people, places, and events, so that on days when the imagination will not boil forth, Didion can summon the remembrances of things past from her notebook and then write.

*Aperçus*: quick insights or surveys.

F. Scott Fitzgerald (1896–1940) chronicled the extraordinary lives of wealthy Americans, especially in *The Great Gatsby* (1925).

**Paragraph 9**

But no. The notebook does not collect other people and events so much as it gathers Didion's reactions to other people and events. The notebook tells Didion about how she was, among the events, not about how the events were, with her looking, describing, and recording them.

"Silk dress": Didion herself is the "unmentioned girl in the plaid silk dress."

**Paragraph 10**

How we act and how we think while we act parallel the notions of appearance versus reality. Here, the reality is what Didion constructs from her notebook, fragments expanded by her imagination into newly minted events, giving old reality a new meaning and life of its own, a fiction.

**Paragraph 11**

The author begins by admitting the obvious, that we are taught a particular way to affect behavior. But in the notebook of our minds we behave in quite another way, directed by "the implacable 'I'." *Pensées* reflections or thoughts.

**Paragraph 12**

If the maker has difficulty with the meaning, even then the meaning remains. Everything in Didion's notebook either is later expanded in her imagination or is a point on her mental compass to remind her where she was or where she is. Nothing is useless that remains in her notebook.

Ambrose Bierce (1842–1914?): American journalist and short-story writer best known for *Devil's Dictionary* (1906), in which he defined *achievement*, for example, as "the death of endeavor and the birth of disgust."

Leland Stanford (1824–1893): Capitalist and politician. Governor of California (1861–1863). Promoted and financed Central Pacific Railroad, western link in transcontinental line. United States Senator (1885–1893). Founded Stanford University.

"Ambergris": a gray waxy substance from the intestinal canal of sperm whales. It used to be the basis for the most expensive perfume extracts until a substitute was synthesized.

**Paragraph 13**

"The Crash:" The Wall Street stock-market crash of 1929.

James Riddle Hoffa (1913–1975?): President of the International Brotherhood of Teamsters (1957–1971). Murder suspected—involved with gangsters; body never found. *Syndicate*: A nationwide network of criminals.

John O'Hara (1905–1970): Journalist, realistic novelist—*Appointment in Samarra* (1934), *Butterfield 8* (1935), and *Pal Joey* (1940).

*Titanic*: A British luxury liner, supposedly unsinkable, which sank after hitting an iceberg in the North Atlantic on her maiden voyage in April 1912, with a loss of 1,517 lives.

**Paragraph 14**

The first exemplar paragraph. The woman who wanted to go back to Paris and the checkout clerk both have their stories, which Didion duly records. Later, upon reflection, she sees how those women's stories are, in themselves, not important. What matters is how those stories have affected Didion. Her aspirations mirror part of each woman's life.

**Paragraph 15**

Didion's keeping this kind of notebook amounts to the psychological process of recording her individuality as she moves from one phase in her life to the next. The value of this process is that it reminds Didion of herself as that self has evolved over the years. Rereading the notes that bring imaginatively to mind the former selves helps to contain the former selves.

**Paragraph 16**

The second exemplar paragraph. Baby Pignatari was a leader in the Syndicate. Our notebooks are for ourselves. The anecdote about the blonde reminds Didion heavily of how time affects other people's looks and fortunes, so strongly that she begins to avoid evidence of how time affects her.

**Paragraph 17**

Writing about the process of keeping her notebook benefits Didion: "It all comes back." She wrote a passage that amounts to an extended notebook entry about the process of keeping a notebook, which in turn led her to remember details of events entered in the original notebook. The process is complete.

## Possible Answers

### *Meaning and Purpose*

1. A diary is an "actual factual record" of what one has been doing. A notebook tells "what some would call lies," as stated in paragraph 7.
2. Students will have varied experiences in keeping journals or notebooks. You might want to discuss what the words *notebook* and *journal* mean to students. They should compare their experiences with some that Didion relates.
3. Didion is talking about the writing process, intuitively. Students need to learn about their own writing process, so that they can better understand and control it and so become better writers.
4. Our notebooks give us away to ourselves, the "implacable 'I'."
5. These statements show Didion's main point: "I tell what some would call lies" (7); "*How it felt to me:* that is getting closer to the truth about a notebook" (8); "*Remember what it was to be me:* that is always the point" (9); "But our notebooks give us away . . . the implacable 'I' " (11); "I suppose that keeping in touch is what notebooks are all about" (16). All these statements are about the self, keeping in touch with the process of who we have been so that we can better understand ourselves in the present.

### *Strategy*

1. The opening is immediate and puts the reader right in Didion's notebook, as if the curtain opens and we see her standing there reading. She doesn't bother with providing a context for what she is saying until paragraph 4. By then the reader is hooked by the details of the little scene in the hotel bar. Didion then backs away from this scene and talks about having written the note. A lengthy explanatory opening about her subject would surely not be as effective.
2. The little stories about the notes tie together the progression of Didion's main points. She expands the context of the notes to lead herself to realize what

she is really doing: remembering, and thereby keeping an account of herself. Paragraph 7 is a good example of this act when she talks about the cracked crab that "makes me see the afternoon all over again . . . that is what it [the incident] was to me." And then in paragraph 8 she solidifies this insight with, "*How it felt to me*: that is getting closer to the truth about a notebook."

3. Didion does in a sense bring the essay full circle by explaining the note about the sauerkraut recipe. But she has also gained insight here by going through the process of the notebook. "It all comes back" (17)—the notebook is about bringing the past back, remembering who she was. And when she makes the sauerkraut "again last night," she suggests there is another story, one that perhaps won't be understood until she can look back later at what she recorded in her notebook.

*Style*

1. Didion's language is informal and conversational, as if she is thinking out loud. She is sharing something quite personal in her notebooks. The transition from paragraphs 7 to 8 shows this thinking-aloud voice. She is conjecturing here about the truth of one of her notes, and then she comes suddenly to a realization—"*How it felt to me*"—in paragraph 8.
2. An "Estelle" is whoever or whatever triggers a feeling of self-pity. It could be "the other woman" as it is for the woman in the crêpe-de-chine wrapper, or any other reminder of an injustice.
3. Students' answers will vary. They might include references to a suntan, sun-streaked hair—whatever else they believe the stereotype includes.
4. A predilection is a preconceived liking, a partiality. A "predilection for the extreme" describes a person who sees or imagines the exotic or extreme in a situation. This is Didion talking about herself as a writer.

# *The Makers Eye: Revising Your Own Manuscripts*

## Donald M. Murray

### Teaching Suggestions

The essay can be approached in a variety of ways. You can treat it, of course, as a fine example of informative process analysis (see pp. 393–396). In the first ten paragraphs, Murray details the skills writers must develop and the problems they must overcome in order to revise their manuscripts. He then details chronologically the process professional writers go through to improve their texts. But you might want to ignore analyzing the essay's form, or combine that analysis with a lesson on revision. The essay could serve as your very first lesson in revision or as a follow-up lesson after the students have completed a paper or two. If this is the case, have them take a paper they have completed earlier and now revise it again following the Murray process step-by-step. The changes may prove instructive.

## Notes

**Paragraph 2**

Peter F. Drucker (born 1909) was born in Vienna and emigrated to the United States in 1937. He has taught in several U.S. universities and authored books on business, technology, and society. He has contributed articles to *Harper's*, the *Wall Street Journal*, the *New York Times*, and *Public Interest*.

**Paragraph 5**

Ray Bradbury (born 1920), an American science fiction writer, is known for his fantastic tales that combine acute social criticism with fanciful science fiction. He is best known for his short story collections *The Martian Chronicles* (1950), *Dandelion Wine* (1957), and *I Sing the Body Electric*! (1969). He also wrote screenplays and plays as well as the novels *Fahrenheit 451* (1953) and *Something Wicked This Way Comes* (1962).

**Paragraph 6**

Nancy Hale (1908–1988), born in Boston, was a painter, journalist, and author. She published nineteen volumes of fiction, biography, memoirs, and many short stories documenting changing upper-class American manners. She was the first woman reporter for the *New York Times*.

John Ciardi (1916–1985) was an American poet, teacher, and critic. He was poetry editor of the *Saturday Review* for many years and wrote numerous essays on the art of reading and enjoying poetry. He published many volumes of his own poetry and made a notable translation of Dante's *Inferno* into idiomatic English to recall Dante's use of the vernacular.

**Paragraph 8**

Eleanor Estes (1906–1988), born in New Haven, Connecticut, was a prolific children's author. She is best known for her earliest work, family stories based on her own childhood.

**Paragraph 9**

Anthony Burgess (1917–1993) was an English novelist and critic. A prolific, versatile, and comic writer, Burgess had an extraordinary facility with language, a talent he admired in James Joyce, the subject of one of his works, *Joysprick: An Introduction to the Language of James Joyce* (1973). Probably the best known of his many novels is *A Clockwork Orange* (1962), in which he envisions a future state terrorized by teenage gangs who speak Nadsat, a language created by Burgess from British and American slang, and Russian.

Roald Dahl (1916–1990) was a Welsh-born fiction and screen writer. He is best known for his macabre short fiction and children's books, the latter including *Charlie and the Chocolate Factory* and *Chitty Chitty Bang Bang*, both later adapted to film. He also wrote the script for the James Bond movie, *You Only Live Twice*.

**Paragraph 11**

Murray here, in a single paragraph, disposes of the minority of professional writers who do not meticulously revise draft by draft. Notice that although their methods may be untypical, they nonetheless include extensive revision.

**Paragraph 17**

Here Murray uses an analogy, comparing a piece of writing structure to a body's supporting spine.

**Paragraph 18**

He uses another analogy here, comparing the amount of information needed to make a point both satisfying and convincing to the amount of garlic needed to make a salad just right. Garlic lovers know there is no such thing as too much garlic.

**Paragraph 24**

Here Murray repeats an idea he stated in paragraph 2: Writers don't know what they think until they actually write about it. The concept is almost totally alien to most student writers.

**Paragraph 28**

Count Leo Tolstoy (1828–1910) was a Russian novelist and moral philosopher. Best known for his novels, Tolstoy also wrote short stories, plays, and essays. Together with another great nineteenth-century Russian novelist, Fyodor Dostoyevsky, Tolstoy, according to many literary critics, made the realistic novel a literary genre that ranks in importance with classical Greek tragedy and Elizabethan drama. *War and Peace* and *Anna Karenina* are probably his two greatest works.

## Possible Answers

### *Meaning and Purpose*

1. Many students might object to Murray's claim that student writers consider their first draft their final draft (1), especially if they do any revision at all. But most will certainly agree that the extensive revision a professional writer does goes far beyond their efforts. Both student writers and professionals share the problem of being overcritical of their work (7).
2. "Normal" readers read what they believe to be a finished piece of writing. Writers, on the other hand, read their own drafts with the possibility of change always in their consciousness (3).
3. Writers must accept both the praise and criticism of others and be suspicious of both at the same time. They must remain detached from their own work in order to work on it objectively (4).
4. It might be worthwhile here to lead the students through these eight elements of writing to make sure they genuinely understand what Murray means by them.
5. Information does not exist for its own sake, but is structured for a purpose, leading the reader to an understanding, a meaning.
6. All of the information in this essay leads the reader to the understanding that for a writer a piece of writing is never complete. It can always be reworked to make it more effective.

### *Strategy*

1. The thesis is stated in the opening paragraph: For a professional writer a draft is just the beginning of writing. Murray restates the thesis, in somewhat different form, in paragraph 10.
2. Ostensibly, Murray is writing an informative process analysis, showing ". . . the sequence followed by most writers most of the time in rereading their own work" (11). But the information is so explicit that it could certainly be used as a guide for revision. If followed, it would be directive process analysis.
3. Murray quotes other authors to give authority to his contention that the biggest part of writing is rewriting.
4. This is another version of the story told about a writer who, when asked what

he thought about a subject replied, "How should I know? I haven't written about it yet." This points up the idea that writing forces the writer to make connections about things that he could never make without going through the writing process, an idea that most beginning writers have a hard time understanding.

5. Murray first establishes the importance of the process for effective writing. He distinguishes between the attitudes of professional and amateur writers, explains how writers must read with a different eye than readers who don't write, establishes a common problem shared by amateurs and professionals, and cites several writers as to not only the importance, but the necessity, of revision. Only then does he describe the typical process itself.

*Style*

1. In these three paragraphs Murray personalizes the revision process to make it more real for the reader. Before this he was speaking in typical terms, and now he shows how he personally applies some of the elements of the process. We think the anecdote of paragraph 27 is particularly effective.
2. Since the thrust of the entire essay is that professional writers feel a near compulsion to revise and tinker with their work continually, it is wholly appropriate for the essay to end without ending.
3. *Journeyman*: a person who has served an apprenticeship at a trade or handicraft and is certified to work at it assisting or under another person; *prolific*: highly productive; *euphoric*: being in a state of happiness, confidence, or well-being; *schizophrenic*: a state characterized by the coexistence of contradictory or incompatible elements; *connotation*: the associated or secondary meaning of a word; *denotation*: the explicit or direct meaning of a word as distinguished by the ideas or meanings associated with it or suggested by it.

# 9 / *Classification and Division*

## *American Regional Costume*

Alison Lurie

### Teaching Suggestions

In the essay Lurie classifies Americans according to their styles of dress and divides the country into five distinct regions that represent these styles. She offers historical, geographic, climatic, political, and economic explanations for the evolution of regional dress. You might begin by asking your students how valid these classifications appear to them. Is an element of stereotyping involved here? Does Lurie take into account other factors that might influence dress? What classifications in dress could be identified at your college or university?

The last question could lead to a discussion of how division and classification help us make sense of complex issues. Both methods separate large subjects into smaller and more comprehensible units. Both methods make large issues easier to understand.

## Notes

**Paragraph 1**

Lurie begins with the immediate claim that America has no typical dress, that the varied histories of various regions have left an indelible mark on styles of dress.

**Paragraph 2**

After establishing where distinctions of regional dress can best be observed, Lurie states her thesis that five distinct styles of dress can be seen in the United States.

**Paragraph 3**

She now explains how styles can be misinterpreted by someone alien to a region. This confusion bolsters her contention that dress styles reflect history, geography, and climate rather than social mores or personal morals.

**Paragraph 4**

Here Lurie begins the paragraph with its topic sentence and then cites examples to establish its validity.

**Paragraph 5**

She again begins with a topic sentence and proceeds with examples. Now, though, the often elaborate dress of the Deep South is contrasted with the severer dress of New England described in the preceding paragraph.

**Paragraph 6**

Lurie uses the first two sentences to introduce her next classification, midwestern dress, and to lead to her topic sentence, the third. After describing midwestern dress, she compares it to dress in New England and the South to even more clearly distinguish it.

**Paragraph 7**

She now describes dress in the Wild West and claims that the language as well as the dress of the Wild Westerners reflects a ranching background.

**Paragraph 8**

First Lurie gives a brief historical background on California's development and then shows how the present reflects the past.

El Dorado was a legendary treasure city in South America sought by early Spanish explorers. By extension, then, it is any place promising great wealth.

**Paragraph 9**

To emphasize the sometimes outlandish California dress, Lurie shows how that dress might be interpreted in other parts of the country.

**Paragraph 10**

Lurie now connects southern Californians with others in the Sun Belt and gives two more examples that distinguish them from those of other regions.

**Paragraph 11**

In the last section of the essay, Lurie explains why some people who live in a region refuse to dress typically and why some styles are popular in all regions. She begins by giving some general examples of people who choose to dress outside the norm.

**Paragraph 12**

She now offers examples.

**Paragraph 13**

Lurie introduces two other factors that influence the popularity of a regional style and offers examples from the past.

**Paragraph 14**

She concludes with an explanation of the current popularity of western costume and gives present-day examples.

## Possible Answers

*Meaning and Purpose*

1. Encourage students to examine their own ideas about what regional American dress is, as well as where those ideas come from and what attitudes they might reflect.
2. Attendees of national meetings generally come from similar occupational and economic backgrounds. Their dress would vary not because of social and economic status, but because of the regions they come from (2).
3. Lurie's thesis is that Americans have five distinct kinds of dress, as she states (2).
4. Regional styles are determined by the region's history and climate and do not reflect moral attitudes. Someone from outside a region may misinterpret the dress of that region by reading moral values into the style of dress (3).
5. She claims that history, local interests, geography, and climate account for the differences in regional dress styles.
6. The current popularity of western costume reflects recent far-right politics and isolationism and a turning away from foreign modes (14).

*Strategy*

1. Lurie's organizational scheme follows the historical development of the United States from the Northeast to the South, the Midwest to the Southwest, and, finally, to the Far West.
2. Lurie's first two subheadings pair adjacent regions, and the two style categories under each are markedly different. The Far West gets its own subheading because it is traditionally big and bold enough to stand alone. California is usually set apart from other regions.
3. Cause and effect.
4. The quotations show that the kinds of dress she describes are reflected in popular and literary culture. These facts bolster the validity of her thesis.

*Style*

1. Some examples: "homogeneous" (1), "factors such as occupation and income are held relatively constant" (2), "laid-back-looking" and "hop into bed" (3). The casual language gives the impression that she's talking about real people.
2. Lurie makes no explicit judgments, but some of her descriptive language sounds opinionated or stereotypical.
3. *Homogeneous*: composed of parts or elements that are all of the same kind; *superficially*: externally or outwardly; *Puritan*: a member of a group of Protestants that arose in the sixteenth century within the Church of England, demanding simpler doctrine and worship and stricter religious discipline; many Puritans migrated to New England; *dandyism*: excessive attention to clothes and appearance; *gingham*: yarn dyed, plain-weave cotton fabric, usually striped or checked; *linsey-woolsey*: a coarse fabric woven from linen warp, or sometimes cotton and coarse wool filling; *dowdier*: to be dowdy is to be out of style, drab, old-fashioned, untidy; *foulard*: a soft, lightweight silk, rayon, or cotton of plain or twill weave with printed design; *sartorial*: of or pertaining to clothing or style or manner of dress; *raffish*: mildly or sometimes engagingly disreputable or nonconformist; *allurement*: fascination, charm; *isolationism*: the policy or doctrine of isolating one's country from the

affairs of other nations by declining to enter alliances, foreign economic commitments, international agreements, and so on; *belligerently*: warlike, aggressively hostile.

# *Three Kinds of Discipline*

## John Holt

### Teaching Suggestions

The essay could be used for discussing both childrearing and learning. The students' own backgrounds will undoubtedly determine their attitudes toward each of the kinds of discipline Holt describes, especially that of Superior Force. Encourage students to give specific examples to back up their opinions, demonstrating that specifics are always needed to be convincing.

### Notes

**Paragraph 1**

Holt begins with examples that immediately illustrate the Discipline of Nature.

"This . . . good teacher": He then shows why this kind of discipline is important in schools: it is a good teacher.

**Paragraph 2**

After explaining the Discipline of Culture, Holt gives examples to show that it works in the real world.

**Paragraph 3**

Holt begins the paragraph using the same format as the last, a brief explanation of the Discipline of Superior Force followed by examples.

He then cautions that this kind of discipline should be used sparingly and goes on to explain why.

**Paragraph 4**

With an extended example of ballet training Holt illustrates how all three disciplines often overlap.

### Possible Answers

*Meaning and Purpose*

1. Holt says that children will "meet and learn" from discipline. His first sentence is his thesis. He goes into detail about three kinds of discipline and how children may learn best from them.
2. Give students time to talk about discipline they have observed and their opinions about it. Encourage them to compare their observations to some of Holt's descriptions.
3. Students will have their own opinions about this statement. Holt's point is that children usually imitate the adults around them and that example is the best teacher. He says, "They watch very carefully what people around them are doing and want to do the same" (2). The evidence he offers is general and perhaps idealistic, but his argument is effective.

4. He believes children are basically good and easily trained, and also that they will naturally strive for the best. The penultimate sentence in the essay illustrates this attitude.

*Strategy*

1. Holt's classification system has to do with the kinds of things in the world outside the self that he thinks impose discipline on children. He chooses nature, culture, and force as three large areas of influence. Another social scientist might choose three other categories, or more than three. Holt's categories result from his own observations and opinions.
2. Paragraph 4 describes where his categories overlap. He doesn't say this is a fourth category, but rather sums up the three and brings them together. In practice, his kinds of discipline don't always occur in isolation. The essay is not imbalanced but balanced by this last paragraph, tied up neatly and brought to an end.
3. Each paragraph contains a series of brief, typical examples illustrating Holt's general statements.

*Style*

1. The names are capitalized because they are formal labels of each division.
2. Holt appreciates the value of all three kinds of discipline while trusting the child to grow naturally without excessive adult interference. He is clearly advocating an approach to teaching in its broadest sense: allow the child to learn from hands-on experiences; provide good examples for the child to imitate; and protect the child from danger, but do not underestimate his or her ability to understand its real nature.
3. *Wheedled*: to have endeavored to influence a person by smooth, flattering, or beguiling words or acts; *contagious*: tending to spread from person to person; *fidget*: to move about restlessly, nervously, or impatiently; *impotent*: lacking power or ability; *novice*: a person who is new to the circumstances in which he is placed; *autocratic*: tyrannical, despotic, domineering; *suppleness*: the condition of being flexible, pliant.

# *Territorial Behavior*

## Desmond Morris

### Teaching Suggestions

Excepting a few who may have had a sociology or social anthropology course, students do not often encounter the social-scientific methods of classification used by Morris. Some say that humankind is not to be treated like other animals. But what of athletes? We classify them like tools—according to their uses, not their intrinsic worth as people. Tribal, family, and personal territories are often thought of as occupying the whole planet, a thought decried by ecologists.

Territory carries responsibility. Do we protect the territory that we display as ours? Or do we ruin it as part of our displaying that it is ours?

While Morris examines territorial behavior, it enlivens the class discussion to add the concept of responsibility to that behavior. Explore the question of whether we should protect for ourselves what is ours alone or whether we should keep our territory in trust. If we keep it in trust, how far are we willing to go to protect it? As far as war? War destroys territory. Are we willing to be constantly vigilant politically to protect territory? And from whom are we protecting it?

## Notes

**Paragraphs 1–5**

Morris begins by dividing human territory into three classifications. Before he expands those classifications, he discusses their sociology. First, he describes the penalties for violating the territories of others. Next, he discusses briefly the healthy reasons for having "owned space." Then he tells how we mark our territories.

**Paragraph 6**

Returning to the first of his classifications, Morris develops it by the strategy of cyclic expansion. That is, he starts at the center, the small group, and expands outward, each circle of expansion larger: The tribe's home base expands, finally, to become the capital city of a nation.

**Paragraph 7**

The nation itself, fixed by borders, holds so many people that individuals begin to lose their tribal identity. They compensate by forming subgroups, social tribes, to gain a sense of belonging, which includes the territorial signals such social tribes agree to use.

**Paragraph 8**

Notice that this classification is as cyclic as the strategy Morris uses to describe it. As the tribe expands, members of the tribe circle back to making efforts to form a subgroup, keeping their own membership small enough to be comfortably identifiable.

**Paragraph 11**

Moving down as they read, from the tribe classification to the family classification, students are occasionally shocked to see the family defined as a "breeding unit" and the family's territory as a "breeding ground." They might be reminded that Morris is not being cavalier with the family unit; instead, he is using the neutral terminology of the social scientist.

Morris's "typical house" is typical for the author's area, but houses differ in this country, according to cost and location. Because his house can be described as "ideal Victorian," students from other kinds of homes might need to be reminded that he is using a model here to represent reality, not to define it.

**Paragraph 12**

Morris's comments on modern architecture can deeply affect students, particularly if they live in apartments, condominiums, or in some older tracts of homes that were built quickly and identically. Teachers often break here, to discuss with their students the ways in which we mark our property as our own, with plants, paint, lawns, fences, pets, trees, and so on. A stimulating question is: "How much do we mark our territory as being comfortably ours before we begin to mark it as a warning to others not to trespass?" It is one thing to build a white picket fence around our house, quite another to build a six-foot chain-link fence, for example.

**Paragraph 13**

So also with temporary territory: Here is a good place to discuss the worth of Morris's comments. Does it really happen as he describes it? Do we stake out territory in the mountains, at the park, the river, the lake, or near the ocean? What happens when our territory is violated? Does it make a difference what kind of people violate our territory? If an old woman and an old man sit quite near our territory, do we feel differently than we would if a teenage boy and girl violated our territory?

**Paragraph 15**

The third classification, the personal space, brings us to the subject many students call the "rights" of the individual. They should notice that Morris is not talking about rights; he is precisely describing the results of socioscientific observations. Determining where we sit and how we protect our personal space is the cultural manifestation of our tribe's territorial habits.

**Paragraph 16**

The higher the density, the less we socially interact. This behavior surprises students until they test its validity by observation.

**Paragraph 17**

Notice the differences between "crowds and crowds": the spectator crowd has a special, collective goal. The rush-hour crowd has diverse goals, a fact that might lead to disputes.

Students are often interested in discussing this observation as it might be applied to driving their cars. Is rush-hour traffic more frenetic because the drivers are focusing on diverse goals? On freeways, expressways, thoroughfares, and toll roads, why does it seem that cars travel in packs, like crowds?

**Paragraph 18**

Adjusting to crowds takes a combination of practice, patience, and observation.

"Space reaction": Morris is discussing *proxemics* here, both sociologically and linguistically. Sociologically, proxemics describes human spatial requirements and the effects of population density on behavior. Linguistically, proxemics describes how far apart people in conversation stand, depending on their degree of intimacy.

**Paragraph 19**

Students from Latin America usually stand closer to each other when talking than students from western Europe. You might want to ask your students to observe proxemics in practice throughout the campus or at their jobs.

**Paragraph 20**

"cocooning": Libraries are sometimes crowded. Workers often are assigned carrels. Students often share apartments with roommates. They all "cocoon," carving out their own privacy in one way or another.

Morris thoroughly discusses by example each part of this classification. Students are often eager to investigate some of these examples. Do your students have their own territories, favorite chairs in the library or favorite tables in the cafeteria? Do they have favorite parking places that they feel territorially belong to them? How do they react when that territory is "invaded"?

**Paragraph 21**

You might want to discuss with students the various methods they use to let others know they have already claimed a space. Do they use the "favored object (20)," the "personal marker," or the "reservation effect"? With what success? Do they have other peaceful ways of claiming their own territory?

**Paragraph 22**

Morris points out that we hear about the exceptions to territorial respect, that most of us respect the other person's "territory," be it the temporary space of a library chair or the more lasting space of a home.

Time permitting, you might want to ask your students whether their city or neighborhood is running out of space that each person or household can call its own. If space is becoming scarce, then you might want to discuss ways of redefining territory or creating respect for territory so that we can keep strife from getting out of hand.

## Possible Answers

### *Meaning and Purpose*

1. Morris's main point is that we are territorial animals, and territory by definition must be defended. The thesis is implicit in a general way in the very first sentence. The fourth sentence in paragraph 3 is the thesis, and the last sentence in paragraph 5 narrows the thesis.
2. The title is neutral-sounding and could signal an academic and informative essay (which this is), or the title could be ironic or humorous, depending on the content of the essay. In other words, the title isn't much help in knowing the content of the essay absolutely before reading it.
3. A number of students mention the bathroom! Some include their place of work (the backroom or storage areas), and others specify attics, basements, garages, and the like.
4. We form subgroups (7) in our large tribal territories to feel a sense of belonging. We choose a "splinter group" to identify with, such as a union or political party.
5. Because so many homes look alike, people have more difficulty displaying theirs as a particular home in an attempt to feel secure and "at home" (12).
6. Morris's words are the neutral terminology of social science.

### *Strategy*

1. Morris discusses the sociology of the three categories of territory, including the penalties for violating someone else's territory, and the reasons for having "owned space" (3). The first five paragraphs give background and definitions so that readers know Morris's basis for classification.
2. The strategy of development is a kind of cyclic expansion. Morris starts with the small group at the center, expands it outward to hunting grounds, and eventually the home base becomes the capital city. When nations become too big for people to feel personal belonging, people circle back to form small groups that they can belong to.
3. Morris talks about the distances at which people stand from each other in conversation and labels three categories: fingertip, wrist, and elbow distance (18). He also discusses how people in crowded places stake out personal space. He calls the strategy "cocooning" (20), and names three kinds: small private office or studio, favored object such as a chair or alcove, and personal markers (21) such as books or jackets. All these subdivisions help organize and order Morris's information so that it is clear and understandable to readers.
4. A home base can be one of a number of areas, depending on the student's perspective. It could be a play area, a favored street corner, one side of a fence, or a car.

### *Style*

1. The tone is formal and academic, and people are labeled clinically—this is a social-science essay. Almost any sentence demonstrates this tone, such

as the first in paragraph 3: "The fact that these upheavals are so rare is a measure of the success of Territorial Signals as a system of dispute prevention."

2. A "pseudo-tribe" is a modern imitation of the historical tribes mentioned earlier in the essay (8). The prefix *pseudo* means "fictitious, pretending, or falsely seeming."
3. Morris's audience probably consists of readers who have read academic writing before, for he doesn't talk down to them. But they are not necessarily social scientists. His language is understandable and readable for lay readers, and he is careful to define his terms in context.

# *Notes on Class*

## Paul Fussell

### Teaching Suggestions

This essay runs counter to the accepted (and unexamined) notions held by some students about our society; therefore, while discussing the essay, many instructors like to ask their students if indeed we have class distinctions in our country. Is it true, as the critic Mary Colum said, that "The only difference between the rich and other people is that the rich have more money"? Encourage students to explore their notions of ethics, where ethics refers to standards of conduct and moral judgment. For example, do people treat each other as equals, regardless of economic, social, or academic status? Ask your students whether standards of conduct, in their opinion, would change according to a person's class, as defined by Fussell. Question your students about whether they have ever witnessed others being treated in a certain way or others treating people a certain way, depending on how people looked or how they dressed.

### Notes

**Paragraph 1**

Fussell quickly sets a tone of mild sarcasm by equating an earlier view of sex with a more modern view of social class, as dirty little secrets. "Dr. Kinsey" is, of course, Alfred Charles Kinsey (1894–1956), the U.S. zoologist who studied human sexual behavior. He co-authored *Sexual Behavior in the Human Male* (1948), and *Sexual Behavior in the Human Female* (1953), each offending a large segment of society over forty years ago. Note the assertion that a person born into one class finds it "virtually impossible" to break out of that class.

**Paragraph 2**

Fussell points out that he is using "perception" to classify, instead of the more usual techniques practiced by social scientists. The word perception as used here refers to using the senses and relying on intuition. The "Class X" list, while humorous, also puts individuals into a class, making that class easily distinguishable.

**Paragraph 3**

Here, after a one-sentence argument against a more traditional method of classification, Fussell begins in earnest to classify while keeping his witty tone—as in the anecdote of the Boston ladies. Inherited money is the main characteristic that sets apart the Top Out-of-Sight Class from all others.

**Paragraph 4**

Fussell connects the very top with the very bottom, pointing out their ironic common features.

**Paragraph 5**

Note that the Upper Middles are *afflicted* with a bourgeois sense of shame, as if that sense of shame were somehow a disease.

**Paragraph 6**

Another characteristic that the Top Out-of-Sight Class and the Bottom Out-of-Sight Class hold in common: Both are nearly invisible. Yet both greatly affect the economy, each in its way.

"claustrated": to be secluded or closed off;

"lamaseries": monasteries of lamas, priests or monks in Lamaism, a form of Buddhism characterized by elaborate ritual and a strong hierarchal organization.

The White House is Fussell's strongest example of one's residence being the measure of one's class.

**Paragraph 7**

Again, the Top and Bottom Out-of-Sight Classes are compared, the comparison leading to an offhand comment about the President, who strives to keep his name in the public eye. Presidential candidates, who often present a program for helping the quite poor, also often receive large contributions from the quite rich.

Note the transition: Compared to the Top and Bottom Classes, the High-and Mid-Prole Classes advertise themselves proudly.

"Hypertrophied": "abnormally enlarged," usually used in a medical description.

**Paragraph 8**

Enclosed entirely in parentheses, this witty aside further illustrates the differences between the classes and moves the reader into the paragraph that follows, which concerns facades.

**Paragraph 9**

Note the tongue-in-cheek introductory sentence, followed by the humorous ranking, in descending order, of seven classes of façades.

The last part of the paragraph accounts for those classes left out of the seven ranks listed in the "façade study."

**Paragraph 10**

Continuing with his short "anthropological study of facades," Fussell points out that materials which are natural and products which are difficult to maintain both signify class.

Sophie Portnoy is the mother of the main character in *Portnoy's Complaint* (1969), a humorous novel by Philip Roth.

*The Preppy Handbook* (1980) amusingly described how students and former students of private preparatory schools looked, dressed, and acted.

Dacron, a trademark, denotes a brand of polyester textile fiber that is strong, wrinkle-resistant, and inexpensive.

**Paragraph 11**

Fussell moves from a consideration of expenses to a consideration of supervision, associating status with how or whether one is supervised. He points out that titles imply class, but they in fact do not define class. Note the comment Fussell makes about a tenured professor; Fussell himself is a tenured professor.

**Paragraph 12**

Constraints, insecurities, habits, attitudes—these are more important than money when classifying groups of people.

"Camp": something that is amusing to the sophisticated because it is so unconsciously artless or self-consciously artificial. For example, a plastic statue of a horse with a light socket coming out of its mouth and a lampshade covering its head, is "camp."

"Shakespeare series": Fussell does not equate the Upper Middle Class with educated taste. Note the irony of structure: The paragraph begins with the Top Out-of-Sight Class, who watches no television programs but who pays people to watch them, and ends with the Bottom Out-of-Sights, who watch television programs but have no choice about which television programs to watch.

**Paragraph 13**

Time helps to define class to the extent that the later one eats—or whether one is in any condition to eat at all—the higher one's class.

**Paragraph 14**

Note the allusion to altitude in the phrase "down there" and the allusion to classes as being on a ladder, in the phrase "down a rung." This paragraph, which targets a person's weight as a measure of class, directly equates thinness with status, and then comes to an aesthetic observation, albeit humorous, that the Proles seem to flaunt their obesity.

**Paragraph 15**

Among the top three classes, plaster casts are worn as the equivalent in status to clothing; they represent a sort of stylishness. Medical bills mean little, just as the cost of clothes means little. Not so with the other classes, however.

**Paragraph 16**

The piece comes full circle, back to paragraph 3. It returns to the opinion that income, how income originates, what one buys and displays with that income, how one acts based on income, and the freedom from pettiness that a significant income brings—these are the major factors that distinguish classes in America. These classificatory gradations show why the American class system differs from the British class system. The British system depends on absolute distinctions between one class and another, based on clearly defined prohibitions.

Vincenzo Bellini (1801–1835): an Italian composer who composed melodic operas including *Il Pirata* (1827) and *Norma* (1831).

W(ystan) H(ugh) Auden (1907–1973): an English-born American poet.

## Possible Answers

*Meaning and Purpose*

1. When students agree with this statement, they usually support their answers by giving evidence from the essay and from their personal knowledge of people they know. When students disagree with this statement, they usually support their answers by asserting that in a free country people can work their way into any class except the highest, where money is inherited rather than earned outright.
2. See paragraphs 3, 6, and 7: The Top and Bottom Out-of-Sight Classes are both "all but invisible." They also strive to retain anonymity. Each class, in it own way, hides. The Top hides from the general public; the Bottom hides from those to whom they owe money.
3. The purpose of this tongue-in-cheek statement is to add humorous credibil-

ity to the essay. Fussell is reinforcing his earlier statement that perception—in this instance, personally passing judgments on façades—is perhaps a more trustworthy way to define classes than is scientific data.

4. This phrase's purpose is to illustrate the trivial attitudes that the top three classes have about their accidents. Other classes have serious on-the-job accidents; these classes injure themselves while at play, and their casts are rarely dirtied. The "honor" is the result of having played hard, not the result of having worked hard.
5. Students' opinions of what is petty and what is trivial will depend on their own backgrounds. Ordinarily, their answers are personal and include such anxieties and problems as worrying about paying for health care, about paying for college, about earning money, about avoiding emotional and physical pain, and about providing for their futures.

*Strategy*

1. Many subjects today, such as fraud in government, obscenity on television, and senseless killings, are more likely to offend than facts about social class. Fussell makes this statement precisely because it so obviously does not offend; instead, it functions as a strategy to "hook" readers, to make them curious enough to read on, to see why Fussell himself believes the subject is offensive.
2. In science and in mathematics, "X" traditionally stands for an unknown quantity or a variable. Fussell shows here that not every class is clearly delineated in a classification system based in part on perception. Class X comprises a mobile group of people who enter and exit a class, "with no permanent location in this hierarchy" (2), never remaining one place long enough to assume a stable identity. Therefore, they represent a group variable, as a social scientist might say.
3. Fussell wants to establish that different classes can have seemingly common features. The mechanic gets dirty from working on vehicles; the dentist gets dirty from working on patients. To that extent, they are equal. What separates them is that the dentist has no supervisor, while the mechanic does. Thus, according to Fussell, the mechanic belongs to a class lower than the dentist's.
4. The answers will vary depending on the student's familiarity with each of the television shows. Fussell is writing to a broad audience. To make his point clearly, he relies here on the ability of that audience to equate his class distinctions with television show distinctions already familiar to his audience.
5. Those six lines of poetry illustrate what Fussell means when he talks of the "absolute prohibitions" that define an English gentleman. This illustration helps the reader to see how Fussell's classification differs so greatly from that in another country.

*Style*

1. The Boston ladies take their hats and their status for granted, to the extent that they appear oblivious to the marketplace. With its stress on *have*, the sentence implies that the hats have always existed; the tone is condescending to the point of unconscious snobbery.
2. *Claustrated* means to be secluded or closed off. The word comes from the Latin *claustrum*, "a bolt, or a place shut in." *Lamaseries* are monasteries of

lamas, who themselves are priests or monks in Lamaism. Lamaism, a form of Buddhism, has elaborate rituals and a strong hierarchal organization. (The word *lama*, from the Tibetan *blama*, means "a chief" or "a high priest.")

3. The ironic comment is that the top four classes are starved by choice, but the bottom two classes are starved by circumstance.
4. The word *vulgar* refers to that which is common to the mass of people in general, suggesting a lack of culture, taste, and sensitivity. The word is from the Latin *vulgaris*, "the common people." According to paragraph 7, the President is a bit vulgar because, unlike the Top and Bottom Out-of-Sight Classes, he keeps his name in the papers as much as he can, mainly because he must appeal to the common people.
5. The word *den* is set off in quotation marks because it is a word used in a special way by Fussell's Middle Class. It refers to any room that the Middle Class wants to call a "den," to mean a small cozy room where one can be alone to read, work, and so forth.

# *Obstacles to Clear Thinking*

## Richard D. Altick

### Teaching Suggestions

Once made aware of logical errors, many students enjoy detecting them in political campaigns and media advertising. They further enjoy correcting those errors. After your students have read this essay, have them bring to class a minimum of ten examples that illustrate the logical errors described in Altick's essay. All of the students can then become involved in discussing the essay and how we are all affected by advertising deceptions based on illogicalities. Such a lesson has a further benefit of preparing each student for writing a classification paper that explores these media deceptions.

If, in your discussion, you organize the student examples into the categories established by Altick in his essay, you will also demonstrate how such organization makes the information more intelligible.

### Notes

**Paragraph 2**

"Among them": a transition that smoothly carries the reader from the first paragraph to the second. Altick is conscientious in his careful use of transitions that link paragraphs.

**Paragraph 3**

"*argumentum ad hominem*": literally, an argument or appeal to the man. Such an argument attacks the appearance, personal habits, or character of the person involved instead of dealing with the merits of the issue at hand: "Devon Delight can't be trusted to make important decisions. She used to be an exotic dancer."

"for example": Altick uses here his first general example to illustrate the fallacy of *ad hominem*. From here on, after he defines each fallacy, Altick presents illustrative examples to make his points absolutely clear.

**Paragraph 4**

"*argumentum ad populum*": literally, an argument or appeal to the people. This kind of argument draws on whatever the people hold dear (e.g., country, religion, family) to sway people by using a favorable label instead of providing reasons.

"name-calling": Attaching an unpleasant label to something or someone can stop people from thinking because they can get caught up in the emotional tangles of the label.

"glittering generality": This fallacy tries to sway people by using a favorable label instead of providing reasons: "A vote for Texas Eames is a vote for the flag."

**Paragraph 5**

"transfer": After showing the negative and positive of one kind of *ad populum* fallacy, Altick now spends a single full paragraph defining another, *transfer*.

**Paragraph 6**

"A common example . . .": The paragraph first gives a general example of *transfer* as seen in politics. A specific example immediately follows, and then Altick carefully explains the logical flaw.

William Jennings Bryan: (1860–1925) American political leader and orator. Bryan was twice elected to Congress (1890, 1892) and won the Democratic presidential nomination in 1896 and electrified the convention with this famous "Cross of Gold" speech. He lost the election to William McKinley by fewer that 600,000 votes. After World War I, his fundamentalist religious beliefs led him to take part in a movement to prevent the teaching of evolution in American schools. In 1925 he served as prosecutor in the celebrated Scopes Trial.

**Paragraph 7**

"The advertiser . . .": Now, after giving examples of the *transfer* fallacy as it exists in politics, Altick presents two general examples (sex and patriotism) and a specific example from advertising.

**Paragraph 8**

"*argumentum ad verecundiam*": literally, argument or appeal to authority. This argument cites the opinion of an "expert" who has no claim to expertise about the subject at hand, thus attempting to transfer prestige from one area to another.

**Paragraph 12**

"Begging the question": As well as the question begging propositions that Altick presents, there are also question begging phrases (sometimes called *alleged uncertainty*) that present something as certain that is open to debate: "Everyone knows" and "It is obvious that" are typical phrases that beg the question.

**Paragraph 14**

"False analogy": a comparison in which the differences outweigh the similarities, or the similarities are irrelevant to the claim the analogy is intended to support.

**Paragraph 15**

"Oversimplication": the fallacy whereby we draw a conclusion while ignoring information essential to the subject. Because we are generalizing from inadequate evidence, the fallacy is also called *hasty generalization*.

**Paragraph 20**

*The New York Times*: Altick's piece ends abruptly because it has been excerpted from a longer work, the same reason that the first paragraph seems to begin *in medias res*. You might point this out to the students with the admonition that the beginnings and ends of their own essays need to be more graceful.

## Possible Answers

### *Meaning and Purpose*

1. Fallacies attempt to by-pass reason and appeal to our emotions.
2. This question will elicit various answers. It could be instructive to have your students explain their own logic for including and excluding fallacies from the two categories.
3. Students should be able to produce a number of examples of the use of *transfer* in advertising.
4. If men are naturally indolent and have limited intelligence (15), they will not automatically demand the truth and will be, thus, easy victims when the truth is distorted or suppressed (17).
5. It is easy to reach erroneous conclusions about important social issues such as race, poverty, and crime when we allow ourselves to be swayed by oversimplifications. Those erroneous conclusions can have harmful effects.

### *Strategy*

1. Most of Altick's paragraphs are developed by examples, both general and specific.
2. Politics and advertising are the most obvious areas where fallacies are purposely used to deceive.

### *Style*

1. Altick uses, for the most part, neutral language. There are two places, however, where he definitely displays his own feelings and thoughts. In the first paragraph he is a bit dismissive when he says that some common thinking errors "can be called 'abuses of logic' only by courtesy." And in paragraph 16 he exhibits a social conscience when he says that "every man and woman has a pressing moral, as well as intellectual obligation to examine the basis of every judgment he or she makes. . . ."
2. *Unwary*: not cautious or watchful against danger; *inductive*: reasoning from specific evidence to a general truth; *deductive*: reasoning from a general statement to a specific instance; *connotation*: the implied meaning of a word; *aspersions*: damaging or derogatory remarks or criticism; *raiment*: clothing, apparel; *auditors*: hearers, listeners; *effulgence*: brilliance, radiance; *fervent*: having or showing great warmth, or intensity of spirit, feeling, enthusiasm, etc.; *august*: inspiring reverence or admiration; *inducing*: leading or moving by persuasion or influence; *invoked*: called for with earnest desire; *pertinent*: pertaining or relating to the matter at hand; *ostensibly*: apparently, evidently; *crux*: a vital, basic, decisive, or pivotal point; *superseded*: replaced in power or authority; *junctures*: points in time, especially those made critical or important by a concurrence of circumstances; *sulks*: remaining silent or holding oneself aloof in a sullen, ill-humored, or offended mood; *hypothesis*: a tentative explanation for an observed phenomenon; *indolence*: the state of having or showing a disposition to avoid exertion; *purge*: to rid of whatever is impure or undesirable; *canvass*: to examine carefully; *innate*: inborn, native; *exigencies*: the need, demand, or requirement intrinsic to a situation; *assiduously*: constantly, unremittingly; *chagrin*: a feeling of vexation marked by disappointment or humiliation; *prominence*: the state of being conspicuous.

# 10 / *Definition*

## *I Want a Wife*

### Judy Brady

#### Teaching Suggestions

Though this essay is two decades old, it still triggers lively classroom discussions about the modern roles of husbands and wives. It can also lead to provocative discussions about today's roles of fathers and mothers.

The essay is written from a feminist point of view, but most people will recognize the duties presented here as fairly accurate traditional expectations. What are the traditional expectations for husbands? Have both traditions changed in the years since the essay was written?

#### Notes

**Paragraph 3**

Beginning here Brady defines a wife by listing expected duties and behaviors.

This paragraph and paragraphs 4–7 present these duties and behaviors in clusters of related items.

The first cluster: caring for the children as well as working outside the home.

**Paragraphs 4 and 5**

The second cluster: housekeeping and cooking.

The third cluster: being emotionally supportive without expecting support in return.

**Paragraph 6**

The fourth cluster: assuming the duties of a social secretary.

**Paragraph 7**

The fifth cluster: being the ideal lover (but respecting the double standard).

#### Possible Answers

*Meaning and Purpose*

1. Let students explore their notions about what being a wife means and where these notions come from. A comparison of their ideas with Brady's should show how traditional or progressive your students are.
2. Repeating "I want a wife" emphasizes the focus of the essay, which is on the elements in Brady's definition, rather than on a simple description. It also sounds demanding, and many men demand that their wives do all the things on Brady's list.
3. Brady's view is that men expect women to assume all domestic duties, so "of course" the duty to care for children stays with the wife after a divorce. The use is sarcastic.
4. No one statement asserts Brady's main point. Instead, her thesis is implied in all her details about what a wife is and does: that it is ridiculous and grossly unfair to expect wives to be superwomen who see to the needs of husbands

and families who do far less work than a wife—and yet they are expected to perform thus. In her last sentence she asks a rhetorical question that implies her thesis.

5. The husband's needs are implicitly stated with the wife's duties in sentences such as, "I want a wife who will keep my clothes clean, ironed, mended, replaced when need be and who will see to it that my personal things are kept in their proper place so that I can find what I need the minute I need it" (paragraph 4). Students may think Brady describes extremes when she stereotypes roles, but students probably know men who are this demanding and self-centered. Stereotypes are never fair, but these serve Brady's point that wives are expected to do far too much for their husbands.

*Strategy*

1. The first paragraph announces the classification "wives" as the subject of the essay, and also establishes Brady's authority to talk about wives because she is one. This opening is strong and direct, and it informs the reader, giving a context.
2. These are possible labels and characteristics: Paragraph 3: label—worker outside the home and primary caretaker for the children; characteristics—organized, fastidious, thrifty. Paragraph 4: label—personal maid; characteristics—neat, good cook, patient. Paragraph 5: label—therapist; characteristics—patient, good listener. Paragraph 6: label—hostess; characteristics—organized, gracious. Paragraph 7: label—perfect lover; characteristics—selfless, responsible.
3. Answers will vary. Students should support their choice of label with statements from the essay. An appropriate label would be sarcastic.

*Style*

1. The expression "A Wife" is capitalized because it is used as a formal label.
2. The word "replace" suggests that a wife is an expendable piece of equipment rather than a person. The word also suggests that husbands are fickle about wives and don't care about who they are, only about what they do.
3. When people are "going on" vacation, they are going together. The person who "goes along" with another person is not altogether that person's equal.
4. The question is rhetorical, which means that it requires no answer—it has already been answered. It emphasizes Brady's sarcastic attitude about what men expect wives to do and her own frustrations about being expected to be such a wife. Questions are effective because they usually address readers directly and provoke thought.

# *Why Men Marry*

## George Gilder

### Teaching Suggestions

When students are asked to write definition papers, love is a popular choice of topic. But the term is so elusive that few of us can do more than repeat a few popular banalities. You might begin a discussion by asking the students to consider why love is such a difficult word to define. One major reason, of course, is that we apply the word so casually to so many situations. But even when we confine our attempts at definition to a limited scope we still have difficulty applying the common definition techniques to this word. Such a discussion may prepare students for a reading of Gilder's essay which approaches the word through a combination of comparison and contrast, cause and effect, description, and process techniques, all done in a rather poetic way.

## Notes

**Paragraph 1**

The short first sentence with its matter-of-fact finality begs to be challenged, but the rest of the paragraph takes the air out of any such challenge by promising to go beyond the image that first comes to mind at mention of "love." The catalog of images begins with complete sentences then moves to fragments as the images pile up faster and faster.

**Paragraph 2**

Gilder continues the catalog related to a popular definition of love, this time focusing on what it would be like to give it up.

**Paragraph 3**

This paragraph introduces the central idea of the essay: that a man will eventually want to settle on one woman and have children.

**Paragraphs 4 and 5**

Here Gilder discusses the nature of procreative love.

**Paragraph 6**

Gilder returns to the cataloging technique to describe the lives of men without love.

**Paragraphs 7 and 8**

These paragraphs move toward a definition of love.

**Paragraphs 9–14**

These paragraphs describe the process of changing from a desire for hunter love to a desire for the deeper meaning of procreative love.

Studs Terkel, radio and television interviewer, has written several books based of oral history including *Division Street* (1966), *Hard Times* (1970), and *Working* (1977).

"Hemingway's hyena": From Ernest Hemingway's short story, "The Snows of Kilimanjaro." As a man lies dying from gangrene, a Hyena, a symbol of death, can be seen and heard on the perimeter of the campsite.

**Paragraph 15**

This paragraph completes the definition of procreative love.

**Paragraph 16**

This last paragraph shows the importance of choosing procreative love.

## Possible Answers

### *Meaning and Purpose*

1. Although the essay may be read profitably by anyone, the primary audience seems to be young men. Gilder wants to convey the power of the desire for procreative love and show that to marry, sire children, and care for a family is a meaningful life achievement.
2. The attractive, but superficial and temporary, side of the unmarried life is described in paragraph 1, but the main point Gilder makes is in paragraph 6.

3. The fundamental reason is for a kind of immortality: to be remembered beyond one's time because one has children to carry life into the future. "The need to choose a particular woman and stay by her and provide for her if he is to know his children and they are to love him and call him father" (paragraph 3); "both partners consciously or unconsciously glimpse a future infant" (paragraph 4); "the couple senses the outlines of a realm that can endure and perpetuate their union" (paragraph 4); "His children . . . they will remember. It is the only hope" (paragraph 15).

   Secondary, but related reasons: 1) being alone and disappointed with life (paragraphs 5 and 6), and 2) the souring of the hunter life (paragraphs 9–12).
4. Children are more important because they will remember him (paragraph 15) and because few are remembered for their jobs (paragraph 12).

*Strategy*

1. Comparison and contrast: paragraphs 1 and 6 and paragraphs 1 and 15.
   Cause and effect: paragraphs 3, 8, 10–12, 15.
   Description: paragraph 9.
   Process: paragraphs 9–13.
2. As students write about or discuss this question, make sure they go beyond "Well, that's my opinion," and cite relevant passages in the essay's text as well as explain their reasons for their conclusions about Gilder's approach. Some students may argue that the essay would be a better example of cause and effect or comparison and contrast than it is of definition. They may be right. It's a good time to remind students that writer's usually use more than one strategy in an essay and the important thing is not to label an essay but to be aware of the possible strategies available to them as writers.

*Style*

1. Other catalogs are in paragraph 6 beginning with "Many more millions . . ." and in paragraph 9 beginning with "One day he looks across . . ."
2. The unborn child is carried in the womb, the infant is suckled at the breast, and being remembered by one's children is a kind of immortality.
3. A woman does not need the roles of husband and father to bear children (paragraph 5) and thus achieve a kind of immortality, but a man does need the roles of mother and wife to achieve the same thing. In the context of this essay, the statement is valid:

   Paragraph 3: "if he is to know his children and they are to love him and call him father."

   Paragraph 5: "a woman can bear a child, but the man is able only to screw."

   Paragraph 6: "There are millions of single men, unlinked to any promising reality, dissipating their lives by the years, moving from job to job, woman to woman, illusion to embitterment."

   Paragraph 10: "His body," "His aggressiveness," "His job" are all failing him.

   Paragraph 15: "this consciousness that he has to struggle to be worthy of her."
4. *Ecstatic*: characterized by sudden, intense feeling; *primal*: first, fundamental; *procreative*: that which brings into being, begats offspring; *sloughs*: conditions of despair, of helplessness; *vapors*: mental depression; *alchemy*: the process of transforming something of little value to something of great value; *morbid*: of

an unhealthy mental state, gloomy; *covenant*: an agreement between two or more persons; *ruttings*: sexual excitements; *purges*: cleanses, purifies.

# *A Definition of Poverty*

## Michael Harrington

### Teaching Suggestions

You might take two tacks with this essay. The first is to pursue Harrington's reasoning paragraph by paragraph. His essay is closely reasoned, carefully connecting one point to another. This close-reading approach can help the student appreciate Harrington's impassioned arguments.

From that reading, a discussion on the validity of Harrington's views might ensue. This kind of discussion usually depends on your students' social status. The affluent, conservative student will have less first-hand knowledge of poverty, of course, and can be brought to Harrington's position by capacity for compassion, by second-hand knowledge, and by Harrington's logical persuasiveness. And, of course, a mixed group of students could lead to a lively discussion indeed.

### Notes

**Paragraph 1**

Harrington begins with a reason for social inaction that he believes to be absurd.

**Paragraph 2**

He shows by examples that current conditions cannot be justified by citing and comparing other times and places.

**Paragraph 3**

He first diminishes such arguments by calling them "abstract," removed from the cruel consequences such justifications have in the real world, and then concludes that "standards of decency" must change with time.

**Paragraph 4**

Harrington now offers his first definition of poverty.

**Paragraph 5**

As his first definition is tied to technological advances, his second involves social standards.

**Paragraph 6**

This paragraph and the two preceding deal in one way or another with psychological suffering by the poor in alienation, pessimism, and despair.

**Paragraph 7**

Harrington concludes this section of the essay by showing that technological and social advances must be made in tandem to avoid human misery.

**Paragraphs 8 and 9**

The next two paragraphs demonstrate that a change some might consider an inroad against poverty (generally higher incomes) may have been bought at too dear a price (the future of our children).

**Paragraphs 10–13**

Harrington's brief, four-paragraph conclusion simplifies and summarizes his definitions of poverty.

## Possible Answers

### *Meaning and Purpose*

1. Harrington's main points are the last three paragraphs.
2. Our perceptions and definitions of poverty are determined by our place in history. The poverty of nineteenth-century England, for instance, would be totally unacceptable now. To argue against social reforms by claiming that the present poor are better off than the poor of another time or place is thus illogical and unacceptable.
3. Comparing the poverty of one historical time to another is purely an intellectual ("abstract") activity that has pernicious consequences in the real world. It allowed nineteenth century conservatives to ignore inhuman conditions among the poor. And twentieth-century conservatives who would be appalled by the horror of nineteenth-century poverty use the same fallacious reasoning to ignore conditions today (3).
4. Families had higher incomes in 1962 when Harrington published *The Other America* than twenty years earlier because more wives were in the work force. The price of this progress may be that children have less care, love, and supervision. Thus, we may have mortgaged their futures—a high price to pay for "progress" (8, 9).
5. Some students may find Harrington's opinions in these paragraphs sexist. Other solutions would be for men and women to share equally the responsibility for taking care of children, and for companies to provide adequate daycare for children of working parents.
6. Any society that has the wealth to eliminate the horrors of poverty and doesn't is spiritually impoverished.

### *Strategy*

1. Paragraph 1 gives the justification nineteenth-century British conservatives used to avoid change. In paragraph 2, Harrington cites similar arguments and implies their fallaciousness. In paragraph 3, he shows explicitly how these arguments are flawed and concludes that our standards of decency must change with time.
2. Each of the definitions can be taken as stipulative. In paragraph 5, Harrington stipulates the "social definition of poverty." Each of the last three paragraphs defines a different aspect of poverty: quality of life (11), psychological (12), and moral (13). Together, these stipulative definitions, and all the other points Harrington makes in considering these definitions of poverty (such as "the social cost of progress" in paragraph 8), constitute an extended definition of poverty.
3. In paragraphs 2–7, Harrington uses the word "this" in the first sentence to clearly refer to ideas just stated. "Finally" indicates (8) that he will make his final point. "Yet" (9) indicates he will now make a distinction from what he has just said. And "all these imponderables" (10) clearly connects the paragraph with all that he has just said.

### *Style*

1. Harrington's tone is formal and controlled, as in these sentences: "Indeed, if one wanted to play with figures . . . United States" (2); "Yet if this book . . . intensifies the exclusion" (6); and "if there is technological advance . . . in

impoverishment" (7). The words in these sentences do not convey strong feelings; they sound academic.

2. "Internal exiles" here means that the poor are members of the society, are internal to the society, but they are outcasts because they "are dispossessed . . . had the will" (5).
3. *Pervasive*: spread through all parts of; *dispossessed*: having suffered the loss of expectations, prospects, relationships, and also disinherited, disaffiliated, alienated; *affluent*: having abundant wealth, property, and other material goods; *imponderables*: things that cannot be precisely determined, measured, or evaluated.

# *Violent Reactions*

## Shari Miller Sims

### Teaching Suggestions

Change brings further change, sometimes not entirely foreseen. Shari Miller Sims carefully and expansively defines aggression, assertiveness, and several lesser but contextually important concepts to show that we should interest ourselves in the possible residue of a major change in traditional (or old-fashioned) society. She uses definition as background information. Her thesis—that more women are accepting violence as a means of expression—is primarily developed with examples and by examining cause and effect.

### Notes

**Paragraph 1**

Sims opens her essay with two journalistic anecdotes, designed to get readers' attention at once by engaging them in lightly detailed particulars from interesting events specifically appropriate to her topic.

**Paragraph 3**

The author contrasts the reactive definition—what the word "violence" suggests to American women—with an academic discovery that violence has become socially acceptable, circumstantially, as a form of communication.

**Paragraph 4**

The paragraph moves from a lexical definition of *violence* to a socially realistic modification of that definition, which includes general examples drawn from life.

**Paragraph 5**

The main topic is introduced here, following the anecdotes and their appropriate definitions, which, combined, form a "hook" introduction, designed to engage readers by piquing their interest.

**Paragraph 6**

Paragraph 4 defines *violence* lexically; paragraph 6 defines it as "levels of violence," drawing attention to responsive violence, particularly in human beings, while showing that society has hitherto denied women the reasons for responsive violence.

**Paragraph 7**

An important reason that encourages women to contain the anger that leads to violence is cultural, as shown by psychological studies in the home, where parents, mostly fathers, tell daughters that anger is "not nice."

**Paragraph 8**

Traditional, male-dominated psychology takes one stance; modern psychology accepts other, more inclusive, possibilities, including a girl's accepting the kind of denial that causes her to have profoundly severe psychological difficulties.

"alexithymic": From "alexithymia," the inability to verbalize feelings.

**Paragraph 9**

In psychoanalytical theory, especially Freudian theory, suppression means pushing down painful memories so that they are not available in consciousness. Psychiatrists believe, however, that these memories may persist in some form in the unconscious, occasionally creating psychological havoc.

**Paragraph 10**

A definitive connection links the inability to master a situation and the onset of violent behavior.

**Paragraph 11**

Notice that the author moves from Lefer's "norms of *civilized* behavior" to her own "norms of *proper* behavior," thereafter introducing the notion of society's control over women's behavior.

**Paragraph 12**

Structurally and muscularly smaller than most men, most women vent their anger verbally instead of physically. Verbally, women and men are more evenly matched.

**Paragraph 13**

Estelle Ramey offers the historical reason that women are often portrayed in literature as being more verbal than physical.

**Paragraph 14**

Sims, with the expert's aid, dispenses with the argument that men are more physically violent just because of testosterone.

"corticosteroids": Hormonal steroids, including the sex hormones, of the adrenal cortex.

Final sentence: Sims preserves her definition by strengthening her argument that how girls are taught, their "socialization," determines their responses to violence.

**Paragraph 16**

Mention how the studies confirm that as we mature, we modify our behavior socially.

**Paragraph 17**

Our views are shaped by our behavior, as that behavior is endorsed by society.

**Paragraph 18**

When socially acceptable learning is changed, behavior is changed in ways that may not have been predicted.

**Paragraph 19**

Recent, socially acceptable learning is reflected in advertising. See also the Virginia Slims cigarette advertisements in magazines, with its slogan directed toward women: "You've come a long way, Baby."

**Paragraph 20**

These examples reinforce Sims's exploratory remarks on how changing social attitude will change social behavior.

**Paragraph 22**

More than 100 years ago, Susan B. Anthony said, in a women's suffrage newspaper, "Make [your employers] understand that you are in their service as workers, not as women" (*The Revolution*, October 8, 1868).

**Paragraph 23**

As used here, *violence* has two meanings: First, it refers to physical force used to injure, damage, or destroy. Second, it refers to unjust or callous use of force or power, as in violating another's rights or sensibilities.

**Paragraph 25**

Unfortunately, socially derived facts can be used politically, to "prove" whatever a clever manipulator of the language wants to prove.

**Paragraph 26**

Notice that Sims carefully includes the results of studies and remarks by specialists. She does not simply make statements about aggression; she lets the experts do that.

**Paragraph 28**

These comments deal with *perception*, sensory experience that has meaning or significance. Because of learning, one understands relationships among objects. When learning includes aggression or violence, then aggression or violence is perceived as part of a relationship.

**Paragraph 29**

G. H. Mead at the University of Chicago early in this century devised a theory linking society, the development of personality, and communication. Mead's statement is famous: To be able to communicate is to be able to "take the role of the other" toward one's own vocalizations and behavior. Nowadays, some people find it possible to take the role of the other, when the other is a fictitious character in film or on television.

**Paragraph 30**

The actions on television shows can be seen as condoning societally centered activities that in fact were not all condoned before those actions were presented on television to a broad spectrum of the population.

**Paragraph 33**

This paragraph opens with a conditional clause, an "if" clause, indicating that all the facts remain to be sifted and examined.

Sims draws a possible parallel, however: That which has been shown in research into violence done by men may also be shown in research into violence done by women.

## Possible Answers

### *Meaning and Purpose*

1. Varied examples of violence are rape, murder, aggression, some sports, fire, child abuse, emotional abuse, and so on.
2. Answers to this question may depend upon your students' degree of social awareness; some examples are alcohol and drugs, firearms, and firebombings.
3. Historically, the "seats of power" include high profile government positions and executive-level management positions. The expression describes any jobs that include the power to make serious, important, far-reaching decisions.
4. Throughout history women have been smaller than men in stature and musculature; they have therefore chosen verbal weaponry as a counterbalance (12).

5. The consequences of violent actions include fear of harming another person and worry about being in a dangerous position, physically.

*Strategy*

1. Sims gives a lexical, or dictionary, definition of violence in paragraph 4. She begins with this narrow but "official" definition before she extends the definition to a larger, and at the same time more specific, perspective.
2. Sims divides her definition into five sections, each with a subheading indicating that section's content. Because she wants to cover so much territory in her definition, from the "basic level" (6) to the "Threshold of Aggression" (30), the sections help organize her information and guide the reading.
3. "Civilized behavior" is behavior that keeps people living together in relative harmony and that most people in a society understand tacitly. "Proper behavior" is temporary behavior that is fitting, seeming, or right for the occasion.
4. These examples help the author to illustrate how women have become more assertive physically and emotionally by gaining a sense of strength.

*Style*

1. The journalistic anecdotes in the first two paragraphs are specific and interesting stories that grab readers' attention and ease them into the topic.
2. Sims has obviously done research on her subject. Her tone is academic and factual, and she quotes numerous authorities—as in paragraph 12—to back her assertions.
3. The pronoun *it* refers to "the portrayal or even glorification of violence in the media," earlier in the paragraph.

# *Who and What Is American?*

## Lewis H. Lapham

### Teaching Suggestions

This essay confronts the current air of discontent that is so pervasive in American life. Many are expressing dissatisfaction with the political parties and with the direction the country is moving. Some are taking politics to the streets instead of the voting booths, and we read of protests, hate crimes, and confrontations full of invective and sometimes violence. Undoubtedly your students have feelings about at least some aspects of the current climate, and this essay may help them to articulate them as well as see them in a larger perspective. Many of Lapham's references to people and events will be unfamiliar to some students. It is hard to say how many of these references must be known in order to understand Lapham's point, but certainly some should be explained. Encourage students, as Lapham does, to be candid in expressing their opinions and emotions. Ask them if they agree with Lapham that honest expression is the first step toward solving these problems. Some may fear that honesty will only fuel the flames. Which position is more in keeping with traditional American values?

Since there is no one definition of "American" in the essay, have your students locate the bits and pieces of a definition that Lapham offers. Can these bits and pieces be put together in one coherent, inclusive statement? With some rewording, we think they can be and encourage you to have your students write a definition based on Lapham's statements in each section.

## Notes

Sir V(ictor) S(awdom) Pritchett (born 1900). British journalist, critic, biographer, and short story writer.

**Paragraphs 1–3**

These paragraphs describe what to Lapham is a disturbing current social and political attitude: The nation has become divided into social, racial, and ethnic factions.

**Paragraph 2**

Jesse Helms: U.S. senator from North Carolina.

**Paragraph 3**

Specific examples to illustrate how political candidates play the politics of blame.

David Duke: Former Grand Wizard of the Ku Klux Klan, a defeated candidate for governor of Louisiana and briefly a candidate for U.S. president in 1992.

Tom Harkin: U.S. senator from Iowa.

Phil Gramm: U.S. senator from Texas.

**Paragraph 4**

"politically correct": a popular, but also much derided term for having the proper (acceptable) views (usually liberal) on social and political matters.

"ice people": According to Leonard Jeffries, a college professor in New York City, Africans are people of the sun and Europeans are people of the ice.

"Who and what is an American?": The rhetorical question moves the essay toward definition. If this question is answered, a definition will emerge.

**Paragraph 5**

Lapham offers a possible reason for this distrust of each other: With the end of the Cold War we may be searching for new enemies.

**Paragraph 6**

"What traits . . .": Another rhetorical question further leads the readers' expectation toward a coming definition.

**Paragraph 7**

This paragraph answers the previous question in a general way and introduces the idea of "false assumptions." Lapham will argue that, in fact, the opposite of these assumptions is what defines an American.

**Paragraph 9**

Cole Porter (1891–1964). American composer of popular music, notably "Night and Day" and "Begin the Beguine."

Lapham's discussion of the first assumption begins with a further, more specific, explanation of the assumption followed by a more lengthy denial of its validity.

**Paragraph 10**

This is a technique frequently used in argument papers: Present your opponent's view and then refute it. (See Persuasion and Argument, pp. 573–682) Lapham will follow this general pattern for each assumption. Each discussion is rich in brief examples.

"divine right of kings": the medieval idea that kings rule by the anointment of God and therefore command unquestioning obedience from their subjects. In England, divine right was brought to an end by the Glorious Revolution in 1688.

**Paragraph 11**

John Quincy Adams (1767–1848): Sixth U.S. president; son of the second president, John Adams. Elected to Congress after one term as president, he strongly promoted antislavery views.

**Paragraph 12**

John Charles Fremont (1813–1890): American explorer and politician. An antislavery candidate for president in 1856.

**Paragraph 13**

The Chinook Indians lived on the northern shore of the Columbia River in the northwestern United States.

**Paragraph 14**

Daniel Boorstin (born 1914): An historian noted for his trilogy *The Americans* (1965, 1968, 1973), *A History of the United States* (1980), and *The Discoverers* (1983). He served as librarian of Congress from 1975 to 1987.

**Paragraph 18**

Wyatt Berry Stapp Earp (1848–1929): A U.S. frontiersman, gunfighter, and law officer.

**Paragraph 19**

Herman Melville (1819–1891): One of America's greatest writers, his best known work is *Moby Dick*, in which the captain of the whaling ship *Pequod*, the obsessed Ahab, pursues the great white whale.

Henry David Thoreau (1817–1862): American writer. A strong individualist, a fact reflected in his best known works, *On the Duty of Civil Disobedience* (1849) and *Walden* (1854).

**Paragraph 23**

An existential premise assumes a self-determining individual accepting full responsibility for his own choices.

**Paragraph 24**

Madame Bovary and Mr. Pickwick: characters in two novels, *Madame Bovary* (1856) by the French novelist Gustave Flaubert and *Pickwick Papers* (serialized 1836–1837) by the English novelist Charles Dickens.

**Paragraph 26**

Daniel Webster (1792–1852): American orator and statesman. He was secretary of state under three presidents: William Henry Harrison, John Tyler, and Millard Fillmore.

**Paragraph 34**

In his concluding paragraphs, Lapham argues that a healthy candor in discussing our differences can come about only through recalling the shared values that hold us together and "our talent for assimilation." (37)

James Fenimore Cooper (1789–1851): American novelist. *The American Democrat* (1838) is one of a series of essays Cooper wrote to criticize the behavior of Americans after returning from a seven-year stay in Europe.

**Paragraph 36**

Atlantis is a legendary island said to have sunk beneath the sea over 10,000 years ago. The search continues.

**Paragraph 38**

Rev. Al Sharpton is a black activist in New York City who served as an adviser to Tawana Brawley, who charged that she had been raped by a Dutchess County assistant district attorney and others.

The last sentence issues a challenge to do the hard work of cooperation instead of taking the easy path of blaming others.

## Possible Answers

### *Meaning and Purpose*

1. Some sentences and phrases that express Lapham's counterassertions: *Group 1*: "We were always about becoming, not being; about the prospects for the future, not about the inheritance of the past" (10); "We are a nation of parvenus" (11); "We were always a mixed and piebald company" (12); "A theme of metamorphosis recurs throughout the whole chronicle of American biography" (14); *Group 2*: "If America is about nothing else, it is about the invention of the self" (18); "a chronic revolutionary and a born pilgrim" (20); *Group 3*: [Americans] insist on . . . decent and mutual respect across the lines of age, race, gender, and social class" (22); "We protect the other person's liberty in the interests of protecting our own . . ." "we value . . . helpfulness, forgiveness, kindliness, and above all, tolerance" (23); [we] "take part in the same idea" and [share] "a common temperament and habit of mind" (26); "the institutions of American government were meant to support the liberties of the people, not the ambitions of the state" and "it was the law that had to give way to the citizen's freedom of thought and action . . ." (27); "My love of country follows from my love of its freedoms, not from my pride in its fleets or its armies or its gross national product" (28); *Group 4*: "The climate of anxiety is the cost of doing business" and "a democracy places (burdens) on its citizens" (33).
2. Each person's definition will be different. You may wish to have the students discuss them in small groups.
3. The sponsors of political campaigns (7).
4. Briefly: to be honest with each other, to recognize our differences and accept them, and to work together without underestimating the challenge of the task. (34–38).
5. He believes in the value and strength of the culturally diverse society but decries the idea of defining ourselves by the group(s) we belong to. Noting that "We were always about becoming," and that we have always been a "mixed and piebald company," he urges us to protect each other's liberty, tolerate our differences, and reflect on what we have in common. He rejects the politics of blame that divides us into factions.

### *Strategy*

1. He begins each section with a further (negative) amplification of the false construction and then refutes it with a barrage of examples.
2. The description of the political climate in his introductory paragraphs is disheartening to say the least. Lapham is establishing such a discouraging view to prepare his readers for his analysis of where our politics have gone wrong.
3. The sheer numbers and the diversity of individuals and examples used become overwhelming, and therefore convincing.
4. Opinions will differ, but we think he has been reasonably successful. This approach allows him to discredit opposing views as he advances his own. Readers may not be left with a definitive statement about the term *American* but

they will have a clear "feeling" for the word. Such a definition may be superior to a more straightforward definition, which may leave readers unmoved. Clearly, too, Lapham's purpose goes beyond definition into argument.

*Style*

1. *Ur* is a combining form meaning earliest or original. As used here, *ur-American* refers to the people who are closest to the original spirit of America.
2. *Centrifugal*: moving outward from the center; *centripetal*: directed toward the center.
3. *Petulant*: showing sudden irritation; *demagogue*: a political leader who arouses the prejudices of the people; *parvenus*: persons who have acquired new wealth or position in society without having developed the appropriate behavior or manners; *piebald*: having mixed patches of black and white or other colors; *candor*: being open and sincere; *cant*: insincere or hypocritical speech.

# 11 / *Persuasion and Argument*

## *The Killing Game*

Joy Williams

### Teaching Suggestions

Portions of this selection are likely to bring vehement denials from some members of the class. If so, you might want to let discussion continue for a time in a freewheeling fashion, then stop to examine the nature of some of the comments of class members. Are they primarily based on logic or emotion? We predict the answer will be emotion, and then it's time to turn directly to the essay itself and see what the balance is between logic and emotion there. Examine Williams's use of emotional words and phrases and ask if a more logical approach would have had greater or lesser impact. Then ask if the students think the nature of the subject itself leads more naturally to emotional arguments or logical ones. Are there other current issues of public debate that are usually argued emotionally? Whatever the outcome of this discussion, you will probably want to leave some time to examine specific sentences and word choices that give the piece its emotional power.

### Notes

**Paragraph 1**

The first four sentences announce the subject of hunting and establish Williams's scornful attitude toward it though no thesis is stated.

The rapid listing of five words for death focuses attention on the seriousness of the subject.

The remainder of the first paragraph begins the attack on the hunters' point of view with the use of emotional words and phrases: "intellectual blather," "fatuous," "philosophical fog," "blow the toes off," "torn apart."

Jose Ortega y Gasset (1883–1955) was a Spanish critic and philosopher best known in the United States for his *Revolt of the Masses* (1930), which expresses his fear of the rising political power of the working classes.

**Paragraphs 2 and 3**

These paragraphs continue the attack on lofty justifications for hunting, dismissing them as the "blather" of "apologists."

Rolston is a professor of philosophy at Colorado State University. "Environmental Ethics" was published in 1987.

**Paragraphs 4 and 5**

These paragraphs reject the idea that hunting is done to provide food.

**Paragraph 6**

Beginning here, Williams shifts from refuting the hunters' arguments to advancing her own: Hunters pursue pleasure (thrills) and power (control or possession).

Mohandas K(aranchand) Gandhi (1869–1948), known for his ascetic way of life and his use of civil disobedience and nonviolence as political weapons in India.

"Beautiful creatures": Note the irony. Apparently the beauty of an animal adds to the thrill of destroying it.

Williams frequently uses the apparent words of hunters to convict them of unthinking cruelty.

**Paragraph 8**

Irony again: These animals are predators, but so are the humans that hunt them.

**Paragraph 9**

A specific example of a concerted attack on a particular predator. The red fox is killed so hunters will have more ducks and pheasant to shoot.

**Paragraph 10 and 11**

Another specific example of hunters protecting "their" game from natural predators.

**Paragraph 12**

The inductive arrangement of the essay leads to a strong assertion (thesis) in sentence 2 that is rephrased and amplified in the remainder of the paragraph.

Note the use of parallel structure and the repetition of the word *time* in sentences 5 and 6. "Time" is echoed in the last phrase of the essay, "check-out time."

## Possible Answers

### *Meaning and Purpose*

1. Obviously, the essay is not addressed to hunters—it would only anger them—though we can easily imagine Williams enjoying the possibility that some hunters may read it. It is addressed to a broader group of nonhunters or only occasional hunters, presumably male, since it first appeared in *Esquire*. Like most argumentative essays, it probably appeals most to those whose opinions it reinforces, but the passion of the argument suggests her desire to change opinions too. It's not a call to action except in the most indirect sense: Someone should make hunting illegal. Evidence to support this answer is in practically every paragraph: the emotional language; the sarcasm; the fact that she never addresses hunters, only refers to them; and the fact that she doesn't outline a plan of action for any reader to take.

2. Hunters say they hunt to relate to Death and Nature, to become a part of nature, for the nobility of the activity itself, and for the less "semireligious" reasons that man needs meat for subsistence and that hunting is a service (ridding an area of predators).
3. Williams says hunters hunt for fun, recreation, play, entertainment, thrills, to make the animals "theirs" (trophies), and to establish dominance and control.
4. The answer depends entirely on the readers, but probably most didn't know that the state bird of South Dakota was imported for "harvest" or about the political maneuvers behind the reintroduction of wolves to Yellowstone.
5. Here, too, the answer is personal. Some may complain that the essay is too intemperate in tone and would prefer a more thorough, logical argument. Others may more readily accept the emotional nature of the issue itself and find the essay convincing because it counters each of the hunters' arguments in turn.
6. The assumption is that life itself is of paramount value and should be left to its natural destiny. Williams comes closest to saying it directly in her last paragraph when she refers to animals as "sentient beings who deserve our wonder and respect." The series "put to death, extinguish, nullify, cancel, destroy" in the first paragraph and the repetition "dead, dead, dead" in paragraph 13 also reflect this assumption.

*Strategy*

1. She includes such quotations either to ridicule and dismiss them as she does with Ortega y Gasset, George Reiger (1), and Holmes Rolston III (2) or to let the words serve as self convictions as she does with Bill Neal (1) and Jack Atcheson (11).
2. Williams has made little attempt to balance logic and emotion. Her argument is emotional, but it proceeds from the assumption mentioned in question 6 under *Meaning and Purpose*. If that assumption is accepted, her emotional defense of it is understandable and more acceptable.
3. The assertion is directly stated in the second sentence of the last paragraph: "Sport hunting is immoral; it should be made illegal." The essay is arranged inductively—all the previous paragraphs make this conclusion inevitable. To state her assertion at the outset would be to risk losing readers who, without having read the other paragraphs, might dismiss the essay out of hand.
4. The words of the hunters, some apparently hypothetical, some identified, some not, have been carefully selected to support her view that their arguments are fatuous, unthinking, or cruel, so she runs no risk using them.

*Style*

1. A variety of adjectives might be used to describe the tone: caustic, mordant, ironic, sarcastic, truculent, scathing, sardonic. Supporting examples will vary.
2. A few examples of each: *Irony*: the hunters' appreciation of beautiful creatures which they then destroy (6); hunters prey on predators, but not for food (8); the state bird of South Dakota, the ring-necked pheasant, was actually imported from Asia to be hunted (9). *Sarcasm*: Mr. Neal "blazed through this philosophical fog" (1); "it's just the cross the 'good' hunter must bear" (3); "supplement their Chicken McNuggets with venison" (5); "We took pictures, we took pictures" (6). *Emotional words and phrases*: "intellectual blather" (1); "pursuit and murder" (4); "rags in the air, shredded, blown to bits" (6); "conned and cowed" and "pampering and coddling" (13).

3. The series in sentence 5 emphasizes the finality and horror of what hunters do and discredits in advance the first quotation: "The kill is the least important part of the hunt." The repetition of "dead, dead, dead" at the end of the essay recalls the opening series and achieves the same effect even more starkly.
4. *fatuous*: foolish or inane; *specious*: seemingly plausible, but actually not valid; deceptive; *atavistic*: the reappearance of a characteristic after several generations of absence; *vermin and varmints*: disgusting or objectionable animals or insects; *abattoir*: a slaughterhouse; *sentient*: conscious, aware, having sense perceptions.

# *What's Wrong with Animal Rights*

## Vicki Hearne

### Teaching Suggestions

A good way to begin discussing this essay is with the title. This title is a clause. It has a subject and a predicate. If it were punctuated with a question mark, then it could lead the reader to believe that she was going to read a defense of rights. For example, if one were to see the essay title "What's Wrong with Capital Punishment?" then it wouldn't be hard to figure out that the essay probably *endorses* capital punishment. On the other hand, if one were to see the essay title "The Wrongs of Capital Punishment," then it would not be difficult to guess that the essay argues *against* capital punishment. Ask your students if the title suggests that the writer is going to endorse animal rights, if the author is not going to endorse animal rights, or if the author probably intends only to discuss animal rights generally. By attempting to answer this question, students will enter into the realm of *ambiguity*, doubtfulness or uncertainty of meaning or intention, learning first-hand that what might seem clear at first glance is indeed often suspect upon reflection.

### Notes

**Paragraph 1**

"Not all happy animals are alike": Note the curious echo of Tolstoy's line in *Anna Karenina* (1875–1877; pt.I, Ch 1): "Happy families are all alike; every unhappy family is unhappy in its own way."

Secretariat: Winner of the Kentucky Derby.

**Paragraph 2**

"emblems": As used here, this word refers to "symbolizing a quality, state, or class; an allegorical picture."

Declaration of Independence: The "inalienable rights" noted in the Declaration of Independence are "life, liberty, and the *pursuit* of happiness," not happiness alone.

"*ex nihilo*": Latin, "out of nothing"

**Paragraph 3**

"Ethics, Aristotle": Here the author refers to *Nicomachean Ethics* by Aristotle (384–322 BCE), in which he writes, "Every science and every inquiry, and similarly every activity and pursuit, is thought to aim at some good" (bk.I, ch.1).

Thomas Jefferson: Third president of the United States (1801–1809)

**Paragraph 4**

"cannot be found in the lexicon": The first clear clue that gives the reader a sense of the direction the essay is going to go.

"they've got it all wrong": Note how smoothly this clause leads the reader into the beginning of the next paragraph.

**Paragraph 5**

Jeremy Bentham: (1748–1832), British jurist, social reformer, and philosopher who wrote *Introduction to the Principles of Morals and Legislation* (1789).

**Paragraph 6**

"iconographic center": The term *iconography* refers to symbolic representation, especially to conventional meanings being attached to an image or images.

"conundrum": anything that puzzles

"apotheosis": Often misused, this term refers to an ideal example, an epitome.

Louis Pasteur: (1822–1895) French chemist and bacteriologist who discovered that certain foods including milk and milk products could be exposed to an elevated temperature for the period of time that it takes to destroy certain microorganisms that can produce disease or cause food spoilage.

"antivivisectionists": people who oppose *vivisection*, the practice of subjecting living animals to cutting operations, especially to advance physiological and pathological knowledge.

**Paragraph 8**

"Ann Landers's column": Ann Landers is a columnist who responds to letters from her readers, that concern their worries or personal problems, which she tries to alleviate or help to solve.

**Paragraph 9**

The last sentence of this paragraph attacks an argument interestingly: Hearne says that Peter Singer and others use their ignorance of animals as argumentative proof of their devotion to animals, a cyclic and therefore meaningless argument at best.

**Paragraph 10**

Notice how vividly Hearne compares the thinking and actions of her Airedale to the thinking and actions of those she describes in paragraph 9.

**Paragraph 11**

"particularly unexamined lives": Compare with this line from Plato's *Apology*: "The life which is unexamined is not worth living."

James Madison: Fourth president of the United States (1809–1817). Noted for his work on the Bill of Rights and for his writings in *The Federalist*.

**Paragraph 12**

"calculus": As used here, the term refers to a highly systematic method of treating a problem.

**Paragraph 13**

"orangutans": In Malay, *orangutan* means "jungle man."

**Paragraph 14**

Again, as was exemplified in paragraph 4, notice how smoothly the last line of this paragraph serves as a transition to the first line of the next paragraph.

**Paragraph 15**

"Rights": As ordinarily denoted, a *right* is that which conforms to some fact, truth, reason, or to some standard or principle.

**Paragraph 16**

Here and in the next paragraph (17), notice the classical use of the analogy, when *analogy* means "reasoning or arguing from parallel cases."

**Paragraph 19**

It develops that "rights" are not only reciprocal but also binding; one cannot have rights without recognizing what supports those rights, which are responsibilities for acknowledging other "animals'" existence.

**Paragraph 20**

"Miranda warning": (Miranda v. Arizona, 1966), a Supreme Court ruling that requires law-enforcement officers to warn a person who has been taken into custody of his or her rights to remain silent and to have legal counsel.

**Paragraph 21**

"Yalies from townies": Hearne lightens her topic for a moment, while at the same time strengthening her point in this paragraph, that dogs recognize reciprocity, as do cats and Hearne's husband (one presumes).

**Paragraph 22**

"elaborate enough": The conceptions that animals have about their "rights" never move to the level of academic abstractions, such as those often embedded in texts and icons.

**Paragraph 23**

"Obedience is reciprocal": Note how often this theme pervades the essay. All that we do and all that is done to us, says Hearne in so many ways throughout this essay, demands of us some sort of reciprocity.

**Paragraph 24**

"Rainer Maria Rilke's account": In *Letters to a Young Poet*, Rilke (1875–1926) says, "Love consists in this, that two solitudes protect and touch and greet each other."

**Paragraph 25**

"Many children": Note the last line, where Hearne comments obliquely and negatively on a common way to "teach" children.

**Paragraph 26**

"correction blocks one path": The author carefully distinguishes between correction and punishment.

**Paragraph 28**

"What a goooooood human": Here the author employs a novel form of personification to make her point.

**Paragraph 30**

"People who claim to speak": What follows, though it might ultimately weaken Hearne's position, is an example of *argumentum ad ignorantiam*, a classic fallacy of noting that an argument is true if it has not been proved false. Whether the argument is weakened or strengthened by this strategy greatly depends on the audience's mood or opinion before the strategy is employed.

**Paragraph 31**

"perfectly my husband's mate": Note Hearne's deft use of analogy in this passage, "analogy" referring to that form of reasoning in which a thing is inferred to be similar to another thing in a certain respect, on the basis of the known similarity between the things in other respects.

## Possible Answers

### *Meaning and Purpose*

1. Answers vary, of course, but no answer should range too far afield from the idea that Hearne strongly equates all living creatures, paying particular attention in this essay to the combination of features shared by dogs and humans. Depending on which parts of the essay the students use for their reasoning, they might illustrate their answers with reference to many of the people named, including Hearne's husband, and to many of her dogs, whom she also names.
2. Relying on students' knowing that we do not have a right to happiness, but rather a right to the *pursuit* of happiness, which she points out at the end of paragraph 3, Hearne suggests that this kind of happiness is abstract, in the realm of philosophy. Animals do not operate in the realm of philosophy.
3. This sentence, according to the essay, has become, knowingly or not, the rallying cry of the kind of animal-rights' activists whom the author deplores. This series of three rhetorical questions cannot be answered, but they can be used to call people to the task of "liberating" animals.
4. Associating her husband with her dogs, as Hearne does several times, makes the point for the reader that she loves both strongly, but not equally. This important point helps the reader to see that love itself does not have a single shade of meaning.

### *Strategy*

1. By using statistics and other recoverable information here, the author points out that "captivity" does not equate with "cruelty." As she illustrates with this information, nature can be crueler than humans.
2. The author would like to leave out the philosophers because they deal with abstractions not appropriate to the topic, which itself is concrete: Either we do keep animals in some sense of *keep*, or we do not. At the same time, she cannot rid herself of the philosophers because, unfortunately, the question of animal rights has evolved into several philosophical questions that must be grappled with; otherwise, the author cannot come to terms with animal rights as they are now conceived, philosophically.
3. Answers will vary to this personal question, with most students agreeing one way or another that one must "give to get." After they have finished reading this essay, students usually agree with the premise that no person can be above another person, but some will argue that dogs and humans do not have enough in common to be thought of in terms of reciprocity.
4. If a "correct" answer exists for this question, then it grows from how closely the student reads paragraph 17. In that paragraph and based on other evidence preceding and following it, *being* need not automatically refer to a person. It can just as well refer to any living creature.

### *Style*

1. As used in paragraph 12, the word *calculus* means "a carefully systematic way or structure designed to solve a problem," or words to that effect.
2. Answers vary depending on how much information the students offer, but almost all answers have a common thread: Hearne intertwines people and dogs to the extent that one can come away from the essay believing, if only

momentarily, that dogs and people have far more in common than previously thought.

3. These two phrases are brief descriptions of the images or icons that certain freedom-for-animals groups use to elicit sympathy for their cause. One can imagine a photograph of a cute fluffy poodle, for example, portraying either helplessness or agony.
4. An *organism* is a form of life composed of mutually interdependent parts that maintain various vital processes. A *species* is a class of individuals having some common characteristics or qualities. Hearne uses these terms to strengthen in her readers' minds the idea of our common, reciprocal dependence upon one another.

# *A Modest Proposal*

## Jonathan Swift

### Teaching Suggestions

We suggest giving students background in Swift's use of irony and Anglo-Irish relations.

Ireland was reduced almost to subjection after the Norman Conquest (circa A.D. 1160) and Elizabeth I's armies finished the job by suppressing Irish rebellions. The English then gave the Irish Catholic nobility's lands to English Protestants in the sixteenth century. Hearing of atrocities by Irish Catholics against English Protestants in the Rebellion of 1641, Oliver Cromwell led an English army, killing thousands of native Irish. By 1653 Cromwell's forces had subjected all Ireland. By Swift's time, 10 percent of Ireland's population was Protestant, controlling 90 percent of the land. This Protestant Ascendancy lasted into the last quarter of the nineteenth century.

Nine years before publication of "A Modest Proposal," the English dropped all pretext of home rule and made the English Parliament Ireland's governing body, the English House of Lords Ireland's Supreme Court. England used Ireland as a source of raw material and discouraged industrial development that could have alleviated abject poverty.

Swift wrote "A Modest Proposal" primarily to protest against the barbaric conditions imposed on the Irish (though he gets his licks in at the Irish as well). Some of the essay's irony is created by the persona Swift adopts, whose voice is steady, rational, disciplined, and interested. Help students see that the contrast between this absolutely logical and reasonable voice and the absolutely mad plan is the key to both humor and gravity.

### Notes

**Paragraph 1**

Paragraphs 1–7 introduce the problems Swift's proposal addresses and some of the calculations on which it is based.

"great town": Dublin, Ireland.

"Pretender": James Stuart. In 1718, many Irishmen joined an army dedicated to restoring Stuart to the crown.

"Barbados": Other Irish, wanting to emigrate, bound themselves as indentured servants to work for a number of years in the Barbados, a West Indies island, or other British colonies to pay for their passage.

**Paragraph 4**

"projectors": planners, people who develop projects or schemes. Swift takes on this persona in the essay.

"shilling": At the time a shilling was worth less than twenty-five cents in today's United States currency.

**Paragraph 6**

Swift uses process analysis here to develop his argument, describing his method of calculation.

"are of towardly parts": Have innate ability.

"Cavan": a county in north central Ireland.

**Paragraph 7**

"three pounds and half a crown": A pound was twenty shillings, a crown five shillings.

**Paragraph 8**

Paragraphs 8–16 present the proposal, more calculations to demonstrate its potential, and a few ideas about how it would work.

**Paragraph 9**

"ragout": A highly spiced French stew.

**Paragraph 10**

Paragraphs 10–15 compose a process analysis, the workings of the proposal. Paragraph 10 itself is cause-and-effect analysis.

**Paragraph 12**

Instead of the narrator's voice here, we get the voice of Swift himself, evident because the narrator has no quarrel with landlords and no sympathy with tenants. The pun on "devour" ironically gives away the stratagem because the humorless narrator would never have punned.

**Paragraph 13**

"French physician": François Rabelais (1494–1553) Swift's favorite French writer and a broad humorist, and thus not a grave author at all.

"among us": The narrator addresses the chief landowners and administrators of Ireland, who are Anglo-Irish (Englishmen who became Irish citizens) and Protestant. His views of Catholicism in Ireland and abroad reflect theirs.

**Paragraph 15**

"artificially": artfully.

**Paragraph 16**

"shambles": butcher shops or slaughter houses.

**Paragraph 17**

Paragraphs 17 and 18 present and reject a possible refinement of the proposal.

**Paragraph 18**

"Psalmanazar": Georges Psalmanazar, a Frenchman who passed himself off as a native Formosan in a totally fictional *Description of the Isle of Formosa* (1705). He became a celebrity of sorts in a gullible English society.

"groat": a coin worth a few pennies. "chair": A sedan chair, on which a person is carried by two men. Swift's own voice surfaces again to attack the costs for "foreign fineries."

**Paragraph 19**

Paragraph 19 dispenses with a possible remaining problem.

**Paragraph 20**

Paragraphs 20–28 describe the proposal's numerous advantages.

**Paragraph 21**

Swift uses cause-and-effect development in paragraphs 21–28. The advantages of the proposal are the positive effects showing that the plan will benefit both the poor (24–26) and the rich (21–23, 25, 27–28). In paragraph 21 Swift attacks the current prejudice against Irish Catholics as well as the motives of many Protestant dissenters from the Church of England.

**Paragraph 22**

"liable to distress": subject to seizures by creditors.

**Paragraph 25**

"receipts": recipes.

**Paragraph 29**

Paragraphs 29–33 anticipate objections to the proposal and dispose of them.

"Therefore . . .": Many of these proposals Swift himself had made in earlier works.

"Topinamboo": A district in Brazil inhabited by primitive tribes and notorious for barbarism and ignorance.

"like the Jews" refers to the fall of Jerusalem to the Romans (A.D. 70), during which time many prominent Jews were executed on charges of collaborating with the enemy.

**Paragraph 31**

"country": England. Swift again allows his own voice to intrude where he says the English may as well eat Irish children, for they are already glad to eat up the nation.

## Possible Answers

### *Meaning and Purpose*

1. The persona writes as an efficient, rational man who sincerely wants to solve the problems of Ireland in a reasonable and humane way. Swift offers real solutions to the problems (29). He voices exasperation, however, that the real solutions have never been tried (30, 31).
2. The essay's persona proposes to kill one-year-old Irish infants and sell their flesh as meat to the wealthy. Because the Irish poor are oppressed by their landlords and have no reliable source of income, they have no way to escape their poverty. His proposal would remedy this social ill.
3. Swift condemns the cruel exploitation and oppression of the Irish by the English.
4. Underneath his irony, Swift pleads for charity and compassion. He sets forth reasonable and compassionate solutions (29).
5. Ask students to try to be serious about answering this question, perhaps in the same rational voice Swift uses.

### *Strategy*

1. By vividly depicting poor women and their children, he creates sympathy for them so that the reader will react with horror to his proposal.
2. Swift, calling his proposal "modest," repeatedly describes the time and care he spent pondering the problem (4), and uses first person with verbs of consideration: "I calculate," "I subtract," "I apprehend," and so on (6). He cites authorities and experts, such as the "very knowing American" (9). He puts forth his proposal with modesty and humility (8, 10). His attitude is respectful throughout: "as I must confess," (15); "although I rather recommend"

(16); "But with due deference" (17). He piously objects to cruelty (5, 17). He refers repeatedly to the good of the nation (2, 7, 19, 21, 23, 29, 33). He carefully lists the advantages of the proposal (21–28). He fears the flesh would spoil if exported (31). And he ironically professes at the end that he wouldn't make a penny from the proposal.

3. The first clue is language that is too outrageous to be taken seriously.
4. The final paragraph serves at least two subtle purposes: Swift takes one last poke at those whose sole motivation is profit, and he aligns himself with the oppressed, the implication being that if he had infants they also would be for sale.

*Style*

1. The livestock expressions dehumanize the Irish poor, making the narrator's proposal more palatable—and Swift's satire more horrifying. These expressions also reflect and thus satirize English attitudes toward the Irish poor.
2. Some students undoubtedly will object to Swift's somewhat archaic language ("increaseth," 11; "how well soever intended" 17), to his formality, and to his often complicated sentences. Others may find that initial difficulties soon fade. Some others may recognize that Swift's formal style perfectly fits the narrator's rather pompous persona.
3. *Importuning*: pressing or besetting with solicitations; *prodigious*: extraordinary in amount; *rudiments*: elements or first principles of a subject; *fricassee*: meat browned lightly, stewed, and served in a sauce made with its own stock; *ragout*: a highly spiced French stew; *prolific*: producing abundant offspring; *papists*: Roman Catholics; *repine*: complain; *deference*: respectful submission or yielding to another's judgment, opinion, or will; *mandarins*: members of an elite or powerful class; *gibbet*: a gallows with a projecting arm at the top, from which the bodies of criminals were formerly hung in chains and left suspended after execution; *desponding*: depressed from loss of hope; *tithes*: the tenth part of agricultural products or income paid in support of the church or priesthood; *vintners*: people who make or sell wine; *farrow*: to bring forth young; *parsimony*: extreme or excessive economy or frugality; *animosities*: feelings of strong dislike; *disobliging*: giving offense or affront to; *inclemencies*: severities or harshnesses of weather; *entailing*: causing.

# *Letter from Birmingham Jail*

## Martin Luther King, Jr.

### Teaching Suggestions

Some students may have seen and heard King speak on television, particularly the "I have a dream" speech, but the 1950s and 1960s civil rights movement will be ancient history to most. Give them some history of the movement before they read the essay.

In 1955, Mrs. Rosa Parks, a seventy-two-year-old black woman, was arrested for breaking Montgomery, Alabama's segregation laws by refusing to give up her seat on a city bus to a white passenger. The outraged blacks organized the Montgomery Improvement Association to boycott the city's public-transit system. King, pastor of a

Montgomery Baptist Church, was elected leader of the Association. In a difficult year it successfully desegregated transportation. King, greatly influenced by the New Testament teachings of Jesus, Thoreau's views on civil disobedience, and Gandhi's principle of nonviolent civil disobedience, then formed the Southern Christian Leadership Conference, which was committed to using nonviolent resistance to accomplish desegregation.

King put Birmingham, Alabama, the most segregated city in the South, in world news in 1963 when he led a campaign to desegregate the city's lunch counters and hiring. To the demonstrations and sit-ins, the Birmingham police responded by turning firehoses and dogs on the demonstrators and jailing King and 2,400 other civil rights workers. Eight local clergymen issued a public letter agreeing with the aims of the movement but deploring the methods used. King's letter is a response to theirs. King uses both logical argument and persuasion to convince readers that his actions are morally compelling. And his argument is complex enough to warrant a paragraph-by-paragraph analysis. You or one of your students might read paragraph 14 aloud to demonstrate its rhetorical power.

In 1964, Martin Luther King, Jr., was awarded the Nobel Peace Prize, at 34 the youngest person ever to receive that prestigious honor. He was murdered on April 14, 1968, in Memphis, Tennessee.

## Notes

**Paragraph 1**

Paragraphs 1–4 explain King's presence in Birmingham, proceeding from immediate and practical causes to more philosophical, ultimate causes.

**Paragraph 2**

The first reason for his presence in Birmingham, he explains, is that he is president of the Southern Christian Leadership Conference, an interstate organization that has business there. He was, therefore, invited.

**Paragraph 3**

The second reason he is there is that injustice is there, and like the Apostle Paul and other religious prophets, he must respond.

**Paragraph 4**

The third reason for his presence is that we are all inextricably related, and injustice anywhere in our society affects us all. King, therefore, cannot be an "outside agitator." He is there because he is needed.

**Paragraph 5**

King uses paragraphs 5–9 to dispose of the clergymen's first objection, their deploring that Birmingham is the site of the demonstrations. Blacks, he explains, had "no alternative." His argument in this section is circular: There must be direct action after three more moderate steps have been taken; those three steps have been taken; there must, therefore, be direct action. The major premise is stated as a given. The minor premise, that all necessary steps have been taken, King fully documents.

**Paragraph 6**

King outlines the "four basic steps" and demonstrates how the first step, establishing that racial injustices exist in Birmingham, has been taken.

**Paragraph 7**

The second step, negotiation, was a failure.

**Paragraph 8**

King describes the third step, self-purification.

**Paragraph 9**

"Having aided . . . no longer": The final step, demonstration, has become inevitable.

**Paragraphs 10 and 11**

In paragraphs 10 and 11 King argues the need for direct action, basing his argument primarily on Socrates.

Socrates (469?–399 B.C.) was an Athenian philosopher.

**Paragraph 12**

Paragraphs 12–14 refute the clergymen's second charge, that the demonstrations are untimely, by demonstrating the opposite.

Reinhold Niebuhr (1892–1971), an American Protestant theologian and philosopher.

**Paragraph 14**

"The cup . . . runs over": With the biblical allusion to Psalms 23:4–6 at the end of this paragraph, King reinforces his point that he is walking "through the valley of the shadow of death" and, because of his faith, "will fear no evil." He thus uses a biblical reference to enforce the point that he is impatient.

**Paragraph 15**

In paragraphs 15–22, King refutes the next objection by the clergymen, that he and the civil rights demonstrators are breaking the law by arguing that it is their moral responsibility to break unjust laws.

St. Augustine (A.D. 354–430) was one of the Latin fathers of the early Christian Church.

**Paragraph 16**

In paragraphs 16–20, King distinguishes between just and unjust laws and offers substantial support to the idea that the laws they are breaking are unjust.

St. Thomas Aquinas (1225?–1274) was an Italian Catholic philosopher and a major theologian of the Roman Catholic Church.

Martin Buber (1878–1965) was a Jewish philosopher and theologian.

Paul Tillich (1886–1965), born in Germany, was an American Protestant philosopher and theologian.

**Paragraph 21**

In paragraphs 21 and 22, King presents several historical examples to justify the idea that they not only have the right but indeed the responsibility to break unjust laws.

Shadrach, Meshach, and Abednego, Jews living in Babylon, refused to worship a golden idol as demanded by the King of Babylon, Nebuchadnezzar. For punishment they were thrown into a fiery furnace. Daniel 3:1–30.

Socrates was tried by the Athenians for corrupting their youth with his skeptical, questioning method of teaching. He refused to change and was condemned to death.

**Paragraph 22**

In 1956, an anticommunist revolution in Hungary was put down quickly by the Soviet army.

**Paragraph 23**

In paragraphs 23 and 24, King digresses from his logical argument to criticize white moderates.

**Paragraph 25**

Here, King takes on the next charge, that the demonstrations "precipitate violence." He shows this position is illogical by again citing historical precedents.

**Paragraph 26**

King addresses the issue of whether the time is right for demonstrations.

**Paragraph 27**

King now answers the final charge, that the demonstrators are extremists, by showing that they are, in fact, taking the middle road that will prevent a "racial nightmare" in the future (paragraphs 27–31).

**Paragraph 30**

"Zeitgeist": German. The spirit of the time; the general trend of thought or feeling characteristic of a period.

**Paragraph 31**

Here King cites several precedents in the history of extremism that have now become respectable.

Amos was a prophet in the eighth century B.C. A book in the Old Testament bears his name. Martin Luther (1483–1546) was a German theologian who led the Protestant Reformation in Germany. John Bunyan (1628–1688) was an English writer and preacher. His refusal to bow to royal edicts banning nonconformist preaching led to his imprisonment from 1660 to 1672.

**Paragraph 32**

King's rebuttal of the clergymen's charge and his argument for direct action end here. Paragraphs 32–44 are primarily devoted to chastising white moderates and the Jewish and Christian churches for being defenders of the status quo.

**Paragraph 43**

"ekklesia": The Greek New Testament word for the church.

**Paragraph 45**

In paragraphs 45–46, King responds to the clergymen's praise of the Birmingham police.

**Paragraph 46**

T. (Thomas) S. (Stearns) Eliot (1888–1965) was a British poet and critic born in the United States. He won the Nobel prize for poetry in 1948.

**Paragraph 47**

King makes the point that the demonstrators, not the police, should have been praised.

James Meredith was the first black to register at the University of Mississippi.

**Paragraph 48**

In paragraphs 48–50, King sarcastically apologizes to the clergymen for taking so much of their "precious time." He also goes through the appropriate formalities for his Jewish and Christian colleagues and "brothers."

## Possible Answers

### *Meaning and Purpose*

1. Jail usually silences and intimidates people, making them powerless. King is not silent or powerless as he puts pen to paper in his jail cell, working for civil rights.
2. King claims that, though mistaken, his critics are "men of genuine good will" and that their criticisms are sincere. They deserve an answer.
3. King outlines the four steps a nonviolent campaign must take to effect social change (6). Negotiation, the second, has already failed. All three first steps have been accomplished, leaving only the inevitable fourth: direct action, or demonstrations.

4. He discusses waiting for racial equality (13, 14). Freedom must be demanded because it is never voluntarily given over by an oppressor (13). He catalogues segregationist human abuses that legitimate immediate action (14).
5. King distinguishes between just and unjust laws (15–22). An unjust law is "out of harmony with the moral law"; is not rooted in eternal and natural law; "degrades human personality" (16); "is inflicted upon a minority that, as a result of being denied the right to vote, had no part in enacting or devising the law" (18). He shows historical and biblical precedents for breaking unjust laws (21, 22). A person who breaks an unjust law but is willing to suffer the penalty expresses highest respect for the law (20).
6. King establishes himself as "in the middle of opposing forces in the Negro community" (27), each of which is an extreme. Then he cleverly puts himself in the same camp as other "extremists" admired by the clergymen he addresses (31).

*Strategy*

1. Emphasizing that he writes from a jail cell, King hopes to create sympathy. He further ingratiates himself by complimenting the audience. He also intimates their importance, for he answers their criticisms, which he would not normally do.
2. King structures his letter around rebuttals to the clergymen's charges. He answers the first in paragraphs 5–9, the second in 10–11, the third in 12–14, the fourth in 15–22, the fifth in 25, the sixth in 26, and the last in 27–31.
3. King appeals to both reason and emotion. He reasons that a law is unjust and democracy thwarted if the minority has no voice in "enacting or devising the law" (18). His language is rational, not emotional. The logic is deductive: if democracy means the people participate in making the law, and a large group of people is denied this right, then the law does not meet the terms of a democracy and is unjust. He appeals to emotion by listing the horrible injustices that blacks suffer every day; he says to whites that the time has come for change (14). His language here is laden with emotion.
4. With sarcasm and subtlety King apologizes to the clergymen for taking too much of their "precious time." And he goes through the formalities appropriate to his "Christian brothers," to reestablish a harmonious relationship with them.

*Style*

1. The periodic sentence that begins "But when you have seen" is masterful. He withholds its full meaning until the last words, keeping the reader in suspense about how the sentence will come out, both structurally and semantically. The 300-word catalogue is organized into eleven parallel subordinate clauses, enforcing order and clarity. Repeating "when" connects the clauses and contributes to the drama in the switch to "then" in the short independent clause concluding the sentence. The long sentence emphasizes how long blacks have waited for justice.
2. King uses metaphors to achieve an eloquent and poetic style and to enhance his appeal to emotion.
3. *Provincial*: having the manners, viewpoints, and so on considered characteristic of unsophisticated inhabitants of an outlying province; *gainsaying*: deny-

ing, disputing, contradicting; *gadflies*: people who persistently annoy or provoke others with criticism, schemes, demands, requests; *millennium*: a period of general righteousness and happiness; *lamentably*: unfortunately; *abyss*: a deep, immeasurable pit or cavity; *anarchy*: without government or law; *elegy*: a mournful, melancholy, or plaintive poem, especially a funeral song or lament for the dead; *incorrigible*: beyond correction or reform; *sanctimonious*: making a hypocritical show of religious devotion or piety; *interposition*: barrier or obstacle; *clarion*: clear and shrill; *laxity*: carelessness or negligence; *mores*: folkways accepted without question and embodying a group's fundamental moral views; *inextricably*: incapable of being disentangled; *scintillating*: animated, vivacious, effervescent.

# *The Shrieking of the Lambs*

## Andrew Klavan

### Teaching Suggestions

Klavan's opinions on the relationship between fictional and real violence is, to say the least, not in the mainstream at the present moment. Undoubtedly many students will react strongly to the essay, some, we suspect, willing to defend his point of view, while others, the majority we venture to guess, willing to attack him. But we would also guess the majority of those students will not have thought out the reasons for their opinions. If this is true, the situation could lead to a worthwhile discussion of the necessity of credible evidence in developing a believable argument. Is Klavan's evidence credible? Is his logic solid, believable? Does he effectively do away with opposing points of view? What evidence can the students gather to support their own opinions?

Klavan's essay is also full of allusions (see the notes to the essay), and a valuable lesson could be given on how well-thought-out allusions can add depth and meaning to what one writes. Attendant to this, of course, is the lesson that the more one has read, the more meaningful any piece of informed writing will be for the reader.

It would also be valuable to use Klavan's essay in conjunction with Stephen King's "Why We Crave Horror Movies" (Klavan and King are in basic agreement—no surprise for two men who make a living writing horror fiction) and Michael Medved's "Denial Behavior," which takes a diametrically opposite point of view, one that Klavan attacks directly in his essay.

### Notes

#### Paragraph 5

"15 minutes": the allusion is to Andy Warhol (1928?–1987, Pop artist and underground film maker) and his pronouncement that "everyone will be famous for fifteen minutes."

Michael Medved: American film critic. His "Denial Behavior," included in this section, argues that film violence has a definite, deleterious effect on society.

*American Psycho*: a novel (1991) by American novelist Bret Easton Ellis. The novel's protagonist, Patrick Bateman, works by day on Wall Street making a fortune. At night he tortures and murders women, described graphically by Ellis.

Catharine MacKinnon: pro-censorship feminist and professor of law. MacKinnon and her colleague, writer Andrea Dworkin, maintain that pornography should not be accorded the same kinds of protection as other forms of speech because it is not speech *per se*. Rather, it is sex discrimination and promotes the subjugation of women.

**Paragraph 6**

Hannibal Lecter: from *The Silence of the Lambs*.

Ice-T: American rap artist. He is a controversial rap singer and film actor who pioneered "gangstra rap" with works that express the rage and fantasies of inner city street life. He outraged many with his 1991 song "Cop Killer."

"sound bytes": refers to 10–15 second video news segments.

**Paragraph 9**

Just William: the innocent looking, middle class, naughty school boy in a series of stories set in England during the first half of the twentieth century.

"Lords of the Flies": refers to William Golding's novel *Lord of the Flies* (1954) in which a group of British schoolboys are stranded on a remote island and gradually degenerate into a savage horde. The novel was adapted to film twice, in 1963 and 1990.

"*What rough beast . . . at last*": lines 20 and 21 of W.B. Yeats' justifiably famous poem, "The Second Coming," in which Yeats expresses his sense of the dissolution of the civilization of his time. Klavan refers to the poem here and other places in the essay. These references are particularly apt considering the subjects of both the poem and essay.

**Paragraph 10**

Martin Amis: (b. 1949) English novelist and journalist. His novels have won widespread acclaim, *The Rachel Papers* (1974) winning the Somerset Maugham Award.

**Paragraph 12**

*Child's Play 3*: the last of three horror films in which a doll named Chucky is really a monster, possessed with the spirit of a dead murderer.

**Paragraph 13**

In this paragraph Klavan demonstrates by specific examples how the British press and politicians grabbed on to easy but irrelevant solutions to explain the Bulger crime, thus ignoring the real issues he lists in the third sentence.

*The Good Son*: a terror film (1993) in which Macauley Culkin, an unremorseful, pubescent sociopath, terrorizes his cousin, and many others.

*Reservoir Dogs*: a sometimes highly praised and often gruesomely violent Quintin Tarantino film (1992) that is a post-mortem dissection of a fatally bungled robbery.

Liberal Democrat MP: a member of the British Parliament in the Liberal Democratic Party, a middle of the road, but minor, party between the conservative to reactionary Tory Party and the liberal to socialist Labor Party.

*My Cousin Vinny*: a film comedy (1992) about a "lawyer's" attempt to defend his innocent cousin and a friend on a murder charge in the deep south. Klavan makes this statement with tongue in cheek, probably.

**Paragraph 14**

"passionate intensity": "The best lack all conviction, while the worst/Are full of passionate intensity," lines 7 and 8 of "The Second Coming."

**Paragraph 15**

This one sentence paragraph is a synecdoche (see *Figures of speech* in the Glossary) in which Klavan has Chucky stand for all fictional violence.

**Paragraph 16**

Plato: a Greek philosopher (c. 427–348 B.C.). Plato aspired to political activity. Dismayed at the inequities of Athenian tyranny, and later at the execution of his teacher Socrates under democracy, he turned toward philosophy in search of an alternative to the unjust and unstable public life of the time. Klavan quotes from his political treatise, the *Republic*.

"Dionysian": Dionysus, the Greek god (Bacchus in Roman mythology) of wine and fertile crops. He was often honored by orgiastic fertility rites, thus the adjectival form of his name indicating recklessly uninhibited, unrestrained, undisciplined, and yes, orgiastic. He represents man's dark side.

**Paragraph 18**

Vaclav Havel: (1936–b) Czech dramatist and poet. Havel became a spokesman for the Czech civil rights movement after the Soviet invasion of Prague in 1968. After Czechoslovakia gained its independence, Havel became its first democratically elected president. He has always been concerned about the relation of language to reality, and many of his works present the crisis of communication as a symptom of deep social malaise.

**Paragraph 19**

"an unfathomable spirit and an infinite mind": Klavan's rather mystical locution seems to refer to a level of mind well beyond the conscious, and may well allude to Carl Jung's "collective unconscious." Most certainly he alludes to Yeats' *Spiritus Mundi* (l. 13) in "The Second Coming," The Spirit or Soul of the Universe, with which all individual souls are connected through the "Great Memory," which Yeats held to be a universal subconscious in which the human race preserves its past memories. It is thus a source of symbolic images for the writer.

"a shadow of the world": Klavan turns Platonic philosophy upside down here. In the "Allegory of the Cave," Plato claims that those things we normally think of as constituting the real world are merely shadows of the ideal forms that lie behind them and that are the true reality. Here, the imaginative transformation of the real world gives us mere shadows.

**Paragraph 21**

*Death Wish*: a 1974 film in which a liberal minded business man's wife and daughter are savagely raped, and his wife dies. This atrocity transforms the previously mild mannered man into a vigilante on the streets of New York.

*Red Dragon*: a novel (1981) by Thomas Harris in which a former FBI agent is called back into service to capture a serial killer, which he does by using the power of his imagination to think like the killer. The psychopathic genius, Hannibal Lecter, who will become a central figure in the later Harris novel, *The Silence of the Lambs*, is introduced as a minor character in this book. *Red Dragon* was made into the movie *Manhunter* in 1986.

*Catcher in the Rye*: a novel (1951) by J.D. Salinger. The book presents two days in the life of Holden Caulfield who has run away from his prep school just before the start of Christmas vacation. He wanders around New York getting himself into a number of wryly humorous adventures. He is a sophisticated, articulate, and amusingly unbalanced adolescent who uniquely represents contemporary youth's dissatisfaction with adult society.

Ceausescu's murderous Roumania: Nicolae Ceausescu was president of Roumania from 1967 until the collapse of Communism in Eastern Europe. His authoritarian regime was particularly brutal.

*Dracula*: the best known novel (1897) by English writer Bram Stoker (1847–1912). The novel is a wild tale of vampires and werewolves. It has been made into several motion pictures and sequels.

**Paragraph 22**

*Psycho*: (1960) Alfred Hitchcock's most notorious film is still terrifying after all these years.

David Koresh: the head of a religious cult that came into conflict with federal law enforcement. The conflict ended with the horrific conflagration in Waco, Texas, in 1994.

**Paragraph 24**

"for taking such pleasure in make-believe acts": here and elsewhere in the essay Klavan attacks the puritanical tendency to deny others the pleasures that one feels personally guilty for. Thus the phenomenon of censorship.

*Thelma and Louise*: a popular film (1991) in which two women friends leave their responsibilities behind to take a short trip, but an unexpected incident turns them into fugitives.

**Paragraph 26**

Agatha Christie: (born Agatha Mary Clarissa Miller, 1890–1976) English detective-story writer, the most widely translated author in English. Her detective novels usually featured her idiosyncratic sleuths Hercule Poirot, a vain but clever Belgian, or Miss Jane Marple, a shrewd and elderly spinster with an endless fascination for murder. Christie had a particular interest in abnormal psychology.

Hemingway: Ernest Hemingway (1899–1962) American novelist and short-story writer. Early in his career as a newspaperman and foreign correspondent, Hemingway was already the craftsman whose terse style, with its dramatic understatement and superb dialogue, was to influence several generations of writers.

Faulkner: William Faulkner (1897–1962) American novelist and short-story writer. Faulkner, who was awarded the Nobel Prize in Literature in 1949, is recognized as one of the greatest of American writers.

**Paragraph 28**

Dickens: Charles Dickens (1812–1870) English novelist, the most popular and considered by many the greatest of England. He became a popular success at the age of twenty-four with the publication of his serialized novel *Pickwick Papers*.

**Paragraph 30**

"Nietzschean": reference to Friedrich Nietzsche (1844–1900) German philosopher, classical scholar, and poet. His philosophy emphasized the will to power as the chief motivating force of both the individual and society.

*The Robber Baron*: We have been unable to track down any film, novel, or story with this precise title. The Brothers Grimm have a folktale entitled "The Robber Bridegroom" in which an old crone hides a young woman in a cellar to have her watch her fiancé and his cutthroat companions dismember another young woman, a fate that would be hers soon. Eudora Welty's first novel (1945) of the same name is based on this tale. The title of Margaret Atwood's *The Robber Bride* is also derived from the Grimm story. There is also a novel by Joyce Brandon titled *The Lady and the Robber Baron*. Which, if any, of these Klavan is referring to, we simply don't know.

Homer: 9th century B.C. Greek epic poet. He is the reputed author of both the *Iliad* and the *Odyssey*. He is traditionally represented as blind, thus "deep-browed."

**Paragraph 31**

Klavan contrasts the theories of experts in this paragraph with what he considers are the real causes that give fiction life in the next paragraph (32).

*Falling Down*: a movie (1993) in which a previously retiring nobody loses control one morning, abandons his car on the freeway, and starts wandering L.A. on an increasingly violent odyssey.

**Paragraph 32**

"*gravitas* . . . catharsis": In his *Poetics*, Aristotle (384–322 B.C.) applies the term *catharsis* (in the original Greek, "purgation," or "purification," or both) to describe that undeniable, if extraordinary, fact that in drama many tragic representations of suffering and defeat leave an audience feeling not depressed, but relieved, or even exalted. This is a literary theory with substance and weight (*gravitas*).

**Paragraph 35**

Medea: in Greek mythology, a sorceress and priestess of Hectate who was involved in several bloody murders, two of whom were her own children.

Caliban: In Shakespeare's *The Tempest*, the deformed, half-human slave of Prospero. The son of the witch Sycorax and a devil, Caliban symbolizes mankind's primitive urges.

St. Francis of Assisi: (c. 1181–1226) Italian monk, founder of the order of Franciscans. The son of a prosperous merchant, he turned at about age twenty-six to a life of asceticism and mysticism, devoting himself to the care of the poor, the sick, and the leprous, as well as to prayer. His approach to religion was characterized by its joyousness and its love of nature. He called both animate and inanimate creations his brothers and sisters, and his preaching to the birds has become a popular subject of artists.

"take them out for a walk": see Stephen King's "Why We Crave Horror Movies" (pp. 351–354).

**Paragraph 37**

Dr. Seuss: (pen name of Theodor Seuss Geisel, 1904–1995) American writer and illustrator of scores of immensely popular, humorous children's books, such as *The Cat in the Hat*, *How the Grinch Stole Christmas*, and *Green Eggs and Ham*.

**Paragraph 39**

Klavan uses an anecdote here to demonstrate how people take a natural delight in fictional gore that is effectively done.

*The Exorcist*: a film (1973) adapted from the best-selling novel of Peter Blatty. In it a twelve-year-old girl's body is possessed by the Devil, and a troubled priest attempts to confront the demon in her—and in himself.

**Paragraph 40**

*Titus Andronicus*: (c. 1590) a tragedy by William Shakespeare (1564–1616). The play is particularly violent, even by Elizabethan standards.

de Sade: Comte Donatien Alphonse Francois de Sade, known as Marquis de Sade (1740–1814), French author. Sadism, a type of sexual perversion in which gratification is found by torturing the object of love, is so called from de Sade whose works first brought such practices to public attention.

**Paragraph 41**

*Time's Arrow*: Martin Amis's seventh novel (1992) in which the narrator is a "passenger or parasite" inside the mind of Tod Friendly who experiences Tod's life in strict reverse order. In this inverted world people walk backwards, absorb excrement, and regurgitate food which they assemble and take to the supermarket. From this point of view, all things become strange and comic, including the Holocaust. For this reason the book was condemned by many. After much controversy, the novel was eventually short-listed for the Booker Prize.

*Goodfellas*: a critically acclaimed 1990 film that presents both the allure and reality of day-to-day life in a Mafia family.

"the Menendez trial": the brothers Menendez, Eric and Lyle, confessed to planning and then carrying out the murders of their parents. In their first trial a hung jury was unable to decide between second degree murder and manslaughter. The jury in their second trial found them guilty of first degree murder. A month later, in April, 1996, they were sentenced to life imprisonment without possibility of parole.

"the Amy Fisher case": as an underage teenager, Amy Fisher had an affair with an older, married man, Joey Buttafuoco, and attempted to murder his wife.

**Paragraph 42**

"graver purposes": Klavan puns here.

**Paragraph 43**

"Rome is burning": alludes to Nero, Emperor of Rome (54–68 A.D.) who was responsible in 64 A.D., according to popular history, for lighting a great fire that destroyed a sizeable portion of Rome in order to see how Troy looked when it was in flames, and then occupied himself musically "while Rome burned." The story is now generally held to be mere legend. But Klavan's allusion adds depth and meaning to the idea that those who see fictional violence as destroying the fabric of society are as apocalyptic and wrong in their vision as those who wrongfully blamed Nero for the destruction of Rome.

**Paragraph 44**

South Kensington: a section of London.

**Paragraph 45**

*Schindler's List*: (1993) the film adaption by Steven Spielberg of Thomas Keneally's best-seller about the real-life Catholic war profiteer who initially flourished by currying favor with the Nazis, but eventually went broke saving the lives of more than 1,000 Polish Jews by employing them in his factory, manufacturing crockery for the German army.

*Mississippi Burning*: (1988) a film based on real-life events in which two FBI agents head a government investigation into the disappearance of three civil rights workers in Mississippi during the summer of 1964.

**Paragraph 46**

Keats: John Keats (1795–1821) English poet.

**Paragraph 49**

Robert Chambers: Better known as the "preppie murderer," Chambers killed a young woman during what could have been a date rape in New York in 1986.

Lorena Bobbitt: was found innocent by reason of insanity after admitting cutting off her husband's penis while he slept.

**Paragraph 52**

Ed Gein: (b. 1906) Wisconsin murderer and necrophile. Gein lived alone on a farm in Plainfield, Wisconsin, after his mother and brother died. He developed a strong interest in the female anatomy and apparently desired to change his sex. Around 1947 he began digging up female corpses from remote graves and bringing them to his farm for experiments. Later he turned to killing women to obtain cadavers. The local sheriff eventually found the skins, heads, hearts, livers, sex organs, etc., of at least fifteen women in Gein's home. He was sent to a state institution for the criminally insane.

**Paragraph 55**

"the sleep of reason": an allusion to the Spanish artist Francisco Goya (1746–1828) and his etching in which a man sleeps with his head on a desk, on which there is the inscription, "The sleep of reason brings forth monsters." The figure is surrounded by nocturnal creatures—bats, owls, and cats—which symbolize the dark forces that continually threaten rationality.

**Paragraph 56**

Carlyle: Thomas Carlyle (1795–1881) Scottish born English prose writer.

"I-and-Thou": Martin Buber (1878–1965), an Austrian Jew, was a philosopher, theologian, and Zionist thinker. His deeply religious world view emphasized the relationship between man and man and between man and God. *I and Thou* (1923), a philosophical treatise that examines these relationships, had a considerable influence on both Christian and Jewish thinkers.

*The Piano*: a film (1993) about love and sex, told from a woman's point of view, and the complications that result when a woman, her daughter, and her piano arrive on a remote New Zealand island for an arranged marriage with a farmer in the late 19th century.

## Possible Answers

### *Meaning and Purpose*

1. Although the idea that fictional violence leads to real violence may be a popular assumption, it has no basis in fact. Michael Medved, says Klavan, may believe it is so, but he has no way of knowing it (40, 46). Klavan, therefore, draws a clean line between belief and knowledge. The judge in the Jamie Bulger murder case makes the same leap of faith as Medved (8–14). And Klavan's Scottish friend who connected the rude and boorish behavior of a movie audience with the violence on the screen has, again, made that same irrational leap (44–45). It is this false causal relationship that blurs fiction and reality when it is a clear distinction that must be made. The distinction must be made clear because in real life real people really get hurt (49). When we blur the distinction between fiction and reality we begin to apply fictional standards to real life situations with disastrous results (49), and we begin to lose our will to defend the sacredness of human life, or as Martin Amis says, "the gentleness of human flesh" (51).
2. The fictional, scholarly journals in *The Silence of the Lambs* can never call the madman, Dr. Lecter, either evil or crazy because they are uncomfortable with moral absolutes (55), and, ironically, reflect the best of us in real life who "lack all conviction, while the worst are full of passionate intensity" (14).
3. Blaming fictional violence is popular because it's easy. Facing the problems of real life (56) can be daunting, and trying to solve those real problems can be overwhelming.
4. With no evidence whatsoever, the judge in the Bulger case speculated that the brutal murder may have been committed because of the noxious effects a horror movie, *Child's Play 3*, had on the two murderous children. The cause-and-effect relationship he suggested had no basis in fact. He made a leap of faith. And the press immediately picked up on the false connection because it was easy to understand.

5. Klavan agrees with Stephen King that all men are potentially violent (see Stephen King's "Why We Crave Horror Movies," pp. 351–354) and that that violence needs to be repressed, and, in turn, that that repression needs a healthy outlet. But for Klavan, this formulation smacks too much of a guilty defense. The enjoyment of fictional violence delights us because it fulfills a deep-seated need. Therefore there's no reason for guilt or defensiveness. But there's every reason for celebration.
6. Klavan argues that would-be censors feel unconscious guilt for enjoying those acts in fiction that would be reprehensible in real life. This is a peculiarly Puritan attitude that Klavan attacks at various points of his essay.
7. Although fiction can make us more human because it allows us to imaginatively empathize with others, it is not powerful enough to transform people's lives. People with hollow lives who turn to violence, among other things, have been hollowed by real life experiences, not by fiction. To fathom the problems of life, we must face those problems head on rather than debate what kinds of fiction people should be allowed to enjoy. Such debate can't solve real problems; rather, it exacerbates the problems.

*Strategy*

1. In one sense, Klavan is condescending to those with opposing views. He implies in paragraph 5, for instance, that any attack on fictional violence is insane. He dismisses opposing views as "nonsense" (6). He labels any argument that insists that fiction can actually cause violence as "homeopathic" (16) and "superstitious fallacy" (17). But while he makes fun of "expert" theories of fictional violence, he very carefully explains why he does so (32). And, while initially dismissive of opposing arguments, he always comes back to admit that his opponents hold on to partial truths, but those truths are indeed just partial explanations of problems and often reductionist (21, 34, 46, 47). In this attitude, he establishes himself as honest, thoughtful, and rational, dispositions not always held by his opponents.
2. Klavan summarizes several opposing arguments in paragraph 5. After calling them "nonsense," he points out some reasons for their popular appeal (6). He then uses the long narrative of the Bulger killing and trial to show that, as in the trial, there is no evidence to show a cause-and-effect relationship between fictional and real violence (8–14). He agrees with his critics that fiction has an effect on real life, but claims that it is far too complex to reduce that relationship to the simplicity of cause and effect. To do so, therefore, is reductionist (21–23). He undermines Michael Medved's argument that the constant barrage of negative images in the media tends to erode values by pointing out that neither he (Klavan) nor Medved actually knows whether or not the connection is true. Using the Bulger case as an example, he questions the validity of that point of view (46). And, finally, he points out that the reasons for the rude behavior of the two audiences viewing *Cliffhanger* reside in their real lives and not in the make-believe on the screen. Besides, he points out, that behavior, though inappropriate and rude, was harmful to no one (47).
3. Fiction, like sex, is profoundly joyful and provides necessary and needed emotional experience (32). Both fulfill deeply personal needs, and, thus, no one has the right to intrude on either (48).

4. All of the paragraphs give the reader visual relief in a longish essay with many fully developed paragraphs. Each summarizes the section of the argument that has immediately preceded it and serves as a transition into the next section.
5. Klavan cites modern authors whose use of violence in their fiction is respectable (26), goes back to Greek myth and drama with Medea (35), and further cites the traditional literature of Shakespeare (*Titus Andronicus*), Stoker (*Dracula*), and de Sade (40).

*Style*

1. The event is "nonreal" because it exists only in fiction, and it is "nonmeaningful" because it, as fiction, has no relationship to real life.
2. When Klavan talks about the fiction that he means to celebrate in the essay, his language is appropriately casual, sometimes slangy, or imitative of the language of horror fiction. When he seriously pursues his argument his language becomes standard, even formal at times.
3. "Trough," a feeding receptacle for animals, is most often associated with pigs. Thus, would-be censors are at least partially motivated by the desire to feed on fame, however fleeting the feast.
4. *Priapic*: suggestive of or resembling a phallus; *plummets*: plunges; *oblivion*: the state of being completely forgotten or unknown; *squeamish*: sensitive, shrinking from contact with; *goading*: prodding, inciting; *posthumous*: occurring after one's death; *jitterbug*: a strenuously acrobatic dance performed chiefly to boogie-woogie and swing, popular in the early 1940's; *coital*: pertaining to sexual intercourse; *jeopardy*: hazard or risk; *estate*: a period or condition of life; *dusted*: killed (slang); *commode*: toilet; *quash*: to put down or suppress completely; *banal*: devoid of freshness or originality; *urbane*: polished, suave, sophisticated; *emblematic*: symbolic; *pundits*: experts or authorities; *distraught*: deeply agitated; *mutilated*: injured, disfigured; *tenuous*: flimsy, weak; *mea culpa*: [Latin, through my fault]: a formal acknowledgement of personal fault or error; *Draconian*: extremely harsh or cruel; *rampaging*: to rush, act, or move furiously or violently; *verities*: truths; *utopian*: founded upon or involving idealized perfection; *Dionysean*: recklessly, uninhibited; *homeopathic*: the treating of a disease by the administration of minute doses of a remedy that would in healthy persons produce symptoms of the disease treated; *template*: something overlayed; *fallacy*: a false or erroneous idea; *isomorphic*: being of identical or similar form, or shape, or structure; *alchemies*: powers or processes of transforming something common into something precious; *sublimate*: to divert the expression of an instinctual desire or impulse from its primitive form to one that is considered more socially or culturally acceptable; *pith*: importance, significance; *literati*: intelligentsia or, more specifically, men of letters; *unfathomable*: incomprehensible; *palliative*: superficial or temporary relief; *specious*: apparently good or right but lacking in real merit; *screed*: a long discourse or essay, especially a diatribe; *jeremiad*: a prolonged lamentation or complaint; *hallelujah*: a shout of joy, praise, or gratitude; *resonant*: resounding or echoing, as sounds; *stichomythic*: closely connected, as when two actors speak alternate lines (as in classical Greek drama); *sociopaths*: those who exhibit asocial or antisocial behavior; *guise*: assumed appearance; *factotum*: a general servant; *mayhem*: a state of rowdy disorder;

*hausfrau*: housewife (German); *risible*: laughable; *peccadilloes*: slight offenses; *gravitas*: substantial, consequential (Latin); *catharsis*: a purification or purgation of the emotions, primarily through art; *palaver*: idle, misleading, or beguiling speech; *expended*: consumed by use; *denounce*: to condemn or censure openly; *expended*: used up; *catharsis*: the purging of emotions or relieving of emotional tensions; *icon*: a sign or representation that stands for its object by virtue of a resemblance or analogy to it; *benevolent*: characterized by or expressing good will or kindly feelings; *nubile*: sexually developed or attractive; *in flagrante*: shortened form of *in flagrante delicto*, in the very act of committing the offense; *goblins*: grotesque sprites or elves that are mischievous or malicious towards people; *menarche*: the first menstrual period of an individual; *evisceration*: the removing of the entrails from, disembowelment; *disembowels*: to remove the entrails from; *geyser*: a hot spring that spews forth hot liquid; *placid*: pleasantly calm or peaceful; *satori*: a sudden enlightenment; *atrocities*: things that are extremely shocking, wicked, cruel, or brutal; *aesthetic*: pertaining to the nature of beauty; *promiscuous*: having sexual relations with a number of people on a casual basis; *mitigated*: lessened in force or intensity; *consigning*: handed over or delivered formally or officially; *corollaries*: immediate consequences or easily drawn conclusions; *ubermensch*: superman (German); *auctorial*: of, by, or pertaining to an author; *atomizing*: to split into many sections, groups, or factions; *humanize*: to make humane, kind, or gentle; *bloke*: man, fellow, guy (informal Britishism); *oubliette*: a secret dungeon, with an opening only in the ceiling, as in certain old castles; *devolve*: to roll down, descend.

# *Denial Behavior*

## Michael Medved

### Teaching Suggestions

The debate over what, if anything, to do about sex and violence in media takes place at all levels of American society. Most students have already given some thought to it and many have formed strong opinions. Recent legislation mandates the development of a V-chip to be inserted into all new television sets to allow parents to control which programs are available to their children. The film industry is frequently assailed for its lack of restraint in producing ever more dramatic and lurid films. A discussion of the V-chip may be a good starting point. Most people favor such a chip at first glance. Parents have a right to control their children's viewing, and the chip makes it easy and automatic. Since such a chip would control others' viewing, not mine, why not? Some have doubts, though, when they learn that the chip, as presently envisioned, is not programmable at the individual set. When it's turned on, it will block all programs that have been given a certain rating. The ratings will presumably be applied by some government or industry board.

If such a discussion sparks some interest, turn to Medved's provocative essay which takes us to the heart of the matter: Does the content of films, television programs, and popular songs influence our social behavior? Medved says yes, and he offers a telling argument: If brief commercials and fleeting product placements influence us, then the much longer exposure to sex and violence must also.

You will probably want to assign this essay along with Stephen King's "Why We Crave Horror Movies" (pp. 351–354) and/or Andrew Klaven's "The Shreiking of the Lambs" (pp. 651–668).

## Notes

**Paragraphs 1–5**

This section sets up the charge and the denial. Some observers insist that violence in entertainment affects behavior. The industry denies any cause and effect connection between the products of the media and social behavior.

**Paragraph 6**

American Enterprise Institute: Established in 1943, the American Enterprise Institute in Washington D.C. sponsors research on government policy, the American economy, and American politics. Its stated purpose is to preserve and to strengthen the foundations of a free society—limited government, competitive private enterprise, vital cultural and political institutions, and vigilant defense.

Jack Valenti (1921–b) This former advertising executive became president of the Motion Picture Association of America in 1966 and the same year was one of the writers of a code for classifying movies which was designed to reflect public values rather than dictate them.

**Paragraphs 6–12**

Medved quotes from four people, giving an overview of the industry's position so he can attack it in his next section.

**Paragraphs 13–16**

Medved states his personal position: media messages encourage destructive behavior and the accumulated effect of these messages cause problems in our culture.

**Paragraphs 17–18**

Although Medved says it is a mistake to concentrate on shocking examples of cause-and-effect connections between media and particular acts of violence, he does devote a rather long paragraph to a recital of some of the most dramatic examples.

**Paragraphs 19–20**

Medved reminds us that his concern is the media's contribution to the general social climate.

**Paragraphs 21–23**

Here Medved insists that research does show a connection between media and behavior.

**Paragraphs 26–27**

Medved dismisses industry sponsored studies as biased.

**Paragraph 28**

He accepts, however, one industry study which supports his views, though he makes no effort to explain why it is valid and the other studies mentioned in paragraph 26 are not.

**Paragraphs 30–43**

In the last section of the essay, Medved reasons that the success of commercials and product placements in programs and films is itself proof that media messages affect behavior. It is a telling argument, though no hard evidence is amassed to support it. He simply reasons that the commercials and product placements are effective or they wouldn't be used. This section is heavy with emotional language.

## Possible Answers

### *Meaning and Purpose*

1. Medved claims that it "exacerbates [social problems] and has become an important contributing factor in many of our current difficulties" (15); that "the most significant problems of the popular culture stem from the pervasive presence of anti-social material" (16); and that it contributes "to a general climate of violence and self-indulgence." (20)
2. Medved does not agree. While he calls such cases "dramatic and disturbing" (19), he recognizes that these incidents usually involve "unbalanced individuals" (17). He says that such attention to dramatic cases only distracts us from the more significant issue: what the pervasiveness of such material does to the rest of us.
3. Yes. He claims that more than three thousand such studies between 1960 and 1992 confirm the connection (22). He cites a report of the Surgeon General of the United States and a 1991 resolution of the American Psychological Association to support his statement (23). He also cites a study commissioned by CBS and conducted by the Survey Research Center of the London School of Economics in which the project supervisor said, "the evidence is very strongly supportive of the hypothesis that long-term exposure to violence increases the degree to which boys engage in violence of a serious kind" (28). He dismisses as biased other studies performed by the entertainment industry itself (26)
4. Medved ridicules the industry's denial, saying that it "contradicts the most basic assumptions of their industry" (30). Product placements and TV commercials are marketed with the assurance that they will influence viewers, yet the industry denies that the larger content of films and TV programs have any influence on behavior.

   He states this contradiction succinctly in paragraph 34: "In short, they have adopted the outrageously illogical assumption that a sixty-second commercial makes a more significant impression than a sixty-minute sitcom."
5. Medved's main point is that we are all affected, in the long-term, by the entertainment industry's "contribution to a general climate of violence and self-indulgence" (20).

### *Strategy*

1. By quoting the president of the Motion Picture Association of America, the chairman of TriStar Pictures, a newspaper columnist, and a popular entertainer, Medved creates for his reader a sense that the entire entertainment industry has a monolithic view. Thus, when he successfully discredits one industry spokesperson, he is successfully discrediting them all.
2. A *straw man* is a weak or imaginary argument that is easy to destroy. In the second section of the essay, Medved claims that the arguments of the four industry spokesmen are really arguments against positions not really taken by those who oppose violence in entertainment. If this is true, the spokesmen's arguments can be dismissed.

   The straw man point is best applied to Teller's statement in paragraph 9.

Teller claims that those who oppose the content of popular entertainment think that "if we stop showing rape in movies people will stop committing it in real life" and that "people are not smart enough to tell make-believe from reality." Medved states that none of the critics he knows take these positions. Therefore, Teller is arguing against a straw man in his attempts to ridicule these critics.

3. It's probably his most effective argument because it points out a logical problem in the entertainment industry's defense: How can some images influence people and others have no effect? It also has a quality of newness because it is an argument seldom heard in this debate. Writers often place their most effective argument last.
4. The first sentence of paragraph 5 concisely states the view of the industry, at least as Medved sees it: 'popular entertainment is by its very nature inconsequential, and . . . no one is seriously damaged by the fleeting images or subtle themes in a movie."
5. The argument about advertising and product placements is presented through reasoning alone. In the absence of hard evidence, notice the increase in the use of emotional language.

*Style*

1. Examples of emotional language abound. Here are a few; students will find additional ones.

   The titles of the first and last sections: "A Cultural Nuthouse" and "The Height of Hypocrisy."
   Paragraph 5 "industry apologists"
   Paragraph 21 "rhetorical tricks"; "laughably bald-faced lies"
   Paragraph 24 "stunning display of corporate arrogance"
   Paragraph 26 "research is regularly dusted off and trotted out"
   Paragraph 28 "equally ludicrous"
   Paragraph 30 "utterly implausible position"
   Paragraph 31 "hired gun experts"
   Paragraph 32 "this nonsense"
   Paragraph 34 "outrageously illogical assumptions"
   Paragraph 35 "bizarre notion"
   Paragraph 37 "absurd internal contradiction"
   Paragraph 42 "naked, gorgeous bodies in transports of passion"
   Paragraph 43 "flagrantly dishonest and lavishly illogical"

2. *Zealots*: fanatics, extremists; *exacerbates*: intensifies, worsens; *pernicious*: hurtful, causing harm; *lurid*: glaringly vivid or sensational, shocking; *conglomerates*: wholes consisting of many semi-independent parts; *moguls*: powerful or influential people; *hypocrisy*: the pretense of having belief, character, or principle that one does not have; *charismatic*: having qualities that give an individual influence over large numbers of people.